THE TENOR: A CULTURAL HISTORY

MATTHEW BOYDEN

Also by Matthew Boyden

The Rough Guide to Classical Music

The Rough Guide to Opera

Opera: 100 Essential CDs

Classical Music: 100 Essential CDs

Icons of Opera

Richard Strauss

Beethoven and the Gothic

For Rachel

Parlo d'amor vegliando, parlo d'amor sognando, all'acqua, all'ombre, ai monti, ai fiori, all'erbe, ai fonti, all'eco, all'aria, ai venti, che il suon de'vani accenti portano via con sé.

Ragueneau Press
7 Friars Mill
Bath Lane
Leicester
LE3 5BJ

hello@ragueneaupress.com
www.ragueneaupress.com

The Tenor: A Cultural History

Matthew Boyden

First Published 2021

Ragueneau Press works within the framework of the Copyright, Designs and Patents Act 1988, and retains all rights for electronic storage and reproduction.

Matthew Boyden has asserted his moral right to be identified as the author of this work.

Jacket Design by Lee Haynes © Ragueneau Press 2021

Typeset in Garamond Pro by Jill Sweet

Front Cover: Franco Corelli (1921–2003), singing "Recondita armonia" from Tosca, at the New York Metropolitan Opera, in 1966.

Back cover: Enrico Caruso (1873–1921), in Pagliacci, photographed by the studio of Aimé Dupont in 1903, the year of his debut as Canio at the New York Metropolitan Opera.

ISBN: 978-1-3999-0017-1

Printed and Bound in the United Kingdom

Contents

	Author's Note	vii
	Preface – Nuts and Bolts	xii
Chapter 1	Boys and Wenches	1
Chapter 2	Prima la parole, poi la musica	22
Chapter 3	The Squawk of a Capon	48
Chapter 4	New Wine, New Bottles	71
Chapter 5	Sovereign's Ransom	86
Chapter 6	Göttersonnenaufgang	114
Chapter 7	Johannes Factotum	144
Chapter 8	Frederick and Victor's Audience with the King	162
Chapter 9	Phrase	189
Chapter 10	Silver Voices	211
Chapter 11	"Mario! Mario!"	241
Chapter 12	A God in Tights	254
Chapter 13	Golden Age	271
Chapter 14	The Poisoned Chalice	300
Chapter 15	Parfum exotique	328
Chapter 16	Sons of Father Russia	354
Chapter 17	Sacred and Profane	376
Chapter 18	How to Fake a Tenor	402
Chapter 19	Glory's Small Change	414
Chapter 20	Epilogue: A View from the Pit	431
	Acknowledgements	457
	Bibliography	459
	Index	467

Author's Note

This is a book about the tenor voice, and tenors as artists; it is about singing also, and the cultures within which the modern tenor has evolved and crystallised as something more than an instrument. It is not a book about opera or music in its generality, or a miscellany of anecdotes or a collection of reviews or an anthology of tributes to the "best" and most famous singers. There are numerous other titles that have done all of these things in different ways, and to varying degrees of success.

It is a book for enthusiasts of singing, new and old, and for anyone interested in knowing more about the tenor as a cultural and musical phenomenon. It is for those who engage with some (or all) of what the "Three Tenors" did, particularly when on their own, and it is for those who want to understand why the tenor voice has achieved such prominence over time, inside and outside the opera house and the concert hall. Although it has been published to coincide with the centennial anniversaries of the death of Enrico Caruso and the bizarrely proximate births of Giuseppe Di Stefano, Mario Lanza and Franco Corelli, it identifies almost 400 individual other singers, as well as hundreds of recordings and films. The narrative reaches well beyond the confines of music history in isolation. Significantly, this book is not about singing in general. It does not speak to the significance or the character of other voices, not least since this volume is the first of four on each of the primary voice types. Where an observation might have applied equally to a soprano, a baritone or a bass, it has been excluded.

Readers will note how the emphasis is in no way cross-cultural; never could it have been. The place of the tenor in world music is sufficiently diverse and fascinating to warrant a separate volume, but time and space – and the relative continuity of the western vocal tradition – have meant that this book's focus is limited to art music and popular song, as both have emerged primarily within Europe and the United States.

Numerous singers are referenced who will be unknown even to serious devotees and collectors; others will complain that someone dear to them has been left out. Inevitably, therefore, it has not been possible within a single volume to consider more than those about whom something meaningful can be written, so that mere quality alone (or favoured status) has not been sufficient to admit a large number of tenors who made recordings or gave celebrated performances. Each of those featured has been included for a reason; whether the reader agrees with these assessments is a construction of taste and prejudice – as it has been for the author.

Record labels and disc numbers have not been included because there are excellent catalogues and databases available digitally and in print. The same is true of the recordings themselves, the majority of which can be heard online through a variety of (mostly) free-to-use services. Similarly, it has been decided not to add pictures because Google will satisfy anyone wanting to see paintings or photographs of almost everyone to whom reference is made.

Opera titles (and the title of any published work) are in italics. Title roles are in plain text. All translations into English are by the author, unless otherwise indicated.[1] While it is unnecessary for the reader to be able to read music, it will be useful to know that a number placed after a note (written as a capital letter) is the expression of (American) Standard Pitch Notation or International Pitch Notation, a method of specifying pitch through the combination of (1) a musical note and (2) a number identifying the octave. In other words, the high B at the end of "*Nessun Dorma*" is a B4; the climactic high C of "*Che gelida manina*" is a C5.

There are numerous references to different types and kinds of tenor voice throughout this book, all adhering broadly to what is known within the singing and opera business as the *fach* system. This emerged in central Europe during the early 19th century in tandem with the emergence of organised and codified Repertory Opera. The word *fach* signifies a range of voices that sit by sub-division within any general vocal category (*i.e.*, soprano, tenor, baritone and bass), after the fashion of the casting of film and theatre actors and directors. At its simplest, John Gielgud's *fach* would have precluded him from being cast as James Bond; Danny De Vito would have failed David Lean's audition for the part of T.E. Lawrence (although he might yet triumph as Napoleon[2]), and Michael Bay would likely achieve little when *Waiting For Godot*.

Richard Boldrey's monumental *Guide to Operatic Roles & Arias*[3] identifies more than 3,500 roles in 1,000 operas; Rudolph Kloiber's *Handbuch der Oper*[4] does something similar. It follows that there are multiple *Fächer* within each voice, a plurality without which a Repertory-*stagione* company presenting numerous operas in a single season with an in-House company would flounder.

As will be seen, no single tenor can do everything – although a couple have had a stab at it – which means that the *fach* system enables the identification of singers' voices according to sound and timbre, range, style and artistry and, even, physical appearance. This last consideration is irrelevant for the most part. Imagine the outcry were a soprano to be judged unsuitable for a role based on her weight, for example, rather than her talents as an actress and a singer?

Particularly where tenors are concerned, there are numerous ways of saying the same thing. A lyric tenor is also *lyrischer* and *leggiero*, depending on the country of the repertoire's origin. A *heldentenor* is also by definition a heroic tenor, and so on. The following terms are used interchangeably throughout, and with good reason – namely that references to *fach* can often cause more confusion than clarity. Tenor *Fächer* is more frequently a function of colour rather than range, which is why Pavarotti remained throughout his career a *tenore-lirico* who proceeded to sing *spinto* roles. Does his having sung *spinto* repertoire mean he was a *spinto* tenor? It does not. Conversely, is Peter Seiffert a *heldentenor*? He is not, which fact does not prevent him from singing the role of Tristan. This issue will crop up frequently, although it is messy to say the least. *Peter Grimes*, for example, was written by Benjamin Britten for the light-lyric tenor Peter Pears; it was subsequently performed (with legendary intensity) by Jon Vickers, a *heldentenor*. So what does the role ask of its performer by way of *fach*?

Author's Note

A passing reference is necessary as concerning the counter-tenor. It might have been appropriate to consider this hybrid voice in a history of the tenor. However, the counter-tenor is being reserved for the second issue in this series of books, for reasons that will become apparent when *The Soprano: A Cultural History* is published in due course.

The following categories make no distinction between the different spellings of "tenor" (with or without an "e", primarily), but it can be assumed that the linguistic origin of a word will determine the repertoire's country of origin.

Comic – character – buffo – charaktertenor
Typical Range: C3 – B flat 4
Typified by: Pedrillo (*Die Entführung aus dem Serail*), Mime (*Der Ring des Nibelungen*), Goro (*Madama Butterfly*), Beppe (*Pagliacci*), Emperor Altoum (*Turandot*)

Light – lyric – leggiero – Lirico – tenore di grazia – lyrischer – lyrique
Typical Range: C3 – D5
Typified by: Ferrando (*Cosí fan tutte*), Tamino (*Die Zauberflöte*), Fenton (*Falstaff*), Nadir (*Les pêcheurs de perles*), Don Ferrando (*Don Pasquale*), Nemorino (*L'elisir d'amore*), the Duke (*Rigoletto*), Rodolfo (*La bohème*)

Spinto
Typical range: C3 – C5
Typified by: Don José (*Carmen*) Manrico (*Il trovatore*), Alvaro (*La forza del destino*), Hermann (*Pique Dame*), Roméo (*Roméo et Juliete*) Des Grieux (*Manon*), Cavaradossi (*Tosca*), Leukiposs (*Daphne*), Drum Major (*Wozzeck*)

Dramatic -- tenore di forza – dramatischer – heldentenor – Wagner tenor
Typical range: C3 – B4
Typified by: Siegmund (*Die Walküre*), Siegfried (*Der Ring des Nibelungen*), Tristan (*Tristan und Isolde*), Parsifal, Otello, Andrea Chénier, Cavaradossi (*Tosca*), Calaf (*Turandot*), Der Kaiser (*Die frau ohne Schatten*), Drum Major (*Wozzeck*)

Finally, a short note on memory. My first experience of opera in the theatre was *Aida*, at Covent Garden in July, 1977. Though still in shorts, I was fortunate to be able to sit through a work that can seem long for people with more years and greater patience than I had then, or now. I can recall the intensity of Plácido Domingo's performance of "*Celeste Aida*", which struck me more forcibly than any of the pomp and circumstance that followed it. His voice operated for me in a vacuum; I cannot draw on anything of detail, but I remember being dragged to the edge of my seat by the resonance and amplitude of the voice – in what struck me at the time as an impossibly cavernous space. Having travelled widely in later years when writing about opera and music, I came to realise there were many bigger, more demanding spaces in which to sing. Even so, my memory of the physical, tactile immediacy generated by Domingo's performance never left me.

Over hundreds of trips to see and hear operas throughout Europe and the United States, I developed an acute sensitivity for the acoustic differences between scale (as amplitude) and clarity (as sung-speech) – a prejudice exacerbated by an early and unhealthy obsession with recordings. Like many other teenagers, I was enthralled by the arrival of Compact Disc and I collected them obsessively. My CD library grew eventually to more than 15,000 titles,[5] half of them of operas and singers. The sale of that collection funded the purchase of my first house. My obsession was lessened by working as a record producer, which afforded me first-hand knowledge of what might be achieved in an editing suite. Over a period of nearly four years I committed serial misrepresentation when making good musicians sound exceptional, all the while noting the parallels between the recording of 60 minutes of music over two or three days and the expectations of models and celebrities when posing for editors and publishers.

I took an unhealthy delight in the interventionism of the studio (and churches, more commonly), relishing a process that made a necessarily profitable virtue of deceit. One award-winning production contained approximately 800 edits. Even more time and effort were committed to the isolation of a "taped acoustic" that owed nothing to what could be heard within the recording space. The sound when captured was on every occasion killed in the service of a truth that allowed performers to sweat without perspiring, slip without falling and speak without stumbling. Matters are at their most seditious when benefitting singers, all of whom hear themselves *very* differently to everyone else. Few people other than, perhaps, Elizabeth Schwarzkopf,[6] have ever delighted in hearing themselves speak or sing – even accepting the primacy of self-analysis as a professional obligation. The modern process of recording is at its most damaging when operating as a memory of something that never happened. The idolatry of a recording in its perfected state memorialises the sterilising of much of the humanity by which singing is defined when experienced or recorded live. This is because the power of a voice resides in its owner's relationship with the acoustic in which he or she is singing, as well as the singer's relationship with stage-colleagues and accompanists. There is an inevitable surfeit of psychological tics from which a singer can suffer, no matter the depths of their (apparent) confidence. Recordings made in the studio – or professionally – are testaments to a questionable slice of progress that can do no more than reach for an ideal that is unattainable by definition. That doesn't mean that recordings are inherently "bad" or to be ignored or jettisoned. The significance they hold for the vast majority of admirers of singing, however (and of tenors in particular) has cultivated an unreality from which subsequent generations cannot escape other than by denial.

For this reason alone I would advocate that anyone reading this book does whatever they can to support the still-living culture of art-music by leaving their favourite studio recordings, as performed by their favourite dead or retired singers, to gather dust on the shelf. Instead, we should all of us seek out the current and the young in live performance so that they might yet be liberated from the chains of

---

5   There are, of course, collectors with 20 times that number.
6   When appearing on the BBC Home Service (now Radio 4) programme *Desert Island Discs* on 28 July, 1958, the German soprano chose eight of her own recordings to take with her to the imagined island – all but one of them featuring her own voice. The exception was the Prelude to the 1956 EMI recording of *Der Rosenkavalier* conducted by Karajan, in which Schwarzkopf nonetheless performed the role of the Marschallin.

Author's Note

a manufactured ideal that can be broken only by looking to the future. It is conceded, of course, that this book identifies and makes positive references to hundreds of recordings; it is a "history", and for such purposes evidence is generally (but not always) a pre-requisite. Noting this fact, any young man turning to a career as a tenor embraces the near-impossible burden of standing on the shoulders of giants whose reputations will survive for as long as their recordings. To an extent, therefore, the next generation will find its voice only if we remember to forget those who sang before them.

It's a curious way in which to begin a history of the tenor – even when noting that the singers who made records are outnumbered disproportionately by those who did not. Where the shadows thrown by the titans of the 18th and 19th century passed as quickly as did their reputations, we have now to wrestle with the permanence of exemplars that prompt the vulgarities of certainty, comparison and ranking. We should, of course, marvel where appropriate at the greatest tenor voices of the past (as we do the finest actors), and we should endeavour to learn from them also where possible – but not if the exceptional causes the normative to become infinitely disappointing.

In the early 1990s I attended two performances of *Tosca* with Pavarotti playing the role of Cavaradossi. On both nights, as he was shot dead by firing squad, the great man leaned heavily against a necessarily robust piece of scenery, lowered himself onto the stronger of his knees and, having steadied himself, rolled onto his side. It took him almost 10 seconds to die from eight musket rounds fired at a distance of 30 feet. Some in the audience sniggered, provoking angry outbursts. This was not a signal moment in the history of opera, but it didn't need to be. It was just another performance from within the professional life of a singer that spanned more than thirty years. I was able then (and now) to remember numerous other performances by Pavarotti in which he was either the most charming or the most musical person in the theatre; if he lacked for verisimilitude as an actor then he had by that stage in his career done enough to weather the unavoidable consequences of age and obesity.

Pavarotti's performances on disc survive him, and his legacy as Cavaradossi will remain discoverable in perpetuity. The same is true of everyone else who has recorded the role, and everyone yet to come. With the recording industry in decline, however, it's possible that the collective memory of the greatest exponents of the tenor craft will diminish to a point that allows for perpetual reinvention and, even, the revival of the art in its purest form – as composition. It is in that ambition that the future of art music, opera and the performing traditions necessary for their continuation needs fully to be invested.

14 February, 2021
Venice

Preface – Nuts and Bolts

*Circa vilem patulumque morabimur orbem
Unde pudor proferre pedem vetat aut operis lex.*[1]

For its 1955 season, La Scala, Milan, had booked its star tenor, Mario Del Monaco, to perform in an opera in which he lost interest only a few weeks before the opening night. Del Monaco informed the theatre's intendant, Antonio Ghiringhelli, that he no longer wished to take part in the scheduled production. Instead, he "invited" La Scala to stage Umberto Giordano's career-defining *Andrea Chénier*. His change of heart was prompted in part by the sudden availability of Maria Callas, who was given just five days in which to learn the role of Maddalena de Coigny.

The opera is celebrated for its one-dimensional French revolutionary setting, an unusual number of arias for the primary cast, and some barnstorming duets – including the work's finale, "*Vicino a te*,"[2] during which Chénier and Maddalena are joined for eternity by the guillotine. There are no fewer than four significant arias for the title role, the best of them Act One's "*Un di all'azzuro spazio*,"[3] in which Chénier is tasked with persuading his aristocratic circle of the significance of the people's struggle, which he frames in terms of love. The aria is hugely demanding, as is the entire role, because it necessitates a voice of Wagnerian scale and an artist with the stamina of an athlete. The *tessitura* of much of the writing sits low in the voice, which is deceptive, since Giordano was a crowd-pleaser; he knew that audiences preferred rising musical narratives with cumulative episodes resolving in long-held high notes. *Chénier* is the most purple of dramas, and thrilling in its musical language. Nothing is made easy for the performers, in part because of the dense orchestration. "*Un di*" is no exception. The aria divides into two repeating stanzas, both of which culminate in thrilling B flat 4s – the second more challenging for the singer than the first because he has been at full tilt for more than five minutes by the time the audience rises to its feet. A tenor can be said to have failed if the music is allowed to continue (as it is meant to) after the aria's final "*d'amore!*".

For all its success, the opera is rarely staged today because there are few tenors capable of doing justice to the title role. Del Monaco was, in some respects, perfect casting, although his Barnum-and-Bailey talent was cultivated to do little more than thrill. He was handsome, but no more than 5' 10" in his shoes. He was given also to

---

1 "We will be delayed throughout this worthless and expanding world where shameful behaviour and disagreements prevent progress." Horace, *Ars Poetica* (ii.132, 135.) Quoted by Burke in *On taste* (1759).
2 'Close to you.'
3 'One day to the blue space.'

posturing, and his dramatic range as an actor veered commonly between the petulant and the pompous. Such was his obsession with raising the roof that he cared more for volume than for tone and expression. Subtlety was sacrificed routinely to excitement – something that La Scala's claque appreciated, and with frenzied enthusiasm. What made Del Monaco so magnificent in verismo – of which *Chénier* is a near-perfect example – was his theatrical sensibility, an innate capacity to judge everything uniquely badly until dramatic demand collided with vocal supply. One of those episodes, and among the most electrifying in the history of recorded opera, occurred on January 8th, 1955, when Del Monaco strutted as Chénier onto La Scala's 30-metre-wide stage like a rooster with teeth. His leather boots, silvered tights, frock coat and thickly-applied make-up would have provoked sniggering in any other context. For La Scala's 2,300 spectators, he was legitimately the cock of the walk.

Appearing on stage with *La Divina*, Del Monaco was charged with meeting the expectations of a good number of Europe's aristocratic and most demanding elite. A recording was made of the performance. It survives as a testament to the thrill of opera as it once was – when it *really* mattered, and then to people spanning every social demographic. It speaks also to the power of the tenor voice to engage in a process of coercive submission. Shortly before 8pm, as he sang out the words "… *non conoscete amor…*" the repeated "*amor*" took him to a thunderous concluding B flat 4. The Tenor strutted towards the orchestra pit, raised his eyes to the gods and hammered out one of the most glorious sounds ever produced by a human being. For all his Apollonian power, however, he missed the B flat by a margin sufficient for the audience – and the conductor, Antonino Votto – to fear that he was either about to split the note or remain beneath it. Failed high notes are collected by cognoscenti as "perle nere," and had Del Monaco not done what he did around three seconds into his culminating B flat, he would have produced one of the blackest pearls of his career.

Falling below the note, and mid-way through the air in his lungs, Del Monaco began to force his tone almost imperceptibly into the resonating chord, such that the once near-lost climax resolved in a staggering, monumental salvaging of the dramatic moment. He capped the note, but only for the briefest of moments, with a perceptible shift in vocal placement, at which point the already charged audience exploded into one of the loudest, most sustained cheers ever heard in an opera house. If the microphones struggled to capture Del Monaco's anvil-hammering voice, they failed absolutely to record the fervour of the crowd's appreciation of it. Maria Callas can be heard in the background attempting to continue with the opera[4] either by reason of professional obligation or because she wanted to redirect the theatre's attention. La Scala was having none of it. For once, the claque and the critics were aligned.

Del Monaco's achievement was something miraculous – either because he failed the note initially or, as is more likely, because he intended to bend the dramatic instant to his will. What makes the episode particularly remarkable is that Del Monaco did not enjoy the easiest top register. He was a dramatic tenor, so everyone was

---

4   Maddalena sings, without irony, "*perdonatemi*" [forgive me]. It can easily be supposed that Giordano and Illica knew precisely what they were doing when having Maddalena interrupt the (hopefully) baying crowd with an apology.

aware that such things compelled near-superhuman effort, strength and focus. The concentration and the courage necessary to do what he did – with Maria Callas standing behind him, and with *l'Europe entière* in the auditorium – cannot properly be understood without considering the pressure to which the Brass Bull of Milan[5] was subjected that evening. The bravura is vulgar, and gloriously so, because Del Monaco sang everything at "11". He marked his territory through carnal vitality – in vibrating homage to Delacroix's diarised confession that "*One never paints violently enough*". Del Monaco understood how any suspicion that he *might* miss the second B flat was sufficient for doubt to be transformed into triumph, a *deus ex machina* that would have been impossible had the audience presumed only confident perfection.

As an aria, "*Un dì*" is among the best, with Luigi Illica's verse meeting head-on the high standards set by Chénier's retro-romanticism. Giordano and Illica's sensibilities were tailored ideally to the role of a poet seeking to persuade a group of unfeeling toffs of the corollaries of unchecked privilege. Chénier submits his reasoning as a romantic cypher – a characteristic rather than a character. The music is written to enable a suitably capable singer to transform the simplistic metaphor and scansion into something irresistibly persuasive. The aria is pure advocacy, therefore – literally and as a narrative – but hearing it done "well" does not mean it is being done effectively. Attainment does not equate in and of itself to success, particularly not in a context wherein another tenor might have hit the B flat full-square while achieving nothing emotional in consequence. There is a Delphic space between the forming of an idea and its presentation – one in which Del Monaco's performance stands apart. The vulgarity of the singing is nullified by the thrill of an occasion that resolves in an amalgam of risk, fear and, ultimately, triumph. It is in this conscious and unconscious recognition of theatrical excess that the tenor voice engages commonly in a physical and technical high-wire, a circus act in which the artist is required to adhere to a character and a narrative without allowing his necessary efforts to get in the way of theatrical and musical truth.

This book is not uniquely, or primarily, about the singer's art, or changes in the perception of artistic integrity – since there can be no agreement on what qualifies as definitive for either. The dissonance flowing from propensity and prejudice renders judgment almost unworkably subjective. There are absolutes, of course – insofar as few would diminish the exemplar status of Caruso, Wunderlich and Pavarotti – but the breadth and variety of voices over time, and the differences between them when singing the same repertoire, compel the isolation of criteria to which analysis can be attached – if only to enable a measure of consistency. The need for precedent is especially urgent when reflecting that many in 1955 considered Del Monaco to be among the least musical people in Italy – the context for which assessment is narrowed dramatically when noting that the Italian pop scene in January 1955 was dominated by Renato Carosone's *Maruzzella* and Clara Jaione's *La Postina della val Gardena*.

Predilection is, of course, a construct for any consideration of singing. Ian Bostridge can no more perform the role of Chénier than Del Monaco was at liberty

---

5   Williams, Jeannie (2007). *Jon Vickers: A Hero's Life*. UPNE. p.165.

to sing Schubert.[6] As such, it is idiomatically certain that forcing square pegs into round holes yields little of value[7] – even when the ill-advised choices of singers prove popular. The prescriptions of taste are inevitable for the reader, therefore, as also the author; whether or not someone listening to Del Monaco likes what he does has no bearing on whether it is any good. The kaleidoscopic range of factors attaching to merit are not the same, therefore, as those applying to preference. Such was Edmund Burke's thesis when holding that it is[8]

> probable that the standard both of reason and Taste is the same in all human creatures. For if there were not some principles of Judgment as well as of sentiment common to all mankind, no hold could possibly be taken either on their reason or their passions, sufficient to maintain the ordinary correspondence of life. It appears indeed to be generally acknowledged, that with regard to truth and falsehood there is something fixed. We find people in their disputes continually appealing to certain tests and standards which are allowed on all sides, and are supposed to be established in our common nature. But there is not the same obvious concurrence in any uniform or settled principles which relate to Taste.

Burke isolated in pleasure and pain the composites for any aesthetic consideration of taste, filtering them through the senses and imagination. His starting point was indifference, from which position of inertia he celebrated the power of music to bring about a state of pleasure. It followed, that a thing was judged to be beautiful or ugly in accordance with the degree of pleasure or pain it caused through the operation of sense, imagination and reasoning. Burke did not have the benefit of hearing Del Monaco thunder his way through a song by Schubert – an experience many would consider definitive of agony. His "logic of Taste" contributes little, therefore, to what many enthusiasts of opera choose to like, since they are either not choosing their preferences at all – any more than did the defendants in *R v Brown*[9] – or they are yielding to an evolving cultural prejudice, of a kind that renders the ugly beautiful. In much the same way that Del Monaco's steam-whistle singing continues to operate for many as a guilty sin, so too are the paintings of Egon Schiele and Francis Bacon beautiful for audiences acclimatised to the changing vernaculars of art and taste. Burke recognised in his essay that

---

6 Which didn't stop him having a crack at it. There are a number of recordings of him murdering "*Ellens dritter Gesang*" [Ellen's Third Song], D. 839, Op. 52, No. 6 (1825) a setting of seven songs from Walter Scott's *The Lady of the Lake*. Better, better known as "*Ave Maria*."

7 The author notes by exception that during the Apollo 13 mission, an exploding oxygen tank compelled the crew to evacuate to the lunar module for the remainder of the trip to the moon and thereafter to Earth. One of the problems requiring a solution was the adaptation of large and cube-shaped CO_2 scrubbers to fittings that were cylindrical and small. Employing plastic bags and cardboard from the mission's log books as a funnel, the cabin air was pumped through the lithium hydroxide using a suit hose, into a fan and then through a sock – all held together by duct tape. See also *La Famille Reed* for a negation of the truism.

8 Burke, Edmund (Second edition, 1759 (2008)). *A Philosophical Enquiry into the Origin of Our Ideas of the Sublime and Beautiful*. Routledge Classics.

9 *R v Brown* [1994] 1 AC 212.

The term Taste, like all other figurative terms, is not extremely accurate: the thing which we understand by it, is far from a simple and determinate idea in the minds of most men, and it is therefore liable to uncertainty and confusion [...] A definition may be very exact, and yet go but a very little way towards informing us of the nature of the thing defined; but let the virtue of a definition be what it will, in the order of things, it seems rather to follow than to precede our enquiry, of which it ought to be considered as the result. It must be acknowledged that the methods of disquisition and teaching may be sometimes different [...] but for my part, I am convinced that the method of teaching which approaches most nearly to the method of investigation, is incomparably the best; since not content with serving up a few barren and lifeless truths, it leads to the stock on which they grew; it tends to set the reader himself in the track of invention, and to direct him into those paths in which the author has made his own discoveries, if he should be so happy as to have made any that are valuable.

It follows that classification is as necessary as it is reckless – so that the consideration of a voice preserved on a recording is able to survive the inevitable chorus of disagreement. No one is able to challenge a contemporary assessment of Enrico Tamberlik, the first Alvaro in Verdi's *La forza del destino* on 10 November, 1862 – because he died in March, 1889, two months before he was able to attend on Edison at the World's Fair in Paris. There is much one might say of what was written *about* his voice, but there can be no consensus by reference to a recording of it. Conversely, everyone is entitled to form a view of the singing of Beniamino Gigli – born almost a year to the day after Tamberlik's death. Gigli made hundreds of recordings, with many taken live from opera houses and concert halls, and he appeared in more than 20 films, all of which allow for an informed assessment by taste and prejudice of his work as a singing actor. Because Gigli and his tutors were taught within traditions that predated recording, it is certain that the generation preceding his was subject to first-hand, purely acoustic influences – just as Leopold Auer learned from Jakob Dont and Joseph Hellmesberger, rather than from cylinders and '78s. It is not possible to learn how to sing like Tamberlik from reviews of his performances – or, even, from reading books and articles by Tamberlik promising to teach readers "how to sing" like Tamberlik. In this sense, and perhaps uniquely, writing about a tenor from before the age of recording equates to "dancing about architecture" – save that one is able to apply criteria of substance to the differences and variabilities that can be determined archivally.

It's worth remembering that everything Tamberlik did sounded very much like Tamberlik. It was an incomparable sound, and he was a unique performer, just as Giovanni Martinelli, Ramón Vinay, Jussi Björling, José Carreras and Jonas Kaufmann can be identified blindfolded. Vocal fingerprints are far from automatic or presumed, however, so that the teaching of technique cannot (and should not) come at cost to the natural character and identity of a voice. Wanting – or trying – to sound like another singer is neither practicable nor realistic, for obvious reasons; but it's meaningful that for every Tamberlik there have been 50 or 100 tenors whose voices have remained unheard, even when listened to. Exponential access to recording devices and opportunities between 1900 and 1940 ensured that literally thousands of singers, and many hundreds of tenors, were able to make recordings, a fact which posterity is tempted to mistake for achievement and "success." The truth is that many of the voices that survive on cylinder, disc and download were second or third rate, with a large number having paid for their shellac wafer of immortality. The evolution of discretion that led from Fred Gaisberg to Walter Legge, and the latter's dictatorship of taste, was a necessary feature of the need to separate wheat from chaff. It is no exaggeration to observe that there has been significantly more fodder than ciabatta. Since the onset of recording it has been difficult, even for those with cultivated ears, to distinguish between the thousands of also-rans, the types who kept the world's opera houses in business for more than three centuries. Collectors and connoisseurs are prone to identifying stones as gems, a feature of context more than conscience. As George Moore discovered before writing his *Confessions of a Young Man*,[10] enthusiasm is never enough. Proximity to talent cannot compensate for its absence.

In his preface to *The Picture of Dorian Gray*, Wilde held that "all art is quite useless" – which prompted one correspondent to ask of the author in April, 1891, where else he might "find developed that idea of the total uselessness of all art?" Wilde replied: "Art is useless because its aim is simply to create a mood. It is not meant to instruct or influence action in any way. It is superbly sterile, and the note of its pleasure is sterility."[11] It was a characteristically Wildean observation, and disingenuous for a man whose life had been taken up with pleasure and the making of instructive statements through art. Where singing is concerned, however, there are a distinct set of largely inarguable sterile criteria for analysis. It follows that any resolution of what qualifies as "good" and "not good" stands on the assignment of prescription, a set of recurring factors where some things can be said objectively to be better than other.

A good example can be found in a live performance from 1967 of *L'elisir d'amore*, filmed and recorded at the Teatro Comunale in Firenze, with Gianandrea Gavazzeni conducting Carlo Bergonzi as Nemorino, Renata Scotto as Adina, and Giuseppe Taddei as Belcore. The staging was little better than that of a high school; the singing of their roles by Bergonzi and Scotto was arguably the most perfect captured by sound and film. There are numerous unforgettable highlights, including Scotto's performance of "*Prendi, per me sei libero*"[12] – with its two unimaginably perfect, floated *fil di voce*[13] high C5s – but it is the transcendent singing of "*Una furtive lagrima*"[14] by Bergonzi that makes this recording a singularly important point of reference.

The aria is well-known – which helps with comparisons, since almost everyone with a voice of the appropriate weight and scale has recorded it. Nemorino has purchased a "potion" with which to steal the love of Adina. It turns out to be cheap red wine sold by a traveling quack; when he sees Adina crying he knows that she has

---

10   1886 in French; 1888 in English.
11   *The Complete Letters of Oscar Wilde* (2000). Eds. Merlin Holland and Rupert Hart-Davis. Fourth Estate. p.478.
12   'Take it, because you are free of me'.
13   Italian composers during the 19th century sometimes marked a passage "fil di voce" [thread of voice] – which extends expressively the principle of *pianissimo*.
14   'A furtive tear'.

fallen in love with him, and he is sure the "elixir" has worked. It is a transcendent moment, and capable of carrying significantly more emotional substance than many are able to give it. It is in B flat minor, with a range from F3 to A flat 4, with a *tessitura* of B flat3 to A flat4. On paper, it presents no obvious challenges, even for a high-lying baritone. The rub lies in the phrasing. Bergonzi's sublime vocal placement, his melancholy palette and range of vocal colour reach far beyond that of anyone else to have recorded the aria. Without suggesting the slightest effort or strain, he approaches each phrase with unique expressive intelligence, fusing words and music so as to elevate what is commonly little more than a pretty tune to the status of high theatrical art.

When the phrase "*Quelle festose giovani Invidiar sembro*"[15] yields to the febrile yearning of "*Che più cercando io vo? M'ama!*",[16] he carries in swell an unbroken line of song that lasts almost 14 seconds. The expressive focus is so total, and the placing of the voice so secure, that Bergonzi is able to submit to the sentiment of Felice Romani's words without yielding once to sentimentality. He is able to place his baritonal tenor at the service of Donizetti's music, so that it is Nemorino, rather than Bergonzi, who fills the stage.

One can marvel at the warmth and power of the voice, the painterly use of *vibrato*, the breath-defying shifts in colour and shape, the whirls of dynamic contrast, and his typically fastidious diction – just as one can marvel at Gavazzeni's sensitive and responsive conducting, and the beautiful rendering of the bassoon solo; but what makes it unique is the apparent ease of the placing and projection of the voice. Bergonzi's successful submission to, and communication of, the aria's emotional sincerity defines both the performer and the performed. Bergonzi is no actor; he never claimed to be. As an artist, however, his translation of feeling through expressive *legato* and word-use is peerless. At the close of the penultimate phrase "*Di più non chiedo, non chiedo*",[17] and having sung the famous 24-note melisma (spanning F3 to A4) with rare delicacy, he approaches the final repetition of the final word of the last line "*Si può morir! Si può morir d'amor*".[18] It is here that Bergonzi's status, and that of his performance, is definitive. The final "*d'amor*" is made up of *two* syllables, and scored as a descending fifth (from F4 to B flat 3). The translation from Italian of "*d'amor*" is '*of* love' (as in 'one could die of love') Bergonzi sings instead the word "*d'amore*", which translates simply as 'love'. In doing so, he is able to accentuate, for dramatic emphasis, a pronounced "eh" at the end of the phrase – a phrase that occupies him for some 18 uninterrupted seconds. He does so on a sustained *diminuendo* that defies technical analysis. The timing is such that he is able to use the final expiration of air from his lungs to communicate the intensity of his feeling, a narcotic effect recognised by the audience, which cheers its appreciation. Bergonzi quite properly milks every last drop, and remains motionless, with his head bowed and his hands folded, for almost as long as the aria took to sing.

---

15 'Those festive young girls she seemed to envy.'
16 'What more could I want? He loves me!'
17 'More I cannot ask, I cannot ask.'
18 'One could die. One could die of love.'

If the parts equate to their sum then it is objectively true that Bergonzi's performance in Florence is as good as can be asserted analytically. That doesn't mean that other performances are not also very fine, or "better" in accordance with individual taste. It is simply that the parts as they can be heard from 1967 memorialise the gamut of expressive ordinance, and enable detailed and repeating comparisons. The toolbox of values employed by Bergonzi was largely the same as those advocated by Garcia, Mozart, Donizetti, Verdi, Wagner and Puccini. It is possible that someone may yet do things "better", without simply doing them differently, but it is unlikely anyone will do so other than in accordance with the values captured by Bergonzi. The constituent elements of this particular performance on that particular night in 1967 qualify as unique for the purposes of any comparative analysis. Because Pavarotti conceded privately[19] that neither he nor Caruso, Schipa or Di Stefano – nor anyone else, in his opinion – had come close to matching the relative perfection of Bergonzi's performance in Florence (which Pavarotti knew well), it is reasonable to suppose that this single four-and-a-half-minute performance of a single aria establishes some of the core values that make tenor singing (if not all singing) an empirical science as well as an expressive art.

It is easy to avoid the candour of objectivity by amplifying difference as a socially inclusive tool for the defeating of elitism. This is, of course, where Wilde's preference for "good writing" is rendered nugatory, since what he and Joyce chose to do with the same collection of words cannot be compared, any more than can the music of Gustav Mahler be set analytically against that of Igor Stravinsky, or Andrew Wyeth's *Christina's World* (1948) brought alongside Mark Rothko's *No. 5 / No. 24* (also 1948). They are incomparable. On the other hand, it is reasonable to observe dispassionately that Bergonzi's 1967 performance of "*Una furtiva lagrima*" is finer in every respect than any recorded performance of the aria by Plácido Domingo. That is not to diminish the art and talent of Domingo; it is simply to acknowledge that the vocal tools employed by Bergonzi were more diverse, more expressive and better suited musically and dramatically to "*Una furtive lagrima*" than those available at any time in his career to Domingo. If it makes any fuming *admiratrice* feel better, Bergonzi's delusional stab at *Otello* in May, 2000, represented the triumph of optimism over age, capacity, reason and accountability.[20]

In his wildly entertaining *Homo deus*,[21] Yuval Harari argued with some force the merits of qualitative analysis – without quite establishing how apples compared with oranges:

> There is an unambiguous hierarchy of human experiences, and we shouldn't be apologetic about it. The Taj Mahal is more beautiful than a straw hut, Michelangelo's *David* is superior to my five year-old niece's latest clay figurine, and Beethoven composed far better music than Chuck Berry or the Congolese pygmies.

---

19 To the author, in London, in 1994.
20 He was able to complete only the first 2 acts of the performance at Carnegie Hall, where no less than Pavarotti, Domingo and Carreras were among the audience.
21 Harari, Yuval (2016). *Homo deus: a Brief History of Tomorrow*. Harvill Secker. pp.257–261.

Harari's denunciation of the liberal-progressive agenda fails in the incomparability of his comparators. Beethoven's Fifth would not have appeased a room of American rock and rollers in 1956, any more than *Roll Over Beethoven* would have secured the approval of the Theater am Kärntnertor in 1824. In the alternative, it would be appropriate to make value judgments as between Beethoven's Third Symphony and Anton Eberl's Symphony in E flat major – both of which were premiered at the same concert on 7 April, 1805. The *Eroica* is an infinitely better work, even if Vienna's critics concluded otherwise at the time. The hierarchy promoted by Harari does not sustain comparative analysis. Singing since the advent of recording does.

More importantly, the values memorialised in 1905, when Victor Capoul made his solitary '78s,[22] were broadly the same values as those celebrated by Bach and Handel, and from which it is possible to isolate qualities that allow for one singer to be thought (and said objectively) to be better than another. On point: Capoul was taught by Alphonse Révial,[23] whose teachers were born in the 18th century. It's a salutary thought that posterity may hear a singer, born in 1839, whose musical grandfather co-existed with Mozart.

The importance of value judgments for singing is not, perhaps, self-evident. Without critical reasoning there would be little merit in recording the same thing over and over again. It would have been possible, for example, to argue in 1939 that Francesco Merli's live recording of *Otello* from La Scala, Milan, was sufficiently remarkable to render the making of further recordings unnecessary.[24] But Merli's performance was in every detail an improvement on the previous recording, from 1931/32, with Nicola Fusati[25] in the title role, so there was good reason for Toscanini to accept NBC's invitation to record him conducting the opera with Ramón Vinay in 1947.

Opera is a living, plastic art form. Its evolution was compelled for the greatest time by shifts in compositional voice, tone and style, and later by acoustics, orchestral forces, socio-politics, technology and fashion. The eventual death of opera as a predominantly creative art form, and its transformation into something re-creative after World War II, led to recording and staging becoming the primary drivers for

---

22   Capoul was a French lyric tenor who created roles for a host of French composers during the 1860s, including Horace in the two-act version of Gounod's *La colombe* on 7 June, 1866, and Valentin in Offenbach's *Vert-Vert* on 10 March, 1869. Capoul was not the first tenor to make records, but he was almost certainly the oldest. His solitary cylinders have much to recommend them, noting as one must that he was deaf at the time of their making. His performance of "*Oh! Ne t'éveille pas encore*" from Godard's *Jocelyn* (which he premiered at La Monnaie, Brussels, on 25 February, 1888) was recorded over 4 takes by Fonotipia in Paris in 1905. Although Capoul's resources are much diminished, his performance is fascinating as a window into 19th century performance practice. See further Chapter 15 below.
23   Louis Benoît Alphonse Révial. 29 May, 1810 – 13 October, 1871. When listening to Capoul, it is well to remember that Révial won first prize in the Conservatoire de Paris singing competition in 1831 – less than 8 months after the first performance, again at the Conservatoire, of Berlioz's *Symphonie fantastique*.
24   Neither the author nor this book advocates the virtue of stereo, or sound quality more generally, as meaningful – *in and of itself*. A bad performance captured digitally will remain always a bad performance. Conversely, one can discern within (and frequently beneath) the worst of analogue technologies talents, values and qualities that transcend the fascism of lucidity. See below Emilio De Marchi.
25   1876 – 1956.

audiences, producers, singers and teachers. This turned opera into a cultural bed-post, with the names of favourite performers of established roles carved into it for archival posterity by enthusiasts and critics alike. Of course, this was true also for the pre-recorded age, when composers of instrumental music were commonly performers also, and recognised in most quarters as both. Composers of opera were reliant on singers from the outset, and many gained from standing on the coattails of celebrity. There were favoured and preferred Florestans, for example, long before Beethoven's death in 1827. Of course, the number of new operas being staged weekly in Vienna and across the German-speaking world meant that any singer tasked with studying *Fidelio* had also to learn a host of other new works to remain in business. The number of new operas being written and submitted in full score for performance until the end of the 19th century is difficult, by modern standards, to fathom. As the appetite for new work declined, and with the popularity of contemporary opera collapsing during and after the 1950s, the status of a singer became determinative. Many forget that the stars of the earliest recording age – including Caruso, Borgatti, Martinelli, Pertile *etc.* – all appeared in premieres, and numerous newly published operas. They were part of a living tradition that calcified only with the repertoire. While many will point to Domingo's striking range of work – spanning 172 roles[26] – he created only one role of significance for a leading composer, *Goya* in Menotti's 1986 opera of the same. Apart from a handful of zarzuelas and some small Spanish-language stage works, his repertoire predated him, and was well-established before he sang it.

During the 18th and 19th centuries it was common for singers to learn hundreds of works with most surviving only for a single performance. These issues are considered in greater detail in later chapters; for now, it's notable that the list of operas studied by the first three "original" Florestans[27] – Carl Demmer, Joseph August Röckel and Julius Radichi – includes many works by composers that no one outside musicology can remember. The scale of the opera business between 1700 and 1900 was industrial, with composers being expected to churn out work in ways that defy euphemism. From among those composers of opera whose names will be recognisable to the casual reader, Scarlatti composed 65 and Telemann more than 50. Handel completed 42, Cavalli 41, Paisiello 110, Salieri 37, Donizetti 75, Rossini 39, Offenbach 102 and Massenet 34. Into the 20th and 21st centuries, 15 operas were completed by Richard Strauss, 16 by Benjamin Britten, 26 by Menotti, 23 by Philip Glass and 8 by John Adams. The sole exception to the law of diminishing returns is Hans Werne Henze, who completed 40 different works of staged musical theatre (including operas) between 1948 and 2008.

For their forgotten part, Wenzel Müller composed 166, Antonio Draghi around 130, Niccolò Piccinni 124, Baldassare Galuppi 109, Rheinhard Keiser more than 100, Pietro Alessandro Guglielmi 95, André Grétry 69, Eduard Ingris 48, and Nicolas Isouard more than 45. If any of these "immortal dead" now sups with the Choir Invisible and looks upon the Earth (as apparently can happen), then one must

---

26   By way of context, Franco Corelli learned and performed almost 40 roles, singing only 27 of them more than once. He made his debut as Don José in *Carmen* (in Spoleto) in 1951, and gave his last appearance in an opera as Rodolfo in *La bohème* (at Torre del Lago) in 1976.

27   Beethoven created three different versions of his only opera, *Fidelio*.

hope that Isouard is otherwise well-occupied and "quench'd by meeting harmonies." Otherwise, he's likely to be disappointed that not one of his operas survived him. It's unclear how many were performed during Isouard's lifetime; considering its brevity (he died before his 34th birthday), his work ethic is conspicuous, even if his music appears not to be.

Everything by Isouard, as by everyone else,[28] required a team of singers, usually of skill and ability. Though a new work might fail to secure popular interest, it was routine for a performer to gain from the exposure. Thanks to the increasingly egalitarian art of performance, value judgements became common currency – requiring little or no insight into the aesthetics, skill and artistry of the composer or librettist. If audiences were not always expert in recognising the genius of a work, therefore, they were at common liberty to isolate the favourite among their singers. By the 1940s, and after the premieres of Strauss' *Capriccio* in 1942 and Britten's *Peter Grimes* in 1945, the number of new operas gaining popular recognition declined dramatically. Inertia was exacerbated by the reluctance of conductors of the first rank to engage with contemporary music – even when the majority had grown up with it. Toscanini could have worked miracles for young composers of the new school(s); aside from providing some support to Samuel Barber, however, he remained culturally atavistic to the end. His great rival, Furtwängler, was not significantly more enlightened. When he first entered into discussions with Gottfried von Einem and Herbert Graf to stage a new production of *Otello* at the 1951 Salzburger Festspiele, he was informed that "modernity" was to appear also on the programme, with a new production of *Wozzeck* by Oscar Schuh, conducted by Karl Böhm. Berg's masterpiece was still controversial, even though it was more than 25 years old in 1951, having been premiered by Erich Kleiber at the Berlin Staatsoper on 14 December, 1925 – three years into Furtwängler's appointment as music director of the city's Philharmoniker.

Furtwängler was antithetical to Berg and his music – although he conducted a good number of contemporary works between 1922 and 1933, including a performance in 1928 of Schoenberg's *Five Pieces for Orchestra* (1924).[29] Neither was he especially attuned to Italian opera. It follows that there was probably another reason

---

28 Certain readers are likely to object that not every opera requires a team of singers. For the sake of completeness, therefore, this is a working list of the exceptions to that rule (with the title followed by the composer): *A Thousand Names to Come* (Jerome P. Kitzke), *A Water Bird Talk* (Dominick Argento), *Before Breakfast* (Thomas Pasatieri), *Bon Apetit* (Lee Hoiby), *Der Langwierige Weg in die Wohnung der Natascha Ungeheuer* (Hans Werner Henze), *Diary of a Madman* (Michael White). *Egon und Emilie* (Ernst Toch), *Eight Songs for a Mad King* (Peter Maxwell Davies), *El Cimarrón* (Hans Werner Henze), *Flower and Hawk* (Carlisle Floyd), *Fugue for Two Voices* (Dinos Constantinides), *Krapp, ou La Dernière Band* (Marcel Mihalovici), *La Voix Humaine* (Poulenc), *Miss Havisham's Wedding Night* (Dominick Argento), *Perséphone* (Stravinsky), *The Harmfulness of Tobacco* (Martin Kalmanoff), *The Italian Lesson* (Lee Hoiby), *The Stronger* (Hugo Weisgall), *The Wild Boy* (Solomon Epstein), *Water Songs* (Solomon Epstein).

29 On May 17, 1933, Alban Berg wrote to his wife to describe a ceremony that had been held that day in Vienna to commemorate the centenary of Brahms' birth: "Furtwängler actually delivered the great address, which made me very depressed all day. It was a Nazi-inspired speech on German music, which, he implied, had found its last representative in Brahms. Without mentioning any names, he betrayed the whole of post-Brahmsian music, especially Mahler and the younger generation (like Hindemith). There was no reference at all to the Schoenberg circle as even existing. It was horrible having to put up with all this and witness the frenzied enthusiasm of an idiotic audience. Idiotic not to realize how the Brahms a cappella choral songs which followed made nonsense of Furtwängler's tendentious twaddle."

for his willingness to conduct *Otello* in 1951. There were actually two. The first was that Furtwängler had heard, and detested, Toscanini's lauded recording of the opera from 1947; the second was the availability of Toscanini's tenor, Ramón Vinay. When taking the impeccably loaded decision to conduct *Otello* in Salzburg, Furtwängler knew that Italian opera was an uncommon pleasure for the Salzburgers. Many reminded themselves that Bruno Walter had staged Donizetti's *Don Pasquale* at the first fully-fledged festival in 1925, and most others accepted the politics of casting Vinay in an opera that Toscanini had known since performing as a rank-and-file cellist at the premiere in 1887. Furtwängler was a petty man, however, and his loathing of Toscanini – the "bandmaster" whose defence of liberty from inside the United States[30] he despised almost as much as his conducting – was enough to legitimise the staging of *Otello* and the casting of Vinay.

For his part, Vinay was predictably humbled to be able to study the role with the two most admired conductors of the 20th century. His operatic career had begun as a baritone in Mexico, in 1938; he retrained as a tenor in 1943 and remains one of a handful of singers to have performed both Otello and Iago[31]. His was a huge voice, with perhaps too wide a *vibrato* and a declamatory quality that some considered better serving of words than music. He was a dramatist also – a genuinely inspired and absorbing physical and vocal actor, with a presence and an intelligence that distinguished his characterisation of the Moor from that of everyone else. For many, his performances remain unequalled, and proof that Iago was wrong when reassuring Cassio that "Reputation is an idle and most false imposition." Many hold Vinay's work for Toscanini in high esteem; for Furtwängler, however, he reached the apogee of what a tenor can achieve dramatically when collaborating with musicians of equivalent (or greater) mind and instinct. The differences between the approaches taken by Toscanini and Furtwängler have been much discussed and are for another book[32]. What emerges from the Salzburg recording made on 7 August, 1951, however, is another exemplar of what it is that makes the greatest tenors great, and why value judgments are vital – even when between performances by the same singer of the same role.

For Toscanini, Vinay is formidable, but not necessarily a creature of revelation. For Furtwängler, however, he mines depths of feeling and reveals vulnerabilities that transcend the sometimes rough tone and harsh placement of the voice. The apotheosis of Vinay's Otello is captured quite properly in the final scene. As he approaches the end of his life, he sings "*Niun mi tema.*"[33] These terminal moments are disclosed through "wonder" VI-IV chords – non-normative VI-IV's interpolated within a tonally-stable structure that are (in essence) parenthetical. Verdi's transition from

---

30 It's easy to forget (and many do) that Toscanini ran unsuccessfully as a Fascist parliamentary candidate in Milan in 1919.
31 Others include Carlos Guichandut – who can be heard in the title role in a 1955 radio broadcast for RAI, conducted by Franco Capuana. He had previously sung Iago opposite Del Monaco in 1950.
32 It will be obvious that the value of a performance is ultimately the sum of its parts, and not individual episodes lifted as "bleeding chunks" from the whole. However, exemplars are, by their nature, isolated – and serve an illustrative purpose that cannot otherwise be achieved through a detailed analysis of every scene and aria.
33 'Let no one fear me.'

E major to C major to E minor is amplified through striking changes in register, dynamics and, of course, sentiment – all of which are (or should be) filtered through the humanity of the tenor's performance. The searing masculinity of Vinay's reading of the phrase "*Niun mi tema s'anco armato mi vede,*"[34] warrants everyone on stage keeping a safe distance. When he sings "*Gloria,*" the VI-IV explosion establishes – as any *parola scenica*[35] should – that Otello has grasped the extent of his self-destruction and all it has cost him. There is no more tragic episode in opera, and Vinay's animal cry shreds the temple veil as well as the last vestiges of Otello's vanity and conceit. For Furtwängler, Vinay manages thereafter to suppress his vast, resonating instrument, bringing a despairing, stumbling pathos to the phrase "*E tu…come sei pallida! e stanca, e muta, e bella.*"[36] The loss of confidence and certainty is lifted briefly by his expressive leaning into the word "*bella*" – a soon-to-fade memory, echoed harmonically and instrumentally by Verdi. Vinay allows Furtwängler to take control of "*Fredda … come la casta tua vita*"[37] during which the conductor accentuates the funeral pulse in the bass-clef. The singer and conductor claw together at the audience's feelings during the lamentations "*Desdemona! Desdemona!…Ah…morta! morta! morta!*", when Vinay's tenderness yields to self-loathing, regret and genuinely Shakespearean introversion.

His final moments ("*Pria d'ucciderti…sposa…ti baicai*"[38]) unfold with a tenderness that swells with motivic reminders of the love duet from Act 1, before he delivers the words "*morendo…nell'ombra… in cui mi giacio*"[39] in near-death tones that approach the intimacy of *Sprechstimme*. The last kiss ("*un altro bacio*"[40]) is never delivered (as the score directs). The resolving D sharp is silent – even if the final syllable of "*Baccio*" is written in Boito's text; Otello is unable to deliver one more kiss, and his life is rounded in failure.[41] Furtwängler's astonishing drawing of pain and pathos from the final bars amplifies the profundity of what has occurred. Few can fail to be irritated when the Salzburger audience undoes the atmosphere by interrupting with applause what should have been absolute silence.

Vinay's talent was often overwhelming, and there were not many roles to which he could apply his voice and intelligence without causing some measure of imbalance. In his memoirs,[42] the Cassio for Furtwängler in Salzburg, Anton Dermota, described Vinay's performance as a force of nature and theatrically overwhelming. Indeed, it was in the admixture of voice and drama that Vinay isolated yet another criteria

---

34 'Let no one fear me, though I am armed.'
35 Verdi's almost single-handed creation of a realistic writing style in nineteenth-century Italian opera was reinforced through a musico-linguistic device that he called *parola scenica* [scenic word]. Its object was a musical syntax in which neither the dramatic intent of the text nor the purely musical intent overwhelms the other. For Verdi, the dramatically effective depiction of a particular feature of experience (a realist theatrical notion) is more important than the mimetic description of the words in musical terms – a romantic theatrical notion apostrophised by *opera seria*.
36 'And thou... how pale thou art! And weary, and mute, and beautiful.'
37 'Cold, even like thy chastity.'
38 'Before I killed thee, wife, I kissed thee thus.'
39 'Now dying ... in the shadow where I lie.'
40 'Another kiss.'
41 Readers may wish to compare Vinay's approach with that of Mario Del Monaco, who never missed an opportunity to sing the final note, and then commonly at forte.
42 Dermota, Anton (1978). *Tausendundein Abend*. Paul Neff Verlag.

for evaluation, namely that not every tenor makes (or needs to concern himself with making) a beautiful noise. This does not equate to a comparison between Del Monaco and Vinay because Del Monaco was capable of singing beautifully, at least in his youth. He chose a different path, one that worked only sporadically. For the curious, Del Monaco's 1954 studio recording for Decca of *Rigoletto* is significantly more deformed than the Jester, and his performance of "*Bella figlia dell'amore*,"[43] in particular, exemplifies the lunacy of having someone perform a role for which they are unsuited musically and by *fach*. Del Monaco could inspire frenzy, but he could not seduce. Being that he was unable to manufacture a genuine *legato*, sufficient to work with (rather than against) the composer, he was by nature stentorian – which is little more than a short-cut to the theatrically dramatic.

For his part, Vinay recognised the difficulty presented by the operation of such a huge voice, and the prospect of him singing anything for the sake of it is almost comical, comparable perhaps to having Rachmaninov accompany an evening of violin works by Paganini and Wieniawski. Vinay's priorities were Wagner's – who wanted to hear a singer speak through music so as to relate audiences in human terms to the often inhuman and sometimes supernatural events on stage. It is well-known that Vinay was coached by Furtwängler – with whom he shared much by instinct. Thanks to the conductor's studied concern for the principle of *parola scenica*, a priority that held word and music in equivalence, the expressive use by Vinay of his voice *on the breath* is often too much to bear. Of course, Vinay was able to rely on more voice and more breath than most; even accounting for these natural advantages his Otello amplifies the capacity of a singer of genius to bring more to a performance than mere song and tone. What Vinay was able to do for Furtwängler raised the craft of tenor singing to something that the conductor considered determinative of the purpose of art – a philosophical dialogue of epiphany that negated the 'superb sterility' of Wildean decay.

Singing is also an art form, in which respect Vinay's achievements for Furtwängler in 1951, and on many other occasions, were tailored to the needs of a dramatic, through-composed opera in Italian from 1887, based on an English play from 1603. The needs, interests and enthusiasms of a stadium audience of 18,000 people under the age of 40 in 1981 were very different. A production of *Otello* would not, for example, have succeeded at the Montreal Forum[44] (and certainly not without amplification), whereas Queen almost brought the roof down when performing what many consider to be their finest (recorded) show. Opera and art music more generally are best experienced in a natural acoustic. One of the thrills of hearing any great voice live and in person is that the singer is able to communicate intimately with his or her audience within a vibrating, resonating cocoon – a space that allows for the fermenting of prejudice. Proximity within a theatre to the power and beauty of the human voice without electronic assistance allows for a levelling of expectation

---

43 'Beautiful daughter of love'.
44 The Montreal Forum was an indoor arena that served as the home of the National Hockey League's Montreal Maroons from 1924 to 1938 and the Montreal Canadiens from 1926 to 1996. The Forum was built by the Canadian Arena Company in just 159 days – and remained a major venue until it was turned into a multiplex cinema. Such is progress.

without which it is impossible to judge how one singer compares with another in the same (or a similar) building.

The value judgments on which this book relies do not presume normative comparisons, therefore, as between the incomparable. That doesn't mean that analysis is not always, and to an often uncomfortable degree, a hierarchical process. The identification of difference is probative of nothing if readers are compelled to isolate and develop their own views without reaching beyond the confines of taste. The distance between taste and discretion is consequential. The former is legitimate in all circumstances and without qualification; the latter compels the identification of evaluative points of reference to which everyone can be subjected equally. It sounds worse than it is, but it is inquisitorially fundamental to understanding the evolution of the tenor voice. In other words, there is no comparing the work of Mario Del Monaco, Carlo Bergonzi and Ramón Vinay unless there is something to compare, whether as between or as against entirely dissimilar voices. Bergonzi and Del Monaco were not equipped (or inclined[45]) to sing German opera, for example, while Vinay was paradigmatically unsuited to Mozart, comparing any of them to Fritz Wunderlich can reveal nothing of value. Outside the opera house and the concert hall, the placing of a voice within a natural acoustic – devoid of amplification – is a different matter entirely.

The author was present, for example, at the Royal Albert Hall on 5 June, 2012, for an "East meets West" classical music gala, with performances by Lang Lang, the Chinese soprano Song Zuying and Andrea Bocelli (supported by the Philharmonia). During rehearsals, when Bocelli was fully amplified, there was an issue with his microphone, and during a full-voice section of "*Di Quella Pira*", from *Il Trovatore*, he was left to sing with the orchestra unaided.[46] He was rendered instantly inaudible. When Franco Corelli and Renata Tebaldi appeared together at the same venue (without amplification) on 9 October, 1973, one of the routine criticisms was that the soloists had been "too loud". The issue is not, of course, whether amplitude is a metric, in and of itself, when a singer is able to meet the expectations musically and theatrically of the work being performed. Bocelli did not, and cannot, sing Manrico's *cabaletta* with anything like the energy, resonance or *squillo* (a bright, trumpet-like tone[47]) compelled by a scene in which the character is informed that his mother is

---

45 It is accepted that Del Monaco sang, on rare occasions, a small number of bleeding Wagnerian chunks in concert, and he is said also to have considered accepting Wieland Wagner's invitation to perform at Bayreuth. For rubber-neckers, there is an exotically terrible performance on film on a concert from 1969 of Del Monaco performing Siegmund's Act I soliloquy from *Die Walküre*, in which he calls out his father's name "*Wälse! Wälse!*". The meter is common, but the tempo (marked "mässig langsam" [moderately slow]), is anything but moderate. The first time around, the first syllable of "*Wälse*" is pitched as a minim G-flat. Del Monaco holds this for 11 seconds. The second cry is the same, but the pitches are a semi-tone higher, *i.e.*, G natural. He holds this for 14 seconds. It is true that Wagner added, somewhat recklessly, a *fermata* over the long note of each bar, but Del Monaco's abuse of the composer's generosity makes absolutely no sense whatsoever – noting, of course, that others have abused the scene almost as senselessly. This is all a matter for taste, even if Del Monaco's German is not.

46 To compound matters, the author's then 12 year-old son was tasked with presenting Bocelli with flowers at the end of the concert (and can be seen doing so on a DVD of the event). He presented the bouquet at belt-height and more forcefully than was, perhaps, necessary.

47 From the Italian verb squillare, meaning "to ring" or "to blare."

shortly to burn at the stake. An amplifier and speakers made no difference, even if they enabled the voice to be heard.

It follows that cutting the voice to the cloth is a key factor – which gets us back to Queen in Montreal. Most would agree that Freddie Mercury was the greatest pop singer of his generation. For many, he stands alone, and the band's performance as it was experienced and recorded on 24th and 25th November, 1981, remains definitive. Montreal was chosen as the location for filming and recording because the audience was said to be louder than in the United States.[48] The band played the same set on both nights, which included many of Queen's best-known hits, as well as a few that had fallen (to an extent) under the radar, notably "Keep Yourself Alive," which receives a performance of blistering theatrical intensity. Mercury's commitment (like that of each of his colleagues) is jaw-dropping in its energy, character, and exhibitionism. There is an overt joy to the concert, with Mercury excelling vocally throughout. It's all genuinely amazing; as an exemplar, "Somebody To Love" stands out.

Written by Mercury when fixating on Aretha Franklin and gospel music, the song was first heard on the 1976 album *A Day At The Races*. The studio version lasts a little over five minutes; the version from Montreal is around seven minutes (six, if one discounts Mercury's improvised pre-amble). Both are in A flat, which means that Mercury is charged with hitting a series of sustained B flat 4s throughout the song, as well as one 9-second melisma forming around a belted A flat during the pre-amble that gives a clear (and unencumbered) impression of the singer's exceptional technical skill and vocal confidence. There is no disputing that this is the highest of theatre, and positively ripe. Notwithstanding the absence of classical finesse, Mercury's tone is unfailingly expressive and emotionally engaging. Even if one looks away – which is never easy to do – the dramatic impulse is tied throughout to his use of the song's words, which he delivers with vitality and expressive articulation. The opening verse and chorus are hypnotically fluid, with Mercury employing substantial *rubato* to achieve an illusory sense of freedom – illusory because Mercury's discipline as a performer is absolute and totemic. The ease of the voice in the bridge – and the common absence of an audible *passaggio* – is unaffected by his dodging of some exposed B flat 4s, because his word-use is sufficiently creative to veer successfully into caricature. After Brian May's perfunctory solo, Mercury's performance of the third verse – with its cultivated use of *vibrato*, declamation and improvisation – ends with an easy but flamboyant high B flat 4. The singer's talent, and the absence of effort that characterise his singing – here and generally – free him to engage with his bandmates as well as the audience of 18,000 during a subdued *ostinato* of "find me somebody to love" that concludes with a transfixing slide from an F sharp to yet another melismatic A flat. During the final repetitions of "find me…" Mercury hits without strain a *falsetto* A flat 5 – G 5 – A flat 5, after which he riffs over Roger Taylor's impressive vocals while hammering out his piano part.

---

48 Which proved to be ironic because the audio was given a dry-mix in production, to give a sense that the band was in the room with the viewer, rather than performing in concert. Audience volume levels were reduced also, which contributed to the misleading impression that the crowd had been bored and unresponsive. Also, "louder" turned out to be less important than "cheaper."

The wonder of this performance is that it is easy to imagine it working naturally, without the need for any backing or support at all. The song is certainly good enough to survive its reduction to a solitary voice with piano, and Mercury's singing – though rough-hewn by classical standards – conveys so much personality that its power resides in the artist's musically-expressed charisma as well as his technical fluency. In this sense, while the song is most definitely *not* its singer (since it has been covered by many others), the singer is here intrinsic to (and probably indivisible from) the success of the song. That has not always been the case, as admirers of Jeff Buckley's recording of Leonard Cohen's "Hallelujah" will testify. It follows, regardless, that Mercury in Montreal succeeds as a singer, first and foremost – and in so doing negates (or, at the very least, diffuses) his status as a composer. Much the same was said by those who heard Beethoven and Paganini play their own works.

While the once-in-a-lifetime talent of Freddie Mercury warrants comparison with no one else, what he brought to his performances by criteria can be applied to the value judgments of anyone seeking to find a voice in a culture where the only certainty is saturation. Each of those identified here by analysis – spanning Vinay's debut in 1938 and Queen's final performance with Freddie Mercury at Knebworth in 1986 – represent variously novel, ugly, beautiful and spellbinding manifestations of tenor singing, as a function of performance. It is not a construction of ease and energy, or *legato* and declamation, or the use of *portamento* and articulation, or breathing and placement, or phrasing and expression, or dynamics and amplitude – or, even, of beauty and sterility. Those archetypes matter, of course, because they are the parts that make up the whole, but the art of tenor singing resides more profoundly in the service of a singer to the genius of a composer, though they may be one and the same. It follows that even when an artist approximates the sublime, one should never be allowed to forget that a singer without a songwriter is the sound of silence.

CHAPTER ONE

Boys and Wenches

The marriage of Aelia Eudoxia to the Roman Emperor Arcadius is said to have been engineered by a court official called Eutropius, whose reputation as a catamite, pimp and body-servant to various Roman soldiers and nobles preceded his elevation to the imperial palace. Eutropius was a European eunuch, and castrated only[1] – as distinct from many far-and middle-eastern eunuchs who endured the triple-whammy of having their penis as well as their testicles removed before puberty. Eunuchs were much valued as high-level political appointees because their inability to have children extinguished any risk of unwelcome dynasties. In most cases, the castration of a child was conducted or authorised by a parent, for whom the prospective wealth and station of a mutilated son held more promise than the uncertain prospect of grandchildren.[2]

Eutropius had come to the attention of the Empress because of what Zosimus,[3] writing almost a century after her death, characterised with Commodusian licence as her "abnormally wilful" desires. Eutropius was not alone in satisfying Eudoxia, whose appetites kept a palace of eunuchs in gainful occupation. Moreover, her interests extended wider than sex. According to Zosimus, the Empress was keen on music, and Eutropius was no singer. She retained instead another eunuch, Brison, as her music-master. Brison is believed to have initiated the use of *castrati* in Byzantine choirs, and within thirty years of the death of Eutropius in AD 399 (and coincident to the Council of Ephesus in AD 431) *castrati* were a common feature of church life for many Christians throughout Europe and the middle east.

With the vestiges of Roman excess colliding with political and ecclesiastical modernity, eunuchs were indulged for private physical pleasure and public veneration. Eudoxia was ostentatiously devout; she provided patronage at great personal cost to numerous Church-led communities, donating gold, and lavish silver crosses with candles to the Nicene bishops. She also made available the services of Brison as choir-master, consequent to which appointment eunuchs became a popular feature of services at the Hagia Sophia. Brison's influence was long-lasting, with *castrati* remaining a feature of liturgical practice until the Fourth Crusade in 1204. North of Rome,[4] the

---

1   In medical terminology, "primary hypergonadism."
2   This vaunted status evolved during the 18th and 19th centuries in Europe, and particularly Italy – where a *castrato* was admirable in public life as a singer first and last. By law and custom, men castrated as children were prohibited from taking Church orders or serving in government and the military. They were "geldings, eunuchs, capons … nature's rejects, nullities of known creation." See Münch, Paul. "Homines tertii generis: Gesangskastraten in der Kulturgeschichte Europas." *Essener Unikate* 14 / 2000. p. 58–67.
3   Zosimus. *The Decline of Rome*. (1967). Trinity University Press. p.18.
4   Until the 17th century, when Naples became the city of choice for castration. However, as Charles Burney discovered, when in Naples the locals blamed Rome, the Romans blamed Florence, the Florentines

castration of boys for musical practice remained exotic and much criticised until the middle to late 16th century, when singers were identified as *soprano maschio*[5] and "*cantoretti.*"[6] The first named *castrati* to be admitted to the Cappella Musicale Pontificia Sistina,[7] in 1599, were Pietro Paolo Folignato and Girolamo Rossini.

The most reasonable question to be asked of (and probably by) all *castrati* was why? The trite answer is that religious practice required it. Matthew 19:12, 28–29 holds that

> there are some eunuchs, which were so born from their mother's womb: and there are some eunuchs, which were made eunuchs of men: and there be eunuchs, which have made themselves eunuchs for the kingdom of heaven's sake. He that is able to receive it, let him receive it.

Quite what the kingdom of heaven had to gain from so costly a gift is unclear; indeed, the majority of catholic priests were allowed to marry and have children until the First Lateran Council in 1123. On the basis that castration was a step too far even for the pious, Paul resolved the issue of women and Christianity by banning them from being heard in churches through the dictum '*mulieres in ecclesiis taceant.*'[8] This questionably Christian injunction compelled adaptation from within the Vatican. Rather than allowing girls or women to sing, however, it was determined that castrating a boy before the age of 11 or 12 was a preferable alternative.[9] In 1589, Pope Sixtus V's *Cum pro nostro pastorali munere* re-formulated the choir of St Peter's to include *castrati*, who replaced both boys and falsettists as the treble line in a standard SATB choir of voices. By 1600, the correlation between castration and singing ability was ubiquitous, if not always justifiably so. Indeed, it was not uncommon for the apparent musicality and vocal talent of a child to disappear with maturity. It is hard to imagine the resentment that such practices caused for an unmusical boy – particularly when he was left knowing that his image would die with him. Shakespeare indulged the stereotype (as well as his love of clanging puns) in *Antony and Cleopatra*, when Cleopatra summons her eunuch Mardian[10]:

---

blamed Milan, and the Milanese blamed Venice. (see generally Clapton, Nicholas (2008). *Moreschi and the Voice of the Castrato*. Haus Books.
5   'Male soprano.'
6   'Little singers.'
7   Sistine Chapel Choir.
8   'Let women keep silent in the churches.' Taken from I Corinthians, 14:34, which provides "Let your women keep silence in the churches: for it is not permitted unto them to speak; but they are commanded to be under obedience, as also saith the law." It falls, of course, to wonder whether the possessive use of 'your' leaves the status of 'all' women (and any woman not falling subject to a man's title) ambiguous. That was not a question for wonder, of course, at least for the majority. Progress, such as it is, has remained painfully slow. In August, 2016, Pope Francis formed the Pontifical Commission for the Study of the Diaconate of Women in the early church. The Commission included twelve "scholars" under the presidency of Cardinal Luis Ladaria Ferrer. In January, 2019, the Commission announced that a report had been submitted to Pope Francis. On 20 June, 2018, Francis announced that there was no conclusive decision, but that he was not averse to ongoing studies. Which was nice.
9   It was often done much earlier, between the ages of 5 and 8.
10 Act I, Scene V.

Mardian
What's your highness' pleasure?

Cleopatra
Not now to hear thee sing; I take no pleasure
In aught an eunuch has: 'tis well for thee,
That, being unseminar'd, thy freer thoughts
May not fly forth of Egypt. Hast thou affections?

Mardian
Yes, gracious madam.

Cleopatra
Indeed!

Mardian
Not in deed, madam; for I can do nothing[11]
But what indeed is honest to be done:
Yet have I fierce affections, and think
What Venus did with Mars.

The practice of castration did not become a significant feature of European cultural life until the first half of the 17th century, when Italian opera made a virtue of the peculiar characteristics of the male soprano. The sound produced was an opiate for the cognescenti, and then for more than 300 years. The reason for their high status is simple enough: an undeveloped larynx left a boy's vocal chords abnormally close to the resonating chambers, which created an often huge sound that was coincidentally revered as sublime, voluptuous and eternally strange. So much so, that the most successful *primo uomi* – notably Carlo Broschi ("Farinelli") and Francesco Bernardi ("Senesino") – were among the wealthiest, most celebrated men of Europe. Accepting that the promise of fame and money was no less great at that time than it is now, posterity still wonders at the follies of greed and ambition that compelled parents to drag their sons to an encounter for which they were wholly unprepared. The "operation," such as it was, entailed the enforced submersion of a boy into a bath of water or milk, while a stranger used a far from surgical knife to remove his testicles, leaving a wound which had to be cauterised by the application of a hot iron so as to avoid the risk of exsanguination and death. Many died, regardless. Those who survived were

---

11   Shakespeare was ill-informed, or uncharacteristically unimaginative. There is *much* a eunuch could do, and then for some considerable time – should he have been so inclined. Moreover, and in practical terms, because of the absent fear of ejaculation and orgasm, *castrati* were in high demand – throughout their careers as singers, and after retirement – as prostitutes. In certain cases, *castrati* earned far more as gigolos than they did as singers. Some have suggested that the prowess of *castrati* was a myth, and that without the requisite hormones, sex was an uncertain business. What is certain is that their appeal as sex toys and objects expired with their celebrity. *Castrati* aged badly. Most became very fat and many were unable to perform even sedentary activities.

fortunate to have access to opium; others had the blood flow to their brains reduced by strangulation.[12] *Visi d'arte* indeed.

The taste for Italian opera travelled widely, with regional churches operating as breeding grounds for darkly aspirational parents – famously so in Naples, where approximately 4,000 boys were castrated annually during the 18th century. One contemporary recorded that[13]

> Most castratos come from the Neapolitan factory, where poverty and the unfortunate lure of profit makes people cruel enough to mutilate children in this way.

Barbers advertised their services without ambiguity: "Boys castrated cheap here." Talent was frequently not its own reward. As a young chorister, for example, the exceptionally musical Joseph Haydn only narrowly escaped being left childless against his will; as it transpired, he lived childless by choice.[14] It is well known that *castrati* were able to develop audible advantages over female singers in volume, breath control[15] and *fioriture* – a word that translates as "blooms" but which in real terms meant "showing off." For musicians, then and now, it identifies the art of ornamentation. A well-trained *castrato* was subjected to at least a decade of brutally enforced study – commencing at around 14 years of age. The primary goals were the sustaining of lines of uninterrupted song for vast spans while engaging in runs, trills, leaps and roulades that transformed singers into superstars that provoked royalty and clergy alike to engage in the deeply insensitive extolment "*Evviva il coltellino!*".[16]

While vocal brilliance became a *raison d'etre* for composers of opera, with floridity emerging as the lodestone value for singers and audiences alike, the ecclesiastical polyphonic tradition evolved with relative modesty. Range was important; tone, expression and phrasing were prioritised – particularly for the Vatican's music masters. In 1638, a member of the *Sistine Capella* (Sistine Chapel Choir), Gregorio Allegri, composed his *Miserere*, a setting of Psalm 51. It was almost immediately the object of rigid Papal strictures, with only two performances allowed annually during Holy Week. Anyone publishing, transcribing or performing the work outside the Vatican was subject to excommunication. Three official copies were made (for the Holy Roman Emperor,[17] the King of Portugal, and the music theoretician Padre Martini[18]), but these were simplified reductions, bastardised to the point of abstraction. The 14-year-old Mozart took it upon himself to do a better job after visiting

---

12 Strangulation was known to interfere with the normal flow of oxygen to the brain. It is now established medically that compression of the carotid arteries and / or jugular veins causes cerebral *ischemia*.
13 Volkmann, Johann Jacob. (1771). *Historisch-kritische Nachrichten von Italien*. C. Fritsch.
14 His marriage was without issue, and he never acknowledged his illegitimate child, Antonio (1783–1855), from his long-running affair with the singer Luigia Polzelli.
15 So flamboyant was the art and skill of improvised ornamentation that competitions were held between singers and instrumentalists to see who could release the greatest number of fireworks without needing to breathe. The singer usually won.
16 'Long live the little knife!'
17 Who kept it in the Imperial Library in Vienna.
18 1706–1784.

the Sistine Chapel on 11 April, 1770 (Holy Wednesday). He heard the *Miserere* just once, in the company of his father, Leopold. Having asked to see the music; he was irritated to learn that it was unavailable for viewing, Mozart returned to his rooms and transcribed the 14-minute score, written for two choirs of five and four voices; he did so from memory.[19] On Holy Friday Mozart returned to check the accuracy of his transcription.[20] Leopold wrote the following day to his wife:[21]

> You have often heard of the famous *Miserere* in Rome, which is so greatly prized that the performers are forbidden on pain of excommunication to take away a single part of it, copy it or to give it to anyone. But we have it already. Wolfgang has written it down and we would have sent it to Salzburg in this letter, if it were not necessary for us to be there to perform it. But the manner of performance contributes more to its effect than the composition itself. Moreover, as it is one of the secrets of Rome, we do not wish to let it fall into other hands….

Leopold's reference to the "manner of performance" is intriguing. The Choir of the Sistine Chapel was populated entirely by male sopranos, whereas the Mozarts' experience in German-speaking territories was of hearing boys and women[22]. The sound and style of the *castrati* was noteworthy, therefore, and it remained so until the 20th century, when the "last *castrato*," Alessandro Moreschi,[23] took part in two sets of recording sessions for the Gramophone & Typewriter Company. The first were produced by brothers Will and Fred Gaisberg on 3rd and 5th of April, 1902. Seventeen usable sides of performances by members of the Sistine Chapel Choir were captured on wax, four of them solos by Moreschi. A recording was also made of a blessing by Pope Leo XIII – head of the Catholic Church from 1878 until his death in 1903.[24] Leo XIII was born Vincenzo Gioacchino Raffaele Luigi Pecci in 1810 – a year before Liszt, and two years before Dickens.

---

19 The following year, he presented his transcription to the historian Charles Burney, who published it in London in 1771 – forcing the Vatican to lift its (now pointless) proscription.
20 In 1831, Mendelssohn completed his own transcription – based on a performance sung a fourth higher than originally intended. This wouldn't have mattered had it not been for the first edition of *Grove's Dictionary of Music and Musicians* in 1880. The first editors used a small section of Mendelssohn's version of the *Miserere* to illustrate the article on Allegri. This was reproduced over many decades and became the accepted version – even though it is *not* the version composed by Allegri and heard by Mozart. As a result, the work's most famous passages – crowned by soaring high Cs - was meant to be a fourth *lower*.
21 Anna Maria.
22 Mozart later wrote several major *castrato* roles in his operas. He even paid tribute to his friend Vincenzo dal Prato in iambic tetrameter: "mio molto amato *castrato* dal Prato."
23 11 November, 1858 – 21 April, 1922. It is believed Moreschi suffered castration as a "cure for a hernia" when he was 12 (in 1870). He joined the Sistine Chapel Choir in the 1870s as First Soprano, having auditioned in front of an entire gathering of every sitting member. Moreschi remained First Soprano until his position was rendered obsolete 30 years later by Pope Innocent XI.
24 2 March, 1810 – 20 July, 1903. He was the oldest Pope (reigning until the age of 93), and had the third-longest confirmed pontificate, behind those of Pius IX (his immediate predecessor) and John Paul II. Leo XIII was also the first Pope to be filmed by a motion picture camera – by W. K. Dickson, whose camera received the Papal blessing during filming.

The second set of recordings was produced, again in Rome, in April, 1904, under the direction of W. Sinkler Darby – a year after the newly ascended Pius X effectively banned *castrati* from the Vatican.[25] The Papal prohibition against a once-revered cultural tradition was not universally welcomed, even though castration had been banned in Italy in 1870. The Vatican's preservation of children against an act that was otherwise sanctioned by the New Testament as meaningful for the "kingdom of heaven" *per ardua*, mattered less to audiences and critics alike than that the highest of the male voices was no longer *ad astra*. This conflicting cultural metric – wherein the mutilation of a child was a cost worth paying – might seem at odds with a contemporary musical culture then defined by the likes of Richard Strauss, Stravinsky, Puccini, Elgar, Nielsen, Ravel, Debussy, Mahler and Schoenberg. It is equally true, however, that Pius X's belated altruism predated Britain's Children's Act by almost six years.[26]

The director of the Sistine Chapel Choir in 1903 was Domenico Mustafà,[27] who had himself been castrated as a child by the "bite of a wild pig."[28] His voice was extremely powerful and he was celebrated for his mastery of the *virtuoso* tradition in which he had been tutored by men whose musical grand-parents had heard Farinelli and Senesino. His vocal range extended at least 2 octaves, from C4 to C6, which gave him the necessary tools for a distinguished career on the stage before his appointment in 1860 by Leo XIII as Director of the Sistine Choir. Mustafà's reputation – and the surviving value of *castrati* as a cultural norm – was sufficient for Wagner to consider casting him as Klingsor for the premiere of *Parsifal* in 1882. When it was pointed out that the emasculated Klingsor was not a castrato, but rather a eunuch castrated after puberty, Wagner reverted to his first choice – the fully intact Karl Hill.[29]

Mustafà's leading soloist, Moreschi, had been a pupil of Gaetano Capocci,[30] maestro di cappella of the Papal basilica of at the Scuola di San Salvatore in Lauro. In 1883, Capocci cast Moreschi as the Seraph for the Italian premiere of Beethoven's *Christus am Ölberge* – bringing him instant celebrity. The master thereafter toured his protégé through the salons of Roman high society, for whom (in addition to gender-fluid material like Tosti's *Ideale* and the Bach-Gounod *Ave Maria* that he recorded for the Gaisbergs) he performed soprano arias from popular operas, including the "Jewel Song" from *Faust*. Quite what Roman society made of the corpulent

---

25 "Effectively" only since the 1903 *motu proprio* doesn't prohibit *castrati*; rather, it provides that "*the high voices of the sopranos and contraltos [...] must be taken by boys*".
26 This delinquent legislation provided finally for the (1) prevention of cruelty to children, the (2) protection of infant life, (3) the assurance of justice for child offenders and (4) the constitutional reform of schooling.
27 16 April, 1829 – 17 March, 1912.
28 It is alarming to note how many genital-mutilating pigs were allowed to roam Italy during the 17th, 18th and 19th centuries. It is of passing relevance that there are almost no records of girls being attacked in similar circumstances. In addition to aggressive pigs, many records noted children being kicked, bitten, born deformed and subject to curatives for colds, disease and a host of other recorded reasons – none of which included "monstrous parents."
29 9 May, 1831 – 12 January, 1893. Also, the first Alberich for *Der Ring des Nibelungen* in 1876.
30 Gaetano Capocci (16 October, 1811 – 11 January, 1898). He was a pupil of Valentino Fioravanti (11 September, 1764 – 16 June, 1837), a celebrated Italian composer of *opera buffas*.

Moreschi singing "*Ah! je ris de me voir, si belle en ce miroir*"[31] is anyone's guess. He was a popular performer, regardless, and more than a match for Gounod's trills and arpeggiation. Although the aria's reach above the stave is commonly no higher than an A4 – with a concluding B4 – the music sits high on the voice and requires considerable agility and lightness of touch. Many have tried to discount Moreschi's recordings because they are bizarre and alien for modern ears; his celebrity outside the Vatican cannot be ignored, however. The ecstatic and spontaneous appreciation of the crowd attending the recording of *Ideale* is consistent with the sort of reaction for which Caruso's appearances became typical. Three years earlier he was invited by the royal family to sing at the funeral of the recently assassinated Umberto I.[32]

For his recording on 11 April, 1904, of the "*Oremus pro pontifice*" by Emilio Calzanera – and noting that he was the only one of the Vatican's six surviving *castrati* to sail the high Cs of Allegri's *Miserere* – Moreschi was joined by the full Choir. The projection of Moreschi's voice in its middle-aged fullness is as mesmerising as the imprecision of the Choir is horrifying. The differences between what would now be considered an *echt* performance of Mozart's *Ave Verum Corpus* and the manner of the Sistine Chapel Choir in the early 20th century are such that the listener is compelled to draw unkind conclusions from what the finest choir in Italy sounded like less than two years after the premiere of *Tosca* in Rome – an opera in which the first Act ends at the Sant'Andrea della Valle, just four kilometres from the Vatican.[33] For a start, the pitching is constantly variable – even accepting the confines of the recording technology – and the respect for bar-lines and ensemble is casual, at best. The striking use of *portamento*, with prominent slides up as well as down, transcends any concern for crispness of word form or placement, and it might be assumed either that the conductor was incompetent or there was no conductor at all. More probably, it wasn't a priority. Indeed, what emerges from this flamboyantly expressive performance is that accuracy and exactitude – the *imprimaturs* of precision as they would be advocated today – were absent considerations. The *ritardando* with which the performance ends was designed to provoke an emotional response; the reliance on what would now be deemed "late romantic" effects draws the attention of the listener to the meaning of the words and the sentiments to which they are making graphic reference:

> Hail, true body, Born of the virgin Mary; Who has truly suffered, slaughtered On the Cross for humanity. Whose side was pierced, Pouring out water and blood. Be a foretaste for us During our ordeal of death.

It would be reasonable for a choir formed of adults to appreciate the seriousness and import of such things for a community immersed in the perception of Christianity as a religion of *pathos* and, lest it go unsaid, compassion. Most modern performances by professionals (whether boys or women) will celebrate the primacy

---

31 'Ah! I laugh to see myself, so beautiful in this mirror.' The aria also contains the potentially awkward lines, for Moreschi as Margherite: "*Est-ce toi, Marguerite, est-ce toi?*" ['Is it you, Marguerite, is it you?']. "*Non! Non! ce n'est plus toi!*" ['No! No! It's no longer you!'].
32 Ravens, Simon (2014). *The Supernatural Voice: A History of High Male Singing*. Boydell Press. p.187.
33 In the Piazza Vidoni, 6 at the politically meaningful intersection of Corso Vittorio Emanuele and Corso Rinascimento.

of clarity and *logos*. It is the difference comparatively between Fernando de Lucia and Benjamin Bernheim. Certainly, when listening to the recordings made by the Sistine Choir for the Gaisbergs, the work of the *Tallis Scholars* speaks of traditions that appear not to have existed before Peter Phillips first revealed them.

Modern prejudices are more problematic still for anyone listening to Moreschi as a soloist.[34] It is inarguably a most unusual sound, and yet his singing is effortless in its placement and the high B4 at the end of *Ave Maria* suggests that he reached a C5, and higher still, without effort. His *evirato* colleagues could no longer do so, apparently – from which it follows that *castrati* did not *automatically* float above the stave, as many presume, or at least not simply because they were "*unseminar'd*."[35] Range and dexterity were trained qualities – even for someone like Moreschi whose speaking voice was (un)naturally high and steely. The sung tone is fluid, and in certain phrases Moreschi's instrument has the purity of a boy soprano with the greater lung power of a man. The sound is otherwise rich, with negligible *passaggio*. For most, any consideration of his recordings is determined entirely by mutations of style, which are sufficiently bizarre to render everything alien – at least on its surface. He is at all times plangent – lachrymose, even – and this characteristic cannot be dismissed as a product of the repertoire because Moreschi sings Tosti's *Ideale* with the same weight of melancholy as he does Mozart's motet. The mournfulness of the lines are further amplified by an histrionic vocal "glot" or "hiccup" for which his singing is archivally unique. It is this feature of Moreschi's art from which the majority recoil.

The dated aesthetic has been misinterpreted as a technical weakness or a symptom of an aging voice; in fact, his glot employed grace notes with purpose, from as much as a tenth below the target note, as a long-standing technique for drawing on the acoustics of the Sistine Chapel. On the other hand, Fred Gaisberg was clear that the horn he was using to record Moreschi took no account of the resonance of the Chapel because the recordings were made in a "salone of the Palace of the Bishop of Rome."[36] Either way, there is no consensus on whether Moreschi's glot was a 19th century corruption of an 18th century *acciaciatura*[37] or simply an accepted mannerism unique to (and co-terminous with) Moreschi.[38]

What is certain is that he was widely admired and because no one else since the invention of recording employed the same weight of glot, and so routinely, it's reasonable to conclude that this was either a tradition common to *castrati* (for which there is no evidence) or Moreschi was indulging an accepted vocal practice that valued exaggerated expressive mannerisms above the "pure" virtue of a seamless *legato*. Indeed, Moreschi's "hiccup" is merely an extreme version of the aspirated consonant

---

34   The performances can all be heard, in a variety of transfers on Youtube.
35   Defined, by reference to *Antony and Cleopatra*, in the *Supplement to Dr. Johnson's Dictionary of the English Language* as "to make barren".
36   Gaisberg, Fred (2010). *The Fred Gaisberg Diaries, Part 1: USA & Europe (1898–1902)*. Ed. Hugo Strötbaum. Unpublished. Available at https://www.yumpu.com/en/document/read/4620641/the-fred-gaisberg-diaries-part-1-recording-pioneers. Gaisberg recorded in his memoirs how he and his team set fire to the building, causing "all the singers [to rush out] panic stricken". pp.112–113.
37   The placement of a note a semi-tone or whole tone above or below the principal note being sung.
38   Again, and significantly, Moreschi had only ever heard himself, and anyone else, sing live – and without the "benefit" of recording.

for which the singing of Beniamino "Gi-hi-li" is remembered, and not always affectionately. The propensity for whining and sobbing was, in fact, common, if not ubiquitous, at the turn of the 20th century.

Less than a week after his recording sessions at the Vatican, Fred Gaisberg travelled by train to Milan, where he recorded ten arias with the entirely modern 29-year-old Enrico Caruso at the Grand Hotel, paying the vast sum of £100 for the privilege.[39] The first surviving disc, cut on 11 April, 1902, was of "*Ah vieni qui… No, non chiuder gli occhi*" from Franchetti's *Germania*, for which Caruso had created the role of Federico Loewe in Milan a few weeks earlier, with Toscanini conducting. When comparing the singing of Caruso to that of Moreschi there is, on the face of it, no common ground; Caruso abjures the vocal emoticons employed by Moreschi – and Gigli, Lauri-Volpi, Masini, etc. – but they are singing within the same tradition, albeit one that Caruso reinvented just days after Moreschi admitted the *castrato* to Gaisberg's wax museum. There is much to compare between those aspiritic tenors who co-existed with Caruso and Moreschi while acknowledging that what are now considered to be aberrant habits were the height of fashion in 1902 – a fashion that Caruso was instrumental in eradicating. Whether or not Moreschi was typical of all *castrati* over three hundred years of evolving practice is less an issue, therefore, than whether audiences in Milan and Rome in 1902 heard Moreschi with the same ears and equivalent expectations. As much would certainly support the universal fanaticism inspired by Caruso from the first because he was entirely novel for an age raised on singing that was not always beautiful and in many cases downright ugly. As will be seen, beauty (as an evolving construct) did not become the singular metric for singing, as it is today, until Caruso re-calibrated expectations. One need not compare Caruso's recordings to those made by Tamagno or any other of the tenor voices known to Verdi and Puccini to appreciate that beauty was not the most important quality for a singer tasked with meeting the dual demands of *verismo* and the modern orchestra. As much is certain from the recordings made by Fernando de Lucia and Caruso.

It was no different for the *castrati*, for whom beauty was not (in and of itself) a reductive value, certainly when accounting for the primacy of virtuosity and the effect of gender-fluidity for audiences more attuned to sexual ambiguity than our own liberal age. The "beautiful" singing of the male soprano Franco Fagioli, for example, is breath-taking, but he is a male counter-tenor, no matter how high above the stave he is able to push his voice. The tone and effect of his singing are always that of a counter-tenor, therefore. While wildly impressive, his performances are also doggedly tasteful, cultivated and balanced for audiences acclimatised to the commonality of beauty. After all, we know what we do of 17th and 18th century *castrati* from contemporary sources; while there are a number of excellent references to confirm what was said about whom, and why, it is *impossible* to know against what and whom comparisons were being made by way of prejudice, at least without yielding to generics. Even so, Moreschi was loved and admired for making a noise that many now consider more deserving of laughter than plaudits. For the sceptical, there are recordings from 1915 of William Pickles, the "Boy soprano of Trinity Church, Pittsburgh," whose voice

---

39   Equivalent in 2020 to around £12,000. The legendary story of this landmark event is entirely that – a legend. See Chapter 8 below.

and performing style are consistent with the singing of just about every other treble of note, spanning the 104 years between Walter Lawrence's recording of "Hear My Prayer" in 1914 and Aksel Rykkvin's recording of "Eternal Source of Light Divine" in 2018. While there are obvious and consistent points of comparison as between trebles over time, the *castrati* and the tenor were divergent – but presumptively only.

The last major operatic role composed for a *castrato*, Armando, in *Il crociato in Egitto*,[40] was written only 36 years before Moreschi joined the Sistine Chapel Choir; the role was performed on a number of occasions by Moreschi's friend and Sistine mentor Domenico Mustafà. The first Armando, Giovanni Velluti[41], was a close friend of Mustafà's and celebrated for creating Rossini's Arsace, Prince of Persia, in *Aureliano in Palmira*. In 1826, Velluti acquired the management of The King's Theatre in London, where he appeared in a wide range of repertoire – in which he excelled thanks to the power and dexterity of his voice. Armando is a male character, as was Arsace. Neither role was scored for a woman, and neither was expected to be sung as women. Indeed, their unchanged status as men (albeit men who sounded "feminine" in the reach of their voices) compelled audiences to engage in a measure of suspended disbelief – accepting, of course, that opera has never exactly been grounded in reality. The blurring of appreciation as between the genders was significant because *castrati* did not perform trouser roles (converse to Cherubino in Mozart's *Le nozze di Figaro* and Octavian in Strauss' *Der Rosenkavalier*) but featured rather as romantic and heroic leads. Vocal equivalence to a woman in tone and pitch did not equate to psychological emasculation, therefore – a feature of 17th and 18th century opera that allowed for men to be engaged on stage in romantic relationships that caused no difficulty for audiences presented with scenarios that were archetypically synthetic.

With the emergence of romanticism during the late 18th century, and thanks largely to the stage works of Gluck[42] and Da Ponte-Mozart, the push for a measure of theatrical authenticity (at least where real-world character and emotion were concerned) began to render the appearance of *castrati* as improbable as their voices. What prepubertal castration took from a child was returned in other, commonly more terrible ways to the man, with victims suffering numerous, easily imagined psychological burdens and struggles and a host of physical effects, which spanned abnormal height and girth, the elongation of the arms and legs, and the deformation of facial features. When writing *Cyrano de Bergerac* (set in the middle 17th century) Edmond Rostand made much of his hero's immersion in libertine culture, and while *castrati* were not "made" in France they were a popular feature of theatrical life in Paris until the middle 19th century.[43] Rostand's juxtaposition of physical deformity, art, tragedy,

---

40   'The Crusader in Egypt.'
41   28 January, 1780 – 22 January, 1861.
42   The first version of *Orfeo ed Euridice* (Vienna) was written for an alto *castrato* (Gaetano Guadagni), the second (Parma) for a soprano *castrato* (Giuseppe Millico); the third (Paris) for a high tenor (Joseph Legros).
43   Even Napoleon, who detested the practice of castration, was so enamoured of Girolamo Crescentini (2 February, 1762 – 24 April, 1846) that he offered the singer the "imperial" salary of 30,000 francs a year to sing in Paris from 1805 until 1812. He made him also a Knight of the Order of the Iron Crown of Lombardy. (Clapton, Nicholas. *Moreschi and the Voice of the Castrato*. (2008) Haus Books). Voltaire's Procurante summed up the common attitude when urging Candide to "swoon with pleasure if you wish

shame and frustrated love would have resonated for any of those whose art was born of life-threatening violence.

Most *castrati* suffered for their art long after their incipient divestment. All ran to fat, thanks to dramatic increases in androgen, with many growing conspicuous breasts. Extremities were rendered hirsute while faces were permanently hairless,[44] swollen and prematurely wrinkled – such that Fred Gaisberg believed that Moreschi was 60 when they met, whereas he was, in fact, 48.[45] Without an Adam's apple, most *castrati* wore tactical cravats (even Farinelli), but no matter how great their disguises most *castrati* were identifiable by sight alone, and rarely to invite kindness and inclusion. The wages of parental sin can rarely have been more costly. Social isolation (or actual sequestration) led inevitably to abuse. A number of *castrati* were homosexual at birth, but others were required to adapt and subjected in consequence to dreadful mistreatment and exploitation. In Chapter 10 of his Diaries, Casanova wrote of one unwilling object:[46]

> We went to the theatre, where the castrato who played the prima donna was a great attraction. He was the favourite pathic [a contemporary term for a catamite] of Cardinal Borghese and supped every evening with His Eminence. This castrato had a fine voice, but his chief attraction was his beauty.

Casanova also recorded a revealing encounter with the Abbé Gama:[47]

> [he] read an incendiary sonnet against the government, and several took a copy of it. Another read a satire of his own composition, in which he tore to pieces the honour of a family. In the middle of all that confusion, I saw a priest with a very attractive countenance come in. The size of his hips made me take him for a woman dressed in men's clothes, and I said so to Gama, who told me that he was the celebrated castrato, Bepino delta Mamana. The Abbé called him to us and told him with a laugh that I had taken him for a girl. The impudent fellow looked me full in

---

or if you can at the trills of a eunuch quavering the majestic part of Caesar and Cato." The word "capon" was used commonly in France to describe *castrati*, and anyone else the user didn't much like. A capon (from the Latin 'caponem') is a cockerel that has been castrated to improve the quality of its flesh for eating.
44   In his translation of Juvenal's *Sixth Satire*, Dryden delighted in his own wit: "There are those who in soft eunuchs place their bliss; / To shun the scrubbing of a bearded kiss; / And scape abortion, but their solid joy / Is when the Page, already past a boy, / Is Capon'd late; and to the gelder shown, / With his two-pounders to perfection grown." Dryden delighted frequently in the eunuch as metaphor, for reasons that concern another book (Horace and Dryden, John. *The Satires of Decimus Junius Juvenalis, Volume 3* (2012) Nabu Press.
45   Gaisberg, Fred (1942; repr. 1977) *The Music Goes Round*. Arno Press.
46   *The Complete Memoirs of Jacques Casanova de Seingalt* (2015). Trans. Arthur Machen. Benediction Classics. p.648.
47   *Ibid*, p.72.

the face, and said that, if I liked, he would show me whether I had been right or wrong…

The best of Casanova's recollections is worth citing in full, since the exchange as he remembers it speaks with sparkling brilliance of the cultural position enjoyed by *castrati* – at least in Italy – during the 18th century:[48]

> I went home, bathed, slept an hour, rose, dressed, and dined pleasantly with the family. In the evening I took the Mengs family for a drive in my landau, and we then went to the theatre, where the castrato who played the prima donna was a great attraction. He was the favourite pathic of Cardinal Borghese, and supped every evening with his eminence. This castrato had a fine voice, but his chief attraction was his beauty. I had seen him in man's clothes in the street, but though a fine-looking fellow, he had not made any impression on me, for one could see at once that he was only half a man, but on the stage in woman's dress the illusion was complete; he was ravishing. He was enclosed in a carefully-made corset and looked like a nymph; and incredible though it may seem, his breast was as beautiful as any woman's; it was the monster's chiefest charm. However well one knew the fellow's neutral sex, as soon as one looked at his breast one felt all aglow and quite madly amorous of him. To feel nothing one would have to be as cold and impassive as a German. As he walked the boards, waiting for the refrain of the air he was singing, there was something grandly voluptuous about him; and as he glanced towards the boxes, his black eyes, at once tender and modest, ravished the heart. He evidently wished to fan the flame of those who loved him as a man, and probably would not have cared for him if he had been a woman. Rome the holy, which thus strives to make all men pederasts, denies the fact, and will not believe in the effects of the glamour of her own devising.
>
> I made these reflections aloud, and an ecclesiastic, wishing to blind me to the truth, spoke as follows –
>
> 'You are quite right. Why should this castrato be allowed to shew his breast, of which the fairest Roman lady might be proud, and yet wish everyone to consider him as a man and not a woman? If the stage is forbidden to the fair sex lest they excite desires, why do they seek out men-monsters made in the form of women, who excite much more criminal desires? They keep on preaching that pederasty is comparatively unknown and entraps only a few, but many clever men endeavour to be entrapped, and end by thinking it so pleasant that they prefer these monsters to the most beautiful women.'
>
> 'The Pope would be sure of heaven if he put a stop to this scandalous practice.'

---

48 *Ibid*. p.648.

'I don't agree with you. One could not have a pretty actress to supper without causing a scandal, but such an invitation to a castrato makes nobody talk. It is of course known perfectly well that after supper both heads rest on one pillow, but what everybody knows is ignored by all. One may sleep with a man out of mere friendship, it is not so with a woman.'[49]

'True, monsignor, appearances are saved, and a sin concealed is half pardoned, as they say in Paris'.

'At Rome we say it is pardoned altogether. 'Peccato nascosto non offende'.[50]

For all the libertine foison and erotic ambiguity,[51] *castrati* were revered until their existence on the operatic stage as heroes and lovers became irreconcilable with early romantic notions of theatrical verisimilitude. It was inconceivable, for example, that Florestan (or, for that matter, Leonora) might have been written for or performed by a *castrato*; it was no less certain that the obsession among *castrati* for ornamentation and technical effect was an increasing nuisance for an art form that was beginning to reach beyond the atavistic absurdities of *dei ex machina*. The training of *castrati* over centuries involved the development of exceptional diaphragm management and breath control; there was no simple *legato* for a 25 year-old peacock who had committed more than half his life to learning how to soar, plummet and machine-gun his way through an opera, the virtuosity of which was more important than the emotional or psychological state to which an audience might have related. An aria saturated by its singer in *coloratura* artifice and *rococo* flamboyance was more often than not left unrecognisable to its composer, who tolerated the abuses of their *gioielli della corona* for reasons of commercial and social advancement.[52] Artistic integrity was rarely a feature of musical relationships in which the beauty or insight of an original work was left decimated by *virtuosita spiccata* (the separation of the notes in a trill[53]) or pointless extremes of dynamics or, most egregiously of all, "portmanteau" interpolations composed by a singer for dropping midway through someone else's opera, after the fashion of a rictus-grinning model in a swimsuit strutting around a boxing ring holding aloft a card to announce the number of the coming round.

Of course, showboating has coloured the entire of music history. Tallis' *Spem in alium*, Beethoven's barnstorming improvisations, almost the entire life's-work of Paganini and Liszt, Strauss' *Eine Alpensinfonie*, Franco Corelli's *diminuendo* at the

---

49   *Contra* Shakespeare, *castrati* were renowned as lovers until the middle 19th century. According to Luigi Tomasini, a violinist and composer (and leader of the Prince Esterhazy-Haydn court orchestra): "They could last long … and would have inspired a taste for Gomorrah in people whose taste is the least depraved."
50   'Hidden sin does not offend.'
51   See Enid Rhodes Peschel and Richard E. Peschel. "Medical Insights into the Castrati in Opera." *American Scientist*, Vol. 75, No. 6 (November – December 1987). pp.578–583.
52   Ravens, Simon (2014). *The Supernatural Voice: A History of High Male Singing*. Boydell Press.
53   For a sense of the utter madness of it all, the curious may enjoy Cecilia Bartoli's magnificent stab at "Cadro, ma qual si mira" from Francesco Araia's *Berenice* ("*Sacrificium: La scuola dei Castrati*"; Il Giardino Armonico (Orch.); Giovanni Antonini (Cond.). Decca (2009; 478 152-1)).

end of "*Celeste Aida*" on 28 April, 1967,[54] and Hendrix' burning of the American flag at Woodstock[55] were all inherently exhibitionist. So too was Moreschi. He was putatively little more than a choirboy, but the acclamation he received inside the Sistine Chapel in 1902 spoke to expectations on the part of the singer that suggested considerable vanity and celebrity. It's easy to imagine the intensity of the appreciation enjoyed by Luigi Marchesi, an 18th century *castrato* with a reputation for pageantry, whose contracts stipulated that he should enter onto any stage, for *any* opera, at the crest of a hill wearing a helmet crowned by six feet of feathers while carrying a sword and a lance. His first words, in every case, were "*Dove sono?*"[56]

For his part, Rossini relished the "purity, the miraculous flexibility of those voices and, above all, their profoundly penetrating accent — all that moved and fascinated me more than I can tell."[57] With his own celebrity, and the success of his music with publishers and opera houses across Italy, the composer began to rail against the "disease" of ornamentation and the infection of his music by artists whose status and vanity eclipsed his own. While gifting the role of Armando to Velluti made commercial sense in 1813 – when, according to Stendhal, the singer was "in the flower of his youth and talent, and one of the best-looking men of his century"[58] – the singer's absurdly convoluted and indiscreet corruptions led to disagreements and a parting of the ways with Rossini. If many now recoil from the melismatic infection of a simple line of song by Mariah Carey, Christina Aguilera and Beyoncé, then Rossini's frustrations with Velluti were greater still – because his concerns were theatrical as well as musical.

Rossini believed in the primacy of opera and singing as drama, in pursuit of which ambition composers across Europe during the first quarter of the 19th century initiated a reformation that would place music at the subservient mercy of words – reversing a polarity that had rendered *libretti* (and dramatic psychology) a hireling during two centuries of the singer's primacy over the composer. Rossini would eventually write out every ornament – a courageous step towards the sort of notational absolutism that would become routine during the second half of the 19th century – but even in 1813 he was attempting to reposition the value of virtuosity as a means towards a narrative end.

Rossini did not forget his roots – or Velluti, with whom he became friends once more after the composer's relocation to Paris – and in 1860 he told Wagner:[59]

> It is impossible to imagine the delightful voices and the consummate virtuosity possessed through lack of something else and through a charitable compensation, by those bravest of the brave. [...] Let's speak first of

---

54   An extraordinary technical feat; recorded live in Cleveland, Ohio, during the Metropolitan Opera Spring Tour.
55   On 18 August, 1969, Hendrix played the "Star Spangled Banner" as part of his set.
56   'Where am I?'
57   Osborne, Richard (2007). *Rossini*. Oxford University Press. p.115.
58   Barbier, Patrick (2001). *The World of the Castrati: The History of an Extraordinary Operatic Phenomenon*. Souvenir Press. p.233.
59   Michotte, Edmond (2016). *Richard Wagner's visit to Rossini, and an Evening at Rossini's in Beau-Sejour*. University of Chicago Press. p.125.

the voice, the instrument formed. Nature, alas, never creates all parts of a voice perfectly, any more than a pine tree gives birth to a Stradivarius. Just as an instrument maker must construct a Stradivarius, so it behoves a future singer to fabricate the instrument he counts upon using. And how long and arduous a labour that is. Among my compatriots, that job formerly was facilitated; in view of nature's refusal to comply, they made castrati. The method, to be sure, was heroic, but the results were wonderful. In my youth it was my good fortune still to be able to hear some of those fellows.[60]

Rossini claimed to believe that the disappearance of the *castrati* had been the "cause of [an] irreparable decline in the art of singing" and it was with gallows humour that he scored his *Petite messe solonelle*[61] in 1863 for "*Douze chanteurs de trois sexes, hommes, femmes et castrats seront suffisants pour son exécution : à savoir huit pour le choeur, quatre pour les solos, total douze chérubins.*"[62] The need for a new kind of *virtuoso* left many of Europe's emasculated elite culturally impotent to boot – but the nostalgia that gripped Rossini in the 1860s had been there from the start of his career. It was this obsessive attachment to song that came to define the era immediately following the decline of the age of the *castrato*, when the tenor emerged for the first time as a definitive musical and cultural voice. It was a bitter irony for many that this transition was facilitated by the *castrati* themselves.

Until the introduction of a financial metric during the early 17th century – calculated initially as a function of duelling patrons and subsequently by the collation of box office receipts – the teaching of singing was regional and mercurial. During the 1600s numerous academies were established throughout Italy, bringing together different disciplines and spanning languages, literature, philosophy, composition and singing. The latter two were interchangeable, and when the first *Solfeggi*[63] were published they were written either by composer-*castrati* or their teachers. The most celebrated were Pier Tosi (author of the *Opinioni de' cantori antichi e moderni o sieno osservazioni sopra il canto figurato,*[64] first published in Bologna in 1723) and Nicola Porpora,[65] whose tutelage at the Neapolitan Conservatorio di Sant'Onofrio and the Conservatorio dei Poveri di Gesù Cristo[66] produced not only the greatest *castrato* of them all, Farinelli, but much of the technical insight that came to define the teaching of singing throughout Italy and, eventually, the modern world. Porpora's career saw him established in Vienna (where he employed a young Joseph Haydn

---

60 It is curious that he should have claimed merely to have heard them in his youth. He wrote one of his greatest roles for Velluti!
61 'Little solemn mass.'
62 'Twelve singers of three sexes, men, women and *castrati* will suffice for its execution: that is, eight for the choir, four soloists, in all twelve cherubim.'
63 Books on the instruction of vocalism and technical training, commonly through sight-read exercises.
64 'Opinions of ancient and modern singers or remarks on figurative singing.'
65 17 August, 1686 – 3 March, 1768. He died in poverty, while Farinelli retired as one of the world's wealthiest commoners.
66 The Conservatorio was founded in 1589 by Marcello Fossataro, a Franciscan friar. Other teachers associated with the school included the philosopher Giovan Vico and the composer Giovanni Pergolesi.

as accompanist[67]), London (where he joined with Farinelli, in competition with Handel's opera company), and Dresden, where he was appointed Kapellmeister by the Elector of Saxony. Sustained by decades of experience as a composer and a teacher, Porpora is said to have required his students to study a single page of exercises for at least five years[68] – at which point they were equipped for any challenge. As much was certainly true of Farinelli.

Both Tosi and Porpora were concerned with ornamentation as a construction of contemporary taste and fashion; they were preoccupied also with breathing, phrasing (with a particular focus on *portamento*), *messa di voce, legato, appoggiato,* word placement and pronunciation.[69] Style was the expression of technique, which is where the *solfeggi* of *castrati* were useful to singers with earth-bound vocal registers. Although the tenor voice, as it is understood today, would not become *il protagonista* until the beginning of the 19th century, there was a clear period during which agility was a transferable skill for tenors as well as male sopranos.

The "bridge" between the two registers was the *haute-contre* – a high, sometimes *very* high-sounding tenor – whose reach to anything above an A4 was achieved in every case in *falsetto*. For this reason, and because many composers were justifiably suspicious of the ubiquity of skill and capacity, a lot of writing for tenors above the stave during the 17th and 18th centuries went un-notated. Composers would tailor a role to a particular singer, who would perform it at the premiere. Few required anything higher of a tenor than an A4. For example, Handel's parts for Francesco Borosoni and Annibale Pio fell within the reach of many baritones (until Handel challenged Borosoni with the role of Bajazet in *Tamerlano*). Mozart was unusual in notating a handful of high Cs (as he did in "*Vado incontro,*" for the first *Mitridate*, Guglielmo d'Ettore), but he otherwise presented his tenors with nothing more demanding than a B flat 4. Haydn relied heavily on his friend and collaborator, Karl Frieberth,[70] for indulgences that did not travel well.

Most of these tenors studied as children with *castrati*, by whom they were taught methods of singing that enabled the mastery of technically challenging repertoire before puberty (with many falling to the knife), but the expressive criteria that became increasingly significant for Gluck, Haydn, Mozart and Beethoven (when writing *Fidelio*) would not have registered with Farinelli as meaningful. As much crystallises when comparing any of the show-stopping music memorialised by the greatest

---

67 Haydn remembered "no lack of [insults] and pokes in the ribs, but I put up with it all, for I profited greatly from Porpora in singing, in composition, and in the Italian language." Gresinger, G. (1975). *Biografische Notizen über Josef Haydn*. Reclam. p.12.
68 (1792 – 1824). Potter, John (2006). "The tenor-castrato connection, 1760 – 1860." *Early Music*, Vol. xxxv, No.1. Oxford University Press. pp.97–110.
69 While diction was important, there is little question that vocal ornament diminished the meaning of a word where a single vowel might be strung out over ten or twenty notes of music. Until the reformations of Gluck, Mozart and Beethoven, the syntactical and emotional value of a poet's writing was subjected at every turn to the fascism of musical and vocal fantasy. There were numerous exceptions, of course, exemplified by Purcell's "When I am laid in earth" from *Dido and Aeneas* – where the setting of the words is indivisible from their spoken meaning and context – but the abuse of poetry by *castrati* in particular was one of the chief causes of the early romantic promotion of the tenor as a viable (and manageable) alternative to the perishable glories of Messiaenic song-birds.
70 7 June, 1736 – 6 August, 1816.

castrati with "*Dies Bildnis ist bezaubernd schön*"[71] from *Die Zauberflöte*. Mozart wrote it for Benedikt Schack,[72] the first Tamino, and he tailored the aria to the singer's voice, such that the first G (which required the aria to be in E flat[73]) didn't push the singer beyond his comfort range.[74] There was no need for it to be any higher because the Queen of the Night held the monopoly on vocal fireworks. Tamino is the opera's emotional centre, and the opening leap from B flat to G speaks of his love at first sight for Pamina.[75] That single interval is heavy with sentiment, and the ensuing music is drafted to communicate the growing profundity of Tamino's love for a girl he has never met. Mozart's language is simple, formed as it is of sighs and surges to communicate the *weltschmerz* of infatuation; it is written also for a tenor with the capacity to articulate a complex and evolving emotional state. The words and their setting are not interchangeable, therefore. One is placed entirely at the service of the other. "*Quell'usignolo*" from Gerolamo Giacomelli's *Merope*[76] contains, however, many more notes than it does words, with hundreds of semi-quavers being attached to a single, unchanging syllable that render words and music representatively independent. The dramatic and theatrical instant and any hint of emotional concentration are lost to the violent discipline of virtuosity.[77] The axiom (attached to many sopranos) that "she might have been singing a shopping list" was commonly true of *castrati*. The same could never have been true of Florestan when singing "*Gott! Welch' Dunkel hier!*"[78] in the metaphysical darkness and isolation of his prison cell.

Castrati were responsible for the training of tenors across Europe until well into the 19th century, including Michael Kelly[79] (the first Basilio for Mozart's *Figaro*, who was spotted while still a treble by Venanzio Rauzzini and trained to maturity by Giuseppe Aprile) and Giacomo David, whose debut was of such note that he was invited only two years later to take part in the inauguration of "La Fenice," singing the role of Eraclide in Paisiello's *I giochi di Agrigento*. With his first appearance in Alessandro Felici's *La cameriera astute* in 1770, and until his last major role-creation, in *Il salto di Leucade* for Luigi Mosc in 1812, David was arguably the most influential tenor during the early history of the voice. He worked alongside the *castrati* Girolamo Crescentini and Gaspare Pacchierotti for avowedly 18th century composers like Paisiello, Bertoni, Cimarosa, Guglielmi and Salieri (with sopranos like Brigida Banti),[80] before transposing during the twilight of his career to roles for Rossini

---

71   'This image is enchantingly lovely.'
72   7 February, 1758 – 10 December, 1826.
73   The opera's (symbolically) dominant key.
74   Branscombe, P. *W. A. Mozart: Die Zauberflöte*. (1991). Cambridge University Press.
75   The aria rises only a semitone higher thereafter, to an A flat.
76   An *opera seria* from 1734 with a libretto by Apostolo Zeno. First performed at the Teatro Grimani di San Giovanni Grisostomo in Venice.
77   It is true that Farinelli was also gifted with music that made a virtue of tone, above anything else – but not routinely. A memorable case in point is Porpora's exquisite "*Alto Giove*," Aci's aria from *Polifemo* (Act III, Scene 5).
78   'God! What darkness here!'
79   25 December, 1762 – 9 October, 1826.
80   She created dozens of roles, including *Alceste* for Gluck in 1795.

– including *Otello*,[81] which he performed alongside Isabella Colbran.[82] David served as a muse for composers between the age of the *castrati* and the advent of "modern" singing, when spectacular but empty virtuosity was transcended by dramatically grounded expression. The reach of David's influence extended through the training of his even more celebrated son, Giovanni,[83] as well as Andrea Nozzari, Domenico Donzelli and Giovanni Rubini.

David's voice was said to be baritonal in its warmth and depth, and while much might be made of this apparently distinguishing feature for a tenor required to meet baroque expectations, Farinelli was able to reach almost as far below the stave as above it. For Leonardo Vinci's 1728 opera *Il medo*, for example, Farinelli was tasked with a range of glass-shattering vocal gymnastics. For the aria "*Navigante che non spera*"[84] he was required to reach well into the baritone register. The aria begins on a B3 below middle C which then drops to an F3 before arpeggiating to a high B4 *above* middle C. The *tessitura* remains bizarrely low until Vinci transposes the main theme to compel the repetition of "*Navigante*," but with the phrase beginning on a low F, which then drops an octave *below* middle C. Giacomo David had to sing almost everything above an A4 in *falsetto*, yet his mastery of *coloratura* (in which he was "able to compete with the castratos in the florid music and far exceed them in his dramatic intensity"[85]) ensured that he kept the gods happy; his status as an artist was such that in 1786 he became the first tenor in the history of Turin's Teatro Regio to be paid more than the *primo uomi* during Carnival season.[86]

Even outside Italy, the tide was turning audibly against the "absurdity" of *castrati* as actors and performers, and the fact that the *castrati* had been largely responsible for training their *completare* usurpers compounded the tragedy of their subversion. In London, for example, Farinelli's divine powers were insufficient to secure him the popular vote, and when John Braham made his debut at Drury Lane in 1796 he was welcomed as a replacement for the "degrading and disgusting form of the castrato" – while at the same time being criticised for "an excessive weight of ornament."[87] Another late century English tenor, Charles Incledon,[88] was admired by Haydn despite the singer's "excessive" trilling in *falsetto* to a high C – and the G above

---

81   A role created by his son, Giovanni, in 1816.
82   2 February, 1785 – 7 October, 1845. A legendary Spanish soprano who created for Rossini the role of Desdemona in 1816 and also *Elisabetta, regina d'Inghilterra* ['Elizabeth, Queen of England'] (1816), Armida, Elcia in *Mosè in Egitto* ['Moses in Egypt'] (1816), Zoraide in *Ricciardo e Zoraide* (1818), Ermione (1819), Elena in *La donna del lago* ['The Lady of the Lake'] (1816), Anna in *Maometto II* (1820), and *Zelmira* (1822).
83   The creator for Rossini of the tenor roles Narciso in *Il turco in Italia* ['The Turk in Italy'] (1814), Rodrigo in *Otello* (1816), Ricciardo in *Ricciardo e Zoraide* (1818), Oreste in *Ermione* (1819), Uberto in *La donna del lago* ['The Lady of the Lake'] (1819), and Ilo in *Zelmira* (1822).
84   'Navigator without hope.'
85   Forbes, Elizabeth. "Davide [David], Giacomo," in (1997) *The New Grove Dictionary of Opera*; Stanley Sadie (Ed.), (Oxford University Press), p.1088.
86   Rosselli, John (1995). *Singers of Italian opera: the history of a profession*. Cambridge University Press. pp.129–130.
87   Potter, John. "The tenor-castrato connection, 1760 – 1860." *Early Music*, Vol.xxxv, No.1 (2006). Oxford University Press. pp.97–110; p.101.
88   1763 – 11 February, 1826.

it![89] When in 1817 William Pearman made his début at the English Opera House as Orlando in Dibdin's *The Cabinet*,[90] he was admired for the beauty of a voice that was otherwise untutored:

> Pearman's falsetto will remind the public of Incledon's, which it surpasses in reach and sweetness. He plays upon it like a flute. His transition to it however from the natural voice is not happy. It is not indeed so violent as Incledon's who, in his leaps from one to the other, slammed the larynx in his throat, like a Harlequin jumping through a window shutter, but it is poor and unskilful; neither does he seem to care upon what sort of words or expression he does it, so as the note is such as he can jump to it.[91]

An imperfect technique was intolerable for audiences weaned on the monstrous regiment of *castrati*, whose swan-song saw them reduced to the birthing of a "new" breed of singer. The traducing of the male soprano was troubling for those unable to accept the tenor as a lead when their vocal armouries were so limited. After Pearman was retained at Covent Garden in 1822, for example, he was roundly judged to be ineffective in a "large" house because his voice carried neither weight nor range. The critic and writer William Oxberry[92] said that Pearman's tenor appeared always to be "smothered"[93], and since his "natural" instrument allowed him nothing beyond an E4, at the top of the stave, he was, in reality, more a baritone than a tenor – until, of course, he resorted to *falsetto*. Audiences were not so easily fooled. If a singer attempted music in a higher than normal register he was required to do so with conviction, something that *falsettists* managed to convey only by way of compromise or, worse, imitation. A "slight" voice was thought incapable of channelling anything of the emotional force for which *castrati* were remembered, even if their legacy was subsumed to (alleged) revulsion. This created a problem for composers struggling to isolate a creative voice worth hearing at a time when verisimilitude began to require "reality" even of dramatic situations that were inherently fantastic.[94] The emergence during the 18th century of female sopranos and, more importantly, mezzo-soprani and contralti, was compensation of a kind, but it was in consequence of pragmatism (and the proliferation of music publishing throughout Europe) that composers came finally to acknowledge how the writing of an opera for a single performance, and often for the pleasure of a handful of aristocrats otherwise distracted by eating, drinking and flirting, was an unsustainable business model.

The shadow of the vampiric *castrato* did not pass quickly, however. The glory of the *ancien* remained consistently *moderne* because of the persisting master-servant dynamic. Composers needed to ensure that new music could be performed other

---

89 *Ibid*; p.102.
90 First staged at Covent Garden in February, 1803, with John Braham, Nancy Storace and Charles Incledon.
91 (1792 – 1824). Potter, John. "The tenor-castrato connection, 1760 – 1860." *Early Music*, Vol.xxxv, No.1 (2006). Oxford University Press. pp.97–11; p.103.
92 (1784–1824). English actor, writer, printer and publisher.
93 *Dictionary of National Biography*, 1885–1900, Volume 44.
94 *e.g.*, Max in *Der Freischütz* and Sir Edgar Aubry in Marschner's *Der Vampyr*.

than by a dwindling supply of male sopranos, thanks in part to the late-18th century shift in gender politics – captured in microcosm by the publication in 1792 of Mary Wollstonecraft's *A Vindication of the Rights of Woman*. Wollstonecraft's petition that women were not *naturally* inferior to men (but should, rather, be accepted as rational beings within a social order founded on reason) was irreconcilable to the practice of castrating boys to enable them to sing as women so as to adhere to an arcane religious injunction by a demented misogynist.[95]

The push towards female emancipation served also to amplify the *extremis* nature of the "other." With the normalisation of women on stage, as well as numerous other previously forbidden arenas, the fractured ambiguities that had allowed for men as well as women to wear powdered wigs, makeup and *haute couture* crystallised previously nebulous and interwoven sexual identities. The coincident embrace of Gothic sensibilities during the twenty years either side of 1800 heightened the symbolic and cultural value of difference as disability – spanning Beethoven's deafness, the vampire's sensitivity to sunlight, the mental and spiritual disease of *Frankenstein*, and Sebastian Melmoth's apparent immortality[96] – and in this respect the *castrato* survived as a metaphor for cultural hubris and social decadence. Honoré de Balzac's novella *Sarrasine*[97] articulated the contradictory sense of wonder and revulsion, shame and pride that characterised the perception of the *castrato* as a painting to be locked in the attic.[98]

Sarrasine is the only son of a wealthy lawyer. Rather than adopting his father's career and his family's wishes, he pursues the life of a sculptor, travelling to Italy where he falls in love with an opera singer, La Zambinella. She becomes his muse, and Sarrasine begins to carve her form in stone. On learning that Zambinella is a *castrato*, Sarrasine attempts to kill the singer and is himself murdered by Zambinella's friends and admirers. Building on Roland Barthes' landmark critical reading of *Sarrasine*,[99] Naomi André has argued persuasively for the lingering sovereignty of *castrati* in 1830:[100]

> the author presents both the body and the voice of the castrato haunting the present and looking back to the past. Though the castrati were not completely unknown in Paris, they never enjoyed the popularity that they had in Italy. Hence, Balzac's use of the castrato not only references an older operatic practice no longer popular, but also cites a foreign

---

95 Objectivity compels an acknowledgment that the Apostle Paul was part of an ingrained racial and religious heritage that tolerated and, indeed, espoused such values. It is equally true that the world has, for the most part, evolved.

96 See generally Boyden, Matthew (2018). *Beethoven and the Gothic*. Verba et Musica.

97 First published in 1830, and later as part of his *Comédie Humaine*.

98 Balzac later wrote a sequel to Maturin's *Melmoth the Wanderer* (*Melmoth Reconciled*), believing as he did that Maturin's novel was as great an achievement as Molière's *Dom Juan*, Goethe's *Faust* and Byron's *Manfred*. Self-evidently, Oscar Wilde (who adopted the pseudonym "Sebastian Melmoth" after emigrating to France in 1897) agreed with this assessment also.

99 First published in 1830, and later as part of his *Comédie Humaine*.

100 André, Naomi (2006). *Voicing Gender: Castrati, Travesty, and the Second Woman in Early-Nineteenth-Century Italian Opera*. Indiana University Press. pp.16–50.

cultural phenomenon that opens up a transgressive realm of fascination and possibility.

Balzac's descriptions of Zambinella's singing are characteristically romanticised, painted brightly to sustain the lust of an aesthete for whom art is the sole metric of value and purpose. That Sarrasine responds as he does to his belated discovery that Zambinella is a man compounds Balzac's dazzling isolation of absurdity in the sculptor's identification of beauty that becomes ugly in the light of a truth that resonates only after its artifice has been revealed. Balzac's greater concern – that all art is by nature deceitful, particularly when "created" through "surgery" – compels the acceptance of Zambinella as beautiful despite and not because of his emasculation. Beauty in this respect is in the ear of the beholder, since the singer's appearance (and until he turns 100) becomes increasingly horrific and symbolically pre-emptive of Dorian Gray's monstrous degeneration in oil.[101]

The air of decay that Balzac attaches to Zambinella's clothing over time is not a trigger for the remembrance of things past, therefore, but a gesture towards their ending. The age and experience by which he is rendered "diabolical" for Balzac is manifestly incapable of being passed onto anyone else. His clothing, his jewels and his voice are co-terminous with his sterility. When Balzac compares his singing to that of Maria Malibran, Henriette Sontag and Joséphine Fodor-Mainvielle – the world's most celebrated female sopranos in 1830 – he places the redundancy of the male soprano in parity with the novelty of contemporary music. Each of those legendary sopranos was made famous by (and helped make famous) the operas of Rossini; just as their talent and brilliance left the male soprano obsolete as a voice, so too did the tenor facilitate the restoration of the heroic and the amorous to the male in form and manner.

Ultimately, grim satisfaction may be gained from the truth that the modern tenor was born of the suffering and genius of the *castrati*. It is equally certain that the apparent novelty of the *bel cantisti* was anything but. Indeed, it can now be seen that the entire history of tenor singing – up to and in some ways culminating with the voices and careers of Franco Corelli[102] and Luciano Pavarotti – was a continuing legacy of the *castrati*. The definitive masculinity of Corelli and the misunderstood celebrity of Pavarotti can be appreciated in their complexity only in their correspondence with the singing, experiences and circumstances of the culture that joined Farinelli to Moreschi, and beyond.

---

101 Wilde clearly relished the conceit, since Balzac draws immense force from the reaction of one of his characters, a Countess, who recoils from Zambinella's appearance when meeting him at the end of his life – only to flee to a painting of Adonis. It transpires that the painting's model was Zambinella.
102 Born on 8 April, 1921 – a year and two weeks before Moreschi's death in 1922.

CHAPTER TWO

Prima la parole, poi la musica

In early 1906 the Gramophone Company invited the actor Sir Herbert Beerbohm Tree[1] to make a series of recordings.[2] The first (by issue number) was of Hamlet's meditation on death, "To be, or not to be." Tree was 54 years old at the time, and by no means the oldest actor of note to speak as Hamlet,[3] but he was the first to do so on record with a grandfather born in the 1700s.[4] Tree's father was christened in 1810 – when it was certain that he, like everyone else, was "heard no more" after his "hour upon the stage"; his own earliest experiences of sound were of voices born when Shakespeare was only recently deceased. Sir Henry first began performing in the 1870s and his acting technique was already considered mannered in 1900;[5] there is a disconcerting singing quality to his voice-acting that many would now regard as overcooked or, worse, insincere.[6] The fashion for intoning Shakespeare – and verse more generally – was thriving when Tree was born. It was cross-cultural as well; a recording of Sarah Bernhardt, Sir Henry's contemporary,[7] reciting two monologues from Act 2, Scene 5 of Racine's *Phèdre*, likewise memorialises the extremes of lyrical extravagance. Bernhardt was 66 years old when she visited Thomas Edison at his laboratory in West Orange, New Jersey, in February, 1910, while touring the United States. Her intonation of verses from Racine's tragedy of 1677 is baffling and bizarre, although some of the breathless urgency can be attributed in part to the technology. She begins:

> "*Oui, Prince, je languis, je brûle pour Thésée.*
> *Je l'aime, non point tel que l'ont vu les enfers,*
> *Volage adorateur de mille objets divers,*
> *Qui va du Dieu des morts déshonorer la couche;*
> *Mais fidèle, mais fier, et même un peu farouche,*

---

1 17 December, 1852 – 2 July, 1917.
2 Five survive; they are numbered E.1312 – E.1316.
3 John Gielgud was 85 when he recorded the same soliloquy to an accompaniment of music by William Walton with the Academy of St Martin in the Fields, conducted by Sir Neville Marriner, in 1989.
4 The Smithsonian holds a recording ("Volta Record 4") of an unidentified male voice reciting the opening lines of "To be, or not to be" from 1885 (green wax on brass).
5 Tree led an interesting life, as part of a fascinating and remarkable family. Among his legitimate grandchildren was the actor Oliver Reed; among his illegitimate children was the film director Carol Reed.
6 This is even more apparent in his recording of Antony's speech over Caesar's body (made in 1906), which teeters on the edge of being sung, with each line moving up the stave until the climax appears to leave him spent.
7 22 or 23 October, 1844 – 26 March, 1923.

Charmant, jeune, traînant tous les coeurs après soi,
Tel qu'on dépeint nos Dieux, ou tel que je vous voi."[8]

The word "*Prince*" is delivered with a quiver that is pitched, if not quite as a note, then with sufficient purpose to allow for similarly contrived emphasis to be applied to the words "*l'aime*" and "*non poin*t" – which Bernhardt modulates to harmonise, with clear intent, the opening reference to Hippolyte. Throughout the episode, it's plain that Bernhardt determined every shift in weight and inflection; each synthesis of sound is heavy with meaning. She dissects the language as might a choreographer the movement of a dancer, subsuming Racine's ruthless hexameter with nerve-shredding intensity. Unlike Sir Henry Tree, whose style has dated horribly, Bernhardt's reading as Phèdre feels modern more than a century later. It was certainly a thing of wonder for her peers. Oscar Wilde attended Bernhardt's first London performance in the role at the Gaiety Theatre on 2 June, 1879, and wrote the following day to Oscar Browning:

> I wish so much you could have been with me last night. Sarah Bernhardt's Phèdre was the most splendid creation I have witnessed [...] she worked the audience to a strained pitch of excitement such as I never saw.

A century later, when Dominique Blanc[9] performed the role for Patrice Chéreau at the Ateliers Berthier (a warehouse operated by the Opéra Comique), the manic and deliberate focus of Bernhardt's reading, with its barely interrupted delivery, had yielded to a halting, almost apoetical intonation. Blanc's spurning of Racine's unrelenting meter spoke more clearly to a 21st century audience. Her use of air and space – with the poetry delivered on the breath, and with little regard for rhyme and meter – corresponded with Chéreau's determined neutering of the remorseless alexandrine couplets. The cast and their director were united in their determination to disrupt the strict 12 / 12 beat, just as episodes of *musique concrète* were employed by Chéreau to separate the drama from its 17th century locus so as to amplify the texture of the words as pure sound. Although Chéreau based his production on an edition of the play with the original punctuation (taken from the first performance in 1677), the language was delivered starkly and, on occasion, violently – even when the characters' hearts were in their mouths.

Conversely, Bernhardt approached Racine's poetry as would a musician. Having introduced herself for the purposes of the recording in an accent that would today be considered perverse in its affectation, her voicing equates to *Sprechstimme*, an expressionist vocal technique somewhere between singing and speaking, made famous by Schoenberg and his *Pierrot lunaire* in 1912. The connection between *Pierrot lunaire*[10] and the "old" school of recitation employed by Bernhardt (and Sir Henry Tree, Lewis

---

8 'Yes, Prince, I suffer in anguish for Theseus / I languish and I long, not as the Shades / Have seen him, of a thousand different forms / The fickle lover, and of Pluto's bride / The would-be ravisher, but faithful, proud / E'en to a slight disdain, with youthful charms / Attracting every heart, as gods are painted.'
9 25 April, 1956 –.
10 Byron, Avior. "*The Test Pressings of Schoenberg Conducting Pierrot lunaire: Sprechstimme Reconsidered*" (2006). Volume 12, Number 1. Society for Music Theory.

Waller, Alexander Moissi,[11] Karl Kraus and a thousand other citizens of the *World of Yesterday*[12]) was formed by the actress Albertine Zehme, a long-time admirer of Bernhardt's. Although the origin of *Sprechstimme* is traced commonly to Engelbert Humperdinck's 1897 opera *Königskinder*, Schoenberg's immediate inspiration was Zehme, who commissioned a cycle of settings of poems by the Belgian writer Albert Giraud for voice and piano. Zehme was obsessed with the artistic and mystical features of recitation (her treatise on the subject, *Die Grundlagen des künstlerischen Sprechens und Singens*, was published in 1920) and in a note titled "Why I must speak these songs" (provided to the audience at her Berlin performances in March 1910 of *Pierrot lunaire*) she wrote:

> The words that we speak should not solely lead to mental concepts, but instead their sound should allow us to partake of their inner experience. To make this possible we must have an unconstrained freedom of tone. None of the thousand vibrations should be denied to the expression of feeling. I demand tonal freedom, not thoughts! The singing voice, that supernatural, chastely controlled instrument, ideally beautiful precisely in its ascetic lack of freedom, is not suited to strong eruptions of feeling – since even one strong breath of air can spoil its incomparable beauty. Life cannot be exhausted by the beautiful sound alone. The deepest final happiness, the deepest final sorrow dies away unheard, as a silent scream within our breast, which threatens to fly apart or to erupt like a stream of molten lava from our lips. For the expression of these final things it seems to me almost cruel to expect the singing voice to do such a labour, from which it must go fourth frayed, splintered, and tattered. For our poets and composers to communicate, we need both the tones of song as well as those of speech. My unceasing striving in search of the ultimate expressive capabilities for the "artistic experience of tone" has taught me this fact.[13]

Zehme's stated concern for the "unconstrained" expressive conception of the voice as an instrument communicating something more than "beautiful sound alone" was written the year after Lotte Lehmann created the Dyer's Wife in *Die Frau ohne Schatten*, and a year before the death of Caruso. There was no shortage in 1920 of beautiful sounds. Of course, the Weimar Republic nurtured convention-shredding – nowhere more so than where beauty was concerned; the evolution of the Second

---

11 Alexander Moissi (born Aleksandër Moisiu on 2 April, 1879; died either 22 or 23 March, 1935) was an Austrian stage actor born in Albania. He was much admired by Ibsen, Wedekind, von Hofmannsthal, Max Reinhardt and many other writers and directors.
12 Krones, Hartmut, "'Wiener' Symbolik? Zu musiksemantischen Traditionen in den beiden Wiener Schulen" in Otto Kolleritsch (ed.) *Beethoven und die Zweiten Wiener Schule*, Studien zur Wertungsforschung 25. Wien-Graz (1992). p.53.
13 Quoted in Simms, Bryan. *The Atonal Music of Arnold Schoenberg, 1908 – 1923* (2000). Oxford University Press (120–21; 235 note 21). The original German text can be found in *Arnold Schönberg, Sämtliche Werke, Pierrot lunaire* (1995). Josef Rufer (ed.) Universal Edition AG and Schott Music International. Section 6; Series B, 24/1. p.307.

Viennese School was characterised by dramatic shifts in ambition and expectation, sufficient for the "ugly" to be painted by the Nazis during the "*Entartete*" exhibitions as normatively Jewish.[14] The sounds produced by the Royal troupe that first performed *Phèdre* at the Hôtel de Bourgogne on 1 January, 1677, would probably have been as alien for Sarah Bernhardt's generation as her 19th century performances are for the 21st – but the key consideration arising from these shifts in expression and interpretation is that, in every case, the process of vocalisation (of voice as sound) has been in constant flux.

Sir Lawrence Olivier broke with the mould of his father's generation (*contra* Gielgud), by meeting the changed requirements of those writers for whom he was able and willing to act. Where Lewis Waller was an ideal husband for Wilde, he would not have suited John Osborne. Olivier, however, could adapt to the role of Archie Rice in 1957, when Gielgud could not – which in no way diminishes the talents of Sir John Gielgud; rather, it emphasises the extent to which voice has always been a construction of text and *context* as well as taste and prejudice. That is not to state the obvious. No one would believe, for example, that the sound of a tenor graduating from the Royal College of Music in 2021 would be recognisable, in any material way, as a tenor trained in London, or that a singer studying in Milan would emerge as an *autentica* Italian performer simply because he or she was tutored in Italy. At its simplest, it is to observe the manifest unsuitabilty of Giovanni Martinelli to German repertoire, while acknowledging coincidentally the absurdity of Jonas Kaufmann performing Gounod's *Faust* – which hasn't stopped him from doing so, of course. It is to recognise that voices, from the earliest, were formed and grounded in geography and by repertoire.

Few students are now required (or able, even) to learn their technique in the company of young and ambitious composers, since there is no platform for them to share. This last occurred materially at the Royal Northern College of Music, and Boulez's IRCAM[15] – both during the 1950s and 60s; it hasn't happened since, and it is unlikely to do so in the future. On the other hand, singers between the 17th and early 19th centuries could be traced by ear alone to their regions and, even, their teachers. Until after the first world war, Jewish tenors and tenors with their roots in Vienna – as obvious examples – were recognisable within a single phrase, in part because of their cultural and geographical origins. Richard Tauber, for example, was *echt* Viennese, and everything he sang communicated that fact, regardless of what he was singing. The same could have been said of Maria Reining and Lisa della Casa in *Arabella* – both of whom located their portrayals of Strauss' *gemütlich* heroines in a tonal and vocal landscape that reached far beyond the corners of the score. It was no less true of Sarah Bernhardt, whose *Phèdre* was comparable in its technical and stylistic form to the legendary performances she gave in Paris as Lady Macbeth in May,

---

14 It is probably unnecessary to remind the reader that most of Schoenberg's followers (including Berg and Webern) were *not* Jewish. As early as 1933, an Austrian gauleiter speaking on Bayerischer Rundfunk characterised both Berg and Webern as Jewish composers, and not to praise them. See Notley, Margaret (2010). "1934, Alban Berg, and the Shadow of Politics: Documents of a Troubled Year." In *Alban Berg and His World*, ed. Christopher Hailey. Princeton University Press. pp.223–268.

15 Institut de Recherche et Coordination Acoustique.

1884.[16] Her *Phèdre* was not the "same" character as Lady Macbeth, but there was an undeniable commonality to the manner in which she used language and tone to communicate her emotional connection to the role she was playing. It follows that her reading of "*Oui, Prince, je languis, je brûle pour Thésée*" would have been comparable by intonation, energy and force to her reading of "*Le corbeau lui-même est enroué.*"[17] However, the power of her performances was located in her use of language, not some artificially grounded method-schooled immersion to character as costume. It is now routine for an actor to be admired for losing themselves to (and within) a role – typified by the (warranted) reverence for Charles Laughton's Quasimodo, Heath Ledger's Joker, and the entire life's work of Gary Oldman. It was previously a more common function of genius for an actor to be able to immerse themselves in the sound and meaning of a character's words while remaining otherwise ever-present. The paradox was not that an actor in the 19th century was thought to be playing themselves by adhering stubbornly to their "voice," but that a voice was capable of firing lightning into a role that could not otherwise be created in truth. Before method acting there was simply "acting," and that skill emerged commonly through the text and its delivery.[18]

This was true for Shakespeare in the 16th century, and for Racine in the 17th. It was most definitely not the case for composers of opera, whose *libretti* until the reformations of Gluck and Mozart (with obvious exceptions, notably Metastasio) were rarely more than frames for the stretching of a canvas. Clemens Krauss and Richard Strauss (or, perhaps, Richard Strauss and Clemens Krauss) satirised the form in their 1942 opera, *Capriccio*, when crafting the sublime pastiche duet "*Addio, mia vita, addio*"[19] for two nameless "Italian Singers."[20] Of course, the theme of *Capriccio* ("which is the greater art, poetry or music?" – captured by the rhetoric of "prima la musica, poi la parole" and its absent question mark) was a topic for debate during the late 18th century, when Salieri composed his opera *Prima la musica e poi le parole*. *Capriccio* dramatizes this dynamic through the story of a Countess torn between two suitors (Olivier, a poet, and Flamand, a composer). The immediacy of these arguments, as they were considered by Corneille and Handel, or Cimarosa and Antonio Sografi,[21] did not provoke any immediate change to the manner in which opera was performed

---

16 For Jean Richepin at the Théâtre de la Porte Saint-Martin, a revered theatre and opera house at 18, Boulevard Saint-Martin, in the 10th arrondissement of Paris. It was here, in 1887, that Bernhardt created the role of *La Tosca* for Victorien Sardou, with a hugely successful initial run of 200 performances. It is the same *La Tosca* that Puccini transformed into an opera in 1900.
17 'The raven himself is hoarse,' Act 1, Scene 5 *Macbeth*.
18 It is accepted that an entire culture of "silent" acting was created during the early 1910s in film, and until the late 1920s. But the emergence of "Classical" Hollywood, French Impressionism, German Expressionism and Soviet Montage *etc.* was (1) driven at all times by text – and writers – and by composers and performers. It is no small paradox that silent film, as art, was never actually silent.
19 'Goodbye my life, goodbye.'
20 For anyone wanting to see it done well, Marco Arturo Marelli's "safe" production at the Wiener Staatsoper in 2014 (conducted with rare theatrical intelligence by Christoph Eschenbach) can be seen on YouTube. The Italian singers are realised to comic perfection by Iride Martínez and Benjamin Bruns. The finest all-round performance on record is Karl Böhm's studio recording for DG, with Arleen Augér and Anton De Ridder, both peerless as the Italian Singers.
21 Salieri's librettist.

and perceived. The defining characteristic for the majority of audiences was the music and its performance, which is where the abuses of the *castrati* became intolerable.

The distinction that came to be made was that a singer's use of words until the late 18th century mattered less than what a singer was able to make of them technically. The capacity to fire off roulades and trills over breath-defying spans of time and patience animated the same impulse to virtuosity that caused audiences to swoon at the feet of Paganini and Liszt. Of course, while there is nothing wrong with sensationalism, it can slide easily into banality, and it was because singers isolated routinely the "unconstrained" expressive conception of the voice as an instrument, communicating nothing more than "beautiful sound alone," that Rossini advocated revolution.

He sought it fifty years before Sarah Bernhardt made her debut with the Comédie Française on 31 August, 1862, in the title role of Racine's *Iphigénie*. Her premiere was unsuccessful, notwithstanding the coaching of Jean-Baptiste Provost[22] and Joseph Samson[23] – voice teachers both born in the 18th century. After the curtain fell on her first night, Bernhardt was met in the wings by Provost, of whom she begged forgiveness. He replied, "I can forgive you, and you'll eventually forgive yourself; but Racine in his grave never will." The influential critic of *L'Opinion Nationale*, Francisque Sarcey, wrote that "she carries herself well and pronounces with perfect precision. That is all that can be said about her at the moment."

A few days later, Bernhardt's aunt held a dinner party. In her memoirs, and with casual understatement, she recalled the guest list including "the Duc de Morny, Camille Doucet and the Minister of Fine Arts, M. de Walewski, Rossini, my mother, Mlle. de Brabender, and I." She continued:

> My mother had dressed me very elegantly, and it was the first time I had worn a really low dress. Oh, how uncomfortable I was! Everyone paid me great attention. Rossini asked me to recite some verse, and I consented willingly, glad and proud to be of some little importance. I chose Casimir Delavigne's poem, "L'Ame du Purgatoire." "You must recite that to music!" exclaimed Rossini when I had finished. Everybody applauded this idea and Walewski said; "Mademoiselle will start again and you could improvise, dear Master." I was delirious. I began again and Rossini improvised a most delightful harmony, which filled me with emotion. My tears flowed freely without my being conscious of them, and at the end my mother kissed me, saying: "This is the first time that you have really moved me."[24] Mama adored music, and what had moved her was Rossini's improvisation. [25]

Bernhardt came to know Rossini during her childhood. She recalled how her

---

22 29 January, 1798 – 26 December, 1865.
23 2 July, 1793 – 28 March, 1871.
24 For readers unacquainted with the details of Bernhardt's life, this reference is as loaded as it would appear. Bernhardt's mother would have given Beowulf nightmares.
25 *My Double Life: The Memoirs of Sarah Bernhardt* (1999). State University of New York Press. p.64.

father used to visit my aunt Rosine's, who was then living at 6 Rue de la Chaussée d'Antin. He was on friendly terms with Rossini, who lived at No. 4 in the same street. He often brought him in, and Rossini made me laugh with his clever stories and comic grimaces.[26]

Another regular visitor to Rue de la Chaussée d'Antin was Adelina Patti,[27] one of the most celebrated sopranos of the 19th century. Her recordings are of exceptional importance because the voice they capture was revered by Rossini, Offenbach, Massenet and Verdi (among many others). Verdi described Patti in 1877 as the "finest singer" who had ever lived and a "stupendous artist."[28] Her talent and celebrity were sufficient for Patti to feature in works by Tolstoy (*Anna Karenina*), Oscar Wilde (*The Picture of Dorian Gray*), Edith Wharton (*The Age of Innocence*), Émile Zola (*Nana*), Jules Verne (*The Village in the Treetops*) and Arthur Conan Doyle (Sherlock Holmes' *Black Peter*). Her recording of "*Casta diva*" from 1906[29] is of particular consequence because she learned the aria with Maurice Strakosch,[30] a pianist who studied singing with (and often accompanied) Giuditta Pasta – the soprano who created the title role of *Norma* for Bellini in 1831. Pasta made her inauspicious debut in Milan in 1816 (in Scappa's *Le tre Eleonore*); her first appearance in Paris in 1821 as Desdemona in Rossini's *Otello* caused a riot. In 1843, Strakosch met the tenor Salvatore Patti (born in 1800) at a music festival in Venice, for whose family and operatic troupe he became tour manager in New York. Nine years later, Strakosch married Adelina's sister, Amalia.[31] From 1859, and until her marriage nine years later, Strakosch was Adelina's primary teacher as well as her manager.[32] During one of Rossini's "Salons de Samedi" she was asked to sing "*Una voce poco fa*," from *Il barbiere di Siviglia*; she did so using liberal amounts of ornamentation. "What composition was that?", asked the composer. "Your own," replied Strakosch. Rossini countered: "That is not my composition; that is Strakoschonnerie."[33]

Rossini was born seven years *before* Schubert. He spent time in the company of Beethoven and Goethe, after whose fashion he became a totem of European and (eventually) world culture. Between 1810 and 1829 (when he retired from the stage with the first performance of *Guillaume Tell*) he completed more than 30 operas for the Italian and French stages that achieved nothing less than the re-invention of the art, publishing, staging and performance of Italian music drama. There are a number

---

26 *Ibid*. pp.11–12.
27 10 February, 1843 – 27 September, 1919.
28 Cone, John Frederick and Moran, William R. (1993). *Adelina Patti: Queen of Hearts*. Amadeus Press. p. 129.
29 Patti did not perform Bellini's *Norma* on stage.
30 15 January, 1825 – 9 October, 1887.
31 Amelia Patti was the oldest daughter of Salvatore Patti and Catarina Barili. Adelina Patti was her sister. In 1852 she married the composer and impresario Maurice Strakosch, who worked for her sister Adelina. Later she lived in Paris were she gave singing lessons. She died there in 1915.
32 Between 1852 and 1854 Strakosch, Amalia, Adelina and Ole Bull toured the United States. In 1856 Strakosch managed his own company, which he merged with Bernard Ullman's troupe in February, 1857. The Ullman and Strakosch Opera Company presented opera at the Academy of Music and toured the East Coast until 1860. The final season was a disaster, and rescued only by Adelina Patti's début.
33 'Cochonnerie' is a pungent French idiom for rubbish. It translates as 'something fit only for pigs.'

of excellent appraisals of Rossini's achievements. One of the finest (and most concise) is by Rodolfo Celletti in his gloriously opinionated history of *bel canto*:[34]

> Mention is often made of 'Rossini's reform,' alluding to the fact that, by writing out in detail the whole of his coloratura parts, Rossini robbed singers of the possibility of improvising or of inserting passages, ornaments, and cadenzas. Aside from the fact that the situation is not exactly like that, the word 'reform' might be used also, indeed most of all, for other aspects of Rossini's operas. Rossini did in fact reform opera, both comic and serious. He reformed it by way of the attractiveness, the breadth, the invention, and the rhythmic impulse of his melodies; the sophistication of his paradoxical views on the comic element as applied to vocalism, to the chorus, and to the orchestra; the new, spicy, brilliant colours of his instrumentation; and the way in which he closed the gap between *opera giacosa* (comic opera) and *opera seria*, in the latter case reshaping the drive of the concerted numbers and finales of acts of the former and giving *opera giacosa* the same florid and sumptuous language as the other. At the vocal level, the advent of Rossini had as its main effect the spread of an approach to singing from which all the countries of Europe benefitted and which literally provided France, for example, over a lengthy period, with executants capable of competing with the Italian singers. Indeed, the years between 1820 and 1840, which most vividly felt the effects of Rossini's presence, represented a Golden Age for vocal art, as had occurred precisely a century earlier during the twenty years between 1720 and 1740.[35]

Rossini's achievement was facilitated by his response to the question posed in different ways by Salieri and Strauss: words or music? His answer did not reduce to "both are equally important," although that was manifestly his conviction; instead, he identified the means by which *parole e musica* might work in equivalence through voice – as a tool for communicating something *more* than the primacy of the performer. Rossini's genius was not located in some narrow "fitting" of music to words since, as he observed more than once, a writer's verse might engage a variety of emotions and mental states to which strict adherence was likely to produce little more than "a mere patchwork" of music.[36] The developing science of language studies did much to address the capacity for spoken and sung language to effect changed responses. The direction of the discourse during the first two decades of the

---

34 *Bel canto* (beautiful song) remains a controversial term for many. It is accepted as identifying music written by (and from the period of) Rossini, Donizetti and Bellini, but it would be absurd to distinguish the principles by which their music was defined (and considered well performed) from the music and performance traditions of Lully, Vivaldi and Mozart, or for that matter Strauss, Puccini and Ravel. Few composers wanted their music to sound other than beautiful – whatever their conception of drama and the dramatic. For this reason, the term is used infrequently throughout this book, and in most cases as a short-hand for early romantic Italian repertoire and performance styles.
35 Celletti, Rodolfo (2001). *A History of Bel Canto*. Clarendon. p.135.
36 *Ibid.* p.136.

19th century led to the emergence in Germany, in particular, of developed Jena-Romantic theorising, with two distinct schools of thought – one (led by Stephan Schütze) that promoted declamation as "the nucleus of melody,"[37] the other asserting that "music should not mirror declamation, but [rather] completely transform it into melody."[38] Schütze was certain that the composition of melody as an art consisted in

> bringing each accent into a melodic course so that a really beautiful melody results, so that it sounds as though the text had given the opportunity for a beautiful melody [...] Strictly, the text is never reproduced in the music, rather only the feeling on which it is based.[39]

The German pre-occupation with sound as science (culminating as it did for the enlightened with the pioneering work of Hermann von Helmholtz) even led to the conceptualisation of the emotional effect of words and music in their conjunction being seismographically attributable to the interaction of replicating waveforms. Rossini was either ignorant of or uninterested in the science behind his art. He did, however, bring an almost surgical talent to his isolation of sense and feeling through melody, with his construction of music and text qualifying as an inversion of

> the Platonic concepts of the Florentine opera composers and very early Monteverdi, or to those of the music-drama of Gluck and the Romantics. Here the singing is the outcome of the words, but respect for the prosody and inflections of the spoken language prevents the melody from spreading its wings. In Rossini, on the contrary, the melody does spread its wings, and its evolutions have an impact on the words, since the emotions of the listener always require, in the theatre, something which has reference to what is happening on the stage. In other words, significant melody gives significance even to words which in and of themselves would not have it.[40]

It was this consideration of the "truth" of sung melody that caused Rossini to detest the acrobatics of Velluti and Patti – though they were separated in their celebrity and pre-eminence by more than half a century; it was this concern for the dramatic, psychological and emotional proximity of text and music that led to his re-invention of opera, and his creation of the modern tenor voice.

The process by which Rossini came to value the metric of a text as highly as its setting was influenced substantively by the dramatic social changes that occurred during the 15 years either side of 1800, when revolution and war politicised all art – written, seen and heard. In particular, the de-stabilised social order and an aggressively expansionist *bourgeoisie* helped drive artists headlong into the jaws of state

---

37 Trippett, David (2016). *Wagner's Melodies: Aesthetics and Materialism in German Musical Identity.* Cambridge University Press. pp. 66–67.
38 *Ibid.* p.66.
39 Celletti, Rodolfo (2001). *A History of Bel Canto.* Clarendon Paperbacks. p.135.
40 *Ibid.* p.135.

censorship.⁴¹ In the Lombard provinces, instructions published in 1818 by the *Imperiale Regia Stamperia* provided a regulatory framework for the Kingdom of Lombardy-Venetia (then still a part of the Austro-Hungarian Empire) that compelled any bookseller and print dealer to keep a register with four categories of material: *admittitur* (works for public sale and distribution), *transeat* (works that could be sold, but not displayed or advertised), *erga schedam* (works that were censored but otherwise available for those with a special permit), and *damnatur* (works fully censored).⁴² The authorities' surveillance of the production of texts and images was reinforced by the strict regulation of printers, with any deviant book, booklet, leaflet, etching or woodcut being subjected to withdrawal or destruction. The range of "offending materials" was extended over time to include the sale of anything transgressive by framers, glassworkers, junk dealers and furniture sellers. In 1833 – four years after the premiere of *Guillaume Tell* – a note in the *Fascicolo Censura* confirmed that "from now on any representation of images, figures and emblems on fabric, furniture and the like to be sold on the market shall be subjected to censorship."⁴³ "Il proibito" extended to the expression of inflammatory political opinions even on private household furnishings – a category that included effigies of national heroes and scenes from famous battles.⁴⁴ The repressions experienced by artisans were no less acute for painters and sculptors, most of whom were terrified of seeing months and, in many cases, years of work forcibly abandoned. Many leaned on history, symbolism and metaphor, as did novelists and dramatists like Alessandro Manzoni, whose *I Promessi Sposi*⁴⁵ was set in 1628, during Spain's direct rule of northern Italy. The work of Vittorio Alfieri and Ugo Foscolo amplified the virtues of fatherland and the evils of foreign tyranny, in most cases with sledge-hammer innuendo, while Giovanni Berchet, Ludovico di Breme, Giuseppe Nicolini, and Silvio Pellico spooled poetry that resonated with moral and social cant.

"Composers are lucky," wrote the Austrian dramatist Franz Grillparzer in a conversation book when "speaking" to his friend Ludwig van Beethoven: "they don't

---

41 The Bourbon Restoration (1815 – 1830) was born of the Congress of Vienna, held by the victorious allies to restore the pre-revolutionary European political *status quo*. The Bourbons returned to Naples, and Joachim Murat declared war on Austria on March 15, 1815. In the Rimini proclamation of March 30 he incited all Italian nationalists to war, but no insurrection occurred. Murat was forced to abdicate in May and executed in October 1815. The Congress of Vienna established the political order in Italy that lasted until unification (1859 – 1870). Francis I of Austria became king of Lombardy-Venetia, which was incorporated into the Habsburg state, and the three aristocratic republics of Venice, Genoa, and Lucca were dismantled. Piedmont was restored, and with it undisputed Austrian rule in the peninsula. Austrian troops were garrisoned in Ferrara, ready to intervene in case of insurrection in the Papal States, and Austria gained further the right to intervene in the Kingdom of the Two Sicilies. The house of Habsburg ruled over Parma, Modena, and Tuscany; and Venetia and Lombardy became, in practice, provinces of the Austrian Empire. Only the Savoy kingdom of Sardinia-Piedmont remained outside the Austrian system designed and imposed on Italy by the Austrian foreign minister Klemens, Fürst (prince) von Metternich.
42 Negri A., Sironi M. (2015). "Censorship of the Visual Arts in Italy 1815–1915." In: Goldstein R.J., Nedd A.M. (eds) *Political Censorship of the Visual Arts in Nineteenth-Century Europe*. Palgrave Macmillan. pp.191–219.
43 Ibid.
44 Dèttore, Ugo (1941). "Le poltrone di 'nonna Speranza,'" in *Civiltà. Rivista dell'Esposizione Universale di Roma, Bompiani*; 21. pp.71–5.
45 'The Betrothed' (1827).

have to bother about the censors" – but, he added, "if only the censors knew what the musicians are thinking as they compose!" One of Beethoven's would-be collaborators, Christoph Kuffner, made a similar comment in another conversation book, noting that, "although words are subject to censorship, the sounds that represent and give force to words are not." The titanic German was untouchable, in most respects, during the 1820s – when he lunched with Rossini[46] but while Beethoven may have been uninterested in writing operas, many others were. The authorities were fearful of the power of musical theatre to provoke extreme emotional responses, and any risk that a work might stiffen the sinews was destined to cause someone, somewhere to become uneasy. Overtly provocative works like *La Marseillaise* were banned during the Restoration, but anything humming with republicanism was likely to compel a visit from a man with a clipboard and a rulebook. The most risk-inherent arena was the opera house, because it provided a forum for the dissemination of ideas to a kettled audience well-placed to discuss what was being said and sung on stage – both after and during a performance. Most European countries after the Congress of Vienna in 1815 were careful to assign artistic and administrative control to government censors, curtailing the elective freedoms of composers, librettists, producers and directors. Some censorship during the first quarter of the 19th century targeted alleged immorality and blasphemy. The guardians of theatrical probity were otherwise concerned with politically-charged material that could be seen and heard as dangerous for the prevailing socio-political order. In short: words mattered. As much was demonstrated by the execution of the Bandiera Brothers in 1844 for inciting rebellion and the unification of the Two Sicilies. They chose for their final words before hanging a direct quotation from Mercadante's opera *Donna Caritea*: "*Chi per la patria muor, vissuto è assai!*"[47]

For Rossini, *libretti* presented an opportunity for the development of modern romantic narratives and dramatic themes that resonated with nationalistic sentiments as well as universal emotional truths. Throughout his life he repeated in a variety of ways his defining belief that expression in music existed not in the manifestation of inner feeling, but in its provocation. In his *L'italiana in Algeri*,[48] for example, Rossini and his librettist, Angelo Anelli, made much of the flag-waving of Isabella's aria "*Pensa alla patria [e intrepido il tuo dover adempi: vedi per tutta Italia rinascere gli esempi d'ardir e di valor]*,"[49] during which the heroine rallies a group of slaves to flee their confinement.[50] The authors' intent resonated in the words and their articulation by a woman stood before an all-male chorus – representing the many, not the few – thereby cementing a mother-child construction that Rossini affirmed in a letter in 1864 in which he attached his life-long support for the Risorgimento to Anelli's libretto for *Algeri*.[51] In Philip Gossett's insightful analysis:

---

46 In April, 1822.
47 'He who dies for the fatherland has lived long enough.'
48 'The Italian Girl in Algiers,' first performed at the Teatro San Benedetto in Venice on 22 May, 1813.
49 'Think about the fatherland and intrepid do your duty: see for all Italy the birth of the examples of courage and value.'
50 In 1819, for a production in Rome, the libretto was amended to "*Pensa* alla sposa" ('Think about the bride').
51 Gossett, Philip. "Becoming a Citizen: The Chorus in 'Risorgimento' Opera." *Cambridge Opera Journal*, Vol. 2, No. 1 (Mar., 1990), pp.41–64.

The music at first is little more than blustery. Even when Rossini reaches the crucial verses, 'You'll see what Italians are worth in the moment of danger,' the choral melody remains almost neutral. Its meaning is subverted, however, by an orchestral tune assigned to the first violins and flute. It is hard not to discern the parody of a melody Rossini could presume his audiences would know well. Though no contemporary critic acknowledges this parodistic quotation of 'La Marseillaise,' there is evidence concerning its reception. In two manuscripts of *L'Italiana* the chorus alone (and not Isabella's following Rondo, '*Pensa alla patria*') is replaced by new music (not by Rossini) to the same words. However seditious textual reference to the worth of Italians might have been, the musical reference, for some contemporaries, was more troubling. Pre-performance censorship of opera (or at least pre-dress rehearsal censorship), after all, even in the most restrictive circumstances, was limited to words. What significance should we assign to this musical quotation? What did it mean to Venetian audiences in 1813? On one level it is a mere witticism, an ironic glance backwards at the unpopular French, who had sacrificed the Venetian Republic to their own political interests, ceding it to Austria in the Peace of Campo Formio of 1797. At the same time, we should not undervalue the impact of French Revolutionary ideals on Italian patriots, even those with bitter memories of Napoleon's invasion. 'La Marseillaise' existed both as a specific reference to Revolutionary France and as a reminder of its ideals. The meaning communicated by Rossini's quotation was not absolute, but rather a function of the changing audience to which its message would be addressed and the changing moments when that message would be received.[52]

Rossini scored the romantic leads for the comedic *Algeri* as a contralto (Isabella) and a tenor (Lindoro). The former he offered to Marietta Marcolini (who created five roles for Rossini between 1811 and 1814); for the latter he turned to Serafino Gentili, a "transition" tenor, who had created roles for Simon Mayr (Amorveno, in *Amor congiugale*,[53] 1805), Giuseppe Gazzaniga (Sandrino in *I due gemelli*, 1807), and Vincenzo Federici (Duarte in *La conquista delle Indie Orientali*,[54] 1808). His was a light-lyric voice, with the necessary range (in *falsetto*) to scale the moderately challenging demands of the role's tentpole arias: "*Languir per una bella*"[55] (a *cavatina* in Act I) and "*Ah come il cor di giubilo*"[56] (a *cavatina* in Act II). A third aria was later introduced to replace "*giubilo*" ("*Concedi amor pietosa*"[57]).

The need for every word to convey cognitive and psychological value was as important for Rossini as was the purely musical effect created by Gentili as a performer; that effect was subsumed inherently to the traditions of the *castrato*. Gentili's voice

---

52 *Ibid.*
53 'Conjugal love.'
54 'The conquest of the East Indies.'
55 'To languish for beauty.'
56 'Ah, like a heart in jubilation.'
57 'Grant compassionate love.'

was sweet, with neither edge nor energy. By intonation – and phonation (the process by which the vocal folds operate through quasi-periodic *vibrat*ion) – he was tasked with producing little more than uninterrupted sweetness of tone. Lindoro's *cantilenas* in *Algeri* require *some* dexterity, but they are otherwise formed by (and limited to) the expressive capacities of an even *legato* – absent force and amplitude. Virtuosity for Rossini as a composer for the post-*castrati* generation was isolated in expressive colour – despite, and not because of, the sort of technical bravura for which Cecilia Bartoli and Juan Diego Flórez are celebrated. The "fact" that Rossini wrote out many of the ornaments he was willing to tolerate on the part of his singers should not detract from his otherwise obsessive concern for the ability of a singer to take the composer's earth-bound music and raise it to the heavens by tone and the evocation of sentiment alone.

Contemporary critics and musicians alike recognised that Rossini's tenors (around 1815) were left in no uncertainty that the absolute value of the words when sung was in the emotional conjunction they formed with Rossini's melodies. That praxis served as a driver for singers as well as audiences. It was of acute consequence also at a time when the illiteracy rate in Italy was greater than seventy per cent. These changes coincided with the romantic movement, which was becoming especially important for a society desperate for heroes with at least one foot grounded in authenticity. The source of opera's power during the early 19th century was located in its transcendence of educational poverty, therefore, so that when the librettist Saverio Salfi wrote that theatres "should be regarded as the greatest of the public schools since [they alone are] capable of rendering public instruction a thing of pleasure,"[58] he knew absolutely what it was that people needed to be instructed in. The evolving conflation of the tenor and the heroic was a function also of the increasingly demarcated Italian bias for the power of the masculine, and the tacit acceptance that acts of violent resistance were the province commonly of the male. The female was "naturally" enfeebled, despite also being swaddled in the sky-blue shroud of Christ's *la perfetta madre vergine*. Notwithstanding her "innate" inadequacy and the originality of her "sin," Rossini's Isabella was still capable of leading men to freedom – and this almost twenty years before Eugène Delacroix painted *La Liberté guidant le peuple*,[59] forty-seven years before the passing of the Casati Law[60] and fifty-one years before Maria Mozzoni wrote *La donna e i suoi rapporti sociali in occasione della revisione del codice italiano*.[61]

When writing his earliest operas, the heroic was not for Rossini a priority – especially not for his tenors. The heroic and the romantic were consigned initially to *castrati* (*Aureliano in Palmira*, for Velluti) and contralti, while the tenor was confined

---

58 Sorba, Carlotta (2012). "National Theater and the Age of Revolution in Italy". *Journal of Modern Italian Studies* 17. p.402.
59 'Liberty Leading the People' (1830; Louvre).
60 Gabrio Casati (2 August, 1798 – 13 November, 1873) was an Italian politician. As Minister of Education, he passed the "Casati law,", which laid the ground for the unitarian Italy mass education system – which established a system for the training of young women as teachers in public schools.
61 'The woman and her social relationships on the occasion of the revision of the Italian Civil Code' (published 1864).

routinely to paternal roles such as Demetrio-Eumene in *Demetrio e Polibio* and Argirio in *Tancredi*. After relocating to Naples in 1815,[62] however, Rossini was required not only to elevate the Teatro di San Carlo's "uber-mezzo" soprano, Isabella Colbran[63] – who dominated the affections of the public as well as the theatre's impresario, Domenico Barbaia – but also the emerging coterie of tenors pushing themselves to the footlights as leading men. Their names survive because of their association with Rossini (and later Bellini and Donizetti) and because they were the first of a new breed of singer that was as popular as it was novel. Many were drawn initially to the flame ignited by Giacomo David, whose work as a teacher as well as a performer distinguished the continuing influence of the *castrati*. The most celebrated was Andrea Nozzari,[64] the evolution of whose voice reflected the changes in compositional and theatrical style around 1800.

Nozzari's professional life began as a *contraltino* in Paris, where he created roles in operas for the 18th century composers Paer, Cimarosa and Paisiello.[65] The high-sitting range of this repertoire contributed to the early ruin of his voice. After a period of re-training, and a contract with Barbaia, he re-emerged as a bari-tenor, expert in mid-voice roles featuring episodic virtuosity. Between 1815 (when he sang the first Leicester in *Elisabetta, regina d'Inghilterra*) and 1823, when he took part in the first performance of Donizetti's *Alfredo il grande*, he created no fewer than eight tenor roles for Rossini.[66] During the same period Rossini composed six roles for Nozzari's sometime rival[67] – and son of Giacomo *père* – Giovanni David.[68] David *fils* had a vocal range of almost three octaves, reaching an F5 (and even, allegedly, a G5), a note that and an A5) – notes that categorised him, in modern terms, as a counter-tenor. He was skilled with florid writing and made much of a *messa di voce* that Rossini came to detest but which kept audiences enthralled, such that many remarked on the uncharacteristic weight of silence that would fall over the house whenever David and Nozzari occupied the stage together. They did so on many occasions, most famously, for Rossini, as Otello and Rodrigo.

Otello, Il moro di Venezia was first performed in Naples, at the Teatro del Fondo,[69] on 4 December, 1816. The San Carlo (built for the first time in 1737) was unavailable

---

62   At the invitation of San Carlo's legendary impresario Domenico Barbaia. Colbran was Barbaia's mistress at the time. She married Rossini seven years later, in 1822.

63   Colbran (2 February, 1785 – 7 October, 1845) studied in Paris under the *castrato* Girolamo Crescenti (2 February, 1762 – 24 April, 1846).– but not for long. Before her 21st birthday she was a European celebrity. For the first of his "Naples" operas, Rossini cast her with good reason as Elizabeth I (*Elisabetta, regina d'Inghilterra*).

64   27 February, 1776 – 12 December, 1832.

65   Castellani, Giuliano. *Ferdinando Paer: biografia, opere e documenti degli anni parigini*. (2009). Verlag Peter Lang.

66   Leicester in *Elisabetta, regina d'Inghilterra* (1815), *Otello* (1816), Rinaldo in *Armida* (1817), Osiride in *Mosè in Egitto* (1818), Agorante in *Ricciardo e Zoraide* (1818), Pirro in *Ermione* (1819), Rodrigo in *La donna del lago* (1819), Paolo Erisso in *Maometto II* (1820), and Antenore in *Zelmira* (1822).

67   Although they were rarely at odds, living up to the Italian idiomatic optimism of *Cane non mangia cane...*

68   Narciso in *Il turco in Italia* (1814), Rodrigo in *Otello* (1816), Ricciardo in *Ricciardo e Zoraide* (1818), Oreste in *Ermione* (1819), Uberto in *La donna del lago* (1819), and Ilo in *Zelmira* (1822).

69   Now the Teatro Mercadante.

because it had been damaged by fire ten months earlier, on 13 February,[70] during a ballet. The original theatre held 1,379 seats. With standing room it accommodated an audience of more than 3,000. Barbaia rebuilt the auditorium as a horseshoe, adding 65 seats, widening the stage and the proscenium to 33.5 metres, and deepening it to 31 metres. For context, the New York Metropolitan Opera (at the Lincoln Centre) has a ticket capacity of around 4,000 – with 3,732 primary seats and 245 standing room places – and a considerably smaller stage than the 1817 San Carlo, at 24 metres in depth and 31 metres in width. On 12 January, 1817, the rebuilt theatre was inaugurated with a production of Mayr's *Il sogno di Partenope*. Among the audience during the first week was the composer Louis Spohr, who recorded:

> there is no better place for ballet and pantomime. Military movements of infantry and cavalry, battles, and storms at sea can be represented here without falling into the ludicrous. But for opera, itself, the house is too large. Although the singers, Signora Isabella Colbran, and the Signori Nozzari, Benedetti, etc., have very strong voices, only their highest and most stentorian tones could be heard. Any kind of tender utterance was lost.[71]

Rossini's *Il moro* is less distinguished than Verdi's *Otello* from 1887. Many who claim to know the earlier work claim also to loathe it – because it's not by Verdi[72] and because of the apparently unforgivable liberties taken with Shakespeare's play by the librettist Francesco Maria Berio[73]. Mary Shelley attended a performance in 1819; she considered the libretto "a wretched piece of business."[74] Lord Byron wrote from Venice the previous year:[75]

> To-morrow night I am going to see 'Otello,' an opera from our Othello, and one of Rossini's best, it is said. It will be curious to see in Venice the Venetian story itself represented, besides to discover what they will make of Shakespeare in music.

Two weeks later, on 3 March, 1828, Byron wrote to the poet Samuel Rogers:

> They have been crucifying Othello into an opera (Otello, by Rossini): the music good, but lugubrious; but as for the words, all the real scenes

---

70   A Tuesday, rather than a Friday…
71   Spohr, Louis (1961). Trans./Ed. Henry Pleasants. *The Musical Journeys of Louis Spohr, Journey to Switzerland and Italy 1815–17*. University of Oklahoma Press. p.176.
72   See, for example, Klein, W. "Verdi's 'Otello' and Rossini's." *Music & Letters*, vol. 45, no. 2, 1964, pp.130–140.
73   The role of Roderigo, a sub-plot in Shakespeare and Verdi, is made prominent, and the drama ends when Otello reconciles with Desdemona and pardons a chastened Iago.
74   Mangini, Nicola (1974). *I teatri di Venezia*. Mursia. pp.86–89.
75   On 20 February, 1818, to his publisher John Murray. Byron was Murray's most notable author, which fact was confirmed by the publisher's decision to pay him more than £20,000 for rights. Their letters are magnificent fun. On 10 March, 1812, Murray published Byron's *Childe Harold's Pilgrimage*, which sold out in five days, leading Byron to observe "I awoke one morning and found myself famous."

with Iago cut out, and the greatest nonsense instead; the handkerchief turned into a billet-doux, and the first singer would not black his face, for some exquisite reasons assigned in the preface. Singing, dresses, and music, very good.

Byron's spite was unwarranted. *Othello* (1603) was itself an adaptation of a short story,[76] and neither Berio nor Rossini had read or seen Shakespeare's play. They based their opera on *Othello, ou le More de Venise*, an adaptation from 1792 by Jean-François Ducis. Critics who bemoan the opera's liberties fail to appreciate that Rossini and Berio were adhering to their source material;[77] notwithstanding the expectations of purists, Rossini's landscape-changing music was enough to cause a sensation. Each of the primary male roles was written for a tenor:[78] Andrea Nozzari (Otello), Giovanni David (Rodrigo), and Giuseppe Ciccimarra (Iago). In addition, Rossini scored three further parts for tenor: the Doge of Venice (created by Gaetano Chizzola), Lucio, and a Gondolier (both for Nicola Mollo). Only three of the opera's nine roles was scored for a voice *other* than a tenor: Desdemona (Colbran; soprano), Emilia (Maria Manzi; mezzo-soprano) and Elmiro (Michele Benedetti; bass).

The work's "Grand" innovations were obvious on the opening night. The thrilling writing for brass instruments, the introduction's novel conjoining of chorus and principals, and the use of dramatic freeze as soliloquy were all striking in their originality. The bedroom scene in Act 3,[79] with its orchestral representation of a storm, has been characterised as the watershed between opera of the 18th century and that of the 19th, while the writing for the leads qualifies as a paradigm shift. In particular, the abandonment of "numbers" is definitive of the full emergence of the romantic movement for Italian musical theatre. In particular, Act 2's almost half-hour ensemble for Otello, Rodrigo, Iago, Desdemona and chorus, beginning "*Non m'inganno*" and ending with "*L'error d'un infelice*" are without precedent in their through-composed fluency – which admitted little room for breath, either from the stage or the auditorium.

The need for dramatic focus and force in the mid-range of the title role's voice-writing represented the genesis of the modern tenor. The once and former *contraltino* Nozzari had to procure an amplitude of tone that was anomalous for contemporary tenors. In the light of the enormous size of the San Carlo theatre, Rossini's demands were ungenerous, at best. The title role is, for the most part, absent technical virtuosity; which left Nozzari little room for vainglorious display while coincidentally compelling a sharper focus on the emotional substance of his character's thoughts and sentiments. The writing for Rodrigo is more traditional in its flamboyance – with

---

76 *Un Capitano Moro* ['A Moorish Captain'] (1565) by Cinthio, a disciple of Boccaccio.
77 Ducis' translations and adaptations of Shakespeare's plays involved the routine rehashing of plots and the renaming of characters. In addition, there had been an attempted revolution in Naples earlier in the year, which sought the establishment of liberal constitutional rule across Italy. Rossini was obliged in consequence to ensure an upbeat resolution, in which the characters' schemes were revealed and the wrongdoers forgiven.
78 Cassio was eliminated completely.
79 Giacomo Meyerbeer wrote that *Otello*'s third act established the opera's reputation so firmly that "a thousand errors could not shake it." He considered it "really godlike, and what is so extraordinary is that its beauties are quite un-Rossini-like. First-rate declamation, continuously impassioned recitative, mysterious accompaniments full of local colour … brought to highest perfection."

a plenitude of high notes and roulades thrown into the mix; his part is striking also for its emphasis on the conjunction of words, music and emotion. The *cantilena* that forms the heart of Act 2's "*Che ascolto*"[80] is especially affecting in its characterisation of Rodrigo's feelings of betrayal, with the audible fluctuations of his broken heart captured in music of tactile pathos.[81] Nozzari's vocal power was formidable. Less than a year after the re-opening of the San Carlo, he was the acknowledged model for the emerging Romantic tenor, an archetype that reached its summit forty years later with the voice and career of Enrico Tamberlik.

Nozzari was the first to attach the tenor to the musical and theatrical conditions of the hero/lover, establishing a polarity that would become routine for Bellini, Donizetti and pretty much everyone else. Rossini's devotion to Nozzari extended to a predilection for his *tessitura*, and with *Armida* (1817) this weakness descended almost to monotony. Of the opera's seven major roles, six were scored for bari-tenors, all of them playing one form or another of romantic-heroic cypher: Nozzari as Rinaldo, Claudio Bonoldi as Gernando and Ubaldo, Giuseppe Ciccimarra as Carlo and Goffredo, and Gaetano Chizzola as Eustazio.

It is tempting to attach Rossini's affection for the bari-tenor to the register's relative ease of vocal production – a facility that made the probable dissemination of Rossini's works more likely. The coincidence after 1815 of theatre-building, publishing, journalism and steam trains – across Europe and, eventually, the United States – resolved an ever-expanding market in which Rossini was far from alone in recognising the need for singers outside Italy to be able to perform roles without the supervision and guidance of the composer. There was little hope of royalties when impresarios were unable to cast a new work in the regions. It was a gradual process, of course – one that saw the separation of the romantic bari-tenor from the *leggiero* tenor voices on which Rossini had otherwise relied for his comic works.

This distinction was brought sharply into focus by *Il barbiere di Siviglia, ossia L'inutile precauzione*, first performed at the Teatro Argentina in Rome on 20 February, 1816. The first Almaviva, Manuel García, was born, appropriately enough, in Seville.[82] He was a chorister at the Catedral de Santa María de la Sede, and through his teachers, Antonio Ripa and Juan Almarcha, he was able to trace his lineage back to Porpora. In 1812, he relocated to Italy where he was taught the mechanics of projection by Giovanni Ansani. Incredibly for a singer who was never anything other than a tenor, García's part in the first Spanish performance of *Le nozze di Figaro* in 1801 was as Count Almaviva. When staging his first *Don Giovanni* in the United States (at the Park Theatre in New York on 23 May, 1826), he performed the title role – with the librettist, Lorenzo Da Ponte, among the audience.[83] On 11 February,

---

80 "*Che ascolto! ahimè! che dici! Ah! come mai non senti / pietà de' miei tormenti, del mio tradito amor?*" ['Listen! Alas! What do you say! Ah! How can you feel no pity for my torment, of my betrayed love?']
81 Rodrigo is shadowed throughout "*Che ascolto*" by a glorious clarinet solo that anticipates Alvaro's apotheosis of miserabilist solipsism in "*La vita è inferno all'infelice …*" in *La forza del destino*.
82 21 January, 1775 – 10 June, 1832.
83 In 1825, García travelled to New York with a small troupe of European singers, which included his wife, his son and his daughter. He announced a season of opera during which, as he put it, "the choicest Italian operas will be performed in a style which he flatters himself will give general satisfaction." Rogers, Francis. "America's First Grand Opera Season." *The Musical Quarterly*, Vol. 1, No. 1 (Jan., 1915). pp.93–101.

1826, García staged (and created the title role in) the first US performance of *Otello*. Edmund Kean was appearing in New York at the same time – as Othello – and commended García and his company on their performance. The audience was in agreement with Kean. According to *The Evening Post*, they were "astonished by his masterly powers, many of whom had no conception that so much tragic effect could be given in recitative." It follows that García was renowned for his work as a lyric tenor (Rossini's Almaviva) while being able at the same time to sing baritone roles (Mozart's Almaviva). *Otello* stood somewhere between the two, although at the time of his first US *Don Giovanni* it is clear that his approach adhered stylistically more closely to Rossini's aesthetics than to Mozart's:

> His voice was no longer at home in the simple melodies of Mozart. He must have a wide field for display; he must have ample room to verge enough for unlimited curvetings [graceful, energetic leaps] and flourishes. It was a maxim with García that no one can ever be a great singer until the voice be a little impaired; that is, that a singer should depend more on his science than on his natural gifts. By his extraordinary skill he has contrived to hide many vocal defects, and in his time obtained the reputation of the first tenor singer in Europe.

The richness and security of García's low and middle voice might suggest that Rossini's casting of García as Almaviva was eccentric, since the role has been performed for more than a century by light-voiced *tenorinis* (such as Tito Schipa, Cesare Valletti and Luigi Alva). It's obvious from his repertoire, however, that García's voice carried unusual weight as well as range. He created Norfolk (*Elisabetta*) for Rossini in 1815, and in Paris he was the first French-staged Lindoro (*L'italiana in Algeri*; 1 February, 1816), Torvaldo (*Torvaldo e Dorliskj*; 21 November 1820), *Otello* (5 June, 1821), and Osiride (*Mosè in Egitto*; 20 October, 1822). In London he was the first Ilo (*Zelmira*; 24 January, 1824), Agorante (*Ricciardo e Zoraide*; 24 March, 1824) and Idreno (*Semiramide*; 15 July, 1824). Between 29 November, 1825, and 27 June, 1827, he staged (and frequently took part in) eighty US premieres – including dozens of works by Mozart and Rossini. According to the musicologist and composer François-Joseph Fétis (who gave the oration at García's funeral when he was buried at Père Lachaise), García was "a deep tenor"; certainly, when first singing for Rossini, it was the amplitude of his baritonal register that attracted the composer. This depth of tone did nothing to dissuade Rossini from tailoring parts for García that rose *higher* above the stave than did the parts he wrote for Nozzari – and García plainly enjoyed fussing with the composer's melodies, as was the fashion at the time. Despite his alleged range, however, he would transpose difficult arias by as much as a third, and was renowned also as a falsettist.[84]

Beyond his status as the first Almaviva, the reach of García's influence was extraordinary. His elder daughter was the legendary mezzo-soprano Maria Malibran[85] (beloved of Bellini and Donizetti); his second daughter was the soprano Pauline

---

84   He was capable of singing soprano parts (after the fashion of modern counter-tenors). Caruselli, Salvatore (ed) *Grande enciclopedia della musica lirica*. (1980) Longanesi & C. Periodici S.p.A. p.506.
85   24 March, 1808 – 23 September, 1836.

Viardot,[86] one of the 19th century's most profligate over-achievers. In addition to Viardot's talents as a composer, she was a muse to Berlioz, Gounod, Chopin, Saint-Saëns (who dedicated *Samson et Dalila* to her), Meyerbeer, Brahms (for whom she gave the first performance of the *Alto Rhapsody*[87] in 1870) and Turgenev (her lover over many years). García's son, Manuel *fils* (or "García II") was a mediocre baritone who became the world's pre-eminent vocal pedagogue. He invented the first laryngoscope, and taught (among *many* others) Jenny Lind, Christina Nilson and, improbably, Sir Henry Wood. He died in London in 1906 – at the age of 101 – having the previous year sat for a magnificent portrait by John Singer Sargent.[88] When delivering a speech in London[89] on 17 March, 1905, at a dinner held in celebration of his 100th birthday, García remembered performing in the United States with his father – who had made his debut as a treble in 1781, eight years before the onset of the French Revolution and five years before the premiere of *Le nozze di Figaro*.

Seven months after García dined in London on *Salmon Sauce Mousseline*, *Aspic de Fòie Gras en Belle Vue*, and *Selle d'Agneau à la broche* (as well as a further five courses and *café et petit fours*), the Spanish-born tenor Florencio Constantino stood in front of a horn[90] and recorded Rossini's "*Ecco, ridente in cielo spunta la bella aurora,*"[91] first performed by García's father 89 years earlier. Almaviva's *cavatina*, in C major, opens with a solo for tenor and guitar, paired with strings and woodwind; between them the poor student and the street musicians he has hired to accompany him attempt to wake the girl he loves, Rosina. It is a sublime, lachrymose invention that captures the painful intensity of young love. The aria's shift in tempo and mood, as Almaviva catches sight of Rosina, resolves in his declaration of love. The laconic elegance is thrilling and disciplined. Both parts of the aria stand on their own – without the need for embellishment, decoration or a *rubato* that is anything less than *tempo*. And yet the tradition since the onset of recording has been to add as much whipped-cream as a conductor's largesse will tolerate – even with Toscanini and Muti asserting their "faithfulness" to the score by adhering oxymoronically to its *urtext*. In this sense only, there is continuity between the end of the 19th century and the 21st. Constantino was born in Bilbao in 1869; he made his stage debut in Brèton's opera *La Dolores* at the Teatro Solís in Montevideo in 1895. Between 1907 and 1917 Constantino sang regularly throughout the United States in an extraordinary variety of roles that spanned Almaviva in *Il Barbiere*, Arturo in *I puritani*, the Duke in *Rigoletto*, Alfredo in *La traviata*, Raoul in *Les Huguenots*, Gounod's *Faust*, Rodolfo in *La Bohème*, Cavaradossi in *Tosca*, Maurizio in *Adriana Lecouvreur* – and *Lohengrin*. Constantino's (heavily truncated) performance of "*Ecco, ridente*" is revealing.[92] He sings with little *portamento*, a quick ("stretto") *vibrato*, and decidedly imperfect pitch. The embellishments

---

86 18 July, 1821 – 18 May, 1910.
87 Rhapsodie für eine Altstimme, Männerchor und Orchester, Op. 53.
88 It can be seen at the Rhode Island School of Design Museum in Providence, Rhode Island, United States.
89 At the Hotel Cecil, demolished in part in 1930 and replaced by Shell Mex House.
90 For the Favorite label. The recording was made in Paris on October 4, 1905.
91 'Here, laughing in heaven emerges the beautiful dawn.'
92 When he recorded the *cavatina* for the second time, in 1909, the speed adopted by whoever was directing the performance was breakneck.

are his own, as is his apparent contempt for bar-lines; the accompanist is commendably sympathetic in adhering to the singer's extravagant *rubato*. The vocal tone is open, easy and varied in its expressive range; he engages in some exceptionally fine *messa di voce* and balletic *fioriture*, with some interesting leaps that make little musical sense, even if they show off the singer's self-evident technical assurance. In short, there is much to enjoy – with a lingering sense that he *might* love Rosina more than himself.

The problem for musicologists is that the history of singing predates recording, which compels a necessary reliance on the inherent subjectivity of testimony. García *fils* was 30 years old in 1835; he wrote his landmark vocal "method" in 1840, shortly before moving to London, where he established himself as a pre-eminent vocal coach. His book (in a later edition from 1905) asks: "What are the principal styles of singing?" He replies:

> In 1723 Tosi recognized three: Stilo da Camera, Stilo di Chiesa, and Stilo di Teatto. In modern times these divisions are not the same, but still there are three principal forms from which all the others are derived, namely:
>
> *Cantoto spianato* – plain style.
> *Canto fiorito* – florid style.
> *Canto declamato*—declamatory style.
>
> Q.   How do you describe the *Canto spianato?*
>
> A.   This, the noblest of all styles (but also the least lively on account of slowness of movement and simplicity of form), is based entirely on the degrees of passion and the variety of musical light and shade. The chief resources of this style (and nothing can replace them) are perfect intonation, steadiness of voice, propriety of timbre, clear and expressive articulation, swelled sounds of every kind, the most refined effects of *piano* and *forte,* the *portamento,* and the *tempo rubato.* This style, although the least favourable to rapid *fioriture,* admits of the use of the *appoggiatura,* turns, and shakes. Other ornaments, if employed, should harmonise with the slowness of its movement and the gentle nature of its expression. It is hardly necessary to remark that though brilliant passages are inappropriate, it is equally imperative to avoid heaviness and dragging. In *cantabile* movements most phrases begin *piano.* Time must be kept, but not accented. In quick movements, on the contrary, time should be marked. These rules are rigorously applied to *Larghi and Adagii.* The other slow movements, such as *Cantabile, Maestoau, Andante,* &c., though retaining a certain gravity, are much modified by borrowing from the florid style.
>
> Q.   How do you describe the florid style?
>
> A.   This style abounds in ornaments. In it the singer may display the fertility of his imagination, and indulge in *roulades, arpeggi,* and rapid

passages of all kinds. The execution should be light and the voice spared. When power and passion are applied to brilliant execution it becomes the *bravura* style.

Q. Are there other modifications of the florid style?

A. There is one called *Canto di Maniera,* created by singers whose voices were wanting in great power, and though sufficiently supple for the execution of all kinds of intervals, did not possess extreme agility. Small embellishments and arpeggiated passages, often divided by syllables and inflections, formed an elegant, delicate style, also known as *Alodi di Canto,* well fitted for graceful sentiments, whether gay or tender.

Q. What is the declamatory style?

A. Dramatic singing. It is nearly always monosyllabic, and almost entirely excludes vocalization. It is divided into the serious and the comic.

García's values, as a singer born only five years after the end of the 18th century, were formed by considerations of emotion, dynamic contrast, intonation, "steadiness of voice" (meaning the avoidance of *vibrato*), clear and expressive timbre and articulation, *messa di voce*, and the "refined" use of *chiaroscuro, portamento,* and *tempo rubato*. Ornaments were to operate *only* in harmony with the written score and the "nature" of the music's expression. Heaviness and dragging were to be avoided, with time being kept but not (other than at speed) accentuated. In short, García was celebrating singing as it was captured on record by Adelina Patti.[93] García's teaching was remembered in writing by his pupils, one of whom, Hermann Klein[94] (an eventual critic for the London *Times*), began his studies in 1875. García's studio occupied the ground floor of the Klein family home in London, so Klein overheard much before becoming a student himself. In 1905 he contributed a preface and notes to the second edition of García's *Hints on Singing*[95] (published in a translation "from French into English"). Two years earlier Klein recalled how

> [T]hough his own voice might tremble with sheer weight of years, he never, to my knowledge, brought out a pupil whose tones were marred by the slightest shade of vibrato. Nor was he at any time guilty of the sin of 'forcing a voice'. I say so with all possible emphasis, because that untrue assertion has been made on various occasions, and it should be contradicted as a libel upon a teacher whose first rule was ever to repress the breathing power and bring it into proper proportion with the resisting

---

93   And by Emma Albani (1847 – 1930) – a student of the legendary tenor Gilbert-Louis Duprez (see further Chapter 3 below). Her recordings confirm that Patti was not atypical stylistically of the period and the genre.
94   23 July, 1856 – 10 March, 1934. For thirteen years, Klein was a vocal teacher at the Guildhall School of Music in London, becoming a lifelong proponent of the methods of Manuel García and helping to edit García's book on the subject.
95   García, Manual (1840). *Traité Complet de l'Art du Chant*. Brandus et Cie.

force of the throat and larynx. The contrary proceeding would have been altogether inconsistent with the system of the old Italian school, whereof García is the last really great teacher.[96]

Constantino does not appear to have studied with García, and he was not "of the old Italian school." His quick *vibrato* is invasive, and palpably more than shade; his short (or absent) *portamento* speaks to contemporary taste as well as a technical limitation – particularly when compared with Adelina Patti, whose 1906 recording of *Norma's* "*Casta Diva*" features almost no *vibrato* (and then only on the repeated high Bs of "*sembiante*" and the final "*ciel*"), as well as a pronounced *legato-portamento*, which is even more conspicuous in her recording of "*Ah non Credea Mirarti*" from *La Sonnambula*. There is a marked difference in the stylistic affectations of these singers, such that the "modern" (Constantino) can be distinguished absolutely from the "old" (Patti). Magnified by his pervasive *vibrato*, Constantino's occasionally forced, almost bleached tone is ugly when compared to that of Patti, who relies more obviously on diction, line and lucidity of tone for effect. Her effortless use of *fioriture* qualifies as a varnish. Dexterity for Constantino equates to marquetry.

In 1904, Almaviva's "*ecco ridente*" was recorded by Fernando de Lucia,[97] a student of Beniamino Carelli.[98] De Lucia is thought by many to be an aftershock of 19th century *bel canto*, and there are hints at a lost age in some of his *sfumando* elegance. He was otherwise a weapon of the *veristi*, and his singing on record is incontestably modern in tone, line and presentation. His 1904 "*ecco*," for example, is coloured throughout by a *vibrato* that was omnipresent only for singers hitting their stride during the final two decades of the 19th century. He makes better use of it than does Constantino, but de Lucia's unrelenting "shake" was divisive, and García and his predecessors entirely detested it. Critics attaching themselves to fading aesthetics considered it an expressive abuse and a barrier to diction. The monochromatic reliance on *vibrato*, after the fashion of Yves Klein's studies in blue, was no less repugnant to the generation of violinists that predated the "Auer"[99] School – personified by Joseph Joachim[100] – because it spoke to an absence of technique and a lapse in expressive discretion. Joachim referred to *vibrato* as an ornament, as it had been during the 18th century, when an unembellished long-held note was thought distasteful. In the first edition of Francesco Geminiani's treatise of 1751, the composer and pedagogue held that violinists should introduce the "close shake … as often as possible to make the sound more agreeable." However, because he marked certain of his scores with indications of where *vibrato* was appropriate, it's plain that his conception of "as often as possible" was paradigmatically "sporadic".

In Robert Bremner's *Some Thoughts on the Performance of Concert Music* (a preface to his publication of Schetky's 6 Quartettos, Op. 6[101]), he held that "where the

---

96   Klein, Hermann (1903). *Thirty Years of Musical Life in London*. The Century Co. pp.370 – 371.
97   1 September, 1861 – 21 February, 1925.
98   9 May, 1833 – 14 February, 1921.
99   Leopold von Auer. 7 June, 1845 – 15 July, 1930. Hungarian violinist and the most successful violin teacher of the 20th century.
100 28 June, 1831 – 15 August, 1907.
101 1777. *Etc.*

beauty and energy of the performance depend upon the united effect of all parts being exactly in tune with each other, [*vibrato*] becomes hurtful." Leopold Mozart compared *vibrato* to palsy, while the Italian violinist Galeazzi advocated in the 1790s that *vibrato* should "be entirely banned from music by anyone equipped with good taste." In 1811, the English violinist John Jousse wrote that "the Tremolo or Close Shake [had] become obsolete," and during the first two decades of the 19th century almost everyone referring to *vibrato* warned against its use other than as a colour, with Baillot's *Methode* of 1803 failing even to acknowledge its existence. In his updated treatise, published in 1834, Baillot revised his earlier silence by writing that, when used frequently, *vibrato* had "the disadvantage of making the melody unnatural and depriving the style of that precious naivety which is the greatest charm of art and recalls it into its primitive simplicity." Almost a century later, in his *Violin Playing as I teach it*,[102] Leopold Auer urged his fellow violinists and students against continuous *vibrato*, although he recognised that the tide was now beating against the sea wall. Significantly, he wrote that *both* singers and string players had

> called into being a plague of the most inartistic nature, one to which 90 out of every 100 vocal and instrumental soloists fall victim, in an ostrich-like endeavour to conceal bad tone production and intonation [...] Those who are convinced that an eternal *vibrato* is the secret of soulful playing, of piquancy in performance are pitifully misguided in their belief [...] Their musical taste (or what does service for them in place of it) does not tell them that they can reduce a program of the most dissimilar pieces to the same dead level of monotony by peppering them all with the tabasco of a continuous *vibrato*. No, the *vibrato* is an effect, an embellishment; it can lend a touch of divine pathos to the climax of a phrase or the course of a passage, but only if the player has cultivated a delicate sense of proportion in the use of it.

The traditions of De Lucia's youth can be traced through his exceptional range of vocal colour and beautifully judged *rubato*. He was confident also in his use of improvised ornaments, which extended to his anachronistic modification of "*Che gelida manina*" when recording Rodolfo's aria in 1917. His occasionally forced tone attached him to a generation that considered amplitude a defining virtue, so that while De Lucia was long associated with the role of Almaviva, he was actively reviled when first appearing in *Il Barbiere* in London – not least for his "excessive" *vibrato*.[103] Despite being only 18 years younger than Patti, de Lucia was in every sense a 20th century tenor – and antithetical in style to the bari-tenors cultivated by Rossini. It is tempting to think that Gaetano Crivelli[104] and Giulio Bordogni[105] – Nozzari's most celebrated bari-tenor rivals – might have sounded in some way like de Lucia (as some have argued), but Rossini's regard for Adelina Patti suggests that the limpid tone

---

102 Published in 1921.
103 Scott, Michael (1977). *The Record of Singing to 1914*. Duckworth. p.124.
104 20 October, 1768 – 16 July, 1836.
105 23 January, 1789 – 31 July, 1856.

and pure line for which she is remembered were consistent with (and comparable to) the sounds produced by García *père* in *Il Barbiere*, Crivelli in *Il crociato in Egitto* (alongside Velluti) and Bordogni when creating Conte di Libenskof for Rossini in *Il viaggio a Reims*.

How might one compare the performance by Sarah Bernhardt of "*Oui, Prince, je languis, je brûle pour Thésée*" in 1906 to that of Dominique Blanc in 2003? They are in every conceivable and measurable sense incomparable. Moreover, it is unlikely there was anything to distinguish between the work of Patti (who was born the year before Bernhardt) in 1906, and Auer's teaching in 1921 as it concerned aesthetics and expressive values. Indeed, Bernhardt and Patti were both products of a culture that placed as much emphasis on the significance of word formation as it did expression. *Declamation* was not the same thing for the early 19th century as *declamatory* (a distinction made repeatedly by García), and where the former would become routine for tenors in the wake of *verismo*, the latter was a colouristic detail – a tool for the addition of emphasis and effect, analogous to *vibrato* and *portamento*. Albertine Zehme's concern for words first, and music either second or (at least) ancillary to the power of non-musical articulation, was Rossini's priority also; it is evident from Patti's recordings and García's teachings that their concerns were directed with equal force towards the expressive value of words *and* music to communicate something more than "beautiful sound alone." It is for this reason that the concept analytically and historically of *bel canto* – as a reductive shorthand for languid or acrobatic melody where sound and technical bravura eclipse (or compensate for the occlusion of) meaning – is a corruption of the very art form to which supposedly it refers. In other words, what passes in the 21st century for *bel canto* on stage and record is for the most part antithetical to the values memorialised by Rossini, Bellini, Donizetti and their singers.

It is no longer possible to hear singers perform romantic opera *without* incessant *vibrato* – or in many cases overt wobbling. Rossini, García *père et fils* and Patti pushed against its ubiquity because *vibrato* will always disguise and interfere with the clarity of the words being sung. This explains why, in part, Patti allowed *vibrato* to colour the high Bs of *sembiante* and *ciel*, because the use of colour did not interfere with the placement cognitively and expressively of the words. It's important to remember also that singers had to present new works on a weekly basis – when the need for clarity could not be compensated for by an audience's long-standing exposure to a libretto, or the addition of surtitles. Everyone can now read in books and online the poetry of "*Casta Diva*"; no-one knew it when *Norma* was first performed in 1831.

Permanent *vibrato* allows for a greater amplitude of tone (*i.e.*, volume). The growth in the size of orchestras and theatres compelled ever larger voices – something for which Rossini was, of course, directly responsible. In early 1822, for example, a sign of the times to come was witnessed in Rome, when the Italian Amerigo Sbigoli was singing the second tenor part in a performance of Pacini's opera *Cesare in Egitto*, at the Teatro Argentina. Sbigoli was sharing the stage with the bari-tenor Domenico Donzelli.[106] Sbigoli's character was required to sing a phrase in imitation of Donzelli. In striving to match his rival's famously resonant instrument he overdid it, pushed

---

106 2 February, 1790 – 31 March, 1873.

himself to his limits and burst a blood vessel in his neck. Sbigoli dropped dead.[107] He had been preparing to create the role of Abenamet in the first performance of *Zoraide di Granata*,[108] Donizetti's fifth opera – which proceeded without a tenor because none was available. Donizetti quickly re-wrote the part for a contralto. A death like Sbigoli's would not have occurred 20 years earlier, when the common loathing of *vibrato*, forced tone and poor diction (and the general preference for elegance and lightness of touch) were hallmarks of a style of singing – and of performance more generally – on which Rossini capitalised to make himself the most successful (and the wealthiest) composer in the history of music to the 1820s. His eye-widening genius extended to his sensitivity to commercial markets, therefore. No other composer was so alive to changes in taste and fashion, or to the need (and potential) for opera to turn a profit. It is not irrelevant that Barbaia had to make his offer to Rossini in 1815 financially as well as theatrically and musically attractive. Accordingly, the composer's contract at the San Carlo guaranteed him 12,000 francs a year and a substantial percentage of the theatre's gambling tables – as well as a large theatre, orchestra and chorus.

When Barbaia signed a contract to take the San Carlo company to Vienna, Rossini was happy to join them for a three-month season – throughout which audiences greeted the composer in what Beethoven's amanuensis, Anton Schindler, described as "an idolatrous orgy." From Vienna, Rossini travelled for a time to London (where he earned the fantastic sum of £30,000), and thereafter, and for the rest of his life, to Paris. His contract with the French government was negotiated during the reign of Louis XVIII, who died in September, 1824 – soon after Rossini's arrival in the city. It had been agreed that the composer would produce one grand opera for the Académie Royale de Musique, and an *opera buffa* or a *semi-seria* for the Théâtre-Italien. The King's death, and the accession of Charles X, changed Rossini's plans, such that his first new work for Paris was *Il viaggio a Reims*, first performed in June, 1825, to celebrate the coronation. It was to be Rossini's last opera with an Italian libretto. The cast at the first night included the soprano Giuditta Pasta as Corinna, Marco Bordogni as Conte di Libenskof, and Domenico Donzelli as Chevalier Belfiore.

Donzelli was already celebrated for singing notes in full voice from the chest to an A below high C, and the power of his new-fangled "tenore di forza" ensured huge popularity while otherwise operating within a limited vocal range that compelled his placing of anything above an A4 in *falsetto*. Donzelli's dark timbre and passionate acting were of considerable value to Rossini in Paris, where the younger generation born after 1800 was repulsed, for the most part, by the anachronism of *castrati*. The blood of post-Napoleonic French audiences ran hot, and the raising in pitch and placement of tenors' chest voices ever higher in the register (thereby delaying the switch to a pure head voice or *falsetto*) generated a more exciting sound, better suited

---

107 According to the diary of Prince Agostino Chigi, the Teatro Argentina held a benefit on 15 February, 1822, for the widow and children of Sbigoli. Six thousand lire was raised. See Weinstock, Herbert (1964). *Donizetti and the World of Opera in Italy, Paris, and Vienna in the First Half of the Nineteenth Century*. Methuen. p.26.
108 On 28 January, 1822.

to the masculated sexuality of Italian opera, and the growing obsession throughout Paris for Beethoven's obsidian slice of romanticism.

Rossini's Parisian career – and his retirement as a composer of opera – culminated in 1829 with the first performance of *Guillaume Tell*. It was fitting that his final stage work (just nine years after his arrival in Naples) should help deliver Grand Opera while at the same time causing (to his instant regret) the first public performance by a singer of that most revered of modern tenorial attainments: "the high C."

CHAPTER THREE

The Squawk of a Capon

In his 1784 essay "*The Stage as a Moral Institution*," delivered to the *Kurpfalzisch Deutschen Gesellschaft*[1] in Mannheim, Friedrich Schiller held that

> The jurisdiction of the stage begins where the domain of secular law leaves off. Whenever justice is dazzled by gold and gloats in the pay of infamy; when the crimes of the mighty mock their own impotence, and mortal fear stays the ruler's arm—then theatre takes up the sword and scales, and hauls infamy before the dreadful tribune of justice.[2]

Later the same year, Nicolas Ledoux completed work on his theatre at Besançon, in which he made visual and architectural reference to his inspiration: the Teatro Olimpico at Vicenza. The exterior of the building was designed as a severe Palladian cube, adorned with a stark neoclassical portico of six Ionic columns. Even before the Revolution, Ledoux's theatre became a focus for the ideals of the Greek *polis* and the Roman Republic. As a romantic, Ledoux abhorred the failure of contemporary theatre design, which he considered disassociative, vulgar and distracting. His functional solution was to create a steeply raked amphitheatre holding more people than the *parterre*, with three semi-circular tiers of seats – without boxes[3] – all rising to the interior's most striking feature, a curving Doric colonnade. The semi-circle was narrower than the stage, and where the first tier met the proscenium it opened onto a bell-shaped plan. Behind this tier ran a sculptured frieze featuring imagery connected with tragedy, comedy and dance. The proscenium arch was wide and formed of a semi-circular barrel-vault, supported by imposing rustication.[4] The interior presented a direct and unmistakable challenge to the *status quo* of European theatrical architecture, which had for two hundred years adhered to the physical and social strata wherein nobles sat in seats and boxes, with the "stalls" retained for standing patrons only.

Ledoux's philosophy was formed by a radical egalitarian belief that theatres might be useful to the community as more than venues for "mere" entertainment, albeit without also challenging established societal hierarchies. Opera Houses had long provided a microcosmic barometer for European class distinctions, and it was not

---

1 Elector's German Society.
2 https://archive.schillerinstitute.com/transl/schil_theatremoral.html.
3 Almost a century before Wagner built his Festpielhaus in Bayreuth.
4 Decorative masonry with a rough or patterned surface. Used typically for ground floor exterior finishes, as a means of contrasting visually with smoothly-finished masonry surfaces known as ashlar.

until 6 March, 1637, that all social classes were able to join together in an accessible cultural space. They did so when the Tron family opened their Teatro di San Cassiano for the first time to purchasers of tickets. This was the first ever 'public' performance of an opera, directed by an impresario with an acute sense of popular taste. Ticketing made theatrical seasons a possibility, which required repertoire and, more importantly, planning – all of which entailed investment. The need for permanent structures and theatrical machines fostered architectural experimentation beyond the prescriptive limitations of Vitruvius and Palladio, such that acoustics and sightlines became an issue when accounting coincidentally for the commercial priority of seating capacity. The value for the titled and the wealthy of the sequestration of the "box" – as an independent space for private use – allowed the privileged to remain so, with a window from which they might observe the people below. In consequence of this Maslowian separation, Ledoux advocated that Besançon include seating and sightlines for all – a radical proposal that would have been rejected summarily had it not been for Charles André de la Coré, the Intendant of Franche-Comté. He consented to follow Ledoux's reformations while ensuring sufficient segregation, with a ground-floor amphitheatre (with seats for the "ordinary" paying public), a raised terrace above them for state employees, and a tier of boxes for the aristocracy. Above this (and where, with some irony, the "gods" now sit) was a tier of smaller boxes for occupation by the middle-class. Access was determined by cost and title.

Ledoux retained Dart de Bosco to expand the wings and scenery apparatus, giving the stage greater depth than was customary and facilitating the re-positioning of the orchestra, the theatre's most striking innovation. Ledoux was initially resigned to the contemporary fashion for placing an orchestra in the centre of the audience:

> They form a circle, the strongest get to the front, the weak remain further away – each takes a place where he can see best, unimpeded by the people around him.[5]

Ledoux was further inspired by an obscure set of memoirs from 1770 by a "De Marette" ("*Memoire sur un nouvel orchestre de salle de spectacles*") in which the author had advocated the placing of the orchestra beneath the stage. He resolved in consequence to regard the instrumental musicians as a voice for placing *alongside* the singers. By hiding the orchestra in the pit, which went partly under the stage and was screened from the audience by a hood, Ledoux prefigured Wagner's Festpielhaus in Bayreuth by almost a century. The addition of a vaulted ceiling below the stage enhanced the acoustic transfer of sound, aligning voice and orchestra in accordance with the innovations of the operas of Gluck and Mozart. Ledoux's design seated between 1,200 and 1,800 – depending on the configuration of the seats, which were smaller and less generous than the 1,100 now installed in accordance with fire regulations. It was huge by the standards of the earliest permanent theatres as survived in Ferrara (1531), Rome (1545), Mantua (1549), Bologna (1550), Siena (1561) and Venice (1565). These were tiny venues comparatively – entirely in keeping with their quasi-domestic purpose.

---

5   Tidworth, Simon (1973). *Theatres: An Illustrated History*. Pall Mall. pp.110–111.

Musical theatre pre-opera was an entertainment exclusively for the aristocracy. Commencing with Jacopo Peri and Monteverdi, the earliest operas were composed as sumptuous accompaniments to weddings, birthdays, and visits from dukes, princes and kings. They were presented by the entitled for the amusement of the titled. The Teatro all'antica[6], for example, was completed in 1590 and allowed for only five rows of seating – sufficient for fewer than 80 people – while the Teatro Olimpico[7] in Vicenza (completed in 1585) could accommodate a relatively vast body of 400. The English architect Inigo Jones visited the Olimpico shortly after its completion and recorded his admiration for the sight lines, the "chief artifice [of which] was that whear so ever you sat you saw one of thes Prospects…"[8] With a small acoustic and only a few hundred seats, most Renaissance theatres required little amplitude either from the singers or the instrumentalists – even over the inevitable chatter that defined common theatrical experience before the end of the 18th century.

Within 10 years of Jacopo Peri's *Dafne*[9] and *Euridice* (the first opera to have survived to the present day[10]), the appetite for musical theatre grew exponentially across Italy. Monteverdi's first opera, *L'Orfeo* (to a libretto by Alessandro Striggio), was composed for the Carnival season of 1607 as a *favola in musica* – an evolved form of the traditional *intermedio*, a musical sequence separating the acts of a spoken play. The need for a "full" band of instrumentalists – and the growing popularity of the form – compelled the building of larger theatres, sometimes for a single event. The Teatro Farnese, for example, was commissioned by Ranuccio I (Duke of Parma, Piacenza and Castro from 1592) to honour a visit to Parma by Cosimo II. Notwithstanding the cost and effort invested in building such a fantastic conceit, Cosimo failed to arrive.

The Farnese[11] is huge – as visitors can discover for themselves to this day. It lies hidden within the vast Palazzo della Pilotta (now a gallery), where it was installed between 1617 and 1618 by Giovanni Battista Aleotti in an enormous hall that had, till then, served as the Palace armoury.[12] The U-shaped auditorium has fourteen rows of seats and was able to accommodate an audience of something between 2,000 and 3,000 people. The seating descends to a point six feet above the ground, which allows for the action to be continued in the arena. This enabled occasional flooding for the hosting of battles "at sea" – as occurred at the eventual inauguration (seven years after Cosimo II's death) in December, 1628, to commemorate the marriage of Odoardo Farnese and Margherita Medici.

---

6   'Theater in the style of the ancients.' Sabbioneta, northern Italy.
7   It was the first free-standing, purpose-built theatre in the modern world, and is one of only three Renaissance theatres still in existence.
8   Laver, James (1951). *Drama: its Costume and Decor*. The Studio Publications. p.76.
9   Completed around 1597, but now lost.
10 First performed in 1600.
11 D'Orazio, Dario and Nannini, Sofia. (2019). "Towards Italian Opera Houses: A Review of Acoustic Design in Pre-Sabine Scholars." *Acoustics* 2019, 1, pp.252–280.
12 Donati, P. (1817). *Descrizione del Gran Teatro Farnesiano di Parma e notizie storiche sul medesimo di Paolo Donati parmigiano architetto teatrale e accademico di Bologna e professore della Reale Accademia di Firenze (Description of the Farnese Theatre in Parma and Historical Information…)*. Blanchon.

Their wedding was celebrated by the performance of a new work from Monteverdi and Achillini – an extravagant opera-ballet, *Mercurio e Marte* – that entailed (among much else) elaborate displays of horsemanship and a denouement in which Neptune flooded the stage and central arena to a depth of two feet. Thanks to the installation of the first movable scenery in theatrical history, the production featured a storm, a shipwreck and fights between sea monsters – a melee resolved only when Jupiter and one hundred of his friends and admirers descended from the eaves on wire. It is recorded that much of Monteverdi's music was lost to the stamping of the audience's feet, so bitterly cold was the ambient temperature.[13]

The Farnese became a model for Baroque theatre by virtue of its size and ambition. Even today, the stage is vast – and of sufficient depth to accommodate ten rows of sliding flats and flies. Such was the audience's distance from the action that a monumental proscenium was installed to divide the stage from the auditorium. This was the first occasion when spectators were provided with a frame through which to observe a theatrical performance – a deep-perspective that mirrored the equally novel concept of a "framed" painting.[14] The addition of a proscenium amplified the distance of the footlights from the audience, which had an obvious and unavoidable effect on the acoustics to which singers had rapidly to adapt. For generations, solo vocalists had been required to fill rooms with audiences of anything between a dozen and, at the very most, a few hundred people. The Farnese was designed for the presentation of spectacular events and episodes that were operatic only insofar as music and singing played a role in the unfolding of the dramatic narrative. By the time Ledoux's theatre opened in Besançon the space was challenging for the majority when staging Gluck and Mozart; it was impossibly huge for *castrati*.

The placement of a voice in a theatre with fewer than two dozen meters of depth and an orchestra of twenty or thirty did not require volume, and Rossini's bari-tenors were happy (for the most part) to make themselves heard in an auditorium that seated 1,000. Increases in venue size required more resonant instruments to penetrate acoustics that were suffocated more often than not by a vast crowd of people draped in layers of cloth.[15] Most obviously affected by the collision between scale and acoustic claustrophobia was the tenor voice. While sopranos and low male voices had enjoyed generations of consistency in training and repertoire, the tenor was evolving rapidly. The higher an early 19th century tenor moved up the stave the less amplitude of sound he was able to generate. Notes from a G or an A natural (above middle C) were performed *falsetto*, a placement that generated little or no penetration. To make matters more challenging still for composers and singers alike, opera houses during the thirty years either side of 1800 became ever larger, with obvious markers for size being the Teatro Regio, Turin (1767; capacity 1,500 – 1,800); La Scala, Milan (1778; capacity 2,500 – 3,500 – with six tiers of boxes); the Teatro Grande, Bergamo (1791; capacity 2,500 – 3,500); La Fenice, Venice (1792; capacity 1,900 – 2,250 – with five

---

13   Tidworth, Simon (1973). *Theatres: An Illustrated History*. Pall Mall. pp.65–68.
14   At a time when most painting (whether on board or canvas) was placed permanently within some form or another of panelling.
15   Berenak. Leo (1962). *Music, Acoustics, and Architecture*. John Wiley & Sons, Inc.

tiers of boxes); and the Teatro Comunale, Trieste (1801; capacity 1,600 – 2,400).[16] Between 1673 and 1763, a tenor at the Paris Opéra would have sung in the Salle du Palais-Royal, which seated approximately 1,200, with three tiers of spectators and a rectangular auditorium. With the singular exception of the Teatro San Carlo, a tenor singing in any of the major Italian theatres between 1673 and 1763 had to be heard by somewhere between 800 and 1,500 people, in an auditorium shaped somewhere between a semi-circle and a horseshoe.

The influence of the Italian increase in scale and capacity on the rest of Europe was self-evident. In 1783, three years before Ledoux's theatre was completed in Besançon, the Théâtre de la Porte-St-Martin opened with a capacity of around 1,800. Nine years later, the Théâtre National de la rue de la Loi claimed a capacity of 1,700. With the opening of the Wiener Staatsoper in 1869, the Palais Garnier in 1875, and the Bayreuth Festpielhaus in 1876, ticketed capacities in most city-based opera houses sailed well past 2,500, while orchestras trebled and, in certain cases, quadrupled in size. This was most obviously true of Wagner's theatre, which was launched with a production of the vast *Der Ring der Nibelungen*.[17] The inauguration of the Garnier Opéra, on the other hand, presented excerpts from Auber's *La muette de Portici*[18] (an opera from 1828), Rossini's *Guillaume Tell* (from 1829), Halévy's *La Juive*[19] (from 1835), Meyerbeer's *Les Huguenots* (from 1836) and the ballet *La source* (by Delibes and Minkus, from 1866) – none of which presumed the parameters of a Wagnerian orchestra.[20] The programme was avowedly passé in its robust attachment to vocalism, therefore, but it was political also, inevitably so in the light of France's recent defeat by the Prussians. The performance of music from *Guillaume Tell* was significant not only because of its revolutionary narrative but because one of the guests of honour at the Opéra on 5 January, 1875, was Gilbert-Louis Duprez,[21] the (now retired) Parisian tenor who created the role of Arnold for Rossini at the opera's Italian premiere forty-four years earlier.

It is no exaggeration to say that Duprez is the most influential tenor in the modern history of the voice. He did not create the role of Arnold for Rossini in 1829, however. That honour went to another Frenchman – Duprez's alleged rival, Adolphe Nourrit.[22] The first performance of *Tell* was presented on 3 August, 1829, at the Salle Le Peletier, which was then the largest theatre in France. When designing the performance space in 1820, François Debret reached little further than a simple rebuilding of the auditorium of the Théâtre des Arts, which was demolished a few

---

16 It is difficult to be precise about seat numbers from before the age of fire regulations and health and safety. In any event, the capacities cited here are necessarily conservative.
17 'The Ring of the Nibelung.'
18 'The mute girl of Portici.'
19 'The Jewess.'
20 As an aside, it is bizarre that not a single excerpt was played from a contemporary work – not even Delibes' recently premiered opera comique, *Le roi l'a dit* (from 1873), or Bizet's *Djamileh* or Saint-Saëns' *La princesse jaune* (both from 1872), or Verdi's *Aida* (from 1871). *Aida* was eventually premiered in Paris, at the Théâtre-Lyrique Italien, Salle Ventadour (with almost the same cast as the Milan premiere), on 22 April, 1876. *Aida* was not presented at the Garnier until 22 March, 1880 – when Verdi conducted a French translation, with Henri Sellier as Radamès and Victor Maurel as Amonasro.
21 6 December, 1806 – 23 September, 1896.
22 3 March, 1802 – 8 March, 1839.

months earlier. Unlike the Théâtre des Arts, however, his finished auditorium was said to be acoustically perfect. So well received was it by performers and audiences that it became the prescribed model for architects when submitting their designs for a new home to the Opéra in 1861.[23]

The Peletier was intended to be temporary[24], and built entirely of wood and plaster – materials that contributed much to the theatre's luminous, benevolent acoustic. Its celebrated resonance was enhanced by the wooden forms on which audiences in the stalls were invited to sit, and – with a stage 31 metres wide, a huge proscenium and an auditorium sufficiently deep for an audience of 1,000 – it was suited ideally to the increasing scale and amplitude of contemporary opera. The Peletier differed from most Italian theatres insofar as it was shorter in height by at least two balconies and shallower from front to back, with a more forgiving curve to the rear of the theatre, such that the audience was brought closer to the stage, from where singers could be heard with unprecedented clarity. The acoustics supported the singers and delighted audiences and composers alike. After Rossini's arrival in Paris, he based himself at the Peletier, from where he oversaw the first performances of *Le siège de Corinthe* in 1826, *Moïse et Pharaon* in 1827, and *Le comte Ory* in 1828.

When completing the score of *Guillaume Tell* during the summer of 1829, it was obvious that the role of Arnold was going to require a tenor with vocal heft as well as dexterity. The phrasing and intervals are a great deal less florid (and require little *fioriture*), but the *fach* sits high in the voice, with two high C sharp 5s, twenty-eight high C5s, and dozens of B4s and B flat 4s). Adolphe Nourrit was Rossini's first and only choice for the role. His father, Louis, had been a well-known tenor at the Opéra, and was loved throughout Paris. It was Louis who introduced his son to Manuel García Père, who trained him for 18 months before his debut in 1821 as Pylades in Gluck's *Iphigénie en Tauride*. In 1826, *fils* succeeded *père* as the principal tenor at the Opéra, a position he held for a decade. Soon after his arrival in Paris, Rossini took Nourrit as his pupil, tutoring him in the principal roles for each of his French operas.[25] Nourrit performed his entire French career in the obliging acoustic of the Salle le Peletier, which suited his García-trained voice to perfection. His success during the first run of *Tell* was attributed to an acute musical and dramatic intelligence and an easy technique that reached D5 in *falsetto*. His insights were much-valued

---

23 On 30 December, 1860, the government of Emperor Napoleon III announced an architectural design competition for the design of a new opera house. Applicants were given a month to submit entries. Garnier's project was one of around 170 submitted in the first phase – at the end of which he was awarded fifth place. As one of seven finalists, Garnier was he eventual winner.

24 It nonetheless remained in use by the Opéra for more than fifty years, staging *inter alia* the premieres of Meyerbeer's *Robert le Diable* (1831), Halévy's *La Juive* (1835), Halévy's *Guido et Ginevra* (1838) Berlioz's *Benvenuto Cellini* (1838), Donizetti's *Les martyrs* (1840), Donizetti's *La favorite* (1840), Halévy's *La reine de Chypre* (1841), Halévy's *Charles VI* (1843), Donizetti's *Dom Sebastien* (1843), Donizetti's *Marie Stuart* (1844), Verdi's *Le prophète* (1849), Gounod's *Sapho* (1851), Verdi's *Les vêpres siciliennes* (1855), Verdi's *Le trouvère* (1857), Wagner's *Tannhäuser* (Paris Version; 1861), Gounod's *La reine de Saba* (1862), Meyerbeer's *L'Africaine* (1865), Verdi's *Don Carlos* (1867), Thomas' *Hamlet* (1868), and Gounod's *Faust* (Paris Opéra Version; 1869).

25 In addition, Nourrit created *inter alia* the roles of Masaniello in Auber's *La muette de Portici* (1828), Robert in Meyerbeer's *Robert le Diable*, Eléazar in Halévy's *La Juive* (1835), and Raoul in Meyerbeer's *Les Huguenots* (1836).

by Rossini, and many others – including Meyerbeer, with whom he reworked the love-duet in Act 4 of *Les Huguenots*[26], and Halévy, for whom he wrote the words of Eléazar's monumental aria "*Rachel, quand du Seigneur*"[27] in *La Juive*.

Nourrit employed what was known as a *voix blanche* – less powerful than the *voix sombrée* – and it was his masterful projection of words and sentiment that ensured his pre-eminence, not least at the Conservatoire de Paris, which appointed him *Professeur de déclamation pour la tragédie lyrique* at the grand age of 25, in 1827. He was, for many, a singing actor – as might be said of Callas and Domingo, for whom the opera house was better suited to lyric-drama than melodrama. Nourrit's concern for words and their placement narratively and musically was obsessive; as a poet and composer himself, he regarded the score as a vehicle for the articulation of thoughts and ideas as well as sentiments. For this reason, his priorities were colour and expression, a characteristically French consideration that set him apart from the less nuanced approach adopted by most Italian singers. This resulted in a certain thinness of tone and timbre. According to Vest:

> The cause of nasality in his voice partly arose from Nourrit's vocal technique, which included singing in *voix blanche* or *voce aperta*, otherwise called open singing... As the pitch rises, the larynx rises. As the larynx rises, the soft palate, or velum, lowers thus creating a nasal sound."[28]

Nourrit had a tendency also to sing in half-voice, for which he was much criticised. Berlioz was present at the first night of *Les Huguenots* and recorded in his review that "The high notes of Nourrit's head voice have very much a feminine sound."[29] It has been suggested that the dynamic markings added by Nourrit to his scores, when accounting for underlying or associated orchestral textures, allude to his singing other than in *falsetto* – in full *sombrée,* therefore. But these notes do not, in and of themselves, counter the observations and recollections of contemporaries (including Henry Chorley and François-Joseph Fétis), most of whom characterised his voice in terms of sweetness and clarity, as opposed to amplitude and excitement.[30] The press were entirely agreed on his good voice, agility, and sound technique. His voice was sweet and *fluté* and reminded one reviewer of the *castrato* Giovanni Battista Velluti....[31] It is difficult to reconcile this assessment with some of the music written for him, most obviously the extraordinary role of Eléazar in *La Juive*.

---

26 Made famous in modern times by Franco Corelli and Giulietta Simionato at La Scala in 1962.
27 'Rachel, when from the Lord.'
28 Vest, Jason (2009) *Adolphe Nourrit, Gilbert-Louis Duprez, and Transformations of Tenor Technique in the Early Nineteenth Century: Historical and Physiological Considerations* (DMA dissertation, University of Kentucky). pp.26 -27.
29 Berlioz, Hector. (1996–2003). *La Critique Musicale*, ed. Cohen and Bongrain, 4 vols. Buchet/Castel. Vol. III. p.217.
30 Smith, Micheal Lee Jr. (2011). *Adolphe Nourrit, Gilbert Duprez, and the high C: The influences of operatic plots, culture, language, theater design, and growth of orchestral forces on the development of the operatic tenor vocal production*. UNLV Theses, Dissertations, Professional Papers, and Capstones. 1273.
31 Everist, Mark (2002). *Music Drama at the Paris Odéon, 1824–1828* (University of California Press). p.3.

First staged in 1835, *The Jewess* remains controversial because of its Shylockian caricatures, and because Eléazar makes the horrifying decision in Act V to allow his daughter to be boiled to death as revenge against his Christian nemesis (and Rachel's *actual* father), Cardinal Brogni – a disturbing snapshot of Protocols that would mature sixty years later with the humiliation and torture of Alfred Dreyfus. The work is a musical and theatrical masterpiece, however, with two immensely rewarding and challenging tenor roles – the second, Prince Léopold, scored for an extremely high-sitting voice. Halévy also created some splendid music for the first Rachel, Cornélie Falcon – one of Berlioz's muses and the brightest star at the Opéra in 1835, a fact openly acknowledged by the House Director, who paid her *twice* what he was paying Nourrit.

The *Air* that precedes Eléazar's tragic wrestling with conscience and instinct is almost shocking in form and context; a good performance can leave an audience in tatters even before the haunting duet for *cor anglais en duo* that precedes "*Quand du Seigneur.*" Nourrit's poetry is among the finest produced for a Grand Opera; it is revealing also of what he demanded of himself as a singer:

> "*Eh bien la mort! Va prononcer ma mort, ma vengeance est certaine!*
> *C'est moi qui pour jamais te condamne a gémir!*
> *J'ai fait peser sur foi mon éternelle haine*
> *Et maintenant je puis mourir!*
> *Mais ma fille!...*"[32]

The language of the aria *propre* is no less affecting; Halévy's lilting music carves out depths of pain and melancholy that few tenors are able to capture without resorting to those temporal and interpretative abuses[33] that commonly undermine the music's metrical ritualism:

> "*Rachel, quand du seigneur*
> *La grâce tutélaire*
> *A mes tremblantes mains confia ton berceau,*
> *J'avais à ton bonheur*
> *Voué ma vie entière.*
> *Et c'est moi qui te livre au bourreau.*"[34]

The poet and the composer attached agonising emphasis to the character's cultural, religious and psychological torture. The range of the aria is considerable, spanning F4 to (a single) B flat 4; the word setting generates haunting emotional resonance, with "*Voué ma vie entire...*" coincidentally draining and lacerating. Nourrit's articulation in performance was as much a source of triumph as his elegance and beauty of tone

---

32 'Well, death! Go pronounce my death, my revenge is certain! It is I who forever condemn you to moan! I made weigh on faith my eternal hatred; And now I can die! But my daughter! ...''
33 The score contains only three *fermatas* – and the celebrated concluding B flat is a creature of habit and tradition, and not written by the composer.
34 'Rachel, when the Lord's Tutelary grace, Entrusted your cradle to my trembling hands, To your happiness I had Sworn my entire life. And it is I who hand you over to the executioner.'

and expression' – a characteristic seventy years later of a number of *echt* recordings, notably those by Léon Escalaïs[35] and Agustarello Affre.[36]

"*Quand du siegneur*" is merely the highlight of a monstrously demanding role remarkable for its emotional span and dramatic craft. Its lyrical profundity was an obvious point of focus for critics and commentators isolating Nourrit's poeticism and sensitivity; many discerned in particular the primacy of *nuance* (as 'shade') in its construction as an admixture of tone, language and articulation. Everyone was agreed on the command of Nourrit's use of words, as well as his sung tone and line. The terminology employed to describe singing during the first half of the 19th century was consistent with the contemporary romantic vernacular. Apart from Berlioz and Wagner, both of whom shifted the dialectic towards analytical precision, most of those who wrote about singing before the 1860s were some way behind E.T.A. Hoffmann's radical re-positioning of music criticism when reviewing Beethoven's 5th Symphony in 1810. Even after Helmholtz's promotion of the concept of "*Klangfarbe*"[37] – the parity between hue and pitch as a function of frequency[38] – writers and composers were reduced to correlating sound and imagery using metaphors that were either imperfect or meaningless. Ambiguity is a legitimate failing of any spoken language, and context will always define expectation. The idea of "force" in pianism, for example, cannot sustain comparisons between the playing of Beethoven by Beethoven or Chopin by Chopin because of the differences between the instruments on which they performed. When recalling evenings spent at George Sand's apartment on the Chaussée d'Antin in Paris in 1839, Liszt described Chopin at his Pleyel as sounding like a "German glass armonica."[39] He recalled additionally the company of Heine, Meyerbeer, Hiller, Delacroix, Sand and Nourrit, who gave the first performance in 1825 of Liszt's only opera, *Don Sanche, ou Le château de l'amour*.[40] His memories of Sand's apartment, with its surfeit of candles, mirrors and satin, form an instant cognitive association on the part of the reader, whereas his comparison of Chopin's piano to an armonica creates irresolvable dissonance. Was he describing the instrument, or the composer's playing? There is nothing to compare between an armonica and a piano, even one from the late 1830s, so it's more than likely that Liszt was paying tribute to Chopin's peddling, which allowed for a fluency and lyricism that transcended the limitations of Pleyel's mechanism.

---

35 Recorded in Milan on 14 November, 1905.
36 Recorded for Pathé in 1910.
37 'Tone-colour.'
38 He observed that, should an F sharp be raised 20 octaves, it would cease to be a sound, and become instead the colour red. See Vennard, William. *Singing: The Mechanism and the Technic*. Carl Fischer (1967). p.151.
39 Kildea, Paul (2018). *Chopin's Piano: A Journey Through Romanticism*. Allen Lane. p.77.
40 'Don Sanche, or the Castle of Love.' Liszt completed the opera as a 12-year old. Nourrit sang the lead at the first performance at the Peletier on 17 October, 1825. The conductor was Rodolphe Kreutzer – dedicatee of Beethoven's Sonata for Violin and Piano, No. 9, Op. 47. In her biography of Liszt, written and published during his lifetime, Lina Ramann wrote: "At the conclusion the applause was boundless; the public called rapturously for their darling and for Nourrit, the singer of the principal part. Then the latter, a tall and stately figure, with an overflowing of amiability, took in his arms the young composer, still small for his fourteen years, and carried him before the audience, whose jubilation was without bounds … that Nourrit […] should have carried him before the public, like a child, gnawed to his inmost heart."

It's impossible to know what Liszt intended, either way – just as it is impossible to conclude from Nourrit's hand-written references to dynamics whether he was singing other than in *falsetto*. There is better evidence for Nourrit's *klangfarbe* in written analyses by his contemporaries, particularly those singers whose careers were established after him. The majority indicate that his voice was defined first and foremost by its *couvert* quality, which means that the octave-leaping B flats (written in the tenor clef as C sharps) in Arnold's aria *"Asile héréditaire"* were delivered either in half-voice or in *falsetto*; the same must have been true also of the concluding C5 (scored as a D natural). Nourrit's Italian bari-tenor contemporary, Donzelli, was praised throughout the 1820s for his singing in "full voice" and a review of his *Otello* from 1823 in the *Allgemeine musikalische Zeitung* (AMZ) held that:

> he has a beautiful, mellifluous tenor with which he attacks the high A in full chest-voice, without once resorting to falsetto, while Signor David rejoices in this higher voice and, on occasion, once ascended to a high F.

Nourrit was competing neither with Donzelli nor David, since he was pre-eminently a French tenor, who adhered where possible to French repertoire. Even though the Peletier was large, it was acoustically perfect also, and he could be heard because his audience was sufficiently interested to want to listen. Nonetheless, *la forza del destino* was beating at his door, and he conceded relatively early the need for greater amplitude to account for changes in orchestral scale, compositional style and theatre size:

> I have come to understand that my future at the Opéra will no longer be like my past, and I have drawn the following conclusions. It would be unwise to count on singing for more than another four years. Despite the raise Duponchel is offering me [...] I have always thought of retiring early enough to make a grand tour of the provinces, the income from which should not be less than a hundred thousand francs [...] Now, will I be able to make that grand tour four years from now? Today all my repertoire is new. The operas with which I now earn money will be old and tired, and between now and then I shall be doing only half the new works given in the Opéra [...] My regular repertoire will be passé, and it could be that between now and then I shall have no new successes [...] All that without taking into account that I shall certainly have lost some of my moral fibre, if only because I will have ceased to be the first and only one, and you know how the public is drawn to the new.[41]

The novelty to which he was alluding was an epoch-defining episode that transitioned into mythology during Nourrit's lifetime – in tragic (albeit misplaced) consequence of his premature death. This "miraculous" event occurred in Nourrit's absence, but it changed his life just as surely as it changed the lives of every tenor and

---

41 Pleasants, Henry (1995). *The Great Tenor Tragedy*. Amadeus Press. pp.15–16.

composer of opera since. On 17 September, 1831[42], during the first Italian performance of *Guillaume Tell*,[43] Gilbert-Louis Duprez performed "*O muto asil*"[44] ("*Asile héréditaire*")[45] When singing the phrase "*Chi mai li guida a me?*"[46] the tenor sang the final repetition of the word "*me*"[47] (an accented C5 quaver, absent a *fermata*, but held by most for as many seconds as oxygen will allow) in "full" voice. A few bars later, during the succeeding "*Corriam, voliam, s'affretti*"[48] he repeated the feat a further seven times, including what must have been a jaw-dropping sound when singing "*Guglielmo per noi non morrà*" above a substantial male chorus and full orchestra.[49] The bravura was exceptional. Considering the setting of so many high Cs in "*Corriam*" it was probably a long time coming also;[50] anyone singing this music *falsetto* could not have been heard above an all-male chorus and brass-heavy orchestra.

Duprez was undoubtedly audible, and from the back of the Teatro del Giglio. In meeting his own challenge, he became the first tenor to sing a "high C" as it has been recognised ever since. The sound he produced was later described by Rossini as "the squawk of a capon having its throat cut"[51] – but it survives as the first reported occasion when a tenor sang (a version of) that Elysian note for which Pavarotti (as the most obvious example) became celebrated during the 1960s and 70s.

The creation of the high C as the "*ut de poitrine*" or "*do di petto*" is the most significant event in the history of the tenor voice. It drove the final nail into the coffin of the *castrati* (who could never have competed with such *outré* masculinity), and it gave rise to a musical and cultural benchmark that remains a universal measure of tenorial ability. Of course, there is a signal difference between a good high C and a bad one, and it is here that the distinction between the chest and head voices comes into focus.[52] The physiology of the C5 is complicated – and still not entirely understood. There are competing schools of thought as to what is involved, with many continuing to refer to the note as being sung "from the chest"; it is better understood, however, as being "from the head" – particularly by those who can sing it. The tradition of isolating three "voices" (chest, *passaggio* and head) has been eclipsed in recent years, with vocal registration more commonly subsumed to laryngeal function and the operation

---

42 At the Teatro del Giglio in Lucca, a 1,000-seat theatre first opened in 1819.
43 As "*Guglielmo Tell,*" in a translation by Calisto Bassi.
44 Followed shortly after by the climactic C in "*Corriam! Voliam!*"
45 Arnold was originally to have been performed in transposition by the contralto Benedetta Pisaroni. After she fell ill, Duprez was called upon by Rossini to sing the role in her place.
46 "*Je viens vous voir pour la dernière fois!*" in the original libretto ['I come to see you for the last time'].
47 As much is certainly true of the *urtext*, and the 1830 edition of the full score published by Schott. It has, regardless, been common for many years for tenors to interpose a final, *final* "dernier" by way of cadence – the irony of which is probably above commentary.
48 "*Amis, amis secondez ma vengeance*" in the original.
49 There is little doubt that even though Verdi claims not to have expected (or wanted) Tamberlik (or anyone else) to sing a high C at the end of "Di quella pira" at the curtain of Act 3 of *Il trovatore*, he must have had an ear to the same since the words of that legendary note are "*all'armi*" – which are also the final words of "*Corriam! Volliam*" which ends also with a male chorus and a long held high C.
50 The seven high Cs of "Amis, amis" remained unmatched until Donizetti outdid his friend with the nine he threw into "*Ah mes amis…*" eleven years later, in *La fille du régiment*.
51 A double-entendre. The capon was both a chicken, and shorthand for a *castrato*.
52 Many continue to refer to the high C as being a chest voice. This is misleading, and the author has adopted head voice throughout to refer to any note that resonates *for the singer* in the head.

of the three most effective physiological resonators: the pharynx, the oral cavity, and the nasal cavity.[53] All of them are located in the head. Many vocal pedagogues now argue against references to the head register, but there is no question that tenors *feel* full-voice notes in the head when singing above an A4 – a categorisation that attaches to resonance and resource rather than register. The controversy over terminology is ongoing, with those opposed to mechanical constructions of the "instrument" being especially vehement in their criticism.

It can be agreed that a pinched or thin sound is redolent commonly of poor technique. A high C ringing with a (necessarily) pronounced *squillo* enables even a lyric voice to be heard in the largest of theatres and over the heaviest of orchestras. For example, Strauss' Leukippos in *Daphne* and Matteo in *Arabella* are well-served by the composer's genius for voicing and texture; both roles are written high on the stave for a lyric tenor, with huge orchestras to boot, but neither can be performed as Strauss intended without a singer generating *squillo* in head voice. Commentators after the fact of Duprez's high C (such as H. Diday and J.E. Pétrequin, writing in the *Gazette médicale*[54]) identified additionally a coincidental darkening in the tone of singers' voices, which they attributed to the lowering of the layynx.[55] Certainly, the process known as "covering" (characterised in tone by a necessarily cautious suppression of vowel sounds) was identified as an expedient method for admitting more tone into the break between the head and chest voices. When applied to the highest vocal register, as it was by Duprez, the technique produced a sound of compelling intensity, one that risked causing serious damage to the vocal organs.

The depth of sound for which Duprez became famous did not inhibit his high C – initially, at least. Indeed, it was recognised universally to be startling in tone and resonance. Whether or not he managed to isolate a *squillo* "ping" as it would be recognised today, brilliance of tone has remained a primary metric ever since. The source of its utility is formed by a peak in the 2 – 5 kHz frequency range, to which the human ear is especially sensitive, and the resonance of these particular harmonics is believed to result from a narrowing of the Aryepiglottic fold, above the larynx, which can facilitate striking clarity and amplification. It is not a question of volume, therefore – a misconstruction that has led many to force and ultimately ruin their voices. Rather, it is the operation of resonance that distinguishes a voice capable of full-voice high notes (vibrating in the head) from singers relying on half-voice, overt covering or *falsetto*. Thanks to post-García developments in studies of laryngeal function during phonation it has been established that the high C in "head voice" causes the vocal folds to vibrate as periodic shakes of the laryngeal cartilage. These are transmitted to the bones in the thorax via the laryngeal depressors, and thereafter to the bony structures in the head through the laryngeal elevators.[56] Singers feel these phonatory sensations as thoracic and facial vibrations when transitioning from chest to head tones – which in turn enables a greater penetration of sound, regardless

---

53 Sataloff, Robert Thayer (2017). *Clinical Assessment of Voice*. Plural Publishing.
54 Diday, H. and Pétrequin, J.E. (1840). "*Mémoire sur une nouvelle espèce de voix chantée*" (*Gazette médicale de Paris*, viii). pp. 305 & 455.
55 See Chapter 12 below.
56 Tarneaud, J. (1933). "Study of larynx and of voice by stroboscopy." *Clinique*. 28: 337–341.

of whether the voice is "greater" in volume. It follows that some "big" voices have proven ineffective in theatres while "small" voiced singers, like Tito Schipa, Georges Thill and Anton de Ridder were audible at the back of La Scala, Milan, even when locking horns with a late-romantic orchestra.

Of course, the audience's delight at Duprez's achievement did not come without cost to the singer. The physical challenge of what was required – at a time when the full voice high C was neither taught nor considered necessary – is impossible to imagine. In his 1880 autobiography, *Souvenirs d'un chanteur*, Duprez recalled how he had been so carried away by "*ces mâles accents, ces cris sublimes*"[57] of "*Asile héréditaire – Corriam!*" that the note happened without any conscious effort. He later added, in apparent confusion, that it had:

> required the concentration of every resource of will power and physical strength. 'So be it,' I said to myself, 'it may be the end of me, but somehow I'll do it'. And so I found even the high C which was later to bring me so much success in Paris.[58]

The attainment was especially remarkable because Duprez was then a stranger in Paris. He made his operatic début at the Odéon in 1825 as Count Almaviva – when only 20 years of age. After three years passing without notice, he relocated to Italy just as Rossini was heading to Paris for a season, performing *tenore contraltino* roles including Idreno in *Semiramide*, Rodrigo in *Otello* and Gualtiero in Bellini's *Il pirata*. The latter generated his first great success – in part because he was averse to (or incapable of) *coloratura*. Indeed, he was manifestly a *leggiero* tenor until falling under the spell of Domenico Donzelli, the bari-tenor whose powerful mid-range voice had done so much to influence Rossini during the 1820s. Even after re-training with Donzelli, the will-power and physical strength to which Duprez referred in his memoirs is credible. After all, he was untrained in the production of the high C – a note that cannot, in the vast majority of cases, come without significant work. Because training can never guarantee its attainment, audiences attach themselves with alacrity to anyone able to hit the note without looking (and sounding) like they are risking *morte per arte*. Few tenors have had the high C "God-given;" some of the finest of the recording age avoided it wherever possible, even when young – notably del Monaco, Bergonzi, Domingo and Carreras. In most cases, downward transposition allows for legitimate compromise because the drama of any full-voice above an A4 is an almost synesthetic aphrodisiac – particularly when accounting for the eternal threat of splitting under pressure. Even Pavarotti cracked when singing "*Che gelida manina*" and when transposing "*Ah mes amis*" in *La fille du régiment* late in his career – with the concluding nine C5s sung as B4s.[59] Most controversially, Pavarotti was booed by the La Scala claque – those diehard fans known in Italy as *loggionisti* – at the opening

---

57 '...the manly accents, the sublime cries.'
58 Quoted in Pleasants, Henry (1995). *The Great Tenor Tragedy*. Amadeus Press. p.166.
59 There is a miserably clear recording of the great man struggling with *La fille*. His courage and professionalism in continuing with the performance can easily bring a tear to the eye.

night of the 1992 season for having failed a single B4 during Act 3 Scene 2 of *Don Carlo*.[60]

So essential is the element of danger to the production of the high C with *squillo* that singers for whom it is apparently easy (most obviously Juan Diego Flórez) can strip the note of its dramatic effect. It is, of course, perverse that a tenor might be punished for mastering the necessary technique – complacency is a bitter by-product of fluency where particularly where virtuosity is concerned – and yet the thrill of the note is bound inextricably to the demands it makes of the singer, whether or not composers like Rossini and Verdi and conductors like Karajan and Muti were inimical to the vanity of its execution. For some, it is the *sine qua non* of vulgarity, because it appeals to the circus tent rather than the agora. It follows that the high Cs when sung by Pavarotti during his 1972 performance at the New York Met of "*Ah mes amis*"[61] owed less to the principle of "l'art pour l'art" than the spandex-stretching antics of Philippe Petit's 1974 high-wire walk between the Twin Towers.

When finally Duprez made his debut at the Paris Opéra on 17 April, 1837, Berlioz wrote an extensive review of the performance which remains the single most important piece of criticism in the early history of the tenor voice,[62] in part because of Berlioz's genius as a writer but also because he knew Duprez's voice from *before* his departure for Italy and studies with Donzelli:[63]

> Last night, Duprez made his first appearance at the Opera; the room was full to the roof, and this crowd may not have been before favourable to an impartial judgment. The memories left by another great artist [Nourrit], who had known how to win strong sympathies and deserve a deep admiration, made the ground slippery for his successor. This loyalty of the public to preserve the memory of the actor who made him experience so many sweet pleasures, so many diverse impressions, is perfectly honourable in our opinion, and must be taken in good part by Duprez himself; for nothing would be more distressing in the eyes of the artist than to see services rendered to art by a distinguished talent, with natural faculties developed by the most serious studies, forgotten overnight without leaving any trace or regret. Nourrit left us voluntarily, despite the most vivid insistence of his many friends and even those of the director of the Opera, who did everything to keep him; it is a misfortune we feel as much as anyone, but which must not put any disadvantage on the efforts of Duprez to console us. The vast majority of listeners were armed, however, in advance against him with cruel prejudice. We were able to convince ourselves of this by listening to the conversations that crossed around us at home and in the dressing rooms. The beginner, it

---

60 On the first syllable of "*salvator*" mid-way through Don Carlo's oath "*Io qui lo giuro al ciel! Sarò tuo salvator, popol fiammingo, io sol!*" ['I swear here before heaven! I will be your saviour, Flemish people, I alone!'].
61 From Act 1 of Donizetti's *La fille du régiment* (1840).
62 Berlioz, Hector (1996–2003). *La Critique Musicale*, ed. Cohen and Bongrain, 4 vols. Buchet/Castel. Vol. I, p.231.
63 On 28 May, 1828, when Duprez contributed to Berlioz's first ever concert as a conductor.

was said, is a cold singer, soulless, without any knowledge of dramatic art, and moreover excessively ugly. A few moments of attention, after the rising of the canvas, were enough to demonstrate the obvious fallacy of these charges. Let's say it right away: Duprez's success was immense. It t the greatest effect of its kind that I have ever seen produced at the Opera.

Before explaining the causes of this enthusiasm, of this nervous quivering of which the whole room was agitated three or four times, let us examine in a few words the career of Duprez and the road which he followed to come, at thirty- and-one years old, to settle with a leap, with such rare happiness, on our first lyric stage [...]

When his manly voice was finally formed [...] Duprez still possessed only a high, flexible tenor, of a soft and graceful timbre, but completely devoid of energy. [...] Duprez, disgusted with his position, but not discouraged, broke amicably his engagement with the director of the Opéra-Comique [...] Passing Florence two years later, I heard admiration of the *Primo Tenore*, Signor Duprez, whose wonderful voice delighted the Florentines. Would it be him, I say to myself? Let's go see. I run to the Pergola theatre; we played the *Sonnambula* by Bellini. I could not paint my astonishment by recognizing in this powerful singer, asked up to three times before the end of the play by an enthusiastic audience, this same young man so little encouraged in Paris. His voice was made; it had become full, strong, biting, of an admirable accuracy, suitable for the expression of lively passions as much as that of the sweetest feelings, and the timbre had further gained in purity, in freshness, in delicious candour. These qualities have only increased since then, and their whole constitutes today a first-rate talent, whose influence on an audience, even if not very favourably disposed, is irresistible: exclamations of pleasure and surprise greeted the duo's sentence in the first act [...] and from that moment the success of Duprez was decided. It was however only a prelude to the emotions that the artist had to arouse before the end of the evening. We have admired in this passage the sensitivity and the method united to an organ of enchanting sweetness; there remained the dramatic accents, the cries of passion. The trio of the second act came, and we heard with a surprise almost equal to that of the rest of the audience, who did not yet know Duprez, the audacious artist singing chest voice, emphasizing each syllable, the so acute nature of the *andante* [...] with a vibrating force, an accent of heart-breaking pain and a beauty of sounds of which nothing until now had given us an idea. A silence of stupor reigned in the room, all breaths were suspended, astonishment and admiration merged in a feeling almost like fear; and in fact, we could have some for the end of this incredible period. But when it ended triumphant, we judge the transport that exploded at the last measure!

[...] The singer rose to a height to which, we who knew him, would never have thought capable of reaching; it was sublime. [...] Then from these two thousand breathless breasts rose one of those acclamations that the artist hears two or three times in his life, and which are enough to make forget many sorrows, to pay long and hard works. [...] This prodigious *grupetto enharmonic*, thrown, always in chest voice, the sharp ground on the natural ground, by the indefatigable singer, screaming that nothing could contain covered, until almost the end of the scene, the choirs, the orchestra and Duprez himself, who could no longer be listened to. This extraordinary effect is the counterpart of that produced eight years ago at the Conservatoire by the first performance of the final of the symphony in C minor.[64] Art cannot and should not aspire to go further. [...] His face has expression, his eyes a lot of fire; as for its size, it is small, it is true; but only remember this: Kean was no taller than him. Moreover, it pronounces in such a way that one word cannot be lost from its role, and we do not believe that it is possible to say the recitative better. But we will come back to it. In the meantime, this is a success for the Opera which many people hardly expected.[65]

Duprez was triumphant.[66] Most critics celebrated the special colour of the tenor's high notes, which were identified as having a unique "effect."[67] Edouard Monnais wrote in the *Revue et gazette musicale de Paris* that Duprez had

A perfectly pure, balanced, and sonorous voice, extraordinary declamation...he sings simply and powerfully, according to his means [...]: '*Asile héréditaire,*' and it is there that his true victory began. This aria is his property, his conquest.[68]

The tenor's success in Paris was absolute. He had honed his talent during years in the huge San Carlo in Naples, so that Berlioz was able to recall in his *Evenings with the Orchestra* how, in consequence of Duprez's "high perfection," the audience [69]

admired the fusion of feeling and of discipline with an organ of enchanting sweetness; there remain to be heard the dramatic accents, the bursts of passion. A number comes during which the daring artist, in chest voice, stressing each syllable, gives out some high notes with a resonant fullness, an expression of heart-rending grief, and a beauty of tone that

---

64 Berlioz is referencing Beethoven's Fifth Symphony.
65 Berlioz, Hector. (1996–2003). *La Critique Musicale*, ed. Cohen and Bongrain, 4 vols. Buchet/Castel. Vol. I, p. 231.
66 Readers might wonder what Berlioz wrote of the rest of the performers that evening. In its totality, he added, almost as a footnote: "The other actors undoubtedly wanted to celebrate their new comrade: they never sang better or showed more verve and ensemble." It was most definitely Duprez's night.
67 Bloch, Gregory W. "The Pathological Voice of Gilbert-Louis Duprez." In *The Divo and the Danseur: On the Nineteenth-Century Male Opera and Ballet Performer. Cambridge Opera Journal*, Vol. 19, No. 1, (Mar., 2007). pp.11–31; p.11.
68 Published on 16 April, 1837. Quoted in Vest, Jason (2009). *Adolphe Nourrit, Gilbert-Louis Duprez, and Transformations of Tenor Technique in the Early Nineteenth Century: Historical and Physiological Considerations* (DMA dissertation, University of Kentucky). p.50.
69 Berlioz, Hector. (1999). *Evenings with the Orchestra*. Trans. Jacques Barzun. University of Chicago Press. p.66.

so far nothing had led one to expect. A petrified silence resigns in the house, people hold their breath, amazement and admiration are blended in a mood akin to fear. There is in fact reason for fear until that extraordinary phrase comes to an end; but when it has done so triumphantly, the wild enthusiasm of the listeners is beyond imagining.[70]

Another critic wrote of his Arnold that he had "A voice that is perfectly pure, even, sonorous; pronunciation that is excellent, declamation that is extraordinary; these are the qualities that first strike one in the new singer."[71] He was, indeed, a new singer, and the Parisian sensitivity to novelty was such that Duprez's *tour de circque* compelled every other tenor – whatever his nationality – to re-appraise the fundamentals of vocal technique. The *Gazette médicale* heralded Duprez as the arrival of a "new species":

> The art of music has recently been enriched by a new species of voice, the discovery of which introduces a new element into the problem of phonation, and which seems to demand a fundamental revolution in the execution and teaching of singing.[72]

One of the first to reach for the gauntlet was Adolphe Nourrit. The story of Nourrit's short life after Duprez's Parisian debut has been redrafted over time to suggest that his suicide in 1839, five days after his 37th birthday, was attributable directly to his inability to match Duprez and his high C. It's a good story, certainly, but the truth is more complicated and interesting. After his triumph in Lucca in 1831, Duprez was all but adopted by Donizetti, who gifted him Ugo in *Parisina* (Teatro della Pergola, Florence; 17 March, 1833), Enrico II in *Rosmonda d'Inghilterra* (della Pergola; 27 February, 1834) and, most significantly of all, Edgardo in *Lucia di Lammermoor* (San Carlo; 26 September, 1835). Before his arrival at the Opéra, therefore, Duprez was a European celebrity, even if he was identified in the French press as "new" and "little-known." International fame was attainable for Parisians only in Paris.

Nourrit's construction of the art of singing was uniquely French, concerned as it was with the primacy of language,[73] elegance of expression and emotional dignity. He was skilled in the arts of costume and make-up, and though given to fat, he was said to transfix an audience with the grace of his bearing. As a musician, his professorial

---

70 It is true that Berlioz's *Evenings with the Orchestra* was a satire – of sorts – and it does pull the wings off Duprez's hubris, which appears to have been considerable. It is well also to remember that Berlioz's point, through the "sunrise to sunset" characterisation of "the tenor's" career, is that the celebrity enjoyed by a singer cannot stand beside the lasting – and death-surviving – art of the composer. In this respect, the author was pricklier than most, with more axes to grind than Odysseus.

71 In the *Revue et Gazette musicale de Paris*. Quoted in Bloch, Gregory W. "The Pathological Voice of Gilbert-Louis Duprez." In *The Divo and the Danseur: On the Nineteenth-Century Male Opera and Ballet Performer*. Cambridge Opera Journal, Vol. 19, No. 1, (Mar., 2007). pp.11–31; p.12.

72 *Ibid.* pp.11–31; p.14.

73 Miller, Richard (1997). "The Role of Language in National Pedagogies," in *National Schools of Singing*. Scarecrow Press. p.176.

concern for enunciation and declamation (advantaged necessarily by the absence of *vibrato*[74]) compelled exemplary pitching, and an intuitive use of *portamento*. The values isolated by the recorded performance of Sarah Bernhardt as *Phèdre* speak to most of what was written of Nourrit. Her renunciation of the artifice of static declamation compelled the use of her entire body for her art, while the "gold" of her voice was celebrated for its expressive range rather than its pure tone – metrics of value and meaning that were applied no less consistently to Nourrit.[75]

Duprez was trained to maturity in Italy, where virility of sound, gesture and emotion were more consistent with the traditions of the Commedia dell'arte than the works of Racine, Molière and Beaumarchais. Corti described Duprez's acting as "exaggerated,"[76] while a critic of *Le Frondeur* identified his undulating gestures, and the bizarre movement of his head, as proof of his having recently returned from Italy.[77] It is true that Duprez sang only in Italian when in Italy, and then in large theatres with imperfect acoustics and noisy audiences. The virtue of a ringing *squillo* tenor voice was an (unrecognised) pre-requisite for theatres with 3,000 people in fitful attendance. The tenorial "ping" was hard-wired by Donizetti to the role of Edgardo – which cannot properly be performed by a light tenor, particularly if the other soloists, chorus and orchestra are invested. Although both Nourrit and Duprez were French, therefore, Duprez was Italian in every meaningful sense.[78] As much is obvious from Edgardo's opening scene in Act 1 of *Lucia* – beginning "*Lucia, perdona…*" (preceding the duet "*Sulla tomba che rinserra*") – which requires the tenor to make himself heard over Donizetti's thrilling writing for strings, with prominent double-bass parts and brass commentaries that would have drowned Nourrit into mime. Certainly, *Lucia* marked a departure for Donizetti's vocal and orchestral language in 1835 – only four years after Duprez hit his first high C in 1831.

While Duprez was *schiacciando come un cappone* in Italy, Nourrit was in Paris preparing to create the title role for Meyerbeer in *Robert le Diable*. The first night, on 21 November, 1831, was a triumph – in part because of the *Pythonesque* "Ballet of the Nuns,"[79] but thanks primarily to Nourrit, whose singing was hailed as miraculous. By

---

74   The issue of *vibrato* is contentious because of its ubiquity on early recordings. However, there is little doubt that for the majority, and until very late in the 19th century, *vibrato* (or the "*tremelo*") was anathema to good taste and technique. For the doubters, who continue to suggest (and they can do no more) that *vibrato* was ubiquitous, there is useful assistance in just about every singing manual published until the end of the century. Sims Reeves, for example (the legendary English tenor who gave the first English performance of Berlioz's *La Damnation de Faust* in 1848, with Berlioz conducting) openly detested the "five out of every six modern singers who are afflicted with it." Reeves wrote this in his "Simms Reeves: On the Art of Singing," which was first published by Boosey's in the year of his death: 1900.
75   Rogers, Francis (1939). "Adolphe Nourrit". *The Musical Quarterly* 25. p.13.
76   Smith, Micheal Lee Jr. (2011). *Adolphe Nourrit, Gilbert Duprez, and the high C: The influences of operatic plots, culture, language, theater design, and growth of orchestral forces on the development of the operatic tenor vocal production*. UNLV Theses, Dissertations, Professional Papers, and Capstones. 1273. p.54.
77   Everist, Mark. (2002). *Music Drama at the Paris Odéon, 1824–1828* (University of California Press). p.8.
78   Pleasants, Henry. (1995). *The Great Tenor Tragedy*. Amadeus Press. pp.164–67.
79   In Act 3, nuns rise from the dead and dance seductively amid the ruins of a moonlit monastery. *Pace* Grand Opera at its grandest.

the end of the 1834 season, he had made almost 100 appearances in the role,[80] which he continued to sing until 1837, when he was replaced at the Opéra by Duprez.

The impact of Duprez's high C in Paris is said to have been psychologically devastating for Nourrit – whose departure from the Opéra was blamed on Duprez's performance as Arnold in full voice in 1837.[81] This is quite simply a fabrication. Nourrit had been planning for some time to relocate to Italy, for a change of scenery and to re-train in the new style of singing. There's little doubt that he knew of, and may well have heard, Duprez in Paris, but stories of his storming from the Peletier in horror are insulting to Nourrit's memory. After all, he was the most celebrated tenor in France, having created numerous landmark roles, including Raoul in *Les Huguenots* in 1836 – then the most expensive production in Parisian operatic history.[82] He was a renowned singer of *lieder* (performing regularly with Chopin and Liszt) and a beloved hero of *la France*. When Nourrit announced his departure from the Opéra, the city organised a glittering benefit gala – for 1 April, 1837, more than two weeks *before* Duprez's debut on the 17th.[83] Meyerbeer had been coaching Duprez to take over the role of Raoul for some weeks (and for which event he composed a new aria for Act V), and on the 11th Henri Duponchel (the impresario who had taken up the general directorship at the Peletier in September, 1835) held a soirée in his apartment to introduce Duprez to the great and the good.

In addition to Meyerbeer, Duprez was welcomed by the Princess Chimay, the Prince and Princess Belgiojoso, Louis-François Bertin (whom Ingres had painted so memorably five years earlier), Louis Viardot, Eugène Scribe, Cherubini, Rossini, Auber, Berlioz, Halévy, and numerous other leading figures of contemporary French and European cultural life. Duprez sang "*Rachel, quand du Seigneur*" from *La Juive*, and two arias from *La muette de portici* – the significance of which (as works created by Nourrit) would not have been lost on the audience. The soirée ended with Liszt improvising.[84] This was a Tuesday evening in Paris in 1837.

After his arrival in Italy, Nourrit endeavoured to adapt to the new style, and he was not unsuccessful, but his aesthetics were ill-suited to Italian taste. As he wrote to friends:

> [...] when you heard me here, [you] were surprised at the change that had taken place in my singing, the surprise not unmixed with a bit of regret. You both observed that in gaining certain qualities (or at least in developing them), I lost others equally essential. Despite the satisfaction

---

80 At the time of Meyerbeer's death in 1864, *Robert le diable* had been performed almost 500 times in Paris alone. The popularity of the work was captured memorably by Degas in 1871. Although the painter liked the opera, he felt it had probably outstayed its welcome some five years after the composer's death – which fact was captured by the painter in the audience member whose indifference to the absurdities on stage is reflected in his use of binoculars to look at patrons to his left.
81 See, for example, Rogers, Francis. "Adolphe Nourrit." *The Musical Quarterly* 25 (1939). p.13.
82 160,000 Fr. See Chouquet, Gustave (1873). *Histoire de la musique dramatique en France*. Didot. p.67.
83 It raised the handsome sum of 24,380 Fr, which ensured Nourrit's trip to Italy was undertaken in appropriate style and comfort. See *The Diaries of Giacomo Meyerbeer: 1791–1839*. p.502.
84 Kahane, Martine (1985). *Robert le Diable: Catalogue de l'exposition Théâtre National de l'Opéra de Paris 20 Juin – 20 Septembre 1985*. Bibiloteque National. p.24.

that I displayed I fully shared your regret, and hoped always that with time I could recover those fine nuances that were the essence of my talent, and the variety of inflection I had had to abandon in order to conform to the exigencies of Italian singing as one hears it today, and as it is effective in Italy.[85]

The *voix sombrée* and the culture of Rossinian bari-tenors left Nourrit sounding underfed and insufficiently masculine. Worse still, compromising to local sensibilities had damaged his art:

I hoped always that with time I could recover those fine nuances that were the essence of my talent, and the variety of inflection I had had to abandon in order to conform to the exigencies of Italian singing [...] To tell the truth, with the Italian inflection that I have cultivated, I have only one colour at my disposal, and I find myself falling into precisely those errors for which we reproach the Italians.[86]

A little over a year after arriving in Italy, Nourrit accepted the inevitable. As his wife explained in a letter to her brother, dated 20 October, 1838:

Adolphe has appeared to be in good health for four days, and that his voice is improving. He has given up the *voix sombrée*, which he had tried to develop, and is now trying to go back to where he was when he arrived in Naples.[87]

Adolphe's good health was fleeting. He was suffering from chronic colitis,[88] which contributed to a severe depression from which he was unable to recover. On 8 March, 1837, Nourrit jumped to his death from the third-floor balcony of his rooms in Naples at the Barbaja Hotel.

Nourrit had wrestled terribly with the huge San Carlo. The theatre's difficult acoustic was compounded by the amplitude of a large orchestra and, most grievously of all, a boiler-room work ethic. The Opéra had always expected much of its singers. After 1835 the culture shifted in tandem with the evolving commercial opportunities – which were intensified by the arrival in Paris of a steam-train service six months before the first performance of *Les Huguenots*.[89] It's clear that Duponchel's bidding contributed to Nourrit's decision to emigrate. Life in Paris was bohemian when compared to Naples and Milan, where the concept of an opera remaining in-diary for 500 performances was neither precedented nor imagined.[90] Duprez's gothic capabilities

---

85 Pleasants, Henry (1995). *The Great Tenor Tragedy*. Amadeus Press. p.73.
86 Pleasants, Henry (1974). *The Great Singers*. Gollancz. p.164.
87 *Ibid*. p. 80.
88 A disease of the digestive system, characterised by the *very* painful inflammation of the colon's inner lining.
89 Dunham, Arthur (1941). "How the First French Railways Were Planned." *Journal of Economic History*. 1.1, pp.12–25.
90 *Les Huguenots* was the first opera to be performed at the Opéra more than 1,000 times – the 1,000th performance being on 16 May, 1906.

were forged by his experiences in Italy, where it was routine for singers to adhere to schedules that would now qualify as unlawful. Duprez, in particular, was known to sing the role of Edgardo five or six times a week,[91] a singer in the 21st century would not be expected (much less required) to perform more than 75 times in a year – around once every five days.

The physical demands of Duprez's schedule are more shocking still when considering the intensifying battle between singers and orchestras. Composers of Grand Opera were the first to treat orchestras independently of singers, which meant less doubling between instruments and voices, and more virtuosity from within the pit. When Nourrit was cast as Pylades in *Iphigénie en Tauride* at the Opéra in 1821, he was required to work with an orchestra with two oboes, two bassoons, two horns and two trumpets in C, timpani, and no more than 14 violins, violas, 'cellos and basses.

Some of the orchestral texture was novel in its density, and to a limited extent Gluck placed the tenor in conflict with the orchestra; the relationship is, for the most part, collaborative, however. Mozart employed a larger orchestra; he scored *Così fan tutte* for two flutes, two oboes, two clarinets, bass clarinet, two bassoons, two horns, timpani, strings, and continuo (harpsichord and cello). Even so, his writing operates to support his singers; vocal lines are often doubled, sometimes in competition but only with darker instruments, so as to enable an even-tempered voice to be heard clearly in partnership with (rather than "over") the orchestra. When performing with a band of between twenty and thirty instruments, a tenor with Nourrit's *voix blanche* would not have struggled to be heard.

By the time Rossini came to score *Guillaume Tell* – just 8 years after Nourrit made his debut as Pylades – his orchestra featured a piccolo, two flutes, two oboes, cor anglais, two clarinets in A, two bassoons, four French horns in G and E, two trumpets in E, three trombones, timpani, triangle, bass drum, cymbals, and somewhere between twenty and thirty strings.[92] The textures are not quite German – and Beethoven's influence is illusive, rather than overt. The dramatic momentum, particularly during Act 4, is nonetheless exceptional in its challenge to any but the most exceptional tenor. The same is true today, which is one of the reasons for the opera's infrequent staging. Rossini understood what he was asking of Nourrit, and "*Asile héréditaire* […] *Amis, amis secondez ma vengeance!*" was more often than not cut for his benefit. It may be presumed that Meyerbeer was no less sensitive to Nourrit's limitations when presenting him with the brutally exacting role of Raoul in *Les Huguenots*. The Act 1 Romance "*Plus blanche que la blanche Hermine*" (which typifies the role with its huge range in pitch, from a baritone register to a C5), the Act 2 duet with Marguerite, "*Beauté divine*," the monumental duet with Valentine in Act 4, "*Tu m'aimes*," and the thrilling Act 5 "*Aux armes, mes amis*" are remarkable moments of musical theatre. For the tenor singing Raoul they are hurdles that require the isolation of a significant weight of tone, with the final act placing him in competition with a full orchestra featuring doubled trumpets and chorus. Every word is expected to remain audible. In his review of the opera for *Le monde*, Liszt wrote that

---

91   Rosselli, John (1984). *The Opera Industry in Italy from Cimarosa to Verdi: The Role of the Impresario*. Cambridge University Press. p.127.
92   Formed as between 6,6,4,4,3 and 8,8,6,5,3.

the orchestral effects are so cleverly combined and diversified that we have never been able to attend a performance of the *Huguenots* without a new feeling of surprise and admiration for the art of the master who has managed to dye in a thousand shades, almost ungraspable in their delicacy, the rich fabric of his musical poem.[93]

He praised Nourrit also, but there is a sense that he did so as an act of generosity for the man who had held him aloft as a boy onto the same stage 12 years earlier. Unlike Nourrit, Duprez was able to spit out his vocal cords when the situation required it – which appears to have been six nights a week after Donizetti presented him with the score of *Lucia di Lammermoor* in 1835. The opera calls for two flutes, a piccolo, two oboes, two clarinets, two bassoons, four horns, two trumpets, three trombones, timpani, triangle, cymbals, bass drum, church bell, and a full complement of strings. Edgardo is not the title role, but his Act 1 duet with Lucia, the quartet and sextet in Act 2, the driving duet with Enrico that opens Act 3, and the recitative and aria that ends the opera, "*Fra poco a me ricovero*," require more of a tenor in terms of amplitude and declamation than anything written previously. This is because of the scoring, which is dense throughout, but also because the role of Edgardo necessitates white-hot passion and psychological disturbance pretty much from the start.

The Grand operatic arms war created by Rossini, Auber, Halévy and Meyerbeer was ended for French composers by Berlioz, whose appetites for orchestral distention were tolerable only because they were sustained by a unique technical and imaginative genius. This first manifested itself on 5 December,1830, with the premiere at the Paris Conservatoire of *Symphonie fantastique*: *Épisode de la vie d'un artiste* […] *en cinq parties*,"[94] The score of the *fantastique* is *sans voix*, but it calls for an orchestra of 90 – a scale dwarfed just seven years later by his *Grande Messe des morts* (or *Requiem*). In addition to a chorus of 80 sopranos and altos, 60 tenors and 70 basses, and a string band of 25 first violins, 25 second violins, 20 violas, 20 'cellos and 18 double basses, Berlioz scored his glorious monstrosity for four flutes, two oboes, two cors anglais, four clarinets in B flat, eight bassoons, 12 horns (four parts, plus two extra in the *Dies Irae*), four cornets in B flat, four tubas, 16 timpani (six pairs, four single), two bass drums, ten pairs of cymbals, four tam-tams, and four *additional* brass choirs featuring four cornets, 16 trombones, two tubas, 12 trumpets and four Ophicleide (a keyed brass instrument similar to the tuba). Berlioz added a single solo vocal part, for tenor ("*Sanctus*").

The *Requiem* was not commissioned formally until 1837, but Berlioz had first conceived of a work "on a grand scale" for massed forces after the instant success of *Symphonie fantastique*. On 30 December, 1831, three and a half months after Duprez sang the first high C in Lucca, and shortly before Berlioz's departure for a period of creative isolation in Italy, the composer wrote to Stéphen de La Madelaine:

---

93 Liszt, Franz. "Revue musicale de l'année 1836" (8 January, 1837). *Le Monde*.
94 Op. 14. *Fantastical Symphony: Episode in the Life of an Artist* […] *in Five Sections*.

> During my exile I will attempt to write something on a grand scale; I will try to realise an immense project that I have been pondering, and on my return we will stir up the musical world in a strange way.[95]

It's unclear whether he had planned a solo movement for tenor this early in the project's design, but had he done so it's obvious he would have gifted it to Adolphe Nourrit. When finally the project came to fruition, Berlioz delivered the score to Duprez as his first and only choice.[96] The premiere on 5 December, 1837, at *Les Invalides* was presented eight months after Nourrit's departure for Italy. Although the *Sanctus* is thoughtfully scored – with the tenor voice lofted above wind and strings only – the context of the work by its grandeur signified the end of the classical period, and the onset of Romanticism at full pelt. Between 1831 and 1837 the modern tenor voice had come into its resolving focus. It would not be the same again.

---

95 Berlioz, Hector (1972). *Correspondance Générale I: 1803– May 1832* [No.'s 1–273], ed. by Pierre Citron. Letter No. 200.
96 Berlioz paid Duprez 300 Fr. for his work – from a project budget of 10,000 Fr.

Chapter Four

New Wine, New Bottles

The practice of Christian worship and music evolved in tandem. It did so slowly. With women "silent in the churches," boys were the solitary resource for treble-pitched voices, with exceptions (or additional support) being provided by men singing *falsetto*. *Castrati* were an Italian curiosity, primarily at the Vatican; well into the 1940s, boys across every social demographic throughout Europe, the British colonial territories and, eventually, the United States were taught to sing at church or in church-directed schools. Until 1791, the government of the United Kingdom required everyone to attend Anglican services at least twice a year (to satisfy, in part, the increasingly Swiftian obsession for statistical analysis). Parliament's oversight was unnecessary, with routine attendance sitting comfortably above 50% of the population until late into the 19th century. Specialist music schools for the training of boys were no less in abundance, although England's celebrated cathedral tradition was well behind the curve established by Charlemagne, and across the Holy Roman Empire. The *Regensburger Domspatzen* (or 'Regensburg Cathedral Sparrows') were formed in 976 for performances by boys and young men only, while a boys' choir was finally established at Westminster Abbey, as a source of training for the country more widely, in 1066. The Dresden Kreuzchor followed suit in 1206. Italy's churches took their lead in the Pontifical Chapel from 1442, and the Vienna Boys Choir which was established in 1489. Scandinavian Chapels became routine throughout the 1500s. The first recorded praise of any English singer was paid to the choristers retained by Henry VIII by a visitor from Vienna who was so enchanted that he wrote that their voices were more heavenly than human, and that they did not chant as men, but gave praise as angels. Phillip II expanded the Spanish Imperial Chapel in 1556, with Elizabeth I and Louis XIV advancing the place and primacy of boys' choirs in England and France throughout their reigns. Peter I invested personally in the development of the choir of the Russian Imperial Chapel in 1689, and from 1750 almost every European composer of note sang as a boy at one time or another in a church or cathedral choir. Bach's work as a chorister was so remarkable that his schooling was given to him free of charge. Haydn sang mass at church from the age of six, as did Gluck, Schubert, Rossini, Mendelssohn and hundreds of others. The battle for musical supremacy between the French, Italians and Germans – and across Europe – was waged through the development of native choral traditions for boys that matched the architectural ambitions of the patrons and supporters of church construction. There are vast statistical resources to support the ubiquity of this correlation.

In 1700, for example, there were approximately 140 active public churches in Venice,[1] when the city's population was approximately 140,000. With a church for every 1,000 inhabitants, the demand for choirs and boys with musical talent as well as soloists capable of performing *concertato* and solo motets generated a significant administrative burden.[2] There was little tension between the sacred and the secular, with the aristocracy being responsible, one way or another, for both until their consolidation was encouraged by the abandonment of clerical status as a requirement for church musicians.[3] With the growing popularity of opera, secular singers were paid to perform at church while clerics were paid to appear on stage. Don Sebastiano Orfei, a tenor, was employed at San Marco (as a member of the Cappella Marciana, the choir and instrumentalists of St Mark's Basilica) while also appearing in a host of operas, including Vivaldi's *La costanza trionfante* (1673) and Varischino's *L'Odoacre* (1687).[4] San Marco was abundantly supplied by *castrati*, tenors and basses – all of whom had, at one time or another, performed as children in the city's churches. The scale of the enterprise was such that boys had to be supplied from out of town to satisfy the demand – particularly noting the coincident rush of theatre construction during the latter half of the century. In 1610, there was a single opera house in Venice. In 1700, there were sixteen theatres in regular operation.

Conversely of course, Venice was a significant cultural hub, and cosmopolitan in its tolerance of secularism. Rome was ostentatious in its piety, with around 700 churches serving the same size population as Venice – which meant there was a church for every 200 residents. The city was less inclined to promote the arts, with only two theatres for the performance of spoken or sung drama in 1700: the Teatro delle Quattro Fontane (1632) and the Teatro Capranica (1679). The Teatro Valle opened in 1726, followed shortly after by the Argentina (home of the first *Il Barbiere*), but the city's apparent affection for musical theatre proved to be a flirtation. At the end of 1786, the Valle was the only theatre open for the performance of opera in Rome.

Prior to 1800, therefore, the Roman demand for singers was ecclesiastical; after 1800, as the influence of the Church began to decline, the taste for popular entertainment took advantage of the resulting vacuum – and not merely in Italy. After the dust had settled on the French Revolution and years of Napoleonic conflict, the rise in Nationalism across Europe had a supressive effect on church building and attendance – although the routine of Sunday services and the tradition of the suburban and village choir endured. The dissemination of printing and publishing and the rise in secular education saw the Renaissance bleed into an Enlightenment that swept away the older values of the Baroque, invigorating a critical spirit framed by the virtues of reason, experience, philosophy and science. During a "century of lights," culture was correlated with progress, destabilising the certainties of form and order to produce a proto-romantic social, political and cultural experience of almost constant

---

1 A handful have been lost, or deconsecrated, while a number of private houses (and Palaces) maintain chapels that have not been made available for public use.
2 Roche, Jerome (1976). "Giovanni Antonio Rigatti and the Development of Venetian Church Music in the 1640s," *Music & Letters* 57/3, 256-67. p.259.
3 Lang, Paul Henry (1941). *Music in Western Civilization*. W. W. Norton & Co., p.464.
4 Termini, Olga (1981). "Singers at San Marco in Venice: The Competition between Church and Theatre (1675 - 1725)." *Royal Musical Association Research Chronicle*, No. 17, pp.65–96; p.67.

flux. The diminution of religious authority for large strata of the population allowed nationalism to thrive, which emerged to take the place of religion as the continent's defining system of faith and guidance. And yet, despite attacks on religion becoming fashionable, even in Rome, families across central Europe and Russia adhered for the most part to a routine in which children were sent to Church every Sunday to sing, whether they liked it or not.

Anyone born after 1980 is probably unaware that there was a time – almost in living memory – when Church attendance in Europe was mandatory, even when it wasn't. The statistical probability of the discovery of vocal talent was coterminous with the number of children learning to sing – which was true even of hamlets and villages, where any conurbation established prior to 1900 had at least three or four large, well-maintained churches. The tenor Giovanni Rubini,[5] for example, was born in Romano di Lombardia, 28 miles east of Milan in 1794. When he sang for the first time as a six-year-old in 1800, his parents had eleven churches from which to choose. The Rubinis were one of 544 families in Romano – which equated to a population of 3,000. With a church for every 270 residents, there was a necessary demand for musical children, and Rubini was noticed almost immediately. He did not remain in Romano for long. Even if a church chose not to maintain a choir (which was rare), or a boy proved not to have a voice, most churches contained organs and pianos, and every village and town operated secular wind and brass bands – a tradition celebrated (and exploited) by most Italian composers throughout the 19th century, for whom the on-stage *banda* was an easy shortcut to colour and character.[6]

The rise throughout Europe of a secular musical culture allowed for gatherings outside the influence of the Church – even when they were held in a church. The general dissociation of Christianity and statehood (promoted as an ideal by the clergy's civil constitution during the French Revolution) and the rise in Nationalism more specifically as a philosophy served to foster many of the same social traits and functions common to religion: namely, the creation of myths of origin, saints and martyrs, holy objects, miraculous places and ceremonial locations and dates. This "transference of sacrality"[7] led to the building of altars to the fatherland[8] – however that was determined – which in turn inspired artists across every medium to articulate their "national" identity, even when there wasn't a nation with which to identify. A huge number of French nationalist anthems urged all *good* patriots to repel the Austrian and Prussian invaders by *"watering the fields with impure blood"* – a sanguinary metaphor that quickly became as routine as La Marseillaise's injunction *"Allons enfants de la patrie, Le jour de gloire est arrivé."*

Painters and composers transferred their attention from religious subjects to social and individuated themes, as is obvious from the trajectory of Delacroix's career. Having immersed himself in the study of Veronese, Tintoretto and Rubens, his first

---

5 7 April, 1794 – 3 March, 1854.
6 Nicoli, Giuseppe (2015). *"Romano e la sua storia […] sulle orme di Damiano Muoni."* http://www.comune.romano.bg.it/attachments/article/539/Romano%20e%20la%20sua%20storia...pdf
7 See generally Ozouf, Mona (1976). *La Fête révolutionnaire* (1789–1799). Editions Gallimard.
8 See generally McLeod, Hugh (2015). "Christianity and nationalism in nineteenth-century Europe." *International journal for the Study of the Christian Church*, 15:1, pp.7–22.

significant works were traditional church commissions: *Vierge des moissons (1819)*[9] and *Vierge du Sacré-Coeur (1821)*.[10] In 1824, his focus shifted dramatically. With the *Scène des massacres de Scio*[11] he achieved his first significant success when revealing on a huge scale the horrors of wartime destruction and desolation visited on the Greek citizens of Chios by invading Ottoman forces. Any French citizen staring up at Delacroix's vast canvas cannot have failed to appreciate the painter's compassion for twenty thousand murdered people, and the forced deportation into slavery of almost every one of the seventy thousand who survived. Persecution of one people by another was now as meaningful to the French as the brutalising of Christ, and Delacroix's impulses inspired him over the next six years to increasingly impassioned articulations of symbolic nationalism, spanning the overtly metaphorical *La Grèce sur les ruines de Missolonghi*[12] (1826), *La Mort de Sardanapale*[13] (1827), and the ultimate and most resonant expression of his convictions: *La Liberté guidant le peuple.*[14] The last of these monumental canvasses was unveiled at the end of 1830 – six months after the "Three Glorious Days" of the July Revolution (26th – 29th), that led to the overthrow of Charles X and the ascent of his cousin Louis Philippe, Duke of Orléans. On 21 October, Delacroix wrote to his brother:

> My bad mood is vanishing thanks to hard work. I have started work on a modern subject, a scene on the barricades […] I may not have fought for my country but at least I shall have painted her.[15]

During those three *glorious* days, Berlioz was sequestered in the Paris Conservatoire writing a cantata (*Sardanapale*) with which he hoped to win the Prix de Rome.[16] In his *Memoirs*, he recalled:

> I dashed off the final pages of my orchestral score to the sound of stray bullets coming over the roofs and pattering on the wall outside my window. On the 29th I had finished and was free to go out and roam about Paris till morning, pistol in hand. A day or two later I was crossing the courtyard of the Palais Royal when I heard a tune I knew well – a dozen or so young men singing a battle hymn of my composition.[17] Unused as I was to this kind of popularity, the discovery delighted me and I pushed my way through to the circle of singers and requested permission to join them. The audience grew steadily and the space round the little patriotic band got smaller and smaller. We barely escaped and fled with the

---

9 'Virgin of the Harvest.'
10 'Virgin of the Sacred Heart.'
11 'The Massacre at Chios.'
12 'Greece on the Ruins of Missolonghi.'
13 'The Death of Sardanapalus.'
14 'Liberty Leading the People.'
15 Unpublished letter, dated 18 October, 1830. In *Eugène Delacroix: Selected letters (1813 – 1863)*. (2001). MFA Publications. p.13.
16 It was his fifth attempt, and his last – because he won.
17 One of the "Neuf Mélodies" to texts by Thomas Moore.

crowd streaming behind us till we reached the Galérie Colbert. There a haberdasher asked us up to a second-floor balcony, where we could 'rain down our music on our admirers' without the risk of being suffocated. We struck up the *Marseillaise*. Almost at once a holy stillness fell upon the seething mass at our feet. After each refrain there was a profound silence. This is not at all what I had expected. On beholding that vast concourse of people I recalled that I had just arranged Rouget de Lisle's song for double chorus and full orchestra, and that where one normally writes 'tenors and basses' I had written instead 'everyone with a voice, a soul and blood in his veins'. After the fourth verse I could contain myself no longer, and I yelled, 'Confound it all – sing!' The great crowd roared out its *Aux armes citoyens!* with the power and precision of a trained choir.

Berlioz's fantastic[18] recollection speaks to the mood of the city, if not reliably to the events as he describes them. His account of the rise in popular democratic zeal is captured sensationally in his arrangement for tenor, chorus and orchestra of *La Marseillaise*, which he completed shortly before the unveiling of Delacroix's *Liberté* in 1830, which appeared only a matter of weeks after the installation of the "July Column" in the Place de la Bastille. The bodies of the victims of the July Revolution were buried at its base, while its top was crowned by a statue representing the spirit of freedom. The ceremony, led by Louis-Philippe (crowned *King of the French* on 9 August), continued with a procession that paused at Notre-Dame Cathedral on its way to the Pantheon, where it concluded with a performance of Berlioz's *La Marseillaise*. As part of the ceremony, Victor Hugo read one of his latest poems, making a discreet allusion to the imminent publication of his vast Gothic-romantic novel, *Notre-Dame de Paris*.[19] The shifting of symbol and metaphor to an avowedly secular purpose was embraced across much of the planet at a time when Catholic Belgians were part of the Protestant Dutch monarchy; Greeks and Bulgarians were part of the Turkish Empire; Ireland was part of the British Empire; Poles and Finns were part of the Russian Empire; and Czechs, Hungarians and Italians were part of the Austrian Empire. It was more than a little ironic that, despite the Church's diminishing influence, the development of Opera from 1830 – and the evolution of the tenor voice – remained for more than a century almost entirely dependent on the surviving cultural attachment to regional church choirs. The biographies of most of the greatest tenors of the 19th century begin with the words "sang in church," just as it had for the *castrati* that preceded them. The difference for families with musical children after 1830, compared to those in 1630 or 1730, was that opera (and music more generally) was now a business from which very large sums of money could be made. The happy collision between industrialisation as the coalface of modernity and the otherwise universal pre-occupation with mythical heroes, medieval legacies and

---

18   In every sense of the word. Indeed, just the thought of the eternally fragile Berlioz carrying a pistol cannot but cause joy as well as incredulity on the part of the reader.
19   On 16 March, 1831.

national languages, gave voice as well as opportunity to the subjected, the suppressed and the peripatetic.[20]

Romanticism from the late 1820s through the 1840s saw the emergence of a new generation of composers whose expectations were, for the first time, global. The building of opera houses in parts of the world accessible only after weeks of travel (such as the Imperial Bolshoi Kamenny Theatre in St Petersburg; 1783) or countries that had only recently come into formal existence (most obviously the United States; 1776), served to escalate both the native ambition for self-invention (particularly north, south and east of Vienna) and the power and influence of impresarios, publishers and singers. *Il barbiere*, for example, was first performed, in Italy, on 20 February, 1816. It did not make its way to London until 10 March, 1818 – more than two years later. Bellini's *I puritani*[21], on the other hand, was first performed on 24 January, 1835 (in Paris). Its London premiere occurred less than four months later, on 21 May *the same year*. The relative expedition with which Rossini's work travelled in 1816, and that of Bellini in 1835[22], cannot be explained away by references to their composers' standing and celebrity. Neither was it a function of geography. The velocity with which *everything* moved around the planet escalated dramatically during the 1830s, and exponentially so after the Warsaw–Vienna railway joined Austria to Warsaw and St. Petersburg in 1848. The speed of copyists and printers was equal in value to the accuracy of instrumental and vocal parts when published. Composers continued to bemoan the inhumanity of publishers well into the 20th century, but the commercial reality was that the entitlement to print a score was also a licence to print money for its authors and their publishing houses. When, for example, Rossini and Colbran arrived in London on 13 December, 1823, they lodged (in the company of their macaw and a chef) in the recently completed Regent Street (at that time the "Quadrant").[23] During their seven-month stay in the City, the couple are said to have earned as much as £30,000 from performances, appearances, royalties and ticket sales – equivalent to something like £3.3m / $4.23m in 2021.

Rossini's extravagant lifestyle magnified the scale of the opportunity. In 1830, and within months of *Guillaume Tell's* first performance in Paris, Bellini and Donizetti[24] had both scored resounding international successes with *I Capuleti e i Montecchi*[25] on 11 March and *Anna Bolena* on 26 December, respectively. Both composers were driven by their mercantile faith in the authenticity of the box office.[26] The German poet Heine described Bellini as "a sigh in pumps and silk stockings"; he was actually red in tooth and claw when it came to the business of opera. After the first run of *Beatrice di Tenda*, he described ticket sales as "the real thermometer of

---

20   McLeod, Hugh (2015). "Christianity and nationalism in nineteenth-century Europe." *International journal for the Study of the Christian Church*, 15:1, p.9.
21   'The puritans.'
22   3 November, 1801 – 23 September, 1835.
23   At No. 90.
24   29 November, 1797 – 8 April, 1848.
25   'The Capulets and the Montagues.'
26   Huebner, Steven (1989). "Opera Audiences in Paris 1830–1870." *Music & Letters*, Vol. 70, No. 2; pp.206–225.

pleasure,"[27] and noted that "an absolutely full theatre is the sign of an opera's reception." For his part, Donizetti developed an almost Le Bron-like sense of the crowd. According to Carlotta Sorba, he would immediately pass

> full details of his triumphs to his correspondents, at least his most intimate ones, including their total box-office receipts, which in his colorful language he called *"denari a bizzeffe"* (gobs of money). Composers, and nearly everyone else, described public reactions – especially extreme ones – with a standard theatrical terminology that seems analogous in its uniformity, strangely enough, to that used to describe performances or musical forms. Spectacles that failed to please were *fiasco* – the worst cases being *fiaschissimo* (big fiascos), which is the term that Donizetti employed for his *Maria Padilla* in Venice. Donizetti, who was a lover of linguistic deformation, referred to great successes ironically as *fiasco coifiocchi* (first-rate fiascos). Less frequently, disasters earned the *disgusto* (disgust) of the public or its *noja* (boredom); these terms were popular but never canonized. Positive reactions generated *furore* (enthusiasm), if not its colorful superlatives *furorone* (as Bellini described the reception of *I puritani*) or *furorissimo* (Donizetti on *Marino Faliero)*.[28]

Bellini and Donizetti were acutely sensitive to their celebrity, and to the alignment of those factors on which their fame was increasingly dependent – most resonantly the agency of the singer. While sopranos and *castrati* had been willing (and able) to travel during the 17th and 18th centuries, they rarely did so for a season, and almost never for a solitary engagement – not least since there was a surfeit of local talent and a dearth of theatres. After 1830 it was feasible and eventually expected that a singer be invited to perform a new opera for an opening run in a city outside its country of origin. By the time Donizetti replaced Rossini in Barbaia's affections in Naples, it was in his mind to write operas for singers who would travel Europe, and to the United States, as ambassadors for his art; it was possible even for a singer to represent the work of a single composer. The first to do so was Giovanni Rubini.

If Duprez was the most famous French tenor of the early Romantic period, then Rubini was its most admired Italian; he remains legendary for being the "only man of his class who deserves to be named in these pages as an artist of genius,"[29] and because of the affection and loyalty he warranted from Vincenzo Bellini. The import of the Bellini-Rubini relationship flows primarily from the brevity, and intensity, of Bellini's life. He died shortly after his 33rd birthday, having composed ten operas in as many years.[30] Rubini created the lead tenor roles in five of them, most famously Arturo in

---

27 Sorba, Carlotta (2006). "To Please the Public: Composers and Audiences in Nineteenth-Century Italy." *The Journal of Interdisciplinary History*, Vol. 36, No. 4, Opera and Society: Part II. pp.595–614; p.605.
28 *Ibid.*
29 Chorley, Henry F. (1862). *Thirty Years' Musical Recollections*. Reprinted, Knopf (1926). p.21.
30 *Adelson e Salvini* (1825). *Bianca e Gernando** (1826), *Il pirata** (1827), *Bianca e Fernando** (1828), *La straniera* (1829), *Zaira* (1829), I *Capuleti e i Montecchi* (1830), *La sonnambula** (1831), *Norma* (1831),

I puritani (1835), as well as forty-five other roles, for everyone from Mercadente and Pacini to Michael Balfe and Sir Julius Benedict. He was important to Donizetti also, for whom he created six roles, including the stupendous Riccardo di Percy in *Anna Bolena* .[31]

Rubini's repertoire was vast (encompassing 147 operas) and his career was prolonged even by modern standards. He made his debut in 1812, at the age of 18, and continued to perform on stage and in concert for thirty-three years.[32] His abilities as a vocalist (rather than as a singing actor) were remarkable by most accounts; they were also *passé* at a time when Donzelli and Duprez were quintessential in their masculinity. Rubini's voice was gossamer even by the standards of García, and the common frame of critical reference was "light" and "veiled," with many complaining of inaudibility, emotional detachment and dynamic asperity. Although Chorley remembered Rubini as an artist of "genius," he wrote of the tenor's London debut that he was "hardly capable, perhaps, of [...] *mezzo forte* or *piano;* for which reason he had adopted a style of extreme contrast betwixt soft and loud, which many ears were unable, for a long period, to relish." His success was attributed to a formidable technique, which allowed him to engage in huge spans of breathless phrasing (in keeping with Bellini's compositional voice) and a range that facilitated a high F above C – albeit in *falsetto*. Anton Rubinstein told the critic Pierre Lalo that he learned his "ideas of noble and eloquent phrasing almost entirely from the example of the great tenor Rubini," while Liszt, when asked how he played with such seamless *legato*, answered that he had "sat at the feet of the greatest singers, the greatest of whom was Rubini."

The composer and his muse first collaborated in 1826, for *Bianca e Gernando*, but their first success came a year later, with *Il pirata*.[33] During rehearsals, Bellini complained that Rubini's singing lacked expressivity, and he urged the tenor to invest his "soul into the character" while using his body "to accompany" his singing "with gestures"; he was to act at all times with his voice – a diktat that Rubini satisfied, in part, by the use of sobbing.[34] Ferdinand Hiller observed more than once of Rubini that he "seemed to be singing tears," and it is clear that his exaggeration of aspirates and certain vowel sounds at moments of acute poignancy had a profound effect on audiences, even though these inflections must have denuded the arched lines of melody of some of their mesmeric force. Bellini plainly approved of these interpolations, and their legacy survived in the shades of unctuous melancholy employed (to varying degrees) by Moreschi, Gigli, Filippeschi, Corelli, *et al.*

It's important to remember that Rubini had to cultivate a toy-box of vocal tricks and effects in the studied absence of ornamentation (which he generally abjured), de-contextualised *fioriture*, or *vibrato*. The style of vocal writing employed by Donizetti and Bellini was almost Lutheran in its simplicity when compared with

---

Beatrice di Tenda (1831), *I puritani** (1835). Rubini created the tenor roles in each of the operas marked with an asterisk.
31 Alfonso in *Elvida* (1826), Gianni in *Gianni di Calais* (1828), Ernesto in *Il giove di grasso* (1829); Idamore in *Il paria* (1829), Riccardo di Percy in *Anna Bolena* (1830), Fernando in *Marino Faliero* (1835).
32 His concert career continued into 1852, just two years before his death aged 60.
33 'The pirates.'
34 Giles, Peter (1994). *The History and Technique of the Counter-Tenor*. Scolar Press, 1994. p.266.

the melismatic vernacular of their predecessors. The need for amplitude rendered lightness of touch in tone and dexterity impractical, therefore, and with increases in volume and a greater emphasis on realism, a tendency towards histrionics widened the gulf between the stately Parisian elegance embodied by Nourrit and Neopolitan *sangue e intestini*. When appearing in *Il pirata*, Rubini did not, of course, have the high C in full voice, and neither did he resort to *vibrato*; instead, he was compelled by Bellini to isolate the emotional substance of his characters through a seam of vocal expression formed entirely of melody.

It's possible to navigate what this meant. Over time, the "Rubini sob" evolved into a *vibrato* that was employed initially to colour single phrases, words, syllables or notes. In 1843, for example, the *Official Gazette* of the St. Petersburg Academy published its review of a performance of *Il pirata*, featuring Rubini, in which the critic noted:

> The last phrase, 'Dei lunghi miei tormenti, del mio tradito amor,' sung with all the strength, all the *vibrato* (qualities which so distinguished the singing of Rubini), moved the hearts of the audience, and for a long time after the curtain was lowered, still sounded in their ears.[35]

Being that *vibrato* was isolated to its use in a single phrase – and distinguished throughout the rest of the review – it is reasonable to conclude that Rubini employed it for passing colour and effect only. In his treatise of 1847, Manuel García states that brilliance of timbre and power of emission confer a voice its natural and credible *vibrati*on – which is supressed so as to allow for its exploitation as an effect. He describes two different manifestations of this "hysteria of the voice" which he finds necessary for powerful delivery. If the agitation is caused by one then the voice can employ a kind of shake; the other produces a grief so vivid that it completely dominates, and the organs of the voice experience a kind of mechanical vacillation. García called this "*tremolo,*"[36] and warned against its routine or indiscriminate use:

> The tremolo should be used to portray the feelings which, in real life, move up profoundly; the anguish of seeing someone who is dear to us in imminent danger, the tear which certain movements of anger or of vengeance draw from us etc. Even in those circumstances, the use of it should be regulated with taste and moderation; as soon as one exaggerates the expression of the length of it, it becomes tiresome and awkward. Outside of the special cases [...] it is necessary to guard against altering in any way the security of the sound, for the repeated use of the tremolo makes the voice tremulous. The artist who has contracted this intolerable fault becomes incapable of phrasing any kind of sustained song. It is thus that some beautiful voices have been lost to the art.[37]

---

35 Marek, Dan H. (2013). *Giovanni Battista Rubini and the Bel Canto Tenors*. Scarecrow Press. p.235.
36 *Ibid*. pp.148–149.
37 Marek, Dan H. (2013). *Giovanni Battista Rubini and the Bel Canto Tenors*. Scarecrow Press. p.235.

García was here referring to Rubini. After years of work, the Italian singer's once-lucid production of tone degenerated during the 1840s into a bleating *vibrato* which many compared to the sound of a goat.[38] It's difficult – and dangerous – to guess at what this was like; there is, however, an obvious point of comparative reference in Alessandro Bonci's[39] recording, from February, 1905, of "*A te o cara*" from *I puritani*.[40] Bonci made his North American debut the following year, on December 3, 1906 – as Arturo – at Hammerstein's Manhattan Opera House, where he was warmly received, and compared (somewhat improbably) to Caruso. Bonci's singing, when judged by this performance, speaks to the tradition into which he was born in 1870 – a mere 18 years after Rubini's death. Some might enjoy Bonci's approach to line, and his lightly floated high C is beautifully delivered; the *stretto vibrato* is otherwise horribly invasive. It's certainly a sound that British and German critics were quick to criticise – while, at the same time, isolating in Rubini's art the *sine qua non* of beauty and refinement, an anomaly that crystallised during the 1870s, in consequence of demand outstripping reply.

During the 1840s, Rubini toured with the horn player Giovanni Puzzi.[41] Their collaboration spanned a repertoire of large ensemble pieces for voice and horn (such as "*Dal tuo stellato soglio*" from Rossini's *Mosè in Egitto*[42]) to arrangements and isolated songs in which Puzzi appeared as Rubini's accompanist.[43] The canzonet "*La potenza d'amore*,"[44] written for Rubini by Tadolini with *obbligato* for horn by Puzzi, entailed languidity and floridity in rhythmic unison, with the sustaining of longer notes exploited for exhibitionist *messa di voce*. When appearing on his own, Puzzi's handbills often promised the performance of contemporary arias "as sung by" the performer who created them – which inevitably included Rubini.

So great was the public's enthusiasm during the first half of the 19th century for celebrity singers that composers took to crafting tributes for those unable to hear their gods in the flesh. Moscheles, for example, composed his *Hommage Caractéristique à la Mémoire de Madame Malibran de Bériot, en forme de Fantaisie*,[45] Op.94b, in 1836. He published the work shortly after the soprano's death, as a means of capitalising on her fame. Of course, his homage was composed for piano (like his *Gems a la* [Giuditta] *Pasta, Fantasia Dramatique*, Op.71a), which subsumed much of Malibran's genius (and her legendary palette of *legato, portamento, vibrato*, declamation, inflection and word placement) to the mechanics of the instrument. When Moscheles created his *Souvenir de Rubini; Fantaisie dramatique pour le Pianoforte, dans laquelle est introduit une Cavatine favorite de l'Opera Anna Bolena*[46] in

---

38 *Ibid*. p. 266.
39 10 February, 1870 – 9 August, 1940.
40 This was one of the tenor's first recordings, produced in Milan for the Fonotipia label.
41 24 May, 1791 – 1 March, 1876.
42 'Moses in Egypt.'
43 Strauchen, Elizabeth Bradley (2000). *Giovanni Puzzi: His Life and Work. A View of Horn Playing and Musical Life in England from 1817 into the Victorian Era (c.1855)*. D.Phil. Music History Somerville College, University of Oxford. p.167.
44 'The power of love.'
45 'Characteristic tribute to the memory of Madame Malibran de Bériot, in the form of a fantasy.'
46 'Souvenir of Rubini; Dramatic fantasy for Piano, introducing a favourite Cavatina from the Opera, Anna Bolena.'

1830,⁴⁷ the tenor was still some years from the height of his fame, and the composer's necessarily hucksterish fluff has provided posterity with no insights into what he might have sounded like. When Puzzi engaged in similar episodes of mimicry, however, he was able to emulate many of the more obviously vocal traits that sustained Rubini's capacity for heightened emotion. These included *vibrato* – a "trick" employed as colour by Pasta, Malibran and the bass-baritone Antonio Tamburini – and exaggerated dynamic extremes, alarming intervals, sustained phrasing (without breath) and a weight of inflection that attempted to capture the voicing of an aria's words.

The theatrical element was not, of course, capable of imitation, so it was said that Rubini had to be seen as well as heard for his talent to be appreciated. Certainly, on 2 December, 1827, the *Gazzetta privilegiata di Milano* observed of *Il pirata*'s premiere run (of 15 performances) that it had "introduced us to Rubini's dual personality as a singer and an actor," and that it "marked the defining performance for the tenor." A few weeks later, in February 1828, *Il pirata* triumphed in Vienna, followed by premieres in Naples, Paris and London. After Rubini's first performance as Gualtiero, Bellini wrote to his friend Francesco Florimo "You have good reason to say that at the entrance of Rubini it seemed to you as if you were seeing an angel, for he said it [the music] with an incomprehensible divineness...."⁴⁸

At the time of his death, Bellini was preparing to refashion *Norma* for Rubini (the role of Pollione having been written in 1830 for Donzelli) in anticipation of the 1835–36 season at the Théâtre-Italien in Paris. The composer had planned to replace the tenor's Act 1 aria and the Pollione-Adalgisa duet with a second tenor aria, while reworking most of the tenor lines – presumably to raise the *tessitura* to better suit Rubini's *fach*. It is meaningful that Rubini required the refashioning of Pollione. In writing the role for Donzelli – and noting its adoption by every *tenore di forza* since – Bellini was plainly seeking a voice of serious dramatic weight. Although Rubini went on to sing the role, and with success in Paris, he plainly struggled with the music's range, which is low for any but the most *robusto* tenor. The Act I aria "*Meco all'altar di venere,*"⁴⁹ and the concluding duets with Norma, "*In mia mano alfin tu sei*"⁵⁰ and "*Gia mi pasco ne tuoi sguardi,*"⁵¹ cannot be sung by the same voice that might perform the role of Arturo in *I puritani*, which is one of the reasons for believing that Rubini committed much of his work during the 1840s into forcing a quart out of a pint pot. The *vibrato* for which he became known may well have evolved in consequence of ill-advised repertoire choices, compounded by the growing scale of orchestras. If Dan H. Marek is right,⁵² and there is considerable evidence to believe that he is,

---

47 Moscheles subtitled most of these tributes as "*pot-pourrits* [...] written in the closest possible imitation [and] from memory" of the voices he had heard. Moscheles, Charlotte (1873 (2014)). *Life of Moscheles, with Selections from his Diaries and Correspondence, by his Wife*. Trans. A.D. Coleridge, vol. 1. Cambridge University Press. p.243.
48 Zucker, Stefan (1997). *The Origins of Modern Tenor Singing*, Bel Canto Society. p.9.
49 'With me at the altar.'
50 'At last you are in my hands.'
51 'Already I take pleasure in the way you look at me.'
52 Marek, Dan H. (2013). *Giovanni Battista Rubini and the Bel Canto Tenors*. Scarecrow Press. pp.100-101.

then Rubini was a Rossini tenor in all but name, and the musical culture that saw the evolution of the bari-tenor – spanning the roles of Otello and Edgardo – made demands of Rubini that neither he nor the vast majority of his peers could hope to satisfy. Many tried, regardless.

Alberico Curioni,[53] for example, created the role of Alberto for Rossini in *La gazzetta* in 1816. He made his London début in 1821 at the King's Theatre as Mozart's Titus and sang in the city until 1837. His roles included Otello, Agorante in *Ricciardo e Zoraide*, King James in *La donna del lago*,[54] Carolino in Mayr's *Il fanatico per la musica*,[55] and Adriano at the London première of *Il crociato in Egitto*[56] in 1825. Seven years later, he created the role of Orombello for Bellini in *Beatrice di Tenda*, at La Fenice, before taking up the role of Pollione, which he performed with Giulia Grisi in her first *Norma* in 1835.

The voice that created Alberto also sang Pollione therefore, and this determination among tenors to keep pace with naturally bigger voices is key to the crises faced by singers like Nourrit and Rubini, and every generation of tenor since. When Curioni sang the title role in the British premiere of *Le comte Ory* in 1829 (created by Adolphe Nourrit on 20 August the previous year), one critic wrote that:

> nearly the whole weight of the performance fell upon Signor Curioni, who [...] appeared to exert himself to the utmost for the purpose of saving the piece from disgrace [...] But his efforts were indifferently supported and his pains ill requited.[57]

The Chronicle reported that "with all proper sense of Curioni's merits [...] he is heard to infinite disadvantage" because of the shift in expectations created by Donzelli's appearance during the same season. The *Examiner* found him to be "more feeble and inefficient than we have ever heard him before,"[58] while another critic lamented "We warned him a long time ago of forcing his voice, but he has persisted in bawling and halooing, till he has destroyed the justness of his pitching."[59] Almost everyone agreed that his intonation was a perennial issue – a classic consequence of a tenor forcing his tone. Of course, Donzelli – who was in London at the same time – was "prodigious"[60] in the amplitude of his voice, and this elemental power caused the eclipsing of Curioni, and just about everyone else. To that end, and like Donzelli and Duprez, many tenors' careers were subjected to the differentiation between distinct vocal phases. Everyone allowed onto a stage after training was equipped by nature with a clear and invariably small and thin voice – after the tradition of the French *haute-contre* and the Italian *tenore contraltino*. Even Rubini, whose sweetness of tone,

---

53   1785 – March 1875.
54   'The Lady of the Lake.'
55   'The Music Fanatic.'
56   'The Crusader in Egypt.'
57   Fenner, Theodore (1994). *Opera in London: Views of the Press, 1785–1830*. Southern Illinois University Press. pp.194–195.
58   *Ibid*. p.195.
59   *Ibid*.
60   *Ibid*. p.197.

line and inflection were legendary, was drawn to repertoire that can only have placed his voice and art under terminal pressure. The virtue of a darkened timbre, coupled with firmly accented diction, nobility of phrasing and vibrant acting, gave rise to the *tenore di forza*, a vocal type that reached its apogee in the 19th century with Verdi's *Otello* and Giordano's *Andrea Chénier*. Even Duprez allowed the taste for scale to cause him to damage his voice, which took an ultimately ruinous toll on his physical resources and musical abilities. According to Berlioz, Duprez's tenor had "hardened" by September, 1838, when he created the role of *Benvenuto Cellini* at the Opéra – only a year after he brought the same House (along with Berlioz) to its feet when singing the first high C outside Italy. Over the ensuing 10 years, and despite some isolated successes, Duprez's singing never recovered and he was forced into early retirement in 1851, after a final run of *Lucia di Lammermoor* at the Théâtre des Italiens. He was 45 years of age.

Although twelve years older than Duprez (who lived until three months before his 90th birthday), Rubini's career continued until 23 March, 1852, when he appeared in a concert in Venice in honour of Count Berthold.[61] Incredibly, for his final public appearance, Rubini shared the stage with Giovanni Velluti – the last of the operatic *castrati*, who had made his debut in 1800 when Rossini was eight, and who created Arsace in *Aureliano in Palmira* in 1813 and Armando in *Il crociato in Egitto* in 1824. Velluti was 71 years old when performing with Rubini in Venice, and it is tempting to identify their appearance together as in some way transitional. The reality, however, is that Rubini's career was co-terminous with that of Velluti, who was a creature of the 18th century. The fact that young composers like Bellini and Donizetti relied so comprehensively on Rubini's talents does not mean that he was a contemporary singer in matters of style, technique and inclination. Indeed, for all that might reasonably be said of his voice, the one absolutely modern feature of his professional life was his itinerary, which saw him travel by sea, railway and carriage across the entire of Europe almost constantly. Thanks to Dan H. Marek's exceptional research,[62] it's possible to see that Rubini subjected himself to gruelling touring schedules while continuing to create new roles until 19 July, 1838 – when he gave the first performance as Fenton in Balfe's *Falstaff*. Between August, 1838, and March, 1852, he appeared (on circuit tours) in Edinburgh, Dublin, Paris, London (with numerous private concerts at Buckingham Palace for Queen Victoria and Prince Albert), most of the UK's major cities (as well as Tunbridge-Wells, Shepton Mallet, Torquay and Preston), Brussels, Amsterdam, Utrecht, Wiesbaden, the Hague, Madrid, Weimar, Coburg, Berlin, Vienna, St. Petersburg, Moscow, Bergamo and Venice. His work ethic was astounding, and his endurance of travel worthy of St Michael's benefaction. He died extravagantly wealthy, leaving his estates in his hometown of Romano to his wife, Adelaide, with strict instructions that she devote a substantial part of their fortune to the building of a gymnasium, a male orphanage and a hospice for elderly musicians. Most of these legacies remain in beneficent operation today.

Rubini was a civilised, sophisticated, intensely musical singer. He was beloved of one of the greatest composers of melody in the history of music, and not just

---

61 Marek, Dan H. (2013). *Giovanni Battista Rubini and the Bel Canto Tenors*. Scarecrow Press. p.393.
62 *Ibid*. p.197.

opera, and he was revered across the entire continent, transcending the peculiarities of cultural and regional taste and expectation. Even though he was the first and most famous of the romantic generation of Italian tenors to secure an international following, he was a remnant of the musical culture and tradition of the *castrati* – as a singer for whom phrasing, effect and colour were more important than volume, resonance and high notes in full voice. In this regard, he was significantly closer in instinct and character to Farinelli and Velluti than to Donzelli and Duprez.

If *I puritani* (1835) and *L'elisir d'amore*[63] (1832) remain the benchmarks for lyric Italian art during the first third of the 19th century, then it is significant that Rubini chose not to sing the role of Nemorino. In so doing, there is a sense that he regarded his art as had the *castrati*, for whom drama was no laughing matter. That Bellinian seriousness of purpose[64] – and the stately dignity and grace that he brought to his performances – ensured his survival as a signifier of a lost age, one that almost pre-dated him. Rubini did not relate to what was happening within earshot – any more than did Bellini. Indeed, it's easy to forget that Bellini was himself the last of an age, even though he was paradigmatically romantic by instinct. He knew Beethoven's symphonies, and was interested in the work of his French contemporaries, but his theatrical obsessions were focussed almost entirely on the primacy of the voice. He was largely uninterested in the orchestra, even his last and grandest opera adheres to repeating formulae, with solo accompaniments reduced commonly to basic string arpeggiations. Judged purely on their orchestral form and detail, Bellini's scores are less inventive than those by Mozart and even Rossini. Ultimately, his priority was the expressive potential in sweeping, occasionally decorated lines of song – which veered between intense drama and aching melancholy. He gave little attention to ensembles and choruses, and threw his energy as a stage director into the accomplishments of his singers – all of whom became associated closely with his work.

In 1836, a year after Bellini's death, Mercadante was invited by Rossini to Paris, where he composed *I Briganti* for arguably the greatest quartet of singers in history: Grisi, Rubini, Tamburini and Luigi Lablache. They were known then (and now) as the "Bellini Quartet" because of their close association with the astronomically successful *I puritani*. Star-power and word association were not enough for Mercadante, and *I briganti* failed almost immediately after the first performance on 22 March. One week later, to the day, an even greater failure was endured by a young Richard Wagner when conducting the premiere of his second opera, *Das Liebesverbot*,[65] a comic work after the manner and fashion of contemporary French and Italian taste. It was woefully under-rehearsed and poorly attended. The first performance was a farce, with the singers improvising in consequence of memory failure, while the second was cancelled after a fight broke out between the husband of the soprano, Karoline Pollert, and the tenor creating the role of Luzio, Ignaz Freimüller. The audience was made up of three people – eight fewer than were named in the cast.

---

63   'The Elixir of Love.'
64   Bellini's ten operas are either determinedly serious or melancholy-sentimental in subject and character.
65   'The Ban on Love.'

Three years later, the first performance of *Oberto, Conte di San Bonifacio*[66] (the first opera by a young Giuseppe Verdi), was a much greater success. For the tenor role of Riccardo, the composer cast Lorenzo Salvi.[67] He was born ten years into the 19th century, and made his debut singing in the premiere of Donizetti's *Il diluvio universale*[68] in 1830 at the San Carlo. He relocated to the opera house in Zadar[69] for the season 1830–1831, before moving to the Teatro Valle in Rome. Verdi knew of Salvi from his acclaimed performances as Otello opposite Malibran and his portrayal of Daniele in the world premiere of Donizetti's *Betly, ossia La capanna svizzera*[70] at the Teatro Nuovo in Naples in 1836. Salvi sang in two more Donizetti premieres, most notably as *Gianni di Parigi* on 10 September, 1839, at La Scala – less than two months before the first performance of *Oberto* in the same theatre, on 17 November.

Verdi did not turn for his debut to an old hand, or an established celebrity vocalist like Rubini. Instead, he entrusted his first-born tenor role to a young singer raised exclusively in the Donizettian tradition of bari-tenorial force and high theatre. Like Salvi, Verdi had attended his local church (the medieval San Michele Arcangelo, in Roncole, near Busetto) from the age of six, where he sang in the choir and learned to play the organ. Because his singing was less capable than were his skills at the various keyboards to which he was given access, Verdi became the official paid organist at the age of eight. 800 miles north of Busetto, Wagner (who was born five months before Verdi) was sent to the Kreuzschule,[71] the ancient boarding school famed for its *Dresdner Kreuzchor*.[72] The School's historically close connection with music was reinforced by the requirement that schoolmasters were musicians as well as educators, and when Wagner sang and played the organ he did so in tandem with most of his peers. For both children, singing – and the new primacy of the tenor as a secular and theatrical commodity – was a pervasive feature of musical and social life for an expanding European population. With the emergence of Verdi and Wagner during the 1840s, the status of the tenor was transformed by composers and audiences for whom the concept of voice extended further than sound. Verdi and Wagner's titanic achievements would transfigure opera for a generation absorbed by political theories and economic systems that transcended the diminishing influence of the Church. While Europe submitted to nationalism, republicanism and proto-socialism, an art form established for an audience defined by primogeniture was re-purposed as a means of communication for peoples in their millions spanning hundreds of kingdoms and cultures. With popularity came ubiquity, however, and the once precious sensibilities that coloured the work of singing angels like Giovanni Rubini underwent a singular and irreversible reformation.

---

66 'Oberto, Count of Bonifacio.'
67 4 May, 1810 – 16 January, 1879.
68 'The Great Flood.'
69 On the Dalmation Coast, modern day Croatia.
70 'Betly, or The Swiss Chalet.'
71 'School of the Cross.'
72 'Choir of the Cross.'

CHAPTER FIVE

Sovereign's Ransom[1]

In 1951 it was decided that the opening night of the La Scala season in Milan should be relocated from 26 December to Saint Ambrose's Day, 7 December.[2] It has been traditional ever since for the theatre to kill the fatted calf and its siblings for the *Versacenti*, whose pearls and diamonds threaten still to outshine the jewels on stage. With the stellar elevation of Maria Callas in 1953, and the devoted attendance of regulars like Richard Burton, Elizabeth Taylor, Ava Gardner, Grace Kelly, Noel Coward, Picasso, Dalí and Bowie, the lifting of the curtain at La Scala became one of the most important dates in the Italian social and cultural calendar. For the launch of the first season of the new millennium (and to commemorate the centenary of Verdi's death), Riccardo Muti conducted a new production by Hugo de Ana of Verdi's *Il trovatore*, starring Barbara Frittoli as Leonora, Violeta Urmana as Azucena, and Salvatore Licitra as Manrico. The most expensive seats heaved with politicians, aristocrats, supermodels, movie stars and billionaires (something the composer would have regarded with disdain and despair). The gods were subsumed to the *loggionisti*.

At the end of the second scene of Act 3, Manrico stepped towards the orchestra for the celebrated *cabaletta* "*Di quella pira.*"[3] Having been informed that his mother Azucena is to burn at the stake, Manrico calls together his soldiers and commands them to rescue her from certain death. The scene is in C major, with a vocal range of E3 to G4, with three optional high C5s – none of them written *ossia* into the score. It has nonetheless been routine for more than a century and a half for tenors to sing the concluding note as a *high* C, and to sustain it for as long as possible (with or without a change in syllable). The orchestration throughout the aria is scored thickly, with the entire ensemble called upon *fortissimo*.[4] It is now usual for "*Di quella pira*" to be transposed, so that the C5s are sung as B4s – and most productions remove one of the verses, so that the tenor (having already sung the lengthy and taxing aria, "*Ah sì, ben mio, coll'essere*"[5]) can get as quickly as possible to "that" climactic note. On 7 December, 2000, Licitra sang *both* verses in C major, but neither of the first two *ossia* high Cs – leaving everyone to expect something roof-raising for the Act's conclusion. Licitra did not sing the high C, however. Instead, he performed the score

---
1 'Il riscatto del sovrano' – a phrase used more than once by Verdi's friends to describe the composer's commercial instincts, and not always kindly.
2 To accommodate Victor de Sabata's scheduled commitments in the United States.
3 "*Di quella pira l'orrendo foco tutte le fibre m'arse, avvampo!...*" ['The horrible blaze of that pyre burned, enflamed all of my being!']
4 Piccolo, flute, 2 oboes, 2 clarinets, 2 bassoons 4 horns, 2 trumpets, 3 trombones, a tuba timpani, triangle, tambourine, castanets, cymbals, bass drum, harp and at least forty strings.
5 'Ah, yes, my love, in being yours.'

as written – and published – with a G where the C might have been. The *loggionisti* exploded into booing and shouting, which was met by hissing and gesturing from the stalls. A single voice from the back of the theatre was heard above every other. Mauro Fuolega, a bank teller, shrieked "*It's the conductor's fault!*"[6] At this point, Muti dropped his baton, turned his back on the stage and rebuked his critic: "Let's not turn Verdi's centennial into a circus."

The conductor's words were ill-chosen and poorly received. The opening night of the La Scala season has more than once been referred to as "*commedia senza arte*"; the event and its cultural status now compare more obviously with the New Year's Day Concert in Vienna than to a Festpielhaus production of *Parsifal* at Bayreuth. Muti's puritanical adherence to the score as written denied the crowd its pleasure, on the painfully earnest basis that Verdi would have disapproved of such low theatre. In amplifying his *urtextual* integrity, the conductor overlooked the cabaletta's *Barnum & Bailey* theatrics while coincidentally failing to account for Verdi's long-standing approval of the interpolated high Cs – after they were first introduced by Carlo Baucardé, the tenor who created the role of Manrico for the composer in 1853.[7] Muti appears also to have discounted the possibility that Verdi's famously black sense of humour, and his well-known distaste for tenors, might have caused him to write the aria in such a way that the silent fourth above G would be musically and vocally logical for performers and audiences alike – as plainly it is – and then on no fewer than three occasions. Verdi was well-acquainted with *Guglielmo Tell*, Act 4 of which contains the most famous high C in operatic history to 1853. The fact that the final C of "*Corriam*" was also scored to the words "*All'armi*" compounds the vanity of Muti's "authenticity."[8]

The composer's more likely reasoning is that the resolution of the tonic, on the 5th of the C major chord (whether by going up or down to a C from G) would have dissipated the tension that Verdi plainly sought to preserve between the third and final acts. Had that been Muti's reasoning, and had he cited the need for the maintenance of dramatic tension harmonically, the claque might have given him the benefit of the doubt. Unfortunately, the conductor's argument[9] was enfeebled by his decision to greatly exceed the published metronome marking for the *cabaletta* (crotchet – 100) and by his addition of pronounced dynamic effects that do not appear in the score.[10] When the chorus and soloist joined together (with Manrico repeating on two occasions the words "*corro a salvarti*"[11]), Muti introduced huge *subitto-crescendi*, drawing

---

6   Jay McInerney, "Milan Notebook: A Night at La Scala," *New Yorker* (Dec. 25, 2000 & Jan. 1, 2001). p.60.

7   Julian Budden claims that Baucardé was the first to add the high Cs—one at the end of the aria and one at the words "*O teco almeno*"—in a performance in Florence in 1855. See Budden, Julian (1978). *The Operas of Verdi*. Cassell. II. p. 58.

8   "*Corriam voliam….*" In *Il trovatore*, Ruiz and the chorus of soldiers sing "*All'armi! All'armi! Eccone presti a pugnar teco, o teco a morir! All'armi!*" ['To Arms! To arms! Here we are, ready to fight with you, or die with you! To arms!']. Manrico's final note is also sung as "*All'armi.*"

9   The conductor was quoted as saying "that he had considered it his duty to honor the composer's intentions by leaving out the high C." Jay McInerney, "Milan Notebook: A Night at La Scala," *New Yorker* (Dec. 25, 2000 & Jan. 1, 2001). p.60.

10   Muti attempted a similar argument in 1982 when conducting *Ernani* at La Scala in 1982.

11   'I fly to save you….'

magnificent fire from La Scala's brass players. It remains entirely thrilling on the live recording, but it is definitely not *come è scritto*. Neither were the wind instruments of the orchestra from the 1850s, nor the strings made of gut, nor the lighting fuelled by oil. The staging was modern and designed – in theory – to inspire the audience to paroxysms of feeling and depths of reflection, rather than to recover the work as it was imagined by Verdi. The absurdity of denying Licitra his bullet-catching moment at the end of Act 3 is that "the *pira*" is merely the best-known example of *Il trovatore*'s otherwise total commitment to the spectacular, a value system that hinged only in passing on the talent – and confidence – of a singer willing to attempt a C5 in full voice while standing above an orchestra of 80 playing *fortissimo*.[12] What Muti was attempting for Verdi *in absentia* would not have concerned the conductor when performing a score by Rossini – or Mozart, for that matter. Neither would it have been a priority for Verdi, who was perpetually disappointed by almost everything when it came to art and his standing as an artist. In this sense, authenticity where singing and the tenor voice are concerned is a fruitless pursuit – particularly from before the age of recording.[13] Whether engaging in imitation or speculation, anyone seeking to define the sound of a singer will fail for the reasons identified by Stendhal when remembering his favourite *castrato*, Crescentini:

> there is no composer on earth [...] whose score can convey with precision [the] infinitely minute nuances of emotional suggestion: yet it is precisely these infinitely minute nuances which form the secret of Crescentini's unique perfection.[14]

The reader might, by way of a thought experiment, consider how to describe their favourite singer's voice, and then by distinction as between that voice and another. The reader might attempt to characterise Caruso's *actual* tenor and then distinguish it from the sound made by Giuseppe Borgatti. Speculation and (where feasible) imitation are rendered impossible by *qualia* and they are pointless in consequence of Verdi's regular endorsement of amendments. He tolerated these abuses despite his standing as the first composer to prohibit contractually the making of changes to his scores. In addition to Baucardé's *ossia* high Cs in *Il trovatore*, there are numerous independently verified accounts of Verdi compromising – a quality that extended to his encouragement of encores.[15] For example, he transposed "*S'incontri la morte*"[16] in *La forza del destino* from C major to B flat – to assist tenors other than the first

---

12 Walter Woolf King was denied his concluding high C when singing the *Pira* as "Rudolfo Lassparri" in the Marx Brothers' hilarious *A Night at the Opera* (1935), albeit under what might be considered unusual circumstances. Purists will want it to be noted that King was actually a trained baritone, not a tenor. His singing voice in the film was dubbed by Metropolitan Opera singer (and native of the Hawaiian Islands) Tandy MacKenzie (10 March, 1892 – 9 November, 1963).
13 See generally, Crutchfield, Will (1983). "Verdi: The Phonographic Evidence," *19th Century Music*, 7; "Performance: Restoring the Color," *High Fidelity*, 33/6 (June 1983). pp.64–6. Also, "Verdi: The Recorded Legacy," *Opera*, 36 (1985). pp.858–66.
14 Freitas, Roger (2000). "Towards a Verdian Ideal of Singing: Emancipation from Modern Orthodoxy." *Journal of the Royal Musical Association*, Vol. 127, No. 2, pp.226–257; p.228.
15 Hepokoski, James A. (1983). *Giuseppe Verdi: 'Falstaff'*. Cambridge Opera Handbooks. p.126.
16 'Meet death.'

Don Alvaro, Enrico Tamberlik – and he adapted some of Radamès' lines in *Aida* for Giuseppe Capponi.[17] Most awkwardly for alleged historicists like Muti,[18] Verdi was critical of conductors adhering too strictly to the music as it was written. Having been informed by Ricordi of a typically metronomic performance by Toscanini, the composer replied:

> When I began to scandalise the musical world with my sins, there was the calamity of the *Rondos* by the *prima donnas*; now there is the tyranny of the conductors of the orchestra! Bad, bad! But less bad is the first.[19]

Verdi travelled widely and he worked with multifarious singers in dozens of cities and countries. The legendary melancholy that possessed him after the death of his family, prior to the premiere of *Oberto,* extended to a perennial dissatisfaction with his performers. On 25 March, 1875, he wrote to his publisher Giulio Ricordi:

> We don't need conductors and singers to discover new effects; for my part, I declare that no one has ever, ever, ever been able, or known how, to draw out all the effects conceived by me […] No one![20]

Verdi's pragmatism facilitated his acclimatisation to the realities of performing practice beyond his immediate control. He accepted that singing styles changed between cities, and he had no option but to adapt to the substantial geographical differences in dialect, pronunciation and pitch. The post-1900 standardisation of A440 (compelled primarily by the business of piano manufacturing) came too late for Verdi to be confident that the demands he was making of his singers in Milan were fair and realistic for the same or different singers in Bordeaux,[21] Berlin, Prague, Stockholm and New Orleans.[22] Pitch standards rose from around A415 during the late 1700s and reached A435 during the 1890s – when his last opera, *Falstaff*, was first performed. It is unlikely to be a coincidence that Verdi disavowed high Cs when

---

17   14 September, 1832 – 6 August, 1889. Remembered today as the first tenor soloist at the premiere of Verdi's *Requiem* on 25 May, 1874. He was to have been the first Radamès also, but illness compelled his replacement by Giuseppe Fancelli (24 November, 1833 – 23 December, 1887).

18   Muti is, of course, no historicist. He has adhered throughout his career to the scale and sound of a modern orchestra, and he has been inconsistent in his approach to a variety of meaningful issues, including repeats. Every performer of the literature of the 18th and 19th centuries has to address the question of whether or not to repeat – as a choice between fidelity to the score and artistic intuition. Muti has made those choices, like everyone else. There is nothing wrong in doing so. In any event, practice has changed since the 18th century, when repeats were mandatory to assist with (1) an audience becoming acquainted with a theme or idea, and (2) to allow for variations in a performer's expressive licence. See MacDonald, Hugh. "To Repeat or Not to Repeat?". *Proceedings of the Royal Musical Association* CXI (1984/1985). pp.121 – 138.

19   Freitas, Roger (2000). "Towards a Verdian Ideal of Singing: Emancipation from Modern Orthodoxy." *Journal of the Royal Musical Association*, Vol. 127, No. 2. pp.226–257; p.228.

20   Chusid, Martin (1979). "Verdi's Own Words: His Thoughts on Performance, with Special Reference to Don Carlos, Otello, and Falstaff". In *The Verdi Companion*, ed. William Weaver and Martin Chusid. pp.144–92; p.183.

21   Grand Théâtre de Bordeaux (1780).

22   The Théâtre de l'Opéra opened in New Orleans in 1859.

writing for tenors.²³ Indeed, the role of Manrico in *Il trovatore* – celebrated for its three *unwritten* C5s – tops out at a single B flat (in the *stretta* that concludes the Act 1 trio²⁴), which the soloist can choose either to sing high or low. Even Manrico's Act 3 aria *"Ah si, ben mio"* extends no higher than an A as written – although a B flat is routinely interpolated, as it was by Licitra when singing the aria for the authenticist Muti. Verdi was not averse to showmanship and virtuosity, which fact emerges from much of his writing for women (consider, for example, Gilda in *Rigoletto* and Lady Macbeth), but it is curious that he should have denied the high C its currency from the outset at a time when it was – in full voice, at least – only three years old.²⁵ The novelty and sensationalism of Duprez's achievement spread fast, but it appears certain that it did not travel well – particularly at first blush. Between 1840 and 1853 it was very much a work in progress, and Verdi appeared uninterested in the ill-formed and the untrained. When Tamberlik – whom Verdi entrusted with the first performance of Alvaro in *La forza del destino* on 10 November, 1862 – informed the composer that the high C was in great demand with the public, he replied: "Far be it from me to deny the public what it wants. Put in the high C if you like – provided it is a good one."²⁶ When Rossini first heard Tamberlik's high C sharp in full voice, the issue of quality was his solitary consideration:

> Now comes Tamberlik. That jokester, wanting ardently to demolish Duprez' C, has invented the chest-tone C sharp and loaded it onto me. In the finale of my Otello there is, in fact, an A that I emphasised. I thought that it, launched with full lungs, would be ferocious enough to satisfy the *amour-propre* of tenors for all time. But look at Tamberlik, who has transformed it into a C sharp, and all the snobs are delirious! [...] fearing a second, aggravated edition of the Duprez adventure, I cautioned Tamberlik [...] to deposit his C sharp [in the cloakroom] and pick it up again, guaranteed intact, when he left.²⁷

During the 1840s and 50s there was a surfeit of Donizettian bari-tenors on whom Verdi could rely without fear of catastrophe. The high C was fine when Duprez was still able to reach it – and Verdi was certainly willing to entrust him with the premiere of *Jérusalem* on 26 November, 1847 – but there was no conveyor-belt of high-C crunching singers available during the first 15 years of his life as a composer of opera. As the most commercial of animals, Verdi was averse to promoting an effect that could not be achieved other than exceptionally, and in any event the characteristics that defined his writing for tenors required a talent for phrasing and voice placement, not pyrotechnics.

---

23   This extends to "*La donna e mobile*" (Act 3 of *Rigoletto*), the end of the second verse of which allows neither for a cadenza or a high C.
24   Corelli was not alone in ending the first act with an interpolated High D flat – when the voice and body have yet to warm up.
25   *i.e.*, since *Oberto*.
26   Budden, Julian (1978). *The Operas of Verdi*. Cassell. Vo. II. pp.98–99.
27   Michotte, Edmond (2016). *Richard Wagner's visit to Rossini, and An Evening At Rossini's In Beau-Sejour*. University of Chicago Press. p.99.

Verdi's legendary sensitivity to the crowd, and to popular taste, extended to his singers. Between Lorenzo Salvi (*Oberto*, 1839) and Edoardo Garbin (*Falstaff*, 1893) he worked with 26 tenors in the creation of his operas.[28] Some premiered more than one role,[29] and over the course of Verdi's nearly half-century career he helped transform the training, sound and status of the tenor as a musical and theatrical phenomenon. These changes were not attributable exclusively to Verdi, of course, but it's possible to identify from the first some obvious shifts in principle and process. For example, in the year of Verdi's birth a tenor would be expected to sing newly written operas on a seasonal basis; from 1840 the number of new operas written and published increased dramatically while the number being staged did not. This was an anomaly because new opera houses were being constructed globally during every decade of the 19th century. With the increasing demand for opera, however, came an escalating cost of supply. The pressure of market forces on impresarios isolated profit as the sole driver for risk-taking. Grand Opera in Paris amplified these challenges for territories where scale and extravagance rendered novelty financially reckless, and with ever larger orchestras and choruses, and an increasing number of seats to fill, economic forces belched the mixed blessing of agency into a market where Bellini's acknowledgment of the box office was commuted by Verdi into the *métier* of art. Much has been written about Verdi's mercantile philosophy. It's sufficient for these purposes to appreciate the composer's "almost frenzied search for the wealth that alone could bring him independence"[30] – a focus against which his friend Streppони cautioned him in 1853 when writing "Sometimes I fear that the love of money will re-awaken in you and condemn you to many further years of drudgery."[31]

The shift in performance and production culture, and the escalating power of publishers, impresarios and agents had a necessary impact on repertoire and quality. Between 1814 and 1840 the operas Rubini had to memorise were composed by Mayr, Paer, Guglielmi, Puccita, Cordelia, Tadolini, Prota, Napoli, Mosca, Pavesi, Fioravanti, Capuzzi, Giuseppe Farinelli, Trento, Coccia, Cordella, Generali, Balducci, Morlacchi, García, Carafa, Lanza, Carlini, Sampieri, Raimondi, Diversi, Conti, Pogliani-Gagliardi, Frasi, Staffa, Riescha, Vaccai, Ricci, Zingarelli, Gabussi, Majocchi, Gnecco, Balfe, Costa and Marliani. The only composers whose names and reputations have survived from his repertoire are Mozart, Paisiello, Mercadente, Rossini, Bellini and Donizetti. From a stable of almost fifty composers, only six are likely to be known to the general reader; more than half the others will be unknown even to experts.

---

28 Lorenzo Salvi, Corrado Miraglia, Giovanni Severi, Carlo Guasco, Giacomo Roppa, Antonio Poggi, Gaetano Fraschini, Ettore Profili, Angelo Brunacci, Jules-Sébastien Monjauze, Italo Gardoni, Gilbert Duprez, Settimio Malvezzi, Raffaele Mirate, Carlo Baucardé, Louis Guéymard, Lodovico Graziani, Carlo Negrini, Emilio Pancani, Enrico Tamberlik, Mario Tiberini, Jean Morère, Pietro Mongini, Giuseppe Fancelli, Francesco Tamagno and Edoardo Garbin.
29 Salvini, Fraschini and Tamagno.
30 Mendelsohn, Gerald A. "Verdi the Man and Verdi the Dramatist." In *19th Century* Music, Vol. 2, No. 2 (Nov, 1978). pp.110–142; p.115.
31 *Ibid*. p. 115.

On the other hand, when Lorenzo Salvi emerged as a tenor of note at the Teatro Carlo Felice in Genoa – where Verdi first heard him sing[32] – he did so in the role of Arnold, for the first Genoese production of *Guglielmo Tell*. Between 1839 and 1842, Salvi was a regular at La Scala, where he sang in the first performance of Federico Ricci's *Un duello sotto Richelieu*[33] in 1839 (as well as *Oberto*, of course) and the House premiere of Donizetti's *La Fille du Régiment* (1840). Previously, Salvi's exposure to new work – and to premieres – attached him exclusively to Donizetti. The remainder of his career was occupied with works by Bellini, Donizetti and Verdi. His first appearances in France at the Théâtre-Italien were as Edgardo in *Lucia di Lammermoor* and Riccardo in *Maria di Rohan*. During the 1840s and 1850s he sang annually at the Royal Opera, Covent Garden, and frequently in the United States, including a celebrated tour in 1851 with the Swedish soprano Jenny Lind. In every case, and throughout his career after 1840, Salvi adhered to a repertoire of operas by three composers: Bellini, Donizetti and Verdi.

Salvi was emblematic of a generation for whom a new role was a lasting commitment. Where a handful of performances had once been considered satisfactory by a composer willing and able to produce more than a hundred operas during his career, Verdi and his peers understood that a new work of even moderate success was likely to outlive its composer. Among the last of what would eventually be considered the "old school" was Gaetano Fraschini,[34] Verdi's favourite tenor and the creator of roles in five of his operas. Fraschini made his debut on 4 April, 1837, at the theatre in Pavia that now bears his name. He sang the light-sitting role of Lord Arturo in *Lucia di Lammermoor*, followed shortly after by Hervey in *Anna Bolena*. Also in Pavia he sang Iago opposite Giovanni David's *Otello*, and for two years he committed to his apprenticeship, devoting himself exclusively to *comprimario* roles by Pacini, Rossini, Mercadante and Donizetti. In short, he appears to have recognised the need to train by increment and through stages, without placing the mechanics of his voice under unnecessary or damaging strain. Before the end of 1840, he was able to undertake the bari-tenor roles of Roberto Devereux and Pollione – with his future wife, Giuseppina Ronzi de Begnis, as Norma.[35]

Between 1840 and 1853 Fraschini was based at the San Carlo in Naples, where he created a large number of roles in operas by Pacini (including *La fidanzata corsa*,[36] *La stella di Napoli*,[37] *La regina di Cipro*,[38] *Merope*, *Romilda di Provenza*,[39] and *Saffo*) and Donizetti (notably Gerardo in *Caterina Cornaro*). He did so while mastering a range of roles by Rossini and Bellini (including *Il pirata* and *Beatrice di Tenda*).[40] In 1845 he created Zamoro in Verdi's *Alzira*, followed three years later by Corrado in *Il cor-*

---

32 Verdi eventually wintered in Genoa for almost forty years, starting in 1853.
33 'A duel under Richelieu.'
34 16 February, 1816 – 23 May, 1887.
35 Migliavacca, Giorgio (2000). "*Gaetano Fraschini: il tenore della transizione da Donizetti a Verdi*" in *Moderne Sprachen* 44. pp.210–211.
36 'The Corsican Girlfriend.'
37 'The Stars of Naples.'
38 'The Queen of Cyprus.'
39 'Romilda of Provence.'
40 *Ibid*. pp.207–232.

saro[41] (1848), Arrigo in *La battaglia di Legnano*[42] (1849), and the title role in *Stiffelio* (1850). In addition, he was successful in productions of *Oberto, Ernani, I Lombardi alla Prima Crociata,*[43] *I masnadieri,*[44] *Luisa Miller,* and *Il trovatore.* He took part in an early production of *Les vêpres siciliennes*[45] in Rome in 1856, singing the role of Henri, and in 1858 he was Gabriele Adorno in the first Neapolitan production of *Simon Boccanegra.* Verdi recognised Fraschini's decade of efforts and attainments by inviting him to create the role of Riccardo in *Un ballo in maschera*[46] on 17 February, 1859. Some criticised his acting as leaden – in probable consequence of his aversion to the lingering taste for histrionics – but Fraschini's success was routine and international.[47] In 1846 he made his debut in Vienna, at the Kaertnerthortheater, singing Chalais in *Maria di Rohan*, followed shortly after by *Ernani, Lucia di Lammermoor* and *Don Pasquale.*[48] In 1843, Fraschini was engaged to appear in the first London *I due Foscari* at Her Majesty's, and twenty years later he gave the Spanish premiere of *La forza del destino* in Madrid. The following year he appeared in Paris at the Théâtre Italien in *Un Ballo in maschera, Ernani,* and *Il trovatore.*[49]

Verdi described him as a "natural Manrico" and praised the warmth and brilliance of his voice; it was described elsewhere as being like "a silver gong struck with a silver hammer."[50] Fraschini retired in 1874, singing Alvaro in *La forza del destino*; he was 58 years old, and still in control of his resources. One of the most striking features of a career that has long since passed into obscurity was Fraschini's ability to continue at full strength into his late 50s. Despite developing an heroic, baritonal *tenore di forza*, he paced himself from the start, and Donizetti and Verdi cherished his ability to sing softly and with subtlety. Fraschini was what has been called a "transitional" tenor because he is said to have bridged the divide between the demands established by Donizetti (as the old) and Verdi (as the new); this is reductive, however. Tenors who became celebrated as Verdi singers long after the alleged "transition" did not abandon Donizetti in consequence of Verdi's unstoppable rise to pre-eminence – any more than did Tamagno, Caruso and Bergonzi give up singing lyrically simply because they were capable of something "more". The area of transition was more obviously compositional, with many inside and outside Italy lamenting the apparently brutal power of Verdi's operas, and the demands they made of singers raised on a gentler diet. It's undeniable that Verdi's writing for voices, and for tenors in particular, was unparalleled in its expressive reach, but critics and audiences were divided over the damage being caused by his marshalling of effect and power to the long-standing lyrical tradition that preceded him. The English critic, Chorley, for example, recalled in 1862 how in the 1840s.

---

41   'The Corsair.'
42   'The Battle of Legnano.'
43   'The Lombards on the First Crusade.'
44   'The Bandits.'
45   'The Sicilian Vespers.'
46   'A Masked Ball.'
47   *Ibid.*
48   *Ibid.*
49   *Ibid.* pp.210–211.
50   Warrack, John; West, Ewan (1992). *The Oxford Dictionary of Opera*. Oxford University Press. p.257.

we were little used to the coarse and stentorian bawling which the Italian tenors have of late affected [… Fraschini] seemed to become more and more violent in proportion as the 'sensation' failed to be excited. But he piled up the agony, *forte* on *forte*, in vain [...] Alas! I already look back to Signor Fraschini as a moderate, if not intemperate Italian tenor, when compared with many who have since made the ears of right-minded persons suffer.[51]

At the same time, the cultural bias towards elegant vocalisation was dismissed as atavistic by many who preferred Verdi's expressive vitality. In London, for example, the novelty attained by Verdi and the so-called "new Italian school" was reviled for undoing the culture embodied by Rubini, with the musical press gnashing its teeth over what was deemed a foreign pestilence. In April, 1848, a reader of *The Musical World* wrote to lament the near-constant attacks to which Verdi was subject in the British press. He noted how rival impresarios had been compelled to recruit their principals from within a cadre of singers largely ignorant of (and untrained in) the traditional repertoire. In other words, it was not a question of finding artists capable of adapting to the new style but, rather, finding artists able to accommodate its progenitor:

> Most of the new importations were entirely unknown in Paris and London; and Paisiello, Cimarosa, Mozart, Rossini, were to them a sealed book: they may have heard of such composers, but could not exactly swear as to the age in which they flourished [...] The school of singing was entirely changed; the elegant, serene simplicity of Mozart was to them a dead letter, the charming vocalisation of Rossini beyond their means, an *appoggiatura*, a *cadenza*, a *mordente*, were discarded as superfluous; delicacy and refinement were abandoned for vigour and energy.[52]

The new school compelled a style of singing that many with longer memories considered a malformation of once-hallowed traditions. It follows that both sides of the argument railed against vocal degradation – with the only consensus being that everything was going wrong in consequence of an unquenchable thirst for novelty. The Editor of *The Musical World* was more than happy to reiterate his opinion that "Verdi was the greatest impostor that ever took pen in hand to write rubbish."[53] It must have been a source of irritation, therefore, that Verdi was enormously and immediately popular across Britain. Talk of "transition" is wasted, in any event, when accounting for the realities of the business of opera internationally.

Verdi caused demand to outstrip supply, and a market when flooded is difficult to preserve against sewage. Tumbrils of second-rate singers were employed by third-rate

---

51 Chorley, Henry F. (1862). *Thirty Years' Musical Recollections*. Reprinted, Knopf (1926). pp.190–191. One can only imagine what he would have made of Martinelli, Del Monaco and Corelli.
52 Zicari, Massimo (2016). *Verdi in Victorian London*. Open Book Publishers. p.90.
53 J. De Clerville, "*Verdi and the Two Operas*." *The Musical World*, 29 April, 1848. p. 276.

regional theatres, where performance standards mattered less than box-office receipts. As George Bernard Shaw noted in *The Perfect Wagnerite*:

> Let us admit that geniuses of European celebrity are indispensable at the Opera (though I know better, having seen lusty troopers and porters, without art or manners, accepted by fashion as principal tenors at that institution during the long interval between Mario and Jean De Reszke).

It was a ransom that *Il sovrano* accepted grudgingly, and in stark contradistinction with Wagner's decision to build a temple on the hill in Bayreuth, where he and his family might better control every last detail of an idealised performance culture. In Bayreuth, a singer was (and continues to be) expected to make a commitment to the Wagner cult that would not have been practicable in any other environment. A tenor retained for a season of Verdi's operas almost anywhere was likely to be invited (and required) to sing works by other composers. Style and substance, in this regard, were mutually exclusive. Whether or not it suited him, Fraschini – the first *Stiffelio* and Riccardo in *Un ballo in maschera* – also sang Ernesto in *Don Pasquale*, an ineffably subtle, lightly-appointed, delicately coloured *opera buffa* that could not now be performed by a tenor cast also as Manrico. Of course, Manrico is a troubadour for whom lyricism is a professional obligation; the role requires lyricism as well as bravura, therefore. Fraschini was far from alone in navigating the consequent extremes of *chiaroscuro*. The most famous exponent during Verdi's lifetime was "Mario," whom Donizetti appointed to premiere Ernesto on 3 January, 1843, at the Salle Ventadour of the Théâtre-Italien in Paris.

Mario was the first superstar tenor to be recognised, idolised and memorialised throughout Europe and the United States. During his glittering career, he earned (and lost) a vast fortune, and achieved the sort of celebrity that would have been impossible a generation earlier. Unusually for the 19th century, his fantastical story is mostly true. He was born Giovanni Matteo De Candia,[54] in Cagliari, Sardinia, on 17 October, 1810, to Savoyard-Sardinian nobility. He inherited the titles *Cavaliere*,[55] *Nobile*,[56] and *Don*,[57] as well as immediate and considerable wealth. He enrolled as a teenager at a military academy (where his fellow students included Camillo Cavour and Giuseppe Mazzini) and he served in the Royal Guards in Turin until the scale of his financial contributions to groups advocating Italian unification led to confrontations with his father, Don Stefano. He was dismissed from the Army in November, 1836, at which point he fled to a fishing village near Nice and lodgings in a cottage belonging to a friend of Lord Byron. Disguised as a fisherman, he travelled to San Lorenzo al Mare and a clandestine meeting with his mother, the Marquess of Candia, who provided him with gold coins, clothing and letters of introduction. Having made his way to the French capital (disguised as a comedian), De Candia was adopted by the Prince and Princess of Belgiojoso, who discovered that he had a fine

---

54 17 October, 1810 – 11 December, 1883.
55 'Knight.'
56 'Nobleman.'
57 'Sir.'

singing voice and introduced him to *le tout Paris*. He became a regular feature of the *soirée* circuit, enjoying the attentions of Liszt and Chopin, as well as George Sand, Berlioz, the Bertins, Alfred de Musset, Balzac, Heine, and Pauline Viardot. He was especially admired by Meyerbeer, who steered him towards a variety of singing teachers, including Louis Ponchard and Marco Bordogni, the latter famed for creating the role of Conte di Libenskof in *Il viaggio a Reims* in 1825. Mario's talents escalated apace, and when finally he made his stage debut as *Robert le diable* on 30 November, 1838,[58] he disavowed his titles and adopted the stage name "Mario." He was 28 years of age.[59] After his debut, Francis Roch wrote that

> Mario is most happily endowed with an exceptionally admirable voice, such a voice as Italy alone can produce or cultivate, and then only in a few individual cases. He spoke our language with great ease and almost without accent, and although he was suffering from the weight of a crushing emotion it was in a firmly modulated, irreproachably correct voice, that the young artist began his first verse [...]. Before he had finished the whole house broke into deep and prolonged applause. If the young artist could have had a moment's doubt of his success, this reception, thoroughly deserved as it was in every way, must have caused even the shadow of it to disappear. Completely reassured by the encouraging sympathy of which he found himself the object, he triumphantly attacked "*La Sicilienne* [...]" and sang the rest of his part with a success increasing with each new song. The bravos which had never ceased throughout the opera, at the last fall of the curtain rivalled peals of thunder, and, recalled by the enthusiastic acclamations of the whole audience, the happy young artist must have understood that a magnificent career was opening before him, and that he had only to march onwards over carpets of flowers. I had the good fortune to be present at this debut. His masters and friends were all jubilant at the instant and genuine success of their protege, and as they all crowded round him with congratulations as he left the stage, Mario modestly answered, 'Well, I hope I have won my spurs.' The next day the Parisian newspapers were full of glowing accounts of the new tenor. I give a quotation from one of them: 'Parisian opera-goers will not be able to appreciate at its full value the treasure of which we have only had a glimpse. The style which obtains on the stage at the Le peletier is not one suitable to Mario. He is not made for German music, still less for French. The howls that our musicians exact from the singers of our operas will never harmonise with the exquisitely pure voice, the fresh intonation, the energetic sweetness, the charming art and vocalisation which makes each note of a *cantilena* or of a *fioritura* fall on the ear as

---

58 To a packed house that included King Louis Philippe, Queen Amelie, and various other members of the extended royal family.

59 There's little doubt that Mario's first performance was one of the most dilatory in the history of opera, an exceptional delay that explains why he was all but untrained when first singing for his supper. The only significant tenor to be older than Mario on the date of his debut was Franco Corelli, who was 30 when he first appeared on stage on 26 August, 1951.

a drop of dew falls on the burning forehead of an exhausted traveller. At the Opera this treasure would be most assuredly wasted. It is for the Italians that he is destined; it is towards being the successor of Rubini rather than of Duprez that the young Mario must aim.[60]

Despite his triumph in Paris, Mario chose not to remain at the Opéra, deciding instead to travel in 1839 to London, at the invitation of the Duke of Wellington,[61] where he triumphed as Gennaro in Donizetti's *Lucrezia Borgia*. While in the capital he met the soprano Giulia Grisi, with whom he would share his life from 1841 and until her death in 1869.[62] After returning to Paris, Mario joined the company of the Théâtre Italien, where he shared the stage with arguably the greatest ever concentration of singing talent: Maria Malibran, Henriette Sontag, Rubini, Tamburini and Lablache.

Mario is said to have excelled in French as well as Italian opera. The nobility of his bearing was as compelling as the grace and elegance of his voice, which was less beautiful than that of Rubini, and not as powerful as that of Tamberlik – but magnetic in its delivery. Eight years after Mario's death, one writer recalled:

> Personal charm and grace, borne out by a voice of honeyed sweetness, fascinated the stern as well as the sentimental critic into forgetting all his deficiencies, and no one was disposed to reckon sharply with one so genially endowed with so much of the nobleman in bearing, so much of the poet and painter in composition. To those who for the first time saw Mario play such parts as Almaviva, Gennaro, and Raoul, it was a new revelation, full of poetic feeling and sentiment. Here his unique supremacy was manifest. He will live in the world's memory as the best opera lover ever seen, one who out of the insipidities and fustian of the average lyric drama could conjure up a conception steeped in the richest colours of youth, passion, and tenderness, and strengthened by the atmosphere of stage verity. In such scenes as the fourth act of "Les Huguenots" and the last act of the "Favorita" Signor Mario's singing and acting were never to be forgotten by those that witnessed them. Intense passion and highly finished vocal delicacy combined to make these pictures of melodious suffering indelible. As a singer of romances Mario has never been equaled. He could not execute those splendid songs of the Rossinian school, in which the feeling of the theme is expressed in a

---

60   Pearse, Cecilia M., and Hird, Frank (1910). *The Romance of a Great Singer: A Memoir of Mario*. Smith, Elder & Co. p.75. Pearse was one of Mario's six daughters. A copy of her book was owned by James Joyce.
61   A family friend who nonetheless refused Mario's request for a military commission.
62   Grisi was involved in an accident after crossing the border into Germany. She spent her last days in a hotel in Berlin, under the care of a Dr. Isabell. She died on 29 November 1869, aged 58. Mario conveyed her body to Paris, where she was buried at Père Lachaise. In an act that many might find repulsive, or worse, Mario commissioned a plain white tombstone with the solitary inscription "*Juliette de Candia.*" Not only was that not his wife's first name (she was christened, and known internationally as, Giulia) but her stage name was never anything but Grisi. Mario's tasteless aggrandisement of his family name was compounded by his use of a stage name throughout his own career.

dazzling parade of *roulades* and *fioriture,* the songs in which Rubini was matchless. But in those songs where music tells the story of passion in broad, intelligible, ardent phrases, and presents itself primarily as the vehicle of vehement emotion, Mario stood ahead of all others of his age, it may be said, indeed, of all within the memory of his age. It was for this reason that he attained such a supremacy also on the concert stage. The choicest songs of Schubert, Mendelssohn, Gordigiano, and Meyerbeer were interpreted by his art with an intelligence and poetry which gave them a new and more vivid meaning. The refinements of his accent and pronunciation created the finest possible effects, and were perhaps partly due to the fact that before Mario became a public artist he was a gentleman and a noble, permeated by the best aesthetic and social culture of his times.[63]

The National Portrait Gallery's collection of photos from the 1860s demonstrates that Mario was not as handsome as he believed himself to be – or, for that matter, as he demanded he appear when painted in the 1850s for a portrait to send to the Mariinsky Theatre in St. Petersburg. Mario's appearance (as well as his life story) became something of an obsession for James Joyce, another Parisian exile, born a year before Mario died. Judith Harrington's elegant analysis of the part played by Mario in *Ulysses* amplifies the correspondence between musical motifs and Mario's work when singing and his appearance.[64] Mario is first identified in "Aeolus," when William Brayden is described passing[65]

statelily up the staircase, steered by an umbrella, a solemn beard framed face? Don't you think his face is like Our Saviour? Red Murray whispered. Our Saviour: beardframed oval face: talking in the dusk. Mary, Martha. Steered by an umbrella sword to the footlights: Mario the tenor. Or like Mario, Mr Bloom said. Yes, Red Murray agreed. But Mario was said to be the picture of Our Saviour. Jesus Mario with rougy cheeks, doublet and spindle legs. Hand on his heart. In Martha. Co-ome thou lost one, Co-ome thou dear one![66]

Joyce was not alone in attaching meaning to Mario's Christ-like appearance. Queen Victoria wrote in her journal that "Mario's head is quite *'une tête de Christ,'*" while Lord Frederic Leighton's drawing of the tenor resembles any number of popular Pre-Raphaelite depictions of Jesus in his Europeanised serenity. Mario's daughter, Cecilia M. Pearse, attested in her biography of her father:

---

63   Ferris, George T. (1891). *Great Singers: Malibran To Titiens, Vol. 2.* D. Appleton and Company.
64   Harrington, Judith. "Mario: The Tenor of His Times." *James Joyce Quarterly*, Vol. 38, No. 1/2, Joyce and Opera (Fall, 2000 - Winter, 2001), pp.219–226.
65   7.43; "In the Heart of the Hibernian Metropolis."
66   U 7.45–60.

If anyone wants to see Mario, let him look at the Christ head on the title page of Chapman's books, which is the archetypal Christ head. The face is like [sic], even to the way of trimming the beard, which must have been suggested to Mario to complete the resemblance. An English gentleman who sat by me said that it had been a subject of universal remark in London, when he came out in the 'Prophete' with his hair parted in the middle and a devout part to perform…[67]

Mario was the first tenor for whom such idolatry became routine; his novelty as a celebrity distracted inevitably from the source of his fame, namely his talent and ambition as a singer. His repertoire was huge and incomparable in its catholicity, even though he created only one significant role – Ernesto. He nonetheless sang in dozens of regional premieres, notably in London, where his following at Covent Garden was canine. Between 1839 and 1871 Mario took part in 930 staged operas in London – an average of thirty nights a season – together with 41 concerts of operatic excerpts. His repertoire over that time provides an insight into the evolution of the tenor voice during the ten years either side of 1850. In addition to Rossini's now standard body of work,[68] Mario sang in operas by Mozart, Cimarosa, Halévy, Bellini (including 14 performances as Pollione and 44 as Arturo), Meyerbeer (spanning 45 evenings of *Le prophète* and 119 of *Les Huguenots*) and Donizetti – who was by far his most represented composer, with 91 performances of *Lucrezia Borgia*, 21 of *L'elisir d'amore*, 32 of *Don Pasquale* and 49 of *La Favorita*. Intriguingly, he took part in only nine performances of *Lucia di Lammermoor*. Thereafter, his range was captured by his work for Verdi. He made his debut in London for the composer in 1846, singing the role of Arvino in *I Lombardi*,[69] followed a year later by Jacopo in *I due Foscari*. Between *Foscari* (1844) and Mario's retirement in 1871, Verdi composed 17 operas; Mario sang only four of them: *Rigoletto* (1851; 53 performances), *Il trovatore* (1853; 28 performances), *La traviata* (1853; nine performances) and *Un Ballo in maschera* (1861; 29 performances). Verdi admired Mario – he presented him with a new *cabaletta* for a production of *I due Foscari* in Paris – and it's clear that audiences adored him. Where his voice sat in terms of weight, range and dexterity is difficult to determine. He sang Almaviva hundreds of times throughout his career – as well as Otello, Pollione, Manrico, Raoul and Riccardo. A tenor suited to Almaviva, Nemorino and Arturo would appear to align with the traditions of Rubini rather than Duprez; but Rubini would not have been heard off-stage singing "*Deserto sulla terra*" in Act 1 of *Il trovatore*, or the reprise of "*La donna è mobile*" in Act 3 of *Rigoletto* – which suggests that Mario was gifted with amplitude as well as elegance. Towards the end of his career he sang in dozens of performances of Flotow's *Martha*, and became a celebrated advocate for Gounod's two greatest successes, *Faust* (in which he appeared in London for

---

67 Pearse, Cecilia M., and Hird, Frank (1910). *The Romance of a Great Singer: A Memoir of Mario*. Smith, Elder & Co. p.156.
68 *La Donna del Lago, Il Barbiere di Siviglia, La Gazza Ladra, Guglielmo Tell, L'Italiana in Algeri, Otello* and *La Cenerentola* – which included 102 performances as Almaviva.
69 *I Lombardi alla Prima Crociata* ['The Lombards on the First Crusade'].

the first of 59 performances in 1864) and *Roméo*, of which he gave the first London performance on 11 July, 1867. His Juliette was Adelina Patti.

The range of Mario's voice was considerable. As much is obvious from the second movement of the *Stabat Mater* ("*Cujus animum*") that Rossini composed for Mario, Grisi, Emma Albertazzi and Tamburini in 1841. At the first performance in Paris at the Salle Ventadour on 7 January, 1842, Mario had no difficulty crowning the D flat 5 – for which there is no *ossia*. If he was able to achieve this in full voice then it's reasonable to assume he had the technique and resources necessary for Rossini, Bellini and Donizetti as well as Verdi and Gounod. In this respect, Mario was the most modern of singers. He travelled the world – with tours of the United States and extended stays in St. Petersburg, where he and Grisi were treated like royalty by royalty (with the Tsar paying his songbirds in gold coins and jewels). He sang largely the same repertoire, night after night, season after season, for audiences intoxicated by celebrity, gossip, status and wealth. His cultivation as an exotic personage of noble birth was sustained by a talent that was appealing to composers as well as audiences, but he was the first singer whose parts were equal, if not superior, to their sum. The popular obsession with Mario as a man of (debatable) beauty and (undeniable) nobility united the classes in a way that had never happened before. Prints and photos of the tenor were made available for purchase in book shops and on newspaper stands, while Queen Victoria was sufficiently admiring to complete a number of pencil-portraits.[70] His popularity was fuelled by stories of immense wealth (estimated at its peak to equate to 600 bullion bars, or something north of £200 million in 2021[71]) and flamboyance, particularly when travelling between the mansions he shared with Grisi in Paris, London and Florence.[72] Most tellingly of all, Mario was for many an amateur – a feature of his artistry decried by George Bernard Shaw, who disapproved of his marked *vibrato* almost as much as his titles. While Shaw raised the brandy of the damned to toast the virtues of "Little Bethel,"[73] Chorley remembered Mario's dereliction with shameless affection:

> The charm of personal appearance and graceful demeanour, borne out by a voice of persuasive sweetness of which can never have been exceeded, has fascinated everyone, the stern as well as the sentimental, into forgetting incompleteness and deficiency, which diligent and thoughtful study might have remedied ere Rubini's successor had been on the stage a couple of years. There has been no desire, no possibility,

---

70 Victoria also mentioned Mario frequently in her diaries, commonly after he attended on her for private concerts at Windsor and Osborne House.
71 Much of this fortune was gone by the end of his life. He sold his considerable collection of painting, sculpture and the other contents of his estate in London before relocating to Italy. They were purchased by the British family of the fiancé of his daughter, Rita, after her death. Most of the paintings he acquired with Grisi were added to the private collection of Sir John Aird, Bart, in whose family (and under the current governance of the 4th Baronet, Sir George John Aird, born 30 January, 1940) they remain to this day.
72 The Villa Salviatino is an exquisite palazzo that is now a boutique hotel, where the most opulent suite costs around €2,000 a night. https://salviatino.com/luxury-hotel-florence-italy/.
73 Shaw had a superb ear but an imperfect memory. He was born in 1856, so the oldest he can have been when hearing Mario sing was 15 – when Mario was 61.

of reckoning with one so genially endowed by nature, with so much of the poet and the painter in his cosmopolitan, and of the nobleman in his bearing. Lines, rules, precedents, comparisons, must sometimes be forgotten: and it is well. Those do not know the least or judge the worst; who fairly surrender themselves to their sympathies – when they cannot help it.... In one respect he arrived at an unlucky time, coming afte Rubini, whose peculiar voice tempted composers to write what no one save Rubini could sing thoroughly. Thus in Signor Mario's singing of *I puritani*, in *La sonnambula*, and *Lucia* there has always been much to desire. Comparison between him and his predecessor was inevitable.[74]

Even the admiring George T. Ferris couldn't resist reminding his readers that Mario was an amateur – but one for whom social class and status qualified as compensation:

he never lost something amateurish, but this gave him a certain distinction and fine breeding of style, as of a gentleman who deigned to practice an art as a delightful accomplishment.[75]

It's unclear what qualified as amateurism, for the British at least, in an age when music colleges were still in their infancy[76] and teachers of singing worked, for the most part, from private rooms. The distinguishing of a professional from an amateur when ability was the only metric for the isolation of success hinged on criteria that were less musical than social. The emerging global middle class, with its pursuit of self-improvement for all, gained much of its momentum from music and art, sustained by a philanthropic attitude to education in the round. As the century progressed, music spread from the churches into homes, schools, the parks and even the streets and squares. Verdi's loathing of the organ-grinders caused him to withhold "*La donna e mobile*" until the last moment before the first night of *Rigoletto* in 1851. 60 years later, Edward VII was compelled to sit through an open-air band arrangement of excerpts from Richard Strauss' most recent opera. After what was presumably an interminable ten minutes, the King applauded politely and asked what had just been played. When told it was from a new work called *Elektra* he replied "be sure never to play it again." By the 1850s almost every middle-class home contained a *tuned* piano, with around 50,000 being produced globally each year.[77] Singing societies sprang up in every town and city throughout Europe and the United States,[78] and choirs were routinely established for junior, infant, day, and Sunday schools. In 1851, Berlioz witnessed the annual service for Charity Children in St Paul's Cathedral, London; he recalled:

---

74 Chorley, Henry F. (1862) *Thirty Years' Musical Recollections*. Reprinted, Knopf (1926). pp.178–179.
75 Ferris, George T. (1891). *Great Singers: Malibran To Titiens, Vol. 2*. D. Appleton and Company.
76 The Royal Academy of Music was founded in 1822 by John Fane and Nicolas-Charles Bochsa. It received its Royal Charter in 1830 from King George IV with the support of the first Duke of Wellington; the Guildhall School of Music and Drama was founded in 1880, and Royal College of Music was established by royal charter in 1882.
77 Ehrlich, Cyril (1990). *The Piano: A History*. Clarendon Press. pp.9–10.
78 *Ibid*. p.11.

Under the dome were piled up, to a great height all round, 6,000 children from the different charity-schools in the city in their different habits and colours [...] You may see this any year, for they are brought to St Paul's, and placed in the same order one day every year, and I think it will be worth your while if you ever come within sight of St Paul's again ... [A]ll the 6,000 children set up their little voices and sang part of the Hundredth Psalm ['All people that on earth do dwell']. This was the moment that I found most affecting; and without knowing exactly why, I found my eyes running over, and the bone in my throat, which was the case with many other people.[79]

Outside the cathedrals, and throughout the majority of working-class communities, curricula were created and disseminated for promulgation by socially improving benefactors and institutions that encompassed intellectual, moral, religious and musical elements. Choral societies, orchestras, brass bands and travelling opera companies – all carried by expanding railway and shipping networks – were soon commonplace, and the infrastructures that produced musically educated and culturally invested people became embedded in the routines and expectations of work, faith, education, politics and self-improvement.[80] The co-incident rise in Methodism and the splintering of evangelical faiths led to an increased commitment on both sides of the Atlantic to hymn-singing across the denominations, and the publication of hymnals and associated music theory and Sol-Fa primers was incorporated into the extensive activities of schools and learning institutes.[81] During the decade after the 1848 Revolutions, almost everyone sang in Europe and the United States, and then almost constantly. In many quarters, there was often something positive to sing about. The supply of tenors born in the 1820s and 1830s peaked during the 1860s, at much the same time as opera reached its zenith as a commoditised art form. Almost every corner of the increasingly civilised world submitted to the musical, theatrical and cultural allure of opera, with access generated through books, journals, domestic-music publishing and photography – as well, of course, as actual ticket sales. Between 1850 and 1900, literally hundreds of opera houses were built across Europe, the United States and (from 1857) South America.[82] The driver for much of this bricks-and-mortar expansion was Giuseppe Verdi.

Between 1862 and 1871, with most of his operas in almost constant circulation, Verdi composed his three grandest works to date: *La forza del destino* (1862; amended 1869), *Don Carlos* (1867; amended 1884), and *Aida* (1871; amended 1872). The latter two works remain problematic theatrically for a host of reasons – not least

---

79 Berlioz, Hector. *Les soirees de l'orchestre* (Paris, 1853), pp.258–61; Trans. C. R. Fortescue (London, 1963), p.203.
80 Palmer, Fiona M. "The Large-Scale Oratorio Chorus in Nineteenth-Century England: Choral Power and the Role of Handel's *Messiah*."
In Lajosi, Krisztina and Stynen, Andreas (2015). *Choral Societies and Nationalism in Europe*. Koninklijke Brill. p.102.
81 *Ibid*. pp.102–105.
82 The first to be opened in South America was the Teatro Colón ('Columbus Theatre') in Buenos Aires, Argentina. The current theatre was built as a replacement and inaugurated on 25 May, 1908.

the intractability of their settings and idioms – while *La forza del destino* hinges on a ridiculous plot that was archaic before the ink had dried. And yet, these intoxicating, psychologically intense narrative contain some of the most extraordinary music written for the stage, and in their dramatic focus they represent the final detachment of Verdi's work from anything that preceded it. They are to Rossini, Bellini and Donizetti what the Ring tetralogy is to Spohr, Weber and Marschner. Each features part-writing of extraordinary range and depth, with music of unparalleled beauty, power and character. Like Mozart before him, and Puccini and Strauss after him, Verdi's skill as a composer during the 1860s enabled him to articulate thoughts and feelings that transcended the words being sung – not to render the poetry moot, or the drama vapid, but to elevate the drama to a point of Shakespearean profundity. All three operas require exceptional *di forza/robusto* tenor voices capable of meeting the challenges of extended scene-writing, spanning solos and ensembles that compel stentorian power and stamina as well as a technique of sufficient security to enable a singer to become an artist.

During Act 1 of *La forza*, the duet for Alvaro and Leonora (*"Ah, per sempre, o mio bell'angiol...Gonfio di gioia hai il core... Infame figlia"*[83]) is written (like much of the role) low on the stave, with numerous shifts in colour, pacing and mood. Verdi submits the character (and the tenor) to emotional and vocal spans that fall only slightly short of requiring circular breathing. The *legato* of the Act 2 duet *"Col sangue sol cancellasi...Le minaccie, i fieri accenti,"*[84] is similarly demanding of lung-power, even if the *tessitura* is mostly baritonal, with only a single B flat above the stave to challenge an actual baritone. In essence, Verdi pitted two baritones against each other, noting as he must have done that any tenor raised during the 1830s would have struggled to be heard. An absence of compassion (or a concern for weight of tone and coloured phrasing above mere *squillo*) characterises Act 3's infamously taxing *"La vita è inferno all'infelice* […] *O tu che seno agli angeli."* The recitative introduction is scored primarily over *divisi* strings, with no brass and only a solo clarinet for company. It is lightly written for the tenor, therefore, whose articulation of Piave's free-flowing verse is absolutely pivotal to the success of a scene in which Alvaro passes beyond the event horizon of solipsism.

The opening bars of the aria require the tenor to hit a rising C4 to A flat 4 ("[…] *che in sen*[…]") – above *pizzicato* strings. It is extremely exposed and demands immense security of vocal placement – as does the descending F octave ("[…]*gli angeli*"). The *cantilena* double-basses, *pizzicato* strings and *obbligato* clarinet present little acoustic challenge to the singer, but the four-bar rising passage (spanning E flat 4 to A flat 4) *"Non iscordar di volgere … Lo sguardo a me tapino … Che senza nome ed esule … In odio del destin"*[85] is written in expansive phrases, without pause, and a *fermata* only on the final syllable. The descending passage is marked *morendo*,[86] so that the tenor is required to manage his breathing without allowing 'fate' to determine the loss of

---

83 'Ah, forever, my beautiful angel […] swollen with joy, your heart is […] Infamous daughter.'
84 'With blood only erased … The threats, the proud accents.'
85 'Do not forget to look down on me, unhappy wretch, who, nameless and exiled, the prey of fate…'
86 'Dying.'

the music's essential shape. When sung by Bergonzi,[87] it can sound easy. It isn't; in fact, it's enormously demanding of a singer's voice-placement and breath-control – technical skills that become yet more relevant in the ensuing "*Che senza nome ed esule ... In odio del destino ... Chiedo anelando ... Ahi misero ... La morte d'incontrar.*"[88] The B flat 4 that crowns the third of the four bars that make up this rising-falling phrase (E flat 4 to B flat 4) is written as a single crotchet in a common-time bar – and then without qualification; however, the aria's two ensuing B flats are marked *tenuto* with *fermata* added to both for emphasis – thereby affording the tenor an absolute discretion to make of these huge expanding-declining phrases whatever he can. As if this were not all sufficiently challenging, Verdi ends the aria not with a descending fifth (as he might have done a decade earlier), but with the final "*Pietà*" resolving as an A flat 4 written over two bars as a semibreve-quaver – with a hairpin *crescendo* to boot. There are few arias in the Italian canon more difficult – or beautiful.

Of course, Verdi had already written much wonderful music for the tenor voice – and there is an obvious precedent for the expressive architecture of "*La vita ... O tu che seno*" in the achingly beautiful "*L'infamie... O mes amis, mes frères*" from *Jérusalem*, composed specifically for Gilbert Duprez by Verdi in 1847. The essence of the writing in *La forza* is its attachment to a character's specific emotional experience as an immediate expression of feeling – even when that experience and expression are formed of the worst excesses of self-pity. Verdi's vernacular fuses hypnotic *cantabile* and declamatory articulation, which in turn compels a diverse palette of vocal inflexion and nuance – with a particular reliance on *portamento* and dynamic contrast for effect. Ultimately, where Verdi redefined the tenor – if not all singing – was in his use of words to place a voice. At every turn and opportunity, he employed the colour of the Italian language to illuminate a melody, and melody to add form and substance to the words. It was because of this invested mutuality that a Verdi tenor is never able to hide behind tone and *cantilena* alone, while "covering" is precluded because it causes a singer to sound constrained or throttled.

When considering the ambit of these mutations, it's reasonable to suppose that Enrico Tamberlik[89] must have had a trumpet of a voice. Verdi would not otherwise have gifted him with the role of Alvaro for the first performance in St. Petersburg in 1862. Even so, it's obvious from contemporary comments and reviews that after his debut in London in 1850, when he was thirty, Tamberlik wasted little time in following the money. His attachment to Verdi, and to crowd-pleasing amplitude, made him a huge star, particularly when interpolating high Cs into *Il trovatore*. However, Chorley's opinion was typical:

> One may tell those of the future that the voice, howsoever effective and in its upper notes capable of great power can hardly be called a charming one – though warm with the south – not regulated by an unimpeachable

---

87 Bergonzi's 1958 recital recording for Decca, with Gianandrea Gavazzeni conducting the Orchestra dell'Accademia Nazionale di Santa Cecilia, has been bettered only for those with differently formed prejudices.
88 'Who, nameless and exiled, the prey of fate, longingly seeks to encounter death, unfortunate that I am!'
89 16 March, 1820 – 13 March, 1889.

method [...] still, there was no hearing Signor Tamberlik during a single act of an opera without being aware that he was a man who could sway his public.[90]

The open criticism of Tamberlik's technique – which extended to a general disdain for his near-constant "trembling"[91] and an imperfect "sense of measurement of time"[92] – was fuelled by his weakness for the crowd. Chorley's criticism that he was technically imperfect was nothing less than a snipe at a lack of colour, and at the tenor's disavowal of (or absent access to) those tricks on which Rubini and Mario had relied for effect. It appears that Tamberlik was something of a blunt tool, even accounting for his ringing high notes, but there were many who were less disciplined still. In his biography of Verdi, Carlo Gatti identified the "new methods of singing developing out of [Verdi's] operas," which he distinguished from the composer's predecessors by noting the increasing reliance on "sobs of grief, shouts of rage, transports of joy; methods that gave full reign to the maestro's passionate feeling." It's difficult to reconcile the musical language of "*O tu che*" to the sound of sobbing and shouting, but not everyone was able to sing like Tamberlik – or, for that matter, Duprez, Salvi and Fraschini.

There's little question that Gatti was identifying a truism that would crystallise only with the invention of recording, namely that the exceptional cannot by definition determine the normative – other than at a distance. The shape of the bell-curve provides that outliers are necessarily a considerable distance from the commonplace. It's equally true that singers of Tamberlik's talent were unable to perform in more than one city a night, which left the regions to acclimatise to inexperienced singers uncultivated in the "new" school. Young tenors raised on Rossini and Bellini were unequipped to cope with the demands of Don Carlo or Radamès, while teachers and singers claiming to be *au moderne* were frequently anything but. Many tenors were reduced in consequence to bawling and howling. The paradigm shift effected by Verdi occurred at such pace, and with such ubiquity, that there was little hope or opportunity for singers to adapt without having to concede to incongruence or obsolescence. Teachers who were not themselves versed in the new school resorted to damning and cursing modernity because it necessitated training they were unable to provide. For once, the emperor's new clothes were truly dazzling – but only when worn by emperors.

During the decade after Verdi cast Tamberlik as Alvaro in 1862, he was one of the world's most popular tenors. For Chorley, his voice was warm but too loud, with ringing high notes and an imperfect technique; he might have been describing Del Monaco a century later.[93] By the 1870s, however – when Tamberlik was in his fifties – a different story was told by George Bernard Shaw. His review of a performance

---

90 Pleasants, Henry (1974). *The Great Singers*. Gollancz. p.171.
91 For a sense of how Tamberlik's bleat might have sounded, there is a delightful point of reference in Bert Lahr's satire of the worst of operatic singing when performing (as the Cowardly Lion) "If I were King of the Forest" in *The Wizard of Oz* (1939). His C4s on "Forest" are ghastly, but far from atypical (even in 1939) of what was deemed to qualify as "bad technique."
92 Chorley, Henry F. (1862). *Thirty Years' Musical Recollections*. Reprinted, Knopf (1926). p.195.
93 Pleasants, Henry (1974). *The Great Singers*. Gollancz. p.171.

of Rossini's *Otello* at Covent Garden, published on 20 June, 1877 (at a time when the struggling playwright was working as a rehearsal pianist), showered praise on Christina Nilsson's Desdemona while setting fire to Tamberlik:

> In order to represent the operatic Othello respectably, a voice and some faculty for acting are indispensable. Signor Tamberlik possesses neither of these qualifications. He sings in a doubtful falsetto and his movements are unmeaning, and frequently absurd. For the C sharp in the celebrated duet *L'ira d'avverso fato*, he substituted a strange description of shriek at about that pitch.[94] The audience, ever appreciative of vocal curiosities, eagerly redemanded it.[95]

A few days later, Shaw provided some context for his opinion, when reviewing a performance of *Il trovatore* with Theodor Wachtel:[96]

> Herr Wachtel's appearance as Manrico, on the 12th, was deservedly successful. His acting and singing were alike excellent. His high C, which he gave three times in the *Di quella pira*, is a genuine note and not, as we commonly hear, a scream. His use of the *mezza voce* is artistic, and is not a device to conceal weakness or total absence of real voice.[97]

Bizarrely, therefore, Tamberlik's high C was either in *falsetto*, or something worse. It was acclaimed regardless, even when Wachtel was capable of "a genuine note." Tamberlik was not in his prime, but it's equally true that Shaw's insights were more than reliable, and then over many decades. It follows that there were marked differences between the best and the worst among tenors, notwithstanding the fact that *both* were popular at the box office. Of course, audience discretion was no less variable than was the quality of the singing. The high C was a focus for ongoing debate even in the 1870s.

Ten years after the success of *Aida* in 1871 and Verdi's retreat into retirement, Giulio Ricordi persuaded the eternally youthful composer to revise *Simon Boccanegra* with Arrigo Boito as librettist. The role of Gabriele Adorno at the first performance of the revised version, on 24 March, 1881, was performed by Francesco Tamagno.[98] Unlike Tamberlik, Tamagno was born into an age when heroic tenor singing was an achievable commodity. He was the first international tenor to graduate from a formally established music conservatory, and the first *not* to work his way through

---

94 Later in the same season, Shaw referred to Tamberlik's Manrico in passing, and observed "[Tamberlik] announces his benefit on the 23rd ins., when he will resume the role of Otello, and give his admirers one more chance of hearing the C sharp which they fondly imagine as a chest note." (1981). *Shaw's Music: The Complete Musical Criticism of Bernard Shaw*. Ed. Dan H. Laurence. The Bodley Head. Vol. I (1876 – 1890). p.161.
95 Shaw, Bernard (1981). *Shaw's Music: The Complete Musical Criticism of Bernard Shaw*. Ed. Dan H. Laurence. The Bodley Head. Vol. I (1876 – 1890); p.136.
96 1823 – 1893.
97 *Ibid.* p.137.
98 28 December, 1850 – 31 August, 1905.

Rossini, Bellini and Donizetti before arriving at Verdi and the contemporary vernacular. After singing in his local church choir, and at his father's tavern, Tamagno enrolled at Turin's Liceo Musicale, founded in 1869 with a legacy from Rossini, who had died the year before.[99]

Tamagno was tutored by the conductor and composer Carlo Pedrotti – an associate and friend of Verdi.[100] He graduated in 1873 and achieved huge success the following year with a sensational performance as Riccardo in *Un ballo in maschera* at the Teatro Bellini, Palermo, on 20 January, 1874. Tamagno was the first tenor to adhere from the beginning of his career to his status as a *tenore robusto/tenore di forza* – outside what continues erroneously to be referred to as the *bel canto* tradition (a progression typified by Fraschini and Mario). Tamagno's repertoire included more than fifty operas, with an inevitable emphasis on Verdi, who helped coach him in numerous roles – most obviously Manrico, Alvaro and Radamès. He also performed a number of celebrated French operas, including contemporary works by Saint-Saëns (*Samson et Dalila*) and Massenet (*Le roi de Lahore* and *Hérodiade*) and he was the first to sing once exclusively lyrical repertoire as a *tenore di forza*, notably *Lucia di Lammermoor, Poliuto, Guglielmo Tell, Les Huguenots, L'Africaine, Robert le diable* and *La Juive*. He created roles for Carlos Gomes (*Maria Tudor*) in 1879, Leoncavallo (*I Medici*) in 1893, and Ponchielli in 1880 (*Il figliuol prodigo*[101]) and 1885 (*Marion Delorme*). In 1884 he was invited for the second time by Verdi to collaborate, for the premiere of the Italian-language version of *Don Carlos*, and three years later, on 5 February, 1887, he created the title role of *Otello* at La Scala, Milan.

Verdi wrote the role of *Otello* specifically for Tamagno. George Bernard Shaw was present for his first performance of the opera at the Lyceum in London, two years after the Italian premiere. In his essay "*How Not to Teach Singing*," written for *The Star* and published on 12 July, 1889, Shaw noted that "Tamagno is original and real, shewing [sic] you Otello in vivid flashes...."[102] At the end of the season, however, he remembered that "his magnificent screaming is henceforth among the *sante memorie* of London amateurs."[103] Two months later, for the *Scottish Arts Review* in September, 1889, he gave a more detailed account:

> Tamagno [is] undoubtedly a quite exceptional artist, whose voice seems to have reached the upper part of the theatre with overwhelming power, though to others some of the current descriptions of its volume seemed hyperbolical. His voice, at any rate, had not the pure noble tone, nor the sweetly sensuous, nor even the ordinary thick manly quality of the robust tenor: it was nasal, shrill, vehement, sometimes fierce, sometimes plaintive, always peculiar and original. Imitation of Tamagno has ruined many a tenor, and will probably ruin many more; but the desire to produce such an affect as he did with *Addio sante memorie!* is

---

99 In 1882 it was re-launched as the *Conservatorio Statale di Musica Gioachino Rossini*.
100 12 November, 1817 – 16 October, 1893.
101 'The Prodigal Son.'
102 Shaw, Bernard (1981). *Shaw's Music: The Complete Musical Criticism of Bernard Shaw*. Ed. Dan H. Laurence. The Bodley Head. Vol. I (1876 – 1890). p.699.
103 *Ibid*; p.711. In an essay titled "*The Opera Seasons and its Lessons*," published on 26 July, 1889.

intelligible to anyone who rightly understands the range of an Italian tenor's ambition.[104]

When reviewing Jean De Reszke's *Otello* in 1891, Shaw informed the readers of *The World* that:

> His Otello will never be like Tamagno's; but he need not regret that, as the same thing might have been said of Salvini. The Italian tenor's shrill screaming voice and fierce temper were tremendously effective here and there; but the nobler side of the Moor, which Salvini brought out with such admirable quietude and self-containment [...] was left untouched by Tamagno. who on this and other accounts is the very last man a wise tenor would attempt to imitate.[105]

As anyone who has seen or heard Verdi's opera will understand, it is technically and emotionally challenging for a tenor, requiring huge reserves of stamina, amplitude, artistry and intelligence. Anyone even attempting the role has to account for the character's unravelling, as he submits to various stages of psychological and emotional decay. His *Lear*-like dislocation, the loss of his mind, and the agony of his final submission to a truth that affords him no redemption, can make sense only if there is more to a performance than mere sound. To understand quite how far Verdi had come as a composer, and to appreciate the scale of his re-calibration of the tenor voice, it's necessary only to consider Otello's first appearance on stage, which reaches far beyond the character's boasting of his defeat of the Turks. In just twelve bars, Verdi paints the portrait of a man devoid of flaw or weakness; he is the absolute master of his destiny and of pretty much everything else. It captures Otello at the peak of the mountain from which he is shortly to tumble. The vocal line's difficulty is established on the third note and syllable of "*Esultate*"[106] – an F (written as an E sharp), which the singer has to amplify above an orchestra of three flutes, two oboes, a *cor anglais*, two clarinets, a bass clarinet, four bassoons, four horns, two cornets, two trumpets, two (of four) trombones, timpani and a string band of around forty – all of them playing together in *fortissimo*. The leading phrase, rising to a G sharp, moves chromatically down the scale to an F below middle C – to convey the Turkish submission to Otello's authority – before "*dopo l'armi*" compels the singer to punch his way to the back of the theatre in the upper-middle of his *passaggio*. The need to juggle the registers – while maintaining an absolute focus of projection and articulation – is exacerbated for the tenor by the need to find *exactly* the right placement to carry the final two syllables of the phrase "*Dopo l'armi lo vinse luragano*"[107] (written on a descending F sharp to E) above the orchestra – without having to cover. Few have been able to do this well.

---

104   *Ibid*; p.768.
105   *Ibid.* Vol. II. pp.401–402.
106   'Rejoice.'
107   'After our arms the storm has conquered it.'

The role is deceptive insofar as much of it sits high in the voice, even though there are no C5s, and only a single grace-note B5, in *"Esultate."* The *tessitura* is exceptionally taxing, particularly considering the amount of time Otello is on stage. It is not (as many claim) baritonal. Indeed, the score is almost surgically tailored to a tenor with a *squillo* ping, as well as weight. The conductor Tullio Serafin recalled of Tamagno: "People think of him as having had an enormous voice, but I have heard much bigger ones. It was the voice's *squillo*, its clear ringing, that was exceptional." A thick or heavy voice will always fail, therefore, as will a tenor with bright tones but no weight to support them.[108] The role is challenging also because the structure is seamless and through-composed; Verdi's orchestrations are the most dense of his career – none of which means that beauty of tone can be sacrificed to acoustic necessity, because Verdi was as concerned with the clarity of Boito's exquisitely formed verse as he was with the transmission of his music. It is not enough for a tenor to be heard, therefore – although that definitely helps during the raging *"Ora e per sempre addio sante memorie"*[109] in Act 2, and the mesmeric oath-duet with Iago *"Sì, pel ciel marmoreo giuro."*[110] Lung power will do nothing to assist a singer if that is all he has when approaching the monologue *"Dio! mi potevi scagliar tutti i mali"*[111] in Act 3, or the final scene in which Otello takes his own life, *"Niun mi tema."*[112] Unless a singer is gifted with lyrical sensibilities and an ear for phrasing, the Act 1 love duet with Desdemona (*"Già nella notte densa s'estingue ogni clamor"*[113]) will descend, as often it does, into farce. There has been good cause for more than a century to wonder why a woman of Desdemona's gentle disposition might love a man whose sole form of expression is yelling.

Verdi survived to the 20th century, but he died before the onset of commercial recording. Tamagno was the first of only two of Verdi's tenor "originators" to step before a horn.[114] It is an eternal wonder that technology has allowed posterity to hear the man who created *Otello* for Verdi with such clarity. The singer's contract with the British Gramophone & Typewriter Company (the first to employ the mechanism of an advance against a royalty[115]) was signed in December, 1902, and the first recordings were made in February, 1903, when Fred Gaisberg attended on Tamagno at his holiday home in Ospedaletti, on the Ligurian coast. A second session was completed in April, 1904, at a hotel in Rome. Tamagno approved 19 sides for release, which were widely advertised with the tenor billed as "the world's greatest." The cost of each two-minute disc equated to a week's average salary. In addition to three excerpts (and various takes) from *Otello*, Tamagno recorded arias from *Il trovatore*, *Guglielmo Tell*, *Il profeta/Le prophète*, *Samson et Dalila*, *Hérodiade*, *Messaline* and *Andrea Chénier*.

---

108 Which explains why Domingo – who did not have an especially "big" voice – was so exceptional in the role.
109 'Now and forever farewell, holy memories.'
110 'Yes, I swear by the marbled heavens.'
111 'God, you could throw every evil at me.'
112 'None should fear me.'
113 'Now in the dense night every sound is silenced.'
114 The second was Edoardo Garbin, who created the role of *Falstaff* in 1893.
115 Gelatt, Roland (1977). *The Fabulous Phonograph*. Collier Books. p.119.

Tamagno was not yet 55 in 1904. Moreover, he approved each of the '78s that were released. They provide an accurate portrait of the artist as a recently young man, in which respect the instrument is manifestly powerful, secure and ringing – with splendid projection. The bright-edged tone, quick but steady *vibrato* and incisive declamation contribute to a sense that Tamagno was formidable in his prime. The sound is more compelling than are the performances, however, which lack style and are entirely absent the sort of phrasing one might have expected of a singer coached by Verdi. Most surprisingly, he abjures *portamento*, with intervals being separated in a manner that causes his voicing to appear rigid, if not actually square; his diction is clear, but often laboured – with little of the colour that might have been expected of music that he was the first to sing. It is difficult not to form the view that Tamagno is, in certain respects, entirely unmusical – particularly when compared with the best of those singers who came after him. Anyone seeking a point of comparative reference might refer to Caruso's recording for Victor of "*Ora e per sempre,*" produced on 28 December, 1910.

Verdi told Ricordi that any tenor at the end of *Otello* should be exhausted – and sound like it – which explains in part why the final cadence of "*Niun mi tema*" is unwritten in the score. This feature of the *urtext* is ignored by Tamagno, just as it would be by Del Monaco. Verdi lamented that dissolution was "a quality lacking in Tamagno – he must always sing in a full voice, otherwise the sound comes out ugly, uncertain, out of tune." The composer reportedly recoiled from the tenor's variable pitching, and begged of the conductor Franco Faccio that he persuade him to sing "something approximating to what I have written." The composer was concerned for the subtlety of his art, and openly condemned Tamagno's ham-fisted approach to *chiaroscuro*: "There are large, long, *legato* phrases [in *Otello*] that are to be sung *mezza voce*, something impossible for [Tamagno]". To Boito he wrote:

> I don't think he could perform the short melody "*E tu come sei pallida*" even less "*Un bacio, un bacio ancora,*" with the right affect […] especially since between the second kiss and the third there are four measures for the orchestra alone, which must be filled with a delicate, moving stage action that I imagined as I was writing the music. It would be a very easy scene for a real actor, but difficult for […] anyone else.[116]

Was Tamagno as good as everyone says he was? For that matter, was Mario? Or Fraschini, Salvi, Duprez, Nourrit, Rubini and Donzelli? It's tantamount to heresy even to hint at the possibility that the stars of the tenorial tradition between 1800 and 1900 were anything less than paradigmatic – in whatever context that criteria might be determined. Yet Verdi and Shaw both thought Tamagno a screamer, and constitutionally incapable of vocal art. As to what can be heard from his recordings, it's not enough to blame the technology – since the same equipment was used by the same producer at the same time for Caruso. The latter's approach to line and phrasing and to word use generally are in diametric opposition to that of Tamagno, and while

---

116 Henson, Karen (2015). *Opera Acts: Singers and Performance in the Late Nineteenth Century.* Cambridge University Press. p.123.

many relish hearing Tamagno as the creator of one of the most important roles in the history of opera, his phrasing – and the placement of his voice – suggest something other than the pinnacle of the art of dramatic singing at the end of the 19th century. Indeed, only the biased could think him comparable creatively to what can be heard in matters of style and substance (rather than mere tone) in performances of *Otello* by Merli, Zenatello, Panizza, Martinelli, Vinay, Vickers and Domingo.

It is here that Tamagno's status as an historical figure crystallises. Firstly, it's necessary to ask why Verdi would turn to someone of whom he had little positive to say, and whose contemporaries thought him, for the most part, a *zuccino*?[117] What then does his status say of the standard of tenor singing generally during the second half of the 19th century? The obvious answer to both questions is that there was no one else to whom Verdi was able to turn. It's inarguable that singing after 1850 had changed rapidly in consequence of the escalation in venue and orchestra size, and that the scale of the commercial market created largely by Verdi placed supply at the mercy of exponential demand. Standards dropped in tandem with experience and expectation. An audience that hadn't heard Nourrit couldn't appreciate the imperfections of Mario, and the audience that heard Tamberlik thought him exciting rather than vulgar. Tamagno was merely the best of what may have been a very inadequate bunch, therefore. The school of singing that predated Tamagno was cultivated over time by Rossini and Donizetti, and incapable of meeting the new requirements of life with Verdi – when the circus of novelty compelled singers to produce scale over substance, and then six nights a week.

Composers did what they could to keep pace, but the number of successful new productions to compete with Verdi between 1851 (with the premiere of *Rigoletto*) and 1871 (with the first night of *Aida*) was surprisingly limited – even though thousands of operas were composed and published. The names of composers producing operas of note in competition with Verdi were, with a few exceptions, routine: Berlioz, Pacini, Mercadante, Meyerbeer, Gounod, Delibes, Offenbach, Saint-Saëns, Massenet and Wagner. Apart from Ponchielli, Bizet, Smetana and Dvořák, Europe's opera houses were dominated by the same small chorus of voices – the loudest of them being Verdi and Wagner. The effect of this transition on singing was self-evident, and much commented on – since the "old" was represented by light voices and by singers pre-occupied with phrasing, word placement and colour. Inevitably, perhaps, the once subtle palette of colour for which the tenor had been renowned was abandoned for something closer to neon. The generation that lurched into the age of recording did so having witnessed the reinvention of the tenor voice. Prized 19th century traditions, evolving over more than two centuries of slowly evolving practice, became archipelagos for the 20th century – when everything remembered other than on record was necessarily superlative.

Woody Allen's *Midnight in Paris* riffs beautifully on the dangers of contingency memory and infinite regress. The film's hero (Owen Wilson as Gil Pender) mythologises the 1920s and the halcyon lives of Zelda and F Scott Fitzgerald, Cole Porter, Ernest Hemingway, Josephine Baker, Alice B. Toklas, Gertrude Stein, Pablo Picasso, Salvador Dalí, Man Ray, Luis Buñuel and T. S. Eliot. He is transported back in time

---

117 Verdi's nickname for Tamagno. Equivalent to "bullet-head."

to experience life with his idols, and the longer he spends in the company of the past, the less satisfied he is with the present. As Pender begins to fall in love with Marion Cotillard's Adriana, an imagined muse to Picasso, he is horrified to hear her eulogise the perfection of the *Belle Époque*. When Pender and Adriana slip further back in history and meet Henri Matisse and Toulouse-Lautrec, they hear them yearn also for a former age. It was ever thus. Allen's commentary concedes that every generation is valuable, whether or not it is appreciated at the time, but the reality as it pertains to the evolution of the tenor voice is that the *actual* standard of singing during the last thirty years of the 19th century appears to have been a constant disappointment for composers and commentators alike. It represented an art in decline. Most of the recordings produced during the first five years of the 20th century do little to counter this conclusion.[118]

Not everyone has made the mistake of thinking the past automatically and presumptively elysian. In his final article on music, "*We Sing Better than our Grandparents!*"[119], George Bernard Shaw railed against the cant of historicist sentimentality:

> As to the robust tenors who came between Mario and Jean de Reszke, the educated and carefully-taught ones sang so horribly that they were classed as "goat-bleaters": Heddle Nash is an Orpheus compared to the once famous Gayarré. The rest were proletarians who had developed stentorian voices as newsboys, muffin men, infantry sergeants, and humble, vociferous cheapjack auctioneers, who mostly shouted their voices away and are forgotten. De Reszke seemed a prince in comparison. When I was first taken to the opera in my boyhood and heard Il trovatore, I was surprised to hear in the second scene a voice from behind the scenes: Manrico singing the Serenade. I asked the adult who had brought me (a teacher of singing). "What is that?" "A pig under a gate." I forbear to rescue that tenor's name from oblivion. Voice production in general is now immeasurably better than it was fifty years ago. Voices so strained by singing continually in the top fifth of their range that they could not sustain a note without tremolo, not keep to the pitch [...]. The notion that Wagner's music broke voices, and that opera voices should sing only that of Rossini, Donizetti, Bellini, and Meyerbeer, has been replaced by the truth that Wagner, Mozart, and Handel, who wrote for the middle of the voice with very occasional high notes for exceptional singers, never broke a properly produced voice. [...] Where we fall short is in roulades, shakes, and gruppettos, which many of our singers simply cannot sing at

---

118 Early recordings of excerpts from *Otello* that are consistently (and sometimes comically) dreadful include pressings by Antonio Arámburo (1840 – 1912), Giovanni Battista De Negri (1850 – 1923), Albert Alvarez (1860 – 1933), and Giuseppe Oxilia (1865 – 1919). There are others, but these give a pretty good impression of the background against which developments after 1900 are best appreciated. There are exceptions to the rule, of course, but *very* few. Among the best is Antonio Paoli (1870 – 1946), who takes ridiculous temporal liberties with the music *come è scritto*, but otherwise sings with terrific character, brilliance and *squillo*.

119 It was published on 11 November, 1950, in *Everybody's Magazine* – eight days after his death at the age of ninety-four.

all […] Let us hear no more of a golden age of bel canto. We sing much better than our grandfathers. I have heard all the greatest tenors […] from Mario to Heddle Nash, and I know what I am writing about; for, like de Reszke, I was taught to sing by my mother, not by García.

The "truth" for Riccardo Muti when conducting *Il trovatore* in 2000 may have been located in playing "*di quela pira*" after the chaotic fashion of the pianist who accompanied Tamagno when he recorded the *cabaletta* in 1903. He might have played the aria in B major, rather than C, and he might have dragged the *tempo*, missed out a verse, and cut the final chorus-driven *stretta* entirely – as did Tamagno. He might also have asked Salvatore Licitra to miss his cues, drag against the bar-lines, sing out of tune, drop notes, employ little or no phrasing and spit out the music in a shrill, poorly-placed *fortissimo*. In Tamagno's "truth" there is an unhealthy measure of authenticity because it's something of which Verdi had been approving (or tolerant) a decade earlier. It was plainly authentic for a tenor said by his record company to be the "world's greatest." In that truth there is another, namely that singers and the musical world more generally were to be much affected by the advent of recording.

CHAPTER SIX

Göttersonnenaufgang[1]

During the 19th century Europe was defined by evolving conceptions of voice, when most forms of intra-societal communication were subsumed after 1791 to symbolism, metaphor and allegory. Outside the galleries of painting and sculpture, the ambivalent transcended the absolute, with Romanticism and Nationalism evolving in tandem to forge narratives more destabilising of the Church's authority than education. The art and science of (proto) semiotics coloured almost every facet of contemporary life. When Napoleon demanded that representations of honeybees be woven into his clothing and his carpets, and doctors first confronted auditory-verbal hallucination, and Schopenhauer presented the world as will and representation, these disparate and secular manifestations of image and meaning operated sub-textually rather than subliminally. The taste for mimetic allusion extended to a pre-occupation with "otherness" that fostered transformative modes of communication. The emergence of trans-national vernaculars, spanning gothic literature (*Frankenstein* and the *Schauerroman*), socio-polemical painting (Jean Gros' *Bonaparte visitant les pestiférés de Jaffa*[2] and Géricault's *Le Radeau de la Méduse*[3]) and romantic-philosophical music (the late works of Beethoven[4]) were directed necessarily at the educated and the privileged; everyone else was captured by popular song, slogans, pamphlets, and penny-literature. The continuing struggles of occupied nations denied their freedom to speak fostered the isolation of identity in ways that ducked persecution and bypassed censorship. When, in 1806, Fichte directed his Thirteenth Address "*To the German Nation,*" his conjunction of language and nationhood resonated for the entire continent:

> The first, original, and truly natural boundaries of states are beyond doubt their internal boundaries. Those who speak the same language are joined to each other by a multitude of invisible bonds by nature herself, long before any human art begins; they understand each other and have the power of continuing to make themselves understood more and more clearly; they belong together and are by nature one and an inseparable whole [...][5] Only when each people, left to itself, develops

---

1 Literally "Sunrise of the Gods."
2 'Bonaparte Visits the Plague Stricken in Jaffa' (1804).
3 'Raft of the Medusa' (1819).
4 See generally Boyden, Matthew (2018). *Beethoven and the Gothic*. Verba et musica.
5 Fichte, Johann Gottlieb (1968). "Thirteenth Address", in *Addresses to the German Nation*, ed. George A. Kelly. Harper Torch Books. pp.190–191.

and forms itself in accordance with its own peculiar quality, and only when in every people each individual develops himself in accordance with that common quality, as well as in accordance with his own peculiar quality – then, and then only, does the manifestation of divinity appear in its true mirror as it ought to be; and only a man who either entirely lacks the notion of the rule of law and divine order, or else is an obdurate enemy thereto, could take upon himself to want to interfere with that law, which is the highest law in the spiritual world![6]

The conjunction of voice and identity was especially consequential for the German people, across every demographic. The huge popularity, for example, of "*Die Gedanken sind frei,*"[7] an anonymous song first published in 1820, was characteristic of the attachment of language to meaning and national sentiment. It first appeared in 1805, in the third volume of Achim von Arnim and Clemens Brentano's collection of folk poems, *Des Knaben Wunderhorn*.[8] For obvious reasons, the subject and substance of the verses (concerning a man imprisoned in a dungeon from which he cannot escape) resonated with Beethoven. The Man asks:

Die Gedanken sind frei, wer kann sie erraten?
Sie fliegen vorbei wie nächtliche Schatten.
Kein Mensch kann sie wissen, kein Jäger sie schiessen
mit Pulver und Blei: Die Gedanken sind frei![9]

The primacy of voice as sound and symbol was an obsessive preoccupation for readers and writers of music criticism after 1800 – particularly in Germany, where Breitkopf & Härtel's AMZ[10] appeared as a weekly magazine between 1798 and 1848.[11] The AMZ was not the only journal devoted to music in Germany, but it was the most widely read. When the final two-act version of *Fidelio* was first staged at the Kärntnertortheater in Vienna, on 23 May, 1814, the AMZ commissioned Amadeus Wendt to write his "Thoughts about Recent Musical Art, and van Beethoven's Music, Specifically His *Fidelio*."[12] The opening of Wendt's extensive review (titled "Higher Musical Art") is typical of the evolving dialectic:

If for all the other arts there is something at hand that, through the magical glance of genius, is lifted for the first time, ennobled and transfigured, from the ground of reality and seems to be placed in the paradise of ideas, then musical art almost seems itself to be conceived in this land, and speaks, like the world spirit, through storm and thunder, as

---

6   *Ibid.* pp.197–198.
7   'Thoughts are free.'
8   'The Boy's Magic Horn.' The poem was considerably older, with overt references in medieval poetry.
9   'Thoughts are free, who can guess them? They fly by like nocturnal shadows. No person can know them, no hunter can shoot them, with powder and lead: Thoughts are free!'
10 *Allgemeine musikalische Zeitung* ('General Musical News').
11 It was abandoned in 1848, and revived between 1866 and 1882.
12 In sections between 24 May and 28 June, 1815.

well as in the gentle breezes of spring and in the whispering waves of grain, a magical language, which is only comprehensible to those whose hearing discloses, not an abundance of outward noises, but the inward parts of the world and the most secret depths of the heart into which no mortal eye can see. The ingenious musical artist is an initiate of heaven; in invisible signs he proclaims his visions, audible to every ear that is open, but not perceptible to everyone. Those less favoured, to whom musical art is, in the exact sense, only sounding art, create for themselves through pleasing combinations of notes a language that strikes the ear easily and comprehensibly, increases the charm of living, and agrees completely with Kant's notorious description of music. For this art can be further called an ingenious play of sensations when the notes are regarded according to the impression they make on the physical senses and are combined, either changed or unchanged, to agreeable effect, with a thoughtful but facile selection of phrases and idioms through which the musical spirit of the times is expressed.[13]

Fidelio's allegorical libretto was second-hand and unoriginal[14] – even after Treitschke's amendments for the third and final version in 1814. The opera's sledgehammer themes of freedom, loyalty and nationhood were considered trite by Wendt because he was unable to attach their psychological resonance to the composer's obsession with the hermeneutics of *L'amour conjugal*.[15] Beethoven's unsuccessful attempts to establish a normal relationship with a woman – even before the deterioration of his hearing – were distilled in the purity of Leonora's Christ-like devotion to Florestan, just as Florestan's Christ-like suffering inspired Beethoven to establish in a single work the fundamental elements of the dramatic tenor voice for more than a century of German opera. It has been reasoned by Maynard Solomon that Beethoven identified more with Leonora than Florestan, a proto-Freudian interpretation that isolates the composer's emotional connection to the power of the feminine, an attachment that would resolve calamitously in the guardianship of his nephew.[16] Others (notably Alan Tyson) have isolated more obvious parallels between the darkness of Florestan's cell and Beethoven's encroaching silence – an allegory of the senses more than sustained by the piercing grief articulated by the recitative and aria "*'Gott! Welch' Dunkel hier.*"[17] It is equally true that Beethoven's opera transformed a routine rescue story into a metaphor for universal liberation, mutating what begins as a domestic drama into a communal *cri de cœur* in which the opera's sociology passes by way of soliloquy and the liberation of an imprisoned community to a choral paean to freedom:

---

13 Senner, Wayne M., Wallace, Robin, Meredith, William (2001). *The Critical Reception of Beethoven's Compositions by his German Contemporaries*, Vol. 2. University of Nebraska Press. No.240. pp.185–222.
14 It was previously set (and then with some success) by *Paer*.
15 The subtitle of Bouilly's original libretto.
16 Solomon, Maynard (1998). *Beethoven*. Schirmer Books. p.199. See also Sterba, Editha and Sterba, Richard (1971). *Beethoven and his Nephew: A Psychoanalytical Study of their Relationship*. Schocken Books. p.111.
17 'God! What darkness here!'

"Heil sey dem Tag! Heil sey der Stunde;
Da, lang ersehnt, doch unvereint.
Gerechtigkeit mit Huld im Bunde,
Vor unsers Grabes Thor erschient."[18]

Like the prisoners allowed briefly into the light in Act 1 ("*O welche Lust*"),[19] Florestan regains a voice that has been denied him by injustice and barbarism. When he first emerges from the darkness at the beginning of Act 2 (singing "*Gott! Welch' Dunkel hier!*"), he has abandoned all hope of action, and his reflection captures simultaneously the collapse of psychological and political integrity. Florestan's separation from his own voice – by experience and as metaphor – results in a visual hallucination and delirium that is resolved only when Leonora appears as his salvation. For contemporary commentators like Wendt, Florestan's first appearance was among the opera's highlights:

> In the introduction we already seem to feel the terrifying arousal of a suffering human soul in the bleak darkness of the deepest prison, the heavy sighs that interrupt the deathlike silence, the cold horrors that flutter through this place; our heart is filled with fear and pity before we catch a glimpse of the suffering one. The curtain opens, and Florestan expresses his feelings and ours in the recitative and in the aria that follows it. Paer wrote an aria for the same situation with *obbligato* violin and viola, a truly good concert aria that, however, apart from the introductory recitative, which is not easy to understand, does not engage the situation nearly as deeply as does Beethoven's composition. What is more, the Italian arranger, in the spirit of Italian theatre poets and composers, did not allow anything but the customary tenderness in familiar phrases to be expressed in this situation. In the German arrangement, the force of religious submission and patience that arise from a clear consciousness is brought significantly to the fore, along with the sorrowful recollection of the wife; this differentiates this scene somewhat from the customary treatment of similar situations. And this is also beautifully expressed in the music, by means of which the terrifying aspects of the situation are moderated in the most noble manner. The composer did not produce an extended concert aria dressed up with brilliant *roulades*, which would only have distracted from the situation being portrayed; he had a much higher goal in mind. A simple and melodious *Adagio* in A flat major, upon which there follows, with the recollection of Leonore, a more agitated section in F minor with arpeggiated accompaniment, which, growing ever slower at the close, is finally given over to the violoncello, and loses itself in the weakly sustained F minor chord, encompasses the entire situation. We seem to hear how, after the final arousal of feeling,

---

[18] 'Hail the day! Hail from the hour; There, long awaited, but not united. Justice with grace, liberty before our grave.'
[19] 'O what a joy!'

which powerfully summoned up memories, the exhausted strength of the terribly suffering man draws, unnoticed, ever nearer to dissolution, which the Italian arrangement only tried to express in a succeeding recitative, apparently in order not to disturb the popular style of the aria.

His vernacular is loaded. The German Beethoven is superior to his Italian rival,[20] whose version of "*Gott! Welch' Dunkel hier!*" ("*Ciel, che profonda oscuritá tiranna* [...] *Dolce oggetto del mio amore*"[21]) is inadequate by comparison. Quite what Wendt was suggesting when invoking "the spirit of Italian theatre poets and composers" is unclear – save that art at its most profound (and, by association, divine) was a "higher goal" attainable only by German artists. Beethoven is praised for producing something other than a "concert aria dressed up with brilliant *roulades*," with his writing for Florestan abjuring the "customary" and the "popular" for something redolent of true "feeling," "strength," "suffering" and "dissolution." Anticipating Schopenhauer's claim that "unless suffering is the direct and immediate object of life, our existence must entirely fail of its aim,"[22] Beethoven's articulation of Florestan's pain can still shock and disturb. Even before he cries out to God, in F minor,[23] the use of angular intervals (especially the tritone) and chromatic tension are employed by Beethoven to render despair as the composer understood it better than most. The recitative begins on a (commonly howled) G4 – marked *piano* – that descends an octave, in parallel with his resignation to the darkness of his confinement. The music's portrayal of isolation is unprecedented,[24] with the language of the recitative employed to characterise suffocation, weeping and mental collapse. Even the glowing phrase "*Das Mass der Leiden*,"[25] and the cantabile of "*in des lebens fruhling*"[26] cannot detract from the purposeful sense of Christ's journey along the *via dolorosa* ("*Und spür' ich nicht linde, Sanft säuselnde Luft?*"[27]). Beethoven was equally determined to place the singer under a measure of stress sufficient for his vision of Leonora ("*Ein Engel, Leonoren, der Gattin, so gleich*")[28] to convey illness and starvation. By setting the aria in the crook of the *passaggio*, and with the rising passages culminating in a series of testing B flat 4s ("*zur Freiheit ins himmlische Reich*"[29]), Beethoven ensured that Florestan's

---

20   Ferdinando Paer (1 July, 1771 – 3 May, 1839). Paer's opera *Leonora* was based on the same story as *Fidelio* (1804). It was first produced a year later. Beethoven owned a copy of Paer's score. Another Italian composer, Simon Mayr, produced his own version in 1805 as *L'amor coniugale*.
21   'Heaven, what profound dark tyranny [...] Sweet object of my love.'
22   Schopenhauer, Arthur (1851). "On the Sufferings of the World," in *The Meaning of Life* (1981). Ed. E.D Klemke. Oxford University Press. p.45.
23   Significantly for Beethoven, F minor was also the key of choice for Bach when writing *Ich ruf zu dir, Herr Jesu Christ* ['I call to you, Lord Jesus Christ'], BWV 639, a bittersweet but profoundly moving choral prelude from the *Orgelbüchlein* ['Little Organ Book'], BWV 599–644. The opening words (which would have been known to Beethoven) are "*Ich ruf zu dir, Herr Jesu Christ, ich bitt, erhör mein Klagen.*"
24   It's worth remembering that *Fidelio* was first performed only 17 years after *Don Giovanni* – while Haydn was still busy at his desk.
25   'The measure of misery.'
26   'In the Spring of Life.'
27   'And don't I sense a gentle, soft-whispering air.'
28   'An angel Leonore! Leonore so like my wife.'
29   '[...] to freedom in the heavenly realm.'

glimpse of salvation would never sound anything less than chimerical. The addition of a solo oboe adds hypnotically to a sense of dislocated reason, with the incessant, nagging tone of the *obbligato* characterising the struggle between sanity and delirium, imprisonment and emancipation, voice and voicelessness. The articulation of faith (in Florestan) and delirium (through the oboe) divides the listener's attention, compelling the tenor to express in sound and word his belief in the triumph of hope over despair.

It is a unique and remarkable invention that compels the drawing of parallels between Paer's approach and that of Beethoven. Of course, any comparison between the Italian and German schools during the ten years either side of 1800 is essentially pointless because there was no "German School." Prior to *Fidelio*, German opera had stalled following the first productions in Vienna of *Iphigenie auf Tauris*[30] in 1781 and Mozart's *Die Entführung aus dem Serail* in 1782 – both at the Burgtheater in Vienna. Aside from the premiere of *Die Zauberflöte* at the Theater auf der Wieden in 1791, little else of note was created in German for German-speaking audiences until the decade 1804 – 1814, and Beethoven's singular operatic obsession.

There is, however, much to compare between the writing by Gluck and Mozart for tenor, and that of Beethoven. The earlier composers scored their works for light, *haute-contre* singers with dexterity and range – as well as ample (if measured) floridity. The writing for Florestan is largely muscular and placed mostly in the same register as Donizetti's operas for Donzelli. It is unsurprising that every single tenor who sang the leading roles in *Der Ring des Nibelungen* and *Tristan und Isolde* after 1900 also placed Florestan at the heart of their repertoire. Melchior, Lorenz, Völker, Hopf, Svanholm, Thomas, Windgassen, Vickers, King, Kollo, Hofmann, Jerusalem and Kaufmann all excelled in Beethoven as well as Wagner because both composers wrote for singing actors with a strong middle voice, considerable declamatory power and German lyricism – precisely those qualities that would distinguish what would become the "*heldentenor.*"[31] Florestan is the first absolute *heldentenor* role, not because of its length (indeed, he appears only at the beginning of Act 2), but because he has to be heard – especially during the final scene, when he is required to rise above an increasingly busy orchestra and chorus, often in ensemble. Beethoven was famously unforgiving as a composer for sopranos, and he is no less ungenerous to his tenor throughout *Fidelio*. His first, on 20 November 1805, was Ignaz Anton Demmer,[32] a singer of the Wiener Hofoper whose musical life began as a chorister at various churches in Cologne. On 4 February, 1791, Demmer and his wife travelled to Weimar, and the patronage of Goethe – whose mother wrote in May that year to inform her son that:

---

30 A revision of *Iphigénie en Tauride*, first performed (in French) on 18 May, 1779, by the Opéra at the Palais-Royal.
31 'Heroic tenor.' The term was not coined by Richard Wagner. In fact, the first recorded use of the term "heroic" when referencing Wagner's operas is from a quote by Berlioz in response to hearing Tichatschek performing in *Rienzi*. Berlioz held that Tichatschek's voice was "elegant, impassioned and heroic." The *New Grove Dictionary of Opera*. Oxford Music Online.
32 Baptised 11 February, 1766 – after 1824. There is some debate as to "which Demmer.". The first Florestan might have been a Friedrich Christian Demmer. It is unclear which. Kurt Dorfmüller, in Beiträge zur Beethoven-Bibliographie, reports a letter from Dr. Friedrich Slezak in which he identifies the first Florestan as Berlin-born Friedrich Christian Demmer.

> Herr Demmer! That's a wonderful man – he played Tamino [*Die Zauberflöte*] with excellence – and our operas have won a lot through him – his wife only performed as Claudia once – you can't say much yet. Last week *Die Zauberflöte* was given two times at such full houses that all the doors had to remain open otherwise one would have suffocated with heat![33]

In addition to Mozart, he created the role of Count Edwinsky for the Viennese premiere of Boieldieu's *Béniovski ou les Exilés du Kamchattka*,[34] of which the AMZ's city correspondent reported:

> A new tenor, Mr. Demmer, who appeared for the first time in the role of the Count, pleased. He really has a strong and pure voice, quite a range, and plays quite well. Even if his technique is not perfect, he tries to make up for it by clear diction, a quality not often found in our singers, especially tenors.[35]

The Vienna correspondent of the *Berlinische musikalische Zeitung* was less generous:

> For a first lover he is no longer young enough, his voice has too little sound and flexibility. But he is understandable, has a good high register, and usually sings with accuracy and expression.[36]

The AMZ further reported that he "almost always intoned flat,"[37] and it's doubtful anyone was surprised, including Demmer, when the composer replaced him with Joseph August Röckel[38] for the first performance of the opera's revision on 26 March, 1806. Röckel lived a remarkably long life, dying in his 87th year – long enough to see the centenary of Beethoven's birth – but he was absurdly young (twenty-two) when being asked to take up the role of Florestan.[39] Röckel's voice cannot have been of any great size or focus since he was, by any standards, entirely untrained; even so, Beethoven's ears were still working in 1806, so he must have heard something to like. Eight years later, he chose experience over youth when gifting the third and final Florestan to Giulio (Julius) Radichi,[40] an Italian-born singing actor who appears to have performed at La Scala during the 1793–94 season, and in Genoa in 1799. The earliest reference to Radichi outside Italy is in the AMZ's Prague bulletin of 1807; the following year he joined the Vienna Court Theatre, where he remained

---

33 Goethe, Katharina Elisabeth (2015). *Briefe*. Vol. I. Palala Press. p.467.
34 'Béniovski or the Kamchatka exiles' first produced in Paris in 1800. The Viennese premiere was presented as *Die Verwiesenen auf Kamtschatka* – which does not translate as "the exiles," but the "referred."
35 *Allgemeine musikalische Zeitung*, Jg. 6, No 45, 8 August, 1804. p.760.
36 *Berlinische musikalische Zeitung* (1969). Ed. Johann Friedrich Reichardt.
37 Allgemeine musikalische Zeitung, Jg. 8, No 15, 8 January, 1806. p.238.
38 28 August, 1783 – September, 1870.
39 He almost outlived his son, August (1 December, 1814 – 18 June, 1876) who became a close friend of Richard Wagner, dying two months before the first *Ring* Cycle.
40 1763 – 16 September, 1846.

until August, 1819 – in his 57th year. Prior to his appearance in 1814 as Florestan, the AMZ complimented his "pure, musical, and extremely flexible voice," which "charmed everyone."[41] Those virtues appear not to have manifested themselves for Beethoven. In its "*News. Vienna*" on 5 June, 1814, the AMZ reported of *Fidelio's* last first night:

> On the twenty-third we saw for the first time at this theatre, to great applause, *Fidelio*, an opera in two acts, newly arranged from the French, with music by L. v. Beethoven. When this opera was twice given at the Theater-an-der-Wien several years ago, it was not by any means able to rejoice in a favourable reception. It is thus all the more gratifying to every friend of art to know that the composer has been rewarded for his tenacious persistence and painstaking revision. That there are yet others who are not completely in agreement with the general judgment may be imagined. Some say that the subject (once again a rescue story) is obsolete, and that after so many similar ones served up almost to the point of tedium […] it must be more repulsive than attractive. Others say that the music, from the vocal point of view, is surely not as original as must have been expected from this master. […] We will leave such controversies to themselves […] One may probably concede to those antagonists that the vocal parts are not always worthy of the most praise, that several reminiscences have crept in, and so forth; the whole, though, remains interesting, and the connoisseur is compensated for a few weaknesses by a number of genuine masterpieces, so that every unprejudiced listener will leave the house satisfied. Apart from the overture—which, newly composed for this purpose, was first given at the second performance—most of the musical numbers were briskly, indeed even tumultuously, applauded, and the composer was unanimously called out after the first and the second acts. […] We would have preferred to see Mr. Wild in place of Mr. Radichi (Florestan); in this way the whole second act would have gained in interest. […] The new overture (E major) was received with thunderous applause, and the composer was again called out twice at this repetition.[42]

The reference to Franz Wild[43] was loaded. Although now best remembered for his celebrated account of Beethoven conducting, Wild was a popular tenor – and one of the first to make a career uniquely in German music. Like everyone else, he began life as a chorister, at Klosterneuburg Abbey in Vienna. In 1804, Wild auditioned for Antonio Salieri, who admitted him to the imperial court chapel. In 1809, he became a member of the Esterházy company in Eisenstadt, from where he was sent

---

41 Senner, Wayne M., Wallace, Robin, Meredith, William (2001). *The Critical Reception of Beethoven's Compositions by his Compositions by his German Contemporaries*, Vol. 2. University of Nebraska Press. No.240. p.181.
42 *Ibid.* p.182.
43 31 December, 1791 – 1 January, 1860.

to the Theater an der Wien. He made his debut on 11 July, 1811, as Prince Ramiro in Nicolas Isouard's *Cendrillon*.[44] In 1813, Wild became first tenor at the Wiener Hofoper, and during the Congress of Vienna he sang on several occasions in front of the "parterre of kings" at the theatre in Erfurt.[45] On 25 January, 1815, he performed Beethoven's song "Adelaide" for the Tsarina, accompanied by the composer in what would be his last public appearance as a pianist.

In 1817, Wild relocated to the Grand Ducal Court Theatre in Darmstadt, from where he toured regularly, performing on a number of occasions for Rossini in Paris. He returned eventually to Vienna, where he worked under contract from 1830 until 1855 – and until the grand age of 64. Count Konstanin von Czartoryski wrote of Wild that he was:

> small, almost as small as Napoleon the Great, but there was something energetic, powerful about his whole personality, and when he sang, his figure grew almost before our eyes. His hair was jet black in youth and in natural curls, his eye fiery and animated, two bushy brows and the sharp-cut features give his noble face the expression of proud masculinity. Wild's voice was second to none. An indescribable enamel and melodiousness combined with a strength and fullness that gave his tone that pithy timbre, that he reached the heart with irresistible power and never forgot the ear that once belonged to him. His lecture, his school, his declamation, gesture and action were of the highest perfection, his enthusiasm swept him and the listener away with him and yet never exceeded the limits of the beautiful.[46]

Czartoryski's account focusses as much on Wild's disposition as a stage actor as on his voice, which is artfully characterised. The "enamel" fluency, combined with "strength and fullness," sustained by a "pithy timbre," all speak to those qualities that would become associated commonly with the finest German tenors.[47] It is in this warmth and richness of tone (equivalent idiomatically to *texture*) that the "German placement" of the tenor voice is distinguished from the Italian school (where *squillo* is a pre-requisite) and the French (where the unavoidable nasality of the language leads no less unavoidably to a pinching of tone). Wild's repertoire, in this respect, is intriguing. He sang fluently in French (Boieldieu and Isouard) as well as German, and he was successful in the bari-tenor repertoire from Italy (in German), including Pollione as well as a number of operas by Donizetti. Most importantly, however, Wild was key to the emerging German operatic school after *Fidelio*, populated

---

44 · First performed by the Opéra-Comique at the Salle Feydeau in Paris on 22 February, 1810.
45 Of this gathering of nobility Baron Friedrich Karl von Tettenborn observed, "In the presence of such a number of ribands it would be hazardous to conclude that they are all due to merit." Auguste Louis Charles Comte de La Garde-Chambonas (2015). *Anecdotal Recollections of the Congress of Vienna*. Andesite Press. p.24.
46 von Czartoryski, Konstantin. *Recensionen und allgemeine Bemerkungen über Theater und Musik*, (1853 – 1855). Bei J. F. Greß.
47 Czartoryski's criteria of value apply absolutely, for example, to the voices of Siegfried Jerusalem and Jonas Kaufmann.

most obviously by Louis Spohr and Carl Maria von Weber. The former did much to inspire the emergence of German musical theatre after 1815, with *Faust* (1816), *Zemire und Azor* (1819) and *Jessonda* (1823), but it was Weber who achieved almost single-handedly the invention of German romantic opera. Between 1821 and his death five years later he completed *Der Freischütz*[48] (a "romantische Oper"; 1821), *Euryanthe* (a "grosse heroisch-romantische Oper") and *Oberon oder König der Elfen*[49] (a "romantische Oper). Two of these operas are named after their tenor lead (the "Marksman" is Max); all three feature prominent roles for tenors singing in German.

Der Freischütz was first staged seven years after the final signing of the Congress of Vienna – and Napoleon's defeat nine days later. Weber's audiences had direct and personal experience of war and its effect on the German-speaking people. When following the hunt in *Freischütz*, and hearing the valve-less horns blaring out calls to arms, many will have had personal knowledge of the Lützowsches Freikorps[50] (or "Schwarze Jäger"[51]), a volunteer force of intellectuals, aristocrats and artists who assisted the Prussian army in fighting Napoleon in the country's dense forests. The characters in *Freischütz* inhabit a world of fantasy and demonology, one painted as an idealised vision of a German past in which hunters lived in pantheistic harmony with the natural order. For the German people, the forest was significantly more prevalent than the city; as a symbol of the unknown and the unconscious, woodland provided as realistic a setting for a national drama as did Beethoven's prison. Weber's drama in *Freischütz* occupies a world in which danger and violence are ever present. Max is in love with Agathe, whom he cannot marry because she is his employer's daughter. Like everyone else at the time, he has to contend with a hierarchical social order – an intransigent horizon that leads him to turn to the Devil. Magic bullets are not a realistic solution, of course, and the opera's denouement reinforces realities that cannot have escaped the attention even of the very young.

The emergence of a romanticised nationalism in Weber's operas, and as it had been articulated by Fichte, fed off the primacy of the German-language as a force for unification. The increasing obsession for German history collided idealistically with the popular taste for fantasy and the fantastic. Diabolical stories like *Freischütz* were especially popular in their provision of extravagant metaphorical canvasses for metaphysical considerations that eclipsed the Italian and French schools in ways that "only" the German people could appreciate. The validation of a progressive national identity, in which the individual was instrumental to a newly collectivised ambition, was driven on stage in almost every case by the presentation of the hero as a tenor. Where Tamino in *Die Zauberflöte* had been a guileless love-interest, and Beethoven's Florestan a damsel in distress, Max and Oberon were entirely heroic. They needed to be, since Weber's approach to the orchestra was revolutionary and far-reaching. Berlioz was profoundly affected by Weber's virtuosity, and in the *Journal des Débats*, on 23 June, 1835, he wrote that "Weber's is a different orchestra, almost as far from Beethoven's as from that of Rossini." It was no exaggeration. For all his invention,

---

48 'The Marksman.'
49 'Oberon, King of the Elves.'
50 'Lützow Free Corps.'
51 'Black Hunters.'

Beethoven's orchestra was classically structured – and civilised in its order. Weber's writing fizzed with nervous energy and an unprecedented range of colour, variety and contrast. Again for the *Débats*, Berlioz wrote on 8 September, 1857, that Weber was

> as great *in Freischütz* as in *Oberon*. But the poetry of the former is full of movement, passion, and contrasts. The supernatural leads to strange and violent effects. The melodic style, harmony, and rhythm have in combination a thunderous and incandescent power; everything conspires to arrest attention. The characters are also taken from everyday experience and have widespread appeal. The depiction of their feelings and daily lives calls for a less elevated style, which is enhanced by exquisite workmanship. This gives the work irresistible charm, even for those minds who disdain musical amusements, and to the general public it comes across in this form as the pinnacle of art and a miracle of inventiveness. [...] The language [...] derives its main charm from harmony, its melodic language is capriciously vague, its rhythms are unpredictable and veiled, and thus often difficult to grasp. It is a language that is all the more difficult for the general public to follow as its subtleties cannot be experienced, even by musicians, without extremely close attention combined with a lively imagination.

Weber took extreme pains to ensure that the "voice" of a work laden with symbolic force should be reflected in the diction of his singers, a priority self-evident from the immense care taken by the composer when asking his singers to confront, and in many cases overcome, an orchestral sound of great density and expressive independence. There are almost no accompaniments in Weber's operas; the orchestra is a voice of its own. Act 1's "*Durch die Wälder, durch die Auen,*"[52] for example, rises no higher on the stave than an A4; the words have to be audible above a large and richly-voiced orchestra. The first to sing the role of Max was Heinrich Stümer.[53] He studied in Berlin with the composer and kapellmeister Vincenzo Maria Righini,[54] and made his debut at the Hofoper as Belmonte in 1811. He was commended for his beautiful voice – which appears to have sustained him in works by Rossini – but in German music he was found wanting. On 21 June, 1823, for example, the *Zeitung für Theater, Musik und bildende Künste* reported of a production of *Fidelio* that:

> Mr. Stümer partially lacks the power needed for the part of Florestan, and replacing him with Mr. Bader would be to the advantage of the opera. Several of the higher notes of each singer seemed to us after some time to be strikingly rough and hoarse, and operas like *Fidelio* are not designed to help a voice out.[55]

---

52 'Through the forests, through the meadows.'
53 1789 – 27 September, 1856.
54 22 January, 1756 – 19 August, 1812.
55 Senner, Wayne M., Wallace, Robin, Meredith, William (2001). *The Critical Reception of Beethoven's Compositions by his German Contemporaries*, Vol. 2. University of Nebraska Press. No. 254. pp.240.

Carl Adam Bader,[56] on the other hand, was described by Fétis as "one of the best tenors in Germany,"[57] although it was conceded that "the partisans of Italian music disputed his title of singer and claimed that he only deserved success for his acting."[58] The distinction between Stümer and Bader was the latter's essential Germanness, because he placed word and gesture above tone – a prejudice that brought him into close alignment with E. T. A. Hoffmann, with whom he worked closely in Bamberg. His success as a uniquely German tenor was considerable, in part because his technique allowed him to satisfy the nativist obsession with word-projection. It would have been impossible for a contemporary Italian tenor to perform "*Nein, länger trag ich nicht die Qualen*"[59] from *Freischütz* while successfully articulating words and music in competition with Weber's orchestra. The uncertain melody and ambiguous narrative architecture would have baffled a tenor pre-occupied by training and experience with linear *ariosi*. It's true that Oberon's "*Seit Frühester Jugend Im Kampf Und Streit*"[60] – with its high B4s (distended commonly by those who can do it) – is better suited in isolation to Italianate voices, but the presentation of the text throughout *Oberon* is for the first time *echt* in its Germanness. This localised quality was amplified yet further with *Euryanthe*, the first entirely German "through-composed" work of musical theatre.

Weber's example was followed by Heinrich Marschner, whose two most successful operas (*Der Vampyr*, 1828, and *Hans Heiling*, 1833) were both located firmly in the romantic-fantastical universe of *Der Freischütz*. One young boy, whose mother was on friendly terms with Weber, was remembered many years later by a school friend for having mounted an amateur production:[61]

> [...] As soon as he saw *Der Freischütz* he absolutely had to stage it. It goes without saying that it was the Wold's Glen scene that struck him as the most suitable in this regard. Pasteboard and glue were pressed into service to make the necessary props. His school friends had to help. Scenery, curtains, fireworks and animals – everything was produced, and my mother particularly admired a large boar with enormous tusks that was rolled along on the board and looked horribly like a Prince of Darkness in person. The performance was to be given at a friend's house. Richard played the part of Caspar, but the Max had not learnt his part and when Richard indicated his disapproval, he first laughed, then called him names, and the others laughed and jeered too.

---

56 10 January, 1789 – 14 April, 1870.
57 *Biographie universelle*, 1, 213.
58 Senner, Wayne M., Wallace, Robin, Meredith, William (2001). *The Critical Reception of Beethoven's Compositions by his German Contemporaries*, Vol. 2. University of Nebraska Press. No. 254. p.240.
59 'No, no longer can I carry the torment.'
60 'In the fight and quarrel since earliest youth.'
61 By Ferdinand Avenarius. Wagner was the step-uncle of Avenarius and his brother, the philosopher Richard Avenarius. *Kunstwart und Dürerbund. Ein Beitrag zur Geschichte der Gebildeten im Zeitalter des Imperialismus* (1969). Vandenhoeck & Ruprecht. p.177

The young Richard's surname was Wagner; his immersion in music and theatre was considered a birthright, as it was for his siblings. His eldest (much older) brother, Albert, was a gifted tenor who abandoned medicine for opera on the advice of Weber; his eldest sister, Rosalie, contracted with the Dresden Court Theatre, while Louisa, his second sister, became an actress. Wagner's mother rented out rooms at their home in Dresden to a stream of celebrated guests, which included Louis Spohr; and his earliest experiences of singing included close proximity to Luigi Lablache and Wilhelmine Schröder-Devrient. The latter became his dramatic ideal, and in Volume 1 of Mein Leben,[62] Wagner recalled Schröder-Devrient's performance as Leonora in *Fidelio*:

> If I look back on my life as a whole, I can find no event that produced so profound an impression upon me. Anyone who can remember that wonderful woman at this period of her life must to some extent have experienced the almost Satanic ardour which the intensely human art of this incomparable actress poured into his veins. After the performance I rushed to a friend's house and wrote a short note to the singer, in which I briefly told her that from that moment my life had acquired its true significance, and that if in days to come she should ever hear my name praised in the world of Art, she must remember that she had that evening made me what I then swore it was my destiny to become. This note I left at her hotel and ran out into the night as if I were mad. In the year 1842, when I went to Dresden to make my debut with Rienzi, I paid several visits to the kind-hearted singer, who startled me on one occasion by repeating this letter word for word. It seemed to have made an impression on her too, as she had actually kept it.

Rienzi was Wagner's first success – although he remembered things differently when speaking to Cosima in 1871:[63]

> Rienzi is very repugnant to me, but they should at least recognize the fire in it; I was a music director and I wrote a grand opera; the fact that it was this same music director who gave them some hard nuts to crack – that's what should astonish them.

Rienzi remained outside the Wagner family's canon until 2013, when it was produced for the first time at the Bayreuther Festspiele by Matthias von Stegmann. Wagner disowned the opera, and it remains a long slog, but it is neither "Meyerbeer's best" (von Bülow) nor "Meyerbeer's worst" (Charles Rosen); in certain respects it prefigured much that was to come. Like its predecessors, *Die Feen* and *Der Liebesverbot*, *Rienzi*'s libretto was written by its composer – a feature of Wagner's despotic aesthetics that isolated the source and substance of his ambition. His preoccupation

---

62 Wagner, Richard (1983). *My Life*. Trans. Andrew Gray and Mary Whittall. Cambridge University Press. p.37.
63 Millington, Barry (1999). "Rienzi: an opera in the grand style"; programme notes to EMI Classics recording conducted by Heinrich Hollreiser.

with the German language as the root of any distinctively German art developed the Goethean obsession with word and identity, an integration that necessitated the re-invention of writing (and of the public's instincts as readers and listeners) sufficient to distinguish German art from that produced by the rest of Europe. Wagner made much of his devotion to Goethe and Schiller – for whom German art was key to the elevation of *das Volk* – but in his essay "The Sorrows and Grandeur of Richard Wagner," Thomas Mann recognised that Wagner's aspirations were for a German art in the sense of *nationale Kunst* rather than *Volkskunst*.[64]

That process began with the German word, and Wagner chose his words carefully. He did so for *Rienzi* no less than for *Parsifal*, but Rienzi was his first title role written specifically for a tenor voice. He was well-acquainted with the singer for whom he wrote it: Josef Tichatschek.[65] Born in Weckelsdorf (Bohemia – now the Czech Republic), Tichatschek abandoned medicine for voice lessons in Vienna with Giuseppe Ciccimarra.[66] After a period in the Kärntnertortheater chorus and solo work in Graz, he was appointed principal tenor in Dresden in 1837. Two years later, Henry Chorley heard Tichatschek in *Euryanthe*:

> Among the tenors of Germany, Herr Tichatschek still bears a high reputation; and few, in any country, have ever crossed the stage with an ampler proportion of natural advantages. He is of the right height – handsome – his voice in 1839 was strong, sweet, and extensive, taking the *altissimo* notes of its register in chest tones. Then, too, he possessed a youthful energy of manner calculated to gain the favour of all who hear and see him. I have heard no one in Germany who was better qualified to sustain the glorious music belonging to the part of Adolar.[67]

In 1843, Berlioz wrote that Tichatschek had a

> pure and touching voice, which becomes very powerful when animated by the dramatic action. His style of singing is simple and in good taste; he is a consummate reader and musician, and undertook the tenor solo in the Sanctus [in Berlioz's *Requiem*] at first sight, without reserve, or affectation, or pretension.

The celebrated bass Karl Formes, remembered singing

> at Dresden with Tiatscheck [he] had a peculiar mannerism in pronunciation; he, so to say, sang his syllables doubly.[68] His color of tone was almost unequaled, quite as perfect as Mario's. In the second act of '*La*

---

64   Mann, Thomas (1985). "The Sorrows and Grandeur of Richard Wagner" in *Pro and Contra Wagner*. Trans. Allan Blunden. Faber and Faber, p.100.
65   11 July, 1807 – 18 January, 1886.
66   22 May, 1790 – 5 December, 1836.
67   Chorley, Henry F. (1854). *Modern German Music*, 2 vols. (reprinted Da Capo Press, 1973), Vol. 1. p.299.
68   It is far from clear what Formes meant by this.

Juive,' when 'Eleazar' prays at the table, and in the same act, in the duo with 'Eudoxia,' 'A chain of gold,' then in the F minor phrase of the curse in the last act, when he asks, 'Recha, my daughter, wilt thou live,' his rendering of these scenes was such, so true, so wonderful, that, after all these years, I am moved when I think of it – so terribly real in 'the curse,' so intense the pain and love in the last-mentioned phrase. [...] His 'Florestan' in 'Fidelio' I have never heard equaled. In the 'Freischütz,' his 'Lives there no God' was almost appalling in its intensity, he made so much of passages which generally pass unnoticed. In Weber's 'Euryanthe,' in the duo between Adolar and Lysar, is a recitative, which was one of his most remarkable performances. In Wagnerian operas, I have never heard his equal; Lohengrin, Tannhäuser, Rienzi – never will his equal be heard.[69]

Rienzi was first performed in Dresden on 20 October, 1842. Wagner had hoped to see it staged at the Opéra, where he would have struggled to find the singers necessary to do justice to his ambition. At the Semperoper, however, Wagner had access to his boyhood heroine, Schröder-Devrient, and Tichatschek, of whom he recalled:

His brisk and lively nature, his glorious voice and great musical talent, gave special weight to his encouraging assurance that he delighted in the role of Rienzi. Heine also told me that the mere prospect of having many new costumes, and especially new silver armour, had inspired Tichatschek with the liveliest desire to play this part, so that I might rely on him under any circumstances.

Wagner worked with Tichatschek for more than six years in Dresden. With the exception of *Der fliegende Holländer*, all of Wagner's mature operas were written after he had come to know Tichatschek's voice almost as well as his own. The stimulus for building his operas around "monstrous" tenor roles can be attributed, therefore, to Tichatschek, who not only had the voice, but the memory necessary for tackling Wagner's epic music dramas. The composer was not alone in marvelling at Tichatschek's capacity for reading and retaining extremely complex music at sight. Wagner was intensely appreciative of Tichatschek's acuity, particularly after the disaster that was *Das Liebesverbot*. The tenor's training with Ciccimarra was typically Italianate, and rooted in the technical foundations that explain, in part, the tenor's longevity. During his first years in Dresden he sang primarily French opera, notably *Les Huguenots*, *Le fidèle berger* (Adam), *Le brasseur de Preston* (Adam), *Le serment*, (Adam) and *Guido et Ginevra* (Halévy).[70] He also sang Weber (Adolar and Max) – and then to great acclaim during the 1842–3 season, during which *Rienzi* was

---

69 Formes, Karl (1891). *My Memoirs. Autobiography of Karl Formes*. James H. Barry. pp.107–08. While Formes may reasonably be believed in this recollection, his autobiography is otherwise of the school of Baron Munchausen.

70 For a detailed account of Tichatschek's repertoire, see Hochmuth, Michael (1998). *Chronik der Dresdner Oper*. Verlag Dr. Kovač.

first staged. Wagner and Tichatschek became life-long friends, and the composer was generous in his memoirs when attaching *Rienzi's* success to his lead tenor:

> When I thus pondered what had really caused the success of my *Rienzi*, I concluded that it was the result of the glorious, electrifying voice of the tirelessly exuberant singer.

Glorious, electrifying and tireless; it may reasonably be said that the last of these qualities was a particular value for *Rienzi* – the first performance of which lasted six hours (with intervals). The title role obligates a tenor to sing for almost an hour. Tichatschek apparently grew in stature and amplitude with each of the five acts, something for which Wagner must have accounted – since the highlight of the role, if not the entire work, is Act 5's extraordinarily beautiful *"Allmächt'ger Vater, blick herab."*[71] The role of Rienzi is the longest for a tenor by Wagner, with the exception of *Siegfried* and *Tristan und Isolde*; it was almost certainly the most demanding of any, in terms of stamina, to 1842. Even Rossini's Arnold sings for fewer than forty minutes. Wagner's admiration for the Italian school – and for what became known as *bel canto* – has been downplayed, and many are happy to forget that he was a lifelong admirer of Bellini, whose melodic genius he held in high regard. Wagner and Tichatschek agreed on the primacy of lyricism, and of melody – which flows throughout each of Wagner's operas. Even though the composer had access to a tenor who appears never to have suffered from fatigue, that tenor was Italian-trained, so Wagner was careful to manage his resources, committing the greater part of the role to the first, second, and fifth acts. *Rienzi* is gruelling only in its duration, therefore, with the composer's orchestrations at this stage in his career proportionate to the size of the available ensemble: three piccolos, three flutes, two oboes, three clarinets, three bassoons, one contrabassoon, four horns, four trumpets, three trombones, a tuba, a harp, timpani, bass drum, cymbal, side drum, tenor drum, tam-tam, triangle and strings. This was still an extravagant orchestra for Dresden in 1842; even so, much of the writing is less dense than in *Der Freischütz*; indeed, at times it is almost cautious, with few cases of singers having to compete with the orchestra in *tutti* or, even, by punctuation. In recitative, the tenor has to sing out rarely, and in ensemble the writing is crafted so that a singer submitting to fatigue can be carried. Though sung commonly by *heldentenors*, the role is only putatively baritonal – with just four D4s and 33 A4s.[72] The *tessitura* is relatively high, therefore, but never florid, and the few declamatory moments are subsumed to a lyricism that speaks to Tichatschek's talents (and his Italian training) as well as to Wagner's prejudices. The composer admitted:

> The special tenor sound of Tichatschek remained decisive for me for all times and may have contributed to the fact that I – which I often regretted later – wrote the leading parts in my works for this type of voice.[73]

---

71 'Almighty Father, look down!'
72 Watson, Brian James (2005). *Wagner's Heldentenors: Uncovering the Myths*. University of Texas. p.65.
73 Hey, Julius (1911). *Richard Wagner als Vortragsmeister*. Breitkopf & Härtel. p.136.

Insofar as he based his writing for tenor on Tichatschek's art, it's certain that the composer's concern for *legato* sustained his obsession for the clarity of his words. Wagner's heroine, Schröder-Devrient, helped shape his acceptance of the *limited* value of *Sprechgesang* – which she employed for dramatic effect when creating the roles of Senta and Venus[74] – and it is common still for audiences (and surprisingly large numbers of musicians) to think of Wagner's music as lacking in melody. His instincts and inclinations nonetheless remained definitively lyrical until the final bars of *Parsifal*. The issue of scale and context that caused the shifting of the "Wagnerian" perspective during the 1860s and 70s was clearly a feature of the composer's thinking in the 1840s. The reluctance of many to concede the lyrical in Wagner's voice-writing throughout *Tristan*, the *Ring* and *Parsifal* is to forget that the composer of "*Amfortas! Die Wunde! Die Wunde!*"[75] also wrote "*Allmächt'ger Vater.*"

Having established the foundations of a near-ideal working relationship with Tichatschek, Wagner's next opera, *Tannhäuser*, was again written for his very particular talents. He met the challenge head on, achieving an extraordinary success for the composer. Of Tichatschek's first performance of *Tannhäuser*, Wagner recalled how the Rome narrative from Act 3 "was delivered with his customary rhetorical amplitude of tone and with such force that it was a joy to hear the accompanying trombones completely dominated by the singer."[76] Tichatschek was not without his flaws, however:[77]

> Hence the need of great moderation and breadth in the conception of the music; first, in order that according to my principle it might prove helpful rather than the reverse to the understanding of the poetical lines, and secondly, in order that the increasing rhythmic character of the melody which marks the ardent growth of passion may not be interrupted too arbitrarily by unnecessary changes in modulation and rhythm. Hence, too, the need of a very sparing use of orchestral instruments for the accompaniment, and an intentional suppression of all those purely musical effects which must be utilised, and that gradually, only when the situation becomes so intense that one almost ceases to think, and can only feel the tragic nature of the crisis. No-one could deny that I had contrived to produce the proper effect of this principle the moment I played the Sangerkrieg on the piano. With the view of ensuring all my future successes, I was now confronted with the exceptional difficulty of making the opera singers understand how to interpret their parts precisely in the way I desired. I remembered how, through lack of experience, I had neglected properly to superintend the production of *Der fliegende Holländer,* and as I now fully realised all the disastrous

---

74 Fischer, Jens Malte (1992). "Sprechgesang or Bel Canto: Toward a History of Singing Wagner." Trans. Michael Tanner. In *Wagner Handbook*, ed. Ulrich Müller and Peter Wapnewski. Trans. John Deathridge. Harvard University Press. p.527.
75 'Amfortas! The Wound! The Wound!'
76 *Richard Wagner: My Life* (1983). Eds. Mary Whittall and Andrew Gray. Cambridge University Press. p.311.
77 *Ibid.*

consequences of this neglect, I began to think of means by which I could teach the singers my own interpretation. I have already stated that it was impossible to influence Tichatschek, for if he were made to do things he could not understand, he only became nervous and confused. He was conscious of his advantages. He knew that with his metallic voice he could sing with great musical rhythm and accuracy, while his delivery was simply perfect. But, to my great astonishment, I was soon to learn that all this did not by any means suffice; for, to my horror, at the first performance, that which had strangely escaped my notice in the rehearsals became suddenly apparent to me. At the close of the Sangerkrieg, when Tannhäuser (in frantic excitement, and forgetful of everybody present) has to sing his praise to Venus, and I saw Tichatschek moving towards Elizabeth and addressing his passionate outburst to her, I thought of Schröder-Devrient's warning in very much the same way as Croesus must have thought when he cried, 'O Solon! Solon!' at the funeral pyre. In spite of the musical excellence of Tichatschek, the enormous life and melodic charm of the Sangerkrieg failed entirely.

Tichatschek was a flawed *imprimatur*. For all his talents as a vocalist, his weakness as a stage actor was fatal for a composer whose conception of the *Gesamtkunstwerk*[78] necessitated the fluent integration of every dramatic element in parity. It's a resonant theme of Wagner's book *Oper und Drama* (completed in 1851) that subordination to a common musico-dramatic purpose began with the word – and the word was Wagner's no less than his music. In 1852, he wrote in his essay "On the performing of *Tannhäuser*" that every cast member should familiarise themselves with the text before even thinking to look at the score. It is to be rehearsed as a spoken play, therefore; only when the expressive sounding of the words is mastered as speech can a singer be fit to consider its performance as opera. Tichatschek grasped these essential elements of text and music, which he studied in private with the composer, and when he sang in the premiere at the Königliches Court Theatre, in Dresden, on 19 October, 1845, the tenor produced for the composer one of the most satisfying performances of his career. He did so by way of compromise, bypassing any sense of Tannhäuser's conflict when torn between the sacred and the profane. This failure to grasp (and convey) the dramatic substance and momentum of the finale of Act 2, "*erbarm dich mein, der ach! so tief in Sünden,*"[79] led to Wagner cutting the passage entirely from the score. Even if Tichatschek was Wagner's model tenor in voice, it was a powerful stimulus – and life-long. In 1871, after completing the score of *Siegfried*, he lamented to the singer:

> When you study *Siegfried*, consider how disgraceful it is that I finished it too late for you. I always heard your voice alone in my imagination, and now who can take your place?[80]

---

78 He employed the term on only two occasions (in his 1849 essays "*Art and Revolution*" and "*The Artwork of the Future*") and then in the novel spelling "Gesammtkunstwerk."
79 'Have mercy on me, oh! So deep in sin.'
80 Letter from Wagner to Tichatschek, dated 20 July, 1871. In Verdino-Süllwold, Carla Maria (1989). *We Need a Hero! Heldentenors from Wagner's Time to the Present*. Weiala Press. p.51.

If Wagner is to be believed (and it would be in keeping with his nature that he was writing what his friend wanted to read), Tichatschek was the ideal not only for *Rienzi*, *Tannhäuser*, and *Lohengrin* – but also *Tristan* (which pre-dated *Siegfried*), Siegmund, Walther and *Parsifal*. It follows that Tichatschek was the singular model for an entire genre of tenor voice, one formed from a combination of values, spanning Italianate *legato*, Beethovenian diction, Weberian declamation and an amplitude that enabled the subjugation of trombones *en masse*. It might be difficult to reason how a tenor whose repertoire included Mozart's *Idomeneo*, Donizetti's *La Favorite*, Meyerbeer's *Le Prophète* and Verdi's *Ernani* might also have sung *Tristan* and *Siegfried* – particularly when there is nothing to suggest that Tichatschek's tenor was especially baritonal – and yet he does appear to be the only tenor with whom Wagner was ever consistently happy. In this regard, his brilliant, penetrating and tireless voice confirmed the origins of Wagner's instincts and the consistency of his expectations.[81]

Wagner's predilections were exemplified by the sublimely lyrical *Lohengrin* – which was, again, composed for Tichatschek. Another tenor, Karl Beck,[82] created the role, however – in Weimar, at the Staatskapelle, on 28 August, 1850. Wagner was in political isolation at the time and unable to assist with the production, which was staged and conducted by his friend (and *Kapellmeister* at the Staatskapelle since 1842) Franz Liszt. Though the opera was an immediate success, Beck was not. In fact, he was fed to the critical lions, with his reputation undone in consequence of the otherwise fêted premiere. Beck had trained as a pastry chef before turning to singing full time. He made his debut in 1838 and worked for a number of years in Prague and Saint Petersburg, at the Bolshoi, where he was highly regarded. In 1848, and after suffering from a prolonged throat infection (on which his declining abilities was commonly blamed), he appeared in Weimar, and secured the position of first tenor. It was obvious that all was not well when Beck requested that Liszt cut the second part of Act III's hypnotic monologue "*In fernem land.*"[83] By all accounts, it might have been better had the first part been cut also. Wagner received reports of Beck's failings while staying with his wife Minna in Zurich, at The Schwann – "watching the clock and closely following the hour."[84] In his memoir, he was careful not to mention Beck by name:[85]

---

81 Wagner considered cementing these through the establishment of a German-language school of singing, which he began to develop with the singing pedagogue Julius Hey. Hey and Wagner later collaborated for the first *Ring* cycle in 1876. In 1885 Hey published the four-volume *Deutsche Gesangunterricht*, which continues (by reduction) to be in common use. Potter, John (2009). *Tenor: History of a Voice*. Yale University Press. p.66.
82 1814 – 4 March, 1879.
83 'In a distant land'; also known as the "Grail Narration." This cut remained in place for almost a century. The second part was not heard at Bayreuth until Franz Völker performed the role in 1936, under the close scrutiny of the Festival's patron, Adolf Hitler.
84 *Richard Wagner: My Life* (1983). Eds. Mary Whittall and Andrew Gray. Cambridge University Press. p.453.
85 He was less considerate of his (then) wife, writing (presumably for the benefit of his current wife) that "I always felt somewhat distressed, uncomfortable, and ill at ease whenever I tried to pass a few pleasant hours in the society of my wife."

The reports received of that first performance gave me no clear or reassuring impression of it. Karl Ritter soon came back to Zurich and told me of deficiencies in staging and of the unfortunate choice of a singer for the leading part, but remarked that on the whole it had gone fairly well. The reports sent me by Liszt were the most encouraging. He did not seem to think it worthwhile to allude to the inadequacy of the means at his command for such a bold undertaking, but preferred to dwell on the sympathetic spirit that prevailed in the company and the effect it produced on the influential personages he had invited to be present.[86]

Beck's career did not recover; when Liszt met him in Prague in 1856 he was managing a coffee shop. The tenor's significance does not, for obvious reasons, attach to his work for Wagner. Rather, he is interesting because of his repertoire, which included *Otello*, *Ernani*, *Robert le diable*, Florestan and Max – as well as a wide range of works for which he was generically suitable. He failed utterly as Lohengrin. Eight years after the opera's first performance, Wagner finally heard the work as he had imagined it – with Tichatschek singing the title role.[87] Tichatschek was, again, his preference in 1867 (though he was almost 60 years old at the time) when Wagner staged an "ideal" production of *Lohengrin* for Ludwig II. The Composer was typically thrilled with Tichatschek's singing during rehearsals; for his part, Ludwig was repulsed by the tenor's appearance and stage-movement (describing him as "the Knight of the Rueful Countenance"[88]) and demanded his replacement. Tichatschek's stand-in was Heinrich Vogl.[89]

Tichatschek had been born in 1807; Beck just seven years later. Vogl was 38 years *younger* than Tichatschek. In terms of repertoire, Tichatschek and Beck were the last tenors to sing Wagner in equivalence with everything else. Vogl was the first of a new breed of tenor defined by a career that began and ended with the music of a single composer: Richard Wagner. As such, Vogl was the first true *heldentenor*. The *Musical Times* on 1 June, 1900, reported Vogl's death (as it did the passing of Hermann Levi, the conductor of the first *Parsifal*, who died a week earlier) and observed in passing that Vogl was successful as a singer of oratorio. Other than Bach, however, the only composer referenced by name was Wagner.[90] In 1868, less than twelve months after the composer's perfected staging of *Lohengrin* for Ludwig II, Vogl was nevertheless overlooked for the role of Walther in the first production in Munich of *Der*

---

86 *Richard Wagner: My Life* (1983). Eds. Mary Whittall and Andrew Gray. Cambridge University Press.
87 In a letter to his friend Wilhelm Fischer (chorus master in Dresden), he wrote on 29 April, 1856: "*T. has at last sang the Lohengrin – gave me great joy! I certainly was not mistaken when, in writing that part, I foresaw that it would be one of his best! Only, what a pity that I could not give a performance of the opera with him, and, instead, must leave it to bunglers to create the part. I willingly believe, that even now Tichatschek is the best in it, and again, willingly would be present when he sings it.*" In *Richard Wagner's Letters to his Dresden Friends*. Trans. J. S. Shedlock. Vienna House. p.409.
88 Newman, Ernest (1947 (1976)). *The Life of Richard Wagner*, Volume IV: 1866–1883. Cambridge University Press. p.77.
89 15 January, 1845 – 21 April, 1900.
90 Vogl did, of course, sing other repertoire – all of it "heavy," including *Otello*, Aeneas in *Les Troyens* and *Benvenuto Cellini* – but he did so relatively infrequently, and to no great effect. He continued to add to his repertoire, including the verismo role of Canio – which he performed four days before his untimely death.

Meistersinger – on the grounds that the composer thought him "totally incompetent." His unsuitability for the role of a man did not preclude him from playing a god, however. The following year Wagner cast Vogl as the first Loge for the premiere of *Das Rheingold* at the Bayerischen Staatsoper, on 22 September, 1869. The following year, on 26 June, Vogl was the first Siegmund in *Die Walküre*, again in Munich. He was 25 years old at the time. Vogl was Loge for the first complete *Ring* at Bayreuth, on August 13, 1876 (although another tenor was cast as Siegmund) and he created both Loge and Siegfried for London's first *Ring* cycle in 1882, conducted by Anton Seidl. After dismissing the general "executive" failure of Neumann's production, the Bayreuth Correspondent of the *Musical Times* asked whether it was necessary

> to admit the enormous talent shown by Wagner in carrying out his ideas? Surely not. The time has gone by for sneering at this man. We may condemn his principles as inimical to the best interests of art, but we must do so with profound respect for the ability with which they are enforced. For my own part I see in the music to the 'Nibelung's Ring' a latter-day phenomenon – a fact as indicative of sturdy life in an age sometimes called limp, as of a restless striving after hitherto unattained good. The only cause for complaint and regret is that Richard Wagner's powerful faculties, controlled by an overwhelming self-consciousness, are devoted to the establishment of a new creed having no support in traditions sprung from the nature of things; no support in the practice of the greatest masters, and none anywhere save from quidnuncs[91], and those who approach the matter on the side of 'philosophy, falsely so-called.'[92]

It's certain the Bayreuth Correspondent had read Wagner's infamous *Das Judenthum in der Musik*,[93] in the course of which the author coruscated Meyerbeer, Mendelssohn and the Jewish people ubiquitously for having insufficient cultural and geographical roots to be able to create great (or German) art, so it's reasonable to delight in the same allegation being directed at *Der Meister*. The Correspondent can be trusted, therefore, when observing of Vogl that he was

> a Loge of the highest class. This artist's impersonation of the subtle Fire-god at Bayreuth, in 1876, made a deep impression, but he has since improved upon it, till now it ranks among the most finished efforts in lyric drama. Herr Vogl sings, or perhaps we should say declaims, as well as he acts, and altogether his performance will be long remembered.[94]

The Bayreuth Correspondent compared Vogl to his replacement in 1876:

---

91 Another word for 'a gossip.'
92 *The Musical Times and Singing Class Circular*, Vol. 23, No. 472 (1 June, 1882). p.323.
93 Published anonymously in 1850, and under Wagner's name in 1869.
94 *The Musical Times and Singing Class Circular*, Vol. 23, No. 472 (1 June, 1882). p.322.

> The Siegfried of Bayreuth exceeded in bodily height him of Her Majesty's Theatre, and would be called a "finer man," but Herr Georg Unger has, in other respects, no advantage over Herr Heinrich Vogl, who played throughout with rare spirit and dignity. He delivered the Sword Song in splendid style, but, as a vocal artist, was heard to best advantage in the scene with Brunnhilde. Here there was singing to be done, and Herr Vogl rose to the occasion, showing himself qualified for the lyric stage [...]. Herr Vogl again commanded admiration by his spirited and appropriate embodiment of the hero, whose native grandeur of soul appeared in all he did....[95]

Writing of Vogl's performance at Bayreuth of *Tristan* on 27 July, 1886, the celebrated critic Richard Pohl held that it was

> a recognized masterpiece. His whole vocal and dramatic conception of the role – with a knightly, noble, yet also gentle tone – is so exceptional, that immediately in his first scene of the first act the characterization of Vogl's Tristan is totally comprehensible to us.[96]

Three years later, however, George Bernard Shaw wrote of Vogl's *Tristan* in London:

> In the third act again Vogl surpassed Charles II, in point of being an unconscionably long time dying. Wagner's heros [sic] have so much to say that if they have not several ways of saying it (Vogl has exactly two – a sentimental way and a vehement way) the audience is apt to get into that temper which, at the English public meetings, finds vent in cries of "Time!"[97]

When Shaw was sent to review the 1889 Bayreuther Festspiele, he wrote that Vogl as Tristan and Gudehus as Walther (in *Der Meistersinger*):

> proved themselves as capable as ever of carrying through two very heavy tenor parts; but though their conscientiousness and intelligence were beyond praise, they are neither young nor youthful (it is possible to be either without being the other), and their voices lack variety and charm.[98]

It is here that Shaw alights on Wagner's eternal problem – and the problem faced ever since by anyone staging the *Ring*, *Tristan* or *Parsifal*. In 1889, Vogl was 44 years old – at which age he was thought to be tired and lacking in "variety and charm." As the singer who created the roles of Loge and Siegfried for Wagner, it might be

---

95 *Ibid*, p.323.
96 "Cosima Wagner's Bayreuth," in *Richard Wagner and His World* (2009). Ed. Thomas S. Grey. Princeton University Press. p.443.
97 Shaw, Bernard (1981). *Shaw's Music: The Complete Musical Criticism of Bernard Shaw*. Ed. Dan H. Laurence. The Bodley Head. Vol. I (1876 – 1890). p.725.
98 *Ibid*. p.805.

assumed that he would qualify in his 40s as the ideal *heldentenor*. Manifestly, he wasn't – because Wagner chose Albert Niemann to sing Siegmund in the first *Die Walküre* at Bayreuth in 1876, when Vogl was still only 31 years old. Niemann was acclaimed a sensation by Lilli Lehmann, and despite his voice being considered finished before that date by Camille Saint-Saëns, he was hailed a decade later – by W. J. Henderson after the first performance on 1 December, 1886, of *Tristan* in New York – for having poured "into the last act […] as he did in the death of Siegfried, the vials of all agonies. He was heart-rending."

Vogl was a fine actor, possessed of a powerful voice. By the standards of his time he was obese, which fact did nothing to dent his exceptional stamina; there are reports of him singing Loge, Siegmund and *both* Siegfrieds on consecutive evenings.[99] He was clearly more declamatory than lyrical, however,[100] and in this feature of his artistry he represented the onset of a Wagnerian tradition – cultivated as much by the music as by the size of the composer's orchestra. A Wagner pit compels amplitude and projection from a tenor as much as (or in place of) clarity and beauty – even if Wagner attached more value to the latter criteria than the former. Indeed, Wagner obsessed over the audibility and dramatic value of his *stabreim*, placing a sign in the wings of the Festpielhaus that read "The big notes will take care of themselves; the little ones and the text are the chief things."[101] The little and the big were scored for piccolo, three flutes (with the third doubling the second piccolo), three oboes, *cor anglais* (doubling the fourth oboe), three clarinets, one bass clarinet, three bassoons, eight horns (with the fifth to the eighth doubling Wagner tubas), three trumpets, one bass trumpet, three tenor trombones, one contrabass trombone (doubling bass trombone), one contrabass tuba, percussion with 4 timpani (requiring two players), triangle, cymbals, glockenspiel, six harps, and a string section consisting of at least 16 first and second violins, 12 violas, 12 violoncellos, and eight double basses. Each part of the cycle makes unique additional requirements – with *Götterdämmerung* calling for five onstage horns and four onstage steerhorns, one of them for use by Hagen. These demands have grown in tandem with the scale and volume of wind and brass instruments since 1900, with modern orchestras generating health and safety litigation as well as increases in amplitude.

The *heldentenor* is well named because Wagner's mature works call for heroic strength and stamina – and a sound (and demeanour) that can be said to be normatively masculine. Wagner more than once used variants of the word *männlich*, and regardless of a character's contextual attachment to purity and innocence, his writing for his leading tenors is in every case determined by the reductive but absolute conception of a "real man." When answering his own question "How should the

---

99 After the death of Schnorr von Carolsfeld, Vogl would became the next Tristan – and he remained the leading interpreter much of the 19th century.

100 Vogl was famously dragged over the coals by Hugo Wolf for "*the most hellish racket of the most unlubricated coach on our potholed pavement.*" Breckbill, David (1992). "Wagner on Record: Re-evaluating Singing in the Early Years", In *Wagner in Performance*. Eds. Barry Millington and Stewart Spencer. Yale University Press. p.161.

101 Shawe-Taylor, Desmond (1992). "Wagner and His Singers," In *Wagner in Performance*. Eds. Barry Millington and Stewart Spencer. Yale University Press. p.15.

masculine voice [...] respond to the challenges presented by today's German art?," he replied:

> Coming from a tradition that privileges physicality and sensuousness, it sees [in German art] only more demands on the [singer's] physical strength and endurance, and the modern singing teacher therefore makes it his priority to produce voices that can meet those demands. It's easy to see how misguided this is, for any male voice trained only to be powerful will, in attempting to respond to the challenges of the new German music [...] soon tire and fail if the singer is not fully alive to the spiritual dimension of those challenges.[102]

Wagner's conception of spirituality was indivisible from that quasi-Christian Teutonism that perceived masculinity as inherently German; in consequence, any sense of maleness was bonded to power and resonance. For Wagner's heroic tenors, this necessitated a baritonal timbre as well as a metallic "ping." It was by this construction that he was inspired to craft the deceitful and wicked Mime in *Das Rheingold* and *Siegfried* as a *high* tenor, a role performed at the first performances in 1869 and 1876, respectively, by Max Schlosser – a celebrated Almaviva.[103] The juxtaposition of a "whining" Mime was, an unsubtle reference to the contemporary (but long-standing) German conception of male Jewish voices as being thin, high and absent masculinity – a prejudice formed in part by the cantorial traditions that had resonated for many years throughout German-language synagogues. The isolation of the "feminised [male] Jew" that would propel Otto Weininger to draft his disturbing and influential *Geschlecht und Charakter (Sex and Character)*[104] in 1903 was pre-empted by Wagner in a number of creative ways, most obviously in Mime's high tenor and Beckmesser's strained baritone in *Der Meistersinger* – the latter set purposefully in opposition with Sachs' bass-baritone and Walther von Stolzing's *heldentenor*.

Wagner's use of a pressurised male voice to convey Jewishness was not lost on Richard Strauss, who did much the same thing when scoring four of his five "Jews" in *Salome* in 1905 as shrieking tenors.[105] The virility of Wagner's heroes was hard-wired culturally and vocally, but the isolation and co-ordination of power and beauty from within the available coterie of singers proved to be as elusive as dark matter. Contrary to long-standing conjecture, true *heldentenors* were as rare in the 19th century as they are in the 21st. The demands of tone, breath control and phrasing compelled by the densest and lengthiest scenes in *Tristan* (such as the Act 2 love duet), *Die Walküre* (most of Act 1), and *Siegfried* (most of Act 3) were without precedent at the time, and they remain unparalleled in the operatic canon – such that anyone capable of pulling

---

102 Quoted in Henson, Karen (2015). *Opera Acts*. Cambridge University Press. p.124.
103 17 October, 1835 – 2 September, 1916. Schlosser also sang as a baritone, but his voice was said to be very light in weight and placement. His career was vast in its length. He joined the Bayerischen Staatsoper in 1868 and remained with the company until 1904 - when he gave his farewell performance singing the Nightwatchman in *Die Meistersinger*.
104 Weininger, Otto (1903). *Geschlecht und Charakter: Eine prinzipielle Untersuchung*. Wilhelm Braumüller.
105 See generally Boyden, Matthew (1999). *Richard Strauss*. Weidenfeld & Nicolson.

a single rabbit from the hat will rarely wear another. Even surviving the experience of learning, rehearsing and performing a tenor role by Wagner is an achievement, as noted in an imagined review from the future by Friedrich Wieck (Clara Schumann's father) in 1853:

> The Tannhäuser was in especially good voice, and in the first act seemed intent upon exhausting his resources, as if he wished to sacrifice himself to his noble mission as an artist. In the last act, however, there was visible and audible fatigue, with conspicuous departures from exact intonation, compensated by vigorous declamation.[106]

The reality of Wagner's expectations was immediate and well-evidenced. Indeed, the most celebrated heldentenor of them all is remembered for having died five weeks after creating the role of Tristan on 10 June, 1865 at the Königliches Court and National Theatre, Munich. Tristan is compared commonly by those who sing it to climbing Everest. By this analogy Ludwig Schnorr von Carolsfeld[107] warrants comparison with George Mallory as well as Edmund Hillary. He was born into a celebrated and talented family of painters; his father, Julius, and his uncle, Ludwig Ferdinand, had both known Beethoven,[108] and Ludwig was immersed in the arts at home as well as the Kreuzschule in Dresden – Wagner's *alma mater*. Although he was at liberty to do anything he wanted, given the family's status and influence, he chose to sing. Incredibly, he did so professionally from the age of 19, making his debut in 1855. He completed his apprenticeship performing the established German repertoire of Florestan, Max, Tannhäuser, Lohengrin and Erik (in *Der fliegende Holländer*), which brought him to the attention of Tichatschek, who informed Wagner in 1856 that he had heard "his successor."[109] Wagner considered Schnorr less perfect vocally than Tichatschek, but he had greater dramatic power and (more importantly) an acute theatrical intelligence. In other words, Schnorr understood the primacy of text and subtext within the organising principle of Wagner's *Gesamtkunstwerk*. Schnorr's voice was renowned for its baritonal colour (Wagner described it as "full, soft and gleaming") and seamless *legato*. He was the Wagnerian ideal, therefore.

Some *heldentenors* have switched from baritone to tenor in the hope of retaining the weight and security of the middle register. This has not always worked, since the *passaggio* for a *heldentenor* (comparable to the *tenore robusto* or *di forza* in Italian opera) sits around F4 / G4. The need for physical strength (which the vast Schnorr had in abundance) assisted with stamina; technique was equally necessary when accounting for some of the higher writing – particularly in *Tristan*. These requirements have often compelled a trade-off between heft and pitching above the stave – with straining and "throatiness" infecting the voices of many alleged *heldentenors* who have been something else entirely. Not much separates the *heldentenor* and baritone

---

106   Pleasants, Henry (1974). *The Great Singers*. Gollancz. p. 227.
107   2 July, 1836 – 21 July, 1865.
108   Ludwig Schnorr sketched the composer in 1809.
109   Newman, Ernest (1978 (1947)). *The Life of Richard Wagner*, Volume IV: 1866–1883. Cambridge University Press. p.453.

*tessitura*s, therefore, such that anything less than sufficiency is likely to be inaudible. *Tristan* is uniquely arduous, with the tenor's score in isolation compelling almost an hour's singing – twice as much as Verdi's *Otello* – and then above orchestrations that present a gruelling challenge of churning, overlaid voicing. Tristan is on stage, for considerably longer also.

During the third scene of Act II, his monologue "*O König, das kann ich dir nicht sagen*"[110] is written high in the voice, and with marked lyricism; when he meets Isolde, and as he cries out her name, every instrument except the trumpets and the harp is joined either forte or fortissimo. Soon enough, and as the couple sing "*O Wonne!*"[111], the trumpets join the fray and all heaven breaks loose. The ensuing love duet is defined by Wagner's bewilderingly inventive orchestrations, which ebb and flow for almost 40 minutes, passing through breath-taking tenderness ("*O sink hernieder, Nacht der Liebe*"[112]) and almost disturbing intimacy ("*So starben wir, um ungetrennt*"[113]) – by way of Brangane's transcendent "warning" ("*Einsam wachend in der Nacht...Habet acht!*"[114]) – before dissolving into a percussive, boiling frenzy that only the most stentorian of tenors can hope to navigate. Both Tristan and Isolde are called upon to surf vast undulating waves of sound while attending throughout to rapidly exchanging and sometimes contrapuntal dialogue, all of it coloured by detailed dynamic markings, pronounced *legati* and forensic word-articulation. None of it can be performed by singers given to wailing, barking or yelling.

It has often been observed that Tristan's monologue in Act III did for Schnorr; this was merely a feature of Wagner's preposterous demands, however. Final rehearsals for *Tristan*'s first night were held over three days from Wednesday to Friday, 7–9 June, 1865. After the premiere, on the Saturday (which the production's conductor, Hans von Bülow, described as "Incredible") there were further performances on the 13th, 19th and 30th. Schnorr performed Erik in *Der fliegende Holländer* on 9 July, and at a concert three days later, conducted by Wagner, he performed extended scenes from *Das Rheingold, Die Walküre, Siegfried* and *Der Meistersinger*. On 13 July, he travelled to Dresden (where he was under contract) and rehearsals for a production of *Don Giovanni*. The following day, physically and mentally exhausted, Schnorr was struck down by rheumatic fever and died from a stroke a week later at the age of 29. His last words were recorded as "Farewell Siegfried! Console my Richard!".[115] Wagner was inconsolable – chiefly at his own loss. As he wrote to King Ludwig:

> He was a fine noble being, consecrated to me, faithful to me. The richly gifted artist became a theatre singer to be of service to me, to be able to further my work [...] I have lost so much.[116]

---

110   'O King, I cannot tell you that.'
111   'O joy!'
112   'Descend, O night of love.'
113   'Thus might we die, that together.'
114   'Alone, waking at night [...] Beware.'
115   Pleasants, Henry (1974). *The Great Singers*. Gollancz. p.229.
116   *Ibid*. p.231.

Schnorr's sacrifice – and his unquestioning devotion to the monstrous Wagner – render the story of the first production of *Tristan* almost as gripping as the opera. The first stagings of the *Ring* in 1876 and *Parsifal* in 1882 generated their own massive challenges, and extra-theatrical dramas, but no one died in the process – and the demands of each role, while considerable, were as nothing compared to *Tristan*. Albert Niemann[117] sang the first *Siegmund,* Georg Unger[118] the first *Siegfried* – in both of the character's operas; Hermann Winkelmann was the first *Parsifal*.[119]

Two of these men lived to see the 20th century; only one of them made records.[120] Winkelmann was a happy choice by Wagner for *Parsifal*. The tenor sang the role at Bayreuth until 1891, and then routinely with Amalie Materna, the first Kundry. He also created Tristan and Walther in London, and in 1883 he joined the Wiener Hofoper, where he remained until 1906, the year before his retirement. He made his first recordings for Berliner and the Gramophone & Typewriter Company, in Vienna, between 1900 and 1905 (at around the same age as Tamagno when he recorded his scenes from *Otello*). In addition to *"Einsam steh'ich und verlassen"* (a translation of *"deserto sulla terra"*) from *Il trovatore* and *"Blickst du mein Freund"*[121] from Act 1 of Smetana's *Dalibor*, he recorded *"Weilten die Sterne"*[122] and *"Morgenlich leuchtend"*[123] from *Die Meistersinger*, *"Dir, Göttin der Liebe, soll mein Lied ertöne"*[124] from *Tannhäuser*, and *"Höchstes Vertrauen Hast"*[125] from *Lohengrin*. Winkelmann's recordings are of a singer chosen and coached by Wagner himself to create the role of *Parsifal* in 1882. They are, for this reason alone, of staggering historical importance, and hugely revealing of what was heard decades earlier at Bayreuth when Levi conducted the premiere.

The passage of time is not without consequence, of course, even if Winkelmann was still performing on stage when he stood before the horn in his early 50s. As the "bravos" after *"Einsam steh'ich und verlassen"* suggest, he was still much admired when doing so. As with Tamagno, it falls to be asked: how good is Winkelmann's singing on record? Judging by his performance of Verdi's aria – in German, of course – the voice is poorly placed, absent focus and imperfectly pitched. The *tempi* adopted suggest that any contemporary performance in Vienna of *Il trovatore* would have run longer than *Parsifal*. The lack of *vibrato* is consistent with contemporary practice everywhere; it is more resonant still for the performance of works by a composer who valued his words

---

117   15 January, 1831 – 13 January, 1917.
118   1837 – 1887.
119   8 March, 1849 – 18 January, 1912. It should be noted that Wagner coached and rehearsed three tenors for the first run of performances. Winkelmann was first, but he was joined on the podium by Heinrich Gudehus (30 March, 1842 – 9 October, 1909) and Ferdinand Jäger (25 December, 1839 – 13 June, 1902).
120   Contrary to popular myth, Winkelmann was *not* the only tenor from the first production of Parsifal to make records. Adolf von Hübbenet (1858 – 17 February, 1903) sang the role of the First Squire in 1882. Winkelmann can be "heard" singing singing two interjections on Mapleson Cylinders as Mime (*Siegfried*) – from a performance at the New York Metropolitan on 19 March, 1901.
121   'Do you look upon my friend.'
122   'The stars remained.'
123   'Glowing in the morning.'
124   'My song shall sound to you, goddess of love.'
125   'You have already to thank me for the highest confidence.'

in equivalence with his music. Wagner's approach to *vibrato* is well-documented. In his scores for *Das Liebesverbot*, *Siegfried* and *Der Meistersinger*, he identified where he wanted *vibrato* – which means he didn't want it ubiquitously. He distinguished between *vibrato* and *tremolando*, which he detested[126] – while applauding (or tolerating) ornaments where they served the best interests of a favoured singer.

Winkelmann employs little *portamento* (although Wagner considered it indispensable to the singing of his music[127]) and despite the presence of a genuine *legato* his phrasing is otherwise rigid and heavy. Apart from a couple of skilful *gruppetti*,[128] the only quality for which his singing stands out is its diction, which is exemplary. The voice is definitely that of a tenor, with only a hint in the closing cadence of baritonal heft. The recording of "*Höchstes Vertraun hast*" is, again, remarkable because it evidences superb word-clarity; the performance is otherwise lumpen and deliberate. Indeed, the phrasing is square and lacking in anything like the sort of expressive beauty for which Wagner yearned. In short, his singing is declamatory and, at times, defined by the sort of heavy-handedness against which Wagner railed consistently. "*Morgenlich leuchtend*" does nothing to alter the general impression of a singer either uninterested in or incapable of the sort of "joined up" phrasing that would become routine from the 1930s. The prevalence of barked word-emphasis in "*Morgenlich*" is especially remarkable, given that this habit provoked Wagner's irritation long before Cosima's inheritance of the Festival in 1886. It is in this detail that her 20-year guardianship of the Festival is evidenced – with Wagner's origin mythologies subsumed to the new Bayreuth School, and an aggressively *regionale Kunst*. In 1892, Cosima collaborated with the choral conductor Julius Kniese to establish principles of pedagogy that prioritised clarity of text and declamation over what Wagner would have characterised with Julius Hey as German lyricism.[129] Unlike her husband, Cosima despised *bel canto* – which she employed as a "term of abuse"[130] – and with Kniese as her adjutant she required every singer performing at Bayreuth to focus on speech over song – something that would become known as *Sprechgesang*:[131]

> Our stage differs from all other operatic stages in Germany in having drama at the centre of all the performances that are given. We look upon as the means, not the end. Drama is the end, and the organ of drama is language […] and if there must be sacrifice at all […] sacrifice rather the music (singing) to the poem than the poem (language) to the music.[132]

---

126 Brown, Clive (1992). "Performing Practice," In *Wagner in Performance*. Eds. Barry Millington and Stewart Spencer. Yale University Press. p.110.
127 *Ibid.* p.110.
128 Turns; they seem oddly out of place in this context.
129 See generally: Parr, Sean M. (2019). "Wagnerian Singing and the Limits of Vocal Pedagogy." *Current Musicology*, 105.
130 Fischer, Jens Malte (1992). "Sprechgesang or Bel Canto: Toward a History of Singing Wagner." Trans. Michael Tanner. In *Wagner Handbook*, Eds. Ulrich Müller and Peter Wapnewski. Trans. John Deathridge. Harvard University Press. pp.524–546.
131 'Speech-song.'
132 Potter, John (2009). *Tenor: History of a Voice*. Yale University Press. p.66.

The primacy of diction over line led to singers "spitting" their consonants with such ferocity that *Konsonanten-Spuckerei* became the preferred vocal mechanism around 1900 for singing Wagner's music.[133] The "Bayreuth Bark" was symptomatic of dilapidation as well as fashion; a singer suffering from age or fatigue will descend commonly to declamation as a means of compensation; consider, for example, the crises faced by Astrid Varnay and Sherrill Milnes. Because Cosima's Bayreuth was the source of a singing style that placed clarity above beauty,[134] Winkelmann's recordings in 1900 communicate little of the aesthetics from which he (like everyone else working on the Green Hill between 1886 and 1906) had been forced to turn by the prescriptions of "new management." It's possible that Winkelmann's work for Wagner in 1882 (when he was 33 years old) differed conceptually with what he did when making recordings in his 50s because he knew that Cosima would likely hear them. Even so, and while accepting the glorious fulfilment of Beethoven and Weber's dreams of a German operatic tradition formed around the primacy of the German language, it is close to inarguable that Völker, Melchior, Lorenz, Windgassen, Jerusalem and Kaufmann have all sung the Wagner excerpts recorded by Winkelmann significantly if not incomparably better. Indeed, the technical and expressive range adopted on record by the first Parsifal suggests that his singing in 1882 of Act 2's "*Amfortas! die Wunde*"[135] was brittle, rigid and wholly disconnected from the extraordinary, surging lyricism flowing from the pit beneath him. It is well-known that Wagner moaned often of his tenors – even the apparently stupendous Vogl – so there was clearly more to the critical consideration of tenor singing in Bayreuth than tone, line and diction. There is a clue in the conductor Anton Seidl's estimation of Vogl's performance of *Parsifal* in Bayreuth on 2 August, 1886:

> He is indisputably the best Parsifal who has ever walked upon the Bayreuth stage [...] His exclamation in Act 3 "*Und ich—ich bin's, der all dies Elend schuf!*"[136] was unquestionably inadequate; it was not strong, emphatic, and grievous enough. I must also admit that the painful, terrible cry in Act 2 "*Amfortas—die Wunde!*" so important to the entire drama, was more gripping when Gudehus sang it this year than when sung on this occasion by Vogl, who evidently needed to spare his voice. What raises Vogl's Parsifal far above that of both his colleagues is the marvellous, pithy way in which he brings out the religious dimension. The individual traits comprising the figure, and certain episodes in the plot, gained a depth and religious solemnity that I have long thought I could only imagine. In his religiosity he had a grandeur, a moral gravitas and noble dignity that raise this character above all other Wagner heroes! The various little acting and singing mannerisms this artist has unfortunately relied on too much of late (though the Munich critics

---

133 See generally: Parr, Sean M. (2019). *Wagnerian Singing and the Limits of Vocal Pedagogy*. Current Musicology, 105. p.58.
134 Spotts, Frederic (1994). *Bayreuth: A History of the Wagner Festival*. Yale University Press. p.99.
135 'Amfortas! The wound!'
136 'And it is I, I, who caused all this woe!'

seem to have overlooked them) were all at once—if I may use a common expression—"blown away": nothing of that kind disrupted the general impression, and a unified, grand, and ideal effect was created. How true to life he was, for example, as the lad Parsifal, his childlike naïveté and vitality! How eloquent his silence during the Grail ceremony! (The clutching at his heart during the most agonized of Amfortas' cries—a detail so significant for the later development of the character—could have been made more noticeable and hence clearer to the audience, however.[137]

Second-guessing what a conductor known to Wagner, and identified as one of "the chosen few," might have said of the performance of a work that he came to know while clinging to the Master's hem is profitless. And yet Seidl's comments attach themselves entirely to Vogl's voice-acting and stage movement, with little of meaning arising from the placement or use, even, of his voice as an instrument to convey what is otherwise portrayed through word and movement alone. There is little against which to measure Vogl's talents when compared to Winkelmann – save that Seidl pays admiring tribute to Vogl's clawing at his chest, a stage action that would become associated with the worst of ham acting fewer than 15 years into the new century. It is eternally tempting to assume that what was done by – and for – Richard Wagner established certainties and touchstones that would never be met or equalled again, just as Liszt remains the greatest pianist in history and Paganini its most perfect violinist. Winkelmann's recordings allow for the isolation of objective criteria against which everything else may be compared, albeit not in absolute equivalence. On point: when performing *Parsifal* in New York in 2013, did Jonas Kaufmann sing the title role more expressively and with greater musical intelligence and technical confidence – so as to reveal more of the psychology of the role and its character through the music – than either Vogl or Winkelmann 131 years earlier? Was Kaufmann's singing more rhapsodic, his voice-placement more secure and his tone more beautiful than *all* of his 19th century predecessors collectively? Is it possible that he reached further towards the suffering imagined by Parsifal during the passage beginning "*Des Heilands Klage da vernehm' ich, die Klage, ach!*"[138]?

With apologies to Wagner: "*Ja, diese Stimme! ... deutlich erkenn' ich ihn.*"[139]

---

137 "Cosima Wagner's Bayreuth," in *Richard Wagner and His World* (2009). Ed. Thomas S. Grey. Princeton University Press. p.452.
138 'The Saviour's lament I hear there, the lament, ah!'
139 'Yes! This was the voice. ... Truly I recognise it'. (Act 2, Scene 2).

CHAPTER SEVEN

Johannes Factotum

"If Raymond Massey offered you a cigarette, it would be a De Reszke[1] – of course!" The same offer was made variously by George Formby, Jr., Henry Hall, Gracie Fields and a host of other performers whose fame was employed during the 1940s to promote a cigarette named after another star long-since extinguished. Jean De Reszke was the first international celebrity to sing opera, a tenor whose name and reputation reached far beyond the arena in which he first became famous. His status as a man of talent and refinement was purchased by a Russian émigré, J. Millhoff, who helped transform the cigarette industry through advertising and endorsement, and by the use of celebrity as a merchantable commodity. Millhoff's use of De Reszke as an actual brand reached its apogee during WW1, when just about every British serviceman smoked De Reszke cigarettes. In peacetime, the company made a compelling case for the sophistication of its product by the use of The De Reszke's status as a man of taste. De Reszke was purported to be "the Aristocrat of Cigarettes [...] blended to cause no harm to the throat and to give pleasure to the discriminating palate.[2] It's a gruesome thought that one of the most revered singers of his – or any – generation should have committed himself over decades to the promotion of a "harmless" pleasure that caused a catastrophic increase in the incidence of throat and lung cancers. Fortunately for De Reszke, he died four years before Fritz Lickint published the first formal statistical description of the connection between cancer and tobacco.[3]

The use and abuse of De Reszke's status and reputation by Millhoff is especially intriguing because the singer retired from the stage in 1904. Sold as "Tenor" ('large'), "Basso" ('extra large') and "Soprano" ('ladies'), the cigarettes were marketed in the United States as "the 'De Reszke' AMERICAN Cigarette, which is recognised in the Trade as the finest cigarette of its kind in England." Elsewhere, Milhoff advertised in Europe and the US on the basis that the sale and purchase of De Reszke products was an internationalist expression of "real solace [and] pleasantly prophetic of the coming Trade Entente between great nations." The values attached symbolically by Milhoff to De Reszke's status over hundreds of adverts and an evolving range of packaging designs were amplified by the implication that "his" cigarettes were smoked in the White House, Buckingham Palace, the Kremlin and the Weimar Reichstag – none of which were to remain *entente* or, for that matter, *cordiale*, for much longer. For

---

1   14 January, 1850 – 3 April, 1925.
2   Imperial War Museum Archive and Research Room. See also Green, Leanne (2015). *Advertising War: Pictorial Publicity, 1914 – 1918*; PhD Thesis (Manchester Metropolitan University (MIRIAD).
3   Lickint, Fritz (1929). *"Tabak und Tabakrauch als ätiologischer Factor des Carcinoms."* Zeitschrift für Krebsforschung. pp.349–65.

many years, the company employed as its personification various illustrations of a tall, thin, Emily-Postian-type that might have looked like De Reszke from across a smoke-addled salon.[4] Milhoff promoted the brand using a cypher for the artist as *Le propre de l'homme* – a commendably sharp decision after the volcanic arrival of the Calibanesque Enrico Caruso. De Reszke was also much less expensive, as a tolerably exotic retiree performing for a generation unable to hear him sing on '78s. As the last significant tenor not to make records, De Reszke's status was uniquely reputational; for anyone not among the relative few to have heard him live, his status as the "world's greatest tenor" was beyond dispute.

De Reszke retired flamboyantly wealthy[5] at the age of 54. He was young to be leaving the stage, even in 1904. He taught sporadically, with success, and his students[6] remembered him with affection and respect. In June, 1922, he was featured in an issue of *Mclean's*.[7] The article was titled "*De Reszke As He Is Today: Romance of This Remarkable Singer Who is Still Active.*" A little unkindly, considering De Reszke was only 72 years old at the time,[8] it began:

> It seems difficult to comprehend that Jean De Reszke, one of the world's most famous singers, and noted as a music teacher of renown, is still with us in the flesh, active and in possession of his faculties....[9]

The article led with De Reszke's reputation as "an extraordinarily heavy smoker" – citing his association "in the minds of many with a cigarette which has been named after him, rather than with his artistic attainments." The narrative collapses into a disgraceful fit of advertorial for Milhoff's cigarettes, which De Reszke's "fellow Slav" is said to have created specifically for the tenor to "smoke with perfect impunity." The PR reaches its ugly nadir when there is said to be

> a sad note in the conversation of De Reszke, with all the sorrow behind. 'My brother,' he said recently, 'is dead and almost forgotten; my son has died and is also almost forgotten; soon I shall be dead and I shall be

---

4   In his splendid comic novel, *An Ice-Cream War* (1982), the Scottish writer William Boyd colours Felix by association: "He took out some books and a cardboard cylinder. From this he removed a coloured poster. It was an offer from De Reszke [sic] cigarettes… one of the brands he smoked. On receipt of six empty packets the poster was sent free of charge. It portrayed a young couple sitting at a table. A slim young man in evening dress leant forward, cupping his chin in one hand his other hand behind him, languidly resting on the seat back, a smoking cigarette held between two fingers. He gazed dreamily into the eyes of an equally slim woman, who leant forward also, thereby causing her considerable bosom to press against the low-cut bodice of her silk gown." Boyd, William (2011). *An Ice-Cream War*. Penguin Books. p.57.
5   Unlike his baritone brother, Édouard (22 December, 1853 – 25 May, 1917), who died in destitution.
6   His most celebrated successes were Leo Slezak, Maggie Teyte and Bidu Sayão. Less well known, but highly talented alumni, included Bessie Abott, Louise Edvina, Claire Croiza, Arthur Endrèze, Vladimir Rosing, Mafalda Salvatini, Clive Carey, Miriam Licette, Edna de Lima, and Isabel Stevens Lathrop.
7   Published at the time as "Canada's National Magazine".
8   By way of contrary example, Gustave Eiffel was still alive in 1922 (having been born in 1832), as was Charles de Freycinet, one-time Prime Minister of France, who was born in 1828!
9   "Reminiscences of Celebrated Singers (A Conversation with Signor Sbriglia)," by Perley Dunn Aldrich (*Etude* Magazine, August, 1906). p.488.

forgotten. The only thing to carry on the name is this,' and he pointed to a box of 'De Reszke' cigarettes.¹⁰

Maclean's quoted the Irish journalist and British politician Thomas "T.P." O'Connor, who had recently travelled to meet De Reszke in Nice:¹¹

> As I journeyed along the sea coast [...] I saw as in a vision the man, and the past of the man, whom I was going to see again [...] For De Reszke had many kinds of glory in those great days of his. His genius as a singer and an actor had about it a dazzling effect almost unprecedented. Who that was ever present at De Reszke's entrance as Faust, as Lohengrin, or in any other of his great parts, will ever forget that strange pause of admiration and of anticipation that brought the whole house to an expectant hush? Except some few great orators, I have never known anybody who had this extraordinary power of De Reszke of producing that sepulchral silence in a vast and excited audience—and everybody accustomed to audiences knows that deadly silence is a far more eloquent manifestation of profound emotion than the most ear-splitting applause.¹²

The article informed its readers in Canada (where De Reszke had not performed) that he was from "an ancient historical Polish family" which enabled him to exist "naturally at home within social portals then inaccessible to the world of artists; he was an aristocrat among the most aristocratic." De Reszke was certainly Polish; he was no aristocrat. In fact, "Jan Reszke" was born to a middle-class family of moderate wealth, but nothing more. His father worked as a state official and sometime hotelier; his mother raised and helped educate the children¹³ – three of whom became internationally successful opera singers. Jan began his singing career as a chorister in Warsaw's St. John's Cathedral; he later studied with the Italian tenor Francesco Ciaffei at the Warsaw Conservatory – where he trained as a baritone. After graduating he studied for almost five years with Antonio Cotogni,¹⁴ whose rigorous attention to the mechanics of voice training – a reflection of his own earlier education – was remembered in 1924 by another student:

> 'For the first year I sang nothing but scales. In the second year, vocal exercises and simple songs. Third year, training in operatic music, chiefly solos. Fourth year, ensembles, duets, trios, etc. Fifth year, training in scenic action, mostly in front of a looking-glass.' This may be to a certain extent too rigid a description, but the fact remains that, as Cotogni said, his master considered him fit for the stage when there was not a single opera in the current repertoire which he did not know backwards, and

---
10   *Ibid.* p.488.
11   In a hilarious slander, born presumably of political and cultural prejudice, O'Connor recalls a visit to De Reszke in France by the "great American tenor" John McCormack.
12   *Ibid.*
13   There were four children in total. Only one, Victor, did not become a professional singer.
14   1 August, 1831 – 15 October, 1918.

when, as he reproachfully added every time I tried to find an excuse for missing a top note, he could be awakened at 3 a.m. and made to give an A-flat mezza voce. Cotogni sang on the stage for over forty years.[15]

De Reszke made his debut using the name Giovanni di Reschi; it was as an "Italian" singer that the British impresario Colonel Mapleson[16] first knew him in London where, as his *Memoirs* record, De Reszke performed the title role in *Don Giovanni* at Drury Lane on 20 July, 1874.[17] The baritone repertoire serviced neither the singer's ambitions, nor popular taste, so he took the commercially and vocally hazardous decision to retrain as a tenor in France. He was accepted by Giovanni Sbriglia,[18] an Italian tenor who performed widely across the United States, Havana, Cuba, and Mexico before retiring in his prime to teach in Paris. As he told an interviewer in 1906:

> I was trained in Naples at the conservatory, under Emanuel Roxas and Busti – the latter of whom died only three years ago – in the strict old Italian school. When we went to the opera, we heard the most perfect models, such as Malibran, Alboni, Fressolini, Tardolini, Lablache, Cortesi, Mario, Rubini, etc.[19]

Through arduous supervision, and fantastic efforts on the part of De Reszke, Sbriglia transformed an averagely capable baritone into the world's foremost lyric-dramatic tenor. It is no exaggeration to say that Sbriglia was as much a phenomenon as his pupil, with a list of alumni that confirms his almost surgical expertise in the training of voices.[20] He wrote no books – believing that nothing written about singing could be of value since "what was good for one was bad for another […] I have no method. I teach people to sing. If the voice is too open, I shut; if it is too shut, I open." There are nonetheless some interesting accounts of his teaching methods.[21] A few months after Sbriglia's death, *Etude* magazine carried an interview with Perley Dunn Aldrich,[22] a student who later became his assistant and accompanist:

> He was eminently a practical teacher. He had very little theory and talked very little. He was not a good musician, played none to speak of on the piano, and, of course, knew nothing of the most modern operas. But

---

15 Mackenzie, Sir Compton and Stone, Christopher (1924). "*Antonio Cotogni's description of his training.*" *The Gramophone* (2). p.202.
16 Name-changing was all the rage during the 19th century. Mapleson sang during the 1850s under the name "Enrico Mariani."
17 Mapleson, James, H. (1966). *The Mapleson Memoirs: the Career of an Operatic Impresario.* Ed. Harold Rosenthal. Putnam. p.99.
18 23 June, 1832 – 20 February, 1916.
19 "*Reminiscences of Celebrated Singers (A Conversation with Signor Sbriglia),*" by Perley Dunn Aldrich (*Etude* Magazine, August, 1906). p.488.
20 The list *includes* Josephine and Édouard De Reszke, Lillian Nordica, Pol Plançon, Mena Cleary, and Sybil Sanderson.
21 *Ibid.* p.488.
22 6 November, 1863 – 20 November, 1933.

he was a real teacher of the voice. He had that rare talent known as the 'vocal gift.' He knew when the voice resonated correctly, and he found original ways and means of causing it to do this. In fact, he was a genius in this one particular line. His teaching was empirical and intuitive. I believe he taught entirely as his intuition bade him, and sometimes this was difficult to follow, for his system would seem changeable to the student. He continually sought after a natural voice, but sometimes he would use unnatural means to gain this end. I mean, he would try to overcome a certain defect before he treated the voice as a whole. For example, I have heard him exercise a pupil vigorously on the sounds tee and tay, with the teeth, on the middle notes, to bring a strong resonance throughout the middle voice. He would use the Concone Fifty Lessons[23] in the same way, making the pupil use sometimes one and sometimes the other of these vowels. When they sang them by the syllables I have seen him change the fa to fee (or tee) for a pupil whose fa was weak and heady. I have seen him carry this same work into the high notes, as far as possible...[24]

Sbriglia directed De Reszke to train physically as well as vocally, encouraging the use of dumb-bells and exercise regimes so as to ensure the strength of the *point d'appui*[25] at the base of the sternum. It was here that a voice was best supported – such that a "strong" singer would be able to perform without fatigue, with an even tone and, theoretically at least, with confidence above the stave. His techniques and insights emancipated De Reszke (and the American soprano, Lillian Nordica, with whom De Reszke's vocal evolution bears direct comparison), thereby allowing him to sing weightier dramatic roles without sacrificing that essential lyricism to which he and Nordica were inseparably attached. Part of Sbriglia's box of tricks was the use of abdominal belts – or corsets – that assisted singers lacking the necessary support, and to help them achieve a sense of breath management for the purposes of phonation and stamina. Sbriglia's corset gave his students something (other than their teacher) against which to push, and to assist with what Italians refer to still as *la lotta vocale*[26] – that contest between the body's natural tendency to collapse as air is expelled, and the resistance mustered in opposition. Because the history of dramatic singing appears to have produced only a handful of tenors likely to be thought athletic outside an opera house, Sbriglia's use of corsets was not without purpose and value – even if it would be abused by those who probably didn't need it.[27] Aldrich remembered that Sbriglia

> often remarked, in his broken English. 'Like you whiz' (whistle). 'Singing on the lips' was another favorite phrase that he used over and

---

23 Giuseppe Concone (1801 – 1861) was an Italian vocal teacher, whose vocal exercises – *solfeggi* and *vocalizzi* – were adopted across Europe, and obsessively so in France where they were published as *50 Leçons de chant*, Op.9.
24 *Etude Magazine*, February, 1917. pp.122–123.
25 'Point of support' – *i.e.*, the diaphragm.
26 The 'vocal struggle.'
27 For example, Lauritz Melchior.

over. This, combined with the strong chest, was the sun and substance of his teaching. For when he wandered afield from these ideas, he came back to them with renewed energy and with wonderful pertinacity. I remember very well a certain *solfeggio* by Guercia that he had me sing with the syllables softly and very rapidly to keep the voice on the lips. '*I fior di labb*i' (the flower of the lips). He would say, over and over. '*Ne pousee pas*' (don't push) when the pupil would force the voice.

Sbriglia taught De Reszke that great voices were unique in their tone and timbre, as well as their operation in matters of style and expression. A singer's fingerprints were inherently physiological, therefore, and the product of a body's resonance as well as the taste and training of the person occupying it. Sbriglia understood that teaching and practice were necessary for the translation of sound through every bone in the torso and the head (from the intersection of the parietal and frontal skull-plates to the lumbar vertebrae of the spinal column) as well as the discipline of breathing and voice placement in the diaphragm. A student's mastery of resonance and conduction was essential to Sbriglia's teaching methods, which focussed on the use of various bodily *chambers* for resonating vocal tone. He rejected the popular obsession with the operation of the vocal cords, which failed absolutely to appreciate the intense physicality of vocalising when done well. A singer's potential range of vocal colour, spanning darkness in the chest and *squillo* brilliance in the head, flowed from the communication of emotional states that crystallised at their simplest as corporeal personality. No two singers can sound the same; it is equally true that many do not sound like anyone at all. De Reszke was said to be recognisable to the visually impaired within a single two-note phrase; that individuality emerged from his control and manipulation of the shape and size of his resonance chambers. The same has been a feature of the success of every acclaimed singer to modern times. Carreras and Pavarotti, for example, both sang beautifully, and from similar expressive platforms, but they sounded nothing like each other. They are nonetheless instantly recognisable, even to those unaccustomed to operatic singing.

In a later issue of *Etude*, Sbriglia was interviewed, with his wife acting as translator. He was asked: "What is the old Italian school of singing?" He answered "The school of Patti, Nordica, Sembrich, De Reszke, Albani, Plançon." In other words, the Sbriglia school. The next question ("Why are there so few singers of the old school?") elicited a more comprehensive answer:

> Because there are so few teachers of the old school of singing. The younger teachers have never studied the old school long enough to understand its principles. The old school began by months of careful work in placing the voice, and then followed three years of *solfeggios* for perfect enunciation. It was only after all this that they attempted the study of the recitatives and airs from the operas. Furthermore, in past years, it was a lesson to go to the theaters in Italy and hear the singers, trained as they were in the finest school of singing and singing only the music which best displayed the '*bel canto*'. But now the teachers find a fine, fresh voice and in six months they have taught him roles by rote, and he

makes his appearance on the stage. At first he attracts attention by the natural beauty of his voice and meets with success. After a short career he disappears entirely, for he knows nothing of either music or the real art of singing. These singers never become fine artists and depend only on their natural gifts, forgetting entirely that it is only by education of these gifts that they can hope for a long and honorable career. With the best voice in the world one cannot hope to become an artist or to preserve the voice unless it has been properly trained. It is like a house without a foundation.

De Reszke studied with Sbriglia for four years.[28] He was almost 30 when he made his debut as a tenor, on 9 November, 1879, as *Robert le Diable*, with his sister Josephine as Alice. Things did not go badly; neither did they go especially well:

> According to some reports he was successful, but newspaper accounts ignored his performance almost entirely. He appeared in *La Favorita* too, with his sister and Gayarre, but was scarcely mentioned. The De Reszke name was writ large in Spanish and Portuguese operatic annals of this period, but it was the vigorous, sometimes almost savage Josephine who was responsible for that, and not her brother. Jean himself wandered far into the valley of doubt during those uncertain days. To his friend and counsellor, Jean Styka, he wrote a letter sorrowfully admitting that he had been 'whistled at,' and that he thought he would leave the stage entirely and not disgrace his father's name.

De Reszke withdrew from performance, and for the next four years he lived with (and off) his famous siblings. In 1899, he wrote to Lilli Lehmann that he had spent "the best years" of his life

> traveling with my sister and my brother, who had engagements at Madrid, Lisbon, Milan, Turin, London and so on. I helped them with my counsel, I heard all the great singers of the period, I compared, I worked at home, without letting myself be seduced by the brilliant propositions which impresarios made me. I should perhaps have continued not to sing in the theater, if Massenet and Maurel had not taken me by force to create *Hérodiade* in Paris in 1884. There began my career as a tenor...[29]

De Reszke forgets himself. He did not create *Hérodiade* (singing the tenor lead of Jean [le Baptiste]). The opera was premiered in Brussels, at La Monnaie, on 19

---

28   Which truth renders absurd the assertion by De Reszke's biographer that his transition from baritone to tenor "he conquered through his own efforts. No teacher could finally achieve what he achieved through his own intelligent perseverance." Leiser, Clara (2015). Jean *De Reszke and The Great Days of Opera*. Sagwan Press. p. 44.
29   *Ibid.* p.42.

December, 1881 – when the honour of singing Jean went to one of De Reszke's leading rivals, Edmond-Alphonse Vergnet.[30] The first Parisian run was staged at the Théâtre des Nations, on 1 February, 1884. The season's final performance, on 13 March, featured all three De Reszkes – Jean, Édouard (as Phanuel) and Josephine (as Salomé). According to De Reszke, he had first come to Massenet's attention the year before, when he and his brother were

> in a music store in Paris, going over some scores in a little back room. Massenet also came into the store. The singing he heard sent him hurriedly to that back room...[31]

When it was announced that De Reszke was to sing in the first French production of *Hérodiade*, one writer noted that:

> It will be Interesting to see the transformation into a tenor of the young baritone, Jean De Reszke. He was, we remember, a charming gentleman, well-bred, distinguished, with a quick intelligence, and was, in addition, a good musician and a lively comedian. If he has really been able to tenorize his voice, one can predict he will appear as an accomplished artist."

Half an hour before the curtain's rising, and haunted still by memories of his Spanish debut five years earlier, De Reszke suffered an attack of nerves and announced he would not be singing. He was talked around by his brother, in the company of the baritone Victor Maurel (who was singing the role of Hérode[32]) – and remained forever grateful for their intervention. De Reszke's success was total, with cheers, ovations and glowing press notices. *The Clairon* was typical in celebrating

> the charm and freshness of his voice, his profound understanding and his diction. I was still under the dazzling influence of the vocal prowess of M. Gayarre, and I must say that, in spite of his immense ability, the Spanish tenor has never given me the delicious sensation which I experienced last night in listening to M. Jean De Reszke; I do not think I am mistaken in predicting a magnificent future for him.[33]

That prediction was cemented by De Reszke's success the following year when creating his only major role – Rodrique in *Le Cid*. The opera was among Massenet's most successful; it is far from being his finest. The triumph of the first performance on 30 November, 1885, was attributed in no small part to De Reszke, who added depth to a role that is bombastic, clichéd and sentimental. His first appearance in Act

---

30 4 July, 1850 – 15 February, 1904.
31 *Ibid.*
32 Maurel's success as Hérode came to the attention of Verdi, for whom Maurel created the role of Iago in Milan three years later.
33 *Ibid.* p.43.

1 is announced by plangent fanfares and an aureate chorus; the tenor has to wrestle with both when singing the doggerel verse beginning[34]:

> *Ô noble lame étincelante,*
> *Pure comme un regard d'enfant,*
> *Combats gardienne vigilante*
> *Et fais l'honneur seul triomphant!*[35]

The opening flurry of leaps and high B flats yields to the expressive, devotional reflection of

> *A Saint Jacques de Compostelle, j'ai voué ma foi;*
> *Il me verra toujours à sa cause fidèle.*[36]

It is in this overt juxtaposition of declamatory power and lyrical sweetness that De Reszke's talent is captured most resonantly. A similar fusion of brilliance and introversion characterised the opera's solitary episode of genius – Rodrigue's Act 3 recitative and aria "*Ah! Tout est bien fini* [...] *O souverain, ô juge, ô père.*"[37] Massenet did not, as many presume, compose the role for De Reszke, since he had been working on the opera for some time when they first met. They did collaborate on its refinement, however, and the line and register of "*Ah! Tout est bien fini* [...] *O souverain*" speak to the core qualities of De Reszke's voice and his use of it. The recitative is lachrymose, intensely poetic and written entirely on the breath; conversely, the main theme of the twice-repeated aria is halting, almost stumbling in its phrasing – with an especially difficult span in one rising-falling phrase between a low E flat and a high A flat 4 ("*au temps prospère et te bé[nis]*"[38]). The secondary 'B' theme is languid when placed at the centre of the *passaggio*, and the writing is generally deceptive in its technical difficulty. It is beyond the means and resources of purely lyric tenors who might be able to reach the climactic B flat quavers (both marked *tenuti*) but not with the heft and bloom necessary to join with the darkly-scored, brass-heavy orchestration as well as a duet with Saint Jacques (baritone), a chorus of "heavenly voices" and a solo violin. The aria is written in such a way that it can (and often does) sound breathless rather than imploring, with the (interpolated[39]) concluding A flat *crescendo* being exploited as compensation by singers for whom the melancholy lines of song have proven too demanding.

Judging by this scene alone, De Reszke was possessed of a sonorous, ringing and flexible voice. Massenet's attention to disparate and fluctuating dynamic markings (with *crescendi* spanning *pianissimo* and *fortissimo* over two and sometimes three-bar passages) confirm what was reported routinely by the critics, namely that De Reszke

---

34 The libretto was admitted to by Louis Gallet, Édouard Blau and Adolphe d'Ennery.
35 'O noble sparkling blade, Pure as a child's gaze, Vigilant fighting guardians, honour the triumphant!'
36 'At Santiago de Compostela, I have dedicated my faith; He will see me always devoted to His cause.'
37 'Ah, it is all over [...] Oh Sovereign, oh Judge, oh Father, always hidden yet always present.'
38 'In time of success, and bless you.'
39 Even in the complete recording of the opera conducted by Eve Queler, with Domingo in the title role, this hollow, artificial effect is hammered home – without the score even hinting at it.

used his exceptional instrument as an artist for whom expression was the end rather than the means. Of De Reszke's first run in London as Radamès, on June 13, 1887, Hermann Klein recalled the performance as being

> one of the most brilliant ever witnessed in this metropolis. It settled the fate of the whole enterprise, as well as that of Jean de Reszke, who instantly became an artist of world-wide fame. [...] So completely was the modest young 'baritone' of the Mapleson days forgotten, that I can scarcely recall a comparison of any sort being made between him and the splendid fully-fledged tenor who now came into the picture. I wrote myself [at the time]: 'This truly great artist once sang as a baritone, but his voice is now unmistakably a tenore robusto. His high notes, produced with ease, and always in perfect tune, are of magnificent quality and resonant as a bell. He sings without a suspicion of the *tremolo*, uses the *mezza-voce* with moderation, declaims with splendid vigour, and phrases with a purity and nobility of expression that never fail to impress.'[40]

It's clear that De Reszke did not (at this time) employ *vibrato*, although his absolute sense of pitch allowed him to attend to details of phrasing and articulation that attached him more obviously to the traditions of Mario than Tamagno. There is ample evidence for this, including the critical perception of Queen Victoria, to whom De Reszke referred in a letter after a private concert at Windsor Castle:

> At her Majesty's request, the concert ended with the duet from the *Traviata*, sung by Madame Albani and myself. The Queen, smiling and full of kindness, approached us and paid us many compliments. Among them she told me that I reminded her of Mario, only that my voice had more power. She refused to believe that I was the elder brother, and this discussion, in which Madame Albani was called upon to arbitrate, greatly amused the Queen. Then, after the customary courtesies, the Queen retired. I found her extremely well, charming in manner, speaking French like a Parisian, and a genuine lover of music.[41]

Between 1885 and 1904, De Reszke was the world's pre-eminent male singer and an international celebrity. He travelled widely – taking full advantage of his fluency as a polyglot speaking Polish, French, Italian, German, English and Spanish – and he was feted in particular by the wealthy and ruling classes. Much was made of his allegedly aristocratic origins, which were attached obliquely to the hereditary credentials established by Mario. His "nobility" was meaningful in different ways, depending on where he was performing. In Britain, where the privilege of title was more valuable than the gold standard, his pretentions led to sneering and humiliation. A wave of cultural prejudice infected one particularly nasty episode, when the

---

40   Klein, Herman. "Jean De Reszke and Marie Brema: Some Reminiscences." *The Musical Times*, Vol. 66, No. 987 (1 May, 1925). pp.405–408.
41   *Ibid*. pp.75–76.

De Reszke brothers were invited (as guests) to a private banquet[42] thrown by Alfred de Rothschild.[43] After dinner, Jean and Édouard were asked to perform. As the cheers died down, the host grandly presented each of the singers with a blank cheque. As one of the world's wealthiest men, and as the owner of his own bank, de Rothschild's gaudy generosity operated as a social insult. As alleged aristocrats, neither of the De Reszke's could have presented the notes for payment. As *mere* artisans they would have been able to charge whatever they liked. The De Reszke's had entered de Rothschild's house through the front door, but only as an indulgence. The cheques were allegedly accepted and returned the following day – blank and torn. Of course, the story was popular among those for whom it served an anti-Semitic purpose, and it was overlooked when Leiser's *schlagobers* life of De Reszke was first published in 1934.[44] The "burden" of Jean's celebrity was nothing of the sort:

> He would sing for hours just to give his friends pleasure, and he enjoyed that; but to agree to be at a certain place at, say ten o'clock in the evening, to be exhibited as a part of the evening's entertainment, that was an idea so distasteful that no amount of money could have induced him to accept such an invitation. Thus, if he could not avoid causing ladies to faint at the opera, he at least was spared the embarrassment of drawing-room gushing, and, for instance, such an experience as befell his famous predecessor Mario. Mario was also a magnificent stage lover, and many women fell under his spell. Once he was singing in a salon in Paris. As he sang the last line 'Come, love, with me into the woods,'[45] a young woman who had been listening in a semi-hypnotic state rose to her feet and tottered towards him, murmuring: 'I am coming.'[46]

Quite so. De Reszke was handsome, talented and *mostly* reliable. His status was such that although his career did not begin until his middle 30s he could have continued without difficulty to sail the gamut of Italian and French repertoire, alternating between his signature roles, Vasco da Gama (*L'Africaine*) Raoul (*Les Huguenots*),

---

42 Held presumably at Halton House, Alfred's magnificent country home in the Chiltern Hills, Buckinghamshire, United Kingdom.
43 Alfred Charles Freiherr de Rothschild, CVO; 20 July, 1842 – 31 January, 1918.
44 Leiser is careful to establish De Reszke's gentile lineage: "One of the most persistent rumors is that of the Hebraic strain in the De Reszkes. 'Did you know that his father was a Jew?' someone will ask, and then, by way of confirmation, add: 'Why, of course; he was a cantor in the synagogue at Warsaw.' Jean did not lack some of the enviable qualities of the Hebrew, but it happens that his father was not a Jew. He and his forefathers were Protestants, and he lies buried in the Reszke plot in the Evangelical Cemetery of Warsaw; but his wife, the mother of Jean and Edouard, was a Roman Catholic, and the children were reared in that faith." Leiser, Clara (2015). *Jean De Reszke and The Great Days of Opera*. Sagwan Press. p.13.
45 It's difficult to isolate what Mario is supposed to have been singing. The last line to which Leiser makes reference is not as the (improbable) anecdote records it. The most likely source is an arrangement of one of Mendelssohn's *Lieder ohne Worte*, Op.62 ('Songs without Words') by Jules Barbier ("*Chanson du Printemps*" ['Spring Song'], beginning "*Salut, printemps, honneur des bois ombreux*" ['Greetings Spring, that honours the shaded wood'], which contains the lines "*au viens aux bois, loins des regards jaloux*" ['come to the woods, far from the jealous looks']. So, a song without words – with words!
46 *Ibid*. p.185.

Jean de Leyden (*Le prophète*), Don José (*Carmen*), Riccardo (*Un ballo in maschera*), Radamès (*Aida*) and the "two Gounods," *Faust* and *Roméo*. With the advent of "Wagnermania," however, De Reszke was presented with an opportunity for which he was not alone in considering himself well-appointed. The composer's death in 1883 had escalated the popularity of his works globally – a designation that now included dozens of opera houses across South as well as North America – and there was a wholly inadequate supply of *heldentenors* to satisfy the demand. If Wagner was unable to find what he was looking for at Bayreuth, then it was probably unreasonable to expect the houses in New Orleans and Buenos Aires to stage *Tristan* and the *Ring* other than in the teeth of compromise.

De Reszke's decision to sing Wagner was informed by certain realities that would become trite by repetition. He was a baritone – first and foremost – who sang tenor roles. Cotogni observed many years later that he "never became a tenor. He was only a baritone with a high enough range to sing tenor notes."[47] In other words, De Reszke was a *heldentenor* who could sing Raoul, Alfredo, Don José and Roméo. When finally he turned to Wagner he achieved something that had escaped almost everyone else – namely the fulfilment of Wagner's ambitions for a lyrical-declamatory tenor, capable of surmounting the orchestra while simultaneously articulating his words and singing his melodies. There have since been hundreds of *heldentenors* without a background as a baritone, but the De Reszke model has remained true ever since, insofar as the greatest Wagner tenors have also sung much else a great deal less Wagnerian. To that end, the tenor that sang the exquisite arietta "*Console-toi, pauvre âme*" from Act 5 of *Roméo et Juliette* was capable also of doing full justice to "*Ho-Ho! Ho-Heil! Schmiede, Mein Hammer.*" With the death of Tichatschek in 1886, Nothung passed to a Polish tenor trained by Italians who spent almost his entire career as a Wagner tenor singing in Britain and the United States. That it took a generalist, performing routinely in French and Italian, to achieve what Germans singing *only* in German could not, was a lesson for those who wished to learn it.

Between 15 May and 21 July, 1888, de Reszke sang 21 performances in London, at the Royal Opera, Covent Garden – including seven as Faust and six as Lohengrin. The following season (18 May – 27 July) he gave 23 performances, with three as Radamès, seven as Roméo, six as Lohengrin and four as Walther von Stolzing. Between 19 May and 28 July, 1890, his stamina and resilience extended to almost thirty performances (equivalent to one every other night) in French, Italian and German, spanning Don José, Faust, Lohengrin, Walther and Roméo. He performed the leads in *Otello* in 1891 and *Werther* in 1894. Two years later he sang his first London *Tristan*, and in 1898 he performed only Wagner, with three performances of *Siegfried*, three of *Götterdämmerung*, seven as Lohengrin, four as Walther and four as Tristan – a schedule that would now be considered ruinous. Notwithstanding the absurdity of the physical and psychological demands presented by De Reszke's schedule, his achievement was miraculous in its reconciliation of the disparate worlds and repertoires of the *tenore lirica-drammatica*, the *tenore di forza* and the *heldentenor*. By transcending the cultural, aesthetic and vocal barriers that separated German opera from the (relative) interaction between the French and Italian, De Reszke embodied

---

47   *Ibid.* p.44.

both the essence of the dilemma facing tenors during the last quarter of the century, and the model of its insolubility. The natural tendency towards specialisation prior to the 1850s was formed of social and geographical parameters, and the relatively small number of cities and composers of decisive consequence. With the rise to pre-eminence of Verdi and Wagner, and the concomitant expansion across Europe and America of theatres, music colleges and publishing houses, the post-1848 realignment of art and aesthetics compelled reasoning that isolated the merits of specialisation for composers, teachers, performers and audiences alike. The *heldentenor* repertoire made specific demands that could not be met by those who, by nature and training, were unable to sing it. Middle-weight repertoire allowed for "one size fits all" voices that liberated would-be De Reszkes to approach everything, without thinking to prioritise the specific stylistic needs and characteristics of a composer's work. In other words, while De Reszke may well have sung Wagner magnificently, it is highly likely he sang everything else in much the same way. His work as a "French" tenor may have featured elements of French style as it was known and taught by pedagogues in Paris; his work as an "Italian" tenor fell broadly within the ambit of what was imagined by Verdi. De Reszke was not an Italian tenor; neither was he French or German. His attention to the needs and requirements of Wagner's essential lyricism cannot have operated in equivalence, therefore, so that Massenet, Verdi and Wagner were all performed as cognates. Something had to give.

Style is not a simile for voice; after more than a century of electrical recording, it has been possible to study the evolving conception of Verdi and Wagner tenor parts in their sovereignty and irreconcilability. There is a striking comparator in the work of Ernest Van Dyck,[48] the Belgian creator of *Werther*, and the first and most famous of De Reszke's contemporaries to straddle the worlds of French, Italian and German opera. Although Massenet composed *Werther* for Guillaume Ibos,[49] it was first performed by Van Dyck in Vienna, on 16 February, 1892 – when he was still able to persuade as a "young poet, aged 23." Van Dyck was not a *heldentenor*, but after studies with the Wagner-obsessed Emmanuel Chabrier he specialised in roles requiring amplitude, notably Berlioz's Faust, Ernest Reyer's Sigurd, Tristan and Siegmund. Van Dyck was chosen by Debussy to give the premiere of *L'enfant prodigue* in Paris, on 27 July 1884. After making his debut as Lohengrin (in the opera's French premiere on 3 May, 1887) he became a student of the conductor and Bayreuth amanuensis, Felix Mottl, with whom he studied *Parsifal*, which he performed for the first time at Bayreuth in 1888. He was thereafter adopted by Cosima Wagner, for whom he became a proponent of *Sprechgesang* at Bayreuth and the Wiener Hofoper, where he remained for a decade. It was because of his status in Vienna that Van Dyck was chosen to sing in the premiere of *Werther* – in a German translation.

For the first productions in French, at the Théâtre de Genève on 27 December, 1892, and at the Opéra-Comique on 16 January, 1893, the title role was played by Ibos. Van Dyck was admired by many outside Bayreuth, although his most committed supporters accepted that a lack of judgment and proper training led to the early ruin of his voice, long before his career ended with performances of *Parsifal* at

---

48 2 April, 1861 – 31 August, 1923.
49 10 July, 1860 – 22 September, 1952.

Bayreuth in 1912 and Antwerp in 1914. His few recordings were produced between 1903 and 1905 for Pathé, Fonotipia and Homophone. Remarkably, one can hear Van Dyck sing "*Pourquoi me réveiller?*" from *Werther*, which he recorded for the Pathé label in London in 1903. It's clear that Cosima's reach extended across the Chanel, since the performance is devoid of lyrical and expressive style – qualities that might reasonably have been expected of a "French" tenor singing music by Massenet. His tone is brittle, overly bright, and absent warmth and colour. His phrasing is without nuance and there is no hint of the bathetic introversion for which the aria is rightly celebrated. Counterarguments that Van Dyck's voice had failed at this stage in his career are negated by the trumpet-like force he brings to the aria's two high A4s. That this ugly strain of singing was now *echt* for Bayreuth is inarguable – not least because his diction is flawless throughout; as a genus of art it was alien to Massenet and French opera, however. Fortunately, Ibos recorded the same aria for Gaumont in 1900 and his singing is a model of its kind. His tone is warm, his breath control exceptional. He employs a light *vibrato* as colour and his creative use of *portamento* carries the words and their meaning with glorious effect. He attends to the score's dynamic markings, and adds a number of his own – with a mechanically impressive *diminuendo* during the rising phrase at the end of the first verse "*Ô souffle du printemps?*" (C sharp – D sharp – E sharp – F sharp). Even if his *rubato* is far from *tempo*, Ibos' clear sense of the aria's theatrical substance, and the character's psychology when singing it, is striking. There is a glorious ease to the entire performance, which pays tribute to his formidable technique and laudable artistic judgment. Ibos sang Wagner as well; he did so within the limits of his voice, never abandoning style to what the Bayreuth School considered to be substance. De Rezske kept his distance from Bayreuth, and the clear difference between his singing and that of Van Dyck characterised the tensions created by the distinct cultural and musical challenges unfolding on either side of the Rhine and the Alps. More than a century later, the number of tenors capable of singing French, Italian *and* German music, and then to the highest of local standards, can be counted realistically on a single hand.

The evolving balance of priorities is apparent from the prevalence of critical reviews during the second half of the 19th century that praised singers for their intonation while ignoring any consideration of the narrow prescriptive requirements fostered by a score and its associated traditions. That De Reszke was able to articulate every word without the need of surtitles, and that he could act before the emergence of cinema, merely compounded his status as a general-purpose singer of exceptional taste and discretion. This was no less true of Plácido Domingo, the most obvious (and arguably the only) tenor worthy of comparison in modern times.

With Wagner's music still relatively new to theatregoers, the critical response to De Reszke's adoption of the Wagnerian mantel was appropriately and justifiably ecstatic. Even "Corno di Bassetto"[50] was an admirer. When, in the delirium of Tristan's death, De Reszke cried out for the last time "*Isolde!*" Shaw, writing for the *London World*, described it as

---

50 G. B. Shaw's sometime pseudonym.

most wonderful; not merely affecting as the despairing and adoring cry of a dying man thinking of the woman he worships, but far more than that. In it one hears not only love but death. It is the mysterious, whispering utterance of a spirit already far away; as if the soul, having started on its dark journey, were compelled by its old and beautiful earthly passion to pause, and to look back down the shadowy vista to the garden of the world that it had left, to the woman that it had left, perhaps forever, and to send down the distance one last cry of farewell, one last dim murmur of love, spectral, magical already with the wonder of another world. Such an effect as this is utterly beyond the reach of anyone who is not a great artist. It is thrilling in its imaginative beauty. It opens the gates as poetry does sometimes and shows us a faint vision of a far-away eternity. Is it possible to crowd such a weight of significance into one word of three short syllables? Jean De Reszke did.[51]

When in 1923 Henry T. Finck quoted Shaw, he added for the unbelieving:

Is it possible for a singer to put so much meaning and emotion into one short word of three syllables? I heard de Reszke do it over and over again. Have we here a glimpse of a future when the art of singing will have reached a much higher general level than it has now ? We may well believe this, when we bear in mind the enormous progress from Rubini's trills to de Reszke's thrills. It indicates the direction in which students must go — the direction of the word " Isolde" as sung by Jean de Reszke.[52]

In 1891, De Reszke sang for the first time in the United States, and between 1893 and 1899 he appeared in every season at the Metropolitan, New York – virtually duplicating his London repertoire. He arrived just as the "all-German" phase had come to an end – such that the company no longer had to perform everything in German, regardless of its original language.[53] The American critics mirrored the view in London – with the consensus being that De Reszke's glowing timbre, grace and refinement were unique on the world's stages. Of his first night (of ten) as Tristan on 27 November, 1895[54], W. J. Henderson wrote for *The New York Times* that

Standing as he had for some years at the top of the lyric ladder, the favorite tenor of two continents has cherished an ambition that beyond all other things demonstrated his worth as an artist. That ambition was to sing Tristan and Siegfried. He will be no more famous with the general public, nor will he be any the greater tenor for having sung Tristan. It is

---

51 Quoted in Finck, Henry T. (1923). *Musical Progress. A series of practical discussions of present day problems in the tone world.* Theodore Presser. p.14.
52 *Ibid.* p.15.
53 Henson, Karen (2015). *Opera Acts*. Cambridge University Press. p.149.
54 With Lillian Nordica as Isolde and Edouard De Reszke as King Marke, conducted by Anton Seidl.

not essential to greatness to be a Wagnerian artist. But M. De Reszke has proved that by adding this role to his repertoire – and in a language new to him – he had the insatiable hunger of the genuine artist to achieve the one grand and noble thing that was left for him to achieve in the whole realm of lyric art.... He is one of the very few who have ever undertaken such a task at this time of life, and after such long schooling in the traditions of the French stage. Whether it is to be set forth today that he has succeeded or failed, he himself must feel the boundless satisfaction of the dramatic artist who has breathed a new atmosphere and who has glowed with the spiritual warmth of a fresh inspiration.[55]

Henderson's assessment of Nordica's Isolde was similarly glowing:

Nothing more beautiful than the close of the *'Sink hernieder'* passage in the duo between her and M. De Reszke has ever been heard here, and certainly it has never been sung better anywhere.

According to Henry Krehbiel in the *New York Tribune*:

Never before have we had a Tristan able to sing the declamatory music of the first and last acts with correct intonation, to say nothing of the duet of the second act [...] Mme. Nordica and M. De Reszke not only sang in tune, they gave the text with a distinctness of enunciation and a truthfulness of expression that enabled those familiar with the German tongue to follow the play and appreciate its dramatic value and even its philosophical purport [...] As for M. Jean De Reszke, his voice was warm and every note he sang a heart-throb.[56]

Six years later, De Reszke was captured singing live on the stage of the New York Metropolitan on cylinders produced by the House librarian, Lionel Mapleson (a nephew of the "Colonel"), using primitive equipment positioned beside the prompter. More than 100 "Mapleson Cylinders" have survived, some much better than others – with numerous subsequent fakes being produced for collectors desperate to hear the "missing De Reszkes."[57] Debates have raged ever since as to which of the many alleged recordings are of De Reszke. Only a handful can be said with any degree of certainty to be genuine, primarily two interrupted sections from Meyerbeer's *L'Africaine* ("O Paradiso," Vasco de Gama's aria from Act 4,[58] and the duet "*Sois ma femme*"), a section

---

55   New York Times, 28 November, 1895.
56   New York Tribune, 29 November, 1895.
57   There are nine other fragments, including excerpts from *Le Cid*, *Les Huguenots*, *Lohengrin*, *Siegfried* and *Tristan und Isolde*. They are all but useless. Conspiracy theorists claim that the British Queen and her family hold private recordings of De Reszke. The same people have not explained why the Windsors won't release them.
58   Recorded on 15 March, 1901, and referenced in Mapleson's diary ten days later: "During this season, have made a fine collection of phonograph cylinders. Melba and Jean De Reszke's voices."

from *Tristan's* Act 2 love duet with Milka Ternina ("*Zu Warte du*" and "*O Wonne*")[59], and a glimpse of "*Mein Herr und König*"[60] from Act 3 of *Lohengrin*. The best of the cylinders ("*O Paradiso*") reflects what was written of De Reszke almost constantly during his career after 1887, and by way of summary after his death by Hermann Klein in 1925:

> the unalloyed perfection of his method (apart, I mean, from the amazing breath-control or his impeccable phrasing), the exquisite and unforced timbre of his voice, the ease of his *sostenuto* – these were things that no singer could have accomplished and maintained for year after if working upon an artificial tension of the vocal cords.[61]

There is a glimmering of flutter *vibrato*, in keeping with contemporary fashion, and some judicious *portamento*; the phrasing is elegant and the tone rich and warm. His breathing, and the pause before the aria's penultimate note, speak to Italian rather than French traditions, as does the overly generous conducting, which De Reszke doesn't hesitate to exploit. Even though the ambient sound is appalling, there's nothing to compare between De Reszke and Tamagno. Where the latter is blunt and heavy, the former breathes the air of other worlds – and the cheering audience knows it. The excerpts from *Tristan* hint at something thrilling, a quality communicated by Walter Damrosch's visceral conducting, which suggests that the building as well as the performers were on fire. The excerpts from "*Sois ma femme*" reveal more of De Reszke's iron-clad technique, including a wonderful vocal flourish that takes him to an easy B flat 4 (from which he descends through a rapid turn and some strikingly focussed semi-quavers) and a splendid *forte* high B 4 which he declaims with furious energy.

It is unfortunate that De Reszke rejected (and ordered the destruction of) the two commercial recordings he made for Fonotipia in Paris in 1905. Regardless, a suggestion of wonder is preferable to a disappointing certainty, noting how posterity has been unkind to some who made recordings that are difficult to reconcile with their reputations. Although De Reszke retired while his voice was still in good shape, his explanation that his health was failing was unpersuasive. After completing his final (uncut) *Ring* cycle in New York in 1899, he ended a remarkable decade with a performance of *Lohengrin* on New Year's Eve, 1900. The turn of the first year of the new century coincided with De Reszke's (privately expressed) decision to retire from the Metropolitan and on 29 April, 1901, a lavish Gala was held during which forty women had to be revived by the use of ammonia.[62] Two thousand people stood behind the (on-stage) orchestra, which was conducted by Walter Damrosch and Franz Schalk, the latter of whom would go on to conduct the first production in Vienna of *Die Frau ohne Schatten* in 1919. The programme harks back to an age that was golden

---

59 Recorded on 13 March, 1901.
60 Recorded 29 March, 1901.
61 Klein, Herman. "Jean De Reszke and Marie Brema: Some Reminiscences". *The Musical Times*, Vol. 66, No. 987 (1 May, 1925). pp.405–408.
62 Murphy, Agnes G. (2016). *Melba: A Biography*. Palala Press. p.162. The Gala was not (as some have reported) a "farewell" for De Reszke.

even when compared to the one that preceded it. It began with a performance of Act III, Scene 1 from *Roméo et Juliette* (with Thomas Salignac and Suzanne Adams as the lovers, and Pol Plançon as Laurent) which was followed by Act 2 of *Tristan*, played in full – with the De Reszke brothers, Nordica and Ernestine Schumann-Heink as Brangäne. After the interval, Nellie Melba sang the "Mad Scene" from *Lucia di Lammermoor*. To acknowledge De Reszke's impassioned devotion to the articulation and elevation of language as dramatic art, the stage was yielded to Sarah Bernhardt and Coquelin *aîné*,[63] who played Leon Gozlan's *short* one-act comedy *La Pluie et Le Beau Temps* (1861).[64] The Gala ended with a performance of Act 3 of *Die Walküre* conducted by Walter Damrosch, with the tireless Nordica as Brünnhilde[65] and David Bispham as Wotan. *The New York Times* recorded the ovations as being "frantic" and "frenzied".

De Reszke resolved his retirement with justification. He was emotionally and culturally out of step with the new school of *verismo*, and he was aware of many young pretenders to a throne he had occupied without challenge for almost 15 years. Shortly after the brothers' return to Britain, Édouard attended Covent Garden to hear a young tenor called Enrico Caruso. When asked for his opinion, he replied without hesitation: "it's the greatest voice that God ever gave to man!"[66] Later that evening, Édouard sent Caruso a note from his hotel, in which he wrote with sanguine perspicacity:

> I never heard a more beautiful voice. You sang like a god. You are an actor and a sincere artist, and above all, you are modest and without exaggerations. You were able to draw from my eyes many tears. I was very much touched, and this happens to me very, very seldom. You have heart, feeling, poetry and truth, and with these qualities you will be the master of the world.[67]

---

[63] Coquelin and Bernhardt had toured the United States in 1900, with enormous success. Their itinerary included the first American production (in French) of Rostand's *Cyrano de Bergerac* (1897) at Broadway's Garden Theatre. In its review of the first night, *The New York Times* reported "The audience was large, but [...] there were a few vacant seats here and there in remote parts of the house. But in quality the audience was exceptional. Fashionable society was largely and brilliantly represented, and there were many men and women of some note in the house whom one does not habitually see at theatrical first night. Naturally such an audience gave gratifying evidence, now and then, of its intelligence [...] The two actors [from a named cast of 28] were recalled with abundant enthusiasm, and the uncommon skill and beauty of their acting were thoroughly comprehended, but not overpraised. This is most rare."

[64] 'Rain and Good Weather.'

[65] Milka Ternina was announced as Brünnhilde; illness compelled Nordica to stand in.

[66] Leiser, Clara (2015). *Jean De Reszke and The Great Days of Opera*. Sagwan Press. p.256.

[67] According to Caruso's wife, Dorothy, her husband had this letter framed. *Ibid*.

Chapter Eight

Frederick and Victor's Audience with the King

When first taking an interest in singing, and in tenor voices in particular, most people ask at some point: how good was Caruso?[1] For many, this equates to interrogating the *Mona Lisa*'s status as the "greatest" painting, or the standing of Beethoven's 5th Symphony as "the most sublime noise that has ever penetrated into the ear of man."[2] Of course, Da Vinci's portrait is not the greatest and, when badly conducted, Beethoven's Symphony in C minor can provoke tedium. Defamers of Renaissance painting and critics of Beethoven as a bloated monumentalist are entitled to their prejudices. The catholic value of a work of art is refracted through Joyce's overheard "rosary of hours, [a] life simple and strange as a bird's life, gay in the morning, restless all day, tired at sundown...." Imagined certainties are transcended only rarely, and throughout the modern history of the tenor voice there has been only one unchallenged reality, namely that since 1902, and the release of his first recordings for what would become EMI, Enrico Caruso was the finest, most perfect and yes, the "greatest" tenor, to sing opera. That reality has been compounded by every critical review, book and recollection to feature in print; even for those who merely know of his status as the *sine qua non* of tenors, it is accepted that he remains the model against which all others are to be measured. Few have reached for their panegyrics contextually – although many continue to attach themselves to Caruso in isolation, in whatever way best suits them commercially.

In August, 2019, Sony Classical released a recording by Roberto Alagna titled "Caruso 1873" – said to be a tribute by Alagna "to the Neapolitan singer he considers the greatest tenor of all time." The press quoted Alagna, who wrote:

---

1   25 February, 1873 – 2 August, 1921.
2   Forster, E. M. (2000). *Howard's End*. Penguin Books. "It will be generally admitted that Beethoven's Fifth Symphony is the most sublime noise that has ever penetrated into the ear of man. All sorts and conditions are satisfied by it. Whether you are like Mrs. Munt, and tap surreptitiously when the tunes come-- of course, not so as to disturb the others--or like Helen, who can see heroes and shipwrecks in the music's flood; or like Margaret, who can only see the music; or like Tibby, who is profoundly versed in counterpoint, and holds the full score open on his knee; or like their cousin, Fraulein Mosebach, who remembers all the time that Beethoven is echt Deutsch; or like Fraulein Mosebach's young man, who can remember nothing but Fraulein Mosebach: in any case, the passion of your life becomes more vivid, and you are bound to admit that such a noise is cheap at two shillings. It is cheap, even if you hear it in the Queen's Hall, dreariest music-room in London, though not as dreary as the Free Trade Hall, Manchester; and even if you sit on the extreme left of that hall, so that the brass bumps at you before the rest of the orchestra arrives, it is still cheap."

"For as long as I can remember, I've felt an almost visceral love and admiration for Enrico Caruso [...] Caruso is part of my life, part of my roots even [...] My great-grandparents knew him in New York. I feel as if I'd known him.". His aim was to "celebrate Caruso, while retaining [my] own vocal identity [...] I respected the Caruso 'style' when making this recording, just as one would respect a composer's style."[3]

According to Sony Classical, Alagna and his conductor, pianist, and arranger Yvan Cassar had

"committed to find a way into Caruso's world, as accurately as possible. They recorded not only in the original languages and keys that Caruso used in his recordings but also tried to match his tempos, his variations, his breaths… They even did everything to recreate the original orchestrations, for instance by including heavier brass, in order to reproduce the atmosphere of the early recordings."[4]

Alagna informed his readers that he was "so immersed in the sound of Caruso" that he "started hearing his voice instead of [his own] during the sessions. [...] I hope this recording will help younger generations to discover or rediscover Caruso's unique artistry. That way his flame will burn forever."[5] Alagna's vanity was eclipsed only by the idiocy of believing that any singer other than Caruso might be able to perpetuate his talent. The notion that an increase in brass resonance might render a digital recording in stereo comparable to a '78 produced in 1904 by the use of a horn in a room with no acoustic was as misconceived as believing that *tempi* and breathing might enable one singer to appear like another. Alagna's immersion in the "sound of Caruso" aimed little higher than imitation; the project collapsed into delusion. One of the songs performed by Alagna, "*Mattinata*,"[6] was composed for Caruso by Ruggero Leoncavallo in 1904. It was dedicated to the tenor, and he was the first to record it– with the composer at the piano. It's a short song, in E major, with a range of C sharp 4 to G sharp 4. The melody was designed to highlight the placement of Caruso's voice, which on record reveals almost no *passaggio*, a warmth of tone that is consistently baritonal, and an effortless *legato* that abrogates metaphor. Caruso's absolute and total otherness is a product of his phrasing. The placement of every syllable, the use of dynamic contrast and the tension generated and released through his use of *vibrato* and *portamento* are unique in recorded history; the end of the final (repeated) line "*Ove non-sei la luce manca, Ove tu sei nasce l'amor*"[7] concludes with a roared E4 that evokes Titta Ruffo at his grandest. Alagna's performance is embarrassed by

---

3 https://www.sonyclassical.com/news/news-details/roberto-alagna-caruso-1873#:~:text=%E2%80%9CFor%20as%20long%20as%20I,Enrico%20Caruso%2C%E2%80%9D%20writes%20Alagna.&text=Alagna's%20aim%20was%20to%20celebrate,would%20respect%20a%20composer's%20style.%E2%80%9D
4 Ibid.
5 Ibid.
6 'Morning.'
7 'Where you are not, there is no light, where you are, love is born.'

comparison, in part because he was stepping into shoes he was un-equipped to fill, but chiefly because Caruso's singing was unprecedented in 1904, just as it has been incomparable ever since.

The *actual* context for any proper consideration of Caruso's impact on opera, and tenor singing more specifically, is 1900 – not 1873. The turn of the 20th century has been the subject of more pathology than almost any other in human history. In 1900 the world was able for the first time to celebrate a new century globally – using technology unimagined in 1800. The telegraph and teletype, the telephone, trans-national rail networks and motor cars redefined the speed with which people were able to communicate with one another – person to person, and through real-time reporting and publishing. The globe was reduced most dramatically in scale by steam shipping. When the García company travelled to the United States in 1825 they did so by "packet" – a journey of almost 60 days. In April, 1838, the *Sirius* delivered 45 passengers from Cork to New York in 18 days. The speed of trans-Atlantic crossings between the 1840s and 1870s improved dramatically; the passenger experience did not. Of the 77 vessels leaving Liverpool for New York between 1 August and 31 October, 1853, 46 delivered the bodies of ticket-holders who had died *en route* of cholera. *The Washington* suffered 100 deaths during a single crossing alone. In 1894, less than a decade before Caruso travelled for the first time to New York, the *RMS Lucania* traversed the Atlantic in a little over five days. On 14 April, 1909, when Caruso sailed from New York to Liverpool on the *RMS Mauretania*, his journey was completed in extravagant luxury and at a constant speed of 25 knots – faster than a trans-Atlantic cruise ship in the 21st century.

Caruso was the first tenor in history to be cast by reference to recordings alone, which were shipped around the world and sold in their millions within weeks of pressing. When he arrived and sang for the first time in rehearsal, the common response among conductors, cast members, orchestral players and stagehands was one of disbelief. As such, while it is easy to consider the scale of his achievement in isolation, it's important to remember that Caruso was one of a large number of tenors performing on the same stages of Europe, Russia and the Americas. It's equally significant that he was not the first choice for every new opera. Indeed, while much is made of Caruso's audition for Puccini (when he is said to have responded "Who sent you to me, God?"), the composer made a conscious decision *not* to engage him for the first production of *Tosca* in Rome.

Contemporary music during the decade following Caruso's debut on 15 March, 1895 – in the now-forgotten *L'Amico Francesco* by the equally unremembered Mario Morelli – was a time of extraordinary resurgence for Italian opera, when hundreds of tenors were competing globally for first-billed status. Caruso was born into relative poverty; his only birth-right was Verdi and *verismo* – with Rossini, Bellini and Donizetti prevailing for the most part as footnotes for historicists. As far as taste and training were concerned, modernity was defined during the 1890s by Verdi's *Falstaff* (1893), Mascagni's *Cavalleria Rusticana* (17 May, 1890), Leoncavallo's *Pagliacci* (1892), Puccini's *La bohème*, Giordano's *Andrea Chénier* (both 1896), Cilea's *L'arlesiana* (1897), Giordano's *Fedora* and Mascagni's *Iris* (both 1898). When Mascagni won the Casa Sonzogno competition for one-act operas in 1889 (with *Cavalleria Rusticana*), seventy-three composers submitted fully orchestrated entries.

Giordano came sixth. *Tosca* was first performed on 14 January, 1900. The following year, almost to the day, Verdi died. Thereafter, Italian composers produced nothing of importance or international note until 1902, when Caruso created the tenor leads in the first productions of Franchetti's *Germania* (on 11 March) and Cilea's *Adriana Lecouvreur* (on 6 November) – both at La Scala, Milan. During the ensuing nineteen years, when Caruso reigned supreme as the "world's greatest tenor," the number of significant operas by Italian composers to be staged more than once slowed dramatically before collapsing entirely. After the unsuccessful premiere of Puccini's *Madama Butterfly* in 1904, nothing of note was produced until 1910, when Caruso created the role of the bandit Dick Johnson in *La fanciulla del West*. Aside from Montemezzi's *L'amore dei tre re*[8] in 1913, Zandonai's *Francesca da Rimini* in 1914, and Mascagni's *Lodoletta* in 1917, the only Italian operas to secure a popular following were composed by Giordano (*Madame Sans-Gene*, 1915) and Puccini (*La rondine*, 1917, and *Il trittico*, 1918). Puccini died three years after Caruso, in 1924, leaving *Turandot* incomplete. There were other Italian composers of opera, and some fine work was produced;[9] for the most part, however, Caruso's career coincided with the decline and fall of Italian music drama. In this context, he made a peculiar virtue of timing, because the contraction of contemporary music coincided with the emergence of recording as the new business of opera.

Beginning with his creation of Maurizio in *L'arlesiana* for Cilea, and ending with Johnson in *La fanciulla* for Puccini, Caruso gave the premiere of only six operas – four of which remain in general circulation.[10] His repertoire was large, spanning 74 roles, and while the majority of these were Italian he championed a number of French works – including *L'Africaine, Les Huguenots, Le Prophète* and, at the end of his life, *La Juive*. He performed the title role in the first US production of *Julien* for Charpentier in 1914, and in 1910 he sang Renaud in the American premiere of Gluck's *Armide* – 133 years after its debut in Paris. His last significant first night was the American premiere of Mascagni's *Lodoletta*, in 1918, with Geraldine Farrar in the title role. His only German operas (which he sang in Italian) were Flotow's *Martha*, Goldmark's *Die Königin von Saba*,[11] and *Lohengrin*.[12] It is eternally disappointing (and bizarre, considering his status as the world's most famous Italian singer) that Caruso appears not to have been invited to take part in a production of Strauss' *Der Rosenkavalier*. Neither did he record "*Di rigori armato.*"[13] Strauss was an admirer of Caruso's talent, and it's inconceivable that he and Hofmannsthal did not think of the tenor when writing the short scene in Act 1 for an 'Italian Singer' – performing in

---

8   'The Love of the Three Kings.'
9   Ferruccio Busoni, Ermanno Wolf-Ferrari, Gian Francesco Malipiero, Alfredo Casella, Licinio Refice, Franco Margola, Luigi Dallapiccola, Ennio Porrino and Nino Rota all composed operas, but none was ever what might realistically be termed popular.
10 The sixth, *Le maschere* ['The Mask'], was a homage by Mascagni to Rossini, and the *buffa* and *commedia dell'arte* traditions. It was premiered simultaneously in six Italian opera houses on 17 January, 1901. Caruso sang in the La Scala performance, with Toscanini conducting.
11 'The Queen of Sheba.'
12 He performed the latter two in Buenos Aires in 1899 and 1901 respectively.
13 The first 'Italian Singer' in the US, Carl Jörn (5 January, 1873 – 19 December, 1947), recorded "*Di rigori armato*" on 11 December, 1911 – just ten months after *Der Rosenkavalier*'s first performance in Dresden; bizarrely, the role's originator, Fritz Soot did not.

Italian. The obvious symmetry – and opportunity – was never acted on, even when Strauss and Caruso were frequently in the same city, and noting Caruso's delightful cartoon from 1910 of the composer holding the severed heads of Salome and (presumably) Klytemnestra.

Outside the opera house, and between 1 April, 1902,[14] and 16 September, 1920,[15] Caruso made approximately 290 recordings – most of which continue to sell on '78, LP, CD and digitally. It has been dogma for more than a century that the gramophone made Caruso, and Caruso made the gramophone, but this is simply not the case. Apart from anything else, it's a platitude that devalues the tenor's titanic work ethic on stage at the Metropolitan Opera in New York where he gave 863 performances, with his first (as the Duke of Mantua) on 23 November, 1903, and his last on Christmas Eve, 1920.[16]

Caruso was uniquely phonogenic because his voice was so perfectly suited to the acoustic recording process – which favoured darker vocal timbres. Many of his '78s sold in vast numbers, but records had been popular from 1899, when the bass-baritone Joachim Tartakov was recorded by William Sinkler Darby. Numerous other Russian singers made records during 1901, including the Figners, Labinsky, Sobinov, Vialtzeva, Nezhdanova and, most successfully, Chaliapin, whose first recordings were produced before Caruso's in January, 1902. The tenor Carlo Caffetto started recording in July 1900, and the bass Nazzareno Franchi followed suit in July, 1901. The French baritone Maurice Renaud made his first recordings in September, 1901 – as did Mario Sammarco, Giovanni Gravina, and Amelia Pinto, all of them colleagues of Caruso's for the first production of *Germania*. Only twenty-two of his recordings were made for the Gramophone Company – the rest for Anglo-Italian Commerce (Zonophone and Pathé) and the American Victor company.[17] Though Gaisberg would not be able to match Victor's later offers of money and publicity, his payment in 1902 of £100 (as sovereigns) to Caruso for just ten arias over a single afternoon in Rome was remarkably prescient – even if the stories told about this event (not least Gaisberg[18]) have little basis in fact. As Peter Martland's laudable detective work has demonstrated:

> The idea of Fred Gaisberg with a bag of gold wandering over Europe as a free-lance recording engineer, doubling up as a talent scout or impresario, recording anyone he felt would make a good recording artist, becomes somewhat absurd. By 1902, he and all the other engineers employed by The Gramophone and Typewriter, worked to predetermined schedules agreed and arranged between London and the branch managers […][19]

---

14 Franchetti, "*Studenti, udite*" ['students, hear me!'] from *Germania*.
15 Rossini, "*Crucifixus*" from *Petite Messe Solenelle*.
16 By way of comparison, Domingo performed 706 times as a singer (and 169 as a conductor) – but over a span of more than twice as many years.
17 See generally Favia-Artsay, Aida (1965). *Caruso on Records*. The Historic Record (Valhalla).
18 Martland, S. "Caruso's First Recordings: Myth and Reality." *ARSC Journal* XXV I ii 1994. pp.192–201.
19 *Ibid.*

As it turns out, Gaisberg did not send the famous telegram demanding monies for payment to Caruso. It was sent by Alfred Michaelis, the Company's branch manager, and it referred to additional singers, all to be paid handsomely. Gaisberg did not receive a reply forbidding him to proceed. Even so, he was certainly among the first to appreciate the dependency of the gramophone on voices of quality as well as celebrity, and securing these was sometimes harder than it should have been. When touring with his equipment through Europe (in 1899) and Russia (in 1900 and 1901), Gaisberg claims to have struggled to promote the virtues of what was dismissed by many as a gimmick:

> It is important to remember what a primitive little affair the gramophone was in 1900 [...] Whenever we approached the great artists, they just laughed at us and replied that the gramophone was only a toy.

There may well be some truth in this, but where Caruso was concerned the tenor was already established before he was recorded by Gaisberg. He was famous in Italy, and his tours to South America, Egypt and Russia pre-empted a contract to sing at Covent Garden shortly after the recording sessions. He was held in high esteem by Puccini, Leoncavallo, Giordano and Franchetti, and his co-stars were united in their admiration – including Melba, Tetrazzini, Chaliapin and Toscanini. If anything, it is surprising that he had not recorded earlier. Either way, Caruso embraced the technology because it assured him a calling card for potential engagements, and because it was *relatively* faithful to the tone and placement of his voice. When negotiating his fees, Caruso retained his pianist, Salvatore Cottone, to speak for him, and the opening run of '78s generated a fortune for the Gramophone and Typewriter Company. Caruso's promotion of the technology also helped persuade other prominent singers to sign contracts, including Antonio Scotti and Emma Calvé.

Caruso's performances for Gaisberg were far from perfect. There are missed entries, failed notes, coughs to clear his throat, and some dubious pitching. The circumstances of the recording sessions were less than ideal, of course. Caruso and Cottone had to perform in a carpeted hotel room with an ill-tuned upright piano that had to be set on a platform of packing cases at the same level as the tenor's head, so that the horn might capture the voice and its accompaniment in relative equivalence. The best and most faithful account of the experience of recording from this time is by Busoni, who recalled having to extemporise a four-minute version of Liszt's 10-minute arrangement of the Waltz from Gounod's *Faust* to cram it into a single take:

> thinking of certain notes which had to be stronger or weaker in order to please this devilish machine; not letting oneself go for fear of inaccuracies and being conscious the whole time that every note was going to be there for eternity; how can there be any question of inspiration, freedom, swing, or poetry?

Imperfections were trivial matters for listeners who were now able to eat, drink and relax at home to the sound of a voice that for once warranted the superlatives. The power, warmth and elegance of his singing were – and remain still – incomparable, which does not mean that there was nothing against which to make a comparison. At a time when there were dozens of premieres for which he was presumptively the first and only option, Caruso nonetheless created just six roles over 26 years. When Puccini was casting *Tosca*, his celebrity was such that he could have called on God to sing for him, and while it's true that he considered Caruso a divine *benefaction*, he nonetheless chose to gift the role of Cavaradossi to Emilio De Marchi.[20] He did so because of his greater experience. Caruso was only 26 years old in January, 1900 – an age when he was still some years from reaching vocal and physiological maturity. De Marchi was twelve years his senior and strikingly handsome; he was possessed also of an exceptionally powerful *spinto* voice. He made his debut in 1886 as Alfredo in *La traviata*, after which he toured Europe and South America singing Don José, Enzo (in Ponchielli's *La Gioconda*) and Faust. Prior to *Tosca*, his only notable creation was in 1895 when singing in the first production of Arturo Berutti's transcription of Nikolai Gogol's *Taras Bulba*. De Marchi made his debut at La Scala in 1898 as Walther, in an Italian-language version of *Die Meistersinger*; it was these performances that persuaded Puccini to cast him as Cavaradossi. Puccini is said to have regretted his decision after hearing Caruso sing the role in Bologna the following November, but this is neither fair nor probable. For a start, Caruso was thought by some to be too raw – crude, even – before he arrived in New York. One of those fortunate to be present in 1903 for that now legendary event, Arthur L. Friedman, lived long enough to be interviewed in his 90s by the *New York Times* in 1973. He recalled:

> I was 22 at the time, and I remember it all quite clearly. I was at the opera that night with a friend who knew a great deal about singing. Of course, the audience was prepared for Caruso — he was well-known abroad, you know —and they gave him tremendous applause. But my friend said: 'He's a hit, but I don't like him. Too crude'. And it was true. Caruso developed all his finesse in New York. He became a very fine artist, but he had no presence when I first heard him.[21]

It's manifestly absurd that Caruso had "no presence" in 1903. It is accepted, however, that he was only 30 at the time, and his earliest recordings do suggest a predilection for throwing the kitchen sink to the wind. A lack of restraint may have bothered Puccini also, a composer with almost surgical theatrical sensibilities, so De Marchi's greater experience gave him the edge – at least in 1900. Puccini also favoured other tenors for later premieres. Giuseppe Borgatti[22] sang the first La Scala Cavaradossi (under Toscanini) on 17 March, 1900, Fernando de Lucia[23] was Covent Garden's choice in 1901 (with Puccini in attendance), and the first night at the Metropolitan Opera on 4 February, 1901, was gifted to Giuseppe Cremonini.[24] De Marchi was engaged to play Cavaradossi at Covent Garden in 1901, and it was his debut role

---

20   6 January, 1861 – 20 March, 1917.
21   20 February, 1973.
22   17 March, 1871 – 18 October, 1950.
23   11 October, 1860 (or 1 September, 1861) – 21 February, 1925.
24   25 November, 1866 – 9 May, 1903.

the following year when he joined the Metropolitan Opera company. While in New York, De Marchi also gave the US premiere of *Ernani* – alongside much-praised performances as Radamès, Alfredo, Manrico, Raoul, Rodolfo, Riccardo, Turiddu, Canio and Don José.

De Marchi made no records, but Lionel Mapleson recorded him on cylinder performing in *Tosca*. It follows that posterity can hear something of the first Cavaradossi singing on the stage of the New York Metropolitan with a full orchestra in an opera he created for Puccini just two years after the premiere in Italy. For historians of the tenor voice, these cylinders are of Grail-like significance because they allow for the sound of De Marchi's voice to be heard in a natural acoustic, which a recording produced in a hotel room could not. It is possible also to hear the conducting of Luigi Mancinelli, which is incendiary and driven in a way that suggests things have not improved with time and technology. From the limited surviving material, the only really useful episode captures De Marchi singing "*Vittoria!*" during Act II. He generates a fantastic, ringing tone that more than validates the composer's instincts. Certainly, it's a more robust voice than that of Fernando de Lucia – the *bel canto* tenor who created the title role of *L'amico Fritz* for Mascagni in 1891. Somewhat improbably, De Lucia transitioned from lyric to much heavier repertoire; for all the beauty of his voice, however, and noting his exceptional technique, De Lucia was no *tenore di forza*. His tone is well supported on most of his recordings, but George Bernard Shaw (among many others) considered him underweight even for Gounod's *Faust*. Neither was his voice especially beautiful; indeed, his *vibrato* is rapid and incessant – with no sense whatsoever that it was being employed as *pigmento* – and he over-indulged *mezza voce*, *falsetto* and, most grievously of all, *fioriture*. He was inclined to adapt scores – including those by living composers – which provoked intense irritation among his contemporaries. Tito Ricordi, for example, wrote to Mascagni that:

> everything possible was done regarding Sig. De Lucia, who during rehearsals accepted all the observations [and] performed as required: only at the last rehearsal had I the – fleeting – suspicion that he was placating us [...]. I sent Toscanini to repeat to him all the recommendations made a hundred times at rehearsals – and the first night De Lucia played a dirty trick and did it his own way! What should we have done? Dragged him out through the wings? [...] Or fired a revolver at him?[25]

De Lucia's adoption of the *spinto* and *verismo* repertoire was a sign of the times, and a reflection of the incremental (and international) demand for tenors after 1900. This is well-illustrated by *Tosca*'s performance history. During the decade after its premiere on 14 January, 1900, Puccini's opera was staged in forty-four countries:

Argentina (Buenos Aires): 16 June, 1900
Britain (London): 12 July 1900
Turkey (Istanbul): 23 August 1900
Brazil (Rio de Janeiro): 13 September 1900

---

25   Potter, John (2009). *Tenor: History of a Voice*. Yale University Press. p.77.

Spain (Madrid): 15 December, 1900
Ukraine (Odessa): 1 January, 1901
Portugal (Lisbon): 29 January, 1901
United States (New York): 4 February, 1901
Greece (Athens): 14 April, 1901
Chile (Santiago): 30 June 1901
Mexico (Mexico City): 27 July, 1901
Egypt (Cairo): 26 November, 1901
Romania (Bucharest): 11 February, 1902
Uruguay (Montevideo): 17 Aug 1902
Germany (Dresden): 21 October, 1902
Cuba (Havana): 13 December, 1902
Puerto Rico (San Juan): 1902
Malta (Valletta): 4 March, 1903
Monaco (Monte Carlo): 28 March, 1903
Peru (Lima): 15 July, 1903
Tunisia (Tunis): 1903
France (Paris): 12 October, 1903
Poland (Warsaw): 7 November, 1903
Czech Republic (Prague): 21 November, 1903
Hungary (Budapest): 1 December, 1903
Paraguay (Asunción): 1903
Costa Rica (San José): 1903
Sweden (Stockholm): 15 February, 1904
Belgium (Brussels): 2 April, 1904
Austria (Graz): 10 June, 1904
Netherlands (The Hague): 22 December, 1904
Russia (St. Petersburg): 20 December, 1905
El Salvador (San Salvador): 10 May 1905
Finland (Helsinki): 20 September, 1905
Venezuela (Caracas): 25 October, 1905
Bulgaria (Varna): 10 May, 1906
Slovenia (Ljubljana): 1906
Switzerland (Geneva): 7 December, 1906
Philippines (Manila): 24 January, 1907
Panama (Panama): 3 November, 1908
Lithuania (Kaunas): November, 1909
Ireland (Dublin): 31 December, 1909
Denmark (Copenhagen): 5 May, 1910
Colombia (Bogotá): 9 August, 1910[26]

The triumph of *Tosca* was not shared by *Madama Butterfly*, premiered on 17 February, 1904. That work's failure was no fault of the first Pinkerton, Giovanni

---

26   Between 1910 and 1919, it was first staged in a further eleven countries: Australia, Latvia, Estonia, Croatia, Yugoslavia (Belgrade), Libya, China (1915), India, Sri Lanka, New Zealand and Japan.

Zenatello,[27] a singing actor with an exceptional, ringing tenor voice who benefitted from rare musical (and general) intelligence. He began his training as a baritone, and it was as a baritone that he made his debut at Belluno in 1898. The following year he switched to tenor roles and made his second debut as Canio in Naples. The richness of timbre formed during Zenatello's early twenties never left him, and the music written for his voice throughout his early career took valuable advantage of this baritonal registration. His first "originator" role was Vassili in *Siberia*, for Giordano in 1903; in the same year he created the role of Init in Antonio Smareglia's now forgotten *Oceàna*. In 1904 he was the first Pinkerton. In 1906 he was Franchetti's Aligi in *La figlia di Iorio* and in 1907 he gave his last premiere, as Lionetto de' Ricci ("Il Fortebrando") in Cilea's *Gloria*. In a gesture of profound generosity and good faith, Puccini retained Zenatello to sing Pinkerton in the revised version of *Butterfly* on 28 May, 1904. On both occasions, the conductor was Cleofonte Campanini – the brother of the celebrated tenor, Italo.

Judging by his recordings, Zenatello was not an obvious choice for Pinkerton. He was essentially a dramatic tenor, and during the 1910s and 20s he became the finest *Otello* of his (and arguably any) generation. As the live recording made of him as a fifty-year-old at Covent Garden in 1926 testifies, his status as the pre-eminent Moor was more than warranted.[28] Pinkerton is a different animal entirely; his lyricism is wholly at odds with the voice captured on record. Where, for example, Bergonzi made a case for Pinkerton being the most perfect *bel canto* role ever written, Zenatello's undeniably thrilling voice is rarely, if ever, beguiling. Indeed, rather than spin silk, Zenatello orates, adopting an approach to word and note placement that would set the benchmark for a generation that adopted an Italianate *Sprechgesang* for *verismo*. This feature of his art is less apparent on his recording of (part of) the love duet from Act 2 of *Butterfly* ("*Vogliatemi bene* […] *bimba dagli occhi pieni di malia*"[29]) with Linda Canetti, from 1911 – just seven years after the premiere(s). While this recording is interesting historically, it is far from persuasive.

That Pinkerton has only a single aria – "*Addio fiorito asil*"[30] (lasting around 2 minutes only) – should not detract from the role's status as Puccini's most complete essay for the tenor voice, more so even than Rodolfo and Cavaradossi. Pinkerton is a thoroughly nasty piece of work, whereas Rodolfo is weak and Cavaradossi and Johnson are vapidly heroic; Calàf rises little above a romantic cipher, even if some of his music is legendary. Pinkerton is a cruel and manipulative womaniser, a rapist in all but name; the insubstantiality of his character colours the monumental Act 2 duet with Butterfly as well as the Act 1 duet with Sharpless ("*Dovunque al mondo*"[31]). It's clear that Puccini was writing for Caruso even if Caruso was not cast for either premiere.[32] The solitary *ossia* high C at the end of the duet would not have challenged

---

27   22 February, 1876 – 11 February, 1949.
28   He retired six years later, in 1933.
29   'Love me. please […] girl with eyes full of malice.'
30   'Farewell, my flowery refuge…'
31   'Anywhere in the world.'
32   He did, however, sing Pinkerton at both the British and New York premieres (in 1905 and 1907 respectively).

Caruso on a good day; the rest is placed firmly in his sweet spot – in and around the *passaggio*. On 9 February, 1905, Puccini wrote to Caruso:

> I learned of Tosca at the Metropolitan and it pleased me so much to hear the echoes of the successes mostly obtained through you and your merits. In London you will sing Butterfly. I hope very much for your collaboration together with Destinn and Scotti.[…] I can hear you, I can see you in that part, which not being so lengthy a one (less work for you to learn it) has, notwithstanding, the need of your refulgent voice and of your art for the purpose of putting the role in its just and efficacious evidence.

Puccini had good reason to consider Caruso as "refulgent," but he was perennially in need of tenors. By 1911, with hundreds of opera houses across Europe and the United States and two or three tenors necessary for each fresh run of performances, the global appetite for opera fuelled an industry for the production and management of talent that would be eclipsed only by cinema during the 1930s. The sums of money earned by Caruso and his immortal soprano, baritone and bass-singing peers were widely publicised and sufficiently draw-dropping for opera to become a recognised route out of poverty, analogous to the boxing ring for many across Europe and the United States. Two years before Caruso's triumph as Dick Johnson in the first production of *La fanciulla del West* in 1910, John "Jack" Johnson[33] – the "Galveston Giant" – became the first African-American world heavyweight champion, initiating a continuing tradition wherein boxing would operate as a mechanism for social and cultural advancement as well as sporting achievement.

Caruso's contemporaries as Cavaradossi were in many cases his predecessors also. To appreciate the scale of the competition it's worth noting the names of *some* of the tenors who recorded for Fonotipia during the first decade of the 20th century: Luigi Longobardi, Fernando De Lucia, Fernando Carpi, Giuseppe Acerbi, Celeste Grassi, Romano Ciaroff-Ciarini, Francisco Vignas, Carlo Albani, Carlo Dani, Chamaemelo Fuscati, Luigi Schenoni, Manfredo Polverosi, Alessandro Bonci, Ode Gillion, José Palet, Obelissima Capelli, Giuseppe Krismer and Giuseppe Borgatti. Outside the arena of the collector and the expert, and apart from De Lucia, only the names of Borgatti and Bonci[34] have survived. Bonci was three years older than Caruso, but like many of his Fonotipia colleagues he had a light voice, incongruous with contemporary taste. He created no repertoire and devoted his long career to performing and recording[35] roles that predated him. Borgatti was a different matter. He was improbably handsome, beautiful even, and physically commanding – qualities that resonated through his singing as a genuine *tenore di forza*; even if he wanted for Caruso's warmth and infinite elegance of line, he was vocally and dramatically thrilling. In 1896 he created the role of *Andrea Chénier* for Giordano, and in 1900 he sang Cavaradossi in the first *Tosca* at La Scala, with Toscanini conducting. Borgatti

---

33   31 March, 1878 – 10 June, 1946.
34   10 February, 1870 – 9 August, 1940.
35   Between 1905 and 1926.

would go on to sing Wagner, and he relished a (brief) career as the finest Italian *heldentenor* of his generation; fittingly, he was the first Italian tenor to appear at the Bayreuther Festspiele, in 1904. Both Cosima Wagner and Hans Richter, conductor of the first *Ring* Cycle, were admirers of Borgatti's voice and theatrical judgment, as was Richard Strauss, who approved of him singing the role of Herod in the first production at La Scala of *Salome* in 1906 – again conducted by Toscanini, with Solomiya Krushelnytska (the "saviour" of *Madama Butterfly*) in the title role.[36] The following year, Borgatti was affected by glaucoma and over the following two years his sight degenerated rapidly. After a final performance of *Tristan* in 1913, and with his voice still in ringing form, Borgatti was forced to retire from staged opera. He continued to sing in concerts, blind in both eyes, until 1928.

Borgatti's fewer than 20 acoustic discs (for Fonotipia [1905] and Pathé [1919]) include some magnificent, era-defining performances, including a necessarily priceless "*Si fui soldato*"[37] from *Chénier*. They testify to an immense, expressive and disciplined tenor voice that was capable of performing "*Una furtiva lagrima*" even after years of singing Wagner. It's clear that Giordano reached further than he might have done in consequence of Borgatti's power-to-lyricism ratio, for which the role of Chénier was written, and the opera is unusual for its surfeit of memorably "floated" music for the tenor lead. In addition to the Act 1 blow-out, "*Un dì all'azzurro spazio*," there are numerous moments of blood-rushing drama and beauty in "*Come un bel dì di Maggio*,"[38] the Act 2 duet for Chénier and Madalena, "*Ora soave, sublime ora d'amore!*"[39] and the lovers' final duet.

Arguably the most remarkable moment in the tenor's score is the Act 2 soliloquy "*Credo a una possanza arcana!*"[40] in which Chénier summarises his destiny as love rather than poetry or soldiering. Giordano's writing is almost *parlando*, such is its elegance when performed by the right kind of voice; the tenor is required to soar above lush, romantically opulent orchestrations[41] as the poet articulates his philosophy through music that sits for the most part in the middle of the vocal register. The fluctuating psychological tensions and fevered emotion culminate in two B flat 4s that need to be delivered with persuasive brilliance at the end of the phrase "*Credi all'amor; Chénier, tu sei amato!*".[42] It is feverishly dramatic, and beyond the resources of the vast majority of tenors – particularly those who fail to engage with the naturally-occurring *portamento* that was hard-wired by the composer to his writing. Where Puccini's Rodolfo in *La bohème* suits a lighter voice – one capable of a C5 at the end of "*Che gelida manina*"[43] (when not transposing from D flat) – Chénier necessitates a dramatic tenor capable of phrasing like a Rossinian when gifted with the

---

36   For Toscanini, Krushelnytska was the "only woman I ever fell madly in love with who refused me." Christensen, Kenneth A. (2014). *The Toscanini Mystique: The Genius Behind the Music*. Xlibris.
37   'Yes, I was a soldier.'
38   'Like a beautiful day in May.'
39   'Now sweet, sublime hour of love!'
40   'I believe in a mystic power!'
41   During the *Credo*, for example, the tenor has to ring out a traffic-stopping F4 when singing the word "*soldato*," and then over the entire orchestra in *fortissimo* – absent only harps and double-basses.
42   'Believe in love; Chénier, you are loved!'
43   'Your little hand is frozen.'

diction of a Wagnerian. The oft-cited "bluntness" of *verismo* – typified by the roles of Turiddu in *Cavalleria Rusticana* and Canio in *Pagliacci* – does not translate to the majority of the repertoire, which is constitutionally lyrical. For all the sobbing and garment-rending interpolated into Tonio's "*Vesti la giubba*"[44] and notwithstanding the fun to be had with the hysterics of Turiddu's "*Addio alla Madre*" (with its invariably convulsive "*Un bacio, mamma! Un altro bacio! – Addio*"), the majority of *verismo* operas benefit as productively from *legato* as do the operas of Bellini. If the ability to hurl out B flat 4s in "*No pagliaccio non son*"[45] will suffice for those concerned only with *squillo*, the rest compels a talent for vocal and physical acting no less demanding than the mature Verdi canon.

It is in this nexus of power, expression and artistry that Caruso's exceptionalist status was located between 1900 and 1920. He was able to sing *verismo* as music drama while adhering throughout to the sanctities of line and articulation; he placed his enormous, kaleidoscopic voice at the service of intimate details as well as searing melodrama. Luigi Lucioni, a resident of Greenwich Village in New York, was 17 years old when he first heard Caruso sing in 1917. Fifty-six years later he recalled as unforgettable "one simple phrase" in *Le Prophète*, "a bit of recitative where [Jean] asks his mother, 'Am I your son?'".[46] Mr. Lucioni heard Caruso on six occasions, and he continued to attend the Met three times a week over the ensuing decades, but even after hearing everyone else who followed during those golden decades, Mr. Lucioni remained adamant that:

> I've never again heard anything like it. He absolutely believed in what he sang. You know, the voice had a beautiful dark baritone quality, but then going up it would suddenly have a burst of sunlight.

He told The New York *Times'* reporter of his friendship with one of Caruso's many "successors," Giovanni Martinelli. One evening at a party together, a guest flattered the tenor that he had heard him outdo Caruso in a recent performance. This irritated Martinelli, who replied: "My friend, you could put me, Gigli and Lauri-Volpi together and still not have a Caruso."[47] If the next generation was unable to compete, many of Caruso's contemporaries were presented confidently as rivals – even when plainly they were not, either because they were outclassed or because they chose to avoid the competition. From the former category, the most entertaining of Caruso's

---

44 'Put on your costume.'
45 'No, I am not a clown.'
46 The scene remembered is in Act 4: "*Eh bien, que maintenant vers moi ton oeil se lève!* [...] *Et vous qui m'écoutez. peuple, levez le glaive! Si je suis son enfant, si je vous ai trompés, Punissez l'imposteur! ... Voici mon sein ... frappez!* [...] *Suis-je ton fils?*" ['Well, let your eyes now lift up to me! ... And you who listen to me. people, raise the sword! [...] If I am her child, if I have deceived you. punish the impostor! [...] Here is my breast ... strike! [...] Am I your son?']
47 The story is told in other ways, albeit by people who were not present to hear him say it. For example: "If you were to put together the voices and talents of Gigli, Pertile, Martinelli, Lauri-Volpi, Schipa and the rest, their combination still wouldn't be fit to kiss Enrico Caruso's shoes." (as told to the author by the celebrated vocal coach Emannuale Morris in 1991).

immediate challengers was the wildly eccentric Spanish tenor, Antonio Arámburo[48] – the model for "il pazzo" himself, Franco Bonisolli.

Arámburo was born into wealth, and he specialised early in dilettantism. He decided eventually to train as a tenor and secured lessons with Antonio Cordero. His debut in 1871, in Milan, led to engagements throughout Italy, and three years later he performed at the Teatro Colón, and thereafter in Havana, Montevideo, Santiago and, eventually, New York. His repertoire included numerous Verdi operas, as well as *Norma*, *L'Africaine*, *Poliuto*, *Lucia di Lammermoor* and *Carmen*.

Arámburo's behaviour on stage was odd from the start. Some attributed it to nerves; others suggested he preferred not to sing sober. The general view remains that Arámburo suffered from a serious but undiagnosed mental illness. He was known to walk out of performances without cause – mid-way through an aria or an ensemble. While singing Edgardo at La Scala he was so angered by the audience's treatment of a debutant soprano (as a replacement for Emma Albani) that he marched from the theatre to his hotel room, where he was discovered by the Intendant in his underwear, frying breadcrumbs on a stove. When implored to return to the theatre, he draped a cloth over his head and began singing Spanish folksongs. Colonel Mapleson remembers Arámburo in an unfavourable light in his memoirs, while acknowledging that he was "a tenor possessing a marvellous voice, who has since achieved European fame":

> A kind of operatic duel was now going on between my two tenors, Campanini and Arámburo. The latter, with his magnificent voice, had quite conquered New York. Being a Spaniard, his own countrymen supported him by their presence in large numbers. But the tenor was displeased at sundry hisses which came from unknown quarters of the gallery, whilst two or three newspapers attacked him without reason. It was the eve of his performance in *Rigoletto* when I was informed that Senor Arámburo and his wife […] had suddenly sailed for Europe […] Early that morning Arámburo had come to me wanting to borrow 300 dollars. At first I refused, but he pressed me, saying that he had 'property in Spain' and that he really needed money to close up certain business transactions. I gave him the money, and this was the last that I saw of him.[49]

During a performance in 1882 as Manrico at the Teatro Real in Madrid, Arámburo learned that King Alfonso XII and his wife, Queen Maria Christina, had failed to attend as assured. He stormed in full costume from the opera house and headed to the city's Plaza Mayor, where he performed "*Di quella pira*" – *a capella*. By the 1890s, Arámburo was unemployable in Europe and so headed to the Americas. Unsavoury reviews in New York did not dissuade him from booking an extensive concert tour of the West Coast of the United States, and when this failed he returned to Montevideo and work as a doorman at the Teatro Solís – where previously he had been cheered on

---

48 17 January, 1840 – 16 September, 1912.
49 Mapleson, James, H. (1966). *The Mapleson Memoirs: the Career of an Operatic Impresario*. Ed. Harold Rosenthal. Putnam. pp.134–135.

stage. If Arámburo is now forgotten as a singer, he is enshrined for eternity in James Joyce's "The Dead":

> Mary Jane led the table back to the legitimate opera. One of her students had given her a pass for *Mignon*. Of course it was very fine, she said but it made her think of poor Georgina Burns. Mr. Browne could go back farther still, to the old Italian companies that used to come to Dublin—Tietjens, Ilma de Murzka, Campanini, the great Trebelli, Giuglini, Ravelli, Arámburo. Those were the days, he said, when there was something like singing to be heard in Dublin. He told too of how the top galley of the old Royal used to be packed night after night, of how one night an Italian tenor had sung five encores to *Let Me Like a Soldier Fall*, introducing a high C every time, and of how the galley boys would sometimes in their enthusiasm unyoke the horses from the carriage of some great prima donna and pull her themselves through the streets to her hotel. Why did they never play the grand old operas now, he asked, *Dinorah, Lucrezia Borgia*? Because they could not get the voices to sing them: that was why.
>
> – Oh, well, said Mr. Bartell D'Arcy, I presume there are as good singers today as there were then.
> – Where are they? asked Mr. Browne defiantly.
> – In London, Paris, Milan, said Mr. Bartell D'Arcy warmly. I suppose Caruso, for example is quite as good, if not better than any of the men you have mentioned.
> – Maybe so, said Mr. Browne. But I may tell you I doubt it strongly.
> – Oh, I'd give anything to hear Caruso sing, said Mary Jane.[50]

Arámburo is essential to any appreciation of Caruso's seismic effect on opera around 1900 and his influence on standards of singing during the thirty years preceding his appearance. Some – chiefly Arámburo – considered Arámburo to be superior even to Tamberlik, but his recordings suggest that anyone thinking this was lip-reading by necessity. He first made recordings, for his own label, in around 1901[51] – towards the end of his career, when Arámburo was around 63 years of age. There are some mesmerising highlights in his performances of "*D'un'alma troppo fervida*"[52] from *Poliuto*, Tosti's "*Ideale*" and "*Solenne in quest'ora*"[53] from *La forza del destino* – the latter in the company of a nameless, long-suffering unfortunate. The star of the show is the pianist, who does a sterling job keeping pace with Arámburo. The duet is among the most bizarre recordings in the history of opera. The baritone is more than capable, but required to stand some metres behind Arámburo, so that the duet operates for the most part as a solo. The missed entries, manic changes of pace and ludicrous *tenuti* (which conjure a mental image of "Tom" playing the piano in *The*

---

50 Joyce, James (1968). *The Dead*. Almqvist & Wiksell. pp.48–49.
51 The suitably concise *Compañía de Impresiones Fonográficas Antonio Arámburo*.
52 'Of a too fervent soul.'
53 'Solemn at this hour.'

Cat Concerto) suggest that performances with Señor Arámburo were chaotic, at best. There is nothing funnier on record than hearing the delusional tenor stumble and shout his way through music he is known to have performed in Milan, at the Teatro Lirico, in 1905, and at the Teatro Petruzzelli in Bari in 1912. But for Arámburo's status as a renowned tenor during the last third of the 19th century he would, for this recording alone, have been consigned to that box of rough-cut gems occupied by Florence Foster Jenkins, the Portsmouth Sinfonia and Steve Mauldin.[54]

There is compensation in Arámburo's tone, which is striking, and he boasts impressive resonance for a man of his years; it's a pleasure also to hear a turn-of-the-century tenor sing without a perennial "flutter" *vibrato* – as was clearly the fashion for singers reaching their maturity during the last decade of the century. His phrasing, such as it his, suggests inebriation, and a startling disregard for the score, presuming he had access to one at the time. There is no expression beyond "con belto," and he makes not a single attempt to vary his dynamics, which remain doggedly *fortissimo*. Having said all of that, the excerpt from *Poliuto* – while surreal – indicates that Arámburo had access to a genuine *legato* in his youth. The performance of *Ideale* is anything but, even if it is well-articulated, and his creative use of *vibrato* is again intriguing for a man who made his debut in the same year as Verdi's *Aida*.

Of those to cross Caruso's path only rarely, neither Borgatti nor Giuseppe Anselmi[55] nor Fiorello Giraud[56] performed in the United States. They were incomparable for audiences in New York , therefore, other than by reference to their recordings. It was inevitable that Caruso's fame would be ubiquitous throughout the United States, where PR was all but invented. Giraud's celebrity flowed uniquely from his creation of Canio in *Pagliacci* on 21 May, 1892 – when he was still seven months from his 22nd birthday. Giraud's voice was splendid; his recordings of the "Flower Song" from *Carmen*, and "*Come un bel dì di maggio*"[57] are both memorably virile,[58] even if his *vibrato* is invasive and the phrasing far from aqueous. Anselmi is another tenor with a near-constant *tremolo* that debilitates his otherwise solid "old school" technique. Most of his recordings reveal an exceptional talent for *mezza-voce*, dynamic contrast and (distended) *rubato*. Depending on the repertoire, his phrasing can be pleasingly lyrical, but the style is often mannered and uneasy. He is inclined to force his tone, especially above the stave, and while he lacked the heft necessary for *verismo* it is still fascinating to hear "*Vesti la giubba*" sung as *bel canto*, with line prevailing over histrionics.

A simple comparison between Anselmi's laboured performance of "*Giunto sul passo estremo*"[59] from Boito's *Mefistofele* and Caruso's recording of the same aria for Gaisberg in April, 1902, reveals the differences between the singers' voices and their

---

54 Mr. Mauldin, a "tenor," is renowned internationally for his hilarious recording of "O Holy Night," which was made yet more famous by Martin Landry's outstanding lip-synched "performance" on YouTube. It is not entirely clear whether Mr. Mauldin's singing is intentionally bad, but bad it most definitively is.
55 6 October, 1876 – 27 May, 1929.
56 22 October, 1870 – 28 March, 1928.
57 Unusually, Giraud sings the climactic phrase "*Darò per rima il gelido Spiro…*" as written, with a G flat, rather than with the *ossia* B flat provided by the composer.
58 Recorded in April, 1904, in Milan – with Caruso's accompanist Salvatore Cottone.
59 'Nearing the utmost limit.'

approaches to phrasing. Caruso was not yet thirty, and his voice was still a long way from reaching its prime; the essence of the haunting, expressive melancholy for which he would become famous is in striking evidence, however, particularly during the aria's seamless closing phrase. Where Giraud and Anselmi both sound as if they are lifting weights, Caruso appears to be doing nothing more than breathing. Indeed, his exceptionally resonant lower and middle registers, and the colour of the voice in its variegation, render the inequalities of the acoustic recording process Darwinian for everyone else. Caruso has been criticised for singing everything *forte*, if not *fortissimo* – and it's undeniable that he approached things differently to his allegedly *bel canto* predecessors and contemporaries, but the recordings speak louder than prejudice, so while Caruso bypassed the taste for technical *minutiae* (such as the extremes of colour and dynamics indulged by De Lucia *et al.*), he rejected the fashion for bloated *rubati*, ill-considered *mezza-voce* and *fioriture*. He was happy to pay lip service to convention, on occasion. In 1908, for example, for his first recording of "*Bella figlia d'amore*" from *Rigoletto*, he sings almost every connecting phrase with an exquisitely limpid *portamento* – all of it plainly considered by the tenor – and he adds a number of unwritten turns, each of them designed to achieve emphasis over effect. Caruso's voice is pure velvet, whereas the later recordings are darker and more powerful, such that the sound equipment struggled to capture the huge and imperious tone. His ability to shape and articulate Verdi's music was extraordinary during the first decade of the 20th century, but so too were his performances of music by the *veristi* and Puccini. In other words, where Caruso's rivals sang Leoncavallo as well as Donizetti and Verdi because the market required it, Caruso performed old and new because he could.

Caruso learned also how to sing for the gramophone, which is where the '78s he made soon after his arrival in New York in 1903 reveal a notable shift in maturity. The Milan sides are relaxed, sloppy even; the 1904–1905 sessions in New York demonstrate unprecedented heights of polished vocal mastery. The early versions of "*Una furtiva lagrima*" are spontaneous and vital; the first New York remake is a jaw-dropping demonstration of the virtues of effortless *legato* and breath control. It's a near-perfect demonstration of that rare fusion of showmanship and artistry for which Caruso was, to that time, unique.

Another would-be rival, Carlo Albani,[60] amplifies the difference between Caruso and everyone else. His recording from 1912 of "*Un di all'azzurro spazio*" reveals yet another ugly *vibrato*, and some heavy-handed phrasing. The voice has scale and intermittent focus, but the tone is one-dimensional, and he appears either to hate the conductor and the orchestra, or not notice their presence. At one point, everyone except Albani appears to give up. Oscar Hammerstein engaged him for the 1908–09 season at the Manhattan Opera, where he made his debut as Manrico. He later made the mistake of carrying out some engagements with the Boston Opera while in contract with Hammerstein; predictably, this resulted in litigation. Albani was arrested on stage, mid-way through a performance. Many of his recordings suggest there were other, better reasons for his incarceration – most of them flowing from his palpable contempt for the score and the conductor. His performance of "*Ora e per sempre*

---

60   1872 – 1924.

addio" re-casts Mario del Monaco as a pedant. His "*niun mi tema*" is positively porcine – and includes not only the silent (and unwritten) E4 with which Otello dies, but a repeat of it for good measure.

The inadequacies of many of those highly regarded tenors who made records around 1900 cast doubt over the reputations of those who didn't. Julián Gayarre,[61] for example, was born four years after his *camarada* Arámburo, but died young in 1890 at the age of 45. He created the posthumous role of Marcello for Donizetti in *Il Duca d'Alba* in 1871, and Enzo for Ponchielli in *La Gioconda* in 1876. He was admired by many as among the greatest stylists of the 19th century. He was a singer of contemporary music also, and towards the end of his career he created the role of Sobinin at the London premiere in 1887 of Glinka's *A Life for the Tsar*. He was able to alternate in the same season between Rossini and (early) Wagner – most famously *Tannhäuser* (of which he gave the first performance in Italy) and *Lohengrin*, which he created for Spanish audiences in Madrid in 1881. Prophetically, he understood the curse of the singer's fate before the advent of recording. In 1880 he wrote to his friend and biographer Julio Enciso Robledo:

> The glory of the theatrical artist is like a dream; a painter, a poet, a composer, they leave their works. What remains of us? [...] Nothing, absolutely nothing. A generation that says to the other: How Gayarre sang! [...] When my throat says: I can't take it anymore, what will be left of Gayarre? A name that will last for as long as those who heard me last, but nothing after that. Believe me, then, my friend Julio, that our glory is not worth, and will not last longer than, the smoke of a cigarette.[62]

What can be established without question is that Gayarre employed a quick and incessant *vibrato* – comparable to that of Albani and Anselmi. Writing of Gayarre's London performances, G. B. Shaw lamented what he considered to be vocal affectations and lapses in judgment – as if, presumably, Gayarre had chosen to sing in this way. Shaw lamented the tenor's "artificial" vocal mannerisms, but Gayarre appears to have compensated for his tone production by its extreme variation. He made a virtue of dramatic dynamic contrasts which, supported by excellent breath control, suggest he warranted comparison in purely mechanical terms with De Lucia. Gayarre did not live long enough to make a name for himself in *verismo*, but his rival, Roberto Stagno,[63] made a successful transition from Rossini, Bellini and Donizetti to contemporary music – and the first performance in 1890 of *Cavalleria Rusticana*. Stagno was popular internationally, and during the 1880s he was one of the first Italian tenors to triumph critically in North and South America, particularly in Buenos Aires and New York. His popularity in the United States was short-lived, however, because he too indulged a pronounced and persistent *vibrato*, which audiences at the Met were not prepared to tolerate. Mascagni was an admirer, since he chose to cast him as the first Turiddu.

---

61   9 January, 1844 – 2 January, 1890.
62   Robledo, Julio Enciso (1891; 1990). *Memorias de Julián Gayarre*. Laida Edición e Imagen. p.86.
63   18 October, 1840 – 26 April, 1897.

Similarly beset by issues relating to *vibrato* was Italo Campanini[64] – a rival to Gayarre, Stagno and Tamagno – whose voice declined early, and before he was invited to create any roles of significance. Not every late-19th century tenor surviving to the 20th, however, sang with a "bleat." The Spanish tenor Fernando Valero[65] made a small number of fine recordings, despite having made his debut in 1878. In 1880 he appeared for the first time at the Teatro Brunetti in Bologna in Ponchielli's *I Promessi sposi*; the following year he sang for the first time in Milan, where he was greeted as "Little Gayarre." He performed widely throughout Europe and Russia (as the first Don José in Moscow) and was cast as Turiddu at the New York Metropolitan Opera opposite Emma Eames in 1891. In 1903 he recorded in London and Milan for Gaisberg; while plainly no longer in his prime, Valero's tone is warm and beautifully placed. His *vibrato* is light and his artistry is among the finest on record from the period when Caruso made his first recordings. The performance of Turiddu's "*O Lola ch'ai di Latti*" is especially musical, as are the two songs by Tosti. The voice is light, albeit nowhere as large as Caruso's; his attention to line and expression are marvellous, and for a singer born in 1856 his performances are among the finest from the period.

There were other tenors worthy of note from the turn of the century – a number of whom made recordings at the same time as the young Caruso, between 1903 and 1908. Eduardo Garbin,[66] for example, was Verdi's (reluctant) first choice as Fenton for the first staging of *Falstaff* in 1893 – just 18 months after his stage debut at the Teatro Comunale on September 6, 1891.[67] Verdi based his decision, in part, on Garbin's success in October, 1892, when he created the role of Don Fernando Guevara in the world premiere of Franchetti's widely praised *Cristoforo Colombo*. Verdi had wanted Angelo Masini for Fenton, but when he proved unavailable the composer coached Garbin personally, in circumstances he described with absent charity to his publisher Ricordi. Verdi complained that the tenor was unable to learn the part in the time available, and he advocated the retention of "a pedant" to teach him the "notes, tempo and clear words well." Verdi further complained of Garbin's habit of spreading his vowels, and his pronunciation more generally. The tenor's recordings between 1902 and 1913 for The Gramophone & Typewriter Company, Fonotipia, and Columbia are alarmingly inconsistent, and many reflect Verdi's concerns – particularly his "*Che gelida manina*" which is, at times, profoundly ugly. There is little phrasing, the *vibrato* is wide and incessant, the tone colourless and the breathing all but amateur. He was in much better voice for "*Donna non vidi mai, simile a questa,*"[68] from *Manon Lescaut*. Recorded in November, 1904, for Fonotipia, this performance reveals a striking upper register, considerable tonal focus and some elegant phrasing to boot. Garbin was popular in Italy, derided in London, and never invited to sing in the United States. Because his reputation as the first Fenton gave him inevitable authority, he was retained for a number of other (now forgotten) first nights by Leoncavallo (*Zazà*, 1900), Spiro Samara (*Rhea*, 1908), Italo Montemezzi

---

64 30 June, 1845 – 14 November, 1896.
65 6 December, 1856 – January, 1914.
66 12 March, 1865 – 12 April, 1943.
67 In Vicenza as Don Alvaro in *La Forza del Destino*.
68 'I have never seen a woman such as this.'

(*Héllera*, 1909), Giocondo Fino (*La Festa del Grano*, 1910), and Ezio Camussi (*La Dubarry*, 1912).

Garbin's variable artistic judgment was typical of many who made records at the time, including Bernardo De Muro (remembered for his absurdist "*Esultate*"), and Francesco Marconi,[69] who utilised an interesting albeit less intrusive Moreschi-sob as a turn for his recording of "*Di pescatore ignobile*" from *Lucrezia Borgia*.[70] Marconi made his debut in Madrid in 1878 at the Teatro Real, singing Faust; ten years later he was retained by Italo Campanini to sing in the first production of *Otello* in New York. Unfortunately for all concerned, the first night was a disaster, and after the second performance Campanini was compelled to take over. Although ill-judged repertoire was pivotal to Marconi's early decline, his recording of "*O paradiso*" from *L'Africaine* contains some marvellous singing; the final few bars are extremely well carried off. It's plain that his efforts were deleterious, requiring more of him than he would have been able to give for the duration of an opera on stage, and it's self-evident that the shadow thrown by Caruso's amplitude did far more harm than good. Of course, Caruso chose not to sing the role of Otello, although he recorded "*Ora e per sempre addio*" and "*Si per ciel*" with Titta Ruffo – recordings considered to be among the finest by a tenor to be released commercially. Of those among his contemporaries to succeed in the role, the Puerto Rican Antonio Paoli[71] was perhaps the most admired, although it's debatable that he warranted the sobriquet "King of Tenors." In 1902–1903, Paoli belonged to an opera troupe assembled by Mascagni that toured the USA and Canada; for the ensuing twenty years he enjoyed a considerable career in Caruso's wake – until the First World War closed Europe's opera houses and Paoli took up his new career as a professional pugilist. After a period of training in Spain, he relocated to England as a prize fighter. To his credit, he was undefeated after five fights, but during the sixth he broke his right wrist and was forced to return to singing. Elvira de Hidalgo, who later taught Maria Callas, recalled:

> No one suspected that Paoli was coming back to the stage; we all knew that he had lost his voice. People were there to see him fail; I saw some guys with tomatoes and rotten eggs, ready to throw them as soon as Paoli made his first mistake. But when he came out singing his initial aria, the public went crazy and stood up in a standing ovation. Paoli's voice sounded like one of those trumpets that you expect to hear in the day of the final judgment. His debut was tremendous. He had to repeat twice every single aria that he performed that night, because the public furiously demanded it. He performed for seven consecutive nights with the theater at its maximum capacity. I attended every single function. Every night he sang better than the night before. I always dreamed to

---

69 14 May, 1853 – 5 February, 1916.
70 It's likely Marconi picked this up from Moreschi and his peers while studying with Venceslao Persichini in Rome at the Conservatory during the 1870s.
71 14 April, 1871 – 24 August, 1946.

sing with Paoli, but I don't think my voice was good or strong enough to sing with him. I think he was the greatest tenor ever.[72]

In 1907, Paoli was the first tenor to record an entire opera when he sang Tonio in a performance of *Pagliacci*, with the composer conducting. To make the recording, the orchestra was placed at the end of the "studio," with the chorus in a semi-circle in front of the gramophone. Paoli stood some 20 feet from the horn – and his voice survives as brilliant, focussed and resonant. Appropriately enough for an undefeated boxer, one of his finest performances on record is of "*Esultate,*" the tenor's entrance at the beginning of Act 1 of *Otello*. It is, as de Hidalgo remembered, a trumpet of a voice – and Paoli uses it well, all things considered. Attractive it is not, however, any more than was the voice of the dramatic tenor Giovanni Battista De Negri,[73] born twenty years before Paoli and Caruso, but who retired after making a handful of recordings for Zonophone between 1901 and 1903. De Negri was among the last Italian tenors to create a major 19th century role – *Guglielmo Ratcliff* for Mascagni in 1895 – although it was his performances as *Otello* that brought him fame and fortune. He sang the role more often even than Tamagno, and Verdi was openly admiring of his abilities as an actor.

Many of the tenors said to be in competiton with Caruso didn't sing his repertoire because he remained throughout his career a lyric tenor with *di forza* resonance. His voice was larger and brighter than any other, but he never allowed the virtues of amplitude to distract him from the cardinal art of phrasing. His attention to warmth of tone, silken *legato* and language-directed *portamento* – for which his singing is quite properly revered – would not be jeopardised even after his voice darkened in 1918, such that it was indistinguishable from many baritones. Caruso's style and his aesthetics as a voice actor defined his work as a singer; many of those to emerge during the ten years either side of his death in 1921 were transitional rather than hereditary, since they were unable to learn from what he had only recently been able to teach. The most important of these was Giovanni Martinelli.[74] He sang as a child in his local church choir and played the clarinet in a military band, where the music director heard him singing by chance. He was sent to train with Giuseppe Mandolini in Milan, where he made his professional debut at the Teatro dal Verme in a production of *Ernani* in 1910. The following year he gave his first performance as Dick Johnson in *La fanciulla del West*, which he sang soon after in Rome with Toscanini. Having succeeded in London (as Cavaradossi) he made his American debut in Philadelphia, and on 25 April, 1913, he portrayed Pantagruel in the premiere staging of Massenet's *Panurge* at the Théâtre de la Gaîté in Paris – almost a year after the composer's death.

Martinelli appeared at the Metropolitan Opera for the first time on 20 November, 1913, as Rodolfo. Two years later, on 25 January 1915, he was chosen by Giordano to create the role of Lefebvre in the premiere at the Met of *Madame Sans-Gêne*, conducted by Toscanini. On 28 January, 1916, he sang in his last premiere – again at the Met – as Fernando in Enrique Granados' *Goyescas*. Martinelli served as a pillar of

---

72 Lopez, Jesus M. (1997). *Antonio Paoli: El Leon de Ponce*. Ediciones Liricas. p.469.
73 30 July, 1851 – 3 April, 1924.
74 22 October, 1885 – 2 February, 1969.

the House for 32 seasons, giving 926 performances of 36 roles, most commonly as Radamès, Otello, Manrico, Don Alvaro in *La forza del destino*; Calàf, Dick Johnson, Arnold in *Guglielmo Tell*, Eléazar, Enzo in *La Gioconda*, Don José, Vasco de Gama in *L'Africaine,* Canio and Pollione. He also sang *Tristan* during the 1930s, but chiefly, it seems, to make a point. In 1967, at the improbable age of 82, he gave a single performance in Seattle as Emperor Altoum in *Turandot*.

Other than Caruso, and with the exceptions of Richard Tauber, Miguel Fleta (who created Romeo for Zandonai's *Giulietta e Romeo* in 1922 and Calàf in *Turandot* in 1926) and Nicolai Gedda, who sang the role of Anatol in the first production of Barber's *Vanessa* in 1958, Martinelli was the last internationally renowned "Romantic" tenor to create a role for a significant composer. He had a powerful, *spinto* voice of ringing brilliance that produced a strong high C in its youth; even so, he was never easy above the stave and he was far from lyrical by instinct. He had none of Caruso's warmth or elegance, and his recordings are marked by an unsteady tone, with an uneven (or absent) *vibrato* that suggested a lack of technique rather than artistic judgment. In 1926 he appeared in a Vitaphone short film at the beginning of the sound era (singing "*Vesti La Giubba*") – a year before *The Jazz Singer* – and in 1927 he was captured by the same company in an extended scene from *La Juive* ("*Ta fille en ce moment*"[75]) with bass, Louis D'Angelo. Martinelli's career overlapped substantially with that of Caruso – and continued for more than twenty years after Caruso's death in 1921. Beniamino Gigli, on the other hand, gave his first performance at the New York Met on 26 November, 1920 – less than a month before Caruso's last.

Between November, 1913, and August, 1921, thousands of tenors took to the word's stages and waited their turn. In all but a handful of cases, it never came. During Caruso's final eight years, the title of the world's greatest tenor was never in doubt. Though he created only a single role for Puccini, and then in the least successful of his major works after *Manon Lescaut*, Caruso was the Puccini tenor of his age, a singer able to stand alongside the composer in matters of talent, charm, success, wealth and celebrity. Indeed, Puccini might have been describing himself when writing of Caruso that he "won't learn anything, he's lazy and he's too pleased with himself."[76] Even when he received bad notices, which happened on occasion, there was usually a clear reason for the criticism. In December, 1912, a review of *Grand Opera Singers of Today*, a recently published book by Henry C. Lahee, was printed in the *Lotus Magazine*, in which

> Mr. Lahee says of the tenor, who dominates Italian opera in New York today, that "of all the singers engaged by Conried[77] at the Metropolitan Opera-House no one ever became so great a celebrity as Enrico Caruso. As an actor and as a singer his art was inferior to that of several of his rivals…. Campanini was a Caruso, a Bonci and a Salvini in one.[78]

---

75 'Your daughter, here now…'
76 Seligman, Vincent (1938). *Puccini Among Friends*. Macmillan. p.119.
77 Heinrich Conried (3 September, 1855 – 27 April, 1909), director of the Metropolitan Opera between 1903 and 1908.
78 "Opera Singers of Today." *The Lotus Magazine*, Vol. 4, No. 3 (Dec., 1912). pp.115–120.

The reviewer was inclined to "explain" that

> the extremes to which the Caruso craze sometimes is carried, is found in the large number of Italians who go to the opera and their demonstrative methods. In Campanini's best days New York had but a small Italian population. Yet Campanini scored many triumphs. They never, however, degenerated into a nuisance as many a Caruso demonstration does.[79]

Henry Krehbiel's vernacular was more eloquent, but no less hateful. Of Caruso's Eléazar he wrote that it qualified as an "inartistic and deplorable catering to the taste of the groundlings."[80] He was writing primarily as a devotee of Jean De Reszke, and thereafter as a critic seeking to forge his independence from Caruso's "internationalist" claque. Krehbiel was describing an immigrant from one of the poorest parts of Southern Italy who nevertheless, during almost two decades in the United States, paid vast amounts of tax to the US treasury – taxes which helped fund the writing of the Immigration Commission's Dillingham report in 1911, in which it was stated without fear of contradiction that

> Certain kinds of criminality are inherent in the Italian race. In the popular mind, crimes of personal violence, robbery, blackmail and extortion are peculiar to the people of Italy.[81]

The Commission's report was racist even by the standards of a country that attached itself without shame to the "Jim Crow" laws for more than four decades after Caruso's death. When, in 1913, he recorded Percy Kahn's version of "Ave Maria" (a Catholic prayer for the intercession of the Blessed Virgin Mary) with violin *obligato* provided by a Ukranian-Jewish émigré (Mischa Elman), it's unlikely that many of those who bought the discs in their thousands recognised the perverse irony of President Woodrow Wilson's having initiated the segregation of federal workplaces that same year. Caruso's sensitivity to his "innate" social isolation, even with all his fame, wealth and influence, is poignant, and it explains in part why he was so offended by criticism of his acting when it was said by certain quarters to lack "class," whatever that was supposed to mean. For the likes of Henry Krehbiel, it meant that he was blue-collar and uncivilised. Stories of Caruso's eating habits (such as his consumption of an entire plate of spaghetti in a single mouthful) and his profligate spending were preferred to tales of his generosity and kindness, and the sheer wonder of his physicality off-stage as well as on it. Indeed, if the spaghetti episode is incredible, it's worth remembering that he was seen on one occasion to put an orange into his mouth and click his teeth. Caruso's vibrancy was repainted as impetuosity. For the likes of Krehbiel, his larger-than-life character distinguished him from the classical restraint and artistic "dignity" of Jean De Reszke. For others, it was nothing more

---

79 *Ibid.*
80 Krehbiel, Henry. "Caruso Sings in *La Juive.*" New York *Tribune*, 5 December, 1919. p.13.
81 Benton-Cohen, Katherine (2018). *Inventing the Immigration Problem: The Dillingham Commission and Its Legacy*. Harvard University Press.

complicated than jealousy. In the *Literary Digest* dated 9 May, 1908, for example, a "foreign visitor" from Paris, André Tardieu, was given column inches to pontificate on America's "Caruso Delusion":

> At the moment it is Caruso who reigns. His prestige is incomparable. He owes it first of all to the enormous price which he charges for his services, for in the theatre the American public admire only those artists for whom they pay dear.... Everything he sings he sings with the same facility, with the same sonorous prodigality – and also with the same bad taste. The Americans are surprised and dumbfounded when they hear this criticism of Caruso. They admit that Caruso may not be particularly artistic, but they do not judge him as he deserves to be judged. In listening to him they forget to study him, and the richness of his voice satisfies them. This, however, is not sufficient for the European, fastidious with regard to style and artistic form.... his American public does not seem to be affected by his deficiencies...[82]

Tardieu's leading criticism was that a "great" artist need not also be a "great" singer. With what appears to be signal personal *animus*, he cited the treatment in the United States of Ernst Van Dyck after he lost his voice, and asserted that "'golden notes' will always appeal to the women." Caruso's popularity in New York was the product apparently of "amiability and his kindliness to newspaper men." Tardieu's loathing for a "fellow" European was not lost on Caruso, and his sensitivity to the media explains in part his profound attachment at the end of his career to *La Juive*. Halévy's opera had long exercised a cross-cultural magnetism for immigrants, whether Jewish or Gentile, and Caruso's connection to the role of Eléazar was understandable to many less sensitive than he to his background as a poor and imperfectly educated "*guappo*."[83] After triumphs at the Met in French opera in 1916 (Saint-Saëns' *Samson et Dalilah*) and 1918 (Meyerbeer's *Le Prophète*), Caruso did not struggle to persuade Giulio Gatti-Casazza, General Manager of the Met, to mount a new staging of *La Juive*. During the summer of 1919, while at home in his Tuscan Villa Bellosguardo,[84] Caruso worked obsessively on the score, transcribing each syllable phonetically. During his many years of almost constant travel he had paid regular visits to synagogues to hear the cantors. When passing through Hamburg, for example, he asked his European agent, Emile Ledner, to join him on a visit to the Bornplatz synagogue in the city's Jewish quarter (the "Grindelviertel").[85] After the service, Caruso explained:

---

[82] *The Literary Digest*. 9 May, 1908. p.688.
[83] *Guappo* (plural: *guappi*) is a hostile term of address adopted during the late 19th century on the east coast of the United States, after its common use by Neapolitans; it translates broadly as thug, pimp, braggart, hooligan and (eventually) mobster.
[84] Now a Caruso museum. It is available also for weddings.
[85] The synagogue on Bornplatz was inaugurated in 1906. It was destroyed during the first night of the *Reichspogromnacht* ("Kristallnacht") in 1938. After the building's demolition in 1939, the site was "sold" to the city.

> I have discovered that the Jewish cantors employ a peculiar art and method of singing in their delivery. They are unexcelled in the art of covering the voice, picking up a new key, in the treatment of the ritual chant, and overcoming vocal difficulties that lie in the words rather than in the music. For this reason I visit the Jewish synagogues whenever I have the opportunity and the time.[86]

When back in New York, he spoke with Yiddish theatre directors and actors, as well as rabbis, to ensure that his portrayal did justice to the detail of Eléazar's appearance as well as his sound and movement.[87] A great deal has been written about this extraordinary production, and with good reason. The conductor was the supremely talented Artur Bodanzky, and Rosa Ponselle was retained to sing the role of Rachel. The audience's reaction on the first night (22 November, 1919) was adulatory; the critics were not far behind:[88]

> Eleazar is a character which gives an opportunity for the full display of his voice and vocal resources. Moreover, dramatically it suits the maturity of the great tenor, who at forty-six no doubt grows a little weary of interpreting passionate and youthful lovers. Paternal affection, religious ecstasy, and overpowering revenge – these are epic passions unfelt by callous youth.

On November 23, 1919, James Gibbons Huneker wrote in the New York *World* ("*La Juive* is Revived"):[89]

> We have seldom heard such expressive singing as Caruso's delivery of his air in the fourth set, 'O Rachel'. Our generation should feel it a privilege to hear this truly great artist sing; apart from his unique vocal organ he is dowered with a musical temperament rarely found in the tenor tribe. His success was tremendous on this occasion, as it deserved to be. His voice was in splendid condition, and Shylock-Caruso bids fair to become one of the sensations of a not particularly promising season. He was called a half dozen times after Act IV.

---

86 Caruso, Enrico Jr. and Farkas, Andrew (1990). *Enrico Caruso: My Father and My Family*. Amadeus Press. p.339.
87 There is a photograph of Caruso in costume as Eléazar, with both hands displaying the Jewish gesture of "*Kohanim*" – formed to represent the Hebrew letter Shin (ש), which has three upward strokes. The letter Shin is here used to mean *El Shaddai* ("Almighty God"), as well as for *Shekinah* and *Shalom*. There are numerous fans of opera who are also "Trekkers", fans of *Star Trek*, in which the same hand gesture is used by the "Vulcan" people. In his autobiography, *I Am Not Spock*, Leonard Nimoy wrote that he based the greeting on the blessing he had seen performed as a child when taken by his grandfather to Synagogue.
88 "Caruso Scores in the Revival of *La Juive*." New York *Tribune*, 23 November, 1919. p.17.
89 "*La Juive* is Revived." New York *World*, 23 November, 1919. p.15

The praise was qualified elsewhere (predictably, from Henry Krehbiel):[90]

> In his impersonation of Halévy's Jew, Mr. Caruso shows a desire to make more of himself than an operatic marionette. He succeeds in doing this in his singing, and strives valiantly towards this in his acting. It is, perhaps, an inherent defect in his individuality which prevents him from sinking himself completely in his part.

If it seems churlish of Krehbiel to have damned the finest tenor of his generation for having too much personality, this was a routine criticism of a performer who was felt by many to align more obviously with Tonio than Eléazar. His transcendence in *La Juive* was absolute, however, and ten of his 47 appearances during the 1919–20 season were as Eléazar, with seven in New York, and one each in Brooklyn, Philadelphia and Atlanta. The nobility, power and pathos of Caruso's portrayal had a profound effect on many, including Ponselle, and few were surprised when *La Juive* was nominated for Caruso's sixteenth season opening, on 15 November, 1920. Richard Aldrich of the New York *Times* described the tenor's final confrontation with Cardinal Brogni:

> Here Mr. Caruso is a tragic actor and discloses resources of tragic power that he has never before disclosed in the same potency. It is a scene that he has evidently studied seriously; and his composition of it in pose, gesture, facial expression… is matched by the poignant intensity of his declamation in the baleful color he imparts to the musical phrase. It is operatic acting of a high order.

It was a fitting assessment of Caruso's working life – one defined by industry, concentration and application, as well as talent and creativity. As a solitary testament to his achievement as Eléazar, he recorded "*Rachel, quand du seigneur*" during his penultimate sessions in September, 1920. The voice that survives is incomparably dark and rich; the phrasing is easy, with Caruso employing an effortless and natural *portamento*, a refined and variegated *vibrato*, and almost no *passaggio*. The word-use is declamatory where appropriate, and the tone is adjusted in its placement and dynamic contours to suit the character's evolving emotional state. The climactic B flat 4 is delivered with the same burnished, golden tone as the rest of the aria, and while it may not be especially French in style, delivery or pronunciation, it is near-perfect in the singer's articulation without strain, compromise or artifice of the corpus of Eléazar's anguish.

Towards the end of the season, Caruso was injured by falling scenery, and suffered terrible pain in consequence. During a performance of *Pagliacci* he was seen to spit blood, and on 11 December, 1920, he was forced to abandon *L'elisir d'amore* mid-act. He managed to get through one final performance of the superstitiously-feared *La forza del destino*, but the following day he collapsed in agony. Pleurisy was diagnosed.

---

90 "Caruso Sings in *La Juive*." New York *Tribune*, 5 December, 1919. p.13.

As he might have wished it, his final complete performance was as Eléazar – on Christmas Eve, 1920; it was his thirteenth appearance in the role. In May, 1921, he returned to Naples to recuperate from a series of operations, one of which included the partial removal of a rib. *En route* to a clinic in Rome, the tenor and his wife Dorothy stayed at the Grand Hotel du Vesuve in Naples,[91] where he died at 9am on Tuesday, 2 August, 1921.

Caruso's two-decade transition from *tenore lirico* to *tenore lirico e drammatico senza rivali* was achieved without cost to his art and artistry. Even at the end of his career, and as he approached his 50s, he was sufficiently secure to undertake Nemorino, Don Alvaro and Eléazar in the same season. Though the voice clearly increased in size and resonance over time, what survives over 18 years of recording is the manner in which he used it – which fact amplifies Caruso's unique status as the first universally accepted measure against which every subsequent tenor could (and invariably did) measure his own expectations and performances. Where De Reszke survived by reputation alone, Caruso's art established certainties that could not be subjected to the ambiguities of prejudice and memory. De Reszke was said to be a finer artist than Caruso by Nellie Melba (who sang with both men), and her opinion is inviolate. For his part, Enrico Jr recalled in his memoir that despite the immense power and fullness of his father's voice, the timbre was defined by an "ingratiating softness" – a quality lost commonly to most "large" tenor voices. No matter how it was remembered and recorded, Caruso's lyricism was nurtured as well as innate; it operates still as a lasting testament to his unfailing judgment and discretion. His passions – while considerable – never undermined his communication of sentiment and empathy, so that his superabundant personality was placed always at the service of the composer's art.[92] Caruso is often described as the first "modern" tenor – because of his commercial and industrial success – and it's reasonable to attach modernity to an artist whose fortune exceeded $100m at his death. Caruso was actually the last of an era, however. He performed in only a handful of premieres, at a time when his influence would have allowed him to do more for the promotion and advancement of contemporary composition than anyone in the history of music. Though his career began during the 19th century, the cult of the celebrity-tenor as "creator" came to an end just five years after Caruso's death, when Miguel Fleta sang the first performance of Alfano's completion of *Turandot*. Other tenors would create roles for other composers, but with the exceptions of Richard Tauber and Peter Pears, all of them would be celebrated for their performances of music from an earlier age.

---

91 The Hotel remains in operation, as the Grand Hotel Vesuvio. The management now claims it had "a moral obligation to name its roof-garden restaurant after Enrico Caruso, since the tenor was a treasured guest of the hotel . He called it his 'Neapolitan home' and after returning to Naples, he spent the last years of his life here." In order of statement: (1) it did not; (2) so was every guest, presumably, (3) there is no evidence for the truth of this statement, and (4) no, he did not. Even so, it's probable that Caruso would have approved of the rampant puffery.
92 In this sense he was aligned closely with Toscanini.

Chapter Nine

Phrase

Puccini's love of hunting, shooting, fishing and smoking[1] was eclipsed only by his affection for women and motor cars. In 1901, he outbid his rival automobile enthusiast, Victor Emmanuel III, when acquiring one of the first De Dion-Buton's – at a time when there were only four in the country. Puccini would go on to purchase a Clément-Bayard, a Sizaire-Naudin, a Fiat 60, an Isotta Fraschini, a La Buire, an Atala, and a Fiat 501. He later invited Vincenzo Lancia to design a car for off-road use, and only a few months later the first Italian cross-country vehicle rolled out of the factory. It was a Lancia, and so had to roll back in with depressing frequency. On 25 February, 1903, while being driven home to Torre del Lago after dinner in Lucca with his future wife Elvira and their son Antonio, his chauffeur flipped their car. Mother and child were thrown to safety, with minor injuries; Puccini was pinned beneath the chassis, which compressed his chest and badly fractured his right leg. Although the composer's recovery was long and arduous he was back on the road and receiving speeding tickets within a year. Many believed Puccini would die at the wheel, but it was his addiction to Toscano cigars and cigarettes that killed him. During the spring of 1924, he bought his last car – a Lambda – in which he drove to the train station in Pisa, from where he travelled to Brussels for the throat operation that would end his life on 29 November, 1924.

Seventeen months later, on Sunday, 25 April, 1926, Puccini's unfinished opera *Turandot* was staged incomplete at La Scala, conducted by Toscanini. Half-way through Act 3, two bars after the words "*Liù, poesia,*" he stopped the performance, laid his baton on the rostrum and turned to face the audience. Toscanini announced "*Qui finisce l'opera, perché a questo punto il maestro è morto.*"[2] The conductor had insisted on the casting of Rosa Raisa in the title role, and the Spanish tenor Miguel Fleta[3] as Prince Calàf.[4] Fleta was a *lirico-spinto*, with a bright but warmly centred

---

1 Approximately seventy cigarettes a day.
2 'Here the opera ends, because at this point the maestro died.' There are different accounts of the words used, including "Here the Maestro laid down his pen."
3 28 December, 1897 – 29 May, 1938.
4 Fleta alternated with Franco Lo Giudice (14 March, 1893 - 8 August, 1990) – a magnificently powerful *tenore di forza*. Lo Giudice was greatly admired by Toscanini and Zandonai, who picked him for the premieres of *I cavalieri di Ekebù* on 7 March, 1925 and *Giuliano* on 4 February, 1928. In March 1929, he appeared for the first time at the Teatro dell'Opera di Roma, singing the title role in the premiere of Giuseppe Mulè's *Dafni*. Although Lo Giudice had a much larger, more resonant voice, Fleta was the greater stylist, and a more musical singer. He did not have the heft necessary for Calàf. Such was Fleta's struggle with the demands of the role that he never sang it again (unlike Lo Giudice – for whom it became a signature role). Incredibly, Lo Giudice lived to see and hear the "Three Tenors" sing "*Nessun dorma*" at the first of their global spectaculars, on 7 July, 1990. He died a month and a day later. His name

voice. His earliest recordings – which *pre-date* his creation of Calàf – testify to the fluency of his technique, typified by a 1922 performance of "*A te o cara*" from *I puritani*, in which his prolonged and ringing C5 suggests he did not struggle with the B4 at the end of "*Nessun Dorma.*"[5] Except, of course, that the B4 that crowns Calàf's third and final "*Vincerò!*"[6] is written as a *semi-quaver* rather than the *semi-breve* as most have sung it. The note is written to be snatched, therefore, rather than sustained – a feature of the opera that, when heard as written, leaves the majority disappointed. The aria's *final* note, an A4 *semi-breve,* is also subject to routine prolongation, although this never works;[7] a conductor can delay the cadence for the B4, but the A4 needs to end with its bar if it is to make any sense harmonically. It is still commonly asserted that the only tenor to adhere in the studio to Puccini's wishes is Francesco Merli.[8] In fact, Richard Tauber recorded the aria in German in 1927,[9] and he makes even less of the B4 than did Merli, singing it as a grace-note. Surprisingly, perhaps, it was the first recording of the aria, by Alessandro Valente (also in 1927), that established the tradition of sustaining the climactic B4 for as long as possible.

When Valente was booked by HMV to record "*Nessun dorma*" (alongside "*Non piangere Liù*"), he was the company's second choice. Fleta's unease with the role was so great that he turned down HMV's invitation to record "his" arias – even though Fleta was a "Red Label" celebrity. Valente was unknown at the time, so his recordings were transformative of his status and reputation. They were produced in London, with Manlio Di Veroli[10] conducting. Valente was immediately acclaimed (like so many others) as the "new Caruso"; he was contracted soon after to sing Canio in the first electric recording of *I Pagliacci*. He cut a handful of further discs, but his career was essentially over in 1927. He disappeared prematurely because he was not the youth he was presumed to be when first working for HMV. In fact, he was only a decade younger than Caruso,[11] which suggests a Brunelesque suspension of disbelief on the part of the audience that heard Valente singing Turiddu at the Hippodrome in 1912 (with Mascagni conducting) when he was advertised as being 17 years of age. Valente remained in England, appearing in music-hall for a number of years as "Alex

---

– and continuing existence – were completely ignored by Pavarotti, Domingo and Carreras, as well as the broadcasters, the record company *Decca*, and everyone else involved in the "Three Tenors" event in Rome.

5   'None shall sleep.'

6   'Victory!'

7   The most absurd example of this particular vulgarity is a recording by the Chinese tenor "Deng" [Xiao-Jun Deng], born 1963 in Nanking. He studied briefly with Carlo Bergonzi, and had a short and unremarkable career. He sang only 23 performances of minor roles (chiefly the Messenger in Aida) at the Met from 1995 to 1997.

8   He recorded the aria twice – firstly in 1927, and again ten years later as part of a complete performance of the opera with Franco Ghione conducting.

9   "*Keiner Schlafe.*"

10 Somewhat bizarrely, Veroli (12 April, 1888 – 21 September, 1960) coached the Welsh-born comic actor, and member of the "Goons," Harry Secombe. When not playing "Neddie Seagoon," Secombe was a fine lyric tenor. For the truly interested, Secombe recorded "*Nessun Dorma*" for Philips in 1958 – as a tie-in for his appearance later the same year in Michael Relph's film *Davy* (in which he performs the aria on stage). Secombe sings more musically, and with more *squillo*, than many better-known full-time operatic tenors.

11 Various sources state that he was born in 1890. However, there is sufficient uncertainty for this "fact" to be challenged.

Vallo." In 1924 he returned to the "operatic" stage as a tenor when he was engaged by Luisa Tetrazzini as a supporting artist for her farewell tour. By the time he came to make his debut recording of the last great aria for romantic tenor by the recently deceased Puccini, he was around forty years of age. Unsurprisingly, therefore, some of what survives on disc is dated because of his indulgence of extreme *rubato* – which is no less debilitating throughout his recording of *"Non pangiere Liù,"* leading to one very audible disagreement with Veroli. Valente's diction is superb (although the openness of his vowels will not be to common taste) and his elegant, lucid phrasing is well supported by the *portamento*-heavy string section of the nameless orchestra. The tone is warm and sonorous throughout; the B flat 4 at the end of *"Non pangiere Liù"* resonates stupendously. It's easy to hear why these recordings were so popular.

A large part of their success flowed from the music itself, rather than its poetry or narrative context. After all, there is something ridiculous in a character promising *"None shall sleep"* while yelling "victory" at the top of his lungs after midnight. The simplicity and focus of the aria's emotional arc, rising at it does to arguably the most thrilling climax in tenorial history, is a genuflection to a musical culture entirely out of step with popular as well as serious musical tastes. Strauss' *Salome* had been first staged more than 20 years earlier, while *Elektra's* vicissitudes were *passé* by the time Schoenberg's *Pierrot Lunaire* was first performed in 1912. Approaches to "voice" in Italy remained largely unchanged throughout the first quarter of the 20th century, with the usual suspects continuing to produce work that remained *fin de siècle* 30 years into the new century. Catalani, Zandonai, Giordano, Mascagni and Wolf-Ferrari stuck to those principles of popular entertainment that would have been recognisable to Verdi, and while Ferruccio Busoni, Gian Francesco Malipiero, Vincenzo Tommasini, Luigi Dallapiccola and Mario Castelnuovo-Tedesco[12] subscribed to *les modernes*, the majority of Italian composers to 1945 adhered doggedly to the country's lyrical traditions. The tenor voice for Italian opera, until the 1950s at least, was a 19th century instrument.

Things took a different course in Austro-Germany, where sixteen weeks prior to *Turandot*'s premiere in Milan, Erich Kleiber conducted the first staging of Alban Berg's *Wozzeck* at the Berlin Staatsoper.[13] The influence of this short but monumental work was a watershed moment for musical art in Germany, and for western lyric culture more generally. The fact that it was played at all is nothing short of a miracle. During the autumn of 1923, Kleiber had seen a piano reduction of the opera (made under Berg's supervision by his pupil, Fritz Heinrich Klein) and in January, 1924, the conductor arranged to meet the composer in Vienna to hear Ernst Bachrich play through the score. Before the beginning of the third scene, Kleiber had resolved to stage the premiere in Berlin.

The work makes unprecedented demands of its cast, chorus and orchestra – a reality driven home by Kleiber's 126 rehearsals. For those who believe (or have yet to be persuaded against the prejudice) that operatic singing is beautiful only when

---

12　Each of those named composed operas, but their musical interests were primarily instrumental and orchestral. The only significant Italian composer from this time not to compose even a single opera was Alfredo Casella.

13　On 14 December, 1925.

normatively lyrical, *Wozzeck* is a shot of adrenaline. The first voice heard is that of the Captain, a *tenorbuffo* – who berates Wozzeck while the private shaves him. There is no obvious musical line, with extreme intervals and manic word-use, entirely befitting the Captain's incoherent thinking. The uneasy atmosphere is amplified through Berg's adoption of Schoenberg's conception of atonality to express emotion, a technique well-suited to an opera pre-occupied with mental dislocation and social alienation. Berg's fluency in this new musical language is breath-taking, and while it's true that atonality would not have suited the *Presentation of the Rose*, it's equally certain that Strauss' sensibilities were disconnected from the realities of life during the First World War, when Berg completed much of the (orchestral) score. Life under Weimar republicanism was more suited to *Wozzeck's* articulation of the rapidly evolving sense of changed identity in post-war Germany. The score abjures the techniques of major–minor tonality, with pitch organised in accordance with a complex structure of leitmotifs; it is only through the repetition of certain note clusters, intervals and chords that continuity and form allow for the work's otherwise impenetrable detail to emerge as cogent. Much to Berg's surprise, *Wozzeck* was immediately successful, such that he was able to subsist for a time on royalties alone. When attempting to explain the opera's popularity, Theodor Adorno credited

> the choice of a text – a fact made much of by the envious. But the music demands so much of the listener, was felt at the world premiere in 1925 to be so excessive, that the text alone… would not have sufficed to overwhelm a restive audience. What people sensed was the constellation between lyrics and music, that peculiarly indicative moment in the music's relation to the topic. Besides, the social effect and authority of any music is by no means directly equal to the understanding it has found. It is conceivable that in the case of Wozzeck… neither the details nor their structural connection were fully understood, but that the phenomenon fashioned by the compositorial force conveyed that force to an audience whose ears would have been unable to account for it in the particular.[14]

Wozzeck is famous for its *Sprechgesang*, an exceptionally challenging style of vocalisation that compels a singer to abandon in every case the essence of their training. No singer was ever taught to run with *Wozzeck* before learning to walk with Mozart, and while many continue to talk of *Sprechgesang* in terms of "continuity," there is nothing contiguous in *Wozzeck's* Andres for a tenor trained to sing Tamino. He is the only one of the opera's three leading tenor roles to be scored for "*Sprechstimme.*" The Captain is scored only for a *tenorbuffo*, which means a singer is required to vocalise the notes as written. During the opening scene, for example, the phrase "*Es wird mir ganz angst um die Welt, wenn ich an die Ewigkeltdenk*"[15] is scored by Berg over four bars of music that span almost two octaves, beginning on a C3, below the stave, and passing through obdurately placed intervals – all notated, but for a single crotchet, as

---

14 Adorno, Theodor (1976). *Introduction to the Sociology of Music.* Trans. E. B. Ashton. Seabury Press. p.74.
15 'It scares me, the world, when I think of eternity' (marked by Berg "Dieselben massigen Viertel").

quavers – that rise to a sustained *pianissimo* B4, which then drops an octave by way of an A3 and an E3. It is exceptionally challenging music – chiefly since, for much of the Captain's role, the notation must be sung as well as "performed."

Different challenges are presented to the Drum-Major, a metaphysically cruel cartoon scored by Berg for *heldentenor* (again *not* identified as "*Sprechstimme*"), and drawn as an unthinking comparator for the more lyrical and vulnerable title-role. Any tenor voicing the Drum-Major's malformed, Karl Krausian cypher must bring an elemental confidence to a character corrupted utterly by his certainties – again spanning huge intervals all hinging on the *passaggio*. Berg's depiction of diseased power resonates in a tenor's ability to perform music of great difficulty without sounding broken or incapable – a working definition for any *heldentenor*. His monstrosity vests in an admixture of the spiritually grotesque and the militarily "heroic"; he is, after all, defined by Marie's terrified flattery as having "*die Brust wi ein Stier und ein Bart wie ein löwe.*"[16] Berg's attack on the perversity of abused authority through vocal malformation is heightened by the stark juxtaposition of Marie's gentle nature which, in turn, amplifies the aberrance of almost everyone around her – particularly the Drum-Major. The shocking close to Act 1, when Marie is raped, having yielded with dreadful resignation ("*Meinet wegen es ist alleseins*"[17]), is all the more horrifying because the Drum-Major is scored specifically as an "heroic tenor" – a man of plumes and medals, a figure of social and cultural authority who knows more of his status than he does of love and compassion. The lurid artificiality of Berg's score was influenced by the contemporary Cosima-fuelled obsession for declamation, a priority made yet more striking by Berg's endlessly inventive orchestral score, without which the opera cannot properly be appreciated; Kleiber's grasp of *Wozzeck's* invention from a piano reduction is entirely fantastic. The dense thematic and motivic web can appear arbitrary; the disjunctions and dissonances are no less prescriptive than the pointillistic genius of *Elektra*, however. Of course, where Strauss' House of Atreus is, for the most part, as lyrical as Mozart's Château Aguas Frescas, *Wozzeck* forces the ear to resolve imprecisions designed to reach considerably further than mere sound.

When composing *Wozzeck*, Berg knew what *kind* of voices he wanted, because he identified the *fach* for each role;[18] he was not acquainted with (or writing for) the artists who would give the first performance – which meant he was required to hand the parts to singers who, in most cases, knew nothing of *Wozzeck's* radical vernacular. Kleiber had been music director at the Berlin Staatsoper since 1923, having succeeded Leo Blech. He was relatively new to the House, therefore, when deciding to stage Berg's opera. He relied heavily on Fritz Soot[19] to create the role of the Drum-Major, and Waldemar Henke[20] in the role of the Captain.[21] Henke began his stage-career as an actor in 1896 – at the Municipal Theatre in Poznan. He trained only briefly as a singer before making his operatic debut in 1898. He spent ten years at the

---

16   A 'chest like a bull, a beard like a lion.'
17   'it's all the same to me.'
18   He added "*Sprechstimme*" to only four of the named cast: Wozzeck, Andres, and the first of the two Handswerksbursche ('Craftsmen').
19   20 August, 1878 – 9 June, 1965.
20   1876 – 1945.
21   24 March, 1876 – *circa* 1945.

Court Theatre in Wiesbaden (1901 – 1911), during which time he performed in the premiere of *Die Barbarina* by Otto Neitzel (1905). He moved to Berlin in 1911 and the Staatsoper in 1918, where he was the Company's leading character tenor, excelling as Pedrillo in *Die Entführung aus dem Serail*, Monostatos in *Die Zauberflöte*, David in *Der Meistersinger* and Mime. In 1911, he was cast as Valzacchi in the Berlin premiere of *Der Rosenkavalier* – none of which can have prepared him for *Wozzeck*. He made a number of recordings, the best of them a charming duet with Hermione Bosetti from Lortzing's *Zar und Zimmermann* ("*Darf eine niedere*"). He also recorded excerpts as Mime, which are fascinating for their heightened *buffo* quality, as well as excerpts from *Lohengrin*, *Die Meistersinger* and *Les Huguenots*. In 1912 – 13 years *before* he sang the first Captain – he recorded arias from Auber's *Muette de Portici* and (unsuccessfully) *Pagliacci*.

Like Henke, Fritz Soot[22] also began life as an actor, in Karlsruhe – where he performed between 1901 and 1907. He studied singing privately while acting, and in 1908 he made his debut at the Royal Opera in Dresden, appearing as Tonio in *La fille du regiment*. He was 30 years of age. The following year he was chosen by Dresden's kapellmeister, Willi Schuh, and Richard Strauss to create the Young Servant for the premiere of *Elektra*. Three years later, Strauss and Schuh invited Soot to create the roles of Faninal and the Italian Singer for the premiere of *Der Rosenkavalier*. In 1918 Soot relocated for four years to the Stuttgart Opera, from where he moved to the Berlin Staatsoper – and the role of the Drum Major. Soot was committed to contemporary music, which included works by Schoenberg, whose songs he performed before it became fashionable to do so. Kleiber took particular advantage of his open mind. In addition to Schmidt's *Fredigundis*, Paul Graener's *Der Prinz von Homburg*, Rangström's *Die Kronenbraut*, Krenek's *Die Zwingburg* and Dessau's *Das Verhör des Lukullus*, Soot sang in numerous Berlin premieres, including Janáček's *From the House of the Dead* and *Jenůfa*, Weinberger's gloriously titled *Schwanda der Dudelsackpfeifer*[23] and, in 1927, Busoni's *Doktor Faust* – in which he sang the role of Mephistopheles. Soot created the role of the Majordomo at the world premiere of Milhaud's *Christophe Colomb* on 5 May, 1930. He was admired as Palestrina by Hans Pfitzner, who invited him to give the first performance in 1931 of *Daz Herz*, and Strauss thought him exceptional as Narraboth and Herodes in *Salome*. Soot sang the latter role in Berlin in 1952, at the age of 73, when he was said to be vocally ageless. For all his modernity, Soot was renowned primarily as a Wagner tenor, and his performances of *Tristan* and the *Ring* with Kleiber in Berlin were considered by many to be superior to anything being heard at Bayreuth. In 1924 and 1925 he was hailed also in London as Siegmund, Siegfried, Tristan, Erik, Walther and Parsifal.

Between 1911 and around 1930, Soot made numerous recordings, mostly for Pathé, Odeon and HMV; they are fascinating because they capture the sound of a *heldentenor* as it was known to some of the most important Wagner conductors of the early 20th century, including Richard Strauss, Kleiber, Muck, Abendroth, Blech and Fritz Busch. His 1922 recording of "*Brünnhilde! Heilige Braut*" from *Götterdämmerung* is typical, insofar as he sings with a ringing tone, lyrical phrasing

---

22 His real name was Friedrich Wilhelm Soot.
23 'Schwanda the Bagpiper.'

and almost no *vibrato*. The vowel sounds are open and the diction is remarkably clear – a concern of Berg's no less than it had been for Wagner – and there is an abiding sense that Soot was easy in his voice. It is eternally frustrating that none of the then-increasing number of European labels thought it useful to record the original cast performing *Wozzeck*.

Berg's popularity was definitively contextual. A large amount of new German music was being recorded during the late 1920s; it just wasn't being written by composers aligned with the Second Viennese School. Indeed, if 19th century opera was dominated by Italy then the 20th century was epicentrally German – on the stage as well as on record. The explosion in musical theatre in Weimar Germany around the time of *Wozzeck*'s first staging was unprecedented, in part because the novel intervention of the State facilitated the creation of hundreds of theatre companies, spanning musical and spoken repertoire. During the season 1928–29 there were approximately 230 companies in Germany – the majority subsidised. There were private theatre companies also – most of them in Berlin; of Germany's 65 private companies, 30 were based in the capital. The rest were formed as *Gemeinnitzige Theater* – literally "theatres for the benefit of the public," operating as non-profit organisations.[24] Twenty-five of these were for touring; 132 were located permanently in a city. These *Staatstheater*, *Landestheater* and *Stadttheater* signified a broad nexus of tradition and financial support, with the largest theatres in Prussia, Bavaria and Saxony having access to significant revenues and fees at a time when there were almost no private sources of funding. Each of the country's 45 cities with more than 100,000 inhabitants was home to at least one *gemeinniitziges Theater*. Just as Orvieto, a small hill town in Umbria, was able to maintain a theatre capable of staging large productions four nights a week, so Neustrelitz (a town of 14,000 people), Bunzlau (18,500) and Coburg (25,000) had theatres in which contemporary German music was performed routinely.[25] In Duisburg, an industrial city with almost half a million residents, 48 different operas and 11 ballets were staged in 1929 alone – many of them newly composed. Even the municipal theatre in Aachen – where the conductor and director of music, Peter Raabe,[26] embraced an often Jewish musical culture that he would do more than anyone else to eradicate during a decade of service to the Third Reich – presented 20 new productions during the six-month season 1929–1930.[27]

The kaleidoscope of repertoire and performances was made possible in part by the increasing availability of tenors able (and willing, more importantly) to reach further than Mozart and Wagner. Between 1916 and 1930, the variety of contemporary music theatre (and tenorial talent) spanned Erich Korngold's *Der Ring des Polykrates* (1916; Karl Erb), *Die tote Stadt* (1920; Richard Schubert) and *Violanta* (1916; Franz Gruber); Alexander von Zemlinsky's *Eine florentinische Tragödie* (1917; Rudolf Ritter) and *Der Zwerg* (1922; Karl Schröder); Franz Schreker's *Der Ferne*

---

24 Führer, Karl Christian (2001). "German Cultural Life and the Crisis of National Identity during the Depression, 1929–1933." *German Studies Review*, Vol. 24, No. 3. pp. 461–486; p.462.
25 *Ibid*. p.463.
26 Raabe replaced Richard Strauss as President of the *Reichsmusikkammer*. For almost ten years, he oversaw musical life for the Third Reich. He was probably fortunate to die in 1945.
27 Strohm, Heinrich K. (1930). "*Binsenwahrheiten zur heutigen Theaterlage*," *Der Neue Weg* 59. pp.134–36.

Klang (1912; Karl Gentner) and *Die Gezeichneten* (1918; Karl Ziegler); Graener's *Theophano* (1918; Franz Gruber); Schoenberg's *Gurre-lieder*[28] (1913; Hans Nachod); Pfiztner's *Palestrina* (1917; Karl Erb); Hindemith's *Neues vom Tage* (1929; Erik Wirkl); and Weill's *Aufstieg und Fall der Stadt Mahagonny* (1930; Hanns Fleischer) and *Der Silbersee* (1933; Ernst Busch).

The changing vernacular was typified graphically by the premiere on 26 March, 1926, of Kurt Weill's first opera, *Der Protagonist*, with a libretto by Georg Kaiser. This tonal but stringent work was first staged on Strauss' home turf, the Semperoper in Dresden, conducted by Fritz Busch. It is scored for a large orchestra and written for singers immersed in the Straussian late-romantic vernacular; the voicing is newly-minted in its quasi-political asceticism. If the vocal score is frequently lyrical it is rarely melodious; enormous technical skill is required by the singers, especially the title role for tenor (created by Kurt Taucher[29]). Weill's music is grudgingly tonal, crafted in apparent fear of the contagion of establishment notions of beauty. Two years later, Weill abandoned contemporary operatic models when writing *Die Dreigroschenoper*,[30] a "play with music."[31] In collaboration with Brecht and Elizabeth Hauptmann (now recognised as a co-author, having written the majority of the text, as well as providing a German translation of Gay's *The Beggar's Opera*[32]), Weill's operetta was an expression of the authors' passionate commitment to left-wing social philosophy – a value-system to which Brecht was more attached than Weill, leading the composer to observe after their parting that he had not wanted to "set the Communist manifesto to music." Their socially critical, culturally diverse and gaudily cosmopolitan collaboration made a virtue of accessibility and affordability. Drawing on jazz and dance-hall, Weill scored the opera for a tiny ensemble of players, all of them obliged to commit to frantic doubling. At the first production in Berlin, seven musicians performed a total of 23 instrumental parts: alto sax (doubling as flute, clarinet, baritone saxophone); tenor saxophone (doubling as soprano saxophone, bassoon and bass clarinet); trumpet; trombone (doubling as bass); banjo (and cello, guitar, Hawaiian guitar, mandolin, bandoneon[33]); timpani-percussion; harmonium (doubling as celesta and piano). The writing for voices was equally attainable. The role of Macheath ("Mackie Messer"/"Mack the Knife") was created by Harald Paulsen[34] – a singing actor whose vocal register aligned with Weill's scoring of the part for tenor. The charismatic Macheath is the first major operatic role for tenor not to be written for an opera singer. Had a *heldentenor* like Soot been cast, then the ensemble would have been lost entirely to his resonance; performed by Waldemar Henke, Mackheath's contaminating, sinister villainy would have been subsumed to a 19th century singing

---

28 Not a stage work, but it contains more theatre than most operas. Hans Nachod deserves a mention for taming the part of Waldemar at the first performance in Vienna on 23 February, 1913, conducted by Franz Schreker.
29 25 October, 1885 – 7 August, 1954.
30 'The Threepenny Opera.'
31 First staged at the Theater am Schiffbauerdamm, in Berlin, on 31 August, 1928.
32 Hauptmann is now believed to have written at least half of the *Mahagonny-Songspiel* (1927) but was not credited.
33 A type of concertina popular in South America.
34 26 August, 1895 – 4 August, 1954.

technique – something even Berg was determined to preserve in his writing for the Captain. Paulsen's performance was sung, but as his recordings testify his delivery was closer to *Sprechstimme* and a style idiomatically typical of German *Kabarett*. Weill, Brecht and Hauptmann knew the work would elicit extremes of opinion – typified by one far from divergent view that it was a "noxious cesspool". Its popularity was driven by a fusion of danger and accessibility, and by the intimacy of the work's scale, and the affordability of its design, and the egalitarianism of its vocal parts. The opera received 4,200 performances during its first year alone – at 50 theatres across Germany, as well as Prague, Budapest and Vienna.[35] The majority of artists cast in the role of Macheath were actors with tenor vocal registers.

Die Dreigroschenoper opens with a "*Moritat*[36] *von Mackie Messer*,"[37] in which Macheath is compared unfavourably to a shark, and implied to be a serial killer, arsonist and rapist. The song is not performed by MacHeath – although many presume it's the character's opening number; rather, it's delivered by a Street Musician. It was a last-minute addition, inserted shortly before the premiere because Paulsen insisted that his character be introduced. At the premiere, it was performed by Kurt Gerron,[38] who also played Jackie "Tiger" Brown (the Police Chief). Weill intended the *Moritat* to be accompanied by a barrel organ, played by Gerron. At the premiere, the instrument failed so the pit orchestra improvised an accompaniment. It was able to do so because the writing was technically facile and repetitious. The *Moritat* is performed over nine repeating verses that span a D3-D4 octave.[39] It's banal and grinding in its simplicity. Little else in the opera places the singers under pressure. Indeed, the music is written for just about anyone to perform. This is especially true of Macheath, whose role is typified by Act 2's "*Ballade vom angenehmen Leben*,"[40] which again adheres to a limited range and provides little to challenge an amateur. It is popular song in all but name. More importantly, any German "tenor" invited to sing Weill's music had to submit to a de-gendered, anti-heroic conception of what was previously the most masculine of German voices. Stefan Zweig despised Berlin's cabaret scene, which he considered poisonous for German social stability. He was especially challenged by issues relating to gender-certainty and sexual propriety:

> All values were changed, and not only material ones; the laws of the State were flouted, no tradition, no moral code was respected, Berlin was transformed into the Babylon of the world. Bars, amusement parks, red-light houses sprang up like mushrooms. What we had seen in Austria

---

35 Success in the United States was delayed by world events; the translation by Marc Blitzstein was staged at Broadway's *Theater de Lys* in 1954. It ran until 1961.
36 'Moral.'
37 'The Ballad of Mack the Knife.'
38 11 May, 1897 – 28 October, 1944. Gerron was deported from Amsterdam to Theresienstadt, where he was forced by the SS to stage the cabaret review, *Karussell*, in which he reprised the role of Macheath. Gerron and his wife were forced onto the final train to Auschwitz and gassed almost immediately, on 28 October, 1944 – the day before Heinrich Himmler ordered the closure of the gas chambers.
39 The role is played by Ernst Busch in Pabst's 1931 film of the opera. Busch played the part of "Tiger" in the original stage production.
40 'Ballad of the Pleasant Life.'

proved to be just a mild and shy prologue to this witches' sabbath; for the Germans introduced all their vehemence and methodical organization into the perversion. Along the entire Kurfurstendamm powdered and rouged young men sauntered and they were not all professionals; every high-school boy wanted to earn some money, and in the dimly lit bars one might see government officials and men of the world of finance tenderly courting drunken sailors without any shame. Even the Rome of Suetonius had never known such orgies as the pervert balls of Berlin, where hundreds of men costumed as women and hundreds of women as men danced under the benevolent eyes of the police. In the collapse of all values a kind of madness gained hold particularly in the bourgeois circles which until then had been unshakable in their probity. Young girls bragged proudly of their perversion, to be sixteen and still under suspicion of virginity would have been considered a disgrace in any school of Berlin at that time, every girl wanted to be able to tell of her adventures, and the more exotic the better.[41]

The depiction of an Otto Dixian world of nightmarish realities, with its doctor's cabinets and blue angels, was a lifetime away from the *Alt Subjlichkeit* of Richard Strauss' Greco-Roman romanticism – to which gemütlich *fantasia* Zweig made his own contribution in 1934 when providing Strauss with an adaptation of Ben Jonson's *Epicoene, or the Silent Woman*, by way of Plautus' satire *Casina*, the *Declamatio Sexta*,[42] and Antonio Salieri's *Angiolina ossia Il Matrimonio*. Six years before *Die schweigsame Frau*,[43] and less than two months after the premiere of *Die Dreigroschenoper* in Berlin, Strauss oversaw the premiere of *Die ägyptische Helena*[44] at the Semperoper in Dresden.[45] Where Weill had scored his eighth opera for seven players, Strauss' ninth called for a *stage* band of six oboes, six clarinets, four horns, two trumpets, four trombones, timpani, four triangles, two tambourines and a wind machine – around 26 musicians. In the pit, he was comparatively restrained, scoring for four flutes (third and fourth doubling on piccolo), two oboes, *cor anglais*, three clarinets, bass clarinet, three bassoons (third doubling on contrabassoon), six horns, six trumpets, three trombones, tuba, timpani, bass drum, tam-tam, snare drum, cymbals, glockenspiel, celesta, two harps, organ, and around fifty strings. Despite reining things in for *Ariadne auf Naxos*, Strauss' continuing power and influence during the 1920s, particularly in Dresden, meant he could ask for just about anything and assume it would be provided. Even so, *Helena* was not a success, with Strauss' dissipation finding a less than ideal bedfellow in Zweig's lumpen, overcooked symbolism. It remains a difficult prospect for any opera company – because of the huge costs and because it makes unreasonable demands of its two lead sopranos (the title role and Aithra).

---

41 Zweig, Stefan (1947). *The World of Yesterday*. Cassell. pp.238–239.
42 A Latin translation of mythological themes from the Greek sophist Libanius.
43 'The Silent Woman.'
44 'The Egyptian Helen.'
45 6 June, 1928.

Helena's tenor lead, Menelas (Menelaus in English), also represents a leviathan challenge for any but the most amplitudinous *heldentenor*. Strauss cast Curt Taucher – Weill's first *Protagnist* – and he appears to have coped manfully with the absurdities of the plot as well as the cacophonous orchestration. Taucher spent his entire professional life from 1920 in Dresden; in addition to Menelaus, he created numerous (mostly forgotten) roles, including Aurelius Galba in Eugen d'Albert's *Die Toten Augen*, and Horace in Schoeck's *Venus*; he sang many other contemporary roles, the span of which reveals something of the fecundity of German musical life during the first third of the century: Max Brand's *Maschinist Hopkins*, Graener's *Hanneles Himmelfahrt*, Schattmann's *Die Hochzeit des Mönchs*, Weinberger's *Schwanda der Dudelsackpfeifer*, Puccini's *Turandot*, Pfitzner's *Palestrina* and *Der Herz*, Mascagni's *Il Piccolo Marat*, and Wolf-Ferrari's *Sly*. Taucher's recorded legacy is bizarrely limited, with only a few discs from the early 1920s for Polydor and Parlophon – made at around the time he first appeared at the Met in New York, where he sang 95 performances of 11 roles – dominated by Wagner's mature canon. From what survives on record, Taucher had a bright, well-focussed tenor; as with so many others, however, expression was sacrificed to the tyrannical absolute of enunciation. Not one of his recordings preserves a genuine *legato* – not even his performance of "*Wie eiskalt ist dies Händchen*" ("*Che gelida manina*"). Puccini would have appreciated the royalties, but he would have recoiled from Taucher's phrasing, which is breathless, square and difficult.

It's hard to believe that Strauss would have appreciated it either. His willingness to tolerate the imperfections of colleagues over whom he had no direct influence was a product of commercial reasoning and practical experience – formed over many seasons as a conductor, particularly at the Bayreuther Festspiele. His correspondence with Cosima Wagner[46] demonstrates the extent to which he submitted to her influence before the "*demented Jewish-girl*" (as he referred to *Salome* in a letter to Cosima in 1905) caused a shift in his working life from conducting to composition. Strauss' letters to Cosima emphasise the balance of his priorities – which hinged at all times on casting and stagecraft. At Bayreuth he had access not only to the widow of his hero, but also the peerless resources (and pockets) of Germany's most sacred theatre. If he developed at any time a philosophy of expectation, it was during his summers with the Wagner family. The availability of the putative best of everything was a clear influence on his conception as a composer of opera. Strauss refused to accommodate either the aria tradition (he produced only two for tenor, over fifteen operas)[47] or the technical limitations of a recording process that favoured works that might (by whatever means) suffer reduction to four-minute chunks. Notwithstanding these obstacles, and without ever abandoning his taste for technical and theatrical excess, Strauss' operas are the second most performed by a 20th century composer. Puccini did not discriminate between male and female voices – writing fastidiously for both. Conversely, few would dispute the truism that Strauss wrote his finest music for sopranos. Where Puccini humiliated and murdered most of his female characters

---

46   *Cosima Wagner – Richard Strauss: ein Briefwechsel* (1978). Ed. Franz Trenner. Verdffentlichungen der Richard Strauss Gesellschaft. Schneider.
47   The Italian tenor's "*Di rigori armato*" (*Der Rosenkavalier*), and Flamand's "*Kein andres, das mir so im Herzen loht!*" ['Nothing else so inflames my heart'] (*Capriccio*).

violently (or in the teeth of suffering, at the very least), Strauss killed only one[48] – Salome, who is assassinated by Herodes' soldiers after she begins to kiss the mouth of the decapitated, still-bleeding head of John the Baptist.[49] Elektra dies from joy (after the fashion of Isolde) and while some of Strauss' other soprano leads are changed by their experiences – notably Die Kaiserin in *Die frau ohne schatten* (who is transformed by her shadow) and Daphne (who is turned into a tree) – none of them dies violated. Strauss reserved his cruelties for his tenors.

His operatic debut, *Guntram* (premiered in 1894), is a bloated love letter to Wagner and his widow, in which his preference for the female voice is unequivocal.[50] Only four of his subsequent operas contain what might be considered "romantic" tenor leads: *Ariadne auf Naxos* (the Tenor/Bacchus), *Die frau ohne Schatten*[51] (Der Kaiser[52]), *Die ägyptische Helena* (Menelaus) and *Daphne* (the rafter-shaking pairing of Leukippos and Apollo). Each of these roles is, in its own way, absolutely sensational; they are also unkindly written, demanding lung-bursting amplitude and resonance when placed (but for *Ariadne*) over absolutely immense orchestral forces. *Die frau ohne schatten*, for example, is scored for 164 instruments (with some doubling) – more performers, therefore, than audience members for the first operas in Italy.

Strauss' first stage success, *Salome*, features 17 roles, eight of them for tenor. Narraboth (the Captain of the Guard) is a superb invention, crafted by Strauss for Rudolf Jäger, a stalwart *heldentenor* at the Dresden opera between 1899 and 1908. In 1901 Jäger polished his enamel on August Bungert's *Nausikaa*, and on 30 October, 1903, he was in the cast that gave the first performance of part of *Odysseus Tod*, Bungert's delusional attempt to outdo Wagner's *Ring*. He went on to create roles for Leo Blech, Hugo Kaun and Eugen d'Albert. Narraboth requires power and stamina, qualities Jäger brought to the other roles for which he is otherwise best remembered – Tannhäuser, Lohengrin, Tristan, Walther and Parsifal. His qualities survive on a scattering of recordings for the Gramophone & Typewriter Company. The voice is far from beautiful; he enunciates well, however, and there is a hint of the phrasing one might have expected of a tenor known also to sing Strauss' *lieder* in recital.

The role of Herodes was created by Karel Burian.[53] Born in Rousínov, in what is now the Czech Republic, he trained privately and performed as a member of the Maisel Synagogue Choir in Prague before making his debut as a 21 year-old in 1891.[54] Strauss considered Burian his first and only choice as Herodes, a fearsomely difficult role that calls for vocalism of sonorous intensity, particularly when lamenting

---

48   Klytemnestra is killed off-stage in *Elektra*.
49   It never seems like an unreasonable decision on the part of the king.
50   Strauss' prejudice is explained in part by the lifelong inspiration provided by the soprano Pauline de Ahna. He wrote *Guntram*'s only soprano role, Freihild, for de Ahna as an early wedding present. *Guntram* was first performed on 10 May, 1894 – with Heinrich Zeller (7 June, 1856 – 9 August, 1934) singing the title role; the couple were married four months later, to the day, on 10 September. Their marriage ended two days before their 56th wedding anniversary, when the composer died on 8 September, 1949, at the age of 85.
51   'The Woman Without a Shadow.'
52   'The Emperor.'
53   12 January, 1870 – 25 September, 1924. He also created roles for Leo Blech (*Aglaja*, 1893), Karl von Kaskel (*Sjula*, 1895) and Arnold Mendelssohn (*Elsi, die seltsame Magd*; 1896).
54   As Jeník in *The Bartered Bride*.

his bargain with Salome – a scene during which Strauss throws the fridge-freezer after the sink and most of the plumbing. The composer's expectations of word-use reach significantly further than anything in Wagner's *stabreim*. The pitching, rhythmic incision and phrasing are necessarily awkward, as befitting a character whose degeneration is exceeded only by that of his wife and step-daughter – a ruined man for whom Salome's actions have genuine and terrifying consequences. Herod's monologue, beginning "*Ah! Du willst nicht auf mich hören*"[55] is among the most remarkable in all music drama. Appalled by Salome's perversion, and submitting to panic and fear, he is reduced to offering her a part of his kingdom, his vaults and, as a last resort, the vilest of anti-Semitic desecrations. Through increasingly ingenious orchestrations, Strauss paints the colours of the jewels and stones proffered by Herod, and the music pours forth with eye-widening invention. The escalating frenzy reaches its climax when the king beseeches in desperation, "*Ich will dir den Mantel des Hohenpriesters geben. Ich will dir den Vorhang des Allerheiligsten geben!*"[56] The third syllable of "*Allerheiligsten*" is delivered as a sustained A4 semibreve-minim, above the full orchestra playing *fortissimo*. It is an extraordinary, ugly moment, particularly when followed by Salome's chilling "*Gib' mir den Kopf den Jochanaan!*"[57] – accompanied only by flutes, clarinets and snare drum.

The vocal registration of Herodes' writing frequently strangles tenors pushed beyond their means, and the need to persuade as a Roman monarch with near-absolute power reduced to begging and pleading can test even the most talented of singers. Strauss' music requires that the performer should sound as if he is approaching the edge of reason and authority – not the limits of his vocal capacity. It's a balancing act that highlights Strauss' dependence on performers able to act as well as sing. Burian triumphed at the first performance, and Strauss supported his subsequent creation of the role in New York in 1907,[58] and for Beecham in London in 1910.

Burian made a significant number of recordings. The best of them evidences a penetrating voice, with a rich, open tone, and a ringing, albeit uneasy top. His recording for The Gramophone & Telephone Company in 1911 of Strauss' song "*Zueignung,*" Op. 10, No. 1, gives a clear impression of what the composer knew and admired of his voice – chiefly its resonance. Burian would plainly have been audible even above Strauss' densest orchestrations. The phrasing is never especially beautiful; the enunciation is splendid, however – notwithstanding some of the worst pianism east of Tombstone's Bird Cage Theatre. Throughout his recordings, Burian's vocalism is avowedly German, and characteristically hard-edged in its rejection of Italianate style. His 1908 "*O Soave Fanciulla*" from *La bohème* with Minnie Nast (the first Sophie in *Der Rosenkavalier*) compares very unfavourably with the recording made the previous year by Caruso and Melba. The latter couple produce an expressive, effortless performance, rich with subtle *rubato*, elegant *portamento* and wide ranging dynamic nuance. Burian and Nast do not. There is almost no phrasing, at least as it prevailed in Italy and France, and the tone is harsh and colourless. The performance

---

55 'Ah! You don't want to listen to me.'
56 'I shall give you the coat of the high priest. I will give you the veil of the Sacrament!'
57 'Give me the head of Jochanaan!'
58 Conducted by Alfred Hertz.

(in German) is nothing short of ugly – and yet it sold widely to those who preferred their *böhmisch* to *bohème*.

Burian's celebrity was international during the first two decades of the 20th century. He created the role of Tristan in the opera's Hungarian premiere, and his appearances at Covent Garden between 1904 and 1914 were said to be among the finest in the company's history. He sang most of the major Wagner roles at the Metropolitan in New York, where he performed for seven seasons, and in 1908 he made his debut at Bayreuth in *Parsifal* – though he sang at the *Festpielhaus* only once.[59] He developed a reputation for excess, which is said to have resulted in his being poisoned by a *tonmeister*, with whose wife Burian had spent too long in rehearsal. In 1920 he mistook a glass of bleach for water. His wounds healed; his voice did not.

One of the vestiges of 19th century German operatic composition was heard in New York just eighteen days after the first performance of *La fanciulla del West*, when Alfred Hertz conducted the world premiere of Humperdinck's *Königskinder* on 28 December, 1910.[60] His second fairy-tale opera was less successful than his first, *Hänsel und Gretel*, but it was warmly received in New York and Berlin, where it was staged the following year by Leo Blech. The opera is pure *Wagneriana*, which would not be surprising but for Humperdinck's reference to themes, ideas and motifs drafted thirteen years earlier for his first *Königskinder*, a melodrama in which he employed a prescient hybrid of voicing, somewhere between singing and speech, with approximately pitched melodies.[61] Many now credit Humperdinck with the invention of *Sprechstimme* – which is something of an irony considering his avowedly 19th century instincts. Indeed, *Königskinder* is as lyrical in its adherence to normative concepts of vocal beauty as is *Hänsel*. The role of the Köningssohn was created by Herman Jadlowker,[62] a gifted lyric tenor born in Latvia and raised in the Cantor traditions of the synagogue. Although his technique enabled him to indulge in *coloratura*, such that he was able to sing Mozart and Rossini with great skill, he developed over time a darker, more dramatic voice – particularly after spending the seasons 1910 to 1912 in the company of Enrico Caruso. During his time in New York Jadlowker sang 89 performances of 14 operas, including *Faust*, *Madama Butterfly*, *La bohème*, *Tosca*, *Pagliacci*, *Cavalleria Rusticana*, *Falstaff*, *The Bartered Bride*, *Der Freischütz* and *Lohengrin*. He also sang the American premieres of Wolf-Ferrari's *Le Donne Curiose*, Ludwig Thuille's *Lobetanz* and Leo Blech's *Versiegelt*. After returning to Germany, Jadlowker's repertoire extended to *Don Carlo*, *Otello* and *Parsifal*. In 1929, he retired to Riga, and the position of principal Cantor at the Great Choral Synagogue.[63] The arrival of the Nazis forced his emigration, and in 1938 he and his family made safe passage to Tel Aviv and Israeli citizenship.

---

59   Burian's memoir, *Z mých pamětí*, was published in 1913; it is largely fluff, but worth reading for the tenor's recollections of Mahler and Toscanini.
60   'King's Children.'
61   Commissioned by Heinrich Porges for a play written by his daughter, Else. It was first staged on 23 January, 1897, at the Munich Court Theatre, with Hedwig Schako as the Goose Girl.
62   17 July, 1877 – 13 May 1953.
63   The city's largest synagogue. The Nazis burned it down on 4 July, 1941 – an episode planned for filming; it was shown in cinemas as part of a Wehrmacht newsreel.

Jadlowker made over 230 recordings, between 1907 and 1927, for Odeon, Victor, Polydor and the Gramophone & Telephone Company. They testify to a beautiful, honeyed and open tone, which he employs with blistering "old-school" technique, spanning magnificent trills, runs and *fioriture* – all of them evidenced by his German-language recording of "*Fuor del mar ho un mare in seno*"[64] from *Idomeneo*. He used very little *portamento* for the time, and his *vibrato* is light and well-judged, with certain passages sung ruthlessly "straight" – as on his 1908 recording of "*Il mio tessoro*" (again in German). Although he performed for the most part in German and French, he was able to sing in Italian, and his time in the United States clearly influenced his approach to phrasing and enunciation, as can be heard on his impressive recording for Victor in 1911 of "*Che gelida manina*." His performance is lifted straight out of the Caruso copybook, with numerous unwritten turns – a common feature of the Italian's singing – and changes in weight and emphasis that cannot have been inspired by anyone else. The aria is transposed down a tone, however, so the high C5 is sung as a B4 – in tune and without *vibrato* but, it must be conceded, less than easily. Jadlowker's uncharacteristically Italianate sound and phrasing are most in evidence on his splendid 1916 recording for the Gramophone & Telephone Company of "*Niun mi tema*,"[65] from *Otello*. The singing is as far from "German" as can be imagined, and this feature of Jadlowker's art clearly appealed to Strauss when he was casting the role of The Tenor/Bacchus for the first production of *Ariadne auf Naxos*.[66]

Having taken things as far as he was comfortable (or capable of) taking them when creating the role of Aegisth for Johannes Sembach[67] in *Elektra*, Strauss' approach to voicing reverted to a lyrical dialectic that would become idiomatically "Straussian" over the ensuing decades, initially with the molten lyricism of *Der Rosenkavalier* in 1911 and *Ariadne auf Naxos* in 1912.[68] More than any other of his tenor parts, with the possible exception of Matteo in *Arabella*, the role of The Tenor–Bacchus is generous to a singer with the lungs for the part. It is written high in the voice, and particularly during the "opera" it is hugely taxing because the small orchestral forces are still Strauss' version of "small." A *fortissimo* is rarely anything less. While *heldentenors* need not apply, the majority do. This is often to be regretted because the role is arguably Strauss' most lyric for tenor voice; it rewards an artist with a *legato* as well as resonance.[69] Although there is no evidence that the composer was disappointed with Jadlowker's work at the premiere in Dresden, he was replaced for the first performance in Vienna – while Maria Jeritza as Ariadne was not.

---

64 Sung as "*Noch tönt mir ein Meer im Busen*."
65 In German as "*Jeder Knabe kann mein Schwert mir entreissen*."
66 The premiere was given in Stuttgart on 25 October, 1912, conducted by the composer. A revised version of the opera was given in Vienna on 4 October, 1916, conducted by Franz Schalk.
67 See Chapter 14.
68 Incredibly, *Ariadne auf Naxos* was not performed at the Metropolitan Opera until 29 December, 1962, when Karl Böhm conducted Leonie Rysanek as Ariadne, Jess Thomas as Bacchus, Gianna D'Angelo as Zerbinetta, Kerstin Meyer as the Composer and Walter Cassel as the Music Master.
69 The most successful include Peter Anders, Rudolf Schock, Helge Rosvaenge, Jess Thomas, James King and Jonas Kaufmann. The Hungarian tenor, Béla von Környey (18 May, 1873–18 April, 1925), sang the premiere of the revised score in 1916.

A *heldentenor* was mandatory for Strauss' next opera – *Die frau ohne Schatten*. The role of Der Kaiser was created on 10 October, 1919, at the Wiener Staatsoper by Karl Aagard Østvig[70] – a mere five years after his debut at the Stuttgart Staatsoper. In 1922, Oestvig (as he was known in Germany) made the first of a small number of recordings, which included Strauss' "*Ich liebe dich*" and "*Zueignung.*" The latter song is passed off well enough; he has a large and resonant tenor – qualities fundamental to performances as the Kaiser; the voice is far from beautiful, however, and it is constitutionally unsuited to Strauss' melancholic eloquence. In fact, the recording of "*Ich liebe dich*" is ghastly – with no phrasing, a spreading *vibrato*, thickened tone, a strained upper register and a pronounced sense of effort that cannot have fulfilled the potential of the Kaiser's music. There are no recordings by Østvig from the time of *Die frau ohne Schatten*, and his voice may well have changed after the initial run; certainly, the rehearsal schedule and his gruelling diary cannot have helped. Either way, on his recordings made three years later, at the age of 33, he sounds like a singer in his late fifties.[71] He retired late from the stage at the age of 44. In 1932 Østvig relocated to Oslo, where he co-operated with the Nazis through his work as director at The National Theatre. He was said to have been more than merely sympathetic to the invading regime, an opinion articulated after the war by the courts, which sent him to prison for collaborating.

Each of Strauss' remaining operas contains memorable music for tenor; his thirteenth, *Daphne*, stands out as a reversion for the composer. It was his first classically-set opera since *Elektra*, and the work might very well have been titled "Apollo," such is the prominence of the tenor lead. Like *Elektra*, *Daphne* is a single act work, and of similar length; it too is based on a Greek myth and scored also for a vast orchestra; it has only five named cast members.[72] Where *Elektra* is dominated musically by the title role and her sister Chrysothemis, *Daphne* is a love letter to its creator, Torsten Ralf.[73] But for Daphne's final transformation into arboreal wordlessness – yet another commentary by Strauss on "*zuerst die Musik, dann die Worte*" – the opera's finest writing is reserved for Apollo. The role contains more to reward a suitably-equipped *heldentenor* than any other in the canon of 20th century German opera; the melodic, thematic and harmonic richness is bewildering, as is Strauss' use of *leitmotif*, which is sophisticated even by his standards. Were it not for the cost of its presentation, and the intimidating demands of some of Apollo's writing (which engages in strenuous interval leaps, sits high on the stave, and compels immense resonance as well as legions of B flat 4s and B4s), *Daphne* would warrant as much popularity as *Elektra*. As a "bucolic" drama, rather than a blood-soaked tragedy, it's not as interesting or as malleable as staged drama, and the narrative and libretto are aggrandising of their

---

70   17 May, 1889 – 21 July, 1968.
71   Østvig was exceptionally talented with new scores; his professionalism and stage presence were clearly sufficient compensation for his barrel-chested approach to line and language. Østvig created the roles of Ein Laienbruder (a Lay Brother) and Giovanni de Salviati in the world premiere of Max von Schillings' *Mona Lisa*, in 1915; on 22 May, 1922, he played the role of the Dwarf in the Viennese premiere of Zemlinsky's *Der Zwerg*.
72   *Elektra* has a larger company of unnamed singers: Elektra's Confidante; Her trainbearer; the Young, and Old Servant; Orest's Tutor, and the Overseer are all nameless.
73   2 January, 1901 – 27 April, 1954.

over-read authors. The music is ample compensation, however. From the transformation scene beginning "*Was furt dich her?*"[74] – when Strauss paints the rising of a full, silver moon and the settling of an enchanted mist through exquisitely layered modulations – Apollo is on stage for almost an hour and singing for most of it. He shares the score throughout with Daphne and, briefly, Leukippos (another splendid tenor role, created at the first performance by Franz Klarwein[75]) but there is little overlap between the voices. The characters communicate almost entirely in exchanges of dialogue – a functional necessity considering the density of the frantically contrapuntal orchestral score. The music following Apollo's declaration of love for Daphne reaches its climax in a scene that likely caused the composer to blush[76]; the indulgences escalate until Daphne refuses both god and man, and Apollo murders Leukippos. This trio (of sorts) contains the most thrilling music Strauss wrote for tenor(s), and when Apollo finally reveals the glory of his life-giving divinity, he does so through music of ravishing sensuality ("*Jeden heiligen Morgen…*") that can fail only with its tenor.[77]

Daphne was first performed on 2 October, 1938, in another Dresden first night for Strauss, this one conducted by Karl Böhm (to whom the composer dedicated the opera). Torsten Ralf took on the horrendous task of finding the voice, and the lyricism, necessary for a god, and we can know that he triumphed because there is a recording from the year of the opera's premiere of "*Götter! Brüder in hohen Olympos!*"[78] – produced in Dresden by HMV. Ralf sings splendidly, meeting the challenge of scale and range without once sacrificing the expressive fluency for which the role is remarkable. Like many other celebrated *heldentenors*, Ralf paced himself when young, during protracted training and studies; he chose his earliest roles carefully, particularly when taking on contemporary repertoire, including originator parts in Sutermeister's *Die Zauberinsel*, Mohaupt's *Die Wirtin von Pinsk*, Schoeck's *Massimilla Doni* and Heger's *Der Verlorene Sohn*. Not until joining the Wiener Staatsoper in 1935 did he take on more dramatic repertoire, including Florestan, Walther, Bacchus, Tannhäuser and Otello. Ralf was greatly admired in London and across Europe, and in November, 1945, the Met cheered him as Lohengrin. During his three seasons in New York, he sang 50 performances of eight roles, including exceptional appearances as Siegmund, Tristan and Parsifal. After years of struggling with Leukemia, he died at the age of 53. Ralf was a magnificent singer, and an artist of exceptional taste and discretion. It was a sign of the times in 1938 that he was one of many of whom the same could be said. Just three months before *Daphne*, Strauss' *Friedenstag* was first performed in Munich with Julius Patzak and Peter Anders singing the tenor leads.

---

74 'What brings you here.'
75 8 March, 1914 – 16 December, 1991. Klarwein was also the first male of the Italian Singers in the hilarious pastiche duet, "*Addio Mia Vita Addio,*" in *Capriccio*. The female Singer at the premiere was Irma Beilke.
76 "*Hörst du, Geliebte, Hörst du, was sie singen? Kennst du den Sinn, Der blühenden Rebe? Wagst du Verneinung Dem Liebesfest?*" ['Do you hear beloved, Do you hear what they sing? Do you know the meaning of The flowering vine? Do you dare negate the festival of love?']
77 'Every holy morning.'
78 'Gods! brothers in high Olympus!'

Strauss ended his operatic career with *Capriccio*,[79] and the role of Flamand (a composer). It is a ravishingly clever and beautiful creation, made perfect by music of delicate sensitivity and humour. Flamand is a character of infinite grace and humanity; Strauss painted him in music that equates at times to the intimacy of *lieder*[80] – a palette that crystallises in the effortless joy of "*Kein andres, das mir so im Herzen loht!*" and his ensuing declaration of tumultuous, unrequited love for the Countess. Flamand was created by Horst Taubmann.[81] Incredibly, Taubmann lived until 1991; Strauss first's operatic tenor, Heinrich Zelle, was born in 1856. Throughout his long life, Strauss worked with some of the finest tenors, to which he had automatic access as the world's most celebrated German composer. As a voluminous recording artist, he might have been expected to work with more tenors than he did, but what survives is treasurable.[82] From 1921, he can be heard accompanying Robert Hutt[83] in "*Breit uber mein Haupt,*" Op. 19, No. 2, and "*Morgen!*" Op. 27, No. 4 – performances of arresting beauty, striking for the singer's tone and line, and important for Strauss' repudiation when playing solo in "*Morgen!*" of the debilitating *faux-rubato* to which Hutt (and just about everyone else since) is allowed to stoop. In 1942 or 1943 (it's not clear which), the composer recorded 14 of his songs at the piano with Anton Dermota, and in September, 1944, Strauss and Patzak broadcast four songs with orchestra. They are exquisite points of reference for the art of singing, and not simply by tenors. Of the large amount of unpublished material featuring Strauss as a performer, the most interesting is a private recording on acetate of excerpts from *Salome*, taken from live performances on 15 February and 6 May, 1942, at the Wiener Staatsoper. Joseph Witt[84] and Joachim Sattler[85] can be heard alternating as Herodes. The sound is poor; the playing and the conducting are stupendous, however. The composer was 77 years old at the time.

When compared to some of their predecessors, it's inarguable that the recordings of Strauss' songs by Robert Hutt, Anton Dermota and Julius Patzak excelled in part because of their proximity to Strauss. The composer wasn't known for biting his lip, and keen attention to his core values is common to each surviving performance – even if Strauss is more generous to Hutt than he would have been to himself. It's self-evident also that the standard of German-language singing during the 1930s

---

79 Purists might argue that it ended with *Die Liebe der Danae* because it was finished before *Capriccio*, and first performed after the composer's death, in 1952. *Capriccio* was nonetheless the last opera that Strauss helped bring to the stage, which means it was also the last opera over which he had artistic (and casting) control.

80 Strauss' acute sensibility for text setting allowed him to satirise old-fashioned Italian forms in the opera's pastiche duet – where the musical shape is purposefully disconnected from the words – with the tenor's part, in particular, intentionally all over the place.

81 14 February, 1912 – 28 November, 1991.

82 There are a number of Strauss discographies available. By far the finest, and most thorough, is that by Peter Morse, entitled "*Richard Strauss's Recordings: A Complete Discography.*" It is unpublished, but widely available on-line.

83 8 August, 1878 – 5 February, 1942.

84 17 May, 1901 – 3 January, 1994. Witt was much admired by Karl Böhm, with whom he collaborated frequently in the studio.

85 21 August, 1899 – 15 July, 1984. Sattler was discovered by Siegfried Wagner, and sang at the Bayreuther Festspiele in 1928, 1929 and 1931. He was admired by Strauss and is remembered for singing the role of Melot in the first complete recording of *Tristan*, in 1928, conducted by Karl Elmendorff.

and 40s was incomparably finer than it had been at the turn of the century. This was a function of statistics as well as training. Throughout the 1920s there was an ever-rising demand for performers and performances, which caused an exponential increase in the number of music schools and academies in every city across Europe, Russia and the United States. With improvements in technology, recordings became affordable for just about everyone, fostering a market-driven ubiquity of opinion from which there was nowhere to hide. Anyone singing out of tune or with an ugly tone, or without thinking carefully about the reach of posterity, was doomed to failure and obsolescence. The aesthetics of popular taste became more pervasive still when the cinema added another source of access and opportunity, such that the business of singing was, by the middle 1930s, firmly and irrevocably international.

Strauss' status as the world's pre-eminent German composer did not mean he was peerless in Austria and Germany. The disconnect between pre-eminence and popularity was thrown into stark relief by the career of Franz Lehár, and the talent of "his" tenor, Richard Tauber. Born in Linz – closer to the Czech and German borders than to Vienna – Tauber sang his first operetta by Lehár in Berlin in 1920.[86] During the next fourteen years he became indivisibly associated with Lehár's works; he did not create all of the composer's tenor leads, but he was sufficiently attached to his music for the hit song from *Das Land des Lächelns*[87] (*"Dein ist mein ganzes Herz"*[88]) to become known as the "*Tauberlied.*"[89] The composer and the tenor worked closely together for many years,[90] a collaboration that bore its first fruit in 1925, with the premiere of *Paganini* in Vienna. Tauber did not sing the role of the titular violinist at the first performance,[91] which was in any event unsuccessful. When he gave the Berlin premiere on 30 January, 1926, however, the public's reaction was frenzied, and the operetta ran for three months. Strauss could only look on and sigh. Tauber had sung the role of the Italian Singer in Dresden for the first time on 1 September, 1913 (with the original Marschallin [Margarethe Siems], Octavian [Eva von der Osten] and Sophie [Minnie Nast]); he went on to perform the first version of Bacchus in Berlin in 1915, and Narraboth in 1916. On 5 October, 1919, he sang his last Strauss role for the first time (the revised Bacchus) and, for whatever reason, Tauber and Strauss never worked together.[92] By 1926 – when Tauber's reputation ensured he needed neither Strauss nor the security of a company appointment – it was too late. It has since been speculated that Tauber's liberal politics caused him to keep his distance

---

86 A tenth anniversary revival of *Zigeunerliebe*.
87 'The Land of Smiles.'
88 'You are my heart's delight.'
89 Eventually, all the hit songs from Lehár's operettas became known as "Tauberlieder."
90 In addition to *Zigeunerliebe*, *Das Land des Lächelns* and *Paganini*, Tauber created roles (or performed) in stagings of *Frasquita* (10 July, 1922); *Der Zarewitsch* (6 February, 1927); *Friederike* (4 October, 1928); *Schön ist die Welt* (3 December, 1930); and *Giuditta* (20 January, 1934).
91 The honour went to the *heldentenor* and silent film actor, Theodor "Carl" Clewing (22 April, 1884 – 15 May, 1954).
92 *The World's Encyclopaedia of Recorded Music* claims that Strauss accompanied Tauber in acoustic recordings for Odeon in two of his songs: "*Freundliche Vision*" and "*Traum durch die Dammerung.*" There is no evidence that these recordings were ever made. Tauber mader the recordings, in 1919, but they were accompanied by Mischa Spoliansky. See Jones, Robert (June, 1970). "The Authenticity of the Alleged Strauss-accompanied Tauber Records." *The Record Collector*, Vol. 19. pp.76–81.

from the composer; this is plainly not the case since Tauber continued to sing his *lieder* during the Third Reich.

Tauber's performances of operetta – on stage and on record – have never been bettered. His repertory reached much further, however, having been raised at home on the music of Mozart, and Mozart remained his guiding light during more than thirty years on stage. In 1913 he made his debut as Tamino in *Die Zauberflöte* – encouraged by his father, then Intendant of the theatres in Chemnitz. A few days later he played Max in *Der Freischütz*, which resulted in a five-year contract with the Dresden Opera, where he was known to (but not favoured by) Strauss. He relocated to Vienna and Berlin, where he specialised in lyric repertoire, notably *Don Giovanni*, *Mignon*, *Faust* and *Carmen*. During this time, Tauber marshalled his considerable vocal resources, which were defined by a golden tone, lyrical sensibilities and exceptional technique. He was referred to by many as the "Viennese Caruso," and there is some merit in the *sobriquet* because Tauber's singing was defined by the same ineffable ease of delivery for which his Italian contemporary was revered. The music simply flowed out of Tauber, without the slightest hint of effort. So remarkable was his feeling for word placement and so soluble his *legato* that he was considered internationally to be the most perfect lyric tenor singing in German – even with his (allegedly *echt*) Viennese vocal tics, namely a rapid *vibrato*, a *portamento* that he employed as a "flick" as well as a "sigh" and a *rubato* that "robbed" in anticipation.

Tauber's most lasting contribution to the tenor tradition was his successful traversing of the "serious" and the "popular" without doing harm to either. His celebrity was entirely earned, through artistic merit, and an integrity that resonates throughout his substantial body of recordings. These convictions fed predilections that mitigated against him singing anything *avant-garde*. Though he was a feature of many of the same companies and performing in the same towns and cities, he sang nothing by Zemlinsky, Weill, Schoenberg, Berg or Webern. He was committed to contemporary music, just not its more challenging developments. In addition to world premieres of operettas by Jan Brandts Buys, Karl Kaskel, Hugo Kaun and Leo Fall, he performed "serious" work by D'Albert (*Die toten Augen*[93] and *Tiefland*), Humperdinck (*Königskinder*), Graener (*Don Juans letztes Abenteuern*[94] and *Theophano*), Korngold (*Der Ring des Polykrates*,[95] *Die tote Stadt*[96] and *Das Lied der Liebe*[97]), Pfitzner (*Das Christelflein*[98]) and Schreker (the Berlin premiere of *Der Ferne Klang*[99] in 1926). He was the first significant tenor to choose between modernity and popularity, or he was at the very least the first to act on a distinction between the two. Kurt Taucher, for example, sang Weill as well as operetta and Wagner. So too did Berg's troopers, Fritz Soot and Waldemar Henke. Hanns Fleischer,[100] the first Fatty der Prokurist in Weill's *Aufstieg und Fall der Stadt Mahagonny* on 9 March, 1930, also sang Bach, Beethoven,

---

93 'The Dead Eyes.'
94 'Don Juan's Last Adventure.'
95 'The Ring of Polykrates.'
96 'The Dead City.'
97 'The Song of Love,' an arrangement of music by Johann Strauss II, premiered by Tauber in 1931.
98 'The Little Elf of Christ.'
99 'The Distant Sound.'
100 8 November, 1890 – 28 April, 1969.

Berg, Webern and Jan Brandts Buys.[101] Tauber's identification as a "popular" singer was as much a construction of perception as reality, therefore; indeed, it was an ontological crisis that would come to define both the separation of the powers (as "serious" and "popular") as well as the generalist presumption that opera singers (and tenors, more specifically) would never again be associated with the performance of works by living composers.

Tauber knew his audience, and was openly manipulative of some of the more sentimental corners of the repertoire – for which reason there has never been a consensus for Tauber as there has been for Caruso. His extraordinary range of tone and expression are comparable nonetheless to Caruso's, particularly noting how Tauber's voice is easily as recognisable in its texture and phrasing. He would even remove his monocle when the circumstances required it. His singing of Mozart was very different to his performances of Lehár and his *lieder* recordings are remarkable for their intimacy, elegance and a use of dynamics as colour. Tauber was always willing and (more importantly) able to control his open-throated resonance where text and music gained from less being more. Memorable examples include his recordings of Strauss' "*Heimliche Aufforderung*"[102] and "*Morgen!*" and a home-made recording from 1936 (with the tenor at the piano) of Schubert's "*Fruhlingstraum.*"[103] His duet with Lotte Lehmann of "*Glück das mir verblieb*"[104] from Korngold's *Die tote Stadt* is frequently cited as being one of the most perfect recordings of the 20th century. The duo gave the Berlin premiere of the opera on 12 April, 1924 – in a production conducted by Georg Szell. They recorded the duet for Odeon five days later, again with Szell conducting, and it is indeed miraculously beautiful. Yet more of Tauber's unique artistry is found in his performance from the same session of the opera's final scene, "*O Freund, ich werde sie nicht wiedersehen.*"[105] The melancholy that Tauber brings to this intensely bittersweet episode is entirely believable; his pushing against the bar-lines amplifies the pathos without diminishing the credibility either of Paul's decision to move on from his former life with Marie, or the music's calculated emotional blackmail. Tauber first recorded "*Dein ist mein ganzes Herz*" on 3 October, 1929. This famous performance is saturated with all the effects for which he was famous and it is delivered with unimpeachable sincerity. If "a heart of stone" was necessary for anyone "to read the death of little Nell without laughing," then Tauber managed to bring persuasive conviction to music that has since been lost to sentimentality. Tauber saw no distinction between the music of Lehár and Mozart; they were branches of the same tree.

Having refused repeated invitations from the United States, Tauber remained in Britain throughout the Nazi regime. He made his debut at Covent Garden as Tamino in 1938, and after the theatres closed he toured the country giving concerts and radio broadcasts, making recordings, conducting and composing operettas. In 1947, he was discovered to be suffering from lung cancer. Despite enduring terrible pain

---

101 'The Rise and Fall of the City of Mahagonny.'
102 'The Secret Invitation.'
103 'Spring dream.'
104 'Joy, that near to me remains.'
105 'O friend, I will not see her again.'

and a collapsed lung, he sang his last operatic performance as Don Ottavio in *Don Giovanni* at Covent Garden on 27 September, 1947 (replacing an indisposed Anton Dermota).[106] Incredibly, a recording was made of the performance, and it's possible to hear Tauber give a peerless account of "*Dalla sua pace*" (sung in German as "*Nur ihrem Frieden*"). Even at the end, his tone is golden, his breath control absolute and his projection effortless. The ensuing applause is delivered by a capacity audience clapping an Austrian singer who made his home in Britain without needing to. News of Tauber's death was broadcast on the radio and on newsreels around the world. It was fitting that many said goodbye to this beloved singer in a cinema – since that was how the largest number of people had come to know him and the very modern world of the operatic tenor.

---

106 The cast on this moving occasion is worthy of note also: Cebotari, Schwarzkopf, Güden, Schöffler, Kunz, Weber and Poell – all conducted by Josef Krips. If anyone is looking to isolate the "good old days" of singing, this would be as good an example as any.

Chapter Ten

Silver Voices

During the Autumn of 1918, as the Great War in Europe was coming to an end, the planet experienced the emergence of a disease that manifested itself as influenza. It proved to be something worse. "Spanish Flu" was virulent, with a mortality rate of 2.5%. One fifth of the world's population was either infected or died, with the most vulnerable group aged between 20 and 40. 28% of Americans were infected, with 675,000 recorded deaths – ten times as many as were lost to the War. The final edition of the Journal of the American Medical Association for 1918 recorded

> a year momentous as the termination of the most cruel war in the annals of the human race; a year which marked the end, at least for a time, of man's destruction of man; unfortunately a year in which developed a most fatal infectious disease causing the death of hundreds of thousands of human beings. Medical science for four and one-half years devoted itself to putting men on the firing line and keeping them there. Now it must turn with its whole might to combating the greatest enemy of all – infectious disease.[1]

The virus killed almost 200,000 in October, 1918, alone. Attempts were made to shut down public life to limit dispersal. Cinemas, theatres and stores were closed; funerals were limited to 15 minutes, and many towns required a signed certificate for entry. Passengers had to be authorised to disembark at railway stations. It was routinely observed to be a "once in a century event," a prediction that proved to be stunningly accurate. When life began to return to normal, studios directed their marketing to cinema owners as a mechanism for commercial and social recovery. In early 1919 the producers Adolph Zukor and Jesse Lasky, of the Famous Players–Lasky Corporation,[2] published a marketing flyer and posters for *My Cousin*, directed by Edward José. It promised "a show that will start the ticket machines whizzing again!"

> Perhaps business has been slack. Perhaps, worse still, your theatre has been closed. You're wondering how to get back the before-the-epidemic crowds. You wish you had a picture that would bring not only the regular patrons, but a heap of new ones – folks who don't usually go to

---

1 28 December, 1918.
2 They would go on to form Paramount Pictures.

motion pictures. In other words, you want to re-open with a crash like a high explosive shell.³

Here's the very picture. Shout out to your town that you're re-opening with – Caruso in his first motion picture.

My Cousin was not the first film to feature an opera singer; it was the first to star history's most famous tenor, however.⁴ Patrons were assured two Carusos for the price of one, since the plot concerned Tommasso Longo (a poor sculptor, played by Caruso) and his cousin, Caroli (a star at the Met, also played by Caruso). This must have seemed like a good idea at the time, and the film-makers clearly delighted in the movie's singular joke, that Tommasso when singing in his apartment has a terrible voice. There was something perverse in presenting a silent film, with a necessarily voiceless accompaniment from a disillusioned pit band, starring the "world's greatest tenor." Caruso might just as easily have played a deaf mute or a taxi driver. The film is valuable only for its preservation of one of the most significant artists of the 20th century playing the role of Canio on the stage of the "Old" Metropolitan. The close shots of him singing "*vesti la giubba*" are fascinating, and evidence the exaggerated facial movements typical of singers at the time; the shots from the stalls capture the crowded stage during the opera's final moments, when Caruso announces "*La commedia è finita!*"⁵ – before rushing to the body of the now-dead Silvio and (apparently) stamping on his head.

At the foot of the marketing poster for *My Cousin*, the name of the Director General of the Famous Players–Lasky Corporation is advertised as Cecil B de Mille, who three years earlier directed the first major film of an opera, *Carmen*, with America's most celebrated soprano, Geraldine Farrar, in the title role. Farrar was the only professional singer cast – which fact might suggest the film was based on the opera. However, Bizet's score was still in copyright, so de Mille based his production on Prosper Mérimée's novel.⁶ It was cheaper for the studio to commission an orchestral score from Hugo Riesenfeld (using themes from Bizet's work), which was performed at the premiere screening. Farrar was cast as an actress, not as a singer, and the success of the film encouraged her to make a dozen more movies, earning her two Stars on the *Hollywood Walk of Fame* in 1960. De Mille's *Carmen* was one of two released that year – the other, starring Theda Bara, has been lost. So popular was the subject matter that sixteen filmed versions were released before the end of 1948.

The blurring of boundaries between media was consistent with the plurality of art and technology during the first quarter of the century, when music and theatre were as transgressive as they were reassuring. The lingering effects of *Grand Guignol* in Paris

---

3   More than a century later, it is especially bizarre that anyone would think to make a positive comparison using the simile of a "high explosive shell" when men were returning daily from a war with "shell-shock" (PTSD). It is more likely that the copywriter knew nothing of combat, than that cinema operators and owners had themselves not survived time in Europe fighting for their country.

4   It was not the last either. He went on to make one more film, *The Splendid Romance*, in 1919, but this too was unsuccessful.

5   'The comedy is finished!'

6   It's worth noting, also, that Bizet's title role was written for a mezzo-soprano, so Farrar would not have performed the opera in any event.

and gender-fluidity in Berlin were caught at their lightest on film by the ambiguous but heightened sensuality of Rudolph Valentino[7] and Wallace Reid[8] (Farrar's Don José). On 18 July, 1926 – a year before the first "talkie" – questions of Hollywood's portrayal of masculinity in the United States provoked the Editor of the Chicago *Tribune* to write:

> Do women like the type of 'man' who pats pink powder on his face in a public washroom and arranges his coiffure in a public elevator? ...It is a strange social phenomenon and one that is running its course not only here in America but in Europe as well. Chicago may have its powder puffs; London has its dancing men and Paris its gigolos. Down with Decatur; up with Elinor Glyn. Hollywood is the national school of masculinity. Rudy, the beautiful gardener's boy, is the prototype of the American male. Hell's bells. Oh, sugar.[9]

Caruso's masculinity in *My Cousin* was not diminished by scenes of "Caroli" powdering his face. Indeed, his appearances as Tommasso are rugged, muscular and sweaty. He glistens with manly endeavour (albeit as a sculptor) and pursues the fragrant waitress, Rosa Ventura, with gusto; his relationship with the "shop boy," Ludovico, is paternal, and never suggestive of something "other." Caruso is emphatically a man's man. Though inaudible on screen, his voice was known by everyone in the cinemas to be baritonal and paradigmatically "male," and the hair on his face and arms was heterosexual and ursine, after the fashion of Theodore Roosevelt rather than Richard Bulger.[10] The private knowledge of Caruso's *many* relationships with women was compounded by the public "scandal" of his alleged sexual assault of a woman at the New York Zoo.[11] So emblematic was the episode that the equally priapic James Joyce borrowed from it for Leopold Bloom's trial in *Ulysses*, and it served as a clear point of reference for the themes of sin running through *Finnegans Wake*.[12]

The juxtaposition of the Italian Caruso (as a man of objective talent) and the Italian Valentino (a cypher for androgynous erotic fantasy) led rapidly to a loss of traction among tenors as a (western) societal focus for masculinity. Neither "man" was accessible to the readers of *Good Housekeeping* and the *Ladies' Home Journal*, of course; given a choice it's safe to say that most women (and presumably men) would have preferred to spend their evenings performing with Valentino *after* hearing Caruso do his thing

---

7   His given name was Rodolfo Alfonso Raffaello Pierre Filiberto Guglielmi di Valentina d'Antonguella (May 6, 1895 – August 23, 1926).
8   15 April, 1891 – 18 January, 1923.
9   Studlar, Gaylyn (1989). "Discourses of Gender and Ethnicity: The Construction and De(con)struction of Rudolph Valentino as Other." *Film Criticism*, Vol. 13, No. 2. pp.18–35; p.18.
10 Bulger and his then partner Chris Nelson founded *Bear Magazine* in 1987. This was predicated on George Mazzei's article for *The Advocate* in 1979 titled "Who's Who in the Zoo?" that characterised gay men as seven types of animal, including bears.
11 Bauerle, Ruth. "Caruso's Sin in the Fiendish Park: 'The Possible Was the Improbable and the Improbable the Inevitable.'" *James Joyce Quarterly*, Vol. 38, No. 1/2, *Joyce and Opera* (Fall, 2000 - Winter, 2001). pp.125–142.
12 Caruso was clearly the model for H. C. Earwicker. It's likely also that Joyce borrowed Bloom's pseudonymous "Henry" and "Enrique" from the tenor.

on stage. The seductive allure of talent was being replaced by plain seduction. The rapidly evolving conception of beauty shifted the metric for singers and audiences alike, and while it's inarguable that the eye of the beholder is a singular conceit, there has always been a consensus – whether the individual likes it or not. Tom Cruise and Brad Pitt are among the most handsome and charismatic men of their generation; the same was also true of Robert Mitchum and Victor Mature, however. During the second decade of the twentieth century, Wallace Reid was dubbed "the screen's most perfect lover" – not its greatest actor. That title went (variously) to Charlie Chaplin and Ronald Colman, neither of whom was "classically" handsome. The "leading man" was required to act, of course, even if the road to a studio contract was paved by beauty more often than talent, which is why John Gilbert, Ramon Novarro, Douglas Fairbanks, William Haines, Richard Arlen and Charles Farrell were cast as romantic leads rather than Caruso and his misshapen contemporaries.

There is ample evidence for Hollywood having disguised its ethnic, cultural and religious mix within an idealised vision of European male beauty.[13] The indeterminate conception of the genders favoured by pre-Raphaelite painters was rooted in 400 years of neutered iconography, with Jesus portrayed almost everywhere except Eisenheim as handsome, tranquil and asexual. Christ's conversion by the Catholic Church and its legions of artists and sculptors was a workable solution for immigrants arriving at Ellis Island. As a strategy for assimilation, the representation of Jesus as a feminised, facially and bodily-hairless man of greater than average height and slender build operated to diminish those distinguishing features that recast the foreign as alien. This amorphous portrayal of physical difference was adopted by Hollywood as a mechanism for camouflage and integration – a process exemplified by the casting of Weissmuller as Tarzan.

In Burroughs' conception, Tarzan is a wild man by nurture, not nature; he is tall and athletic, handsome and tanned. He is also clean-shaven, after the manner of Caravaggio's *Supper at Emmaus*. When Jonny Weissmuller appeared for the first time as Viscount Greystoke in *Tarzan the Ape Man*, in 1932, few thought him anything less than central casting. He was 6'-2" and breathtakingly attractive. He had fabulous hair. Though absent menace, Weissmuller was sufficiently muscular to carry "his" woman to safety; his ambiguous European descent was balanced by a solid American Christian name.[14] When calling to the animals he did so using a baritonal-tenor to form a signal made of an interval of a third, spanning an E to a G – with an alternating soprano-pitched yodel to render Tarzan binary for those preferring Valentino to Caliban. There are numerous accounts for the origins of the call – with Weissmuller claiming it for himself, and the family of the tenor Lloyd Thomas Leech asserting his status as the source of the male-voiced sounds. Either way, Weissmuller's Tarzan was closer to the male ideal than was Giovanni Martinelli, a contest that was over before it began.

---

13 Winokur, Mark (1987). "Improbable Ethnic Hero: William Powell and the Transformation of Ethnic Hollywood." *Cinema Journal*, 27.1. pp.5–22.
14 He was born Johann Weißmüller, as a Banat Swabian, an ethnic German population in the south-eastern part of the Kingdom of Hungary.

On 5 August, 1926, Warner Brothers presented the first screening of *Don Juan*, a romantic epic directed by Alan Crosland, starring John Barrymore. It was the first feature-length film to use Warner's Vitaphone "sound-on-disc" system, with a synchronized score and sound effects. Because the film had no dialogue it qualified still as "silent." As if to make a point, and to set Barrymore in opposition with Valentino, *Don Juan* features the most kissing in mainstream film history; Barrymore locks lips with Mary Astor and Estelle Taylor on no fewer than 127 occasions. The premiere was held at the Warner Brothers Theatre in New York and preceded by an hour of short films that included solos by Anna Case (an Edison recording artist, said to be "the most beautiful woman in grand opera") and Giovanni Martinelli, the latter singing "*Vesti la giubba*." Robert E. Sherwood wrote that Martinelli "proved to be extraordinarily impressive." In his *Memoirs*, the tenor recalled:

> When I heard Caruso at the Metropolitan… I realized I would have to do something to make my own interpretation a bit different. I went to Leoncavallo and asked for his help. The composer of Pagliacci looked at me in amazement and a bit of disgust. 'Martinelli,' he laughed, 'you ask me for help when you have the greatest Canio of my dreams at the Metropolitan to watch. Go ask Caruso for help'. I worshipped Caruso, but hesitated to ask. Apparently Leoncavallo wrote to him about my request because Caruso invited me to attend his rehearsals.

The difference on which he alighted appears to have been one of *tempo*, chiefly. His Vitaphone performance is possibly the slowest recorded – expiring at three minutes and 8 seconds, where Caruso, for the first of his recordings in 1902, was lighting his cigar after just over two minutes.[15] This decision appears to be something that Martinelli opted not to share with the conductor, since the orchestra is more than once heard to attempt an entry which Martinelli was determined to delay. For all its *longeur*, the singing is magnificent, with ample *squillante*, no audible cover from his chest voice through the *passaggio*, exceptional breath control, and some splendid alveolar trilling. He is less lyrical than Caruso – there is a clear separation between line and declamation – and the tone is bright and not always easy. Moreover, the aria is by no means performed as a soliloquy; Canio's anguish is real but indulgent, a quality self-evident from his deliberate mispronunciation of words for effect. For example, Martinelli changes "*ta applaudira*" to "*DA applaudira*," no small difference where *legato* is the priority. Elsewhere he makes a studied use of *vibrato* (including its negation) to emphasise the character's shifting feelings and sentiments, and he throws in more aspirates than anyone except perhaps Gigli so that "*ridi*" becomes "*riHi del duol…*". His use of an apparent hiccup was a purposeful glottal interruption employed by tenors raised on *verismo* that enables the collation of pressure in the larynx to facilitate its subsequent release as resonance without using the thorax to force the diaphragm.

---

15   For his recording in 1904 he took his time, finishing at two and a half minutes; in 1907 he found a middle ground, at two minutes and 20 seconds.

Martinelli is comfortably built, with an absurd curly wig that makes him look suspiciously like Harpo Marx – whose first film with his brothers, *Animal Crackers*, appeared just four years later. The tenor is not a handsome man, and certainly not when compared to John Barrymore; audiences still attended in their droves to see and *hear* the Metropolitan Opera's *primo uomo* – so often, in fact, that James Agate had cause to write: "I suppose that someday I will be able to enter the theatre without hearing Mr. Martinelli bellowing but that day is not yet."[16] A little over two weeks after *Don Juan* and Martinelli made their Vitaphone debuts, Rudolph Valentino died at the age of 31, on 23 August, 1926. Those mourning the loss of his beauty and sensuality did not look to the opera house for compensation. Hollywood was adept, regardless, at spinning plates, and there was ample room for stars of the Met on film – particularly after the technology allowed for real-time synchronisations of sound and picture. Not everyone relished seeing opera singers up close. Aldous Huxley – who was known to like neither the cultural phenomenon of cinema nor its mass-oriented achievements – wrote a frothing polemic for *Vanity Fair* in July, 1929, in which he brought Old Testament fury and confident racism to the "nauseatingly luscious" *Jazz Singer*:

> To what lengths this process of decay has gone was very strikingly demonstrated by the next item on the programme, which was the first of that series of music-hall turns, of which the dreadful jazz band had been the last. For no sooner had the Singer and Mammy of Mine and My Baby disappeared into the limbo of inter-cinematographic darkness, than a very large and classically profiled personage, dressed in the uniform of a Pierrot, appeared on the screen, opened his mouth very wide indeed and poured out in a terrific Italian tenor voice the famous soliloquy of Pagliacco [sic] from Leoncavallo's opera. Rum, Tum, TiTum, Tum; Rum-ti-ti, Tum, Ti-Tum, Tum—it is the bawling-ground of every Southern tenor and a piece which, at most times, I would go out of my way to avoid hearing. But in comparison with the jazz-band's Hebrew melodies and the Jazz-Singer's jovialities and mammy-yearnings, Leoncavallo's throaty vulgarity seemed not only refined and sincere, but positively beautiful, exquisitely and sublimely noble. Yes, noble; for after all the composer, whatever his native second-rateness, had stood in some sort of organic relation, through a tradition of taste and of feelings, with the men who built the Parthenon and the mediaeval cathedrals, who painted the frescoes at Arezzo and Padua, who composed the Magic Flute and the Choral Symphony.[17] Whereas the Hebrew melodists, the muffin-faced young Nordics with their saxophones and their Swanee whistles, the mammy-songsters, the vocal yearners for Dixie and My

---

16   Parker, David L (Summer / Fall 1980). "Golden Voices, Silver Screen: Opera Singers as Movie Stars." *The Quarterly Journal of the Library of Congress*, Vol. 37, No. 3/4. pp.370–386; p.371.
17   Huxley does not say anything of the Vitaphone recording – released at the same time – of Efrem Zimbalist and Harold Bauer performing the second movement (*Andante con variazioni*) from Beethoven's Sonata for Violin and Piano No. 9 in A major, Op.47 (the "*Kreutzer*"). He would doubtless have disapproved of the cuts, and the performers' liberal interpretation of the marking "*Andante*."

Baby are in no perceptible relation with any of the immemorial decencies of human life, but only with their own inner decay—the psychical putrefaction of those who have denied the God of life and have abandoned their souls, already weakened by the hereditary malady of Christian spirituality and scientific intellectualism, to the lifehating devil of the machine.[18]

Huxley was probably unaware that the views from his ivory tower were framed between adverts for a European ferry company boasting proudly that "French Line Officers and Stewards converse in English" and Sulloway Golfing Stockings, said to be "guaranteed not to shrink." Elsewhere, he railed against the

apocalyptic close-ups of individual performers gigantically enlarged[19]… singing and at the same time registering the emotions appropriate to the musical circumstances… the human countenance smiles its six-foot smiles, registers soulfulness or grief, whimsicality or libido with every square centimeter of its several roods of pallid mooniness… opens and shuts its thirty-two inch eyes… the spectacle was terrifying.[20]

Huxley might have suffered an embolism had he stuck around to see the direction in which the custodians of high art were turning their talents. Vitaphone obliged Frances Alda, for example, to follow her performance of "*Ave Maria*" from Verdi's *Otello* with "*The Star Spangled Banner*" and "*The Last Rose of Summer*," while Ernestine Schumann-Heink[21] programmed Schubert's "*Der Erlkönig*" with "*Danny Boy*" and "*By the Waters of the Minnetonka*." Martinelli's dozen shorts included a memorably dreadful performance of Tosti's Neapolitan song about missing Sorrento ("*Torna a Surriento*") while dressed as a gondolier punting along a canal in an absurdist torch-lit reconstruction of Venice. Huxley would not have liked it one bit. Other films include Martinelli singing "*Estrellita*" in a "Spanish" garden, and a hilariously misplaced rendering (with *obligato* whip-cracking) of "The Life of a Gypsy," with the tenor dressed as a wagon driver in a camp populated with "native" dancers.

By the summer of 1929, six hundred Vitaphone films were being screened in seventeen hundred theatres across the United States. For all their popularity, short films aged badly, and the public tired of watching opera singers perform bleeding chunks absent anything more thrilling than "mere" singing. The ante was most

---

18   Huxley, Aldhous (July, 1929). "Silence is Golden." *Vanity Fair*. pp.72–73.
19   On this issue he was in good company. The critic Ernest Newman famously railed in one especially outspoken essay against the horrors of being able to see inside the mouths of singers from whom a good distance should otherwise have been routine.
20   *Ibid.*
21   15 June 1861 – 17 November, 1936. One of the most significant contraltos of the 20th century. She performed regularly with Mahler and was a regular at Bayreuth, performing for Cosima and her son from 1896 until 1914. Her thirty-three year career at the Metropolitan Opera began in 1899. In 1909, she created the role of Klytemnestra in *Elektra*. The singer didn't like the opera, and the composer didn't much like the singer. During rehearsals he was heard to berate the conductor, Ernst von Schuch: "*Louder! I can still hear Madame Schumann-Heink!*"

definitely upped when the decision was taken to film Emmy Destinn performing in a cage with fourteen lions – the same Emmy Destinn who created the role of Cio-Cio San for audiences in London, and Minnie in the world premiere of *La fanciulla del West* in 1910. In 1932 *Madame Butterfly* was filmed "straight" by Paramount, with Cary Grant as Pinkerton and the Bronx-born Jewish-Russian-Romanian Sylvia Sidney playing the Japanese title tole. It was successful, but there was no great rush of films based on operas. Instead, studios re-positioned the value of "serious" singers by building them into films with little or nothing to do with opera. It was this hybrid vehicle that carried one of the most beloved opera singers of the 20th century to an international celebrity that not even Caruso had enjoyed.

Beniamino Gigli[22] was widely marketed as "Caruso's successor." This was nonsense at the time and it remains so a century later. He was a lyric tenor, with a much lighter voice than his predecessor; his attachment to weightier repertoire, particularly on record, did not entitle him to sing it, and it's remarkable that his career lasted for as long as it did considering his tendency to force a quart out of a pint pot. Gigli made his debut in October, 1914 (as Enzo in Ponchielli's *La Gioconda*); within just four years, and before his 29th birthday, he had triumphed in Palermo, Naples, Rome and Milan. He appeared for the first time at the Metropolitan Opera on 26 November, 1920 – less than four weeks before Caruso's last performance in New York. The timing was not coincidental. Three years earlier Fred Gaisberg had written to his brother:

> [the conductor] Sabajno will be writing to you about a new tenor named Gigli who has been singing in Rome and here [in Milan] and making an awful hit. I have heard him and today I made a test of his voice. I tell you he is wonderful and don't hesitate o follow Sabajno's advice about securing him because he is going to have a great career. You can describe him as a 2nd Caruso except he has greater vocal flexibility. It is a real lyric voice than rings out all over the place and give [sic] you the impression of illimitable [sic] reserve. He is about 24[23] and robust health average height and shows extraordinary intelligence for a tenor. Columbia have already made him an offer so we are not alone in the ring. We lost Schipa and for goodness sake don't let us lose Gigli.[24]

The Gaisbergs got their man, and Gigli made his first recordings for HMV in 1918. When writing his memoirs, the tenor recalled being introduced by Mascagni to Carlo Sabajno,[25] who invited him to hear a recording of Caruso singing "*Com'è gentil*" from *Don Pasquale*. Gigli claims not to have heard a gramophone recording previously, so his introduction to the technology was atypical. His reaction was not; he embraced Caruso's voice as a revelation. Sabajno invited Gigli to make a test pressing, and when hearing his own voice for the first time he recalled:

---

22 20 March, 1890 – 30 November, 1957.
23 He was 27 years old at the time.
24 Martland, Peter (2013). *Recording History: The British Record Industry, 1888 – 1931*. Scarecrow Press. p.316.
25 Carlo Sabajno (1874 – 1938). From 1904 to 1932, he was the Gramophone Company's chief conductor and artistic director in Italy.

> What was even stranger was the affinity of tone that I could plainly hear between the record of mine and the Caruso… It left me wondering. What had maestro Sabajno wanted to imply by the juxtaposition?[26]

This was unfiltered vanity. There is little to compare in the tone of either singer, and even less in their art. It's true that Gigli's voice was naturally formed and (initially at least) effortless; at times, it could be remarkably beautiful. His innate, unschooled musicality – described by the uncharitable as *incolto* – did not always equate to good taste, and his singing was characterised by a number of traits that would become synonymous with the Gigli style, and irritating by repetition, notably a predilection for sentimentality and cheapened emotional gestures. His tendency to interject aspiratically into words and phrases that gained nothing by it became his calling card, and an easy cliché. Unlike Caruso, however, he was technically capable of engaging in expert *messa di voce* – those long, drawn out dynamic shadings for which he was celebrated on both sides of the Atlantic – and some of his early recordings are exceptional for their warmth, ease and instinct.[27]

Gigli's 1918 recording of "*Cielo e mar*"[28] from *La Gioconda* is typical of his voice in its youth. The sweet timbre and fluid, *portamento*-heavy line during the first verse yields during the second to some spirited attacks and an open-throated, darkening timbre. The final B flat 4 resonates superbly with pinging *squillo*. Made at the same time (and with the same technology) as Caruso's later recordings, it's obvious that Gigli's voice is more sky than sea; it plumbs no depths and dances over the surface of Enzo's turbulent emotions. The use of the "Gigli sob" and some *very* plastic *rubato* cannot compensate for a nagging sense of artificiality – something that would colour his work as the first Italian tenor to become a star of screen as well as stage.

His earliest filmed appearances were for Vitaphone in 1926. He is seen and heard singing a "Programme of Concert Favourites" – four slices of the white-bread repertoire that would keep him in jam and butter for thirty years: "*Mirame Asi*," "*Bergère légère*,"[29] "Come, love, with me" (sung in English), and "*O sole mio*."[30] Gigli was not a handsome man. By 1930 he had gained considerable weight, and for the rest of his life he would carry all before him, even when wearing a corset. While Gigli never grew as large as Pavarotti, his pear-shape figure prevented him from doing more than navigate a stage, whatever the dramatic context. Martinelli was better looking; so too was Peter Lorre, and while Martinelli was taller, neither he nor Gigli was able to traduce the developing truism that tenors were short, fat and better heard than seen. In 1933 Gigli was filmed for the first time in Britain by Pathetone News – as "the World's Greatest Operatic Tenor" – performing "Handel's *Largo*" on the stage

---

26   Gigli, Beniamino. *The Memoirs of Beniamino Gigli* (1977). Arno Press. p.85.
27   In January, 1921, and like so many others, Gigli jumped ship to Victor. He returned to HMV in 1931 and recorded for the company every year thereafter, until his retirement in 1955.
28   'Sky and sea.'
29   Jean-Baptiste Weckerlin's 'Light Shepherdess' was a favourite song of Gigli's. It was part of the "public's request" programme at the sixty-five-year-old old tenor's final appearance in Carnegie Hall, on 17 April, 1955. The recording of that concert testifies to the singer's ill-health and (by this stage) the *very* light placement of his voice.
30   Bizarrely, he sings the songs other than in the order indicated in the opening credits.

of London's Kingsway Hall surrounded by record company men in stiff collars. The performance is less striking than Gigli's posture when singing, which causes him to appear like a Grecian urn, with his elbows held stiffly away from his sides and his head pushed backwards into his neck. There is not the slightest hint of theatrical sensibility – something for which he was criticised in New York, where his status paled beside Caruso's.[31] It was thus a stroke of Olympian good fortune that he should have been cast in middle-age, in 1935, by the director Augusto Genina as the star of the German film *Vergiss mein nicht*,[32] starring Magda Schneider as Liselotte Hessfeld, a disillusioned young secretary who falls in love with Enzo Curti, a widowed opera star. The film is as sentimental as the singing, and for the sweetest of teeth only. The British rights were bought by Alexander Korda, who passed the making of the English-language version to his brother, Zoltan, who utilised *Forget Me Not* as a vehicle for his wife, Joan Gardner. Joan was 24 years younger than Gigli, and 19 years younger than her husband. The British version is more spumescent, even, than the original, and its winsome tale of frustrated love more than returned its investment.

Many other musical films were made in 1935, but none called on "serious" opera singers. The most irreverent, *A Night at the Opera*, was released on 15 November to leviathan receipts. The Marx Brothers' film is incredibly funny and more than competent musically, with excellent performances from the rival tenors, Allan Jones and Walter Woolf King – neither of whom was a professional opera singer.[33] The blurring of the lines between popular and serious repertoire was captured in the mixture of material, spanning the film's hit song "*Alone*" and a range of highlights from *Il trovatore*. The fact that Gigli wasn't definitively superior as a singer to Allan Jones was not lost on film-makers keen to ensure that audiences were presented with entertainments to which they might relate through language and repertoire. Choice became a commercial virtue, with hit musicals throughout the year featuring talented singers, and lots of tenors – all of them performing material that was recognisably and accessibly "local" and original. Hollywood produced *George White's 1935 Scandals*, Busby Berkeley's *Gold Diggers of 1935*, and *Reckless*;[34] in Europe, the Austrian-Hungarian *Ball at the Savoy* and the British *Music Hath Charms* achieved box-office success while being operatic only in scale. The only significant musical of 1935 to engage with "serious" artistic traditions was the French-German production *Light Cavalry*, based on Franz von Suppé's 1866 operetta.

Two years later, one of the most widely admired tenors of the 20th century (albeit incidentally) struck gold when singing "*The Trail of the Lonesome Pine*" in *Way Out West*. Harry Carroll's song from 1913 was performed by Oliver Hardy and Stan Laurel, with support from The Avalon Boys. Hardy was born in 1892. He determined

---

31   Gigli resigned from the Met in 1932 over money – having refused to take a pay cut. The Met's general manager, Giulio Gatti-Casazza, released this fact to the media, claiming that Gigli was the only Company member to refuse to accept less money. This was only partly true. A number of other singers had refused also, and Gigli's offer to sing a number of concerts for free, by way of compensation, was never made public. Worse still, Gatti-Casazza had given himself a significant pay rise in 1931, so that his grandiloquent gesture of paying himself less was perceived as noble when it was anything but.
32   'Forget Me Not.'
33   See further footnote 12 in Chapter 5.
34   Starring Jean Harlow, William Powell and a 15-year old Mickey Rooney.

at a young age to train as an operatic tenor. His voice was light, beautifully placed and exquisitely delivered, such that it was ideal for film and recording – most remarkably when performing "Lazy Moon" in *Pardon Us*[35] (1931), and "*Shine On Harvest Moon*" in *Flying Deuces* (1939). One of Hardy's most treasured memories was making the journey by train to Atlanta as a teenager to hear Caruso.[36] His glorious performance of the chorus in "*Lonesome Pine*," with its nuanced *rubato* and elegant *legato*, is ruined by Laurel when miming to the voices of the bass Chill Wills and (after being struck on the head with a mallet by Hardy) the soprano Rosina Lawrence.

Hollywood's growing love affair with popular song caused opera to become increasingly marginalised in the cinemas – at least in its more serious form. Before Chuck Jones introduced a new generation of Americans to opera through cartoons like *Long-Haired Hare*, *The Rabbit of Seville*, and *What's Opera, Doc?*, the "high" artistic culture of opera was employed more frequently as colour than content. Stan and Ollie's appearances as "Stanlio" and "Ollio" in the 1933 film *The Devil's Brother* was based very loosely on Auber's 1830 opera *Fra Diavolo*, while *The Bohemian Girl*, which the duo released in 1936, was based even more loosely on Balfe's work of the same name. It is described in the opening credits as "A Comedy Version," although neither of the characters played by Laurel and Hardy appears in the opera. Their 1940 film *Swiss Miss* is "about" a composer of opera – played by Walter Woolf King of Marx Brothers' fame.[37] Nothing even faintly operatic appears in the film, however.

The situation was different in Europe, where opera remained contemporary, particularly after 1933. In the light of his success with *Forget Me Not*, and the Italian production *Non ti scordar di me*, Gigli appeared in a series of mostly German-made films, beginning with *Ave Maria* in 1936. During the next eight years, he was the musical and romantic focus in thirteen popular films: *Du bist mein Glück*,[38] *Die Stimme des Herzens*,[39] *Mutterlied*,[40] *Dir gehört mein Herz*,[41] *Giuseppe Verdi*,[42] *Marionette* (1939), *Der singende Tor*,[43] *Casa lontana*,[44] *Musica di sogno*,[45] *Mamma* (1941), *I pagliacci* (1943), *Lache Bajazzo*,[46] and *Silenzio, si gira!*[47] The last of these was released on 2 October, 1943. It follows that Gigli not only performed for the Axis powers during the Second World War, he did so for the Nazi regime during the Reich. It's an unpalatable fact – one entirely forgotten on 8 October, 1997, when the Metropolitan Opera unveiled a bust of Gigli in memory of his 12 years in New York between

---

35 Though the context is entirely comic and devoid of malice (and noting the film was made in 1930), it is unfortunate that this scene involves Stan and Ollie wearing "blackface."
36 McIver, Stuart B. (1993). *Dreamers, Schemers and Scalawags*. Pineapple Press. p.37.
37 Woolf returned as the villain, Beecher, in *Go West*, in 1940.
38 'You Are My Joy,' 1936.
39 'The Voice of the Heart,' 1937.
40 'Mother Song,' 1937.
41 'My Heart Belongs to Thee,' 1938.
42 1938. Gigli was cast as Raffaele Mirate (3 September, 1815 – November, 1895), the first Duke of Mantua in *Rigoletto*.
43 'The Singing Gate,' 1939.
44 'Distant home,' 1938.
45 'Dream Music,' 1940. Also released as *Ritorno*.
46 'Laugh, clown,' 1943.
47 1943.

1920 and 1932. Fine speeches were delivered in tribute to Gigli's performances for charitable causes, while Licia Albanese and Gabor Carelli remembered his talent as an artist and his warmth as a man.

Gigli was nonetheless the first and most famous Gentile tenor to achieve the sort of fame and influence that allowed him to choose where he wished to live after the signing of the Rome-Berlin Agreement on 25 October, 1936, and again after Mussolini and Hitler made their Pact of Steel on 22 May, 1939. Gigli chose to make his home in Rome. There can be no question that he was a collaborator. His voice, his reputation and his celebrity advantaged fascism and fed the Reich's propaganda machine, even as it was repudiated by Toscanini and so many others. Goebbels and Hitler were desperate to demonstrate the superiority of German and Italian art and culture after the flight (and murder) of those "degenerates" and "cowards" who were either unfit or unavailable for the Nazis to exploit. Photographs of Gigli shaking hands with Hitler and Goebbels may now embarrass those for whom the politicisation of art is in some way a distraction, but the facts survive regardless: Gigli was the most celebrated Italian tenor of his age and he submitted to its darkest episode as an apolitical *naif*. For all his alleged intelligence, he is said to have recoiled from political debate, and he was never a Fascist by formal allegiance. He was nonetheless granted (and accepted) honorary membership of the Party in 1932. The many defenders of Gigli and his conduct fail, perhaps, to remember that while he lived as one of the regime's pre-eminent cultural figures, many of his colleagues died in consequence of its vile brutalities. What price Gigli's reputation when weighed against the murders of the pianist Mario Finzi, the composer Leone Sinigaglia and the painter Gino Parin?

Gigli's apologists assert his "tacit" detachment from Nazi Germany after 1936 while acknowledging presumably that he and the La Scala Company performed in Munich and Berlin in 1937 as overt supporters of a militarised Hitler rather than as ambassadors of a brokered peace. His defenders fail to account for the associative value that his film work, recordings and performances generated for the Axis powers, year on year. In 1936, for example, Goebbels wrote in his diary of a concert in Berlin by the London Philharmonic Orchestra:

> Beecham conducts in a very vain and disagreeable way, and what's more it's superficial. His orchestra's strings sound very thin, lacking precision and clarity. Putting Beecham in the same class as Furtwängler is like comparing Kannenberg[48] with Gigli. Only Berlioz's Roman Carnival and a Dvořák Rhapsody made any impression; the Haydn symphony seemed downright boring. The evening dragged on. It was painful, as one had to clap out of politeness. Also the Führer was very discontented. How high Germany's musical culture stands in contrast, what with the Berlin Philharmonic and Furtwängler![49]

---

48 Hitler's chef; renowned for singing popular songs.
49 Goebbels, Joseph (2001). *Die Tagebücher von Joseph Goebbels*, ed. Jana Richter, Part 1, 1923–1941, Volume 3 (March 1936 – February 1937). K.G. Saur Verlag GmbH). pp.250–251.

High German culture reached considerably further than Rome, and attempts to distinguish between Gigli's patriotism and his nationalism, when he was at liberty to travel without encumbrance as one of Italy's most famous musicians, operate as defences of the indefensible. Gigli knew nothing of the complexities of Furtwängler's circumstances, just as surely as he failed to live up to Furtwängler's example when the conductor risked his own life and that of his family to protect the lives of many of his persecuted Jewish colleagues, as well as the integrity of German culture. On 1 April, 1933, eleven musicians sent an open cablegram to Hitler to protest "the Hitlerite persecution of musicians, composers and conductors."[50] The signatories were the conductors Arturo Toscanini, Bruno Walter, Frank Damrosch, Serge Koussevitzky, Artur Bodanzky, Alfred Hertz and Fritz Reiner; the pianists Ossip Gabrilowitsch and Harold Bauer; the violinist Charles Loeffler; and the composer Rubin Goldmark. Their message deplored the Nazi's treatment of artists in Germany for political and religious reasons, and articulated the forlorn hope that

> such persecutions as take place in Germany at present are not based on your [Hitler's] instructions, and that it cannot possibly be your desire to damage the high cultural esteem Germany, until now, has been enjoying in the eyes of the whole civilized world.[51]

The New York *Times* published the cablegram the day after it was sent. The accompanying article cited a letter from Gabrilowitsch to Toscanini, in which the former expressed his belief that any protest sent to Hitler would "remain without any appreciable results" unless the conductor gave his name to it: "There is only one man who could protest effectively…."[52] Gabrilowitsch had been bitterly opposed to the use of the title "Your excellency" in the letter's address to Hitler, and he warned Toscanini of the consequences were he to fulfil a scheduled engagement to conduct at Bayreuth that summer:[53]

> Two years ago (1931) when you left [Bayreuth] in disgust and anger, you were reported in a newspaper interview as having expressed yourself very sharply against Hitlerism. This year (1933) you are returning to [Bayreuth] when Hitlerism is at the climax of its triumph. Do you not think that this must be interpreted by the whole world as an expression of your approval of Hitlerism?[54]

Of course, Gigli was one of many tenors not to find himself conflicted. Ferruccio Tagliavini was the first Italian tenor to perform in the United States after Mussolini

---

50 "Toscanini Heads Protest to Hitler: He and Ten Other Musicians of World Fame Ask End of Persecution of Colleagues." New York *Times*, 2 April 1933, 1. p.29.
51 *Ibid.*
52 *Ibid.*
53 Toscanini cancelled his performances at Bayreuth, where he was replaced by Richard Strauss. See Boyden, Matthew (1999). *Richard Strauss*. Weidenfeld & Nicolson.
54 "Toscanini Heads Protest to Hitler: He and Ten Other Musicians of World Fame Ask End of Persecution of Colleagues." New York *Times*, 2 April 1933, 1. p.29.

banned overseas appearances by Italians in 1940; years later, he was keen to remember having made his "American debut" when performing for the troops that liberated Italy. Yet Tagliavini was also one of the first to leave the United States before the War in consequence of his outspoken fascist convictions – the sincerity of which inspired him to spend most of 1935 and 1936 in Africa as a volunteer fighting for the ill-fated Fascist cause.[55] Tagliavini was an extremely musical light-lyric tenor, expert in the *coloratura* of Rossini and the languor of Bellini with the heft when necessary to sing Verdi, Puccini and Massenet. He was close friends with Mascagni, who considered him the ideal *Fritz*. His exceptional technique ensured a stage career that spanned 1938 to 1970, and a further decade in concert. Tagliavini made an amazing number of recordings, some of which are very fine – particularly his surviving work for RAI. His voice was light, refined and expressive; he was also an accomplished actor, with a particular flair for comedy. Tagliavini made seven films between 1942 and 1958 – *Voglio vivere così*,[56] *La donna è mobile*,[57] *Ho tanta voglia di cantare*,[58] *Il barbiere di Siviglia*,[59] *Al diavolo la celebrità*,[60] *Anema e core*,[61] and *Vento di Primavera*.[62] The best known is Mario Costa's US TV film *Barbiere* (for which Deems Taylor[63] was credited as writer), starring Tito Gobbi as Figaro. Although Tagliavini was talented, he was never able to escape the shadow of his primary rival, Tito Schipa.[64]

Like Tagliavini, Schipa was known to be more than sympathetic to fascism before the war (not least through his close friendship with Achille Starace), when he earned the sobriquet "Mussolini's tenor." It was an unfortunate association for arguably the most extraordinary *tenore di grazia* of the first half of the 20th century. Schipa's voice was a marker for silk merchants. It was not large, or coloured by *squillo*; it was wonderfully clear, however, such that every beautifully articulated word could be appreciated even in the largest of theatres. The slightly granulated tone, ease of placement and elegance of projection were unique at the time; they are positively freakish by modern standards. Unlike Gigli, Schipa was an artist – a painter in song for whom every word and phrase was an opportunity for expressive licence. He could elevate the simplest and most banal of sentiments to a pitch of sophistication of which Gigli could not have dreamed – in part because Schipa was raised (and trained) in a formal tradition of which Gigli knew nothing. Like pretty much everyone else at the time, his earliest musical experiences were as a child singing in his church choir, and as a member of the chorus in local opera productions. He was trained as a teenager by Alceste Gerunda[65] – with whom he studied for five years. Gerunda

---

55 Kraemer, Richard H. (2010). *The Secret War in the Balkans: A WWII Memoir*. Author House. p.92.
56 'I Live as I Please.' (1942).
57 'Women are Fickle.' (1942).
58 'Anything for a Song.' (1943).
59 'The Barber of Seville.' (1947).
60 'To Hell with Celebrity.' (1949); released also as *A Night of Fame*.
61 'Heart and Soul.' (1951); released also as *My Heart Sings*.
62 'Spring Wind.' (1958).
63 The writer of *Fantasia* (1940).
64 27 December, 1888 – 16 December, 1965. Most sources give his date of birth as 2 January, 1889, but his birth was not registered until 2 January of the following year. The name given to him on his birth certificate was Raffaele Attilio Amedeo Schipa.
65 1847 – 1917.

was "old school" and would beat Schipa during their first two years together if he was heard to sing anything other than scales and exercises. Such was the ruthlessness of Gerunda's schooling that Schipa was able to make his debut only weeks after his 20th birthday, on 4 February, 1909 – as Alfredo in *La traviata*. His international career was launched four years later, with appearances across South America, and in 1916 he appeared for the first time at La Scala. Within three months of his triumph in Milan, Puccini chose him to create Ruggero Lastouc in the world premiere of *La Rondine* – Schipa's only apparent origination. Five years later, while in the United States, Schipa recorded Alfredo's "*Lunge da lei per me non v'ha diletto! … De' miei bollenti spiriti*"[66] from *La traviata*. His performance is miraculous, and emblematic of Schipa's unusually heightened sensibilities. For the phrase "*Qui presso a lei, Io rinascer mi sento, E dal soffio d'amor rigenerato, Scordo ne' gaudii suoi tutto il passato*"[67] he spins a near seamless thread which he transforms when singing the words "… *lei, Io…*", dipping lightly below the first note and adding a syllable to the second. Schipa creates an unmistakable sense that Alfredo is aware that the past is not entirely forgotten. The shadows cast by this remarkable piece of writing – where words and music are psychologically and emotionally symmetrical – are made darker still by Schipa's breath-taking *diminuendo* when delivering the rising phrase to a crowning *pianissimo* A flat for the words "*gaudii suoi*." The technical brilliance is employed for a calculated dramatic purpose – in service to the libretto, the narrative and the character's emotional state. It is a technical feat that overcomes the vanities of its source.

The role of Ruggero was premiered in New York by Gigli in 1928, in which year he also recorded "*Lunge da lei … De' miei bollenti spiriti*" from *Traviata*. It's *vero* Gigli, and a pleasure for the tenor's even tone and expansive *rubato*. Unlike Schipa, however, who was able to tap a rainbow of colours of which most of his contemporaries were insensible, Gigli approaches everything with a largely consistent weight of tone, the usual "Gi-hi-li" sob, and some frankly prosaic phrasing. It would be routine in its uniformity – but for a single, stupendous exception to his own rule. During the aria itself, and when singing the phrase "*quasi in ciel … Dal dì che disse…,*" Gigli ignores the semi-quaver rest immediately after "*ciel*" (written as a crotchet) and in an effortless *mezza-voce* he descends without breathing to the semi-quaver B flat for the word "*Dal*". It is nothing short of magical – a moment of unqualified perfection that taps an intimacy inimical of the tenor's often lazy reliance on tone. Of course, the moment emerges independently of the score – indeed, it openly ignores the composer's specific instructions. For that reason alone it is pure affectation. It's a stunning reminder, regardless, that when at his best there were few better than Gigli.

Schipa and Gigli were often compared with one another. During the 1930s, however, their repertoire separated them, with Schipa remaining true to his *leggiero* anatomy and Gigli pushing well beyond his resources to take on dramatic roles, rarely with success. Schipa's first film, *Tre uomini in frak*,[68] was released on 30 June, 1933, in France. It concerned the predictably contrived tale of Marcello, a tenor fearful of performing in public, whose friends design a scheme in which a stand-in appears on

---

66 'There's no pleasure in life when she's away! … My passionate spirit.'
67 'I feel myself reborn, Revived by the breath of love, Forgetting the past in present delights.'
68 'Three Lucky Fools.' Also released as *L'amore che canta* ['The Love that Sings'].

stage while Marcello sings from behind the scenes. Of course, before the credits role he triumphs over his anxieties. The film was directed by Mario Bonnard, famed for his spectacular (and part-censored) *I promessi sposi*, based on Manzoni's nationalist novel of fatherland and occupation, and released in two versions (in French and Italian) in June, 1933 – a month after the Nazis began staging mass book-burnings for the media, and two weeks before the German government enacted the *Gesetz zur Verhütung erbkranken Nachwuchses*[69]. During his tour of the avowedly anti-Fascist Australia in 1937, Schipa ended his recitals with the Fascist salute. Two years later, he declined an invitation (and a fee of $1,000[70] for each appearance) from a coalition of Italian-American groups to perform a dozen concerts to raise money for the Anti-Fascist movement in Italy. On 23 February, 1939 he wrote:

> I am sorry that I cannot sing for Loubet; but you MUST understand my situation; and my relationship with Achille Starace in Italy and all authorities there. And you know the purpose of the benefit for which Loubet asks me to sing for. Not tell anybody the reason; tell that I cannot come to New York or some other excuse; but don't ask me the impossible.[71]

Schipa's second, *Vivere*, was directed by Guido Brignone and marketed as much for its title song by Cesare A. Bixio as for Schipa's performances – which are exquisite. Between 1938 and 1945, he appeared in five films – all of them successful in Italy and Germany.[72] After the war, Schipa played Gilbert Duprez in *Il cavaliere del sogno* (a biopic of Donizetti, 1947) and *I misteri di Venezia* (1951) – both of them forgettable – and he appeared as himself in *Follie per l'opera*[73] and *Soho Conspiracy* (1950). His return to the United States after the war was predictably controversial. On 13 March, 1947, the gossip columnist Walter Winchell wrote a "Portrait of a Nazi" – in the form of a syndicated "Memo to the State Department" – containing revelations about Schipa's (first) wife and children, all of whom had supported the Allies and Italian resistance in defiance of Schipa. Winchell pulled no punches:

> In January this reporter charged that Tito Schipa, the opera singer, was a Fascist. We added that we suffered nightmares when the U.S. Govn't allowed him to return to our shores … He was an intimate friend of Benito Mussolini… Whenever he met Italians in this country he immediately expressed his great love for Il Duce, going to great pains to describe the wonderful things Big Mouth was doing for Italy. In 1935 he told the

---

69 'Law for the prevention of offspring with inherited disorders.' To make lawful the compulsory sterilisation of citizens suffering from a *long* list of allegedly genetic disorders.
70 Approximately $18,500 in 2021.
71 Quoted by Walter Winchell in The Longview *News-Journal* (Texas), 13 March, 1947. p.5.
72 *Vivere ancora* ('Live again,' 1945); *Rosalba*, 1944; *In cerca di felicità* ('Looking for happiness,' 1944), *Terra di fuoco* ('Land of Fire,' 1939), *Chi è più felice di me!* ('Who Is Happier Than I?', 1938).
73 'Mad About Opera.' (1948).

American press that "Mussolini was grand, Italy grander, and everybody but silly England must see that Italy's destiny was to expand."[74]

If Schipa was Italy's pre-eminent lyric tenor during the 1930s and 40s, then Giacomo Lauri-Volpi[75] was its most charismatic. He was born Giacomo Volpi (adding "Lauri" to distinguish himself from two other tenors with the same name) and orphaned at the age of 11. He was highly intelligent, a polyglot in Classical as well as Romance languages, and unusually well-educated even for the time.[76] He trained as a lawyer in Rome, singing as an amateur in his spare time. After winning second place in a singing competition, he abandoned the law and academia for voice training with Antonio Cotogni – the same Cotogni that had trained Jan De Reszke. His studies were interrupted by (distinguished) service as a Captain during the First World War, and when he returned to Italy at the end of 1918, Cotogni was dead. Lauri-Volpi made his debut as Arturo (in *I Puritani*) at the age of 27 on 2 September, 1919. With characteristic *chutzpah*, he did so as "Giacomo Rubini" in part because he was able without appreciable effort to ring out genuine high C5s, D flat 5s, D5s and, in rehearsal, E flat 5s. On hearing him crown a D5 in Rome in 1920, Luisa Tetrazzini was heard to observe, "My God! He can sing nearly as high as I can!".[77] Within three years, and after triumphs in Rio, Buenos Aires, Trieste, Genoa, Bologna, Madrid, Barcelona, Monte Carlo and Milan (La Scala), he performed at the Met in New York. By the time of his first appearance at Covent Garden, in 1925, as Andrea Chénier, Lauri-Volpi was Europe's most celebrated *spinto* tenor and one of its most infamous *prima uomi*. His combustible nature provoked confrontations with performers, managers, and even audiences. The Romanian soprano, Stella Roman, recalled a *Rigoletto* in Italy during which Lauri-Volpi performed "*La donna e mobile*" in *mezza-voce* – for no obvious reason. He littered the performance with *fioriture*, and when the audience registered its disapproval as only Italian audiences can, the tenor marched to the footlights and demanded that the conductor repeat the aria. He sang it again, this time as expected – save that he sustained the clipped D flat in the cadenza for several beats. The audience cheered, at which point Lauri-Volpi picked up the Duke's prop deck of cards and threw it at the audience. They in turn began to throw whatever they could at the tenor. Lauri-Volpi spat openly at the stage and then the stalls – past the now empty podium – and marched to his dressing room.[78]

Unlike the majority of his rivals, Lauri-Volpi was tall, handsome and athletic. When arriving in New York for the first time, the waiting press was given a taste of what to expect when he walked from the *SS Duilio* wearing a white satin *camiciotto* with crimson piping that revealed more of his chest than was appropriate or fashionable.[79] The swagger and vanity were warranted. He looked magnificent in

---

74 Winchell, Walter, in The Longview *News-Journal* (Texas), 13 March, 1947. p.5.
75 11 December, 1892 – 17 March, 1979.
76 He wrote a number of books on music and vocal training, many of which were published, including *Cristalli viventi* (Rome, 1948), *Voci parallele* (Milan, 1955), and *Misteri della voce umana* (Milan, 1957).
77 Drake, James A. (1981). "Ecco! Il Leone!: Giacomo Lauri-Volpi and the Metropolitan Opera, 1922–32." *Italian Americana*, Vol. 7, No. 1. pp.45–64.
78 *Ibid*. p.60.
79 *Ibid*. p.45.

thigh-length boots and the brilliance and ease of his voice, and its resonance above the stave, provoked wild enthusiasm. He was not the first tenor to plead to the dubious virtue of distended and inappropriate high notes; he was arguably the first to get away with it – famously so when creating the role of Calàf for the first Met production of *Turandot* in 1926. Two years later, during a performance in Philadelphia of *Il trovatore* with Rosa Ponselle as Leonora and Giuseppe Danise as Count di Luna, things got out of hand. The Philadelphia *Inquirer* delighted in reporting how:

> In the first scene of the first act, everything rippled along melodiously. Then came the second scene, Lauri-Volpi as Manrico, playing heavy lover to Miss Ponselle…. His rival is Giuseppe Danise, a Count, and [is] not so successful at the romance stuff. Danise is a baritone. They are in a garden. Leonora discovers by lifting a mask that the Troubadour is none other than Manrico. Thereupon the Count challenges him to a duel. The scene ends with the trio rising to the D-flat region. That is, Leonora and Manrico hit that note. It is usually held for two beats. Sometimes three. On this occasion Miss Ponselle and Mr. Lauri-Volpi held it for five together, but Lauri-Volpi kept on going and continued for three more beats to establish a record. No other prima donna ever suffered this experience on the Metropolitan Opera House stage. She thought with lightning alacrity. To conceal her embarrassment, she plunged into the action of the opera, fainting to separate the two duelists. But Lauri-Volpi was oblivious to her ruse. It all happened so swiftly. The audience burst into applause – Miss Ponselle broke into tears. As the curtain dropped, Miss Ponselle fainted. That was in keeping with her part, to many it seemed a realistic bit of acting…[80]

Lauri-Volpi had neither the style of Schipa nor the tone of Gigli – of whom he was pathologically hateful and jealous; Martinelli was more resonant and Aureliano Pertile (see below) had infinitely better judgment. He nonetheless presented a complete package for audiences feeding at the cinemas on Gary Cooper and Nils Asther. Surprisingly, considering his profile and unblinking narcissicm, he made only a single film during his prime, *Das Lied der Sonne*[81] – ostensibly a vehicle for the tenor to perform scenes from some of his most celebrated roles. It's fortunate he was filmed at his best because he was poorly served by studio recordings and his voice declined noticeably during the 1930s, in consequence of over-use and poor repertoire choices. In *Das Lied*, directed by Max Neufeld (who the following year directed *Ein Stern fällt vom Himmel* starring Joseph Schmidt), his performance of excerpts from *Gli Ugonotti*[82] is thrilling for its gleaming tone and resonant projection. Not everyone will warm to his rapid *vibrato* and peculiarly drawn-out *legato*, which employs pronounced *portamento* (both rising and falling) with insufficient punctuation, but the

---

80   *Ibid*. pp.57–58.
81   'Song of the Sun.' (1933). Also released as *La canzone del sole*.
82   Meyerbeer's *Les Huguenots*.

squillo ring and amplitude are magnificent. The same is true of a live recording from 1930 of "*O muto asil,*" which conveys a voice of clarion power and easy delivery.

Lauri-Volpi remained with the Met until 1933 – when he too was caught up in the Gatti-Casazza pay-cut fiasco.[83] After returning to Italy he was elevated by Mussolini and the *Fascisti*, though his political sympathies were comparatively innocuous. For this reason, many within the party considered him an unreliable ally.[84] Whenever possible, he retreated to Spain with his Spanish wife, and in 1940 he made plans to return to the United States and another stint at the Met. Before he could leave the country, however, war in Europe dragged him back into national service and a ceremonial appointment, with the rank of Colonel. His co-existence with fascism was sufficiently detached for Lauri-Volpi to be welcomed back into Britain and Portugal in 1946, and in France, Belgium, Denmark and Sweden in 1947 – although his voice was by now a shadow of its former glory. Lauri-Volpi continued to sing publicly into his 70s. At the age of 81 he released a recording of operatic arias when plainly he should not have done. For many, he is best remembered for his friendship with Franco Corelli, with whom he was often compared, for a variety of reasons.

Lauri-Volpi's weakness for indulgent *tenuti* and high-wire *tessitura* was lapped up by the public and condemned by the critics. Conductors were increasingly unhappy also, at a time when interpretation (as a metric for "re-creative" rather than "creative" art) had eclipsed composition as the driver for opera. This *Querelle des Bouffons* metastasised in the visceral and mutual loathing of Furtwängler and Toscanini – with the former advocating a metaphysical construction of the score as a point of departure and the latter memorialising the Note as gospel. Toscanini's allegedly strict adherence to the principle of *come è scritto* was a reaction to laziness and vanity on the part of singers, orchestras and conductors. Indeed, the "art" of conducting in Italy was in its infancy when Toscanini directed the first performance of *La bohème* in 1896, whereas *fin de siècle* Vienna, Berlin and Paris had been nurturing the concept of performance as philosophy for nearly a century, building on foundations laid by Schiller, Schopenhauer, Schumann and (practically) Louis-Antoine Jullien and Édouard Colonne. With the horizon being stretched further still by the expansionist values of Florestan and Eusebius, and with Liszt's status as a pianist and a conductor superseding his genius as a composer, the emergence of interpretative *savants* like Hans von Bülow, Hans Richter, Hermann Levi and Arthur Nikisch was weaned on the novelty of recording. Comparison now infected the incorruptibility of transience. "*If only you had heard…*" was replaced by "*would you like to hear?*" – an outcome that resolved in recordings becoming a value system for the creation of the canonically impossible. The *Mysterium fidei* cultivated by the unseen and the unheard – with Rubini, Duprez and Nourrit being the most obvious candidates for conjecture – fell to the analytically subjective "certainties" of cultural prejudice. "Furtwängler's Beethoven" could now be said by his acolytes to be "better" than Toscanini's; Schipa's

---

83 Gatti-Casazza asked a number of the Company to sign a written protest against Gigli's absent co-operation. Lauri-Volpi was delighted to do so, but because of difficulties with the House over new roles, and because he genuinely hated living in the United States, he left the Metropolitan at around the same time as his nemesis – albeit more discreetly.

84 He kept a distance from the Party in Italy, but in Spain, and during almost 30 years of life in the country after the war, he supported Franco.

"*Suzel, Buon Dì*" from *L'amico Fritz* was superior for his admirers than Gigli's – even though there was a recording from 1917 of the first Fritz, Fernando de Lucia, singing the duet, rendering all others inadequate "by definition." Of course, there is no inherent virtue in a performer being the originator of a role – many singers were far from ideal *in loco parentis*. Particularly in Germany, therefore, Toscanini's ambitions were perceived by many as vacuous because his fidelity to the score was really little more than a reaction to generations of bad and lazy practices. In any event, the "ideal" of fealty is achievable only when the vanities and extravagances of singers are curtailed or extinguished. In this respect, it was the composer that expired, not his frustrations. These were transferred to the new gods of the art of performance – conductors.

Toscanini's favourite tenor before the war was Aureliano Pertile.[85] A fine musician, Pertile created leading tenor roles in Felipe Boero's *Tucuman* (1918), Boito's *Nerone* (1924), Wolf-Ferrari's *Sly* (1927), Constantino Gaito's *Ollantay* (1926), and Mascagni's *Nerone* (1935).[86] At his best, he had a powerful, ringing voice as well as a keener appreciation of dramatic articulation than most of his peers, including Lauri-Volpi. He was expert at *verismo*, with a muscular voice that had considerable dramatic punch – something admired by Toscanini, who worked with him regularly during his decade's reign as the leading tenor at La Scala between 1927 and 1937. His often limpid phrasing – well evidenced on his 1924 recording of "*Queste ad un lido fatal*" from Boito's *Nerone* – was undone by a rapid *vibrato* during the first half of his career; by the time he came to record for Telefunken in the 1940s it had spread badly. Pertile was renowned as Otello. He first sang the role in 1937 – in his early 50s – and only accepted the challenge because his voice was approaching its end. His recording of "*Niun mi tema*" survives, regardless, as a testament to one of the most thoughtful dramatic tenors of the 20th century.[87]

Pertile was highly regarded without him needing to make feature films.[88] His sincerity as an artist enhanced his reputation as a "singer's singer." In German-speaking territories (a fluid taxonomy after 30 September, 1938[89]), cinema and opera audiences overlapped significantly. For the Viennese, in particular, music was heard almost everywhere – at home, in the open air, in *Kaffeehäusen* and *Heurigen* along the Prater, and the city's many concert halls, churches and opera houses. The ease with which musical theatre was annexed by cinema amplified the unusual degree of pollination between the progressive and the popular[90] – not least since Vienna was well-resourced to supply its cinemas with musicians. In 1920, there were 163 cinemas in Vienna, 26 as part of a society and three formed as *Arbeiterheime*.[91] The

---

85   9 November, 1885 – 11 January, 1952.
86   There is publicly available footage of Mascagni conducting *Nerone*, with Pertile, at La Scala.
87   Yes, he too sings the final note, to which he adds some sobbing and a final sigh.
88   This was an unlikely option considering his *brutta* appearance.
89   When Great Britain, France and Italy signed an agreement that allowed the Nazis to annex the Sudetenland (the northern, southern, and western areas of what was then Czechoslovakia).
90   It's worth remembering that during the 1920s, when he was engaging with free atonality, Public Modernist No.1, Arnold Schoenberg, made arrangements of songs by Schubert and Sioly, and also waltzes by Johann Strauss II, for small bands formed of a mix of single strings, wind instruments, mandolins, harmonium and piano.
91   'Worker's homes.'

Arbeiterheim in Ottakring had an audience capacity of 2,000. In 1920, the city's cinemas provided 50,833 seats[92] and employed 554 musicians – not always proportionately. Mutoscope, for example, filmed a scene from Donizetti's *La Fille du régiment* in 1898, which was accompanied live by a band of between 10 and 20 musicians. Pathé produced a version of *Faust* in 1905 that was closer to Goethe than to Gounod, and in 1909 two different versions of *Rigoletto* appeared, one in France, the other in the United States. Each was adequately served by a similar sized ensemble, but chamber resources were wholly inadequate for Edison's production of *Parsifal* in 1905 – released only two years after the opera's North American premiere in New York, when it was performed with an orchestra of around 100.

The circumstances were very different when *Der Rosenkavalier* was made into a silent film in 1926 and first shown at the Semperoper in Dresden (where it had made its debut in 1911) on 10 January.[93] Strauss' demands were met head-on and by routine. He conducted the Staatskapelle orchestra at the first screening[94] – although a last-minute re-edit knocked everything out of sync so that the composer was compelled to lower his baton on twenty occasions.[95] *Der Rosenkavalier* was directed by Robert Wiene,[96] the revolutionary director of the expressionist masterpieces *Das Cabinet des Dr. Caligari*[97] and *Raskolnikow* (1923). At the Berlin premiere, the audience's ovation was reserved for the Jewish Wiene, which Strauss was seen to acknowledge without smiling – forcing the composer to yield the stage to the director. One reviewer, having observed the scene, wrote:

> We have to judge here as film people and not as musicians. And we have to say that we liked the film far better than the opera in Dresden… [Wiene] has created a splendid achievement that needs to exist through, not only as an 'illustration' to Strauss's music, i.e. as a dependent appendix, but which should also be a success everywhere as a film.[98]

The emergence during the Weimar Republic of opportunities for Jewish artists was not excluded by cinema, and the meaning of (and association between) "Jewish modernisation" and "Jewish integration" were positive in their diversification of opportunity and identity, and negative for the resentment they caused for those who considered the concept of a "pure" German community meaningful. The tension

---

92   *Filmbote*. Jan. 1920, Nr. 1. p.10.
93   Jung, Uli and Schatzberg, Walter (1994). "The Silent *Rosenkavalier*: A Film by Hugo von Hofmannsthal, Richard Strauss and Robert Wiene." *Modern Austrian Literature*, Vol. 27, No. 2. pp.77–89; p.81.
94   The film was well-received at its Berlin premiere at the Capitol Theater on 16 January, 1926. This time Strauss was in the audience to hear his music being conducted by the experienced film composer and conductor Willy Schmidt-Gentner, who rearranged the music *again* to achieve synchronisation – this time successfully.
95   *Ibid.* p.81.
96   27 April, 1873 – 17 July, 1938.
97   'The Cabinet of Dr. Caligari,' (1920).
98   Jung, Uli and Schatzberg, Walter (1994). "The Silent *Rosenkavalier*: A Film by Hugo von Hofmannsthal, Richard Strauss and Robert Wiene." *Modern Austrian Literature*, Vol. 27, No. 2. pp.77–89. p.82.

between "symbiosis" and "submission" was transcended whenever Jews were able to relinquish their particularities by assimilation – something Wiene achieved when asserting his status as a Protestant in his Viennese university and accommodation records between 1894 and 1925, and by filming *INRI* in 1923. It's unlikely that Wiene would have identified as a Christian had Jews not suffered prejudice for being Jewish, any more than Mahler's application to become Music Director of the Wiener Hofoper would have been processed without his "converting" pre-emptively. It's accepted that these cultural practices were informed by social as well as political and historical pressures – a praxis of transnational influences and voices that was at its most integrated when being sung. A tenor could be Jewish while singing Wagner, just as a gentile was at liberty (before 1933, at least) to perform the role of Eléazar in German. The question of the "Jewish voice" crystallised literally and metaphorically after film ceased to be silent, when Jewish writers, producers, directors, designers and performers were able to collaborate openly, albeit as a "*noxious bacillus.*"[99]

Thanks to the long-standing (and consistent) traditions of the Cantor or *chazzanut*, synagogues had for more than 150 years provided a ready and highly-trained line of tenors across central and eastern Europe – most productively in Austria and Germany. Nomenclature ensured that it was possible to hide, to an extent – particularly when gentile Germans utilised names that were not traditionally German.

One of the first Jewish tenors to make a success of the transition from stage to screen was the popular Austrian-born singing-actor Alexander Girardi.[100] His short films of songs by Gustav Pick and Edmund Eysler[101] are as Viennese as Sachertorte, albeit less digestible. It's a question of taste, of course, but the alveolar trilling, shrieking laughter and exaggerated mannerisms of the supposedly drunk Girardi in "*Fiakerlied*"[102] can be of interest only to curators. His first and only feature film, *Der Millionenonkel*, was formed of a selection of his most famous scenes, including arias from *Der Verschwender* and *Die Fledermaus*. It set the tone for a wave of opera films, produced either as extant scores or as new works written specially for the screen. A number of productions were made as "*Gesangsfilme*"[103] – notably *Sonnige Träume*,[104] *Das Zauberlied*[105] (1914) and *Wo Die Lerche Singt*.[106] Cinema's full potential as a

---

99 Hitler, Adolf (1943). *Mein Kampf.* Houghton Mifflin. Ch. XI: Nation and Race. "This, however, has nothing to do with nomadism, for the reason that a Jew never thinks of leaving a territory that he has occupied, but remains where he is, and he sits so fast that even by force it is very hard to drag him out! His extension to ever-new countries occurs only in the moment in which certain conditions for his existence are there present, without which – unlike the nomad – he would not change his residence. He is and remains the typical parasite, a sponger who like a noxious bacillus keeps spreading as soon as a favorable [sic] medium invites him. And the effect of his existence is also like that of spongers: wherever he appears the host people dies out after a shorter or longer period."
100 5 December, 1850 – 20 April, 1918. Girardi's father was Italian, having emigrated to Graz in the 1840s. Ironically, the origins of his surname were Old German – Gerhard, meaning "spear-brave".
101 From his operetta *Künstlerblut.*
102 Produced by the splendidly named "Duskes Kinematographen-und Film-Fabriken GmbH und Messters Projektion GmbH."
103 'Singing films.'
104 'Sunny dreams.' (1921).
105 'The Magic Song.' (1914).
106 'Where The Lark Sings.' (1918).

vehicle for operatic tenors was not exploited, however, until the emergence during the 1930s of the Jewish tenors Richard Tauber and Joseph Schmidt.[107] The former established box office benchmarks with *Ich glaub' nie mehr an eine Frau*,[108] *Ein exotischer Fürst*[109] and *Das Land des Lächelns*.[110] He later headlined several popular musical films in England, having emigrated to avoid being imprisoned or murdered by the Nazis. The best of them was *Blossom Time* (1934), in which Tauber played Franz Schubert; the least successful was *Pagliacci* (1936) – for which Tauber was paid a fee of £80,000.[111]

Schmidt's voice was as fascinating as his biography – which is unique in the modern history of the tenor voice. Through radio and film, he was the first European tenor to succeed in opera without having performed in one on stage. He had little choice in the matter because, at four foot eleven inches, he was by some way the shortest, least physically present tenor of the 20th century. When Leo Blech first heard him singing he was bowled over. While shaking the tenor's hand, the conductor exclaimed "It's a pity you're not small…", to which Schmidt protested "But I am!" "No," replied Blech, "You're not; you're too small."

The "Pocket Caruso" was born in Davideny, in a district of the Bukovina province of Austria-Hungary; this became part of Romania after World War I and, later, a part of Ukraine. His musical roots were unusually diverse, so that he could speak (and sing) in multiple languages – including Hebrew, having studied for a time at the Czernowitz Synagogue.[112] Schmidt made his local debut in 1924 singing a recital of arias and songs; his success led to three years of formal study in Berlin with Hermann Weissenborn. He completed his first professional engagement when replying to an advert by a Berlin radio station for a tenor. He was perfect for the radio; though his voice was essentially light it was warm in its focus, and appeared richer than it would have done without a microphone. His broadcast debut was as Vasco da Gama in *L'Africaine*, in 1929. He went on to sing Rodolfo, Eléazar and Idomeneo; in 1933 he was cast in his first movie, *Ein Lied geht um die Welt*.[113] Directed by Richard Oswald for a German production company, and produced on location in Venice, the film's narrative hinged (as did most of Schmidt's films) on his diminutive stature, telling a version of Schmidt's life to date. He plays "Ricardo," a penniless operatic tenor (in 5-inch Cuban heels) who succeeds on the radio while failing in love. Bizarrely, and perhaps unwittingly, Joseph Goebbels was said to have applauded vigorously at the film's Berlin premiere in 1933, and Rochus Misch claimed after the war that he would "hear from Hitler's study the fine voice of the Jewish chamber singer, Joseph Schmidt, whose gramophone records the boss loved so much."[114]

---

107   4 March, 1904 – 16 November, 1942.
108   'Never Trust a Woman.' (1930).
109   'The Land of Smiles.' (1930).
110   'End of the Rainbow,' (1930).
111   £5.6m / $6.8 at the time of writing. The film was a famous box office failure.
112   Built in 1873, the synagogue was confiscated and closed by the Soviet government in 1940. It is now a cinema.
113   'A Song Goes Round the World.' He filmed it again a year later…
114   Misch, Rochus (2014). *Hitler's Last Witness: The Memoirs of Hitler's Bodyguard*. Frontline Books. p.6.

Before the end of the year, Schmidt relocated to Austria to avoid Nazi persecution. His next three films were produced by Austrian companies: *Wenn du jung bist, gehört dir die Welt*,[115] *Ein Stern fällt vom Himmel*[116] and *Heut' ist der schönste Tag in meinem Leben*.[117] Because the director, Richard Oswald, was declared an enemy of National Socialism (a justified allegation), *Ein Stern* was denied a permit in Germany; *Heut' ist* was first shown in Slovenia in 1935. Schmidt's last film was the British-produced remake of *Ein Stern* (as *A Star Fell From Heaven*).

Schmidt's life after 1935 is a litany of bad decisions and worse luck. He had travelled to Palestine the year before (giving concerts of cantorial music, songs and arias) but chose to return to Austria, where he remained until moving to Brussels. In 1937, he toured the United States, performing in Carnegie Hall with Grace Moore, only to return to Europe and another relocation, this time to Paris. Shortly before the outbreak of war, Schmidt bought tickets to sail to the United States; he never made it because someone impersonated him at the dock and stole his passage. The boat sailed without him. Even before the Anschluss, Schmidt's virility and talent as a performer and his beauty as a man had been problematic for the Nazis, who persecuted him through the media and made his working life increasingly difficult. It's possible he was tolerated initially because his size conformed with the Nazi's racist consideration of Jews as physically inadequate; he was not tolerated for long, however. Schmidt gave his final public appearance at a benefit concert for refugees in Avignon, on 14 May, 1942. He then became a refugee himself, making his way to Zurich and sanctuary with friends. Because he was determined not to violate the laws of a country that appeared to have given him a home, he reported himself as an "illegal" to the Swiss police, who sent him directly to an internment camp in Girenbad. During his incarceration, and while his application for asylum was being processed, Schmidt was forced into hard labour. This led to him being hospitalised at the Kantonsspital in Zurich. Two weeks later he was released, and while walking past the Waldegg Inn he was taken ill again. As he rested on a couch, Schmidt suffered a heart attack from which he died shortly after. He was 38 years old.[118] The camp arranged for his burial at the Friesenberg Jewish Cemetery near Zurich, where much later a headstone was laid with the inscription "*Ein Stern Fällt.*"[119]

Schmidt's films and recordings constitute an indelible legacy. They capture the often wondrous vocal gifts of an artist of rare technique and sensibilities with a range and dexterity that enabled him to engage in sophisticated trilling, endless *legati*, and ringing high C5s and D5s. His voice was rich in colour, bright, focussed and eternally easy – without the slightest hint of strain or effort. He applied equivalent artistry to everything, whether a popular song, a *hazzan* or an aria. This is well-reflected in the sequence in *Ein Lied geht um die Welt* where he sings "*O paradis*" (as "*Land so wunderbar*"), and his performance of Hans May's title song for "*Heut' ist der schönste Tag in meinem Leben.*" The fluency of both performances brings these apparently disparate

---

115 'When You're Young, the World Belongs to You.'
116 'A Star Fell from Heaven' – re-made in Britain in its English translation.
117 'Today is the Most Beautiful Day of My Life.'
118 He was buried the following day at the Israelitischer Friedhof Unterer Friesenberg in Zürich.
119 'A Star Falls'. It should more accurately have read "*Ein Stern ermordet*" ('A Star Murdered').

vernaculars into striking proximity – just as his duets with Grace Moore (a "popular" artist subjected to grotesque prejudice in the United States) made Puccini's music accessible to audiences who might otherwise never have heard it. The plots of Schmidt's films are habitually European, insofar as they are a great deal less sentimental than their American counterparts, with sombre and often obsidian narratives better suited to the "impossibility" of a small Jewish man being taken seriously as a love interest. *Ein Stern*, for example, tells the story of a temperamental film singer, the failure of whose voice leads to a (more gifted) student (played by Schmidt) substituting for the star – after the manner of Cyrano and Christian. Schmidt proceeds to lose the girl to the man in whose place he has performed. The film ends unhappily. The same was true for Schmidt, whose life was emblematically nasty, brutish, and short. Even so, Hobbes' celebrated axiom from *Leviathan* contains two other descriptors for a life lived outside society – solitary and poor – and Schmidt was neither. His social contract prevailed in ways that the Nazis could never have anticipated. He survived the Reich on record and film, and his life and career established almost single-handedly the entitlement of a classically-trained tenor to exist in ways and through media that would have been impossible but for the quality of his voice and the depths of his artistry. In short, Schmidt legitimised the right of a singer of opera to exist outside the opera house.

Not every opera star transitioned to celluloid; not every "opera star" was known for singing opera. The Irish tenor John McCormack[120] is remembered as one of the most popular tenors of the 20th century. His hundreds of recordings and concert tours made him a huge fortune, such that he appeared not to need the money offered by film studios. He performed in just three movies, all of them as himself: *Wings of the Morning* (1937), *Song o' My Heart* (1930) and *Love Never Dies* (1928). In each he sang only popular song. McCormack made his debut in 1906 at the Teatro Chiabrera, Savon, on the Ligurian coast; the following year he became the youngest principal tenor at Covent Garden, singing Turiddu in *Cavalleria rusticana*. In 1909 he relocated to the United States, where he sang as an Italian tenor, making records of arias and songs in French and Italian. His success was considerable, although he engaged rarely with new repertoire – a singular exception being his creation of the role of Lieutenant Merrill in the world premiere of one of the New York Met's greatest disasters: Victor Herbert's *Natoma*, with Mary Garden in the title role. McCormack was subsequently engaged by Nellie Melba to tour Australia, as the star tenor for the Melba Grand Opera Season. In 1917, McCormack took American citizenship and devoted himself to concert-giving – although he didn't leave the stage entirely until 1923. His popularity was second only to that of Caruso, and he made similar sums of money. He owned lavish apartments in London and New York, and between 1925 and 1937 he leased the vast Moore Abbey in Monasterevin, County Kildare, from the 10th Earl of Drogheda. After filming *Song o' My Heart* in 1930 he acquired Runyon Canyon, a huge house in California where he was feted by Hollywood's elite, including Errol Flynn, Will Rogers, Charlie Chaplin, John Barrymore, Basil Rathbone and Ronald Colman. McCormack retired for the first time after a concert at the Royal Albert Hall in London in 1938; a year later he returned to performing

---

120   14 June, 1884 – 16 September, 1945.

in support of the war effort until his declining health forced him to abandon singing in 1943. McCormack's celebrity has obscured his friendships with many significant men and women of letters, most importantly James Joyce,[121] who was himself a tenor of training and talent. The writer had considered a career as a singer when returning to Dublin from Paris in April, 1903, and five months later Joyce's brother, Stanislaus, recorded in his diary that

> Jim's voice, when in good form, has a beautiful flavour, rich and pure, and goes through one like a strong exhilarating wine. He sings well.[122]

In March, 1904, Joyce spent several evenings with McCormack and Richard Best, a Dubliner who was interested in the Feis Ceoil, a musical contest held annually in Dublin.[123] McCormack persuaded Joyce to enter the competition that year, where he was awarded the Bronze Medal. McCormack had won the gold medal the previous year, on 18 May, 1903.

McCormack was a lyric tenor – with a smooth, easy tone and acute dynamic sensibilities. His exceptional breath control enabled him to sing Mozart and Handel like few others, and his technical skill was sufficiently impressive to warrant his infamous putdown of Bing Crosby: "all you need today is a cardboard megaphone and a little nerve and then to stand near a microphone and fake a thing they call singing." Certainly, for all its lyricism, McCormack's voice conveyed great resonance also. In the words of Stanislaus Joyce, "When McCormack has been singing *piano* and he lets out his voice in its full power, it gives you a bang on the ear."[124]

As late as the 1920s, when the publication of *Ulysses* was already sending shockwaves across several continents, Joyce's wife Nora told Ettore Schmitz:

> I've always told him that he should give up writing and take up singing. To think he was once on the same platform with John McCormack.[125]

That platform was the Antient Concert Rooms in Dublin, where Joyce and McCormack joined various others on 27 August, 1904, for a "Grand Concert." The *Evening Telegraph* of 29 August reported that Joyce was "the possessor of a sweet tenor voice" and "sang charmingly." McCormack was "the hero of the evening," however, receiving especially generous notices because the concert was announced as "his last public appearance in Ireland."

Like Joyce, McCormack wrestled with his relationship with Ireland, as a proud Irishman and an émigré to foreign lands. Similar issues troubled Tauber and also

---

121 See generally John, Scarry. "James Joyce and John McCormack." *Revue belge de philologie et d'histoire*, tome 52, fasc. 3, 1974. Langues et littératures modernes - Moderne taal-en letterkunde. pp.523–536.
122 Joyce, Stanislaus (1971). *The Complete Dublin Diary of Stanislaus Joyce*. Ed. George Harris Healey. Cornell University Press. p.4.
123 Ellmann, Richard. *James Joyce* (1959). Oxford University Press. p.156.
124 Joyce, Stanislaus. *The Complete Dublin Diary of Stanislaus Joyce*, ed. George Harris Healey (1971). Cornell University Press. p.36.
125 Ellmann, Richard. *James Joyce* (1959). Oxford University Press. p.572.

the British-born Alfred Piccaver,[126] who shared Tauber's mantle as Vienna's most beloved tenor. Piccaver appeared in only a single film – *Abenteuer am Lido*[127] – an Austrian comedy directed by Richard Oswald and released in October, 1933. He plays Gennaro Mattei, a singer persuaded out of early retirement by the untrustworthy Nora Gregor's Evelyn. The film contains some fine singing, and is additionally memorable for an appearance by S. Z. Sakall, who went on to play Carl, the waiter in *Casablanca*, and Schwab, the lecherous Broadway producer in *Yankee Doodle Dandy* (both 1942). Piccaver's life story is unusual. He was born in Lincolnshire and emigrated with his parents to Albany, New York, where he took American citizenship. He sang as a treble in Albany's thriving St. Peter's Episcopal Church, and took developed lessons before enrolling in 1905 at the Metropolitan School of Opera. Heinrich Conried recognised his potential, and in 1907 he travelled to Prague for further studies that resulted in a contract with the Deutsches Landes-Theater. He made his debut on 9 September, 1907, in Nicolai's *Die lustigen Weiber von Windsor*[128] – to universal acclaim. Piccaver resisted the consequent temptation to specialise in operetta. Indeed, his repertoire never veered widely from Mozart, Flotow, Gounod, Verdi, (early) Wagner and Puccini. In 1910 the aging Mattia Battistini invited Piccaver to Vienna, where he became a full member of the Hofoper company. He made his debut there on 6 September, 1912.

Piccaver's technique was studied, though he enjoyed neither an easy high C5 nor an especially comfortable B4; these limitations contributed to infamously crippling stage-fright. In his phrasing, however, he came as close as any of his peers to the young Mischa Elman – with whose ubiquitous *portamento*, flexible sense of time, and seamless *cantilena* Piccaver's art compares. Puccini considered Piccaver his "*ideal Rodolfo*," and the tenor's extensive discography – spanning *lieder* as well as opera – testifies to heightened expressive sensibilities and exceptional judgment. He was at all times *tastefully* Viennese, rejecting the idiosyncrasies of Tauber and his imitators. The city embraced him like few others, particularly after he refused lucrative offers from the United States; even after a financial dispute in 1931 caused the Staatsoper to terminate his contract, he remained a prominent feature of Viennese musical life. Piccaver returned to Britain in 1937, months before the *Anschluss*, and he went "home" in 1955 for the re-opening of the Staatsoper – never to leave again.

By the standards of the 1930s and 40s, Piccaver's career was almost provincial. His quiet ambition placed him in opposition with one of his passing rivals in Vienna, Jan Kiepura,[129] the first operatic tenor to become more famous for his work in concert and on film than for his performances in the theatre. Kiepura was born in Poland, where he completed only two years of serious training before making his debut in Lvov, as Faust, in 1924 – at the absurdly youthful age of just 22. In 1927 he made his city debuts in Budapest, Berlin, Vienna, London, Stuttgart, Munich and Prague; he sang in the first Viennese run of Korngold's *Wunder der Heliane*.[130] Ten years later

---

126   5 February, 1884 – 23 September, 1958.
127   'Adventure on the Lido.'
128   'The Merry Wives of Windsor.'
129   16 May, 1902 – 15 August, 1966.
130   The role was created in Hamburg by Carl Günther (2 November, 1885 – 9 September, 1958).

Korngold failed to sign him for the premiere of *Die Kathrin* because Kiepura had by then moved with the money and joined the Met. In 1928 he signed a three-year contract with La Scala, where his repertoire was broadly *spinto*, in part because of the virility of his voice but also because he was athletic, handsome and wildly charismatic. He looked the part as Calàf (which he sang in the opera's first run in Vienna[131]) and Cavaradossi, and he was able to play the roles on stage so as to suggest that Turandot and Tosca might have had good reason to fall in love. A number of live recordings survive that qualify as exceptional (including a "*La donne e mobile*" from the 1930s that is a masterclass in breathing, *messa di voce* and inflection). The primary rule for Kiepura, however, was that he sang everything in full voice, all of the time. There's no denying the appeal of this sort of open-throated, free-wheeling vocalism; it can be tremendously exciting, and his unaffected, almost naïve talents as a communicator made him a perfect fit for cinema.

In 1930, he made his first sound film,[132] *Die singende Stadt*[133] – alongside Brigitte Helm,[134] (best remembered for her roles as Maria/the Maschinenmensch in Fritz Lang's *Metropolis*). Over the next two decades Kiepura appeared in around twenty films,[135] some of them in the company of equivalent talent. *Mein Herz ruft nach dir*,[136] for example, was written by Emeric Pressburger – the writer-director of *A Matter of Life and Death*, *The Life and Death of Colonel Blimp* and *The Red Shoes* – while *My Song for You*[137] (1934) was directed by Maurice Elvey, the most prolific director in British film history. Kiepura's straddling of the operatic and lighter repertoires was effortless. In *My Song for You*, for example, he brings commitment and authenticity to the title song by Mischa Spoliansky and Frank Eyton as well as luxuriant performances of Gounod's "*Ave Maria*" and "*Celeste Aïda*" – the latter during an amusing backstage sequence. Kiepura was Jewish, and after he and his wife, the Hungarian-born soprano Marta Eggerth, read the daubing on the walls, he accepted Edward Johnson's invitation to join the Met – at $500 a performance. His first night, as Rodolfo, on 10 February, 1938, raised the audience to its feet and his fee to $800. Kiepura did not sing often at the Met, and by 1942 his film career in the US had stalled.

The following year, he and Eggerth were invited to star in a new production of *The Merry Widow* (in English) at the Majestic on Broadway. Kiepura was given an ultimatum by the Met's long-serving assistant general manager (and talent scout) Edward Ziegler: if he sang *The Merry Widow* on Broadway he would not sing at the Met again. Kiepura chose Broadway, and the production ran for 322 performances.

---

131 He sang Calàf at the second performance – after the fifty-three-year-old Leo Slezak was "gifted". the opening night.
132 His first movie, in 1926, was the silent Polish-produced *O czym się nie myśli* ('What you don't think about') released as 'The Unthinkable.'
133 'The Singing City.'
134 17 March, 1908 – 11 June, 1996.
135 The number is imprecise because he more than once made the same film twice (in different languages).
136 'My Heart is Calling'; made also in French as *Mon cœur t'appelle* – directed by Carmine Gallone.
137 The US remake of the same film made *twice* previously as *Ein Lied für Dich* in Germany (1933) and *Tout pour l'amour* in France (1933).

Broadway exercised a huge draw and paid significantly more than the opera houses, albeit not as much as Hollywood. When the Veronese tenor Nino Martini[138] emigrated to the United States in 1929, he did so having been discovered while performing in Paris by Jesse Lasky, who engaged him for several Italian-language speaking roles in short films. Martini had studied with Maria Gay and her husband Giovanni Zenatello, and when not making films he performed at the Met for 12 years and appeared often on the radio. His first American film, *Paramount on Parade* (1930), was an "all-star" revue – presented by the ubiquitous Lasky – with Martini in extraordinary company, including Clara Bow, Maurice Chevalier, Gary Cooper, William Powell, Warner Oland, Eugene Pallette, Fay Wray, Jack Oakie, Kay Francis and a more than usually excruciating turn by Mitzi Green. Martini made a small number of recordings (infamously an "unreleased" 1933 "*Credeasi Misere*" from *I puritani* which does more to curl the toes even than Mitzi Green), and his only significant complete performance on record was as Ernesto in *Don Pasquale*, opposite the exquisite Bidu Sayão. The best of his films are *Here's to Romance* (1935), *Music for Madame*, (1937) and *The Gay Desperado* (1936) – the last of which contains some genuine comedy, notwithstanding the extravagant racism. At one especially absurd point in the film, Martini is called upon to sing "*Celeste Aida*" with a band that is forced by a stereotypical "Mexican bandit" to improvise Verdi's music at gunpoint. Martini's voice had warmth, and he carried it well; he was not especially musical, however, and for all his energy he lacked discipline and charisma. The critic Otis Ferguson dismissed him as "little more than a voice."

Like Martini and Schmidt, the lyric tenor James Melton[139] was a success on radio before he appeared in movies. One of his first, a ten-minute short called *The Last Dogie* (1933), presented him singing cowboy songs while performing rope tricks. It can be presumed that a lasso was thought to make him more of a man. When appearing in his first full-length feature, *Stars Over Broadway* (1935), Melton played a singing porter; the film was, however, little more than a revue, so that his performances of "*M'appari*" and "*Celeste Aida*" made as much sense dramatically as did Busby Berkeley's dance numbers. Melton had a fine tenor voice, as a live recording from 1944 at the Metropolitan of" *Tu che a Dio spiegasti l'ali*" demonstrates. For his next two films, however, the arias were dropped for popular songs like "*September in the Rain.*"

In less than two decades, the times had changed beyond recognition. Shifting concepts of gender and identity, the rapid erasure of the lines separating serious from popular entertainment, and the isolation of art music from contemporary concerns all contributed to the rise of film's popularity as a dominant form of entertainment, diminishing if not supplanting the opera house as a cultural touchstone. Public taste and commercial reality cultivated a new landscape in which masculinity was formalised and popularity was legitimised. The first twenty years of tenors on film proved that the greatest singing was not often produced by the best or most handsome actors. Gigli, Schipa, Martini, Tauber and Schmidt were foils, not leading men. Indeed, the tenors of the late 19th and early 20th centuries could not have hoped to reach

---

138   7 August, 1902 — 9 December, 1976.
139   2 January, 1904 – 21 April, 1961.

or appeal to a generation of young people characterised by the emerging hoard of "Bobby-Soxers." On 10 January, 1945, the New York correspondent of *The Guardian* newspaper in London saw the future when reporting that

> The United States is now in the midst of one of those remarkable phenomena of mass hysteria which occur from time to time on this side of the Atlantic. Mr. Frank Sinatra, an amiable young singer of popular songs, is inspiring extraordinary personal devotion on the part of many thousands of young people, and particularly young girls between the ages of, say, twelve and eighteen. The adulation bestowed upon him is similar to that lavished upon Colonel Lindbergh fifteen years ago, Rudolph Valentino a few years earlier, or Admiral Dewey, the hero of Manila Bay, at the turn of the century. Mr. Sinatra has to be guarded by police whenever he appears in public. Indeed, during the late political campaign he broke up a demonstration for Governor Dewey, the Republican candidate, merely by presenting himself on the sidelines as a spectator. (Since Mr. Sinatra was an ardent supporter of President Roosevelt, some unkind people suggested that he had done this from political motives.) His earnings, including songs on the wireless, gramophone records, appearances in motion pictures and engagements in theatres and night clubs, are in the neighbourhood of $1,250,000 annually. His mail runs into thousands of letters daily; he cannot put his nose out of doors without careful precautions in advance. Many thousands of his 'fans' have never seen him in the flesh but have only heard him broadcast or seen him on the films, where, incidentally, he is not particularly successful. Psychologists have written soberly about the hypnotic quality of his voice and the remarkable effect upon susceptible young women. Because he wears a polka-dotted bow tie hundreds of thousands of young people of both sexes wear a similar tie. The teen-age girls who constitute the main part of his audience also wear short white half-hose, and are therefore called 'bobby-sox girls' or, more simply, 'bobby-soxers'.

Sinatra was a baritone. He nonetheless represented the now-definitive confluence of masculinity and music – with which opera singers, for all their talent and training, were no longer aligned. That would remain the case, with one brief and entirely fantastic exception.

Chapter Eleven

"Mario! Mario!"

Between October, 1929 – when the US stock market imploded – and September, 1945, when Japan surrendered formally to the Allies, the United States experienced a period of social and cultural upheaval unprecedented since the Civil War. Sixteen years of domestic and foreign tribulations produced a reaction during the late 1940s and 50s that all but re-invented the way in which the media, in particular, portrayed what it was to be American, and how the United States wished to be perceived at home and abroad. Potent amnesia clouded the country's reflection on its status as a nation formed of immigration; dramatic increases in anti-Semitism during the interwar period crystallised in the normalisation of the Ku Klux Klan, the activism of Henry Ford, and the hate-mongering of Father Coughlin. The identification of Jews as Bolsheviks and the passing of parallel legislation hostile to the diaspora was compounded by the public acceptance of African-American subjugation. The cultivation of "all-American" values was escalated by a sense of white pre-eminence and superiority that allowed the metrics of Cold War division to characterise the unassimilated as alien. In the case of flying saucers, this was literal and metaphorical. Beam-spitting tripods, "things" from other worlds and "bodysnatchers" were not designed to render the unknown and the incomprehensible merely different – since difference passed no judgment and allowed no prejudice. The escalating sense of "otherness" populated by "greens," "greys" and men in black fostered detachment and fear rather than curiosity and wonder. A population force-fed a near-constant diet of social probity and Christian order was encouraged to regard anything non-conformist as threatening and dangerous. This sense of barbarian malignance extended to cultural mores and particularities – manifested in details of appearance, practice and language. The abnormality of "deviant" sexualities, aesthetics and philosophies were coterminous with *Entartete kunst und kultur* and disseminated as dystopian nightmares, set for the most part on a contemporary Earth, and usually within the United States – where "invasion" was as likely to originate from Russia as from Mars.

The effect of integration was pernicious in its whitewashing of immigrant cultures, so that God-fearing Protestants were happy to embrace the tenors Jan Peerce and Richard Tucker because they were tolerably Jewish, while Elvis Presley made hard-driving rockabilly and rock and roll acceptable for those unable to stomach the "blackness" of Big Joe Turner and Fats Domino. Long before John Lennon declared "Before Elvis, there was nothing," Sam Philips lamented that, "[but for] a white man who had the Negro sound and the Negro feel, I could make a billion dollars."[1] Elvis' acceptable form of gyrating masculinity – relished without shame by the young, and

---

1   Miller, James (2000). *Flowers in the Dustbin: The Rise of Rock and Roll, 1947–1977*. Fireside. p.72.

in secret by the old – was entirely unthreatening, particularly during his career as a film actor. In *Jailhouse Rock* (1957), for example, there are glimmers of "traditional" American machismo; the film is otherwise redolent of a masculinity formed of homosocial bonding. For all the presumed eroticism of the Elvis masque, his films are antithetical to the butch social constructionism that typified 1950s Americana. His shy, deprecating manner on screen was impossible to reconcile with his strutting priapism as a singer. Rather than appearing threatening or aggressive, as many in the conservative media painted him, Elvis' masculinity as an actor was almost platonic, even in the supposedly "shocking" *Kid Creole* (1958). The fraternal, vulnerable Elvis is a caricature of the boy next door, just as Doris Day, his cultural sibling,[2] managed to be both attractive and sexless when compared to the celluloid-melting sirens of the 1920s, 30s and 40s. The apple-pie and picket-fence unrealities satirised by Gary Ross' enchanting *Pleasantville* (1998) were aspirational markers for the world as white America wished to be seen. It was an America remembered a decade later by Thomas Pynchon in *The Crying of Lot 49*, a chimera that presented the clearly homosexual Liberace as an idealised bachelor because he was gifted, charming and from nowhere more exotic than Wisconsin – qualities that enabled him to persuade hundreds of thousands of Americans to open bank accounts simply by looking directly into the camera and saying that they should do so.

This racist, sexist and fraudulent environment was tailor-made for Alfredo Arnold Cocozza,[3] a second-generation immigrant, whose parents travelled to the United States from the Abruzzese-Molisan region of south east Italy. Alfredo's mother's maiden name was Lanza; her first name was Maria. Appropriately enough, Alfred was born in Christian Street, Philadelphia, in 1921 – the same year, and just six months before, Enrico Caruso died. The young man's raw, natural voice was apparent shortly after it broke, when he sang in local operatic productions in Philadelphia for the YMCA Opera Company. In 1940 he was recorded privately, at the age of nineteen, singing "*Vesti la giubba*," "*Che'lla mi creda*" (an aria he did not record again), "*Torna a surriento*," and "*E Lucevan le stelle*." His speaking voice is immediately recognisable when introducing the recording as a 20th wedding anniversary gift for his parents. The performances are fascinating, for a host of reasons. He is clearly untrained, and there are some serious issues with placement and breathing; the *vibrato* is very fast, particularly above the stave – and he forces the tone almost constantly. Even so, the voice is richly cast for someone so young, and his phrasing is instinctive and often musical. Most impressive of all is his diction, which was a priority from the outset.

In 1942 he was introduced to Serge Koussevitzky, Principal Conductor of the Boston Symphony Orchestra, and one of the most influential men in American music. He provided the 21 year-old Cocozza with a full scholarship to the Berkshire Music Center at Tanglewood, Massachusetts, where he made his formal debut as Fenton in a performance in English of Otto Nicolai's *The Merry Wives of Windsor* on 7 August, 1942. He studied the role with the conductors Boris Goldovsky and Leonard Bernstein. Cocozza was now Mario Lanza, a name-change compelled by the apparent

---

2   See, generally, Duffett, Mark (2001). "Caught in a Trap? Beyond Pop Theory's 'Butch' Construction of Male Elvis Fans;" *Popular Music*, 20(3). pp.395-408.
3   31 January, 1921 – 7 October, 1959.

difficulty for many when pronouncing his given name. The New York *Times* hailed Lanza as having "few equals among tenors of the day in terms of quality, warmth and power." He sang two performances as Fenton at Tanglewood, and a single evening of Act III of *La bohème* with Irma González as Mimi. War intervened, as did his marriage on 13 April, 1945, to Betty Hicks, the sister of one of Lanza's army friends.[4] In October, 1945, Lanza was booked as a stand-in for Jan Peerce by CBS and their radio program "Great Moments in Music." Over the next four months he sang selections from works as varied as *Otello* and *The Student Prince*. The recordings that survive attest to Lanza's improbable vocal maturity at the young age of 24; the love duet from Act I of *Otello* (with Jean Tennyson) further confirms that there was no one in the background advising or training him to preserve his resources.

Lanza was fortunate to catch the ear of Enrico Rosati,[5] an Italian singing teacher remembered for his classes at the Accademia di Santa Cecilia in Rome, where his students included Gigli and Lauri-Volpi. In the United States Rosati tutored Frances James, Karin Branzell and George London. The latter remembered how, before working with Rosati, Lanza's voice was

> unschooled but of incredible beauty, with ringing, fearless high notes…. Rosati directed him to singing more lyrically, with less pressure, to good advantage.

Fifteen months later (during which time Rosati prepared Lanza for a performance of Verdi's Requiem with Arturo Toscanini that never happened) the tenor had acquired a much finer sense of line, an easy high C, exceptional breath control and probably the most perfect diction of any tenor to make records. Lanza's voice was a natural *Lirico-spinto*, with a range from low A to high D, an open, quasi-baritonal colouring in the middle and lower registers, and a capacity for wide-ranging dynamics. Rumours and suggestions that he was a "studio" tenor only – without the amplitude necessary for performances in a theatre – were (and remain) untenable. George London, arguably the most resonant bass-baritone of the 20th century, and Lanza's partner for dozens of performances as part of the "Bel Canto Trio," stated more than once that Lanza's natural vocal endowment was greater than any other known to him. The tenor was not, and would never become, a technical or disciplined singer, but he left Rosati's supervision with a voice that was sufficiently relaxed, fluent and individual to sustain a career, of sorts. When reviewing a performance at Chicago's Grant Park in July, 1947, the *Tribune* observed that

> a multitude of fine points evade him, [but Lanza] possesses the things almost impossible to learn. He knows the accent that makes a lyric line reach its audience, and he knows why opera is music drama.

---

4   They married in a civil ceremony, and remarried on 15 July, 1945, in a Catholic church. They would have four children: Colleen, Ellisa, Damon and Marc.
5   9 June, 1874 – October, 1963.

His voice was as idiomatic as those of Caruso, Gigli and Schipa; it was shortly to make him more famous than all of them. Between July, 1947, and May, 1948, Lanza, George London and Frances Yeend performed as Columbia Artists' "Bel Canto Trio," giving almost 90 concerts across the United States, Canada, and Mexico. Lanza's decision not to submit to the routines and rigours of an opera house career has long provoked more commentary than cogency; the reality for Lanza as a singer in his late twenties – less than three years after the end of WWII, with working-class immigrant parents and a young wife to support – was that he was offered life-changing sums of money for singing arias and songs in concert. He was also at liberty to perform just about anything he wanted – which included numbers from musicals as well as scenes from *The Magic Flute, Faust, Simon Boccanegra,* and *I Lombardi*. The Trio was an enormous success, and on 28 August, 1947, Lanza was conducted at the Hollywood Bowl by Eugene Ormandy in three operatic duets with Frances Yeend (including "*Parigi, O Cara*" from *La traviata* and "*Bimba dagli ochi*" from *Madama Butterfly*) and three solo arias, notably "*Una furtiva lagrima*" and "*Un di all'azzurro spazio.*" Sitting among the audience was the film producer and head of MGM, Louis B. Mayer.

The following morning, Albert Goldberg wrote in the Los Angeles *Times* that Lanza possessed the

> sort of tenor voice that nearly every operatic stage in the world has been yearning for, lo these many lean years…. Lanza's is the warm, round, typically Italian type of voice that caresses every graceful phrase and makes the listener breathe with him as it molds each curve of the melody.

It is significant that Lanza was hailed as a "typically Italian type of voice." Although called Mario Lanza, he was identified constantly as an American. As almost every interview from the time makes clear, he was a natural-born citizen of the United States, who spoke as an American, dressed as an American, served as an American, and was as "American" in his appearance as George London[6] and Frances Yeend. What that meant in 1947 fell necessarily to context. In October of that year, hearings of the House Un-American Activities Committee supervised the persecution of eleven "unfriendly witnesses" from within the movie industry – with Bertolt Brecht alone in answering the questions put to him. The "Hollywood Ten" were condemned for their silence, and black-listed until swearing their denunciation of Communism. The Senate's definition of "Un-American" allowed for the smearing of everything else – and for the evolving repositioning of what qualified as definitive and what did not.

Lanza's integrity as a citizen was unquestionable. His tooth-white all-American values were promoted in performance by a flair for schmaltzy commentary and winsome dialogue; his ability to speak to his audiences, whether on stage, by radio or in interview was compelling for a population made fearful of the aggressive, sweaty animalism typified by Stanley Kowalski in *A Streetcar Named Desire*. Tennessee Williams'

---

6   Although, of course, London was a Jewish second-generation Russian, born George Burnstein to U.S. naturalised parents.

play was first performed on 3 December, 1947 – with Marlon Brando dominating the stage as he would the screen four years later. His seismic portrayal of the immigrant experience in late 1940s America was antithetical to Lanza's polished, emasculated wholeness. Unlike Kowalski, Lanza was representatively sober and good-natured. He went to church on Sundays and loved his parents as a dutiful son. He didn't sweat, or lose his temper and break things. Lanza was handsome but with nothing of Kowalski's masculine sensuality and less still of Brando's ambiguous beauty. His cherubic face and square body were utilitarian and unerotic. On and off the screen, he played a character who appeared to know nothing of sex, joining with the hygienic Betty only to produce equally sanitary children. He sang American songs by natural-born citizens in crystalline American English alongside arias from operas that had neither to be translated nor explained, other than in generalised sound-bites, redolent of Stokowski's hilarious introduction on television of his arrangement of "When I am laid in Earth" from *Dido and Aeneas* as "a work that everyone knows, and everyone loves." "Everyone" no more knew Purcell's masque from 1680 than they did the sonnets of Shakespeare. What "everyone" knew was that Stokowski had probably worked with Purcell, and poetry had meant something to the Founding Fathers.

Lanza's performance with Ormandy in Hollywood survives on record, as does the audience's applause and whistling – a sound not commonly associated with the appreciation of high art. Of course, this was not high art – any more than was Lanza an opera singer. It was entertainment after the fashion cultivated by American radio, with time and opportunity allowing for banter and advertising. In 1948, Lanza sang Pinkerton in a production of *Madama Butterfly* in New Orleans. It was his first professional, fully staged performance. His second appearance in the run proved to be his last in costume in an opera house.[7] In May, 1949, Lanza made his first commercial recordings, one of which ("*Che gelida manina*") was voted Operatic Recording of the Year by the US National Record Critics Association. Four months later, he appeared in his first film, with fourth billing[8] – behind Kathryn Grayson, José Iturbi, and Ethel Barrymore. Louis B. Mayer had obsessed over Lanza after seeing him sing with Ormandy, and *That Midnight Kiss* was the first issue of a seven-year contract with MGM. Lanza went on to perform regularly with Grayson, in concert and on radio; it was significant that he should have been paired with another "opera singer" untrained in opera – although MGM did their best to mould her in anticipation of what was expected of her career.

Grayson and Lanza's radio broadcast recordings reveal much of the culture into which Lanza had been dipped by Hollywood. "Popular" numbers would be introduced with "banter," followed by Mantovani-esque arrangements of show tunes like "They didn't believe me" from *The Girl from Utah*. Their voices were suited ideally to the sentimentality of the music, with swooping *portamenti* and quivering *vibrati* conveying the implicit authenticity of their characters' feelings. Not a single sung note is struck other than with (or after) a slide. It was questionably tasteful for many at the time; it remains so seventy years later. The grotesquerie of Lanza and Grayson

---

7 Lanza agreed to return to New Orleans in 1949 as Alfredo, in *La traviata*, but MGM's contract intervened – even though it allowed him six months a year to pursue other projects.
8 "*Introducing Maria Lanza.*"

singing the music of Rubens and Jones pales against their assault on what the compere identifies as "the Addio" from *Lucia di Lammermoor*.[9] The entirely ridiculous *tempo* adopted by the conductor Johnny Green alludes to the pressure of advertising, while Grayson's concluding F6 (which ranks among the most excrescent sounds to rupture the ear of Man) punctuates the extent to which the MGM machine was uninterested in a market schooled or interested in opera and singing.

As with Joseph Schmidt's films before him, *That Midnight Kiss* adhered closely to Lanza's personal story by having him play an (American) tenor from Philadelphia, Johnny Donetti, trying to make it big. During filming, Lanza spent time in the company of Iturbi, who is likely to have shared some of his anxieties about becoming a Hollywood star – if only because Lanza's first film would be Iturbi's last. The pianist had been warned that the "fripperies" of his films were damaging to his "serious" career as a pianist and a conductor, typified by the scene in *Anchors Aweigh* (1945) when Iturbi and Sinatra take an axe to Tchaikovsky's First Piano Concerto, with the crooner making a case for the song transcription by Freddie Martin ("Tonight we love"). Although Lanza maintained throughout his ten years in the limelight that he was preparing to commit to a career as an *actual* opera singer, his personal life from 1950 was sufficiently Rabelaisian to allow for little more than survival.

Numerous books and monologues have been devoted to the extremes of Lanza's life in Hollywood. Some are gaudier than others; none of them is pretty. The truth falls somewhere between his victim-status as a vulnerable *ingenue* given to insatiable appetites and his portrayal as an idiot-monster – abusive, foul-mouthed, drunk and cruel. If just some of the stories told of his behaviour are accurate, it's remarkable that he managed to perform anything at all. Certainly, it is a testament to his character (and his long-suffering, frequently humiliated wife) that he was able to submit to the barbarism of the studio system for as long as he did.

Initially, at least, Lanza's sales and successes ensured he could do no wrong. When his second film, *The Toast of New Orleans,* was released in 1950 (again with Grayson, this time with shared billing), the cinemas were heaving for weeks, while his in-film recording of "*Be My Love*" became the first of three consecutive million-selling singles. That recording is arguably the most perfect made by a tenor of a show tune. The line, the phrasing and the resonance are jaw-dropping – as is, of course, the miraculous diction. There is an even more impressive (live) recording of "Overhead the moon is beaming" from Act 1 of Sigmund Romberg's *The Student Prince*, which further demonstrates the tenor's easy range and the prominence of his American accent when singing in English – a feature of his art that carried unconscious significance for an almost exclusively white, middle-class audience.

Both performances resonate with confidence, as was typical of Lanza when singing popular songs. He knew he was the most complete tenor to sing this repertoire, and while there have been more impressive tenors, as singers and as musicians, in this particular field of American dreams Lanza was peerless. He has remained so ever since. Lanza's triumph can be explained in part by the absence of competition. During the late 1940s, the urgent and inflammatory propagation of "homegrown" talent coincided with an explosion in the appetite for Technicolor musicals. The era was

---

9 "*Verano a te sull'aure*" ('They will come to you on the breeze.')

saturated with productions of increasing skill and sophistication, in which the singing of the leads was frequently a minor consideration. Before Lee Marvin and Clint Eastwood demonstrated the compensatory merit of charisma in *Paint Your Wagon* (1969), Hollywood musicals made a popular virtue of Wagner's *Gesamtkunstwerk* – ensuring that being able to hold a tune was sufficient when acting; dancing, timing and physical beauty were the dominant metric for a studio's renaissance dialectic. The invention on display in the best-known of the musicals released while Lanza was making films warrants no commentary; the titles speak for themselves: *Annie Get your Gun* (1950), *An American in Paris* (1951), *Show Boat* (1951), *Singin' in the Rain* (1952), *The Band Wagon* (1953), *Gentlemen Prefer Blondes* (1953), *Calamity Jane* (1953), *Kiss Me Kate* (1953), *Seven Brides for Seven Brothers* (1954), *A Star is Born* (1954), *White Christmas* (1954), *Guys and Dolls* (1955), *Oklahoma* (1955), *The King and I* (1956), *Carousel* (1956), *High Society* (1956), *Funny Face* (1957), and *South Pacific* (1958).

If Fred Astaire was unable to sing or act (although he could "*dance a little*"[10]), then Lanza's limited skill set, crowned by a magnificent head of eternally Dapper Dan'd hair, isolated him when in the company of people who could do literally anything.[11] That included not over-eating and drinking – vices that caused Lanza's minders, as well as his corset, such persistent strain that he was subjected to often brutal and dangerous treatments to force his weight-loss. These are said to have included long periods of induced sleep and drip-feeding, and the injection of urine from pregnant mothers. The 1950s were indeed an age of wonder.

Woody Allen was not thinking specifically of Mario Lanza when he wrote the role of Warner Purcell for Jim Broadbent in *Bullets Over Broadway* (1994); on the other hand, Purcell's tendency to over-indulge when anxious, stuffing his pockets as well as his face with chicken, pies and cakes, suggests Allen knew something of Lanza's infamous struggles with stress-eating. This was prompted in part by the wages of fame. Lanza suffered from acute feelings of inadequacy brought on by his perennial obsession with returning full time to the opera house. His confidence when performing show tunes was warranted but so too was his insecurity when singing almost exclusively Italian arias and ensembles. Lanza understood he would never be taken seriously by critics as an artist until he committed to the operatic stage and abandoned Hollywood.

It was no small irony that MGM's roaring lion throughout Lanza's brief time with the studio was named Tanner. In his 1905 play *Man and Superman*, Bernard Shaw articulated through his character, Tanner, the ruthlessness of the "true" artist's focus:

> The true artist will let his wife starve, his children go barefoot, his mother drudge for his living at seventy, sooner than work at anything but his art. To women he is half vivisector, half vampire. He gets into intimate relations with them to study them, to strip the mask of convention from

---

10   According to Hollywood folklore, a report on Astaire's sceen test for RKO Radio Pictures recorded: "Can't sing. Can't act. Balding. Can dance a little."
11   Lanza dances with Grayson in *The Toast of New Orleans*. He was good enough to admit in interviews at the time (many of them on the radio with Grayson) that it was not his strong suit.

them, to surprise their inmost secrets, knowing that they have the power to rouse his deepest creative energies, to rescue him from his cold reason, to make him see visions and dream dreams, to inspire him, as he calls it. He persuades women that they may do this for their own purpose whilst he really means them to do it for his. He steals the mother's milk and blackens it to make printers' ink to scoff at her and glorify ideal women with. He pretends to spare her the pangs of child-bearing so that he may have for himself the tenderness of fostering that belong of right to her children. Since marriage began, the great artist has been known as a bad husband. But he is worse: he is a child-robber, a bloodsucker, a hypocrite, and a cheat. Perish the race and wither a thousand women if only the sacrifice of them enable him to act Hamlet better, to paint a finer picture, to write a deeper poem, a greater play, a profounder philosophy! For mark you, Tavy, the artist's work is to shew us ourselves as we really are. Our minds are nothing but this knowledge of ourselves; and he who adds a jot to such knowledge creates new mind as surely as any woman creates new men. In the rage of that creation he is as ruthless as the woman, as dangerous to her as she to him, and as horribly fascinating. Of all human struggles there is none so treacherous and remorseless as the struggle between the artist man and the mother woman. Which shall use up the other? That is the issue between them. And it is all the deadlier because, in your romanticist cant, they love one another.

Lanza's behaviour aligned routinely with Shaw's unforgiving simulacrum; rarely, if ever, was it in the service of art. For all his yearning for a life on the acoustic stage, his practical philosophy was that of an entertainer rather than an opera singer, and it was in part because of the dearth of exceptional tenors in the United States during the 1940s that Lanza's elevation made such acute commercial sense. With the war clearing the country's Houses of many of its European visitors, the stable of native operatic tenors in the United States was occupied by a small coterie defined primarily by reliability. The exception to that rule was Jan Peerce,[12] one of the two most prominent – and talented – Jewish tenors of his generation. The other was his brother-in-law, Richard Tucker.[13]

Peerce was born Jacob Pincus Perelmuth, in Manhattan, a year after his parents emigrated from Poland. He was immersed in music at home and through the Synagogue, where good connections led to lessons with Joe Bogash, a Philadelphia-born coach who changed his name to "Giuseppe Boghetti" and later taught a host of American stars, including Blanche Thebom, Helen Traubel and Marian Anderson. Peerce's obsessive practicing helped form an iron-clad technique that was the envy of most. It sustained a Trojan work ethic and a reputation for conscientiousness that helped make him a syndicated star on the radio before he made it to the stage.[14] It was

---

12   3 June, 1904 – 15 December, 1984.
13   See Chapter 13 below.
14   It is amusing that the indisposition of one of the most reliable singers of the 20th century should have given Lanza, one of the least reliable, an early break.

through the radio that Peerce was "discovered" by Toscanini, who heard him singing Wagner. After a famously brief audition the conductor all but adopted him as "his" tenor. Their collaboration was one of the first to be traced routinely on record. They first worked together on 6 February, 1936, for a broadcast from Carnegie Hall of Beethoven's 9th Symphony – with Vina Bovy, Kerstin Thorborg and Ezio Pinza.[15] The surviving recording captures Peerce's resolute vocal characteristics – with a strong line, powerful resonance and largely unchanging dynamic. His *vibrato* is quick, and the phrasing stiff – qualities that characterised his singing into his late 70s. There is footage of him recording "*Questa o quella*" from *Rigoletto* in 1982, with the Beersheba Chamber Orchestra and Mendi Rodan; it's scarcely credible that he was 78 years old at the time; he sings like a man easily forty years younger. Peerce's legacy with Toscanini included four complete operas: *Fidelio* (1944),[16] *La bohème* (1946), *La traviata* (1946), and *Un ballo in Maschera* (1954). The conductor's ruthlessness will remain eternally controversial; it's clear, however, that Peerce joined with Toscanini in his literalist expectations. The "dry" phrasing and unfailing discipline were an idealised admixture for an aesthetic in which self-denial and the denigration of ornament and indulgence were as important as tone and technique.

Fortunately, Peerce was able to tick every box, although he was no stylist. His recording of *Faust* with Monteux (1955) is as French as Inspector Clouseau – and indistinguishable in matters of line and voicing from his Pinkerton (Ormandy; 1948), Bacchus (Leinsdorf; 1958) and Don Ottavio (Böhm; 1957). Toscanini relished Peerce's professionalism, and their collaboration was unique insofar as the tenor was claimed to be the only singer with whom the conductor never lost his temper. Peerce's exceptional qualities as a man and an artist, devoid of vanity and ego, were insufficient to compensate for his essentially unmusical approach to his craft. Pretty much everything was delivered *con belto*, almost as if the robustness of his technique caused him to forget there was more to singing than tone. The first of his 337 performances at the Met is a case in point. The surviving recording of "*Lunge da lei* [...] *De' miei bollenti spiriti*" from *La traviata* on 29 November, 1941 (conducted by Ettore Panizza) is impressive, but unrelenting and absent expression. The rigid phrasing and incessant *mezzo-forte* are draining, even if the audience clearly thought otherwise at the time.

With the exception of his rival Richard Tucker, Peerce's competition is now largely forgotten, although the best produced some excellent work. Richard Crooks[17] made his debut at the Met in 1933 and sang 77 performances – a third of the number given by his predecessor (as an American citizen) Edward Johnson.[18] Crooks' voice was often beautiful, and his many recordings and TV work (memorably as one of the *Voices of Firestone*) ensured considerable popularity until his early retirement in

---

15   Peerce recorded the Symphony in the studio with Toscanini in 1952 for RCA, when the conductor was 86 years old.
16   He also recorded *Fidelio* for Westminster in 1961, with Knappertsbusch conducting. This is one of the most bizarre recordings in history, so slow are the tempi. It is a testament to the professionalism of Peerce and his colleagues that they are able to adhere to the conductor's questionable judgment.
17   26 June, 1900 – 29 September, 1972.
18   22 August, 1878 – 20 April, 1959.

1945. Charles Kullman[19] made his debut at the Met in 1935, where he sang 421 performances of a bewildering range of work. His voice was essentially light, like every other tenor at the Met during this period, and he pushed it hard to accommodate the demands of Edward Johnson, who was appointed the Met's general manager in 1935. Kullman's work ethic was not lost on audiences, who admired and liked him because of his willingness to commit to the needs of the House at a difficult time. His first role was Faust, followed by Alfredo in *La traviata* (of which there is an interesting recording with Bidu Sayão and Leonard Warren from 1943). Four years later he appeared in the film *Song of Scheherazade* as Lorin, a singing ship's doctor and friend of Rimsky-Korsakov. Over the next 25 seasons, Kullman jumped between the differing requirements of Ottavio, Don José, Pinkerton, Walther, Avito in *L'amore dei tre re*, Manrico, Eisenstein in *Die Fledermaus*, Tannhäuser and, even, Parsifal. He shared his burden with Kurt Baum,[20] the only tenor from this period to build a career at the Met who was not born in the United States. Baum gave the first of his 354 performances at the Met in 1941, when he appeared briefly as the Italian Singer in *Der Rosenkavalier* – interpolating a high D flat with the allegedly written permission of the composer. Baum's repertoire was more expansive even than Kullman's, in part because his voice was larger, with a genuine *spinto* "ping." It was never beautiful, however, and he sang pretty much everything with the same stentorian disregard for dynamics, phrasing and colour as Peerce. Thomas T. Hayward[21] is now all but forgotten; he nonetheless gave 334 performances at the Met, making his debut in 1945. He was born Thomas Albert Tibbett – a cousin of Lawrence, the most celebrated American baritone at the time – and during his 12 seasons he gave solid if uninspiring service to the House, much of it when covering for Jussi Björling.

The long seasons of rehearsals and performances endured by stage tenors, and the years-long regimes of practice and training, were inimical to Lanza, who was psychologically and emotionally ill-equipped to commit to an opera house. Though he was more gifted naturally than many of his American peers, Lanza's inability to make the sacrifices necessary for a stage career was obvious from every corner of his life. Even *The Great Caruso* was undermined by Lanza's lazy reliance on forced tone and expressive vulgarity. With a guarded nod to the hostility of the subject's widow, Dorothy, the opening credits make it clear that the script was never likely to err on the side of biography:

> The events, characters and firms depicted in this photoplay are fictitious. Any similarity to actual persons, living or dead, or to actual firms is purely coincidental.

The Great Caruso is Lanza's best film and largely terrible when measured against the musicals with which it was competing. For his many fans, of course, it was a masterpiece, and it hammered the box office – coming fourth in the US behind *Show*

---

19   13 January, 1903 – 8 February, 1983. On 8 December, 1939, he changed the spelling of his name to Kullman.
20   15 March, 1908 – 27 December, 1989.
21   1 December, 1917 – 2 February, 1995.

Boat; *David and Bathsheba* and *Quo Vadis*. It was a triumph in the UK also, where it sold more tickets than any other film in 1951, the year of its release,[22] riding a wave of nostalgia for the now-absent G.I.s. It's not necessary to isolate Lanza's incongruities of style and technique; they are obvious by comparison, and there is something almost tragic in his attempt to draw sincerity from the wretched dialogue. *The Great Caruso* nonetheless became the reference point for *tenorissimo* perfection for a generation of American audiences uncaring of, and oblivious to, the weekly radio broadcasts from the Met. If Lanza's Caruso was coincidentally innocuous and sentimental for the British, in the United States it portrayed the acceptable face of assimilated immigration. US audiences uninterested in the neorealist masterpieces of Roberto Rossellini, Vittorio De Sica, and Federico Fellini were able to embrace Italian romanticism through the watery eyes of second-generation outlanders, consecrated by the likes of Frank Sinatra, Dean Martin (Dino Paul Crocetti), Perry Como, Tony Bennett (Anthony Dominick Benedetto), Frankie Laine (Francesco Paolo LoVecchio), Bobby Darin (Walden Robert Cassotto), Julius La Rosa, Jimmy Durante, Rose Marie (Rose Marie Mazzetta), Connie Francis (Concetta Rosa Maria Franconero), Carol Lawrence (Carolina Maria Laraia) and, of course, Mario Lanza.

While American filmmakers working at Rome's Cinecittà studios churned out sword-and-sandal clunkers and romantic dramas, such as *Roman Holiday* (1953), Lanza introduced domestic audiences fearful and suspicious of the foreign and the alien to sanitised slices of *autentica Italiana*. During one memorably toe-curling interview in 1949,[23] Grayson referred to "those Lanza pizza-parties…." Simmons responded "Pizza? You mean that Italian bread with a highly-seasoned tomato and anchovy sauce on it?" Lanza jumped in "that's it! About once a week… we all get together for a pizza party; we eat it hot from the oven, with plenty of crisp celery and then, boy, can we sing!" It's difficult to imagine Lanza eating celery. The audience lapped it up, regardless, just as they did *Three Coins in the Fountain*, nominated for Best Picture at the Oscars in 1954, starring Rossano Brazzi – with an instantly recognisable but uncredited Frank Sinatra performing the title track.

For reasons that none of his biographers can agree upon, Lanza's career as a film actor with MGM was interrupted in 1952 – during pre-production for *The Student Prince*. The tabloid press blamed Lanza's escalating weight, such that he was unable to fit into his costumes.[24] The rift is said by others to have occurred as a result of a fight with the director Curtis Bernhardt who, during the sound recording, asked Lanza to tone down the emotionalism – his character was royalty after all. Lanza considered Bernhardt's opinion irrelevant, though he had directed *Le vagabond bien-aimé*[25] with Maurice Chevalier in 1936. This provoked an ultimatum from the tenor. When asked to choose between Bernhardt and their star, to Lanza's considerable surprise MGM

---

22   12,400,000, when the population was 50,000,000. France was also in love with Hollywood, where the box office was won by the ridiculous spectacular *Samson and Delila*, starring Victor Mature and Hedy Lamarr. Both *Samson* and *Caruso* were produced by the ubiquitous Jesse L. Lasky. He has much to answer for.
23   When promoting *The Toast of New Orleans* in 1949, with the uber-sycophant Dick Simmons.
24   Stern, Michael (1964). *An American in Rome*, Random House. p.287.
25   'The Beloved Vagabond'.

stood by its director.[26] Filming proceeded in 1953 with the English actor Edmund Purdom playing the Prince – and S. Z. Sakall making his final appearance on film, as Joseph Ruder. Lanza agreed to his voice being used for Purdom to lip-synch during the musical numbers, and by an indirect route, and without MGM capitulating, Lanza got his way as concerning Bernhardt. The production ended up being directed by Richard Thorpe.

Lanza reacted badly to his dismissal, and for more than a year he submitted to undiagnosed alcoholism and binge-eating. His film career resumed in 1955 with *Serenade*, for Warner Bros., with a solid cast that included Joan Fontaine and Vincent Price.[27] His singing of arias from *Der Rosenkavalier*, *Fedora* and *L'arlesiana* is solid enough. Licia Albanese appeared as Desdemona to Lanza's unpersuasive Otello, and later recalled:

> I had heard all sorts of stories about Mario. That his voice was too small for the stage, that he couldn't learn a score, that he couldn't sustain a full opera; in fact, that he couldn't even sing a full aria, that his recordings were made by splicing together various portions of an aria. None of it is true! He had the most beautiful *lirico spinto* voice. It was a gorgeous, beautiful, powerful voice. I should know because I sang with so many tenors. He had everything that one needs. The voice, the temperament, perfect diction…. Vocally he was very secure. All he needed was coaching. Everything was so easy for him. He was fantastic![28]

In May, 1957, Lanza relocated to Italy and *Seven Hills of Rome* (1958); he returned also to giving concerts. On 24 November he appeared as the closing act at the Royal Variety Show, at the London Palladium. When the compere addressed the live and broadcast audience he used language approved by Lanza and his manager, Leslie Grade, to introduce "A star of many opera stages and a great star of Hollywood."

When he walked on stage, wearing a tuxedo that appeared to have been tailored to a filing cabinet, he had only hours earlier emerged from a two-day drinking binge.[29] His long-time conductor, Constantine Callinicos, was seen to mouth almost every word of each number to Lanza, as he had done throughout rehearsals.[30] Lanza was in complete control, however, and his performance of *"Because You're Mine"* showed him working his audience like a puppeteer. The premature applause spared him and his cummerbund having to dwell too long on the song's concluding B flat, and when he spoke "to the English people" (coincidentally insulting his viewers in Scotland, Wales and Northern Ireland) he did so to "say hello" rather than "Son qui!", as does Mario Cavaradossi when acknowledging Tosca's calling of his name at the beginning of the Act 1 duet. Lanza proceeded to sing *"E Lucevan Le Stelle,"* and as the applause died down he told his audience, which numbered Queen Elizabeth II, "You're

---

26   Cesari, Armando (2008). *Mario Lanza: An American Tragedy*, Baskerville. p.168.
27   The Maltese actor Joseph Calleia appeared as "Maestro Marcatello". In 2012, the Maltese tenor, Joseph Calleja, recorded an album for Sony titled *Be My Love - A Tribute to Mario Lanza*.
28   Cesari, Armando (2008). *Mario Lanza: An American Tragedy*. Baskerville. pp.201–02.
29   Mannering, Derek (2005). *Mario Lanza: Singing to the Gods*. University Press of Mississippi. p.154.
30   *Ibid.*

certainly terrific." He concluded his set by singing "The Loveliest Night of the Year," which closed with a dozen dancers, most of them taller than Lanza, twirling on stage. His performance ended with another ringing B flat 4, delivered with sweat falling off him like Seabiscuit.

In 1958 Lanza toured the UK, Belgium, the Netherlands, France and Germany – achieving largely positive reviews, despite cancelling frequently. He completed some recording sessions, including the describably awful *Lanza Sings Christmas Carols*, and the soundtrack for the unfortunately-titled *For the First Time* – his last movie. Lanza had been ill, on and off, for months, and in April, 1959, he was levelled by a heart attack and pneumonia. He was admitted in September to Rome's Valle Giulia clinic for another round of weight-loss treatments. This proved too demanding, and on 7 October, 1959, Lanza suffered a pulmonary embolism and died at the age of 38. Five months later, his wife Betty committed suicide, leaving their four children orphaned.

Mario Lanza's story is not a happy one. It is inherently teachable, however. He was the most famous "opera" singer in history to that time; but for the "Three Tenors" he would be the most famous *ever*. His flaws and weaknesses cannot detract from the raw, untamed value of his voice – which at no time equipped him for the status and acclaim of an opera singer. That was Lanza's most violent pain – and the price he paid for celebrity and money. During the *Seven Hills of Rome*, the truth of Lanza's career was captured in a hideous episode in which he imitated Louis Armstrong performing "When the Saints Go Marching In." It is the musical equivalent of "blackface," and unpalatable even for the 1950s. Lanza's medley of impressions includes Perry Como, Frankie Laine and Dean Martin. Like these "pop" contemporaries, Lanza was an Italian-American entertainer, but where the "Rat Pack" and their associates would dance to their own tunes, Lanza was an almost servile reminder of the widespread and ingrained hatred and suspicion of those with allegiances to cultures formed outside the United States. Lanza remains the poster-boy for *Pleasantville* America. He is an icon for a society defined by advertising, television, prudery, juvenile delinquency, household technology, the resurgence of evangelical Christianity, state-sponsored racism and a construction of American civilisation that was neither fair nor accurate. Plácido Domingo and José Carreras liked to claim that Lanza and *The Great Caruso* had inspired them to become opera singers. There may have been a grain of truth in their saying so – but they didn't say it in their native Spain, or in Italy, where the pantheon contained real deities.

CHAPTER TWELVE

A God in Tights

When taunting Jesus in the wilderness, the first two of Satan's alleged temptations do not appear especially tempting. The third – "all the kingdoms of the world, and the glory of them" – raised the stakes dramatically, although the impossibility of his delivering on the offer, and his acknowledgement of Christ's status as the offspring of Satan's creator, rendered it uncompelling. When imagining the Devil's manipulations of Faust, Goethe isolated the psychological crisis in his petition to Mephistopheles for *"die Welt im Innersten zusammenhält."*[1] It is not a simple transaction. Goethe introduces a Job-like impulse to their dialogue when wagering with Faust that he will be able to satisfy his curiosity – a prospect more terrifying even than the loss of the Scholar's immortal soul. While Goethe's hero is saved and redeemed, Thomas Mann's Leverkühn[2] endures syphilitic mental, physical and spiritual ruin, and most subsequent treatments of the mythology of the "man at the crossroads" have ended comparably badly.

The Devil's pursuit of a price on earth when removing the promise of eternity in heaven has touched many for whom fame and success were cyclically destructive. Niccolò Paganini[3] is a case in point, insofar as his diabolical talents could not save him from drug and alcohol addiction, disease and financial ruin.[4] A century later, the blues guitarist Robert Johnson[5] took his guitar to Dockery Plantation at midnight. The Devil is said to have played Johnson's instrument and given it back to him, together with his infernal talent. Johnson was a man of constant sorrow and dead at the age of 27 – famous and certain to be remembered. The cemeteries are brim-full with similarly snuffed-out genius. In order of youth, Georg Büchner (23), John Keats (25), Richard Gerstl (25), Percy Shelley (29), Franz Schubert (31) Srinivasa Ramanujan (32), Wolfgang Mozart (35), Théodore Chassériau (37), Vincent Van Gogh (37), Caravaggio (38) and Blaise Pascal (39) all ran their course prematurely.

A precipitous death is insufficient to cast lives less ordinary as diabolically-influenced. For the Devil to work his deceptions, a signatory's improvement needs to be miraculous; they must suffer by reason of the transaction's purpose – after the cruel and tragic fashion of Midas and his golden touch. In the modern history of the tenor voice there is one such character, a man whose talent was matched toe-to-toe by the

---
1 'The true essence of the world.'
2 In *Doktor Faustus: Das Leben des deutschen Tonsetzers Adrian Leverkühn, erzählt von einem Freunde* ('Doctor Faustus: The Life of the German Composer Adrian Leverkühn, Told by a Friend'; 1947).
3 27 October, 1782 – 27 May, 1840.
4 Paganini lost his fortune when failing to make a success of a casino in Paris in 1836.
5 8 May, 1911 – 16 August, 1938.

misery it caused him, a singer so extraordinary, unusual and unique that he can be imagined shaking hands with *Il diabolo* at an "incrocio" in Ancona.

Franco Corelli[6] is surprisingly little remembered outside the shrinking community of opera fans. This is especially curious when accounting for the breath-catching force of his appearance and the supernatural scale of his voice – which emerged almost overnight when he was already past his 30th birthday. Corelli had sung in his youth, and at church as a boy. He was uninterested in training, or in a professional career as a singer; after university he worked for a number of years as a *nibelheim* in local government. During his middle 20s he took a handful of lessons, which he abandoned for a close study of recordings by Caruso, Lauri-Volpi and others. In 1949 he was encouraged by friends to enter the Maggio Musicale voice competition in Florence. Corelli was alone in progressing through the rounds – making it all the way to the finals where, appropriately enough, he sang "*Giunto sul passo estremo*" from Boito's *Mefistofele*. Later the same year he met with Arturo Melocchi,[7] the teacher of the tenors Gastone Limarilli[8] and Mario del Monaco, to both of whom he conveyed successfully the "lowered larynx" technique. Corelli received lessons second-hand from another Melocchi student, the baritone Carlo Scaravelli. In January, 1950, Corelli entered the Spoleto voice competition and fared badly; in 1951 he registered with the Lirico Sperimentale competition – again in Spoleto – where he sang the infamously difficult "*Celeste Aida.*" He later recalled:

> That day was blessed by, what can I say – a Grace. Never in my life did I manage to sing that aria like I sang it then. That *romanza* ends with a high B flat, and I shall never forget the B flat that came out of my throat.... there was no end to it. I never managed to sing it like that again, but I won the contest with it.[9]

Corelli was booked immediately to sing Radamès. He nonetheless managed to persuade the Festival to allow him to make his debut in the lighter role of Don José, and on 6 September, 1951, Corelli made his stage debut in *Carmen*. Just 19 months later, on 9 April, 1953, he opened as Pollione in *Norma* with Maria Callas in the title role. In 1954, Corelli made his debut at La Scala, Milan, at the cherished season opening (7 December), performing the role of Licinio in *La vestale* – again opposite the recently slimmed Callas in a production directed by Visconti.[10] Corelli was 34 years old and had by this stage in his career been singing professionally for three years.

---

6   8 April, 1921 – 29 October, 2003.
7   9 December, 1879 – 25 October, 1960. Melocchi was an odd, Leland Gaunt-type figure who nonetheless enjoyed a near-spiritual reputation as one of only two teachers at the Liceo Rossini to refuse to join the Fascist Party. Melocchi's anti-Fascist values compelled him to leave the country, and not until 1947 was he allowed back to the Liceo Rossini.
8   29 May, 1927 – 30 July, 1998.
9   Seghers, René (2008). *Franco Corelli: Prince of Tenors*. Amadeus Press. p.46.
10 Corelli later recalled: "Visconti was the one who wanted me as Licinio. He had heard me a few months before in Rome, in *Norma*. I should better say "seen" than "heard." Visconti was looking for a classical, beautifully sculptured athlete who would resemble a gladiator or a Roman general to put next to Callas. That was certainly one of the reasons he selected me, though not the only one. But even if it was,

This narrative is unique in the history of the tenor voice. It is widely accepted by those inclined to an opinion that between 1954 and 1967 Corelli was the world's most complete dramatic-*spinto-tenore di forza*. He was, in fact, the man and the artist that Mario Lanza had dreamed of becoming, and it was probably a blessing in disguise that Lanza (who was born only a few weeks before Corelli) died before the younger man's now legendary debut at the Metropolitan in 1961. Lanza was 5 feet 7 inches tall (1.7m) and given to fat; Corelli was 6 feet 2 (1.87m), muscular and improbably athletic. He was also the most beautiful tenor to be photographed or filmed, a man so handsome that Graziella Sciutti remembered attending a rehearsal during the late 1950s at the Rome Opera[11] when the soprano with whom Corelli was performing had cause to faint. Sciutti rushed to her aid, and her dressing room, where the soprano explained that the episode had been brought on by her proximity to "that man … that voice…." She continued, "I have just committed adultery, and we didn't lay a finger on each other."

There are numerous photographs of Corelli in the public domain, and a large number of video clips, only a handful of which are mimed. The live footage includes a complete performance of *La forza del destino* (from the San Carlo, Naples, in 1958, with Renata Tebaldi, Ettore Bastianini and Boris Christoff, conducted by Molinari-Pradelli) as well as various TV appearances, a good number of them in colour. There is little to distinguish the live from the dubbed performances because Corelli's titanic voice came to him as naturally as his beauty. He was often said to have the looks of a film star, and it would be difficult to counter the proposition that he was as handsome as any actor in the history of cinema. A mimed clip of him performing "*Non piangere, Liù*" from *Turandot* is a case in point. His physical presence is astonishing; he appears during the phrase "*sarà domani, forse solo al mondo…Non lo lasciare, portalo via con te!*"[12] as an amalgam of Gary Cooper and James Garner. The clip captures Corelli's lantern-jaw, the pronounced *buccinator* muscles in his face, the huge laryngeal prominence, and his enormous mouth; it records also his unusual hands, notable for their finger length and the *diastrophic dysplasia* that caused his thumbs to bend backwards. The soprano Gigliola Frazzoni remembered how when singing *Chénier* together

> he turned towards me after having embellished the *romanza* ["*In di all'azzurro spazio*"] and he would say those lines: "Udite, non conoscete amore?". He would [sing] them in a way that gave me gooseflesh, and I would be transformed. He would drug me. I was hypnotised by his way of handling the sentence and by his hands…. I was a passionate person by nature, but he would charge me, he would give me more…[13]

I was convinced that physical beauty is an advantage for an artist and it should be put to good use, just as any given vocal qualities, a certain temperament, or a fine high C-natural should." *Ibid.* p.97.
11   In conversations with the author. Sciutti was not herself rehearsing, but a guest only.
12   'It will be tomorrow, perhaps only in the world … Don't leave it, take it away with you.'
13   Boagno, Marina and Starone, Gilberto (1996). *Corelli: a Man, a Voice*. Atlantic Books. p.219.

Corelli grew into his features with time, and even at the age of 50, when he can be seen in clips performing songs with piano in Hamburg, he is a magnetic presence. Between 1964 and 1968, Corelli was a regular on the *Ed Sullivan Show*, and he made numerous appearances on the *Voice of Firestone* and the *Bell Telephone Hour* shows between 1959 and 1966. Among the surviving footage, there is a compelling performance of "*E lucevan le stelle*" which gives a good idea of the tenor in his prime. The scene was filmed in colour and it makes much of his oft-observed ability to fill a pair of tights, reminiscent of Beecham tapping Rudolf Nureyev on the crotch with his baton and asking "what have you got in there boy, a teapot?"

Corelli was never tempted to appear in narrative cinema; instead he made five studio films of signature roles – all of them mimed: *Pagliacci* (1954), *Turandot* (1958), *Carmen* (1956), *Tosca* (1956) and *Andrea Chénier* (1973). Only the last of them is in colour. Each captures Corelli's intense physicality and something of the erotic animation he inspired in audiences and colleagues alike. He was married for more than forty combustible years to Loretta – a soprano who sacrificed her career to support her husband – while developing internationally a reputation for sexual appetites that would have alarmed a bonobo. There is a library of anecdotal evidence that he seduced many of his co-stars, chorus members, secretarial staff, administrators, press officers, agents, spouses, realtors and financial advisors, as well as legions of significant and insignificant others. He appears throughout to have been unambiguously heterosexual, after the fashion of Errol Flynn rather than Rock Hudson, and at a time when sexual identity was just starting to allow for liberal forces that tolerated the representation and occupation of more fluid states of mind and body. Unlike Caruso before him, Corelli was everything he appeared to be – long before he opened his mouth.

If he warranted the attention he so frequently enjoyed, then Corelli's diabolical pact resolved in a voice that remains now, as it was at the time, freakish in its amplitude, resonance, placement, colour and range. Many who heard him regularly in the theatre commented that studio recordings did no more than approximate the power of the instrument when heard acoustically. More can be gained from live recordings, therefore, where there is a sense of connection with the resonance of the venue and the relationship between the voice and the orchestra, chorus and other soloists. There is a useful exemplar in an audience-produced recording of a 1967 performance in Cleveland of Corelli singing "*O Holy Night*" in typically idiomatic English. Even when marshalling his tone, to ensure a veneer of balance between the tenor and the 70-piece orchestra, the fight is unequal. As he concludes the carol, with the penultimate six syllables of "*O Night Divine*" (performed in E major as E – F sharp -B – B – A – G sharp), Corelli's octave leap to the B4 "[div]*ine*" releases a flood of sound, glistening with a prism of overtones, that renders the orchestra mute and the audience ecstatic. In London, in July, 1961, Corelli was recording an album of Neapolitan songs with Franco Ferraris and the Philharmonia for EMI. At the end of "*O sole mio*" he interpolated a high C of such thrilling resonance that the orchestra all but dropped its instruments and burst into cheers and applause. The take was lost, and although a recording was made and released, the resulting high C was not "*that*" high C. An earlier album with Ferraris, again for EMI, of French and Italian arias contains a performance of "*A te o cara*" from *I puritani*[14] which features a phrase that is crowned by another ringing, gold-plated high C of almost impossible abundance. It ranks among the most remarkable sounds made by a human being. Were it not for substantial live-recorded evidence to the contrary, it might be thought to be a fabrication of post-production technology, or a construction of voices after IRCAM's fusion of a male contralto and a female soprano for Gérard Corbiau's 1994 film *Farinelli, Il Castrato*.

The impossibility of Corelli's voice at the height of its perfection, around 1960, cannot be exaggerated. No-one else has come close to approximating the juxtaposition of baritonal weight to an unattenuated extension that allowed for an apparently effortless ascendance to high C5s, C sharp 5s and, even, D5s. The absence of a material *passaggio* amplified the sense of unreality that characterised his colossal resonance – for which the power source was an admixture of exceptional strength, a diaphragm that might have been formed of graphene and a mastery of the "lowered larynx" technique taught by Melocchi. Like his San Carlo predecessors, Corelli was naturally a baritone. He might have remained so but for his Freudian obsession for self-examination and a training regime analogous to the breathing techniques marshalled by freedivers. The lowered larynx is a physical-mechanical process, employed previously by Donzelli and Rossini's bari-tenors; it has been used, to an abbreviated extent, by many others. In its illimitable use by Corelli, it equates to beatification.

The larynx (referred to commonly as the "voice box") is an organ below the point where the pharynx divides into the trachea and the oesophagus; it helps regulate breathing and the production of sound while protecting against food aspiration. The larynx houses the vocal folds and manages pitch and volume – essential to spoken and sung phonation. The position of the larynx shapes the acoustic space above it – namely the "throat." This "shaping" is key because it affects the operation of resonance and determines resulting changes in character, tone and range. The larynx detrudes when yawning, and what Melocchi taught, and what Corelli learned, was the ability to control its rising and falling, so that even when moving up the scale, and through the *passaggio*, the voice (and resulting tone) remain open. Lowering the larynx increases the space in the pharynx, achieving a lower frequency harmonic boost, and commensurately deeper, warmer tones – free of constriction and tightness. The operation of "source filter interaction" (the influence of resonance on vocal fold function) is complex physiologically[15]; in essence the effect of the lowered position is to facilitate the relocation of the voice from the chest register to the head. Where many tenors "cover" through and above the *passaggio*, Corelli was putatively capable of transcending the contraction of the extrinsic laryngeal (supra hyoid) muscles – freeing the tone and allowing for exceptional breath control and air management. In short: he was able to ensure that the larynx did not rise with an ascendance in pitch.

Of course, a raised larynx is not in itself a negative; it will allow for a brighter (but necessarily thinner) sound, for the obvious reason that a reduced resonating space in the pharynx creates a narrower "reed" through which the air can pass. Corelli did not

---

14 Recorded in June-July, 1961.
15 Titzeb, Ingo R. (2008). "Nonlinear source–filter coupling in phonation: Theory." *The Journal of the Acoustical Society of America*. May; 123(5). pp.2733–2749.

sing everything with a lowered larynx; his "neutral" position was lower than normal, however, so that even when soaring to a high B4 or C5 his "brilliant" tonal quality carried substantially greater weight, warmth and resonance. Ultimately, Corelli's technique facilitated the eradication of chronic muscle tension – his freedom from which meant he was able to focus on the more expressive and meaningful values of breathing, line, phrasing and articulation. The colour and amplitude of his singing were augmented by a sense that everything appeared (and sounded) effortless. It wasn't; or, rather, it didn't come without cost.

For the opening of the 1960 season at La Scala, Corelli was engaged to sing the title role of Donizetti's *Poliuto* with Maria Callas as Paolina. This signalled that Corelli was now the world's leading dramatic Italian tenor – whatever Mario Del Monaco might have made of that statement.[16] The programming of this rarely staged work carried substantial baggage. Corelli had made his name performing repertoire that was entirely beyond the reach (or outside the remit) of most *tenore di forza*, including Achille in Gluck's *Iphigenia en Aulide*, Enrico di Braunschwig in Spontini's *Agnese di Hohenstaufen*, Licinio in Spontini's *La vestale*, Sesto in Handel's *Giulio Cesare*, Gualtiero in Bellini's *Il pirata*, and Handel's *Hercules* (*Eracle*). *Poliuto* was written for the newly sensationalised Adolphe Nourrit (who never sang the role). Donizetti had completed the score for Nourrit's debut in Naples. It was banned by the censor because of its Christian subject matter. The tenor's feelings of betrayal were acute, and contributed inevitably to his suicide in March, 1839. The premiere was delayed until 30 November, 1848 – seven months after the composer's death – when the title role was created by Verdi's then favourite tenor, the first Manrico, Carlo Baucardé. Subsequent productions of *Poliuto* were scarce – and mounted commonly for a "star" tenor to show off, most famously Tamberlik and Tamagno. Both Gigli (1940)[17] and Lauri-Volpi (1948) were past their best when taking up the challenge. Corelli and Callas[18] were at their absolute peak, however, when La Scala defied debt and a national financial crisis to engage the two most expensive singers on earth for what was still a little-known work of inconsistent quality. By 1960, Corelli had performed many of the operas for which he would become most famous: *La forza del destino*, *Don Carlo*, *Il trovatore*, *Pagliacci*, *Andrea Chénier*, *Tosca* and *Turandot*. Corelli and Callas had appeared together frequently, in productions of *Il pirata*, *La vestale*, *Fedora* and *Norma* – and they were widely heralded as the most glamorous and physically beautiful stage couple in contemporary opera. They were well-suited to each other vocally also – with Callas having the force and focus of voice, and the dramatic presence and sheer personality, to match Corelli scene for scene. It's true that Callas was also instrumental in forcing EMI's hand to pay the massive sums demanded by Corelli for an exclusive contract. Negotiations began in 1959, and resolved in a three-year term (beginning 7 August, 1959) wherein EMI was compelled to record four of eight "reserved" works: *Aida*, *Il trovatore*, *Cavalleria Rusticana*, *Pagliacci*, *La Forza*

---

16   In 1954 Del Monaco's claque were motivated to insult Corelli by referring to him as "PeCorelli"- the "Sheep" – because his *vibrato* at this stage in his career was very quick.
17   It was a performance during this production that inspired Giuseppe di Stefano to devote himself to his studies as an aspirant tenor.
18   Leyla Gencer replaced Callas for the second run of performances.

del destino, *Norma*, *Tosca* and *Otello*.[19] At this stage in his career, he had performed all but the last of these works on stage. He had yet to appear at the Metropolitan, however – something considered by EMI to be a condition precedent for successful record sales in the United States. The first night of *Poliuto* was observed at the time to be one of the most sensational in La Scala's history. The house was filled with roses and celebrity, royalty and money. Black market tickets changed hands for the price of a new sports car, and the hopeful queued overnight and in denial for returns.

Though Callas had gained a few pounds since *La vestale*, she remained hauntingly beautiful and in matters of dramatic talent the finest operatic soprano of the century. Because she was not the opera's lead, and to compensate for the stentorian excesses of Corelli and the evening's Severo, Ettore Bastianini, Callas pushed her voice harder than she needed to, but the surviving broadcast recording attests to a once-in-a-lifetime event. Corelli's opening number, "*D'un' alma troppo fervida*," is marked by golden tone, some exceptional dynamic control and a miraculous, fluid line. The latter quality was achieved in part by his surgical use of *portamento*, a quality that caused most of what he sang to appear melancholy, if not actually lachrymose. Particularly after 1960, it coloured almost every passing note, such that attack was achieved only by *sforzandi* or phonetic articulation.

If his first aria suggested nerves, then they had evaporated by the second act, when his singing of the recitative and aria "*Sfolgoro divino raggio*" demonstrated his supremacy as the most complete dramatic-*spinto* Italian tenor since the invention of recording. Corelli's declamatory power and the ease with which he soared about the stave exceeded probability, while his phrasing was as breath-taking as his breathing was implausible. The huge expressive range and overwhelming expanse of tone demonstrated abilities that by their incomparability approximated the preternatural. When, finally, he let loose the aria's tooth-rattling C5, neither the fully-stocked La Scala pit nor the bellowed ecstasy of the 3,600-strong audience could drown him out. It's quite simply one of the most thrilling and awe-inspiring episodes in the history of opera – recorded or otherwise – and a uniquely perfect illustration of why the art form provokes such frenzied extremes of emotion. The cheering and curtain calls at the close of Act 3 proceeded for almost as long as the act itself, and in an unusual gesture of acknowledgment from the House, the orchestra remained in its seats, joining with the acclamation rather than rushing to their cars and *taverne*. The critic of the Paris Match knew what he had witnessed, and wrote of Corelli:

> His joy is understakable. Sure, he owed this break to Callas, but he is the one who has won everything in this opening night, during which he redirected his competitors Mario del Monaco and Giuseppe di Stefano back to their earthly realms. With all the vanity and the egoism that is a tenor's own, he has taken all and everything.[20]

---

19 As it was, he went on to record all of them except for *La forza* and *Otello*. Much has been written about Corelli choosing not to sing *Otello*, much of it in error. Corelli did in fact agree to record the opera in 1962 – when he was 41 – but a musician's union dispute in London prevented the sessions from proceeding, and the project was never resuscitated.

20 Seghers, René (2008). *Franco Corelli: Prince of Tenors*. Amadeus Press. p.193.

He was triumphant, for certain, but colleagues and intimates were aware that he suffered from nerves; more than once he had to be dragged forcibly to the wings when the strain of expectation became too great. Corelli's torment was diminished to an extent by study and practice; the happy, cheerful and good-natured young man remembered from before 9 April, 1953, was dispossessed by the terror with which he lived throughout his performing career. The price paid by Corelli for his talent was the misery generated by never knowing for how long it would survive. There are numerous stories of him suffering fits and episodes of hysteria when pacing his dressing room, of his vomiting from the anxiety brought on by the sounds of an audience applauding the arrival of a conductor. His fear of not being able to do what everyone expected of him, year on year, was psychologically ruinous, and with no hope of children (an early bout of mumps having left him infertile) he obsessed over his voice like Gollum his "precious." He would tape each performance and, after signing record covers and programme booklets for fans, and while his colleagues and friends headed to dinner, he would retreat to his room to study the evening's performance, making notes that served only to worsen his dissatisfaction.

He was capable of relaxing, on occasion. On 21 January, 1967, Corelli was persuaded to remain on stage at the Teatro Regio in Parma, following a thrilling performance of *Tosca* (which was also recorded, preserving a 12-second, single-breath A sharp 4 for the three syllables of "*Vittoria!*"[21]). His claque managed to get an upright piano wheeled out, and Corelli agreed to perform a single encore: "*Core 'ngrato.*" The crowd was already tightly-wound, and Corelli's visceral performance prompted more than one evangelical outburst – silenced angrily by *la folla*. Corelli's singing is impressive after the fashion of a man dragging a passenger jet with his teeth; it is a calculated, physical display of Barnum & Bailey prowess, employing astonishing *mezza voce*, expansive *rubato*, *diminuendi* and Farinellian breath control. The astonishing *diminuendo* for the phrase "*Tu nun'nce pienze a stu dulore mio, tu nun'nce pienze tu nun te ne cure*"[22] causes an audible intake of breath from his admirers; the concluding B flat 4 provokes a roar that is as thrilling as the note that inspired it. The performance owes nothing to the musical traditions of Neapolitan song – any more than did his recordings of *canzone* for EMI – save that Corelli's doleful phrasing is tailored perfectly to the solipsism of Riccardo Cordiferro's words "*pecchè me dici sti parole amare; pecchè me parle e 'o core me turmiente, Catarì?*"[23]

His fixation with his voice, and the racheting of his highly-strung nature in tandem with the pitch and intensity of his success, produced a thoroughly earned reputation for volatility. There are countless anecdotes of absent control and lost temper, when his own expectations failed to meet those of his audience. On 13 February, 1960, he sang Manrico for the first time at the San Carlo in Naples. At the end of the

---

21 There is a revealing comparison to be made between the reaction of the Parmanese to Corelli's "*Vittoria*" in 1967, and the British response to a similarly extended "*Vittoria*" in 1958, at Covent Garden. In Parma the audience all but rips out the furniture; in London there is no reaction at all. The conductor of the latter performance, Sir Alexander Gibson, told the author over dinner at The Garrick in London that he believes Corelli lost consciousness briefly as a result of the aria; certainly, the surviving recording confirms he stumbled immediately following the A sharp 4.
22 'Words that leave me shuddering? You do not think of the pain I feel, You do not think.'
23 'Why do you tell me only words of bitterness, why only things that torment me, Catarì?'

second act, with the cast taking their curtain calls, a member of the audience, Mario Improta, shouted directly at Corelli "*Va via!* ('Get out!')" – a term reserved more commonly for dogs. The tenor fixed his gaze on the source of the insult and ran off stage. He leapt up the stairs to the public corridors, his shield still in his hand. A local policeman, Pasquale di Constanzo, saw what was happening and attempted to interrupt the tenor's progress. Corelli fought his way past the officer and into the crowd outside Improta's dress-circle box. He ripped open the door and lunged for his critic; both men were saved by di Constanzo, who managed to remove Corelli to prevent the need for his arrest. As he was being pulled away, he yelled at Improta "I will wait for you outside!" Incredibly, after a 50-minute delay, the performance continued and Improta and Corelli prepared themselves for a bare-knuckle fight in the street outside the theatre. The brawl was prevented, and peace was declared.[24]

Many considered Corelli too much: he was a *prima donna*, overly expensive and a narcissist of mythological proportions – opinions that crystallised after his relocation to New York in 1961. His combustible relationship with EMI – which resulted in numerous lost and abandoned recordings and a famously destructive relationship with Callas' favourite conductor, Georges Prêtre – and his notoriously explosive tactics when at the Met, were compounded by frequent cancellations and a reluctance to engage with the publicity machine that was misread as proof of a selfish and unkind nature. In the February, 1961, edition of the Italian fashion magazine *Arianna*, Corelli was quoted as saying

> On stage I am a lion, but before… what a terror! The audience thinks of me as an operatic character, bold and confident in life as on stage. But I am very timid. And from this shyness stems the fear: a terrible fear of the confrontation with the public, a fear which consumes my nervous system and makes me approach the performance as a battlefield. Yet, once I step out of the shadows behind the scenery and the lights of the stage surround me, my nervous tension miraculously vanishes and a supreme serenity infuses me, I could even call it a state of grace, which makes me lucid and aware of my performance at all moments. These are the only truly happy moments of my days, where no worries, no doubts, and no uncertainties cross my mind.[25]

The source of his unhappiness was more than a function of expectation. In many ways, Corelli's career and his reaction to it were defined by its roots – which were solidly 18th and early 19th century in repertoire. His initial training enabled arguably the most resonant tenor of the 20th century to sing music by Gluck, Handel, Rossini, Bellini and Donizetti – and then without ducking the high notes with which even *leggiero* tenors struggled. The prospect of losing those notes caused Corelli to live in an almost constant state of anxiety. He did not record a complete opera by any of these "early" composers (because EMI knew they were never likely to sell), and after 1965, and with a single exception, his repertoire reached no further back than

---

24 The two men ended up becoming firm friends.
25 Seghers, René (2008). *Franco Corelli: Prince of Tenors*. Amadeus Press. p.193.

Verdi.[26] His initial public triumphs with earlier work – and *Poliuto* most obviously – were followed by private study (and home recordings with piano) of the Duke in *Rigoletto* and Arnoldo in *Guglielmo Tell*. Corelli's private recording of the latter role, with its dozens of high C5s and C sharp 5s, has not been released. It has been heard, however. He doesn't sing in full voice, which is itself fascinating in a close, domestic acoustic, but it is extremely impressive and he experiences no difficulty with the limpid phrasing, extended breathing and voice placement. In June, 1965, he travelled to Paris where he completed the first session *only* of a recording with Callas – and Georges Prêtre – of duets that was abandoned either because Callas' voice was completely exhausted and inaudible when placed beside Corelli, or because Corelli behaved like a child, was unprofessional and inherently unmusical. The latter opinions were disseminated widely by Prêtre, who despised the tenor then, and forever after – ensuring that Bergonzi got the job as Cavaradossi when Callas re-recorded *Tosca* in Paris for EMI later that year. The repertoire for the failed recording of duets is noteworthy; in addition to routine excerpts from *Aida*, *Un ballo in Maschera* and *Don Carlo*, they undertook to record "*Fini ... me lassai*" from *I puritani*; "*Vieni! Cerchiam pei mari*" from *Il Pirata* and "*Donna! Malvagio! ... Lasciando le terra*" from *Poliuto*. Even in 1964, and acting clearly in homage to the repertoire trajectory of his friend and part-time adviser Giacomo Lauri-Volpi, Corelli was still attaching himself to repertoire that bound him to a lyric tradition for which, in many respects, he was unsuited. Of course, the tailoring of a voice to "its" repertoire was then, and remains now, the negation of entropy. Corelli's capacity to sing work that he should not have been able to sing equipped him to transcend the traditional boundaries dividing dramatic tenors from lyric.

Arguably the most extreme example of this desegregation was his performance as Raoul in *Gli Ugonotti*[27] at La Scala in May and June, 1962. Corelli was clearly in thrall to Lauri-Volpi, and the staging of Meyerbeer's most challenging role for tenor was an obvious gesture to a tradition that reached through Lauri-Volpi to Nourrit, Mario, Tamberlik and De Reszke. The role presents numerous opportunities for *tenorissimo* acrobatics, and Corelli's ocean liner voice was required to operate as a *vaporetto* – particularly during the infamously demanding Act IV duet "*Dillo ancor.*" The resulting performances (one of which was recorded and is widely available) were sensational – thanks in no small part to the equally astonishing work of Giulietta Simionato as Valentina. The duet – with Corelli's endless soaring B4s – produced an hysterical reaction, and even today the 20-minute ovation enjoyed by the couple at the end of the act is the longest (mid-opera) in the history of La Scala.

So great was Corelli's attachment to the dramatic-lyric repertoire that he agreed to commit to preparing for a recording of *I puritani* with Joan Sutherland.[28] That he was able to undertake such a challenging role for a *tenore di forza*, including (presumably) the high F in "*Credeasi, misera.*" isolates the nexus of Corelli's status as an operatic tenor. For all his monastic asceticism as a student of his own voice, and despite his routine correlation by critics to Nourrit and Duprez, Corelli's quintessence during

---

26   *Lucia di lammermoor.*
27   *Les Huguenots* (Meyerbeer).
28   A project that failed tragically to materialise.

the early 1960s was more obviously analogous to the position enjoyed by *castrati*. The unreality that characterised his performances aligns manifestly with the sounds and reactions produced by Moreschi and his forebears. This atmospheric dissociation did not protect Corelli against accusations of vulgarity, any more than it did Farinelli and Senesino. Like these paradigmatic song-birds, Corelli was given to renaissance levels of self-indulgence when at his most assured; even his critics were silenced by his overcooked "*Vittoria,*" his "impossible" uninterrupted *cantabile* in "*E lucevan le stelle,*" the concluding *diminuendo* B flat 4 of "*Celeste Aida,*" the endless high B4s (and C5s when not transposing) of "*Di quella pira,*" and the gladiatorial battles with Birgit Nilsson when outdoing each other in *Turandot*.

These incomparable gestures to the metaphysical all hark back to a time when vocal display was an end in itself. The emergence of romantic melodrama did not dispose of the public's affections for stylised and isolated display, associated commonly with the *castrati*. Every role played by Corelli was a lover or a fighter, or some fusion of the two – which helps explain, in part, his lifelong attachment to the title role of *Chénier* – and yet his abnormal technique and the extraordinary sounds he was able to produce (frequently without needing to breathe) aligned him to the emasculated peacocks of the 17th and 18th centuries through Velluti to Moreschi. He could act, insofar as he was able to operate beyond X marking the spot, but his range was limited to a repertoire that required a slim gamut of romance, melancholy and variations on a theme of exaggerated tension. He traded neither in ambiguity nor charm. In his natural and unnatural separation from the median, he owed more to Farinelli than to the musico-dramatic heroes imagined by those composers for whom romanticism represented a shift towards the purposeful conception of art as a collegial expression of a developing cultural identity. Corelli's work was defined for the most part by isolation and exceptionalism, therefore. Tebaldi, Callas, Leontyne Price, Simionato, Scotto and Freni were capable of matching him, but none exceeded him – not even Nilsson, who acknowledged Corelli's greater resources. Of course, lung power is not a form of art. It is, at best, a tool for the re-creation of inventions by composers and dramatists, and an act of abeyance on the part of performers who should, in theory, place the composer's needs above their own. Callas' artistry extended to her sensitivity to the orchestra, as well as the conductor and her colleagues, such that she would vary her tone and voice placement to account for the changing harmonies and colours from within the pit.[29] Corelli was oblivious to such niceties. As such, the excesses of his work were almost anti-theatrical, albeit never anti-climactic.

For many of his admirers, Corelli's focus on Corelli was consistent with their own disregard for anyone else on the stage. This was observed by Noel Coward in his diary for 12 March, 1961, when he wrote of a performance by Corelli during his debut production at the Met in New York:

---

29   Rosen, Charles (2002). "Operatic Paradoxes: The Ridiculous and the Sublime." In *Freedom and the Arts: Essays on Music and Literature*. Harvard University Press. p.287.

> On Monday I took Coley[30] to *Trovatore,* Price again, more marvellous than ever, also Franco Corelli. Beautiful voice, very handsome and very delighted with himself.[31]

Corelli's resonating eroticism was vocally and physically ostentatious. It was redolent psychologically of the belief among women religious that Christ had only to think of them to cause their insemination. He did not invent the coquetry of the perverse – opera is emblematically ridiculous in form and nature, after all – but Corelli's performing philosophy was masturbatory, and a negation of Shaw's catechism that "Opera is the story of a tenor and a soprano who want to go to bed with each other, and a baritone who wants to stop them." Corelli was happy and most fulfilled in his own company, apostrophising the construction of an art that operated as a platform for the communication primarily of himself.

Throughout the 1960s, when his fame in the United States was inimitable, Corelli was an obvious focus for the attention of many in the gay community, but even here his appearance made him an exception to the otherwise common rule that tenors sounded better than they looked. The identification of the soprano as the "Queen's Throat" made sense for Wayne Koestenbaum, as it does for any gay man or woman seeking a generative, repeating stereotype where the odds were good, if not better, that a singer might appear as beautiful as they sounded. As Koestenbaum idealised it:

> By the twentieth century, homosexuality already meant more than just sex acts or desires shared by bodies of the same gender. It implied a mileu and a personality, flamboyant, narcissistic, self-divided, grandiose, excessive, and devoted to decor. These stereotypes have shaped behaviour, and have been reinforced by gay people when they have made the transition from enduring their preference, to choosing it.[32]

Corelli's beauty was unattainable – just as Farinelli represented an ideal at a distance. Both men were magnificent "creatures" because they were phenomenal midst a community that was already exceptional. A gay man might approach female sexuality without fear of violence or aggression or – more importantly – rejection, whereas

> The diva helps him escape the shame with which society has characterized his inadequate response to the female anatomy. At last he can find genuine passion for a woman, not merely as a mother or a nanny, but as an erotic object, for the sexuality embodied – or disembodied – in her voice.[33]

---

30 Cole Lesley. From 1936, "Coley" was Coward's dresser, but eventually became his secretary and amanuensis.
31 Coward, Noel (1983). *The Noel Coward Diaries*. Macmillan. p.466.
32 Koestenbaum, Wayne (1993). *The Queen's Throat: Opera, Homosexuality, and the Mystery of Desire*. Poseidon Press. p.85.
33 Rosen, Charles (2002). "Operatic Paradoxes: The Ridiculous and the Sublime." In *Freedom and the Arts: Essays on Music and Literature*. Harvard University Press. p.286.

Despite – or, perhaps, because of – his priapic heterosexuality, and considering the common knowledge that he was no more likely to cause a pregnancy than was Farinelli, the height of Corelli's voice and cheekbones cast him as alien even for the alienated; while many may have fantasised replacing Mirella Freni as Juliet when being seduced by Corelli's Roméo, it was easier to submit to the romantic tumefaction of Gounod's music because the man singing it was implausible in his appearance *as an opera singer*. Whither fantasy when traduced by reality? The tension between the real and the unreal was exacerbated further by Corelli's transcending of the normative expectations of tenor voices when singing anything above an A flat 4. During his performances of *Poliuto* in 1960 with Leyla Gencer, Corelli threw in a handful of D5s that caused even seasoned opera-goers to rock on their heels. The security, confidence and power of the tenor's head notes – compared by Cristina Deutekom to the launching of the Saturn V – were *petitis décès* for the initiated and transgressive for everyone else. The traditional tenor praxis compelled that anything above a B flat 4 was anticipated (and delivered) in the teeth of jeopardy and tension. Anyone who has been to the opera regularly will have had cause to experience acute feelings of empathy whenever singers have suffered cracked or missed notes. These *perles neres* occur for tenors in most cases when voicing above an A4. Other than in exceptional circumstances, audiences share in the drama of apprehension. Farinelli occupied an exalted state, wherein every note – no matter its reach or difficulty – came to him with apparent ease. Corelli was no different, insofar as he robbed his audiences of an essential element of the tenor's art – even if, psychologically, it cost him more dearly than any outside his circle can have realised.

The deaths of Sbigoli in 1822 and von Carolsfeld in 1865 were merely extreme examples of the consequences of a tenor's superhuman efforts, which is where Corelli and Farinelli before him were perceived by their admirers as supernatural. They were their own masters also – charging eye-watering sums for doing what they could choose *not* to do. In John Locke's philosophy, the "father or prince"

> hath an Absolute, Arbitrary, Unlimited, and Unlimitable Power, over the Lives, Liberties, and Estates of his Children and Subjects; so that he may take or alienate their Estates, sell, castrate, or use their Persons as he pleases, they being all his Slaves, and he Lord or Proprietor of every Thing, and his unbounded Wil their law.[34]

Corelli was his own Estate, and it was accessible uniquely on his terms – as Rudolph Bing learned at the Met all too often, over many exhausting years together. When Farinelli was invited by Elizabeth Farnese, wife of King Philip V of Spain, to help reverse her husband's "total dejection of spirits, which made him refuse to be shaved, and rendered him incapable of attending council or transacting affairs of state,"[35] he sang the same collection of songs, night after night. He was paid in silver –

---

34 Locke, John (1967). *Two Treatises of Government*, Ed. Peter Laslett. Cambridge University Press. pp.166 and 305.
35 Thomas A. King (2006). "Restoration and Eighteenth Century." *Studies in English Literature, 1500–1900*, Vol. 46, No. 3. pp.563–583; p.565.

staggering amounts of it.[36] Corelli was well-remunerated also[37] – $4,000[38] a night by the Met in 1964 and $7,000 a night by La Scala[39] – and on occasion he would require his fees to be paid in cash before agreeing to sing, which had then to be delivered to the tenor's dressing room stuffed into carrier bags.

At the end of the 1737 season, Farinelli travelled from London to Madrid where:

> Philip appeared at first surprised, then moved; and at the end of the second air, made the virtuoso enter the royal apartment, loading him with compliments and caresses; asked him how he could sufficiently reward such talents; assuring him that he could refuse him nothing. Farinelli, previously instructed, only begged that his Majesty would permit his attendants to shave and dress him, and that he would endeavour to appear in council as usual. From this time the King's disease gave way to medicine; and the singer had all the honour of the cure.[40]

Farinelli's "honour" made him one of the richest entertainers in history, and one of the most narrowly appreciated. The same points of reference continue to be rolled out, most of them originating with the assessment of his colleague Giovanni Mancini:

> His voice was thought a marvel, because it was so perfect, so powerful so sonorous and so rich in its extent, both in the high and low parts of the register, that its equal has never been heard in our times.... The art of taking and keeping the breath, so softly and easily that no-one could perceive it, began and died with him. The qualities in which he excelled were the evenness of his voice, the art of swelling its sound, the *portamento*, the union of the registers, a surprising agility, a graceful and pathetic [melancholic] style.... The successes which he obtained in his youth did not prevent him from continuing to study; and this great artist applied himself with so much perseverance that he contrived to change in some measure his style and to acquire another and superior method, when his name was already famous and his fortune brilliant.[41]

---

36 Charles Burney cited the London *Daily Post* for 26 September (1737?): "Advices from Madrid inform us, that his Catholic Majesty has settled a pension of 14,000 pieces of eight on Signor Farinelli, to engage him to stay at the court, besides a coach, which the king will keep for him at his own charge." In Thomas A. King (2006). "Restoration and Eighteenth Century." *Studies in English Literature, 1500–1900*, Vol. 46, No. 3. pp.563–583; p.578.

37 On 3 March, 1968, Corelli appeared on the Ed Sullivan Show before an audience of 30 million. He was preceded immediately by *The Muppets*, who ended their set by throwing fake $100 bills at the audience and across the stage – onto which the plainly incredulous Corelli stepped to sing (live) Torelli's song "*Tu lo sai.*"

38 $32,000 at the time of publication.

39 $56,000 at the time of publication.

40 Thomas A. King (2006). "Restoration and Eighteenth Century." *Studies in English Literature, 1500–1900*, Vol. 46, No. 3. pp.563–583; p.565.

41 Clapton, Nicholas (2005). "Carlo Broschi Farinelli: Aspects of his Technique and Performance." *British Journal for Eighteenth-Century Studies*. pp.323–338.

This account might have been written of Corelli 230 years later – in every canon by which the *castrato* and the tenor are remembered. Of course, nothing is said by Mancini of what Farinelli did, or did not achieve, in the service of the music he performed. He is little more than a Mechanical Turk, therefore. In Thomas A. King's gloriously acidic analysis of Farinelli's achievement in Madrid:

> Surprise aroused wonder, the first of the Cartesian passions and foundation of the body's motions, its appetites and aversions…. Post-Cartesian theory held that music cured melancholia by its mechanical vibration of the body machine; the particular efficacy of the castrato's voice was its power to penetrate…. Harmonizing the motion of bodies Italian singing achieved an aural exchange in Spain, consisting in the king's and his eunuch's oint reenactment of positions of authority and patronage. Farinelli's cure of Philip's melancholy represented a homeopathic exchange between two non-useful bodies…[42]

Corelli's body remained useful until it wasn't. As he approached his 50th year the superstructure that supported his titanic instrument began to fail him, and in 1970 his *vibrato* began to widen, though never to a point of ugliness. In 1971 his voice gave way during the famous *diminuendo* B flat 4 at the end of "*Celeste Aida*"; more problematic still was the darkening of vocal tone and its increasing resonance, such that it was difficult to pair him with singers capable of operating as something other than a shadow puppet. Audiences and critics continued to implore him to sing *Otello*. Instead, he turned during the late 1960s to French repertoire – Gounod's *Roméo et Juliette* and Massenet's *Werther* at the Met, and *Carmen* in Florence, all sung in French. As evidenced by his ghastly studio recording of *Carmen* with Karajan, Corelli's French was only slightly less *pesante* than his English, and his approach to French style was positively xenophobic. His use of shading and tonal variance was artificial, with his exaggerated *portamento* and over-aspirated consonants obliterating the intrinsic and fundamental relationship between line and language. Bing cast Mirella Freni as Juliette, and while she had on occasion to spit out her vocal cords she was more than persuasive; the EMI recording produced in June, 1968, contains some splendid moments, but it speaks to a voice in decline; the tone is increasingly harsh and the placement a battle of wills and force of technique rather than, as once it was, speech remade as song.

In January, 1971, Corelli appeared for the first time at the Met as Edgardo in Lucia di Lammermoor. The resulting performances were grotesque; many wondered how long he would (or should) continue. Corelli didn't need the money – for the season 1970–71 the Met paid him $168,975[43] – but his voice was his life, and after Bing retired from the Met in April, 1972 – commemorated by a Gala at which Corelli taunted his fans by singing the love duet from *Otello* with Teresa Zylis-Gara – he began to plan for retirement. Eventually, after three unwelcome performances as

---

42 Thomas A. King (2006). "Restoration and Eighteenth Century." *Studies in English Literature, 1500–1900*, Vol. 46, No. 3. pp.563–583.
43 More than $1m at the time of publication.

Macduff – a bizarre decision on his part, explained by rumours that he was obsessed with the star of the show, Grace Bumbry[44] – Corelli closed down his diary. He appeared in costume for the last time at the Festival Puccini in Torre del Lago, as a fifty-five year old Rodolfo, on 13 August, 1976. His voice was still resolute, but far from beautiful, and he ended his career with his reputation just about intact.

Corelli's standing as the most complete *spinto* tenor of the 20th century – even if for little more than a decade – has been acknowledged by everyone from Christa Ludwig, Leontyne Price and Luciano Pavarotti to Herbert von Karajan, Leonard Bernstein and Antonio Pappano. His place in the history of opera is as unique as his voice, therefore, but his shadow has since proven suffocating for any tenor singing "his" repertoire – an outcome similar to that achieved by Farinelli. In 2019, Piotr Beczała[45] gave a masterclass at Carnegie Hall during which he coached a young Argentinian tenor, Jose Romero, in De Curtis' "*Tu ca nun chiagne.*" Beczała was then in his tenth season at the Met – singing one of Corelli's roles, *Adrianna Lecouvreur*. He interrupted Romero's performance to correct his breathing and observed:

> We are all like that! We are all listening to Franco Corelli sing like that, thinking 'how is he doing that,' you know? You know Franco Corelli was like that [he holds his hand up to indicate Corelli's height] and he was an athlete. He could move this piano with one finger! We are not like that. We have to work…

The audience laughed and Romero's face collapsed. Of course, Corelli worked hard – harder than most; that abiding sense of a Faustian pact, of a talent so "easy" that it cannot have come other than supernaturally, continues to colour both his reputation and considerations of his recordings. The best of them were made live. In the studio, his voice was simply too huge and, according to EMI's Peter Andry, "a total bloody nightmare" to record.[46] There are numerous legendary live performances doing the rounds, the best of them capturing Corelli's debut at the Met on 27 January, 1961,[47] as Manrico – conducted appropriately enough by Fausto Cleva, with Leontyne Price making her Met debut also, as Leonora. Equally impressive are his first Met Calàf, recorded just two months later, with Nilsson as Turandot – conducted by Leopold Stokowski[48] – and his Manrico for Karajan in July, 1962, at the Salzburger Festspiele (again with Price). These performances – by everyone involved – approach perfection. For all the high-octane bravura, however, one of the most revealing highlights (beyond the unblinking fearlessness of "*Di quella pira*" and "*Nessun dorma*") occurs in Scene 2 of Act IV of *Il trovatore*, when Manrico sings:

---

44 Seghers, René (2008). *Franco Corelli: Prince of Tenors*. Amadeus Press. p.421.
45 28 December, 1966.
46 In conversations with the author.
47 There is a better quality recording available of the second performance in the run, on 4 February.
48 One of Corelli's two favourite conductors, the other being Karajan.

> "*Se m'ami ancor, se voce di figlio, ha possa d'una madre in seno, ai terrori dell'alma, oblio cerca nel sonno, e posa e calma.*"[49]

It is a potentially unremarkable phrase – a simple bridge to Azucena's grim intimation of mortality, "*Sì, la stanchezza m'opprime, o figlio.*"[50] As written, "*oblio cerca nel sonno, e posa e calma*" would sound clipped and perfunctory (if sung in time) because of the semi-quavers in the third of the phrase's three-bars, but Corelli's *cetacean* breath control allows him to draw out the words "*nel sonno, e posa*" in a single, exquisite line, unbroken for 12 magical seconds.[51] In many performances, the moment is cursory; in Corelli's hands it is tender, intimate and unforgettably persuasive. It was the product of a centuries-old philosophy first memorialised by Farinelli in the 18th century – and summarised by Corelli the year before his death at the age of 82 in 2003, when he observed how

> Each year you understand the mystery of the voice a little better and only after many years can you begin to understand where your voice can go. Then you start thinking of interpretations, possible colours that you can give it. Before going to sleep I spend hours just thinking about my voice, about the ideal road to take. Singing must pursue you, must live inside you and blossom. Those few hours on the stage don't do the job, it is the constant research in between, the discipline, the never ending sacrifice.[52]

---

49 'If you love me still, if a son's voice has power in a mother's breast, seek oblivion in sleep from the spirit's terrors, and rest and calm.'
50 'Yes, weariness overcomes me, my son.'
51 He was unable to repeat the effect for Karajan, of whom Corelli was unashamedly in awe.
52 Seghers, René (2008). *Franco Corelli: Prince of Tenors*. Amadeus Press. p.206.

CHAPTER THIRTEEN

Golden Age

The first complete recording of an opera, Verdi's *Ernani*, was released in 1904 by HMV – on 40 single-sided discs. Many have since questioned why one of Verdi's lesser known works was chosen for this honour; others have wondered who bought them – noting their enormous cost and combined weight. The "long-playing" (LP) record was launched in the United States in 1948 by Columbia Records. It allowed for half an hour of music to be heard without a break, and then on hardy vinyl rather than brittle shellac. In 1949, Decca adopted the LP ahead of EMI – in mono; in 1954 the sound engineers Arthur Haddy, Roy Wallace and Kenneth Wilkinson developed the "Decca tree," a stereo microphone system for recording large orchestras and operas. RCA Victor was the first company to record in stereo, in the United States, in March 1954. Decca was the first to release a stereo recording of a work of classical music, conducted by Ernest Ansermet, with the *Orchestre de la Suisse Romande*.[1] Stereo introduced two-channels to create a soundscape that transformed the recording and reproduction of orchestras, with instruments separated during playback as if on a stage or in a pit. "High Fidelity" was capable of approximating something that approached the live experience. For opera fans unable to afford theatre tickets, or for those who lived too far from a city (or a country) with an opera house, recordings were a life-changing resource. By 1950, "record players" were pollinating living rooms globally, and even before the revelation of stereo the hour-long capacity of an LP allowed for the majority of operas to be stored on only three or four discs. The commercialisation of stereo was delayed until 1958, when Columbia, Mercury and RCA sold stereo equipment as well as records[2] – building on a violently shifted cultural objectivity wherein performance compensated audiences for the post-war collapse in the writing, publishing and popularity of new art music.

The LP revolution coincided with a remarkable period in the history of opera performance, fomented by an accident of timing that enabled musicians trained before the war in the company of composers to capture their work in idealised performances. The roster of conductors active during the 1950s who made complete opera recordings of historical importance is a fantasy league for the nostalgic, with merely the obvious being the "Old Guard" (born in the 19th century[3]) spanning

---

1 The bizarre programme was made up of Nikolai Rimsky-Korsako's *Antar*, Alexander Glazunov' *Stenka Razin*, Balakirev's *Tamara*, Liadov's *Baba-Yaga*, *Kikimora* and Eight Russian Folksongs, and Debussy's *Le Martyre de Saint Sébastien*. Recorded in Geneva between 13 and 28 May, 1954.
2 It is well to remember that anyone wanting to play a stereo recording had to buy equipment to play it.
3 Although he continued to work until shortly before his death in 1962, Bruno Walter never conducted a complete recording of an opera in the studio. The closest he came to doing so (other than in "fragments")

Barbirolli, Beecham, Böhm, Busch, De Sabata, Furtwängler, Gui, Kleiber, Klemperer, Knappertsbusch, Krauss, Leinsdorf, Mitropoulos, Munch, Reiner, Santini, Serafin, Toscanini and Votto. The vanguard (as those born during the first 15 years of the 20th century) included Cleva, Cluytens, Erede, De Fabritiis, Fricsay, Gardelli, Gavazzeni, Giulini, Karajan, Kubelik, Leinsdorf, and Molinari-Pradelli.

The opportunity to make complete opera recordings with these exceptional conductors was embraced by every major label. Hundreds of still-sensational albums were produced – frequently out of fear for a conductor's age and health. Furtwängler and Clemens Krauss both died in 1954 (with the latter having recorded only a single opera in the studio, *Die Fledermaus*). In the same year, De Sabata retired – having recorded only *Tosca* in the studio.[4] Two years later, Erich Kleiber, Hermann Abendroth and Guido Cantelli were all dead – the latter, dreadfully, at the age of 36. Toscanini died in 1957. The rush to enshrine the work of the finest conductors to disc resulted in a body of definitive recordings, featuring a stellar concentration of singers. A catalogue of recordings for the years 1951 to 1966 would contain more "historic" performances than any other. Certainly, when compiling one of its periodic lists of the "Greatest 100 recordings" in 2015, the *Gramophone* magazine nominated 21 operas – of which 13 were produced between 1951 and 1966.[5]

Recordings from this period document the voices of immortal tenors in "golden age" collaborations: Di Stefano and Callas, Björling and Milanov, Del Monaco and Tebaldi, Tucker and Merrill, Gedda and de los Ángeles, Corelli and Nilsson, Bergonzi and just about everyone. This period is unusual for the quality and distinction of the singing and also the profusion of exceptional talent in the pit. The transformation of orchestral standards after the war reached unprecedented levels of excellence during the 1950s and 60s – typified by Walter Legge's gauntlet-throwing creation of the Philharmonia. These improvements were welcomed by conductors whose talents were formed in most cases through their work with composers who were otherwise singular in their creative focus. The "old guard" helped coach many of the singers whose artistry blossomed after 1950; some listened more closely than others. The best of the work produced during the 1950s and 60s is probably the best there has been. It was during this period that claques were first able to form and operate beyond the confines of the theatre. Recordings served as reliquaries for enthusiasts and devotees whose attachment to their heroes was capable of something proximate to objectivity. Though Decca and RCA's engineering was palpably manufactured it was more accurate and revealing than the '78s and broadcasts with which listeners had previously to be satisfied. LPs allowed for the forensic analysis of a performance – a process much enhanced by John C. Koss' invention of stereo headphones in 1958. The emergence of audiophilia as a dialectic as well as a disease was at its most revealing when applied to voices that were recorded before the war, as well as after.

---

was his famous recording of Act 1 and Act II, Scenes 3 and 5 from *Die Walküre* with the Berliner Philharmoniker and Lotte Lehmann and Lauritz Melchior for EMI, on 22 and 26 June, 1935.

4   Purists will note that De Sabata came out of retirement just once, in 1957, to conduct at Toscanini's funeral.

5   One was produced in 1931 (Elie Cohen's *Werther* with Georges Thill) and four during the 1970s.

Among the golden age of tenors, this shift from mono '78s to LPs and, eventually, stereo was straddled most completely by the careers and recordings of Jussi Björling[6] and Giuseppe Di Stefano.[7] Björling was born in Sweden in 1911; he was a celebrity while still a child. His father, David, was an accomplished singer and his son's first teacher. Jussi's brothers, Olle and Gösta, were professional singers also and the family performed together as "Björlingkvartetten" (the Björling Male Quartet). He made his public debut in 1916, at the age of five – in the same year that Caruso first recorded "*O Sole Mio*" and "*Santa Lucia.*" He gave his last performance in an opera, as Faust, on 1 April, 1960 – three years after Plácido Domingo made his debut. The family toured for more than a decade, and while he was still a teenager Björling appeared for the first time on the radio. In 1928 he enrolled at the Royal Swedish Academy of Music in Stockholm, where his training progressed so rapidly that he was able to make his stage debut at the Royal Swedish Opera on 21 July, 1930. His memory and work ethic enabled him to perform 53 different roles over eight years. Having begun with Mozart, Rossini and early Verdi, he worked his way up to *Faust*, Vasco Da Gama in *L'Africaine*, Rodolfo in *La bohème* and Florestan in *Fidelio*. He performed in the Swedish premieres of *La fanciulla del West*, *Il tabarro*, *Arabella* and *Prince Igor*. The voice in 1937 – when he was still in his twenties – was a phenomenon, albeit raw and unschooled. Its placement is recognisable for its fast and relatively wide *vibrato* – a feature exacerbated by his tendency to force the instrument to the point where he would sing sharp on anything above an A4. Björling's technique was bullet-proof, as evidenced by an early recording of "*Ch'ella mi creda*"[8] in which he takes without difficulty the aria's final line, "*Ah, tu della mia vita [mio solo fior!]*"[9] with only a single breath – before "*mio*". The uninterrupted phrase is delivered as required by Puccini – "*Con grande espressione, esaltandosi, col viso quasi sorridente*"[10] – but *not* as written: there is no slur joining the *fermata'd* B flat ("*Ah*") to the following A flat ("*tu*"). Puccini did not expect even Caruso to meet such a challenge; indeed, Domingo and nearly everyone else has had to breathe at least twice during the same phrase – before "*della*" as well as "*mio*".

Björling's pre-war recordings are treasured, as are the live recordings he made after his debut at the Met on 24 November, 1938. Many consider his broadcast from 1940 of Beethoven's *Missa solemnis* and Verdi's Requiem (both with Toscanini) to be highlights; in neither performance is he comfortable, however. The Beethoven is especially incongruous, thanks to the conductor's rigidity and the inappropriately operatic atmosphere. Far better is the splendid recording made at the Met on 8 December, 1940, of *Un ballo In Maschera*, with a sensational performance by Zinka Milanov as Amelia. The conductor, Ettore Panizza,[11] generates hair-raising momentum, while working closely *with* his singers to allow them to breathe in tandem with the music. The tenor's tone is mellow, improbably sweet and plangent when necessary

---

6   Johan Jonatan "Jussi" Björling (2 February, 1911 – 9 September, 1960).
7   24 July, 1921 – 3 March, 2008.
8   Recorded in September, 1937.
9   'Ah, you of my life my only flower!'
10 'With great expression, exalted, with an almost smiling face.'
11 Born in 1875, Panizza was much admired by Puccini and Richard Strauss, but he made very few studio recordings.

– unforgettably so during the Act II duet "*Teco io sto,*"[12] which Panizza drives towards Milanov and Björling's climactic high C like a (sixty-five-year-old) man possessed.

The war confined Björling's appearances to Europe, with legendary successes in the UK and at home. Circumstances prevented him from making his debut in Paris, and he sang only a handful of performances in Italy – an anomaly considering his fame and popularity. Björling's career at the Metropolitan after 1945 was uneven because of his infamous drinking habits and consequent unreliability. This caused his relationship with Rudolf Bing near-terminal strain, so that he appeared often at rival American Houses, notably Chicago and San Francisco. During the 1950s he made a series of recordings for RCA, some noticeably better than others. Björling was a *lirico-spinto* tenor; for those who heard him in concert as well as the theatre he was more gifted as a performer of songs with piano than as a singer of opera. His inclination to force his voice was enhanced on record, increasingly so when taking up repertoire for which he was unsuited. His first project (*Il trovatore*) in 1952 was solidly cast (with Milanov and Leonard Warren in blistering if occasionally blunt form); Björling's tone is strained and harsh, with a metallic quality made colder still by the engineering. "*Di quella pira*" is sung in key; the performance is otherwise characterised by a measure of tension *non come è scritto*. The 1953 *Cavalleria Rusticana* (again with Milanov) and *Pagliacci* (with de los Ángeles as Nedda, Leonard Warren as Tonio and Robert Merrill as Silvio) should have been spectacular; unfortunately, the voices were ill-served by the recording and the performance was eclipsed in any event by EMI's production from the same year, with Serafin conducting Callas, Di Stefano, Gobbi and Panerai. *Manon Lescaut* (1954, with Licia Albanese in the title role) and *Aida* (1955, with a dreadfully below-par Milanov, Warren, Barbieri and Christoff) contain memorable moments. Neither recording is likely to be heard on a desert island.

Björling's fortunes improved in 1956 when he recorded *La bohème* with de los Ángeles and Merrill, conducted by a 77-year-old Sir Thomas Beecham. This is plainly one of the finest recordings ever made; certainly, it is the tenor's best work in the studio. The cast join together beautifully and, despite some lumbering *tempi*, the aging conductor generates exceptional energy and engagement from Björling. The resulting performance is believable, and frequently unbearable in its intensity. It was a perfect moment for the tenor – a summary representation of his abilities at their best, when his resources were matched absolutely to the music, his colleagues and the conductor. There is a pronounced and discernible sense of character, therefore – the appearance of a staged performance notwithstanding the absence of an audience. The same cannot be said of the *Rigoletto* recorded by Björling later the same year (although Merrill is excellent in the title role) or the *Tosca* produced in 1957, which is a day-light plane-crash without survivors. Decca-RCA's *Cavalleria Rustican*a, with Tebaldi and Bastianini, conducted by Erede, is solid fare – and despite his voice sounding worn and tired Björling unearths one or two truffles, including an exquisite *pianissimo* at the end of the "*Siciliana*". Björling's Turiddu is an angry caricature for the most past, and almost entirely unsympathetic. One can easily imagine Rina Corsi's relief when he bids his final farewell.

---

12 'I am with you.'

Björling's recording of *Turandot* in 1959 paired him with his compatriot Birgit Nilsson, alongside Renata Tebaldi as Liù. Erich Leinsdorf drags the score badly, and there is an exhausting absence of momentum. Björling was now singing in "Living Stereo," but his voice lacked the weight necessary for the role, particularly when stood beside Nilsson, who leaves him all but mute at the end of "*In questia reggia.*" The tension in Björling's voice, and his *vibrato* in particular, now coloured everything – such that even his *cantabile* was robbed of elasticity and expression. The tenor's final complete opera recording was as Pinkerton in 1960, with de los Ángeles as Cio Cio San, and Mario Sereni in idealised form as Sharpless. Gabriele Santini does his best; he is indulgent of his lovers, however, who sound more mature than was intended by the composer. In Björling's hands, Pinkerton is aggressive and arrogant, an approach that fails spectacularly during the duet, which is febrile and overfed. His phrasing is square and hard-edged, and he barks his sweet nothings at de los Ángeles. It's hard to imagine anyone responding positively to his dead-voiced enunciation of "*Vieni!*". RCA decided for some reason to leave in his concluding high C5 – which is thinner than the partitions inside Butterfly's home. The tenor singing Goro, Piero de Palma, is consistently more seductive than Björling, and he's playing a marriage broker.

Björling's last studio recording was produced in Vienna between 12 and 19 June, 1960. It proved to be prophetic. The tenor part of Verdi's Requiem suited him, and he was sufficiently in awe of Fritz Reiner to do as he was told. The Hungarian monolith oversaw a virtuoso and often clinical performance that nonetheless contains some sensational music-making. The Wien Philharmoniker and the chorus of the Gesellschaft der Musikfreunde are transcendent; Björling fed off the youth, energy and discipline of his colleagues Leontyne Price, Rosalind Elias and Giorgio Tozzi. It was a magnificent swan-song for a tenor whose death at the age of 49 of *cardiomegaly* was mourned globally as a tragedy. That it was, but his career was longer than most and more meaningful for its trajectory and product – because of when and how it was formed.[13]

Björling cut his first discs in 1929, his last 31 years later. Throughout those decades he listened to his own voice almost as frequently as did his audience. As Harald Henrysson's discography demonstrates,[14] he spent literally hundreds of days – well over a year of his life, in fact – in the studio. Between 1929 and 1960 his sense of his own voice was forced upon Björling with unrelenting propinquity. Not a single year passed without him being recorded, one way or another. He was, in consequence, the first tenor able to trace his voice in detail across the span of his entire career,[15] and he was one of the first to trace the progress and history of his contemporaries and predecessors.

Björling was the product of a remarkable family, born into an equally remarkable culture – one that prized art almost as highly as technology. Where the two bisected resolved a game of solitaire, in which Björling's self-awareness operated as

---

13 Anyone keen to explore Björling's work in greater detail should acquire Stephen Hastings' exceptional *The Björling Sound: A Recorded Legacy* (2012). Boydell & Brewer.
14 Henrysson, Harald (2014). *A Jussi Björling Phonography*. Svenskt Musikhistoriskt Arkiv.
15 As an adult.

his undoing, submitting him as the source of a sound he could hear and analyse to a host of psychological stresses unimagined by De Reszke and his predecessors. For Björling, however, the evolving technology became the end as well as a means because he – like every other opera singer to make records after the emergence of the LP – was competing with himself.

The most invasive and destructive effect of recording as a technology is its isolation of those failures and flaws that only the performer can hear. Björling's demons – coincidentally summoned and exorcised by his drinking – were as much a product of his acoustic relationship with his own voice (because he was also able to analyse it when silent), as they were a function of the pressures of performing in public. His characteristic forcing of tone was the manifestation of his need to do more, of the narcotic of bigger being better – of amplitude substituting for song and sensibility. Recordings delivered spectra of sin and inadequacy that operated as the price of entry to Olympus while coincidentally diminishing the primacy of acting skill and dramatic focus on stage.

LPs were no less toxic for audiences. The difference between the best seat in the House and an armchair with headphones was more than the difference between edited perfection and the tactile, immersive fallibilities of the unpredictable. For those interested only in singing, a night at the Opera is commonly disappointing – if not something worse – by reason of the expectations formed by recordings being neither realistic nor repeatable. The engineered sound of Karajan's opera recordings from the 1960s and 70s is astonishing; it is also grotesque in its deception.

Engaging with live performance is more than a listening process – particularly when opera throws so much else into the mix. It's true that Björling did not add much to opera's multisensory value as an art form best experienced in the flesh. His limitations as an actor were recognised at the time. Seeing a tenor achieve on a stage what a producer with a razor-blade is able to manufacture in a window-less, rubber-walled room involves visual cues as well as social and emotional stimuli that compound the physical proximity of musicians working together. Live music is necessarily immersive, and distracting of somatic and psychological symptoms – insofar as performance cannot be fully appreciated in person without movement or an admixture of extra-musical variables arising from the location of a ticket-holder's seat, the temperature of the space, the infinite psychological tensions within and between the performers, and the genuine imperilment of contact with people for whom a theatre is indistinguishable from their living room.

Listening to music in a purely auditory form, isolated from the gestures inherent in its creation, is a modern phenomenon. Even for the visually impaired, live performance remains intensely human and interactive. One can imagine the force of the olfactory experience during a Schubertiade, notwithstanding its romanticised commemoration by Moritz von Schwind. Research has demonstrated how multisensory *simulacra* are more engaging than those that draw on a single sense. They tend to be more immediate, vivid and direct for the listener, with a heightened perception of interaction feeding impulses that owe nothing to music.[16] Live theatre

---

16 Finnäs, L. (2001). Presenting music live, audio-visually or aurally: Does it affect listeners' experiences differently? *British Journal of Music Education*, 18, 55–78. See also Coutinho, Eduardo, and Scherer, Klaus

is also more obviously temporal when perceived visually.[17] In 2008, psychologists compared modes of presentation and investigated the objective physiological expression of emotional responses to music by measuring electrodermal activity.[18] Twelve musically trained women aged between 20 and 25 were allocated to one of three short audiovisual (AV), audio only (AO) or visual only (VO) excerpts from a work for solo clarinet by Stravinsky. These were repeated ten times for each participant, with 30-second intervals between each repetition. Electrodermal amplitude for the AV presentations was significantly higher than the sum of electrodermal responses to the AO and VO presentations. The AV response was self-evidently more than the sum of its parts, realising a potent property formed of bimodal interaction, highlighting the implications of seeing as well as hearing the musician perform. In 1983, Lucanne Magill Bailey conducted a seminal study comparing live and taped recordings of the same songs and musicians. The live group reported significantly less tension-anxiety, greater vigour and improvements in attitude and mood when compared to the recorded group after just 25 minutes of music. Bailey concluded the force of "human elements" in live performance, spanning body language, acoustic-spatial vocal resonance, and other subtle communications between musician and audience.[19]

None of this is to state the obvious. The majority of those who have left the "Greatest Hits" albums of *Queen* (1981) and *The Beatles* (1982) on repeat did not hear either band perform in concert; even those who "heard" *Queen* at "Live Aid" in 1985 were, for the most part, sufficiently distant from the stage to be compelled to watch the band on a monitor just as the rest of the planet was watching on television. The disconnect between the artist and the music – and its reproduction (inside Wembley stadium and as a broadcast) – did not affect the performers or the manner of their performance. For Jussi Björling, however, and for many other tenors during the 1950s, the process and commercialisation of recording as the primary vehicle for the dissemination of musical art was positively Gothic. Records ceased during the 1950s to exist as an accessory and became instead a *deus ex machina* by which a performer might no longer exist in the flesh. The Adam of these labours was Giuseppe Di Stefano.[20]

For Italians in particular, Di Stefano's voice was God-given; his use of it was one of the miracles of the age. Born in Sicily in 1921 – just three months after Corelli and six months after Lanza – he moved with his parents to Milan, where he joined a local church choir and later enrolled in a seminary to study for the priesthood. He was honest enough to accept in later life the improbability of this early attachment to divinity, which was interrupted in any event by a profane meeting with a local

---

R. (2016). The effect of context and audio-visual modality on emotions elicited by a musical performance. *Psychology of Music*.
17   Levitin, Daniel J. and Tirovolas, Anna K. (2009). Current Advances in the Cognitive Neuroscience of Music. *Annals of the New York Academy of Sciences*. Annals of the New York Academy of Sciences. 1156: 211–231.
18   Chapados C., and Levitin D.J. "Modal interactions in the experience of musical performances: physiological correlates." *Cognition*. 2008, 108(3), 639-651.
19   Bailey, Lucanne Magill (1983). "The Effects of Live Music versus Tape-Recorded Music on Hospitalized Cancer Patients." *Music Therapy*, Vol.3, Issue 1. pp.17–28.
20   24 July, 1921 – 3 March, 2008.

seamstress. The Church's loss was music's gain, although opera was not his first love. Di Stefano made his debut singing popular songs for audiences at movie theatres between films, using the pseudonym Nino Florio. Around the time of his 18th birthday, he received formal tuition from the baritones Luigi Montesanto and Mariano Stabile. The latter was famed for his style and skill with comedy. He was renowned also for his diction – of which quality Di Stefano took careful note. With the outbreak of war, he served in the Italian army, which assigned him to an infirmary. In most subsequent interviews he claimed to have been saved from the Russian front by his regimental commander, who allegedly gave him a medical dispensation to preserve his voice. Di Stefano was inclined to tall tales, and this one was no exception.[21]

In late 1943, he made his way to Switzerland, and after a period of internment was invited to sing on local radio. He came to the attention of a wealthy and older Russian lady, who asked him to record a selection of arias and songs. It was rumoured that his fee of 50 francs for each recording was rendered for more than singing.[22] Di Stefano was also fortunate to come to the attention of the Romanian-born conductor Otto Ackermann, who taught him how to sing with an orchestra and how to read a score. Di Stefano performed a number of complete operas for Radio Lausanne, with Ackermann, including *L'elisir d'amore* (on 3 September, 1944[23]) and *Il tabarro* (on 12 or 18 February, 1945[24]). The excerpts from *L'elisir* are sensational. His diction is flawless, such that every syllable is carried with crystalline precision – without ever impacting on his effortless *cantabile*. Though light, the tone is cut from velvet, and he demonstrates consistent judgment in the placement of his voice. On the other hand, the opening of "*Hai ben ragione*" from *Il tabarro* is all over the place, and a clear sign that he was still finding his feet; once he recovers himself and the music, however, the aria is delivered by Di Stefano with refulgent tone and the easiest projection. Discretion was in abundance throughout the first five years of his career – when he was unrivalled in the Italian lyric repertoire. Recordings of his work in 1947 and 1948 attest to a voice of exceptional fluency and beauty. There are some *very* open sounds – with almost no covering – and the *passaggio* is overcome rather than managed. The joining of his *legato* to arguably the most perfect diction of any Italian tenor of the 20th century was barely precedented, and certainly not on record. His instinctively musical personality, prismatic colour palette, breath management and elegance of line are impaired only by a hint of absent control when singing above an A4. The performances of *Manon* (1947 and 1948), *Rigoletto* (1948), and *La traviata* (1948) are genuine, and consistently superb – at least as far as Di Stefano is concerned.

He made his debut at the Metropolitan Opera in February, 1948 – as the Duke in *Rigoletto*. Critics fell over themselves to praise the tenor's tone and timbre, which many compared to Gigli while accepting his analogous (and distinguishing) purity

---

21   In numerous interviews, Di Stefano noted that most of his regiment never returned. That bit may well be true. The real reason for his remaining was that he was frequently ill, and something of a liability for his fellow soldiers.
22   His "patron" was also an illustrator, and Di Stefano modelled for her as a "prince." The drawings have survived.
23   Recorded and released as excerpts broadcast by Radio Lausanne 3 September, 1944.
24   Shaman, William (1999). "*More EJS: Discography of the Edward J. Smith Recordings – Unique Opera Records Corporation.*" Greenwood Press. p.163.

of style. In his memoirs, Sir Rudolf Bing recalled of Di Stefano's broadcast debut in *Faust* how the tenor's *diminuendo* on the high C5 at the end of "*Salut! Demeure*" was "the most spectacular single moment in my observation year…. I shall never as long as I live forget the beauty of that sound."[25] Di Stefano's *annus mirabilis* was 1949. Recordings survive of *Il barbiere di Siviglia*, *Falstaff* (conducted by Fritz Reiner), *Faust* (conducted by Pelletier), *La favorite* (conducted by Cellini), *Gianni Schicchi* (conducted by Antonicelli), *Mignon*, *Der Rosenkavalier* (again with Fritz Reiner), *La traviata* (Antonicelli) and *Werther* (Cellini). Each performance demonstrates the unfiltered sunlight that was Di Stefano's voice in its prime – caught, by way of a snapshot, in his sublime rendition for Reiner of "*Di rigori armato.*"

In 1951 Di Stefano sang with both Renata Tebaldi and Maria Callas – the two leading Italian-repertoire sopranos of the age. They were incomparable in their work, with differing allegiances and attachments to repertoire and colleagues; their infamous rivalry was inflamed by claques and promoters. Tebaldi was renowned for her collaboration with Del Monaco, who also worked with Callas – albeit less frequently.[26] For her part, Callas was attached initially to second rank tenors like Kurt Baum, Cesare Valletti,[27] Mario Filippeschi,[28] Gianni Poggi,[29] Francesco Albanese,[30] and, for a single performance,[31] Daniele Barioni.[32] If each of them was talented on occasion, by any standard Callas' proximity shifted the metric of expectation. She even found herself partnered with the aging Lauri-Volpi – for a *Trovatore* in Naples on 27 January, 1951. Callas relished being the centre of positive attention on stage; advice and instinct steered her towards the commercial virtue of successful partnerships, which were likely to sell more records – particularly after the failure of her *La Gioconda* in 1952 for Cetra with the underwhelming Poggi.

The emergence of Di Stefano provided Callas with a partner who was capable initially of meeting her in equivalence after her re-education by Tulio Serafin as a singer of early 19th century repertoire. Their first performances together in *La traviata* in South America had been exceptional; by the time they came together for *I puritani*, however, it was clear that Di Stefano was overworking his voice. Arturo is a brutal role even for the most secure of singers – and Di Stefano was never trained to forge what Rubini would have understood to qualify as a technique. The live recording from May, 1952, at the Palacio de las Bellas Artes in Mexico City, features accordingly a number of moments where his once easy reach to a high C compels effort, palpably so for the duet "*Vieni, fra questia braccia.*"[33] He and Callas are clearly bouncing off each other, and Di Stefano's alveolar trilling and *messa di voce* are thrilling, as

---

25 Bing, Rudolf (1972). *5000 Nights at the Opera*. Hamish Hamilton. p.145.
26 On record, there are sensational live performances of *Turandot*, conducted by Serafin in Buenos Aires (1949), and an *Aida* from Mexico City conducted by De Fabritiis (1951); their most celebrated collaborations, all in 1955, were *Andrea Chénier* (conducted by Votto on 8 January) and *Norma* (conducted by Serafin on 29 June and by Votto on 7 December).
27 18 December, 1922 – 13 May, 2000.
28 7 June, 1907 – 25 December, 1979.
29 4 October, 1921 – 16 December, 1989.
30 13 August, 1912 – 11 June, 2005.
31 *La traviata*, on 6 February, 1958, with Mario Zanasi as Germont.
32 6 September, 1930 –
33 'Come into these arms.'

is the sweetness of the voice; even in 1952, however, it was beginning to sour. The coincident performances of *Lucia di Lammermoor* were more successful. The recording from 10 June, 1952, is almost as noisy as *I puritani*; but the singing warrants unfettered applause seventy years on. The duet "*Sulla tomba*" speaks to his chemistry with the multi-textural Callas, as well as the value of joining such paradoxical voices in music that gained from juxtaposition.

On the back of their work together in 1952, and because there was no one else in whom the label could invest long-term,[34] Walter Legge chose to sign Di Stefano as Callas' putative partner for EMI. The initial recordings were released in 1953, beginning appropriately enough with *Lucia di Lammermoor* and *I puritani*.[35] Less appropriately, Di Stefano recorded *Cavalleria Rusticana*[36] and *Tosca*, the latter with Callas in the title role and Tito Gobbi as Scarpia, conducted by Victor De Sabata. Millions of words have been expended on evaluating the virtues of this performance, among which many count the beauty of Di Stefano's voice. However, he was not then, and would never become, a Cavaradossi – particularly when partnered by singers whose resonance and dramatic artillery could not help but expose Di Stefano as undernourished. De Sabata's searing conducting and La Scala's indulgence of Puccini's rich-hewn scoring exacerbated Di Stefano's absent *squillo*. The Act 1 duet reveals Callas at her most complex, with a heart-stopping breadth of vocal and phonetic colour that resolves an unfair comparison with the unfocussed Di Stefano.

Walter Legge admitted he was not an expert in Italian opera; his ears were better than most, however, and while keeping Di Stefano occupied he used other tenors for repertoire that required larger, more resonant voices. In 1954, he paired Callas with the lymphatic Filippeschi for *Norma* and he favoured the brittle Tucker as her Alvaro in *La forza del destino*. When Callas looked back to Rossini with *Il turco in Italia* – an opera for which Di Stefano's voice might have been created – she was partnered with Nicolai Gedda. Di Stefano was again overlooked for Gedda when Callas recorded *Madama Butterfly* with Karajan in 1955; by the time they were reunited for *Rigoletto*, Di Stefano was casting himself as a romantic *spinto* tenor. With a single exception,[37] both his theatre roles and his recordings reached well beyond the repertoire for which his voice was suited by nature. Di Stefano was in overt competition with Mario Del Monaco (whose recording of *Cavalleria Rusticana* in 1953 established his reputation as the world's leading dramatic Italian-repertoire tenor) and Richard Tucker, who joined Callas for her recording of *Aida* in 1955.

At the same time, Callas was working in the theatre with Corelli, with whom she sang *Norma* for the first time in 1953 and *La Vestale* in 1954. Between 1952 and 1956, Björling was achieving huge numbers for RCA in the United States, with Gedda snapping at his heels for EMI. Mario Del Monaco's recording career exploded with hugely successful Decca productions of *Manon Lescaut* and *Otello* in 1954, *La Forza del Destino* in 1955 and *Il Trovatore* in 1956. By the time Di Stefano returned to the studio in 1955 he had heard all but the last of these LPs, which he studied

---

34   Del Monaco had by this time signed to Decca.
35   The first three albums were conducted by Callas' mentor, Tulio Serafin.
36   They recorded *Pagliacci* in 1954.
37   *L'elisir d'amore* with Hilde Gueden and Fernando Corena.

before undertaking his own recordings with Callas of *Rigoletto* (1955), *Il trovatore* (1956), *La bohème* (1956), *Un ballo in Maschera* (1956), and *Manon Lescaut* (1957). When released from his contract by EMI, Di Stefano jumped to Decca and productions of *La Gioconda* and *La forza del destino* in 1957 – both with Milanov and Warren. The following year he recorded *Lucia di Lammermoor* in stereo with Renata Scotto and Ettore Bastianini for Ricordi. Di Stefano barked his way through most of these sessions, struggling painfully even with the assistance of an editor's blade.

By 1958, the "sad augurs mocked their own presage." He was increasingly yesterday's man, a fact much inflamed by the enormous publicity generated on 27 March by a performance of *Traviata* at the Teatro Nacional de São Carlos in Lisbon, when Callas partnered with a young Spanish tenor, Alfredo Kraus.[38] In the same year, Decca released an album of 14 tenor arias with Carlo Bergonzi (conducted by Gianandrea Gavazzeni), the wonder of which signalled the arrival internationally on record of a once-in-a-lifetime artist. By 1962, when Di Stefano made his last recording of a complete opera[39] – a tragically awful *Tosca* for Decca with Leontyne Price and Giuseppe Taddei, conducted by Karajan – his voice was in tatters. He was 41 years old.

In his repertoire choices on stage and in the studio, and noting the clear parallels in chronology and context, Di Stefano's international career began in 1952 and was over in 1958; it traced a path of studied self-destruction with only a single comparator.[40] He was criticised (and sacked) by Rudolph Bing for his high living and contract breaches, and by many others for his low habits, which spanned smoking, gambling, womanising and a general lack of professionalism wherein he neither cared for, nor attended to, the preservation of his voice. It is true that many other singers have lived badly without building their own gallows; the root of Di Stefano's undoing was located more precisely in his inability to accept the limitations of the scale and amplitude of his instrument – particularly when in the studio. Its natural beauty and effortless placement before 1951 would have survived had he adhered to his *fach*, and exercised self-control when allowing for the maturity of time, training and experience. Instead, Di Stefano was drawn to the celebrity and wealth enjoyed by his bigger-voiced rivals – an arms war that Di Stefano could never have hoped to win. His feelings of inadequacy were escalated brutally after the ascension of Corelli, Gedda and Bergonzi, and there are numerous stories of Di Stefano losing his temper (and refusing to sing) when seeing their names, and that of Del Monaco, in brighter lights than his own. His competitive streak undermined his judgment so completely that by 1955, when he recorded *Rigoletto* with Callas, he was a shadow of the Duke that survives from Mexico just seven years earlier (22 June, 1948). His recording of *Il trovatore* in 1956 was a professional embarrassment for EMI as well as Di Stefano; he should never have been allowed to sing this repertoire, far less some of the more demanding work to which he turned his increasingly withered hand over the next twenty years. The nadir of this degeneration was his appearance with the Pasadena Opera Company on 31 March, 1966, as Verdi's Otello, although

---

38 This performance was recorded also.
39 Not including his bizarre appearance as Prince Sou-Chong in Lehár's *Das Land des Lächelns* – in German (1967).
40 See chapter 17 below.

his ill-fated performances in 1964 at La Scala as Rienzi,[41] conducted by Hermann Scherchen, warrant a dishonourable mention. Di Stefano was not the first tenor to squander his talent; he was the first to do so as a victim of modern times, however. The moral of his story is obvious – although it has been ignored by many of his heirs and successors.

Different lessons were ignored when taught by his rival, Mario Del Monaco, a controversial figure, adored and abjured in equal measure. For his unblinking admirers he was the most thrilling *tenore di forza* of the century. For his critics he was a clownish brute, a singer devoid of song and the embodiment of vulgar excess. Neither position is absent evidence. Del Monaco's use and abuse of a "lowered larynx" should not have allowed him to keep singing as he did – and those who have tried to copy him have failed in every case but one.[42] He nonetheless kept the show going for decades, bringing audiences to their feet and colleagues to their knees because he was willing to hold onto notes for longer than necessary or appropriate, and capable of doing so night after night on more than 2,000 occasions over thirty years on stage. His infamous approach to Wagner is a gruesome case in point; another was exemplified in 1972 when he sang "*Esultate*" in Gran Canaria – at the age of 57 – such that he was able to complete "*Dopo l'armi lo vinse l'uragano*" in a single breath-defying, 16-second phrase. That he continued to sing like this into the 1970s was a testament to his Herculean construction of the Melocchi method, which equated for Del Monaco to the inverse of "chugging" – whereby the air was forced from his diaphragm and past his teeth without interruption. His technique was a steam-punk collection of physical and psychological neuroses. Magda Olivero recalled how, when performing *Francesca da Rimini* together at La Scala

> he explained his whole vocal technique to me. When he finished I said, 'My dear Del Monaco, if I had to put into practice all the things you've told me, I'd stop singing right away and just disappear'. The technique was so complicated: you push the larynx down, then you push this up, then you do that – in short, it made my head spin just to hear everything he did. We recorded *Francesca* excerpts together. Francesca has a beautiful phrase, '*Paolo, datemi pace*,' marked '*piano*,' and then Paolo enters with '*Inghirlandata di violette*,' which also should be sung softly, delicately. Instead, Del Monaco was terrible – he bellowed the phrase! When he listened to the playback he exclaimed, 'I can't believe it! After that soft poetic phrase I come in and what do I sound like – a boxer punching with his fists!' He recorded the phrase again, but the second attempt was more or less the same because he was incapable of singing *piano*. He was furious with himself because he wanted to. He tried everything, but his technique would not permit him to sing softly since it totally was based on the muscles.[43]

---

41 Di Stefano sang three performances on 4, 6 and 9 June, 1964.
42 Lando Bartolini. See Chapter 17 below.
43 Nuzzo, Ferruccio (2003). "Mario Del Monaco." *Tenors in Opera*. Opera Magazine Ltd. p.20.

There is a photograph of Del Monaco recording *Otello* with Karajan in Vienna in 1961, in which he can be seen standing approximately a metre and a half from the microphone, having adopted the pose of a fencer lunging at an unseen opponent. His right arm is outstretched, his left is behind his back. His jaw is dropped, his teeth fully exposed and his eyes raised heavenwards. It is the physical expression of concentrated, animalistic effort, as was typical of a man who sang almost everything above the stave with his eyes raised to the ceiling. It is rumoured that Del Monaco's wife egged him on, standing in the wings yelling *"Louder, Mario! Louder!"* but Del Monaco did what he did as a subscriber to the *verismo* tradition, as a specialist in sound and fury. He was authentically southern, and alien to the northern cosmopolitan fantasy of Fellini's *La dolce vita*. He employed an entirely natural vocal range for a native Italian speaker with a Neapolitan father and a mother of Sicilian descent, modelling a "hypertonic prosody" that exacerbated the absence in the Italian language of a phonemic distinction between long and short vowels, while heightening the length of the vowels in stressed open syllables at the end of intonational phrases. This could come across as "barking", but it was entirely consistent with his speaking voice, even though he was born into an affluent, well-positioned family. For anyone wishing to experience the limits of Del Monaco's practical range as a tenor, there is sufficient evidence in his recital recording for Decca of *"La mia letizia infondere"* from *I Lombardi*, with the Orchestre National de l'Opéra de Monte-Carlo, conducted by Nicola Rescigno. Oronte is telling Giselda of his divinely-infused joy, and of how he perceives her as an angel of purity and virtue. In Del Monaco's conception, Oronte might as well be reacting to the onset of gout or hemorrhoids. His phrasing is hard and broken; the tone is delivered in a constant *forte* with an uneven placement; there is no *legato* or a hint of musical intelligence. It is shapeless, angry singing.

Though Del Monaco was not a Verdi tenor, his career was dominated by *Otello*, which he claimed to have performed on more than 400 occasions. The actual number was closer to 220. By the 1970s his approach to the most dramatically challenging of Verdi's roles for tenor was misshapen by his own Quasimodean standards. He would shout, yell, bark, howl, shriek and bellow his way through music that had been designed to characterise complex human states of mind and feeling. Del Monaco's monochromatic approach to his art was to ignore anything but the pitch of a note, and then with no great consistency. He was incapable of *fioriture*, *messa di voce*, *legato*, dynamic colour or a variegated *vibrato*. *Pianissimi* were as Kryptonite. His diction was atrocious; indeed he cared little, if at all, for the work of the librettist. What passed for phrasing was delivered more often than not in splinters and, most remarkably of all, he had a limited extension that in practical terms reached no higher than a B4. Across more than 100 live recordings in current circulation, there is not a single example of him singing a solo high C, although there are five legitimate high Cs when in the company of a soprano. Even in the studio, there are only two *bona fide* solo high Cs (for *"Di quella pira"* in *Trovatore* for Decca, recorded in 1956).[44] Famously, the high

---

44   His *"Che gelida manina"* for Decca in 1952 was manipulated.

Cs from his 1949 performance of *Turandot* with Maria Callas are forged – although the Cs in the studio with Borkh are genuine.[45]

His tone was often sensational, and capable of cracking the plaster in even the largest operas houses. For all the genuine *squillo* ping of his voice during the 1950s and early 60s, its placement was such that the prioritising of volume over texture and line afforded him an emotional range that ran the gamut of A. He was incapable of subtlety or ambiguity, and his blustery approach to his own charisma brought him closer to Donald Wollfit's Lear than to David Suchet's Fool. His approach to love was primordial, and he gave not the slightest hint of a character's nature or evolution. Every role sounded like every other. His Duke of Mantua for Decca's nihilistically cynical *Rigoletto* in 1954 ranks as one of the ugliest, least thoughtful performances of anything, ever; it is as if Otello has wandered drunk into a bourgeois wedding from which he has been banned. The original album cover featured a photograph of the tenor with his chest puffed out, and the names of his "supporting cast" relegated to the status of small print. They were probably in hiding. Bad as his Duke is, it is nothing compared to his *Carmen*, conducted by Thomas Schippers (1963). Decca's producer, John Culshaw, apparently fell to despair when learning that Del Monaco would be singing Don José. The resulting "performance" qualifies as an overt assault on the French language, style and sensibility. It might have been worse. And it was, as an infamous pirate recording of a *Carmen* from the Bolshoi testifies: everyone on stage sings in Russian, except for Del Monaco, who alternates between a brutalist form of French and Bane-like Italian. Judged by these indelibly ghastly performances, he can reasonably be identified as the least musical tenor of the first rank to survive on record.

It is here that the rub lies. Mario Del Monaco was undeniably of the first rank – particularly when compared to the many before and after him who claimed to be *tenori di forza* when they were not. It's accepted that he did not unpack his heart with words; it was the sounds he made that drove audiences to delirium. The truth of Del Monaco as a thug is undeniable, however; there is too much evidence to argue anything else. Naturally, there were exceptions to the rule, sufficient to allow for a kinder assessment of his reputation as a Brass Bull in a china shop. The live recordings of *Andrea Chénier* with Callas (1955); his Enzo for Decca's magnificent *La Gioconda* (conducted thrillingly by Gavazzeni (1957/8), featuring the finest account of the Act 2 duet with Laura on record[46]); his *La Fanciulla del West* with Tebaldi (which boasts atypical expression when he sings "*No Minnie non piangete*"[47]); and his *Otello* for Karajan are among the most impressive performances of the century. Of anything. Callas famously observed that "it's not enough to have a beautiful voice," and if that was true of Callas it was no less true of Del Monaco, who worked his instrument like

---

45 He ducks the *ossia* version of "*No, no Principessa altera*" – as did Di Stefano. Of course, Corelli delighted in taking the high C, and then often with contemptuous ease – both live and in the studio. For those keen to experience stupefaction, his 1958 recording with Previtali is a good starting point.
46 The section beginning "*Laggiu fra le nebbe remote*" has him singing (briefly) in half voice. On the other hand, his "*Cielo e mar*" is classic Del Monaco, featuring an admixture of clumsy and vulgar phrasing, with passing moments of beauty, including a stunning *diminuendo* at the end of the first verse.
47 'No Minnie, don't cry.'

a block of tamahagane steel. Of course, Callas benefitted from piercing insight and intelligence where Del Monaco did not. He relied on weight of tone for expression – an approach that succeeded with a *very* limited number of roles – most obviously Canio and Calàf. His recording of the latter for Decca in 1955, with the incendiary Turandot of Inge Borkh, features unsurpassed vocalising that operates as the sum of its parts, with his steam-hammer voice reaching little further than sound. Ultimately, the only role where Del Monaco's indulgence for amplitude was routinely successful was *Otello*.

The context for that assessment began with the role's creator. Tamagno had many fine contemporaries and successors, including Giovanni De Negri[48] (who came out of retirement to record "*Ora e per sempre addio*" and "*Niun mi tema*," with an alarmingly honky-tonk pianist), Francisco Viñas[49] (who recorded "*Ora e per sempre addio*" in 1907) and Augusto Scampini.[50] Scampini had the greater instrument, and among pre-LP voices he is closest to Del Monaco in delivery – as can be heard from his 1911 recordings of "*Esultate*" and "*Niun mi tema*." Del Monaco's immediate predecessors were the Chilean baritone-turned-tenor Renato Zanelli[51] and Francesco Merli.[52] Zanelli died from cancer at the age of 42; his surviving recordings attest to a large, somewhat burly voice, with less *squillo* than Del Monaco and a more refined sense of line, articulation and diction – memorably so in the Act 1 duet he recorded with Margaret Sheridan. For many, Merli was the finest Italian *Otello* of the century. The live recording of "*Esultate*" from 1939 captures a huge voice of sensational dramatic locution, while the recordings of the Act 1 duet in the studio with Claudia Muzio in 1935 and live from Trieste ten years later with Renata Tebaldi speak to unusually elegiac, lyrical sensibilities.[53] For all his flaws, it is undeniable that Del Monaco's first appearance as *Otello* in 1950 signalled the emergence of something incredible, and both of his studio recordings for Decca have much to recommend them. The second version, from 1961, is sonically overwhelming; Karajan's conducting and the playing of the Wien Philharmoniker are revelatory in their precision and dramatic articulation, and Del Monaco is on his best behaviour throughout. The Austrian conductor's authority was sufficient to compel artistry from the tenor, so that while the love duet is never beautiful, and much of the bleakness of "*Dio! Mi potevi scagliar*"[54] is lost to clamorous bluster, there is more music in this performance than any other by Del Monaco. Of course, he is at his most believable when tearing into "*Ora e per sempre*" and "*Si per ciel*" which is pretty much all his audience could want or hope for.

---

48 30 July, 1851 – 3 April, 1924.
49 27 March, 1863 – 14 July, 1933.
50 1880 – 1939.
51 1 April, 1892 – 25 March, 1935.
52 27 January, 1887 – 12 December, 1976.
53 Recorded in Trieste on 30 December, 1945. The excerpts are poorly recorded, but interesting regardless. Merli was 58 at the time; he sounds considerably younger – attesting to his famously exceptional technique. This performance qualifies as Tebaldi's debut on record – at the age of 23. The performance is important also for its capturing of an orchestral sound that was soon to be killed off. The conductor Edmondo De Vecchi is now little remembered, but the playing of the orchestra is extravagantly lyrical, with wonderfully formed *portamento*.
54 'God, you could reject me.'

Del Monaco was not without rivals in the role. Lesser known singers who can be heard on recordings of complete performances include José Luccioni[55] and Carlos Guichandut.[56] The most widely respected interpreters were Jon Vickers and Ramón Vinay, both of whom brought immense vocal power and charisma as well as art to their interpretations. The American tenor James McCracken[57] recorded the role with Barbirolli for EMI in 1967, with mixed results – in part because of the weak casting, which included Dietrich Fischer-Dieskau impersonating an Italian baritone singing Iago. McCracken's alveolar trilling, some distended emoting, and the sound engineers' atrocious tolerance of the tenor's apparent tendency to wander around the studio mid-scene is at its worst in *"Dio! Mi potevi scagliar"* and *"Niun mi tema."* His performances of these challenging scenes defy repeated listening. McCracken had a powerful if odd voice, which could be most unpleasant when under pressure – inviting one observer to comment of a particularly overwrought performance: "John Wyndham didn't know the half of it." While the thick, chest-heavy texture of his voice conveyed effort as well as drama, he was an extremely fine actor, and persuasive in ways that Del Monaco would not have registered. There were numerous other pretenders to the "big tenor" throne during the 1950s. Galliano Masini,[58] José Soler,[59] Gino Penno,[60] and Bruno Prevedi all had fine voices; each pushed harder than their resources allowed – in Penno's case to a point where he lost his voice completely during an *Il trovatore* at the Met in 1956, prematurely ending his career in America and, soon after, internationally.

The golden age of tenor voices reached further than chandelier-rattling belters. The lighter, more lyrical spectrum was well served by artists with impeccable techniques and instincts – all of whom hit their stride in tandem with the LP during the 1950s, albeit without securing the lifeline of a record contract. Giacinto Prandelli,[61] for example, was a supremely musical singer, as his relatively few recordings of French and Italian repertoire testify; his naturally sweet voice was thin above the stave, however, and coloured during his 30s by a wide *vibrato* that infected his memorably elegant sense of line. The live performance from Naples on 3 July, 1954, of *Traviata* with Tebaldi, conducted by Serafin, evidences each of these characteristics in abundance. Gianni Raimondi[62] is remembered for a beautiful albeit somewhat bland voice. He achieved early success, partnering Callas in 1952 in a revival of Rossini's *Armida*, and again at La Scala for his début in 1956 as Alfredo. He worked often with Visconti (famously as Percy in Donizetti's *Anna Bolena* in 1957) and Zeffirelli (singing Rodolfo opposite Mirella Freni's Mimi in 1963 for the legendary production conducted by Karajan) and throughout his long career he adhered for the most part to high-lying roles, such as Arnoldo in *Tell*, Arturo in *I Puritani*, Fernando in *La favorita*, Edgardo in *Lucia di Lammermoor*, and the Duke in *Rigoletto*. Prandelli still recorded more

---

55 14 October, 1903 – 5 October, 1978.
56 4 November, 1914 – 27 September, 1990.
57 16 December, 1926 – 29 April, 1988.
58 7 February,1896 – 15 February, 1986.
59 22 February, 1904 – 30 August, 1999.
60 8 December, 1920 – 8 February, 1998.
61 8 February, 1914 – 14 June, 2010.
62 17 April, 1923 – 19 October, 2008.

than Carlo del Monte,[63] a Catalan tenor remembered for just two LPs – both of them entirely magnificent.

Del Monte's career is an anomaly. He was born Helenio Barjau Vallmitjana, and enjoyed early successes using that name singing Arturo opposite Callas as Lucia and Di Stefano as Edgardo. Leading roles followed, including celebrated performances as Manrico. He was championed by Victoria de los Ángeles, with whom he recorded a beautifully-voiced and characterful Rinuccio for EMI in 1958, with Tito Gobbi as Gianni Schicchi (conducted by Santini), and an effortless, lachrymose Alfredo in 1959, with Mario Sereni as Germont, conducted by Serafin. After completing the latter recording he lost the use of an eye during surgery, the effect of which damaged his confidence, particularly on stage. His career in Spain was undermined further by his Republican affiliations and sympathies. During the 1960s he fulfilled regular bookings in Europe and Mexico, specialising as the Duke in *Rigoletto*, Hoffmann, Pinkerton, and Rodolfo – none of which he was invited to record. His work in the studio was limited thereafter to Zarzuelas, notably a series of dubbed film soundtracks under Torroba for EMI-Hispavox – most impressively Jacinto Guerrero's *El huésped del sevillano*; Jesús Guridi's *El caserío*, and Amadeo Vives' *Maruxa*. In 1967 Philips engaged him to contribute to an anthology of Zarzuela, conducted with energy and character by Igor Markevich. Del Monte's voice was extremely beautiful, with a light *vibrato* and a rich and consistent tone throughout the range; these qualities are obvious from his exceptional performances of Rinuccio's *"Firenze è come un albero fiorito,"* and Alfredo's *"Lunge da lei… De' miei bollenti spiriti."*

If it is a tragedy that Vallmitjana/Del Monte did not make more recordings of the lyric repertoire, then the same could not be said of Nicolai Gedda,[64] who recorded almost everything. Gedda's career was launched in 1952 by EMI's Walter Legge – just weeks after his debut in April, singing the little-performed and infamously challenging high-tenor role of Chapelou in Adolphe Adam's *Le Postillon de Lonjumeau* at the Stockholm Royal Opera. Legge cast him as Dimitri in EMI's now-legendary Russian-language recording of *Boris Godunóv*, with Boris Christoff singing all three bass roles. Though the orchestra and chorus were French, they were conducted by Issay Dobrowen, a gifted Russian-born Norwegian émigré who had directed the first German performances of Mussorgsky's opera in Dresden in 1922. Like everyone else, Dobrowen hailed Gedda as a sensation, and his performance as Dimitri has not been improved upon. Gedda was a polyglot, fluent in at least seven languages – including Russian. His linguistic talents were a huge value at a time when opera houses and record companies were determined to perform and record operas as written, or conceived, at least. Before the end of his first year as a professional singer he was under contract at La Scala, and chosen by Karajan to record Bach's Mass in B minor. The beauty, ease and expressive range of Gedda's gleaming tenor, joined to an eternally curious mind, compounded an almost immediate reputation for versatility and reliability. His resolute technique and easy *tessitura* equipped him to sing as often in concert and recital as in opera. His even tone and fastidious style also gave him considerable advantages in *lieder*, the intimacy of which had a profound influence on

---

63 25 January, 1923 – 15 September, 2000.
64 Born Harry Gustaf Nikolai Gädda (11 July, 1925 – 8 January, 2017).

his approach to performing opera. His song repertoire extended widely, across composers and languages, much of it preserved in an extensive catalogue of recordings spanning Schubert, Strauss, Poulenc, Tosti, Tchaikovsky and Rachmaninov.

Gedda made his debut at the Paris Opéra in 1954 (as Huon in Weber's *Oberon*), Covent Garden in 1955 (as the Duke in *Rigoletto*), and the Metropolitan on 1 November, 1957 – as Faust, a role for which he became internationally celebrated. His career at the Met was one of the longest – his last performance being given on 11 November, 1983 – and included his creation for Samuel Barber of the role of Anatol for the premiere of *Vanessa* in 1958. He later sang the first Kodana for the premiere of Menotti's *The Last Savage* in 1964. Gedda also performed and recorded an extensive repertoire of lighter music, well beyond the obvious pillars of Offenbach, Johann Strauss and Lehár.

Because he made records from the outset – and then into the 21st century – Gedda learned quickly to work to the best advantage of the recording process. Where Di Stefano and Del Monaco were tolerated by conductors, Gedda's professionalism and cosmopolitan nature were pursued across continents by Karajan (who conducted his debut at La Scala as Don Ottavio in *Don Giovanni* as well as recordings of *Die Fledermaus* and *Madama Butterfly* two years later), Louis de Froment (*Orphée et Eurydice*, 1956), Cluytens (*Faust*, 1954 and 1958; *Les Contes d'Hoffmann*, 1964), Mitropoulos (*Vanessa*, 1958), Matačić (*Die lustige Witwe*, 1962), Krips (*Die Entführung aus dem Serail*, 1966), Prêtre (*Carmen*, 1964, *Werther*, 1968 and *La Damnation de Faust*, 1969), Klemperer (*Die Zauberflöte*, 1964; Bach, B minor Mass; 1967), Schippers (*La bohème*, 1963), Molinari-Pradelli (*Rigoletto*, 1967), Gardelli (*Guillaume Tell*, 1972), Colin Davis (*Benvenuto Cellini*, 1972; *La Damnation de Faust*, 1973), Boult (*The Dream of Gerontius*, 1975), Rostropovich (*Lady MacBeth of Mtsensk*, 1979) and Bernstein (*Candide*, 1991). In May, 2001, he sang the role of Emperor Altoum for Chandos' English-language *Turandot*, and two years later the High Priest in *Idomeneo*, for the same company, again in English. There was almost nothing Gedda didn't sing – excepting *verismo* and Wagner. He performed *Lohengrin* in Stockholm in January, 1966 (a production that survives on record), and he accepted an invitation from Wolfgang Wagner to repeat the role the following year. Scheduling issues prevented him from appearing at Bayreuth, and Gedda thereafter neither sang at the Festpielhaus nor in a Wagner opera – and not for the want of offers. His production-operatic repertoire was otherwise vast, and embraced works by Rameau, Gluck, Mozart, Haydn, Schubert, Weber, Lortzing, Cornelius, Rossini, Bellini, Donizetti, Verdi, Auber, Meyerbeer, Berlioz, Bizet, Offenbach, Gounod, Massenet, Lehár, Liebermann, Puccini, Kálmán, Enesco, Hahn, Debussy, Tchaikovsky, Mussorgsky, Rachmaninov, Prokofiev, Korngold, Pfitzner, Richard Strauss, Stravinsky – and many, many others. In recital and in concert, Gedda's repertoire is yet greater still, with the only omissions forming around his aversion to the Second Viennese School and contemporary music after 1950.

Gedda was tall, attractive and comfortable in his skin. He was the antithesis of many of his bigger-voiced contemporaries in his dedication to his art and the preservation of his voice. His instinctive understanding of style worked across different periods and genres, although his catholic abilities were broader than the timbre of his voice. It was not a "warm" instrument, especially after 1970, and while his performances of romantic French repertoire have been lauded universally, it is also true that he was not a Gallic stylist – at least when compared to the best of his French-born contemporaries. Gedda's good taste made him ubiquitous; it is equally certain that some corners of the operatic canon are at their best when at their most vulgar. It's a difficult path to tread, and an audience's frenzy is provoked commonly by vocal exceptionalism that places technique at the service of expression. During his youth, Gedda's style was clean, precise even. It could also be cold, notably so in Italian opera. This is not to criticise his art in its considered form; it is merely to amplify the cost that has sometimes to be paid by rigour and temperamental discipline. When compared to the best of his peers, Gedda's voice was not intrinsically beautiful, and considering his enormous range of style and sensibility it was inevitable he would fail to be all things to all people. Everyone has their favourite singers, and no one can subscribe to a single artist for everything – assuming that anyone other than Gedda was able to turn to so much so often. Birgit Nilsson recorded Mozart, but no-one seriously believes she was suited to the role of Donna Anna (which she recorded with Leinsdorf in 1959 and Karl Böhm eight years later) any more than Ramón Vinay should have performed Don José in *Carmen,* as he did for Stokowski and Leinsdorf in 1946. When Nilsson closed the Rudolph Bing Gala in 1972, with the final scene from *Salome*, the roar that crowned her performance announced the wonder-struck audience's recognition of one of the greatest voices in history, as well as a unique symmetry between the singer and the sung. At a time when Björling, Corelli, Del Monaco and Di Stefano were exceeding the boundaries of taste and technique, Gedda's pillars of wisdom refreshed palates sullied by vocalism that placed the composer hierarchically at the mercy of the singer – a polarity that Gedda was known to despise. It was for this reason that many wanted Gedda to sing *Werther* at the Met, rather than Corelli – who was unlikely to think of Massenet, Goethe or the sorrows of his character before his own.

Dispositional priorities determined a creative environment in which singers, conductors, producers, directors, designers, costumiers and administrators had to wrestle with artistic decisions such that a performance might exceed normative expectations only when first having placed them under strain. If a software programme were to "sing" the majority of opera as written, then the resulting "performances" would adhere strictly to the written meter, without *rubato, portamento,* shaped phrasing, inflection or vocalisation – in other words, *senza espressione.* Unsurprisingly, therefore, the difference between a performance defined by its "good" taste and one said to be definitively "bad" can occupy the same space as the extraordinary and the exceptional. The conspicuous divergence between authorial intention and performed reality operates to free an artist to express themselves as well as the composer and the librettist. This can produce the aesthetically aberrant and the absurd – typified across the tenorial canon by the repeating of arias at the behest of an audience yelling "*bis*"[65] or the indulging of a fifteen-minute ovation mid-scene.[66] Thomas Nagel characterised

---

65 Classic exemplars include Corelli repeating "*Nessun dorma,*" and Franco Bonisolli repeating "*Di quella pira.*" The latter would also add high Cs to "*No, no Principessa altera*" in *Turandot.*
66 Domingo's performance of the "Improvviso" in *Andrea Chénier* in 1981 at the Wiener Staatsoper is an obvious case in point.

the absurd as "a conspicuous discrepancy between pretention or aspiration and reality,"[67] a perceptual conflict that admits endless backflips in which aural and visual sensation can tolerate extreme abuses of prevailing taste. A non-operatic example would be the embrace of distended "Gypsy-Hungarian" practices for Monti's *Czardas* that would be tolerable for a performance of Brahms' Hungarian Dance No.5, but not for the same composer's Concerto for Violin.[68] The context of appreciation is changed where the "high" artistic principles attached to one work are allowed to slip for another – if only by concession. Nicolai Gedda's unimpeachable judgment when set against the self-aggrandisements of some of his contemporaries distinguish by this analogy between a performance of almost anything by Ivry Gitlis and the work of Sarah Chang. It is for the audience to decide which they prefer; it is for the performers to determine which approach best serves them and the music.

The production of what is sometimes referred to as "bad art" allows for the absurd and the bizarre to become normative, which explains in part the success of tenors who recoiled from objective or faithful recreations of a score as written. Those grubby and imperfect features that define the human in all art are amplified by the context of appreciation, just as Marcel Duchamp's *Fountain* provoked outrage for how it was "made" and where it was shown. Opera is littered with works of limited artistic virtue that have profound aesthetic value – commonly so across the *bel canto* and *verismo* repertoires – to which end the opportunity for display and coquetry is analogous to a peacock fanning itself without risking its delivery to the dining table. Nicolai Gedda did not treat the stage as a runway; he existed outside the abnormative matrix of bad taste and absurdity. There is no doubt that his refinement of mind and voice was counterintuitive to the form and purpose of much of his repertoire, and if beauty is eternally subjective then so too is discretion. Though many who frequent the Opera adhere outwardly to the parameters of discernment, most yearn secretly for the tenor to sustain the high C at the end of "*Di quella pira*" or the crowning B of "*Nessun dorma.*"

Resolving these issues is challenging because of the significant disconnect between the absurdity of content and performance. Verdi's hunchback sings some of the most beautiful music written for a baritone; the character "I" in Schnittke's *Life with an Idiot* does not. *Le Grand Macabre* articulates in extreme sonic modes the excesses being portrayed on stage, with Ligeti cutting his cloth to Michael Meschke's model. Strauss' famous observation that his scores for *Salome* and *Elektra* were "well-suited" to their subject matter was typically evasive and disingenuous, and yet in 1907 a correspondent wrote to the New York *Times* denouncing *Salome* as a "detailed and explicit exposition of the most horrible, disgusting, revolting, and unmentionable features of degeneracy… that I have ever heard of, read of, or imagined." The music's lyricism was buried beneath degeneracy, which presumably caused the same critic to recoil from the Isenheim Altarpiece and Velasquez's *Pinturas Negras* but not, conversely, Caravaggio's far-more disturbing *Death of the Virgin*. Something similar has

---

67 Nagel, Thomas (1979). "The Absurd." *Mortal Questions*. Cambridge University Press. p.13.
68 There are good arguments to suggest that this is mistaken. Would Stéphane Grappelli have played Brahms' music as he wanted to hear it (as opposed, for example, to the manner of Yehudi Menuhin *et al*)? Probably.

always been written about the temporarily shocking; the same can be observed of singing when there is a perceived superabundance of character and identity. Can Del Monaco be accused of lacking character? Probably not. Can it be said of many of the tenors to have thrived during the golden age of the 1950s and 60s? It certainly can.

Another tenor for whom categorisation was an eternal issue was Gedda's contemporary at the New York Metropolitan for 17 years, Richard Tucker.[69] Tucker made his Met debut on 25 January, 1945; he was a contemporary also of Giovanni Martinelli (who gave his last performance at the Met on 24 March, 1946) and Luciano Pavarotti, (who gave his first performance on 23 November, 1968). Among leading tenors at the Met, Tucker gave the greatest number of performances (738) with the exception of Caruso (863) and Martinelli (926).[70] He sang for the last time at the Met on 3 December, 1974 – when he succumbed to a heart attack while resting in his dressing room, before a concert with Robert Merrill in Kalamazoo, Michigan. He was 61 years old. On 11 January, 1975 the New York *Times* reported:

> The funeral for the 60-year-old[71] tenor who died of a heart attack Wednesday in Kalamazoo, Mich., marked the first time in the 90-year history of the Metropolitan Opera that a funeral for a singer was held in the opera house itself. The honour has only been accorded to two ether persons associated with the Metropolitan, both of them general managers. They were Leopold Damrosch… and Heinrich Conried, the general manager who brought Enrico Caruso to the Metropolitan and who died 1908… His coffin was placed in the middle of an almost bare stage, where he had been scheduled to sing "Cavalleria Rusticana" last night. It would have been his 504th performance in New York.[72] The coffin was flanked by huge bouquets of chrysanthemums in the autumnal colours of brown and gold, and on the left of the stage six ballroom chairs from the first act of "La Traviata" were set up, for the participants in the ceremony. The orchestra was taken up by practically every member of the opera company and by such figures in government and the arts as former Mayor John V. Lindsay and his wife and Sir Rudolf Bing, former general manager of the Met. A few minutes after 10 AM., a hush fell upon the house and Mr. Tucker's widow, Sara, dressed in black with a black veil on her head, was led in, weeping. She was escorted by her three sons, Barry, David and Henry. Rabbi Mordecai Waxman of Temple Israel in Great Neck [Long Island], where Mr. Tucker worshipped, read from Isaiah, and Cantor Benjamin Siegel intoned the Psalms.[73]

---

69   28 August, 1913 – 8 January, 1975.
70   Completists will want to note that the singer to have appeared most often at the Met was also a tenor. Charles Anthony performed 2,928 times on the stage of *both* Met Houses, between 6 March, 1954, and 28 January, 2010. It should be noted also that if Plácido Domingo's work as a conductor is added to his work as a singer, then Domingo is third on the list, with 706 appearances on the stage and 169 from the pit.
71   He was 61.
72   Also wrong.
73   New York *Times*, 11 January, 1975.

Among the guests were Robert Merrill, Roberta Peters, Anna Moffo, Risë Stevens, Licia Albanese, Leontyne Price, Eleanor Steber, Jerome Hines, Kurt Baum, Cyril Ritchard, Wilfred Pelletier, Maria Jeritza and Franco Corelli. Tucker was loved by colleagues and audiences alike, and he remains a national treasure in the United States. There are good reasons for this. He was an unusually decent and uncomplicated man, particularly for an opera singer. Like Gedda, he cared for the art and its audience – priorities that were obvious from his commitment in rehearsals as well as during performances. He was also an all-American star, adhering throughout his career to the United States, and the Met in particular. Of the more than 130 available recordings of Tucker performing in complete or excerpted operas (the majority of which are live), only three are of performances at La Scala; two of those are "studio" recordings for EMI.[74] There is a single recording of Tucker in a complete role in London – *La Juive* at the Royal Festival Hall on 4 March, 1973. Even though Tucker travelled, his career as a pre-eminent Franco-Italian tenor during the 1950s and 60s was as American as biscuits and gravy. Or, rather, a salt beef sandwich from *Katz's* on East Houston Street. Tucker was Jewish and defined to a great extent by his pride in his ancestral culture and religion. He did a huge amount for Jewish causes – contributing directly to the cantorial tradition, which he served in the Synagogue and on record. His operatic work was influenced by the *Hazzunah* but his singing was otherwise wholly secular. It is for this reason revealing of the American tenor tradition immediately after World War Two.

Tucker's only real teacher was Paul Althouse,[75] a gifted tenor-contemporary of Caruso's, whose 30-year career was the first of note for an American tenor without European training or experience. Althouse was initially a lyric tenor who retrained as a *heldentenor* after visiting Bayreuth in 1925. That transition was never fully realised. He was a musical singer, as his recording as Waldemar for Stokowski of Schoenberg's *Gurre-lieder* in 1932 evidences, but he was not a true heroic tenor because his tone lacked the weight necessary to achieve the Wagner-sound for which he yearned. A similar discrepancy marked Tucker's emergence as a *spinto* tenor when he made his debut at the Met as Enzo Grimaldo in *La Gioconda* with Emil Cooper conducting. It's debatable that Tucker should have been singing such heavy-weight repertoire so early in his career, particularly noting the essential lightness of his voice as it was recorded in 1941. In 1945 the sweetness of his timbre survives on a broadcast recording from 29 July of the "Westinghouse Radio Show." He is introduced as "the sensational new Metropolitan opera tenor," and he sings a mix of popular and operatic material. The standout is a performance of "*La fleur que tu m'avais jetée*" from *Carmen*, which resonates with virility and style. There is no gesturing and, even with the least amount of *portamento*, his *cantabile* is extremely beautiful. It is the voice of a virile lyric tenor.

His first decade at the Met bound him to a number of resolutely 19th century conductors, notably Emil Cooper, Fritz Reiner, Giuseppe Antonicelli, Fritz Stiedry, and Arturo Toscanini – who cast him in 1949 as Radamès for a televised concert performance of *Aida*. The approval of a conductor known to Verdi in a role for which

---

74 *La forza del destino* (1954), conducted by Tullio Serafin, with Maria Callas as Leonora; and *Aida* (1955), again with Serafin and Callas. The live recording from May, 1969 (of excerpts only) is of *Luisa Miller*, conducted by Francesco Molinari-Pradelli.

75 2 December, 1889 – 6 February, 1954.

he was vocally ill-equipped was contrary to the best interests of Tucker's naturally lyric instrument, and despite one or two anomalies (*Zauberflöte* and *Così fan tutte* for Stiedry in 1951 and 1954) his repertoire after 1950 placed him in direct competition with Del Monaco and Corelli, interchanging between *Il trovatore*, *Don Carlo*, *Simon Boccanegra*, *Un ballo in maschera*, *La forza del destino*, *Don Carlos*, *La Gioconda*, *Cavalleria Rusticana*, *Pagliacci*, *Manon Lescaut*, *La bohème*, *Tosca*, *La fanciulla del west* and *Andrea Chénier*.

His voice was bright in tone, and *spinto* only with a push, a necessary investment on Tucker's part that resulted in a certain stiffness vocally, such that his naturally warm and round tone was disabled over time by tightness. In 1957 he made an unusual and probably unexpected recording called *The Art of Bel Canto*. The collection of songs was period appropriate; it was also left-field and little-known at the time. The accompaniments were arranged by Thomas Z. Shepard for the Columbia Chamber Ensemble, and they add in their incongruity to the curious atmosphere. The diminished scale of the enterprise allowed Tucker to relax, vocally and in himself, and the results are exceptionally pleasing – particularly noting his predilection after 1955 for monochromatic belting and an Italianate affectation that saw him adding linguistic and prosodic tics that played no part either in his education or his culture.

The effect is analogous to the distinction between "Original Pronunciation" and "Received Pronunciation" for those studying and performing the works of Shakespeare. The latter is as it was spoken by Olivier and Burton; the former is as it is believed to have been spoken by Richard Burbage, Will Kempe, Henry Condell and all the King's Men. It's not simply a question of accent – although that is a consideration. Rather, the idiosyncrasy is formed of a host of linguistic emphases and effects that arise from the language as it is written. Shakespeare's Sonnet "Let me not to the marriage of true minds" ends with the lines:

> Within his bending sickle's compass come;
> Love alters not with his brief hours and weeks,
> But bears it out even to the edge of doom.
> If this be error and upon me prov'd,
> I never writ, nor no man ever lov'd.

At its simplest, the tail rhymes "*come*" and "*doom,*" and "*prov'd*" and "*lov'd*" can function as cadences only if they are forced into equivalence. It's clear they *did* rhyme for Shakespeare, but RP has rendered OP an affectation – with the couplets failing as verse when spoken in a modern voice. What advantage, other than rhyming circuitry, does OP provide an actor used to speaking in RP? Is the actor's talent changed for the better by their pronunciation of the words, save that their meaning is changed? These questions were particularly relevant for immigrant communities in the United States, grimly so during the 1950s. Like many other non-European tenors, Tucker subscribed to Italian-language vocalisation by way of impersonation. He was an American tenor singing Italian opera "like an Italian" while not speaking the language. In 1955, for example, he recorded the role of Alvaro in *La forza del destino* for EMI – with Callas[76] and Tagliabue, conducted by Serafin. He colours his far-from-perfect pronunciation

---

76   Tucker made his debut in Verona with Callas.

using Italianate enunciation, with liberal alveolar trilling, some light sobbing and a palette of emphasis that was *veramente Italiano* only at a distance. It is the operatic equivalent of Marius Goring's[77] Conductor 71 in Powell and Pressburger's *A Matter of Life and Death*. There's nothing wrong with that, in and of itself, but Tucker's experience as a non-European tenor singing European music set a marker for the post-war shift in identity politics, wherein voices functioned metaphorically as well as acoustically. The recalibration of vocal identity as cultural appropriation is an evolving and problematic arena of discourse. The "right" of one to use the voice of another has been exploited over centuries to facilitate the silencing of the other. Tucker had little option but to impersonate "an Italian tenor," annexing as an American a school of vocalism with which he was unacquainted in its spoken and written forms. His approach to Verdi and *verismo* was inauthentic, therefore; it had by necessity to reach further than the sound and articulation of the phonemes he was singing. Of course, it would be absurd to blame Tucker for having been born in Brooklyn (accepting that many continue to damn Dick Van Dyck for not playing Bert in *Mary Poppins* as a "true" Londoner), and yet Tucker's singing could never be anything more than Italianate, as a façade for the pretence of "authentic" expression.

If Tucker's burden has been shared by many, across languages and cultures, it was unusually problematic for tenors required (and expected) to live up to the RP of Italian opera post-*verismo*, rather than adhering to what can be known and heard from early recordings of the OP employed by the singers who created much of it. This is an anomaly best explained by the technology of recording. Like every other singer considered in this chapter, Tucker was raised on Caruso's '78s; unlike Di Stefano, Del Monaco and Corelli however, his introduction to the phonology and cadence of the Italian language was through song rather than speech. Indeed, his nascent linguistic experiences were limited to Yiddish, Hebrew and English, a plurality of obvious value characterised more by consonants than by vowels. Ultimately, the commonalities of Italian opera and the Italian language are indivisible in matters of style and technique. Having been introduced to Italian music drama through recordings, Tucker's approach to performance wanted for linguistic and cultural context. Meaning was sublimated to the purely musical principles of tone and line, with expression formed of effect and emphasis. He was required in consequence to assimilate as an outsider by imitating foreigners – a paradox of belonging that owes more to the *American Dream* of Salvador Dalí than Norman Rockwell. Though Tucker was among the most popular and beloved American singers of the 20th century, he stood alike in dignity with Del Monaco, Corelli, Gedda, Di Stefano, and Björling in his prompting of extremes of devotion, apathy and enmity. They still do. Opera singers die; their claques do not. Critical and popular opinion was united for only one Italian-repertoire tenor to emerge during the 1950s.

Carlo Bergonzi[78] was unusual in his hallowed status, being recognised by conductors as well as colleagues, audiences and critics. His only professional misstep was to remain too long on the stage, ending his career in 2000, ten years too late, with

---

77 Contrary to presumption, Goring was British, having been born and raised on the Isle of Wight – although he made a habit of playing French and German characters on stage as well as film and television.
78 13 July, 1924 – 25 July, 2014.

an ill-fated concert performance at Carnegie Hall of *Otello*, just two months before his 76th birthday.[79] He began his career, as a baritone, in 1948 – singing Rossini's Figaro in a monastery with a "single-strings" band for a fee of 2,000 lire, insufficient at the time to cover his food and travel expenses. He went on to sing a wide range of baritone repertoire until deciding to retrain as a tenor. He made his second debut in 1951, as Andrea Chénier at the Teatro Petruzzelli in Bari. It was fortunate for Bergonzi that 1951 was also the 50th anniversary of Verdi's death; within weeks he was cast by Carlo Maria Giulini as Jacopo in Verdi's *I Due Foscari* for a broadcast performance by RAI. He also performed at a stellar commemorative concert at the Colosseum in Rome, and further broadcast performances of *Giovanna d'Arco* and *Simon Boccanegra*.

Two years later Bergonzi debuted at La Scala and on 13 November, 1956, he gave the first of 324 performances at the Met, as Radamès.[80] By 1958, conductors and intendants were fighting over his diary. Record companies were also beating a path to his door. Having realised that Del Monaco was unsuited to large swathes of the mainstream repertoire, Decca booked Bergonzi to record an album of arias with Gavazzeni that remains one of the two or three most perfect by a tenor in stereo. One of its marvels is the performance of "*La vita... O tu che seno agli angeli*" from Act 3 of *La forza del destino*. The score directs the recitative to be sung "*tristemente, ma con forza*,"[81] which admits a range of colour and tone that reaches far beyond mere melancholy. Of course, the aria begins in low dudgeon, with Alvaro confessing his bitter, despairing philosophy ("*La vita è inferno all'infelice. Invano morte desio!*"). Bergonzi's phrasing of these words would sustain a seminar on the art of singing, passing as it does from rage to grief in just five bars of music. When Alvaro remembers the struggle of his ancestors against tyranny ("*Della natal sua terra il padre volle*"[82]), Bergonzi adheres to the score's direction "*con semplicità*"[83] while respecting the carefully weighted scansion so that when articulating in angry defiance ("*I miei parenti Sognaro un trono*"[84]) he does so by increment, enhancing the tension in his voice by the quickening of *vibrato*, the opening of tone and the dragging of *portamento*. It is a calculated act of service to the composer and the poet.

The aria itself is famously challenging. Bergonzi takes the horrid rising leap in the first bar from C to A flat without difficulty, covering and then opening the tone wonderfully for "*angeli*." His genius is fully realised during the first of the long rising phrases for which the aria is celebrated, beginning with "*Non iscordar di volgere*."[85] His breathing here, and the richness and ease of vocal tone, are astonishing. Bergonzi's formidable technique allows him to take his time, while conserving his amplitude for

---

79 With the Opera Orchestra of New York conducted by Eve Queler. Among the audience was Luciano Pavarotti, Plácido Domingo, José Carreras, Sherrill Milnes, Licia Albanese and Anna Moffo. The performance was a disaster from the start, and he withdrew before the start of Act 3.
80 His Met career ended with a concert performance on 27 April, 1996 – 7 months before his 40th House anniversary.
81 'Sadly, but powerfully.'
82 'From his native land the father wanted.'
83 'With simplicity.'
84 'My parents dreamed of a throne.'
85 'Don't forget to turn.'

"*Che senza nome ed esule.*"[86] The following phrase takes the tenor through "*Chiedo anelando, Ahi, misero*"[87] which he shapes with balletic control and style, so that the entire five-bar phrase unfolds as an uninterrupted stream of consciousness, even with Bergonzi snatching the lightest of breaths. The span written into the music materialises with power and elegance, without the line suffering imposition; a similar expressive logic colours the "*Pieta*" section of the aria, with Bergonzi employing the most seductive, linear *portamento* of any tenor on record. For the final phrase-repetition "*Leonora mia, Pietà,*"[88] he approaches the final B flat 4 (the only one to be marked *tenuto*) in a seamless phrase in which he manages to isolate yet more tone, the thrill of which is judged perfectly to allow the ensuing (and marked) *morendo* its full effect. The aria's concluding A flat 4 is delivered again with a measured increase of tone, with a trademark quickening of the *vibrato* in its tail that would send shivers down the spine of a mannequin. In short, Bergonzi sings the aria as it is written – amplified by vast resources of imagination, expression and *chiaroscuro* that raise the already wonderful to something close to miraculous. It is the measure of how best to sing this music.

Also in 1958, Decca paired Bergonzi with Tebaldi and Serafin for recordings of *La bohème* and *Madama Butterfly*. Everyone will have their favourites; it's easy nonetheless to reason objectively that these recordings are unrivalled. For a start, it's not a one-man show – Bergonzi's colleagues are the pick of the finest singers on Earth at the time, with Tebaldi as Mimì, Gianna D'Angelo as Musetta, Bastianini as Marcello, Cesare Siepi as Colline, Renato Cesari as Schaunard, Fernando Corena as Benoît and Alcindoro, and Piero de Palma as Parpignol. The recording's collegium is obvious from the first scene, which announces a performance rather than mere assembly. The recording's character is coloured by Decca's distinctive early stereo and Serafin's peerless attention to orchestral colour and detail, a value to which the entirely Italian cast subscribes by instinct. That's not nationalist cant; it's a simple recognition that the ensemble is speaking as well as singing its own language. The performance is striking also for the cohesion of vocal timbre, which can be reduced to the simplistic rubric of "big." There are no thin or reaching voices here; indeed, the panoramic richness might be thought too much for characters supposedly starving and cold; those seeking ascetism or verisimilitude should look elsewhere. Bergonzi's part in the production is akin to perfection. The voice is a hearth of warmth and colour, beautifully managed so that he produces not a single ugly or imprudent sound; the extension is fluid, with little or no *passaggio*, and his enunciation is evocative and lucid, amplified as it is by his variegated *vibrato*, which oscillates in texture, animation and emphasis depending entirely on word use, phrase structure and melodic shape. His expressive *portamento* and diction facilitate a genuinely elastic *rubato*. Every word is joined to the music, a quality that feeds Bergonzi's sumptuous *cantabile*. It is here, in his phrasing, that the tenor's accomplishment is nothing short of wondrous. Indeed, it's easy to conclude mid-performance that Bergonzi's art as a tenor is the most comprehensive since the invention of recording.

---

86   'Who, nameless and exiled.'
87   'I ask in longing, Ah! Misery.'
88   'My Leonora, pity….'

The same can be said of his Pinkerton. His characterisation is everything that Puccini hoped for when writing the role – to which end it's the closest comparator in stereo to what can be heard on '78s of Caruso; the warmth and amplitude are plainly analogous; so too is the vitality of the phonation and the elegance of the phrasing – which is fluid, articulate and dramatically coherent. The Act 2 duet has never been sung more beautifully – and certainly not by Bergonzi, when he re-recorded the opera for EMI in 1966 with Barbirolli and Renata Scotto. It is the only performance that persuades absolutely that the couple might actually share in each other's feelings, even if only for that one *"dolce note, tutto estatico d'amor."*[89]

Thanks to his early training, Bergonzi's first two complete studio recordings evidence a voice that is perennially burnished and easy; there is no hint of strain or effort. He is able to speak through song. Even when engaging in *messa di voce* and extremes of dynamic shading, the beauty of the tone allows for the music to rise above its singer, which is pivotal to isolating the wonder of Bergonzi's unique talent. His high Cs do not resonate as did Pavarotti's, and some miss that *squillo* ping; his voice still rang magnificently above the stave and it did so without the tone over-reaching the moment or the character and its context. For all the awe-inspiring beauty of the voice, Bergonzi sings the roles of Rodolfo and Pinkerton as Puccini wrote them, with neither vanity nor self-promotion. They are definitive in their objectification of eloquence and authenticity.

When these immortal recordings were released, Serafin was 80 years old. He continued to work on stage and in the studio (later conducting Bergonzi in *Il trovatore* for DG) with Decca managing the interests and ambitions of younger conductors keen to make legacy recordings in stereo. Between 1959 and 1966 Bergonzi made endlessly imaginative contributions to a series of flawless productions, beginning with Karajan's incandescent *Aida*, featuring Tebaldi in the title role, Simionato as Amneris and Cornell MacNeil as Amonasro. Bergonzi was in sensational, aristocratic form as Radamès – although he did not do for Karajan what he did for Solti and Schippers at the Met in 1963 and 1968 when singing *"Se quel guerrier… Celeste Aida"*.[90] Bergonzi's effortless juxtaposition of masculinity and introversion, and his spinning of the purest of *bel canto* threads, culminates in a *morendo pianissimo* on the concluding B flat of the final line *"un trono vicino al sol"*[91] that was, for want of a better word, impossible. The vast majority of tenors sing the whole aria, far less its final note, *forte*, or thereabouts – including Björling, Di Stefano, Del Monaco and Tucker. Corelli was alone among Bergonzi's contemporaries in being able to shade the line as the composer intended. Bergonzi was also able to produce the necessary *spinto* fireworks during Act 3's *"Tu, Amonasro! Tu! il Re?"*[92] to match the hair-raising brass and timpani of the Wien Philharmoniker, and throughout *"O terra addio"*[93] his extraordinary breath management allowed him to salvage lines sacrificed by most to over-singing. His isolation of interior feeling and poetic expression are unaffected

---

89 'Lovely night, in an ecstasy of love.'
90 'If only I were that warrior… Heavenly Aida!'
91 'A throne near the sun.'
92 'You Amonasro! You, the King!'
93 'Goodbye world.'

by histrionics and cheap theatre, so that he was able to bring a different tonal and emotional emphasis to every word and phrase.

For all the magnificent vocalism, and that from the entire cast, it is Karajan's show – sonically and orchestrally; there was a similar sense of authority emerging from the podium in 1961 when Solti conducted Bergonzi as Riccardo in *Un ballo in Maschera*, with Nilsson as Amelia. It's another unique performance, fascinating in its diversity and complexity – the culmination of which in Act 3 begins with the recitative "*Forse la soglia attinse,*"[94] in which Bergonzi teases out each of the character's passing contradictions when yielding ("*Senza un addio, l'immenso Oceàn ne separi*"[95]) to dejection ("*e taccia il core*"[96]) and despair ("*Ma se m'è forza perderti*"[97]). Bergonzi's artful introspection gives way to one of the most thrilling episodes in the opera, when Riccardo hears the ball-room music and is presented by Oscar with a letter from "*Ignota donna.*"[98] He sings:

"*Sì, rivederti, Amelia, E nella tua beltà,
Anco una volta l'anima D'amor mi brillerà.*"[99]

There is more expression in Bergonzi's performance of this brief episode than in the entire careers of some tenors; the range of texture, shape, colour and nuance is awe-inspiring in its technical skill and dramatic effect. This *lieder*-like attention to detail, joined to Bergonzi's sun-lit tone, characterised his recording as Alfredo for Sir John Pritchard and as Manrico for Serafin in 1962. Heretical though it might be for many, Bergonzi's Manrico is the finest on record – even when compared to that of Corelli, whose voice was near impossible to record. He does not have the bull-fighting ring of Corelli, but he's not far off – and Bergonzi finds more of the character in music that is more often performed in a permanent *forte*. Bergonzi's infinite artistry does not mean he has to compromise for "*Di quella pira,*" which is hammered out in key, and with roof-raising C5s.

1965 was an especially remarkable year for Bergonzi. He recorded a sumptuous *Cavalleria rusticana* with Karajan (DG), a startling *Don Carlos* for Georg Solti (Decca), and an exquisite *Lucia di Lammermoor* with Prêtre (RCA). The latter is especially significant because it captures a genuine *spinto* bari-tenor with the requisite warmth of tone, power and range (to an E flat 5 in duet with Anna Moffo) to warrant reference to Duprez, Nourrit and Donzelli. The force of nature released for "*Qui, di sposa eterna fede*"[100] and "*Io di te memoria viva*"[101] consecrate the tenor's unique and innate feeling for line on the breath, with each phrase delivered with an unshakeable sense of propriety, if not also inevitability. His *annus mirabilis* continued with a searing *Luisa Miller* for Cleva (RCA), and a re-drawn, multi-dimensional *Pagliacci* for

---

94 'Perhaps she has reached home.'
95 'Let the great ocean divide us, with no farewell.'
96 'And keep your heart silent.'
97 'But if I must lose you.'
98 'An unknown lady.'
99 'Yes, to see you again, Amelia. As I look upon your beauty, once again my heart will burn with love.'
100 'But that vow is not broken.'
101 'I remember you alive.'

Karajan (DG). Between 1966 and 1967, he re-recorded *Un ballo in maschera* with Leinsdorf (RCA), *Ernani* with Schippers (RCA), *La Gioconda* with Gardelli (Decca) and another *Traviata*, this time with Prêtre (RCA).

Noting all of these achievements, and considering that he was not yet a decade into his career in the studio, Bergonzi's work as a recording artist was essentially over at the end of 1967. Between 1969 and 1988 he recorded just six compete operas, none of them comparable in quality to their predecessors.[102] He recorded additionally all of the tenor arias from Verdi's operas for Philips, too late for an over-worked voice and an under-exercised body. The project was successful musically; like most other retrospectives, however, it was an exhausting and largely meaningless endeavour that suffered from an absence of context and purpose, and served to highlight as many flaws as it did strengths. Bergonzi continued to perform into his late 70s, and there are more than 100 live recordings to evidence the compromised value of his longevity as the most musical tenor of the 20th century.

The 1950s and 60s represented a renaissance of operatic performance around the world. The near total collapse in contemporary operatic composition was aggravated by the coalescence of forces spanning the rise to dominance of musicals and cinema, the crowning of über-conductors, the emergence of the LP and the gilding of stage directors and producers. It was an age that transformed opera as a largely re-creative art form, with gods and demigods on both sides of the Atlantic atoning for the death of originality. The part played by well-funded record companies was controversial at the time, particularly with sound engineers re-imagining the theatrical experience for audiences never likely to identify their deceit first-hand. Posterity is nonetheless indebted to the label-directors who recognised the artistic and commercial opportunity of long playing records in stereo. The resulting catalogue of wonders preserved some of history's most precious voices at a time when there was more money to be made from popular songs on three-minute '45s with comparably fleeting shelf-lives. The performers and performances saved on the hundreds of complete opera recordings produced during these halcyon decades did not fade into obsolescence, as many feared they might. But if the Age of Kronos survived its passing, then the age of Zeus would burn more brightly and end more decisively.

---

[102] *La forza del destino* with Gardelli (1969, EMI), *Lucia di Lammermoor* with Schippers (1969, EMI), *Attila* with Gardelli (1972, Philips), *I masnadieri* with Gardelli (1975, Philips), *Oberto* with Gardelli (1983, Orfeo), *Adriana Lecouvreur* with Bonynge (1988, Decca).

Chapter Fourteen

The Poisoned Chalice

Anyone interested in Wagner has their favourite *heldentenor*. Anyone loathing Wagner knows what a *heldentenor* is supposed to sound like. Even those who have never heard an opera by Wagner are likely to recognise Mel Blanc as Elmer Fudd in *What's Opera Doc*, Warner Bros.' glorious cartoon from 1957, in which Fudd's hapless Siegfried pursues Bugs Bunny as Brunnhilde through a visually spectacular parody of Wagnerian clichés. Chuck Jones later claimed to have taken "the 'Ring of the Nibelungen' music and crushed it down to six minutes." Neither assertion was accurate. The cartoon lasts seven minutes and there are only two quotations from the *Ring*: the "Ride of the Valkyries" from *Die Walküre* (to which Elmer sings the words "*Kill da wabbit!*") and the horn call from *Siegfried*, used for the line "*O mighty warrior of great fighting stock – what's up doc?*". For the rest of the cartoon's score, the composer Milt Franklyn stole from *Der Fliegende Holländer* (for the opening storm scene, in which Elmer-Siegfried warns the audience to "*be vewwy quiet*" because he is "*hunting wabbits!*"); the Overture from *Rienzi* (to accompany Elmer chasing Bugs); and *Tannhäuser*'s Overture, "Pilgrims' Chorus" (for "*O Bwünnhilde, you'w so wuvwy*" and "*Return my wuv*"), and "Bacchanal," (for Elmer and Bugs' ballet and closing scene).

The cartoon's introduction sees Siegfried conform in shadow puppetry to the caricature of the Wagnerian hero as it was perceived by the mostly Jewish-immigrant designers, artists, musicians and performers whose culture and people had only recently been targeted for mass extermination. If Elmer's shadow form is vast and muscular, then his power over the elements brings him closer to Wotan (or Thor, in our Marvellist times) than to Siegfried. The absurd use of his "spear and magic helmet" to demonstrate his powers befits what would turn out to be Elmer's final cartoon appearance, one in which he gets the rabbit only to regret doing so.[1] Bugs' final line – "So what did you expect in an opera? A happy ending?" – is misplaced for a parody of Wagner's music dramas, most of which do, indeed, end "happily."

Chuck Jones' high-thinking cartoon is the best-known Wagnerian narrative-satire[2] – a genre surprisingly thin on the ground.[3] More esoteric is Thomas Mann's *Wälsungenblut*,[4] a disturbing take on *Walküre*'s incestuous sibling relationship (with characters named Sieglinde and Siegfried) that tears at the then-contemporary rise

---

1 And for only the third time in his film career.
2 Distinguishing satires after the fashion of Anna Russell's stand-up/take-down of the *Ring der Nibelungen*.
3 See generally *The Cambridge Companion to Wagner's Der Ring des Nibelungen* (2013). Eds. Mark Berry and Nicholas Vazsonyi. Cambridge University Press. pp.325–329.
4 'Blood of the Walsungs,' a novella written in 1905 and published in 1921.

in Jewish self-hatred. Mann's normalisation of the Wälsungs' heroic qualities as "merely" abnormal was adopted by Anthony Burgess when writing his public-school Nibelungen novel *The Worm and the Ring*, in which a fantasy-revealing diary functions as the stolen treasure. More recently, Elfrede Jelinek did something similar with *Rein Gold*.[5]

The reduction of the hierarchy of gods, heroes and dwarves to bourgeois, socially-recognisable commonalities did not, of course, level the playing field for those purely musical elements that make Wagner's mature works as difficult for performers as for audiences. It's possible for Wagner's dramas to be relatable as narratives, but it's impossible to do the same for his music. The mature scores are definitively monstrous, compelling vast resources and near-impossible feats of endurance from singers who have, by definition, to meet Olympian entry-requirements.

Readers with established prejudices will be able to name at least one of their preferred *heldentenors* from live performances and recordings. Some will be able to name a dozen; others more than fifty. Certain of these favoured artists will tick multiple boxes – depending on the role. A perfect Wagnerite given to honest reflection will accept that few have ticked *all* of the boxes spanning a *heldentenor's* hierarchy of needs. The number to have done so with the passing of the decades is accepted universally to have been in decline since before the emergence of the LP. Now that the recording of opera as a cultural epoch has come to an end, there is a limited opportunity for isolating the finest *heldentenor* of the modern age without having to compromise the metrics for analysis. In other words, Vilhelm Herold,[6] Erik Schmedes, Leo Slezak and Jacques Urlus[7] may have been the finest Wagner tenors during the first decade of the twentieth century, but that assessment can be made by reference only to an imperfect selection of cylinders and '78s, as well as the testimonies and experiences of colleagues.

Almost three decades passed after 1900 before the first "complete" recording of *Tristan und Isolde* – with Albert Coates conducting the LPO and the English *heldentenor* Walter Widdop[8] and Göta Ljungberg in the title roles. During the ensuing decade a further 10 recordings were produced – conducted by Karl Elmendorff at Bayreuth (1928); De Sabata at La Scala (1930); Artur Bodanzky at the Met (five performances between 11 March, 1933, and 2 January, 1937), and Fritz Reiner and Sir Thomas Beecham with the LPO (in 1936 and 1937 respectively). All but two of these recordings featured the same Tristan – Lauritz Melchior.[9] The exceptions were Renato Zanelli (for De Sabata) and Gunnar Graarud[10] (for Elmendorff). Though little-known, the Norwegian-born Graarud was one of the most musical tenors to sing Wagner, and his work at the Staatsoper in Berlin between 1924 and 1926, and in Vienna between 1929 and 1937, was hailed as contiguous with the "Master's tradition" pre-dating the Bayreuth Bark. In October, 1927, Graarud created the role of

---

5 'Pure Gold' (2013).
6 19 March, 1865 –15 December, 1937.
7 6 January, 1867 – 6 June, 1935.
8 19 April, 1892 – 6 September, 1949.
9 20 March, 1890 – 18 March, 1973.
10 1 June, 1886 – 6 December, 1960.

the blinde Schwertrichter[11] for the premiere of Korngold's *Das Wunder der Heliane* in Hamburg. His Tristan is the work of a tenor, and "light" in the sense that Zanelli's voice was "dark." There is no baritonal heft, and he struggles with much of the second act; his phrasing and diction are exceptional, regardless. Graarud was unlucky to find himself lost to the shadows thrown by Max Lorenz (widely thought to be the finest German-born *heldentenor* of his generation) and the yet more suffocating presence of his Scandinavian rival, Melchior, who dominated and re-defined the *heldentenor* landscape over two decades of tireless work after 1924, the majority of it in the United States. The Danish Melchior continues to be regarded by many as the finest *heldentenor* to make records. In what way was he the finest? The measure of success and attainment remains fluid when there is such an abundance of recorded material to which objective reference can be made. On point: there are now more than 170 published audio recordings of *Tristan*, in various forms of completeness. Before agreeing on whether there was a single magi more worthy of note, it's necessary to pick up where Winkelmann left off.

Parsifal was first performed in 1882. Hermann Winkelmann was thirty-three years old at the time. He started singing Wagner's operas during his late twenties, when his voice was still maturing. The instrument did not crystallise until at least the age of 30 because the human body doesn't "settle" until that age, when the thyroid, arytenoid and cricoid cartilages begin to ossify (that is, become rigid and bone-like). Until these structures are capable of holding the vocal cords in place, the *passaggio* is vulnerable to stress and over-work. Certainly, there is a well-evidenced correlation between a singer's longevity and their careers beginning late. For tenors, this process of deferment is achieved also by early study and performance as a baritone.

The physical mechanics involved cause the tightening of the thyroid cartilage and the narrowing of the vocal folds while coincidentally shortening the distance between the folds and the cricoid cartilage; this causes the muscles connecting the *vocalis* to relax and thicken, a process that can result in cracking and the loss of tone for impatient singers forcing their voices pre-ossification. The larynx continues to harden during a singer's 30s, as the arytenoids dry out – a process that continues for most people into their 60s. As the larynx lowers (naturally over time) there are concomitant changes in testosterone, which add to the thickening of the vocal cords and the darkening of a singer's timbre. It is routine in consequence for lyric voices to become dramatic over time – as evidenced by Peter Seiffert and Jonas Kaufmann. In short, anyone starting out as a *heldentenor* in their 20s is unlikely to remain so beyond their 30s.

By the time Winkelmann made his recordings at the turn of the century he was in his fifties and considered past his best. At much the same time, recordings were made of a "German" tenor who was born just nine months after Brahms, and who made his stage debut a matter of weeks after Wagner completed the score of *Die Walküre* on 27 December, 1854. Gustav Walter[12] was a Bohemian tenor who studied as a young man with Franz Vogl. He sang leading roles in Vienna for more than 30 years, specialising in Mozart and the lighter end of the Wagner spectrum. He created

---

11 The 'Blind Chief Justice.'
12 11 February, 1834 – 31 January, 1910.

the role of Assad for the world premiere of Karl Goldmark's *Die Königin von Saba* in 1875, and after retiring from the stage in 1887 he toured Europe as a *lieder* recitalist, premiering numerous songs by Brahms and Dvořák – to both of whom he was an important figure. He gave the first performances of Brahms' *Liebeslieder-Walzer* and Dvořák's *Cigánské melodie*; the latter were dedicated by the composer to the tenor. Walter was well known to Wagner as Lohengrin, and as Loge in *Das Rheingold* and *Die Walküre*. In 1862 he gave the first concert performances of "*Nothung, nothung, neidliches Schwert*" (the "Forging" song rom *Siegfried*), with Wagner conducting; eight years later he sang Walther in the Viennese premiere of *Die Meistersinger*. For all that, he was overlooked by the composer in 1865, 1868, 1876 and 1882; he was excised in consequence from the lexicon of Wagner's "creators." In 1905, at the age of 71, he made three recordings: "*Leb wohl, Mignon*"[13] from Thomas' opera of 1866;[14] the second of Brahms' 6 *Lieder*, Op. 86 ("*Feldeinsamkeit*"); and "*Am Meer*" from Schubert's posthumous *Schwanengesang*. It catches the breath to realise that one is listening to a singer known to (and liked by) Wagner, Dvořák and Brahms.

His performance of "*Am Meer*" speaks directly to a mid-19th century tradition and is fascinating for all the right reasons. The song begins with the words "*Das Meer erglänzte weit hinaus Im letzten Abendscheine*";[15] they are preceded by an augmented sixth chord, the dissonance of which establishes the ambiguity of a song that toys with a tonic C major chord (rather than the dominant) as well as the uncertainty of the narrator's emotional state. Heine's poem echoes the tears of a man whose mind has been overtaken by yearning and rejection; his grim acceptance of his betrayal is captured in music of stark juxtapositions that Walter reveals through singing of heartfelt poetic melancholy. His tone is warm and well-placed; more compellingly, it is his phrasing, and the liberties he takes with the meter, that persuade. Walter's heavy use of rising as well as falling *portamento* is compelling also for its authenticity, and his use of colour and dynamics provides dispositive evidence for the elegance and delicacy that Wagner and Brahms expected of their singers – and their tenors in particular. This kind of singing is now extinct, and many would think that a good thing. Yet Walter's art is innately expressive and reveals a sense of naturalness in its articulation of feeling as sung-speech. The recording is one of the most important artefacts in the history of music because of Walter's standing as a relic reaching back almost two centuries, and his proximity to the composer of *Der Ring des Nibelungen* – and because his singing is prescriptively *cantabile*.

It's difficult to reconcile Walter's pronounced artistry to the work of the "Bayreuth Barkers" or to much of the German tenor singing recorded during the first quarter of the century. Walter was not a *heldentenor*, insofar as he did not commit to the heavyweight Wagner repertoire and had retired before Richard Strauss composed his first opera. He nonetheless sang much of the same repertoire (including Florestan), and since he approached each of the pieces he recorded in much the same way – emphasising line above letter – he can be isolated from the sphere of Bayreuth's influence *after* Wagner's death in 1883. To that end, Walter's recorded legacy is more valuable

---

13   '*Adieu Mignon,*' from Act 2, Scene 1 of *Mignon*, by Ambroise Thomas.
14   Which opera Walter sang as his final performance in Vienna in 1887.
15   'The sea glittered far and wide in the sun's dying rays.'

even than Winkelmann's – or that of anyone else until the Melchior-Lorenz-Völker revolution of the late 1920s.

The resulting disconnect is meaningful for what can be heard from the early 20th century, because it compels the revisiting of what a *heldentenor* is *supposed* to sound like. In the alternative, it allows for a reconsideration of the common ideal (formed and voiced by Melchior) since only a *very* few *heldentenors* have come close to meeting it. Melchior began his career as a baritone; he was adamant after retiring that the stability and resonance this formative experience gave him qualified as a pre-condition for success in the "heavyweight" German repertoire. Few *heldentenors* have begun life as baritones, however – even though Melchior's logic is inarguable. Wagner did not use the term *heldentenor*, after all. He employed the Rossinian "*tenorbariton,*" which addressed as much the range of the repertoire as the weight of tone considered requisite. Embracing Wagner's concern for melody and clarity, Melchior was preoccupied with the sung line, but like the morbidly obese Schnorr von Carolsfeld he too was a singer first and foremost; most thought him incapable as an actor. So rudimentary was this aspect of his art that he was compared by directors to a cat, insofar as a spotlight had only to point to where he was meant to stand and he would follow it. How might a complete inability to play a role, or live and breathe a character, align with the *Gesamtkunstwerk*? To that end specifically, Melchior was not the ideal *heldentenor* because his performances on stage separated the craft of singing from its theatrical context and impulses. It's true that Melchior's work on record is nothing short of miraculous in its power, resonance, reach and tone. On the other hand, his diction was commonly sloppy and his attention to note values ductile; his phrasing was given routinely to solipsism and effect. He was admired for his amplitude and stamina – a tirelessness which made him the most reliable Wagner singer of the 20th century besides Hans Hotter and Birgit Nilsson. He could sing for hours (albeit with substantial cuts) without yielding audibly to fatigue. This freakish reserve of power endeared him to conductors keen to encourage their orchestras to play to their fullest, including Toscanini, who gifted him the nickname "*Tristanissimo.*" Francis Robinson compared Melchior to Niagara Falls, while Beecham and Walter both identified his primary strength as being able to keep pace with Kirsten Flagstad – the same oddly faint praise that was extended to Corelli and Bergonzi for being able to sing upwind of Nilsson.[16]

Negative criticisms of Wagner's operas highlighted their length and the stamina required to perform them, especially for tenors. The frothy Viennese anti-Wagnerite Eduard Hanslick held that "It would be hard to find music more unvocal, more unsingable, than is to be found in *Tristan und Isolde,*"[17] while Tchaikovsky said of the same opera in 1876:

> To keep singers all these hours singing melodies that have no autonomous existence, but are merely notes belonging to the symphony (in spite of lying very high, these notes are often drowned in the orchestral

---

16 Curiously, Del Monaco sang *very* rarely with Nilsson. It was routinely a match made in Hell.
17 Hanslick, Eduard (1988). *Hanslick's Musical Criticism*, Ed. Henry Pleasants (Dover Publications). p.224.

thunder), this is certainly not the ideal at which modern musicians should aim.[18]

Bizarrely for the author of operas in which melody is often well-disguised, Tchaikovsky later wrote of *Die Walküre*, "There is not a single broad, complete melody which allows the singer to blossom."[19] This consensus has done much to feed the value of the stentorian above the lyrical, even though Wagner's music is as lyrical as any other. The same routine nonsense was applied to Strauss' early operas, even noting (as did Strauss) that *Der Rosenkavalier* was less overtly lyrical (bar for bar) than either *Salome* or *Elektra*. The value of a tenor with a capacity for phrasing as well as amplitude was largely forgotten between the death of Wagner and the early part of the 20th century, when conductors began to break with the prevailing taste by encouraging line above declamation. The first and most prominent to do so was Gustav Mahler. He worked with (and helped train) some of the most important German-language tenors of the first decade of the century, notably Johannes Sembach,[20] Erik Schmedes[21] and Leo Slezak.[22]

Sembach began his vocal studies in 1899 as a baritone (when he used his birth name Semfke). He later abandoned serious opera for operetta and vaudeville at the Apollo Theatre in Berlin, where he recorded "*Komm doch*" by Josef Strauss in 1904 – the year in which he auditioned for Mahler in Vienna. The performance adheres primarily to the style of the day, insofar as it is largely if not consistently awful, an assessment advanced by the additional curse of his whistling for much of the recording. Incredibly, he made his debut as Moser in *Die Meistersinger* on 13 November, 1904; unable to free himself from the shadows thrown by Schmedes and Slezak, he left Vienna at around the same time as Mahler, in 1907, and moved to Dresden where he was much valued, not least by Richard Strauss. He soon became one of the world's leading *heldentenors*, performing regularly in the *Ring*, *Tristan* and *Parsifal*, the latter role also serving as his first at the Metropolitan Opera in 1914. Sembach's recordings of music by Wagner evidence a quick and incessant *vibrato*, which makes it difficult to appreciate his other qualities.

Erik Schmedes was another baritone-turned-tenor. Born in Denmark, he studied in Paris, Berlin and Vienna before falling briefly under the influence of Pauline Viardot; she encouraged him to train as a baritone, and between 1891 and 1897 he enjoyed a largely uneventful career as "second baritone." He was encouraged to retrain as a tenor by Ernst von Schuch – Strauss' conductor in Dresden – after testing himself singing "*Plus blanche que la blanche Hermine*" from *Les Huguenots* on the House stage. Schmedes was summoned in 1898 to the Wiener Hofoper by Mahler, for whom he auditioned as a recently transitioned baritone from Dresden. During his train journey, and while studying the "Grail Narration" from *Lohengrin*, Schmedes

---

18 Bartlett, Rosamund (1999). "Tchaikovsky and Wagner: A reassessment". *Tchaikovsky and His Contemporaries: A Centennial Symposium*, Ed. Alexander Mihailovic (Greenwood Press). p.107.
19 von Meck, Galena (trans). Eds. Garden, Edward & Gotteri, Nigel (1993). '*To My Best Friend'; Correspondence Between Tchaikovsky and Nadezhda von Meck, 1876–1878*. Clarendon Press. p.88.
20 9 March, 1881 – 20 June, 1944.
21 27 August, 1868 – 23 March, 1931.
22 18 August, 1873 – 1 June, 1946.

caught the eye of an elegantly dressed lady, with whom he engaged in conversation. They agreed to meet at the Schiller monument two days later. The following day, as he was walking into Mahler's office at the Opera, Schmedes almost walked into the elegant lady from the train, who turned out to be Anna von Mildenburg,[23] a scion of Cosima's at Bayreuth.[24] Nothing came of their attraction, although they sang as lovers together on hundreds of occasions during Mahler's decade in Vienna. Schmedes' arrival coincided with Mahler's first *Ring* cycle – and the first of note to be performed without Winkelmann. Schmedes was, in essence, Winkelmann's successor in Vienna; his debut as Siegfried on 11 February, 1898, came as a disappointment to Mahler, however, who refused either to look at him during the first performance or take him to dinner after.[25] At the same performance, the role of Mime was sung by the tenor Julius Spielmann, with whom Mahler was especially disgusted:

> He cuts his own throat... and I'm going to fire him immediately. He's already ruined by the sloppy habits of the theatre routine. The worst thing about his performance is his Jewish jargon. No doubt, with Mime, Wagner intended to ridicule the Jews (with all the traits he bestowed on them – excessive humility and greed – the jargon is textually and musically so cleverly suggested) but for God's sake, it must not be exaggerated and overdone, as Spielmann does it, and in Vienna at that, at the K.K. Hofoper. This is sheer folly, a welcome scandal for the Viennese. I know of only one Mime... and that is myself... you wouldn't believe what there is in that part nor what I could make of it.[26]

Mahler was cleaning the stables of bad habits and traditions; he was pleased with no-one except, it seems, Mildenburg. Mahler worked hard with Schmedes for the first night of *Götterdämmerung* (which was, for Mahler more successful) and Schmedes went on to become Vienna's most beloved tenor, even when performing controversial repertoire.[27] His many recordings reflect his repertoire in Vienna, where he gave 1,129 performances of forty-two roles between 1898 and 1924. His repertoire was dominated by Wagner, with 129 performances as Lohengrin, 64 as Loge, 67 as Siegmund, 77 as Siegfried, 73 as Siegfried in *Götterdämmerung*, 58 as Tannhäuser, and 73 as Tristan. He also sang 69 performances as Canio – none of them, judging by his recordings of "*Scherzet nur immer, doch eines schont*"[28] (1906) and "*Jetzt spielen ... Hüll dich in Tand*"[29] (1907), especially Italianate.

---

23 de la Grange, Henry (1995). *Gustav Mahler, Volume 2, Vienna: the Years of Challenge*. Oxford University Press. p.112.
24 She famously made only a single recording (from *Oberon*), and it is extraordinary. Her range and power are manifest, as is the striking absence of *portamento*. She sings with almost no *vibrato*.
25 *Ibid*.
26 *Ibid*. p.112.
27 Most obviously the premiere of Zemlinsky's *Es war einmal* on 22 January, 1900, with Mahler conducting. He also sang frequently at Bayreuth between 1899 and 1906 and created the role of Pedro in the US premiere of Eugen d'Albert's *Tiefland* in New York with Emmy Destinn on November 23, 1908.
28 "*Un tal gioco credetemi*."
29 "*Vesti la giubba*."

The majority of Schmedes' recordings of Wagner's music were made during his time with Mahler. Each demonstrates that he had a trumpet of a voice, just as surely as they speak to a stiffness in phrasing and a style that was strangely absent of character. Mahler was no literalist; like Toscanini he detested the sloppy and lazy behaviour of singers reluctant to commit to thorough preparation. His performances of *Tristan* with Schmedes and Mildenburg remain legendary, as does the conductor's punishing rehearsal regime. It's frustrating that for all the recordings made by Schmedes, no one thought to invite Mildenburg to join him in the studio; she was hailed universally as Mahler's finest Isolde, even if many thought her more masculine even than Schmedes. A good indication of the state and health of the *heldentenor* vocally during the first decade of the century can be found in Schmedes' last recording of "*Nur eine Waffe taugt*" from *Parsifal*, produced in 1908 – after nine years in Mahler's company. His diction is wretched and the tone is uneven, with an irritating *vibrato* and little expressive variation. There is no *schwung* to the singing, which is deliberate and shapeless. He was nonetheless the most celebrated *heldentenor* of the first decade of the 20th century, which seems incredible when noting the near-constant marvels achieved by Mahler with his orchestra. The composer's attention to colour, momentum and texture were apparently lost on Schmedes, whose singing is simply (and for the most part) loud. It's accepted that he was considered a finer actor than vocalist, though his apparently magnificent appearance in Paul Czinner's 1919 silent film *Inferno* is lost. The questionable value of his art on record is still difficult to reconcile to the famously high standards of the perfectionist Mahler.

Something similar must be conceded of Schmedes' rival, Leo Slezak, who arrived at the Vienna Opera in 1901. For his audition he proposed to sing sections from *Lohengrin*. Before he could begin, a voice from the stalls called out "I warn you, if you drag it, you can go to the devil!"[30] Mahler loathed slow *tempi*, as a rule – which makes the abuses of some conductors when performing his symphonies doubly grotesque. Slezak had a reputation for self-indulgence, as evidenced by his spaghettified recording of "*Morgenlich leuchtend*" from *Die Meistersinger*. The Moravian-born tenor had a lighter voice than Schmedes, and so was able to take on broader repertoire – without ever committing to *Tristan*, the *Ring* or *Parsifal*. Slezak made regular appearances as Lohengrin, Tannhäuser and Walther (roles to which he brought a keen sense of line and expression) and on record at least he is elegiac rather than heroic, and closer in spirit and substance to the work of Gustav Walter than to Winkelmann. He too uses less *portamento* than might have been expected of the time, but he phrases well, memorably so when performing *lieder* by Strauss, with which he takes often monstrous liberties.[31]

It would be unrealistic to suggest that any of these early-century tenors warrants comparison with the best of their successors, a triumvirate of whom emerged during the late 1920s and 1930s to change the measure for considerations of what a *heldentenor* might sound like: Lauritz Melchior,[32] Franz Völker and Max Lorenz. Melchior

---

30   *Ibid*. p.351.
31   The best (and worst) of these is "*Ständchen*" and "*Zueignung.*"
32   20 March, 1890 – 18 March, 1973.

studied with Anna von Bahr-Mildenburg,[33] Ernst Grenzebach (Lorenz's teacher) and the legendary bass-baritone Friedrich Schorr. He made many recordings, the best of them in 1935 when he joined Lotte Lehmann for Act 1 of *Die Walküre*. This almost impossibly perfect performance was conducted by Bruno Walter – three years before the Anschluss and 34 years after the conductor made his debut as Mahler's assistant at the Wiener Staatsoper, in September, 1901. Melchior's vocal structure is bizarrely resonant and secure. The tone is easy, virile and ringing; his *cantabile* is remarkable. He credited Schorr with helping him sing below *forte*, and the results are nothing short of definitive, even if his pronunciation and fidelity to note values are anything but. After his first night at the Metropolitan Opera in New York, W. J. Henderson wrote that

> most of the essentials of song interpretation… go into details [when] describing Mr. Melchior's art as revealed last night. There was beauty and quality throughout the scale. There was an unusual and extremely finished use of head tones, which added immensely to the delicacy and polish of a style distinguished by fastidious choice in the means of expression. There was an exquisite sense of the melodic line and an admirable justice of phrasing. Indeed, in the artistic structure of the phrasing one perceived the mastery of a singer who was able to spin the tone through long and sustained utterances with confidence born of technical certainty and with a conviction of the purpose of the composer.[34]

If one accepts the common assessment that Melchior made the most magnificent sound of any *heldentenor* in the history of opera, then it's reasonable that he should be crowned alongside Caruso as the most perfect of "German" tenors. And yet Melchior's disrespect for rhythmic precision, to which the tenor's blue-pencilled scores admitted both knowledge and concern, was sufficient for his most devoted admirers to admit that golden tone and tireless energy did not realise the ideal *heldentenor*. His absent abilities as an actor would have been enough for Wagner to draw stumps; for Walter Legge in 1927 he was "xylophonic" – an axiom for a tenor with a pinched and thin tone above the stave. Melchior was not, in consequence, the "ideal" *heldentenor* – even though for many he remains unrivalled. After Melchior's death in 1973 Harold C. Schonberg claimed that:

> the Heldentenor species died with him. Certainly nobody since Melchior's retirement has begun to approximate the glory of that voice… he had the most heroic voice of any singer of his day and, it could well be, any singer of history.[35]

---

33 Despite her initial attraction to Erik Schmedes, Anna Mildenburg married the writer, playwright, director, and critic Hermann Bahr (19 July, 1863 – 15 January, 1934), adding his name to her own.
34 Emmons, Shirlee (December/January 1990/91). "Lauritz Melchior: Heldentenor for the Ages." *American Music Teacher*, Vol. 40, No. 3. pp.14–17 and 64–66.
35 Schonberg, Harold C. (1981). "The Heldentenor Species Died with Melchior." In *Facing the Music*. Summit Books. p.315.

It's inarguable that his voice was "heroic"; it's equally true that Wagner's mature roles for tenor demand more than mere heroism. The third act of *Tristan*, for example, is intended to convey the unhinging of a mind as a precursor to the transcendence of the physical; Wagner knew when writing the opera that it would leave any but the most robust of singers defeated by exhaustion. Since he knew more about voices than any composer of the 19th century, with the exception of Verdi, his expectations were rational and formed of the ambition that a singer might mirror vocally a character's natural and physical arc. The aberrant Melchior was as fresh when singing "*Wie, hör' ich das Licht? Die Leuchte, ha! Die Leuchte verlischt! Zu ihr, zu ihr*"[36] in Act 3 as when singing "*Isolde! Geliebte!*"[37] in Act 2 – a feature of his art that most identify as a value because it *sounds* so entirely wonderful. Melchior understood the rules of the game, of course, noting as he did that:

> Most of [the Heldentenor roles] are very long, and the voice is not used as in Italian opera, where there are arias and you sing only the melody with the orchestra underneath – oom-pah-pah, oom-pah-pah. In Wagner you are part of the orchestra, and there are no breaks for applause after arias. And the big climax always comes at the end of the opera.[38]

Melchior recognised how the operation of the voice as an instrument within Wagner's orchestra placed inevitable emphasis on the virtues of stamina and volume – such that his writing for *heldentenor*, when isolated from the multi-vocal fabric, loses much of the vast palette of colour, contour, emphasis and character poured by the composer into his word-settings. The physical demands compelled by the pre-requisite of audibility – as an alternative to comprehensibility – was a routine criticism of Wagner's enemies. Hanslick wrote that:

> It is obvious that his method of composition is diametrically opposed to that used by all the old masters. Vocal melody was ever their first and decisive consideration; the accompaniment (free of complex) was subordinate [...] In Die Meistersinger the vocal part alone is not only non-independent, it is non-existent! The accompaniment is everything, an independent symphonic creation, an orchestral fantasy with an accompanying vocal part.[39]

Melchior credited his superhuman abilities to having trained first as a baritone, a line of reasoning adopted variously by Schmedes, Sembach and Melchior's Swedish rival, Set Svanholm.[40] Unusually for a tenor, Svanholm was a sophisticated musician as well as a tenor; before turning full time to his voice he enjoyed early success as an organist, conductor and choral director – a period that included a terminal

---

36 'What? Is it the light I hear? The torch, ah! The torch is extinguished! To her! To her!'
37 'Tristan. Beloved.'
38 Fitzgerald, Gerald (28 March, 1970). "Speaking of Wagner." *Opera News*, Vol. 34, No. 22. p.8.
39 Hanslick, Eduard (1988). In *Hanslick's Musical Criticism*, Ed. Henry Pleasants. Dover Publications. p.120.
40 2 September, 1904 – 4 October, 1964.

confrontation with the young and characteristically ill-disciplined Jussi Björling. In 1929 he obtained the prestigious position of Cantor in St. Jakob's Church in Stockholm, which he retained until 1950. Svanholm made his debut in 1930 as a baritone (singing the role of Silvio in *Pagliacci*), and it was as a baritone that he joined the Swedish Royal Opera company in 1932. After five years of sharing the stage with questionably heroic tenors in Stockholm, Svanholm retrained and made his second debut in February, 1936 – in a performance of Beethoven's Ninth Symphony. Seven months later he sang Radamès in Verdi's *Aida*. He began to perform Wagner in 1937, initially as Lohengrin, and over the next three years he appeared as Tannhäuser, Siegmund and both Siegfrieds. In her memoirs, Kirsten Flagstad wrote "For me there was only one Siegmund… that was Set."

Like Torsten Ralf, Svanholm was popular in Germany during the Third Reich, as a member of the Staatsoper in Berlin, and for Heinz Tietjen in Bayreuth between 1931 and 1944. He sang for a decade at the Met from 1946, as Melchior's self-evident successor. His intelligence, musical sophistication and scrupulous respect for the score distinguished him absolutely from Melchior. There are few commercial recordings (his Loge for Solti and Decca stands out), but there is a library of live material that isolates his preference for thoughtful vocalising over seething declamation. His voice was ringing rather than "big," and prone to imperfect pitching – qualities shared by two of his primary German rivals, Ludwig Suthaus[41] and Bernd Aldenhoff.[42] Both were "natural" tenors (although the former was misidentified as a baritone while still a student), and both were praised for caring more for the science of stagecraft than the Great Dane. Suthaus is remembered chiefly for his (live) Siegfrieds with Furtwängler at La Scala in 1953, and for his Tristan, recorded in June, 1952, for EMI with Flagstad as Isolde. The latter remains a controversial recording – particularly for those acquainted with Furtwängler's work from before and during the War.[43] Suthaus' singing is never beautiful; his dislocation during the third and final act is stunningly well done, however, particularly when framed so viscerally by the conductor and the Philharmonia.

None of these fine artists learned much from Melchior – though each recognised his talent and stature. They looked instead to a tenor who failed to persuade when first auditioning for Cosima and Siegfried Wagner at Bayreuth during the late 1920s. After the death of mother and son, within four months of each other in 1930, Siegfried's widow, Winifred, anointed Max Lorenz Europe's most revered *heldentenor*.[44] Hs reputation throughout the rest of the world was clouded by the suggestion that he owed his success to Melchior's departure for the United States,[45] and because

---

41   12 December, 1906 – 7 September, 1971.
42   14 June, 1908 – 8 October, 1959.
43   Notably the 1941/43 Vienna performance with Lorenz and Konetzni. What survives of the conductor's work with *Tristan* from before the end of WWII is considerably more intense than the studio recording. It is accepted that Furtwängler did not enjoy the process of recording, which didn't help, but his confidence after 1945 was unavoidably affected by de-Nazification.
44   10 May, 1901 – 11 January, 1975.
45   There is no evidence for this prejudice. In addition to Völker, Joachim Sattler (21 August, 1899 – 15 July, 1984) appeared in 1928, 1929 and 1931 as Siegfried in the *Ring* at Bayreuth, and in 1930 as Tannhäuser in Siegfried Wagner's production. He was also the first Tristan on record, for Karl Elmendorff

he was Hitler's favourite singer. Having made his debut at the Semperoper in 1927, where he was cherished by the city's music director, Fritz Busch, he moved two years later to the Berlin Staatsoper where he remained until 1944. Lorenz appeared also at the Met between 1931 and 1934 and from 1933 at Bayreuth, where he gave his last performance in 1954. In 1953 he created the role of Josef K for the premiere of Gottfried von Einem's *Der Prozess*. Like Völker, Lorenz remained in Germany throughout the War; neither man was sympathetic to the regime – and Lorenz had good reason not to be. Though married from 1932 to his Jewish manager, Charlotte ("Lotte") Appel, Lorenz was homosexual. This truth was known to Lotte and the Nazis – both of whom looked the other way. However, when Lorenz was dragged before the magistrates for being found in the "company" of another man (a young conductor), Goebbels informed Winifred Wagner (the widow of the composer's son, Siegfried, who was also gay), that the tenor was no longer suitable for the Festival. Winifred replied that the Festpielhaus would have to be closed in consequence, because Bayreuth was lost without him. Lorenz was allowed to remain. The regime was less accepting of Lotte's race, and in 1943 the SS arrested her and her mother for deportation to Theresienstadt. Lotte was able to telephone Olga Göring, Hermann's sister, who called on her brother to leave the Lorenz family alone. On 21 March, 1943, Göring announced that Lorenz and his family were under his personal protection; they remained so until the War's end.

Hitler was known to adore Lorenz's singing, and the tenor was a clear influence over the Führer's aesthetics, particularly when performing as one of the knights – *Lohengrin*, *Tannhäuser* and *Parsifal*. When painting *Der Bannerträger* in 1935,[46] Hubert Lanzinger depicted Hitler as a messianic figure clad in gleaming armour, with the Nazi flag billowing behind him; his iconography was influenced by Heinz Tietjen's Bayreuth productions with Lorenz. It has been suggested with malice that the Führer liked Lorenz because of some inherent or supressed homosexual urges on his part, and that Lorenz's sexuality was manifest from his singing. It's undeniable that there was an unusual and probably inherent emotionality in his art as a *heldentenor*, and his lachrymose tone and phrasing were far from typical at the time, but the notion that this was attributable to his being gay is troubling. Stereotyping was *en vogue* for those who attacked Lorenz during the Reich, and many have damned him since for being other than a "proper" German tenor because he failed to live up to the robust Bismarckian manliness embodied by Johann Winckelmann, Prince Philipp of Eulenburg, Ernst Röhm, Stefan George and Thomas Mann. The Weimar acceptance of *Anders als die Andern*[47] was anathema to the Nazis, for all the reasons summarised by Otto Weininger in *Geschlecht und Charakter*. Lorenz represented the paradoxical nightmare of a gay man singing the *über männliche* roles of Tristan, Siegmund, Siegfried and Parsifal. His often sensual phrasing, open tone and extravagant articulation transcended Wagner's unequivocal heterosexuality and reached well beyond

---

in 1928. More popular still was August Seider (11 February, 1901 – 18 November, 1989), who triumphed often in Bayreuth and Salzburg. He was another tenor much admired by Strauss and Furtwängler.
46 'The Standard Bearer.'
47 It was the first German film ('Different from the Others') released on 30 June, 1919, directed by Richard Oswald and starring Conrad Veidt and Reinhold Schünzel. The first German film to portray homosexuality sympathetically.

the confines of Cosima's *sprechstimme*. Even now, many recoil from Lorenz's singing of Parsifal, as if his emotional glorification of the music causes in some way the feminizing of the role. It's accepted that he did not often sing below *forte*, and that his *vibrato* began to spread earlier than it should have done. More controversially still, he indulged Italianate devices that raised eyebrows outside the German-speaking world. His 1942 recording of "*Allmächt'ger Vater*" from *Rienzi* is carnal in its melancholy, with numerous slides, aspirates and sobs. He holds the final syllable of the line "*Du wandeltest des Volkes Schmach, zu Hoheit, Glanz und Majestät!*"[48] for far longer than it's scored, and he follows it with a sobbing "*O Gott [vernichte nicht das Werk]*"[49] that is both excessive and profoundly effective. Unlike the bullet-proof Melchior, Lorenz's performances of Wagner's music were coloured by vulnerabilities to which plainly he related; his performances admit a passionate expansiveness that was absent entirely from those by Melchior. There was nothing sensual about Melchior, as a singer, an actor or a man.

Expression was Lorenz's priority, so that he was willing to make musical sacrifices – dragging, straining, swooping and declaiming to achieve extreme points of emotional connection that reached well beyond the otherwise routine pre-occupation with amplitude. It was a value system shared by his regular conductor and friend, Furtwängler, who can be heard conducting him in 1943 in a Bayreuth performance of *Meistersinger*. It's one of Furtwängler's finest recordings; it's one of Lorenz's worst. Equally disappointing is his performance as Siegfried for Furtwängler's La Scala *Ring* (accepting that he was only 48 at the time). Fortunately, their surviving *Tristan* from 1941-3 is magnificent, thanks in no small part to the Isolde of Anny Konetzni and the preternatural playing of the Berliner Philharmoniker.[50] The collegial burdens of recording as a process caused many 19th century conductors acute anxiety, especially Furtwängler, whose conception of music was antithetical to "takes" and editing. His infamous struggles when recording *Tristan* are a case in point, because the "chunking" of music that extended vast temporal, psychological and metaphysical spans offended his sense of musico-dramatic time, and triggered his constructions of *Nahören* (as a 'near-sighted sense of the present') and *Fernhören* (as 'sound from afar').[51] The conductor's attachment to "far-sighted sound" necessitated a constant and often violent interaction between *Nahören* and *Fernhören* that resolved in the experience of an operatic or symphonic work as perpetually unstable. Furtwängler's identification of intersection as a collision between the present and the future (in his capacity to anticipate the arc of a composer's structural thinking) operated as a form of dual

---

48 'You changed the humiliation of the people into nobility, splendour, and majesty!'
49 'O God, do not destroy the work.'
50 It should be mentioned here that much has been made of an incomplete recording from 1942, in Vienna, of *Parsifal* conducted by Knappertsbusch. Some have claimed this to be of the infamous production conducted in 1933 by Richard Strauss upon his replacing Toscanini, who had refused to perform in Bayreuth as part of his campaign against the Nazi regime. The recording is plainly of Lorenz, but the performance is from 1942, not 1933. There are no authentic recordings of Richard Strauss conducting at Bayreuth. The composer's family in Garmisch-Partenkirchen has many, of course, but none has been made publicly available.
51 See *Wilhelm Furtwängler: Notebooks, 1924–1954* (1995). Trans. Shaun Whiteside. Quartet Books; and *Wilhelm Furtwängler, Ton und Wort: Aufsätze und Vorträge 1918–1954* (1955). Brockhaus.

directionality, and Furtwängler's attachment to the mystical drew him to singers with a comparably romantic sense of line, breathing and phrasing. It was here that Lorenz and Furtwängler were ideally suited – in the realisation of the philosophy of the tenor's namesake Alfred Lorenz, to whose "periodisation" of music and performance the conductor made frequent reference.[52] If Lorenz's expansive phrasing and his routine yielding to expressive tension were not always tasteful, they were ineluctably authentic.

Lorenz was also prized by Victor De Sabata, who can be heard conducting him in *Tristan* at La Scala in 1948, with Kirsten Flagstad as Isolde, and by Richard Strauss, who thought him unrivalled as Menelaus in *Die Aegyptische Helena* and Bacchus in *Ariadne auf Naxos*. There is a magnificent live recording of the latter from 1944, staged as part of the composer's 80th birthday celebrations, with Maria Reining in liquid-golden form in the title role. Also available is footage of Lorenz dressed in Lederhosen rehearsing the "*Preislied*" at Bayreuth. From within the cramped acoustic of the rehearsal room it's possible to appreciate something of the ringing power and projection of his voice. He was spared de-Nazification after the War because he refused to collaborate politically. Like Furtwängler, he was a proud German who believed in the primacy and eternity of German art; remaining in the country during its darkest time, as a gay man married to a Jewish woman, presented Lorenz with an opportunity to achieve something decent – even if only by surviving. The tenor Waldemar Kmentt claimed subsequently that Lorenz helped many Jewish people escape or hide; regardless, Lorenz could not have fled himself because his wife was prevented from travelling and her safety depended on his willingness to sing. Lorenz's life and reputation were scourged by Hitler's affections. Of course, the Führer also liked sweets and pastries, sweets and frosted cakes, afternoon tea, and dogs; the paintings of Hans Makart and Franz von Stuck; the symphonies of Bruckner; the operettas of Lehár; and the films of Walt Disney and Charlie Chaplin. None of those "things" had a say in Hitler's predilections. They existed independently of their association with the venal, the ignorant and the destructive; they did not submit in their concordance with the banality of Hitler's aesthetics. Unlike Peter Anders, who reciprocated the Nazis' affections, Lorenz was emotionally and culturally opposed to Nazism and simply unable to leave Germany. He nonetheless emerged from the War with his reputation and character intact. Both Hans Hotter and Dietrich Fischer-Dieskau considered him to be the finest *heldentenor* of the century. The critic John Steane did not agree, dismissing Lorenz by saying that he "began well but seems to have developed into a vocally coarse representative of a school we do not want to see revived."[53] Steane didn't identify the detail of that school's charter.

If Lorenz was not the "perfect" *heldentenor*, he was one of the most beloved – particularly among his many students. After retiring, he became a mentor and a teacher to the next generation of Wagner tenors, which proved to crystallise in the Americas. Lorenz's pupils included Jess Thomas[54] and James King[55] – the two finest *heldentenors*

---

52 Lorenz, Alfred. (1924 – 1925) 'Betrachtungen über Beethovens Eroica-Skizzen (Ein Beitrag zur Psychologie des Schaffens); *Zeitschrift für Musikwissenschaft*, Vol. 7. p.420.
53 Steane, J. B. (2000). *Singers of the Century*, Vo. 3. Duckworth. p.75.
54 4 August, 1927 – 11 October, 1993.
55 22 May, 1925 – 20 November, 2005.

native to the United States during the 1950s and 60s.[56] From north of the border, Canada produced the leviathan Jon Vickers,[57] while Chile spawned Ramón Vinay,[58] the vocal and dramatic correlate to Beowulf or Grendel, depending on which role he was singing and which voice he was using.

Vinay was a most unusual figure in the history of the tenor voice, for whom there are no comparators on record. He made his debut as a baritone in Mexico in 1938 and his second debut, as a tenor, five years later – achieving immediate success in the heavy, dramatic repertoire. His portrayal as Otello was legendary before he'd completed his first "*niun mi tema.*" On live recordings he can be heard singing the role for Toscanini (1947), Busch (1948), Furtwängler (1951), Cleva (1951), Santini (1952), Stiedry (1952), Kubelik (1955) and Beecham (1958). In 1962 he reverted to baritone roles[59] and gave landmark performances as Iago[60] – one of which was recorded with Mario Del Monaco in the title role.[61] The resonance of their singing of "*Si per ciel*" is tooth-loosening and wildly exciting. The Dallas audience bears appropriately noisy witness.

As Otello, and as a *heldentenor* specialising in Wagner, Vinay was a force of nature, with a massive voice that was darkly menacing and capable of freakish intensity. He had a vibrant high C, although his repertoire made little use of it, and while some still dislike his wide *vibrato* there were ample compensations in his exceptional diction, declamatory power and expressive nuance. He was magnificent as Tristan, in which role he can be heard with Fritz Reiner at the Met on 9 December, 1950 (with Helen Traubel as Isolde), and the role of Kurwenal seventeen years later at the Philadelphia Academy of Music, conducted by William Smith.[62] At Bayreuth he was recorded as Telramund for Sawallisch (with Jess Thomas as Lohengrin), Tannhäuser for Keilberth, Parsifal for Clemens Krauss and Knappertsbusch, Tristan for Jochum and Karajan, and Siegmund for Krauss and Keilberth, the latter as part of the first *Ring* cycle to be recorded in stereo. Vinay brings a tragic grandeur to each of these performances; he is unlike anything else on record. It has been suggested that he never really stopped singing as a baritone (and he was capable even of bass parts), so that the quality of the voice is never truly that of a tenor. Indeed, his declamatory power was antithetical to the lyricism that would otherwise characterise the *heldentenor* internationally after 1960 – as typified by Jess Thomas.

Thomas was one of the finest Strauss tenors of his generation. He made his debut in 1957 singing the role of the Italian Tenor in *Rosenkavalier*, his performances (and recordings) as Bacchus in *Ariadne auf Naxos*, Menelaus in *Die Aegyptische Helena*, and the Emperor as *Die Frau ohne Schatten* are widely recognised to be exceptional. His

---

56   Honourable mention should be made also of Jean Cox (16 January, 1922 – 24 June, 2012) and Richard Cassilly (14 December, 1927 – 30 January, 1998).
57   Jonathan Stewart Vickers, (29 October, 1926 – 10 July, 2015).
58   31 August, 1911 – 4 January, 1996.
59   There have been unwarranted comparisons between Vinay and Domingo – who began as a baritone and reverted to baritone roles after decades as a tenor. Domingo chose wisely never to sing as Iago.
60   On what proved to be his final performance on stage, Vinay (who was singing Iago) appeared for Act 3 as Otello…
61   Conducted exceptionally well in Dallas by Nicola Rescigno, in 1962. It is Vinay's only recorded performance as Iago.
62   25 January, 1967.

voice was not especially large but it was bright enough to be heard over the most populous of orchestras, memorably so at Bayreuth and the Met, where he gave the first of 109 performances on 11 December, 1962. His engagement by Wieland Wagner at the Festpielhaus was particularly significant because he was the first American to be accepted in Europe as a *heldentenor* capable of competing with the best of the Festival's German artists. It helped that Thomas, like James King, studied in Germany, where he learned to speak the language natively, and his earliest successes were in Karlsruhe, Vienna, Zurich and Berlin. In 1961 he joined the Bayerischen Staatsoper where, two years later, he sang the Emperor at the Theatre's reopening. He was invited also to perform at the inaugurations of the rebuilt Deutsche Opera in Berlin and the "new" Met in New York, where he created the role of Octavius Caesar for Samuel Barber at the premiere of *Antony and Cleopatra*. He was invited to sing at Bayreuth just two years after his debut in *Rosenkavalier* – which fact Thomas appeared to have forgotten when telling an interviewer shortly before his death that

> One shouldn't do it [sing as a heldentenor] too soon ... a young heldentenor should sing all the Puccini and Mozart roles. [...] I was given good advice not to do them too early in my career.[63]

Wieland was a gifted *dramaturg* and knew what he was doing when throwing *Parsifal*[64] and Hans Knappertsbusch at Thomas. To be just four years into his career and singing Wagner's most complicated tenor role on Wagner's stage, with Hans Hotter as Gurnemanz, suggests that Thomas was right to assert that successful singing was "10% voice, 10% hard work, 10% luck and 70% healthy nerves."[65] The lyricism of Thomas' artistry on the two surviving recordings of *Parsifal* from 1961 and 1962 is apparent throughout the performances, as it was when he sang Siegmund and Siegfried for Karajan in the studio. As a Wagner tenor, Thomas' phrasing was inclined to rigidity, partly because he sang without *portamento* and too much *vibrato*. His articulation of "*Amfortas! Die Wunde!*" From Act 2 and "*Nur eine Waffe taugt*" from Act 3 of *Parsifal* was "pure," after the tastes and sensibilities of Knappertsbusch; it was dry also. He had a tendency additionally to force his tone, particularly when "Kna" flashed his cufflinks. Ironically for a tenor who espoused the virtues of "*piano* singing," and who argued that "to sing *piano* is the [key] to singing Wagner," Thomas did not do so very often, and certainly not in accordance with Wagner's markings. It's arguable that Thomas failed his other declared value system, namely that voices were

> a function of personality.... you can't teach a voice.... singing should never be taken away from speech.... they are identical in a way.

It would be unfair to suggest that Thomas was bland. When compared to Windgassen, Vickers and King, however, his singing wanted for character, such that

---

63   He made this observation a few months before his death from a heart attack in 1993.
64   The invitation was extended two years before he appeared, because Bayreuth like everywhere else booked its singers well in advance.
65   Canadian Broadcasting Corporation interview, 1990.

his concentration on the notes as written denied them their full expressive potential. Thomas was a known – and infamously invested – rival to Corelli at the New York Met (a contest that was over before it began), and in matters of vocal personality his production of tone operated at the cost of complexion. His recognition of the *locus* of a singer's vocal identity (when comparing speech to song) was to identify the essence of what he (and most other) *heldentenors* have lacked since the 1960s. Where Sarah Bernhardt, Laurence Olivier, Richard Burton, Judy Dench and Fiona Shaw can be recognised instantly from their use of language in its isolation (rather than by their accents or tonal resonance), so the finest Tristans and Siegmunds stand out because of their weighting and shaping of individual words *within* phrases. The freedom to develop the diagnostics of a singing voice is gifted by the degree to which the mechanics allow for it. The more resolute a singer's technique, the greater the potential for expression. Whenever a *heldentenor* struggles with the fundamentals of projection and placement, the resulting vocal character can appear distilled and sound intimidated; art is rarely articulate when subjugated to the operation of endurance. For his part, Thomas was defeated by his own discretion and by the need to be heard, considerations necessarily at odds with the writing and dramatic context of his repertoire. Act 1 of *Die Walküre*, for example, calls for extravagant heroics at its close. The demands reach considerably further than mere tone, however. During the "*Winterstürme,*" Siegmund's words resonate in the elegiac music; he has a host of cues spanning "*mildem Lichte,*"[66] "*Wunder webend er sich wiegt,*"[67] "*weit geöffnet lacht sein Aug,*"[68] and "*Keim und Spross entspringt seiner Kraft,*"[69] Wagner characterises each "pivotal" word through music that can be sung according to its phrase – or articulated as it might be spoken (as with the leap to "*ent[springt]*"). There is so much more for a tenor to reveal when he is technically secure in his voice, therefore, as evidenced by the incremental passage:

> Im Lenzesmond leuchtest du hell;
> hehr umwebt dich das Wellenhaar
> was mich berückt errath' ich nun leicht
> denn wonnig weidet mein Blick.[70]

Wagner's phrase markings, and the use of repeating clusters, are designed almost priapically to convey the emergence of the siblings' lust, and in Siegmund's metaphors (of music as well as words) the tenor needs to be able to preserve the character's virility while remaining believably attractive. Melchior (who was described by Rudolph Bing as "a walking sofa"[71]) was essentially an oratorio performer when on stage, whereas Thomas was a fine actor and physically attractive. Vocal opulence and incarnate beauty have rarely been wrapped in a single bow, and yet Siegmund is

---

66 'tender radiance.'
67 'weaving wonders, on he floats.'
68 'widely open laughs his eye.'
69 'bud and shoot spring up by his might.'
70 'Beneath spring's moon shines thou bright; wrapped in glory of waving hair / what has ensnared me now, well I know, in rapture feasts my look.'
71 Steane, J.B. (1992). *Voices, Singers and Critics.* Duckworth. p.73.

compelled to persuade as a lover as well as a man of sword-wielding action. When, finally, he reveals himself and tears Nothung from the tree ("*Siegmund heiss' ich und Siegmund bin ich!*"[72]), the music calls for the grandest tenor voice imaginable. The contrast with the preceding lyricism must be absolute, without the tenor yielding to barking or wobbling, so that when finally he crowns the scene with his A4 (for "*Wäl*[*sungen Blut!*]"[73] Wagner's coda is allowed to operate as a continuation of (and preamble to) the siblings' intermissionary love-making. Jess Thomas was not that man.

In the isolation of an ideal, arising as it does in an amalgam of phrasing, expression and amplitude, the *heldentenor* as a voice type was fixed for many by the emergence of two entirely remarkable Siegmunds: James King and Jon Vickers. Vickers' long career began in Canada during the early 1950s. He enjoyed a series of triumphs at Covent Garden between 1957 and 1961 singing *Don Carlos* for Carlo Maria Giulini, Aeneas in *Les Troyens* and Walther in *Meistersinger* for Kubelik, and Florestan for Klemperer (each of which was recorded live). After making his debut at Bayreuth (as Siegmund, for Knappertsbusch) he enjoyed a series of legendary collaborations with a string of avowedly 19th century conductors, including Knappertsbusch, Klemperer, Serafin and Böhm. He was revered by each of them, not least because of his Protestant work ethic. Much has been written about Vickers' farming background and his "rural" religious convictions, the fervour of which caused him great difficulty when singing certain of Wagner's roles. His Christian austerity undoubtedly shaped his stage presence, and he was roasted publicly after withdrawing from a production of *Tannhäuser* in 1976, having concluded that Wagner's opera was a "strike at the very root of the Christian faith." Unlike Eric Liddell's refusal to compete on a Sunday at the 1924 Paris Olympics, however, Vickers' justification for repudiating *Tannhäuser* was inconsistently applied to the rest of his repertoire choices, which included the overtly blasphemous *Parsifal*, the mass-murdering Samson [*et Dalila*], the incestuous Siegmund, and the violently misogynistic Canio, Otello and Don José. As an extremely difficult man himself,[74] Vickers was adept at playing brutal, controlling men; his imposing physical stature and alarmingly resonant dramatic voice ensured that he was matched among his contemporaries as Otello only by Ramón Vinay and Mario Del Monaco, and in Wagner only by Vinay and King. He shared much of Vinay's primitivism, and joined with the Chilean in his talent as an intensely powerful stage and vocal actor – although he was hopeless when attempting to convey romantic love. There was a pressing sense that submission was a given, whether or not it was consensual or reciprocated. He threw himself into performances with such unchecked physicality that

---

72 'Siegmund call me, for Siegmund I am!'
73 'Volsungen blood.'
74 Vickers' famously difficult nature extended to humiliating singers who did not know their own roles as well as he did, and included momentous confrontations with conductors, famously George Solti, with whom he clashed so often that he was adopted by the orchestra of the Royal Opera House, Covent Garden as their mascot. The horn player Alan Civil (who joined with most of his orchestral colleagues at Covent Garden in detesting Solti) told the author that Vickers threatened on one occasion to feed the conductor his score so that he might do to it what he was doing to the music. He was equally intolerant of ticketholders. Mid-way through a performance of *Tristan und Isolde* in Dallas in 1975 he stepped to the footlights and yelled at a member of the audience: "Stop your damned coughing!!!!"

it was routine for his colleagues to take their bows marked by bruises. His iron-clad technique allowed him to conjure a striking, often extreme palette of vocal colour without jeopardising the stentorian force with which he could rattle fillings at the back of the very largest of Houses. He compared to Vinay in grandeur, and like Vinay his singing was never especially beautiful – for all its textural variety. Vickers was capable of affecting beauty – but only in German music. He neither phrased nor articulated the French and Italian repertoire (other than Otello and Aeneas) to the best of its potential, and his greatest non-German success was in an opera by an English composer.

Benjamin Britten loathed Vickers' portrayal of *Peter Grimes*, for a host of reasons beyond the tenor's rampant homophobia. The application of a voice blasted from granite to music that had been written for Peter Pears was problematic for some, including Britten. Where Pears had identified an ethereal, inarticulate creature, neither victim nor villain, Vickers apostrophised rage and conflict, resonating the character's internal landslide through sounds and gestures of intimidating physical force. The intensity of the rural preacher was miraculous when it captured the "terrors and tragedies" of Slater's fearsome creation, and transcendental during the largely unaccompanied second scene of Act 3 ("*Grimes! Steady*"), which ranks among the most profound achievements of any tenor in the history of opera.[75]

When asked to isolate the most indelible memory of his life on stage, the baritone Thomas Allen answered "Vickers' Grimes." The scale of the voice was beyond characterisation, and masculine in a way that might have united Richard and Cosima in their discrepant pursuit of a lyrical *heldentenor* capable of articulating the poet's *stabreim* while satisfying the composer's longing for maleness. For Allen it was a construction of pathos and Old Testament fury, tapped by a singer whom he considered among the most "complete" of the century. Vickers' stage career came to an end during the late 1980s, with performances conducted by a generation born after the Second World War. He agreed in 2001 to a belated debut at London's Wigmore Hall (to commemorate his 75th birthday), where he recited Tennyson's *Enoch Arden* with incidental music for solo piano by Richard Strauss. One critic wrote of the performance that "He speaks as he once sang, with a mixture of delicacy and raw power. His voice remains beautiful, its bronze tone undimmed by age."[76]

By modern standards, Vickers was a phenomenon – and widely recognised as such. James King, however, was largely unknown to any but the interested, and to collectors specifically of recordings of music by Wagner and Strauss. He was one of the last genuine *heldentenors* to have begun professional life as a baritone – in 1949. Seven years later he retrained as a tenor, working closely with his idol, Max Lorenz. King sang for the first time as a tenor in 1960, with the Saint Louis Municipal Opera; he sang for the last time as a baritone in May, 1961, with the San Francisco Opera as Escamillo with Marilyn Horne as Carmen. The following year he performed with the Deutsche Oper in Berlin and for the Salzburger Festspiele. In 1963 he sang for the first time at the Wiener Staatsoper. Wieland Wagner snapped him up for the 1965

---

75 The video recording of Elijah Moshinsky's 1981 production for Covent Garden would be enough to secure his reputation as one of the finest singing actors of the century.
76 Tim Ashley in *The Guardian* on 24 February, 2001.

Bayreuther Festspiele, and Rudolph Bing engaged him as Florestan for a first night at the Met on January 8, 1966. King later recalled:

> I didn't sing any Wagner until I was thirty-eight years old. The following year, in '63, I sang my first *Lohengrin*, and then at age 40 I sang my first *Walküre*. That was my second Wagner. I was 42 for my first *Parsifal* and that year, too, I sang my first *Flying Dutchman*. I was about forty-five years of age when I sang my first Walther von Stolzing.

It's important to accept, as did King, that he was no actor. He was a large man who moved uneasily around the stage. His talents were located in an unusual fusion of power and stamina to a highly developed musical intuition. King was possessed of that chimerical balance between baritonal weight (with a vocal openness through the *passaggio* that required little covering) and a range that enabled him to strike a B4 with ease. As a Strauss tenor, King had few rivals. He set Metropolitan opera records for the most performances of Bacchus in *Ariadne auf Naxos* and the Emperor in *Die Frau ohne Schatten* (a role he created for the Met when it staged the opera for the first time). He was loved by Karl Böhm, for whom he performed (and recorded, live) the role of Apollo in *Daphne* in Vienna in 1964, alongside the miraculous Leukippos of Fritz Wunderlich. He was filmed performing the same role for TV – again alongside Wunderlich – this time conducted by Keilberth, with the cast miming to a pre-recording. King was Siegmund for Solti's Decca *Ring* in the studio, but his finest performances of that role were for Karl Böhm at Bayreuth in 1967. Fortunately, Philips recorded this legendary cycle, and it has not been surpassed. King's phrasing and articulation make more of Siegmund's music in Act 1 than any other performance in stereo, and the sheer wonder of his tone when at full tilt is an entirely guiltless pleasure. He was recorded as Parsifal at Bayreuth in 1969 (conducted by Horst Stein) but sadly never as Tristan; there is a live recording from 1972 of the second act with the Boston Symphony Orchestra and Eileen Farrell as Isolde, conducted by William Steinberg, which alludes to what might have been.

King sang Italian roles (including Canio, Manrico, Radamès, Otello and Calàf), but King understood that his talents vested with German parts, many of which he learned with Lorenz.[77] Even during the final years of his career, his stamina never failed him, as was obvious from his vanquishing of the brutal *tessitura* of Bacchus in *Ariadne* at the Met in 1988 – when 63 years old. It was suggested at the time, and without malice, that King was one of the few tenors capable of going toe-to-toe with Jessye Norman, even if she had the advantage in reach. There's good evidence for his exceptional gifts from the surviving telecast. King excelled also as the Drum-Major in Berg's *Wozzeck* (for Vienna in 1981, Covent Garden in 1984 and the Metropolitan in 1990), as Florestan (frequently with Böhm, and memorably on record) and as

---

77 In a "Conversation with Bruce Duffie," James King recalled: "Max Lorenz I met in 1964, when I was doing my first *Walküre* in Bayreuth. I went to him to get training and coaching in the role, and we really hit it off. He was wonderful, and I've never seen a person act roles any more powerfully than he did. He would demonstrate things to us and to me, and he was incredible.... Max's voice was somewhat lighter than mine. It was not a Melchior sound, but he was the poet of heldentenors.... no tenor ever did a better job because he was like a poet himself. He was brilliant in this way; he was a real born theatre man."

Paul in Korngold's *Die Tote Stadt*, in which role he was filmed in Berlin in 1983. The final scene of the latter performance ("*O Freund, ich werde sie nicht wiedersehn*"[78]) reveals King at his most distinctive, eloquent and poignant. The tone and its ease of projection are amplified by the elegance of his phrasing as he soars over Korngold's everything-but-the-kitchen-sink orchestration; his *very* judicious use of a barely audible "catch" (akin to the lightest of sobs) when finally he decides to "leave" the stage adds considerably to the force of this heart-breaking episode.

It's difficult not to feel as if King took the *heldentenor* with him when saying farewell to Frank and Marie. The European school of "heroic" singers that followed Lorenz was formed entirely of "natural" tenors – which is not to suggest there was an absence of exceptional voices available after 1940; rather, compromises had to be made to allow for the absence of what Wagner was seeking from his idealised *tenorbariton*. If the German tenor school after the war was formed of extraordinary talent, the majority of tenors adhered to the lighter end of the vocal spectrum, performing *lieder* as often as opera. The best of them were Julius Patzak, Peter Anders, Anton Dermota and Rudolf Schock. Each of these supreme artists pursued a path characterised primarily by lyric sensibilities, as they had been understood by Gustav Walter and Karl Erb.[79] The chief difference between each of them and Max Lorenz, for example, was amplitude. Anders[80] began as a lyric tenor, and prevailed as one of the most perfect of the 20th century. In 1938, he was invited to join the Bayerischen Staatsoper, where he sang in the world premiere of Richard Strauss' unironically titled *Friedenstag* ('Peace day'). Hitler was in the audience, and although he denounced the work's pacifist sentiments, Anders retained his preferred status as an "Artist of the Third Reich." Between 1940 and 1945, Anders was based in Berlin, at the Staatsoper, where he worked enthusiastically for the regime. His repertoire until he left Berlin in 1948 was dominated by Belmonte, Tamino, Lyonel, Hans, Hoffmann, Leukippos, Alfredo, Eisenstein and Rodolfo. In 1949, he began to take on heavier roles including Florestan, Max, Tannhäuser, Lohengrin, Walther[81], Siegmund, Radamès and Otello.[82] Many thought his ambition misplaced; the complete recording of his broadcast as Lohengrin from 1951 (conducted by Richard Kraus) suggests otherwise. Anders was not a *heldentenor*, and could never have been. He was an exceptional musician, however. This is well evidenced by a broadcast recording from 15 February, 1942, of four songs by Richard Strauss with Wilhelm Furtwängler conducting the Berlin Philharmoniker.[83] When listening to Anders' performances of these glorious songs, it's easy to believe they could not be improved upon. His uninterrupted shaping of the opening phrase of "*Waldseligkeit*" would be "impossible" but for the performance having been recorded live.

---

78 'O friend, I will not see you again.'
79 13 July, 1877 – 13 July, 1958.
80 1 July, 1908 – 10 September, 1954.
81 There is a precious recording of Anders singing Walther from Acts 1 and 2 of *Meistersinger* from Covent Garden in 1951, conducted by Beecham.
82 There are various recordings of excerpts from *Otello*, all of which indicate that less was better than Moor.
83 "*Waldseligkeit*" Op. 49 No. 1; "*Liebeshymnos,*" Op. 32, No. 3; "*Verführung,*" Op. 33, No. 1, and "*Winterliebe*" Op. 48, No.5.

Anders was in competition with Rudolf Schock,[84] a sometime film star and performer of light music who also sang Walther at Bayreuth in 1959. Improbably, he was also a cast member for the first performance at the Wiener Staatsoper of Berg's *Lulu*. Also competing were Julius Patzak[85] (who performed in the premiere of *Friedenstag*, as well as Orff's *Der Mond* and von Einem's masterpiece, *Dantons Tod*) and Anton Dermota[86] who, though born in modern-day Slovenia, became a huge favourite of audiences in Vienna. Dermota also took on heavier roles at the end of his career, including Florestan; to that end, he was first and last a lyric tenor, a fact he accepted with eternal youthfulness when singing the role of Ein Hirt[87] for Carlos Kleiber's studio recording of *Tristan* in his 70s. Little remembered, despite his talent, was Anton de Ridder,[88] a Dutch lyric tenor who first learned to sing while working as a diamond cutter in 1947. He performed regularly in coffee houses and music halls, developing an easy, bright and beautiful lyric voice; in 1954 he was awarded a scholarship by the Amsterdam Conservatory, where he studied with Jan Keizer. In 1956 he relocated to Germany and Austria – and the ministrations of Karl Böhm. His work on record and in the theatre with the admiring Böhm created a superb legacy, treasured by collectors.

The greatest shadows were thrown during the late 1950s and early 1960s by the most beautiful German tenor voice since records began. During his grotesquely brief life, Fritz Wunderlich[89] re-aligned expectations of what a German tenor might achieve in matters of tone, articulation, expression and technique. He was rare in uniting critics and colleagues alike, attaining through his peerless art a measure of near-perfection sufficient to negate prejudice, vanity and envy. A story is told of a Gala performance at Covent Garden of *Der Rosenkavalier*, for which Wunderlich was engaged as The Italian Singer. Her Majesty Elizabeth II was in grudging attendance – forewarned that the opera was to last well over three hours. As the Queen settled into her comfortable chair in the Royal Box, she began to nod off. No one dared wake the monarch, but 40 minutes into the first act Wunderlich walked on stage and began to sing "*Di rigori armato.*" As he did so, the guest of honour woke and leaned forward, transfixed by what she was hearing. After the short scene was finished, the monarch asked of her host: "Who was that?" When told Wunderlich's name, she enquired "When does he come back?" to which she received the disappointing reply "he doesn't." The Queen observed simply, "Oh dear" and returned to her slumber. There is no confirmation for this tale. It's believable, regardless.

Wunderlich began his life as a musician playing the horn, professionally so for five years between 1950 and 1955. It's widely accepted that his exceptional breath management was attributable to these formative years. Wunderlich's first significant opportunity as a tenor came in 1959, when Karl Böhm engaged him to sing the role of Henry Morosus for a Salzburg production of Strauss' *Die schweigsame Frau*.[90]

---

84 4 September, 1915 – 13 November, 1986.
85 9 April, 1898 – 26 January, 1974.
86 4 June, 1910 – 22 June, 1989.
87 'A Shepherd.'
88 13 February, 1929 – 9 July, 2006.
89 26 September, 1930 – 17 September, 1966.
90 'The Silent Woman.'

The warmth of Wunderlich's voice, and his effortless scaling of the role's *tessitura* impressed everyone – particularly the humourless and irascible Böhm, who forced a bidding war over the tenor's overworked diary. In the audience for Wunderlich's performance as Morosus was Herbert von Karajan. As the curtain fell, the conductor walked to the tenor's dressing room and offered him a permanent contract with the Wiener Staatsoper. Wunderlich declined; days earlier he had accepted a position in Munich.[91]

Wunderlich was a natural and unusually powerful lyric tenor. His technique was flawless, which enabled him to specialise in Mozart. When singing "*Die bildnis ist bezaubernd schön*" from *Die Zauberflöte*, Wunderlich was able to walk without effort through the opening phrase's treacherous rising major 6th (B flat 3 to G4) with which Mozart characterises Tamino's breathless wonder at the beauty of Pamina's portrait. The marked *piano* dynamic (necessary for conveying the profundity of the character's feelings) adds to the huge technical challenges, which are compounded by the aria's *tessitura*, which sits on the fulcrum of the *passaggio*. Tamino repeats the words "*und ewig wäre sie dann mein*"[92] three times (three being the opera's mystical-Masonic number); Mozart emphasises the text using an ascending line that culminates in an A flat 4 – requiring exceptional breath control from the singer. Wunderlich not only made light work of the necessary placement, but added escalating passion to each repetition so that his feelings might be believable while adhering to the classical order and clarity on which the success of Mozart's writing depends. Wunderlich's facility for endless, golden lines of song was joined ineffably to the soul and intensity of his character's feelings – a summary, in short, of everything to which he turned his voice, whether in opera or concert.

Wunderlich's *annus mirabilis* was 1964 – much of it recorded. Having nailed the Italian Tenor for the duet (with Lucia Popp) in *Capriccio* for Georges Prêtre, he created a sensation, again in Vienna, as Leukiposs, in a production of *Daphne* that made a good case for the opera being one of the composer's finest. Wunderlich proceeded to triumph in the title role of Pfitzner's *Palestrina*, conducted by Robert Heger, before heading to the studio to record Tamino for Böhm. It was clear to many at the time that Wunderlich was evolving, and then at speed. He had sung David in *Die Meistersinger*, the Steuermann in *Der fliegende Holländer* and Walther von der Vogelweide in *Tannhäuser* – the latter two on recorded performances conducted at the Berlin Staatsoper by Konwitschny. He died before taking up *Lohengrin*, the traditional portal to the mature Wagner repertory. Towards the end of 1964, and having sailed through *Palestrina*, the 34-year old Wunderlich recorded Mahler's *Das lied von der Erde* with Christa Ludwig and Otto Klemperer.[93] Notwithstanding the

---

91 Karajan and Wunderlich worked together often – but never in the studio. There are two live recordings, a *Don Giovanni* from Vienna (1963), and a performance of *Die frau ohne Schatten* (with Wunderlich singing Erscheinung eines Jünglings) from 11 June, 1964. The second recorded performance from that run (from 17 June) does not (as some have claimed) feature Wunderlich, but rather Ermanno Lorenzi.
92 'and forever then she would be mine'.
93 Christa Ludwig recorded two movements in February, 1964, and the rest in July, 1966. Chaos reigned in consequence of Walter Legge's dissolution of the Philharmonia in March, 1964. Wunderlich was booked to record his movements in September, 1964. His sessions were cancelled, and displaced by the orchestra's players reformation as the New Philharmonia.

eternal debate, and accepting the poetical insights of Patzak's celebrated recording with Ferrier and Walter, Wunderlich's singing of Mahler's songs is almost superhuman. The ringing splendour of the voice is of a different order, a quality made all the more special by the expansive phrasing, expressive diction, dynamic shaping and articulate character. In the first movement ("*Das Trinklied vom Jammer der Erde*"[94]), Wunderlich's separation of the repeating words as they descend tonally and harmonically ("*Dunkel ist das Leben, ist der Tod*"[95]) floats this monstrously difficult writing; his technique is sufficiently absolute to admit not only a natural *cantabile* sensibility, but a considered responsiveness to poetry, with Wunderlich eternally alive to the imagined "*Vogel im Baum.*"[96] The sense throughout his work of sung poetry is no less striking on the live recording, also from 1964, with Dietrich Fischer-Dieskau and the Bamberg Symphony, conducted by Joseph Keilberth. The voice heard on both these performances is not that of a Mozart tenor. It reaches considerably further in scale and amplitude, transcending the extravagances of Mahler's kaleidoscopic orchestrations. Wunderlich was aware of the strength and the size of his tenor, and he understood the risks of taking on heavier repertoire. In an interview with Egloff Schwaiger, he observed:

> I think you are born a lyric, dramatic or heroic tenor. As he gets older – say, forty-two or forty-three – a lyric tenor may go over to singing heavier roles, but this is not inevitably the case. It is possible to make the voice heavier and more robust by working it harder, but then its light character, the pliant *bel canto*, is gone.[97]

When asked "Where do you think your limits lie?" Wunderlich replied:

> I have set the light Italian parts, such as Rodolfo in *La bohème* or the Duca in *Rigoletto*, as my limits for the next ten or twelve years. Rodolfo is really an exception, and I can only include him because Puccini composed his melodies in a manner so kind to the voice that a strain seems audible that is in reality just a natural vibration of the voice. Puccini's melodic gift ensures that the high notes simply come of their own accord. A good example is the final high 'c' in Rodolfo's aria '*Che gelida manina*'. It is one of the most easily reached top notes in the tenor repertoire, because it arises from a melodic phrase in a completely natural way. You simply have to open your mouth, and it is there. Verdi's high notes are much more precariously placed, because they often involve large intervallic leaps. Verdi makes great demands on vocal agility and hence vocal endurance. Puccini is a composer who accommodates singers, while in

---

94 'The Drinking Song of Earth's Sorrow.'
95 'Dark is life, dark is death.'
96 'Bird in the tree.'
97 Gerdes, Daniel Jon (2011). *The Legacy of Fritz Wunderlich: One Performer's Perceptions of Selected Discography*. A Treatise submitted to the College of Music in partial fulfilment of the requirements for the degree of Doctor of Music. p.27.

Verdi singers have to accommodate the composer. For this reason my limit is higher in Puccini parts than in Verdi.[98]

Many were surprised that Wunderlich prevailed so completely as Palestrina – a sombre role performed by numerous celebrated *heldentenors*, including Schmedes. A little over five years after his debut as Tamino, therefore, he was on the road to Florestan, Lohengrin, Tannhäuser and Walther. For many, it was presumed he would one day sing *Parsifal*. In reality, he was equipped naturally – and more so than any other German tenor of his generation – to grow into Tristan, Siegmund and Siegfried. His darkening timbre, natural warmth and clarity of tone, supported by Wunderlich's exceptional diction, assured him equal success in oratorio and *lieder*. He committed to recital repertoire only late in his career, in partnership with his friend Hubert Giesen; his interpretations of Schubert's *Die schöne Müllerin*, Schumann's *Dichterliebe* and the songs of Richard Strauss demonstrate the extent to which Wunderlich was able to fuse tone and word without either suffering in equivalence. He was no less adept with operetta and "light" music, as evidenced by his riotous, open-throated renditions of Agustín Lara's "*Granada.*"

Wunderlich's death was entirely avoidable. He tripped when descending the stairs of his house and fractured his skull; he died the following day in hospital, aged 35. At Schubert's funeral in 1828, Grillparzer announced "*Der Tod begrub hier einen reichen Besitz, Aber noch schonere Hoffnungen.*"[99] This was no less true of Wunderlich: the *heldentenor* that never was.

For all that might have followed him, what proved to be was largely disappointing. The leading German tenors of the immediate post-war years to succeed in the heroic repertoire would not have been *heldentenors* by the standards of earlier generations, either because they were too lyrical, or because they lacked personality, or because they simply couldn't be heard. Hans Hopf[100] was something of a blunt instrument, lacking charm as well as gravity. He made his debut at Bayreuth as Walther in 1951 and took up Siegfried for Wieland Wagner between 1960 and 1963; he is nonetheless best remembered for having sung the tenor part in the legendary performance from 1951 of Beethoven's 9th at the Festspielhaus, conducted by Furtwängler. Günther Treptow[101] was a fully paid-up member of the SA and Nazi Party – even after the discovery in 1934 of his mother's Jewish heritage. Treptow was banned from performing until Joseph Goebbels granted him a dispensation on 6 June, 1935. His Nazi-tainted past was no bar to his being picked for the 1951 Bayreuther Festspiele, and many others after. Far more impressive was Ernst Kozub,[102] a genuine and thrilling *heldentenor* who appeared during the late 1950s to warrant references to the "cusp of greatness." A live recording from 1965 of *Die Walküre* at Covent Garden (with Solti conducting) more than supports John Culshaw's wild enthusiasm for engaging him as Siegfried for Decca's *Ring* cycle. Bizarrely and inexplicably, however, the tenor refused (or failed

---

98 *Ibid.*
99 'Here Death buried a rich treasure, and even richer promise.'
100 2 August, 1916, Nuremberg – 25 June, 1993.
101 22 October, 1907 – 28 March, 1981.
102 24 January, 1924 – 27 December, 1971.

in any event) to learn the role for the sessions in 1962 and was replaced by Wolfgang Windgassen.[103] Kozub burned his career in consequence, while securing Windgassen's reputation when he became the first Siegfried in studio-recorded stereo.

Windgassen was already an old hand at Bayreuth when singing for Culshaw and Solti. As the son of a celebrated tenor, he was fortunate to enjoy significant opportunities at the start of his career – which began on record in 1948 with a broadcast performance (still available) of *Pelléas et Mélisande* from Stuttgart. He was invited to perform at the reopening of the Bayreuther Festspiele in 1951, where he sang Parsifal for Knappertsbusch, and Froh in *Das Rheingold* for Karajan (both recorded). He appeared annually for Wieland and, after Wieland's death in 1966, for Wolfgang until 1970; he was the Festival's longest serving tenor (over 19 consecutive years) until Siegfried Jerusalem completed his 20th. Of Windgassen's 89 available complete or excerpted performances on record (from between 1948 and 1973), only 16 were of operas by composers other than Wagner. Just three were recorded in a studio – including, of course, his turn as Siegfried for Decca. In addition to his work with Knappertsbusch, Krauss, Keilberth, Böhm and Karajan, Windgassen sang Loge and Siegmund for Furtwängler at La Scala in 1953, and performed frequently with Cluytens, Jochum, Boulez, Sawallisch and Carlos Kleiber (for whom he gave one of his last recorded performances as Tristan at the Württembergische Opera in Stuttgart on 22 April, 1973). If Windgassen was intensely musical, then his vocal tone was unsteady and lacking in consistency and focus. He benefitted greatly from a light *vibrato*, which helped him articulate Wagner's words with early-century clarity.

Even his most devoted supporters would concede that Windgassen was better suited vocally to *Lohengrin* and Walther than to *Tristan* and the *Ring*. He nonetheless brought acute artistry to these roles, particularly when singing them for Karl Böhm. When, in Act 3 of his 1967 performance of *Siegfried* (during the "Heil" section of his vast duet with Brünnhilde) the tenor drops into 9/8 and sings *"ass ich das Aug' erschaut,"* Windgassen's reach to the A sharp on "Aug" is radiant with joy; when singing the three-note descending cadence (A sharp – G – F) for the concluding words *"das jetzt mir Se*[*li-gem lacht!*]*"*[104] he makes the best of the (written) *fermata* in tandem with some outrageous but winning *portamento*. The effect is unforgettable, and highly distinctive – even though he is, throughout the opera, overwhelmed by Nilsson. With every performance by Windgassen and Nilsson of *Siegfried*, there was a bitter sting to her delivery of the words *"Du wonniges Kind!"*.[105] Windgassen's guttural projection of *"O Weib,* [*jetzt*] *lösche den Brand!"*[106] is striking in its unorthodoxy, as is his poetic delivery of Wagner's barely singable doggerel[107] *"Dich lieb' ich: o liebtest mich du! Nicht hab' ich mehr mich: o, hätte ich dich!"*.[108] Windgassen's light touch is particularly valuable in the long sections of fugal writing for the tenor and strings, during which his voice keys instrumentally with the violin and 'cello counterpoint. He makes much of the cyclical *"Sei mein…,"* and he digs through Procrustean depths

---

103   26 June, 1914 – 8 September, 1974.
104   'Now I behold those eyes, bright stars which laugh on my joy!'
105   'O innocent child!'
106   'O maid, you started the fire!'
107   Even non-German speakers will appreciate the reference to William McGonagall.
108   'I love you: did you but love me! Mine I am no more: were you but mine!'

to reach for his thrilling and elegiac articulation of the four-note (B flat – D – F – B flat) clarion injunction "[*Heil der Welt*], *der Brünnhilde lebt!*".[109] For a singer with a voice cast for much lighter repertoire, Windgassen's achievements at Bayreuth were sensational, famously and eternally throughout the still-unsurpassed *Tristan* with Nilsson and Böhm, recorded in 1966. After his retirement, a sign was posted briefly to the doors of the Festspielhaus announcing "Theatre closed until a heldentenor is found." Of course, if Windgassen was not the only *heldentenor* working in Germany, there were pitifully few others from which to choose, which was a disaster when considering the number of theatres capable of staging first-class productions of Wagner's operas after 1955.

The best of Windgassen's mostly anodyne contemporaries was Fritz Uhl.[110] His only immediate successors were Spas Wenkoff[111] and René Kollo.[112] The century rounded with Peter Hofmann,[113] Reiner Goldberg[114] and Siegfried Jerusalem.[115] Uhl, Wenkoff and Goldberg were journeymen. Kollo made many recordings and was popular; he was no *heldentenor*, however. Neither was Hofmann, although he had the advantage of being the imagined physical embodiment of Siegfried and Tristan. All of Windgassen's German-school contemporaries and successors were essentially "forced" lyric tenors. Only Jerusalem was able to produce the resonance and the art petitioned by Wagner; in his isolation he can be appreciated as the last true *heldentenor* of the 20th century – adhering to a tradition that passed through Slezak, Lorenz and Walter rather than Winkelmann, Schmedes and Melchior. Like Wunderlich, Jerusalem's career began in the pit, as a bassoonist. Though taking singing lessons at the time, he surprised many by standing in for an unavailable Franco Bonisolli in 1971, when due to perform in the orchestra for a televised production of *Der Zigeunerbaron*. Jerusalem was 31 years old at the time. The late start to his career as a tenor contributed to the preservation of his voice over more than 25 years of unfailing commitment to the most demanding repertoire in opera. In fact, it's a testament to his training, patience and judgment that he did not hit his stride until his late 40s, when he sang Loge (1988), Siegfried (1990) and Parsifal (1992) for James Levine at the Met, and Parsifal (1989), Siegfried (1991) and Tristan (1995) for Barenboim at Bayreuth.[116] He was the model of Wagner's axiom, "Learn how to sing Mozart. You will then be able, without harm to your voice, to sing my operas."[117] Jerusalem sang Mozart successfully, albeit infrequently, after making his debut at Bayreuth in 1977 in the smaller, lighter voiced roles of Froh (*Das Rheingold*) and Ein junger Seemann[118]

---

109 'Blessed the world, where Brünnhilde lives!'
110 2 April, 1928 – 21 May, 2001.
111 23 September, 1928 – 12 August, 2013.
112 20 November, 1937 –
113 22 August, 1944 – 30 November, 2010.
114 17 October 1939 –
115 17 April, 1940 –
116 This distinguishes the horrible studio recording with the Berliner Philharmoniker (with much the same cast as appeared for the incendiary performance from Bayreuth), demonstrating the value and virtue of recording live performances – even if Heiner Müller's production was more oratorio than opera.
117 Rene, Schoen and Eugenie, Anna (1941). *America's Musical Inheritance – Memories and Reminiscences*. G.P Putnam. p.71.
118 'A Young Sailor.'

(*Tristan*). He relocated to Lohengrin and soon after to Parsifal and Walter. In Vienna he took on Siegmund, alongside Jessye Norman, and in 1988 he was cast as Siegfried at Bayreuth. There are serious problems with Barenboim's *Ring* cycle (as recorded), but Jerusalem is not among them. The granularity and warmth of his voice, together with its bright and easy tone, are propelled for the most part by an irrepressible *schwung* – so that the undeniable absence of baritonal weight never becomes an issue. Indeed, Jerusalem was alone in approximating Wagner's lyrical-poetical tenor ideal between 1975 and 2010. That ideal killed many more careers than it preserved. The list of survivors is short; the list of victors is positively sparse. In 1966, Martin Bernheimer declared:

> The world of Wagnerian tenors is in crisis. In the international community of singers there may be five or six performers who can even get through these roles, and then usually with the help of a sympathetic conductor, an editor's scissors, and some cleverly executed vocal cheating.[119]

At much the same time, John Culshaw recalled that "The Siegfried situation was the bane of opera houses all over the world, because there was only one Siegfried: Wolfgang Windgassen."[120] After Winckelmann, and between Gustav Walter and Siegfried Jerusalem, the evolution of the "German" tenor voice, and the *heldentenor* in particular, has seen the fracturing and re-positioning of expectations. The definitive strengths of the few have been separated from their manifest weaknesses, just as compromises had to be made once King and Vickers had hung up their "spears and magic helmets." The truth so far as Wagner's operas are concerned is that there is no ideal. Every one of those singers isolated in this chapter failed in some manner or detail to meet the expectations created by Wagner, culturally and through his scores. The construction of an archetype, as it was ridiculed by Warner Bros., isolated qualities and values that ask so much of an individual that the collective is commonly damned before anyone can truly save it. The roll call of those who were said to be the "next great thing" is littered with casualties who fell to an event horizon of hubris and conventional wisdom, and yet the chewing up of tenors by the Wagner machine is inevitable for any major cultural city keen to remain relevant. Even small Houses now routinely stage Wagner and Strauss. They cannot be expected to present *heldentenors* formed of ideals that operate outside the possible and the normative, and it may yet be recognised that even the best have been the least incapable of a necessarily mortal bunch.

---

119   Bernheimer, Martin. "The World of Wagnerian Tenors," *Los Angeles Times*, March 10, 1966, quoted in Emmons, Shirlee (1990). *Tristanissimo: The Authorized Biography of Heroic Tenor Lauritz Melchior* (Schirmer Books). p.315.
120   Culshaw, John (1967). *Ring Resounding*. Viking Press. p.126.

Chapter Fifteen

Parfum exotique

The "open" letter was an important dialectical means of social dialogue in France during the 18th century. Addressed to a specific recipient, these pamphlets voiced positions between authors, commonly in cultural, political and scientific arenas – culminating in modern times with the war of words between Bernard Shaw and Ernest Newman over Strauss' *Elektra*. One of the most productive of all French debates was published in January 1761, during the Seven Years' War, when Voltaire attacked Deodati de' Tovazzi's *Dissertation sur l'excellence de la langue italienne*.[1] The primary *gloire de France* for Voltaire was her language. Deodati did not agree and complained that Italian was insufficiently valued in France (and across Europe). Attacks on Italian for "*its lack of energy*"[2] were unacceptable when noting its superiority "*to all other languages*". Across six lengthy articles, Deodati isolated the areas in which French was inferior to Italian: *abondance, netteté, flexibilité, harmonie, noblesse* and *énergie*.[3] He cited and analysed individual words and passages, presenting Ariosto, Dante and Tasso as exemplars of linguistic flexibility and expression. In his "*Réponse*," Voltaire paid tribute to the beauty, clarity and harmony of French while criticising the limited range of word endings in Italian. Voltaire was especially proud of French poetry, which he memorialised through tributes to individual writers as evidence for the nation's significance as a cultural and (with ill-disguised bellicosity) military force without compare.

Language for Voltaire equated to national identity; its power was transcendent of borders. He correlated contemporary French decadence with the failure of France's armed forces; this loss of cultural prestige was a loss for which language compensated as a form of expression and by way of a solution. The tension between French and Italian cultural achievements remained acute long after Voltaire's death in 1778; during his lifetime he did what he could to resist Italian dominance by contributing to a number of projects that attempted to present French musical theatre as equivalent, if not openly superior, to Italian – even when it had been composed by Italians. In 1765, for example, Charles-Simon Favart wrote a libretto for Egidio Duni's *La fée Urgèle, ou Ce qui plaît aux dames*[4] – an opéra comique (or *comédie mêlée d'ariettes*, as it was known) based on Voltaire's *Ce qui plaît aux dames*[5] and Chaucer's "The Wife of

---

1 Iverson, John R. (Spring, 2000). "Voltaire's Militant Defense of the French Language." *Romance Notes*, Vol. 40, No. 3. pp.313–324.
2 *Ibid*, p.317.
3 'Abundance, sharpness, flexibility, harmony, nobility and energy.'
4 'The Fairy Urgèle, or What Pleases Women.'
5 'What the ladies like.'

Bath's Tale." This medievalist fantasy was first performed on 26 October, 1765, at a cost of 20,000 livres,[6] with the role of Robert, "un chevalier," performed by the tenor Clairval.[7] In his memoirs, the Irish tenor, Michael Kelly, recalled seeing Clairval as Blondel, the role he created for the first performance of André Grétry's opéra comique, *Richard Cœur-de-lion,*[8] on 21 October, 1784:

> I always thought it Grétry's masterpiece. Clairval, the original Blondel, gave the air of "*O Richard! O mon Roi*!" with great expression. His acting in the scene, when he heard the voice of Richard from the prison, was electrifying: his joy, his surprise, at having found his king, the trembling of his voice, his scrambling up the tree to let Richard hear his voice, and the expression altogether, made an impression on me that never can be effaced: and while I remained at Paris, I never missed going to see him.[9]

Clairval was of huge importance to Grétry, for whom he created roles in *Le Huron* (1768), *Zémire et Azor* (1771), *Les mariages samnites* (1776), *L'amant jaloux*[10] (1778), and *Aucassin et Nicolette* (1779). He was valued also by the chess-player and composer Philidor, who engaged him to create the title role in his setting of Fielding's *Tom Jones* in 1765. Clairval was an *haute-contre* – a tenor higher in range that the *taille* (equivalent to a high baritone) that came to prominence in France with the operas of Lully, eight of which (out of 14) were written for *hautes-contre*. The voice was characterised by a significant range that compelled the routine use of *falsetto*. The origins of the *haute-contre* date back to the establishment of the Académie Royale de Musique in 1669, and the ambitions of the poet Pierre Perrin, who determined the creation of a novel synthesis of French poetry and music as a mechanism for the projection of national character. The voice was certainly ambiguous where gender was concerned, with many tenors playing *travesti* parts (such as the title role in Rameau's *Platée*). Marc-Antoine Charpentier (himself a high tenor), Rameau and Gluck all made regular use of the voice. Gluck wrote his main *hautes-contre* roles for Joseph Legros,[11] a singer renowned for his "unusually brilliant and flexible upper register, particularly from top F to B flat."[12] Gluck recoiled from Legros' limited expressive palette and thought him incapable as an actor. He recoiled also from his failure to articulate as he might the words of his poets. Legros was the Company principal, however, and entitled as of right to every leading role. He secured in consequence the glory of being the first Achilles in *Iphigénie en Aulide* and Orphée in the premiere of the Paris version of *Orfeo ed Euridice*, for which Gluck transposed the title role as he wrote it for the *castrato* Gaetano Guadagni. Gluck exploited Legros' ringing upper register; he transposed the duet in Act III from G to F to take full advantage of Legros' high

---

6   Almost $1,000,000 in 2020.
7   Jean-Baptiste Guignard (27 April, 1735 – 1795).
8   'Richard the Lionheart.'
9   *Reminiscences of Michael Kelly: Of the King's Theatre, and Theatre, Volume 1*. (1826). H. Coburn. p.290.
10 'The Jealous Lover.'
11 7 or 8 September, 1739 – 20 December, 1793.
12 Howard, Patricia, ed. (1981). *C. W. von Gluck: Orfeo*. Cambridge University Press. p.72.

Cs, while ensuring some (potentially) thrilling D5s for Orphée's lamentation "*Soyez, soyez sensibles, L'excès de mes malheurs*".[13] That Legros could navigate the *haute-contre* stratosphere is well documented; so too is Gluck's loathing of Legros' tendency to shriek. During one clearly stressful rehearsal, the composer addressed Legros with undisguised contempt:

> My good sir, it is intolerable: you always scream when you should sing, and when it is a question of screaming, you don't. Think at this moment neither of the music nor of the chorus, but scream with just as much anguish as if someone were sawing through your bone. And, if you can, realise this pain inwardly, spiritually, and as if it came from the heart.[14]

According to Hector Berlioz, when rehearsing Orphée's first aria in Act II, at the gates of Hades, Gluck called out "Be good enough to moderate your clamour. By the very devil, they don't cry out like that, even in hell!"[15] The rehearsals paid off. Legros was hailed "as one of the most prominent miracles wrought by the enchanter Gluck."[16] During the following nine years, Legros appeared in all the French operas by Gluck, taking the roles of Admetus in the revision of *Alceste*, Renaud in *Armide*, Pylades in *Iphigénie en Tauride* and Cynire in *Echo et Narcisse*. Over time, and thanks to Gluck's tireless harassment, Legros established the model of the "modern" French tenor – which appears from what was written at the time to have operated modally as a quasi-spoken voice.[17] Modal singing is broadly characterised by the interplay between the active thyroarytenoid muscles and bulges in the vocal fold medially below the vocal folds connecting to the arytenoid cartilages. This interaction creates a thicker, deeper *vibrat*ing structure, of particular value in speech-singing and *falsetto* registers. Legros' range was typical, spanning C3 to D5, and his tone was said to be vibrant in its resonance. Pierre Jélyotte,[18] one of Rameau and Lully's favourite *hautes-contre*, was much praised for the power of his high register, although high tenors working in *falsetto* were not typically resonant. The skill of the art was in ensuring the clarity of words that do not, as a rule, sound well in *falsetto* – a complaint made routinely by Rossini, who wrote roles in French for *haute-contre* protagonists in *Le Comte Ory* and *Le siège de Corinthe*.

Tenors in France during the 18th century were required to perform as much as singing actors, as artists for whom the polarities of music and speech were uncertain as the distinctions between French and Italian theatre and language. Gluck would not have advocated shrieking had he not been seeking something more than "mere" song. With these polarities, as stabilised by a German,[19] Gluck's ascendance

---

13 'Be sensitive, The excess of my pains.'
14 Howard, Patricia, ed. (1981). *C. W. von Gluck: Orfeo*. Cambridge University Press. p.72.
15 *Ibid*. p.91.
16 *Ibid*. p.72.
17 Bernardoni, Nathalie Henrich (February, 2006). "Mirroring the voice from García to the present day: Some insights into singing voice registers." *Logopedics Phoniatrics Vocology*. 31: 3–14.
18 13 April, 1713 – 11 September, 1797.
19 There has been much debate since before Gluck's death as to the composer's nationality – and his native language. Gluck's student in Vienna, Antonio Salieri, recorded in his memoirs that his first language

in Paris provoked a *querelle des Bouffons*[20] between the supporters of French opera, after its reformation by Rameau and Rousseau, and an Italian faction for whom Neapolitan opera, and the work of Niccolò Piccinni, were pre-eminent. The physical location of "French" opera was Paris, and in particular the Opéra (for serious dramas with recitative rather than spoken words), the Opéra-Comique (for works in French, with speech), and the Théâtre-Italien (for operas by Italian composers). The fence was jumped by Gaspare Spontini and Luigi Cherubini, who specialised in French operatic forms, with uneven success and popularity. The latter was painted by Ingres with the composer sat in front of Terpsichore. She stands behind him with her right hand extended above his head. Large parts of the Muse were painted for Ingres by his German-born pupil, Henri Lehmann, who used a chemical in the oil paint to prevent drying so that Ingres might complete the image to his satisfaction.[21] This caused the oil to crack with time, which produced an extraordinary effect wherein the pigment introduced the symbolism of *ancien et archaïque*. For the composer of *Medea*, this temporal drama made piercing narrative sense: Cherubini's work after 1815 was eclipsed entirely by the evolving romanticism of Rossini, whose pre-eminence in Italy and, eventually, Paris opened the door for many to the emerging vernacular of romanticism.

Ingres held Cherubini in the highest esteem; he related also to the Italian's status as a cultural outsider. In 1817 Beethoven had declared Cherubini to be the greatest living composer; by the end of 1830, the Italian's adherence to classical tradition had left him out of step with the dominant taste for the *bel cantisti* – in much the same way as Ingres was eclipsed by Delacroix and his followers. Ingres and Cherubini were profoundly gifted artists whose work aged dramatically by context. The Classical–Romantic dichotomy was never more extreme than for those unwilling to embrace the "noise" of the *Chasse aux lions*[22] and *Benvenuto Cellini*.[23] When the latter failed after just four performances in September, 1838, Berlioz resigned himself to the curse of the foreign, with which he (as a French composer) was unable to compete. An obsession with French identity as it was expressed in words and through art was an abiding obsession for Ingres as well as Berlioz, as a painter for whom "language" was a lifelong pre-occupation. A violinist of some skill, Ingres was hateful of Italian music – notwithstanding his passing friendship with Paganini – and his devotion to Gluck and Mozart was never threatened by the music of Berlioz and his French-born peers. In his Memoirs, Berlioz conceded with touching generosity:

> This resemblance between my opinions and those of M. Ingres on the subject of several serious Italian operas by Rossini is not the only one that I can honour myself with. However, it does not prevent the illustrious

---

was Czech, and that he spoke German only with effort. Salieri mentions that Gluck jumped between languages when speaking, namely Czech, German, Italian and French.
20   'Quarrel of the Jesters.'
21   Tinterow, Gary (1999). "*Paris, 1841–1867*". In *The Portraits of Ingres: Image of an Epoch*. The Metropolitan Museum of Art, New York; the National Gallery, London; the National Gallery of Art, Washington D.C. pp.378–386.
22   Series of seven paintings by Delacroix (1849–1861).
23   Opera by Berlioz (1838).

author of the *Martyrdom of Saint-Symphorien* from looking at me as an abominable musician, a monster, a robber, an antichrist. But I sincerely forgive him because of his admiration for Gluck. Enthusiasm would therefore be the opposite of love; he makes us love people who love what we love, even when they hate us!

Ingres' battle with his native critics (in which frustration he was joined, ironically, by Berlioz) pushed him into the arms of his German cousins, which included the eternally cosmopolitan cultural polyglot, Franz Liszt, whom Ingres painted in 1839. Ingres was unambiguous when writing coincidentally *"Music! What divine art! Honest, because music has its manners too. Italian music only has bad ones, but German!"*.[24] When Paganini performed in Paris at the Théâtre des Italiens on 10 April, 1831, Ingres attended – having drawn the violinist's portrait in 1819 – in the hope of hearing the man with whom he had played Beethoven's quartets. His pleasure in Paganini's *legato* was described by his student Amaury-Duval[25]:

> From the moment the first deep, low notes flowed from his instrument, we understood whom we were dealing with, and M. Ingres began to express the pleasure he was feeling in a series of admiring gestures....[26]

Once the violinist began to appeal to the cheaper seats, however, Ingres' reaction changed dramatically:

> When Paganini launched into one of those exercises of prestidigitation, those *tours de force* that have inspired an utterly ridiculous school, M. Ingres's brow darkened, and, his anger rising in... proportion to the public's enthusiasm, he soon could not contain himself: "That isn't him" he said. I heard his feet stamping on the floor with impatience, and the words turncoat and traitor spilling from his indignant lips.[27]

The "ridiculous school" was the empty vessel of virtuosity for its own sake; Paganini's treachery was to have abandoned German music for Italian – chiefly his own. There was a necessary correlation for Ingres – and French audiences more generally – between his acrobatics and the vocal *effluvium* of tenors given to showing off. The floridity and alleged flippancy of Italian music when sung or played on the violin was an easy target for French audiences seeking something meaningful – which Paganini, Rossini, Donizetti and Bellini were able to provide only to a limited

---

24   '*La musique! Quel art divin! Honnête, car la musique a aussi ses moeurs. L'Italienne n'en a que de mauvaises: mais l'allemande!*' In Ingres, *Ecrats*; p.89. The irony of Ingres' prejudices would have cut Berlioz deeply, since his third opera, the comedy *Béatrice et Bénédict*, was written in 1862 for a theatre in Germany, where audiences were more responsive to innovation.
25   Eugène Emmanuel Amaury Pineux Duval.
26   Tinterow, Gary (1999). "*Paris, 1841–1867*". In *The Portraits of Ingres: Image of an Epoch*. The Metropolitan Museum of Art, New York; the National Gallery, London; the National Gallery of Art, Washington D.C. p.227.
27   *Ibid.*

extent.²⁸ Paganini, in particular, was walking in the shadow of Giovanni Battista Viotti, whose debut in Paris in 1782 (when Paganini was just two years old) caused a sensation. Viotti was one of the first to use the newly designed "Tourte" bow, which allowed for more expressive articulation, dynamics and fluency. It was something of an irony that Paganini's celebrity among his composing-performing peers originated with his exceptional *cantabile* – to which Viotti and the *famille* Tourte contributed much – while his celebrity was formed almost entirely by the crackle and pop of music that was paradigmatically *staccato*. Viotti's legacy was to produce almost exclusively Franco-Belgian talent, famously Pierre Rode, Pierre Baillot, Charles-Auguste de Bériot and Henry Vieuxtemps – each of whom managed to absorb something of Paganini's showmanship and theatricality while cultivating a native voice independent of any other.

Before the effect of Gilbert Duprez's "squawk" could properly be digested and regurgitated, French tenors were as used to singing in Italian as French. All of them employed *falsetto* – a necessarily feminised vocal tone that attached the singer to the *hautes-contre* and, in turn, the *castrati* whom they had replaced. One of the most successful was Alexis Dupont.²⁹ He studied initially in Paris, graduating from the Conservatoire in 1818. After five years of theatrical engagements he suffered a technical crisis and headed to Italy to complete three further years of training in Italy. A few months after his debut at the Opéra in 1826, as Pylades in Gluck's *Iphigénie en Tauride*, Berlioz chose Dupont to sing in the premiere of his cantata *La Mort d'Orphélie*³⁰ at its (failed) examination performance for the Prix de Rome in July, 1827.³¹ Twelve years later, he was again Berlioz's choice to create the tenor role in

---

28 At the end of Chapter 24 of his *Mémoires*, Berlioz applauded "heart and soul our great painter Ingres, when I hear him say when speaking of certain works by Rossini: 'It is the music of a dishonest man.'"
29 1796 – 29 May, 1874.
30 'Death of Ophelia.'
31 Berlioz's imagined conversation between two of the judges (in Chapter 23, "L'huissier de l'Institut – Ses révélations" of his *Mémoires*) is worth repeating in full:

"*Je vous l'ai déjà dit, vous avez le second prix, et il ne vous a manqué que deux voix pour le premier. Quand M. Dupont a eu chanté votre cantate, ils ont commencé à écrire leurs bulletins et j'ai apporté la hurne. Il y avait un musicien de mon côté, qui parlait bas à un architecte et qui lui disait: Voyez-vous, celui-là ne fera jamais rien; ne lui donnez pas votre voix, c'est un jeune homme perdu. Il n'admire que le dévergondage de Beethoven; on ne le fera jamais rentrer dans la bonne route.*
'*Vous croyez, dit l'architecte? cependant...*
'*Oh! C'est très-sur; d'ailleurs demandez à notre illustre Cherubini. Vous ne doutez pas de son expérience, j'espère; il vous dira comme moi, que ce jeune homme est fou, que Beethoven lui a troublé la cervelle.*
'*Pardon, me dit Pingard en s'interrompant, mais qu'est-ce que ce monsieur Beethoven? il n'est pas de l'Institut, et tout le monde en parle.*
'*Non, il n'est pas de l'Institut. C'est un Allemand: continuez'.*"

"'I told you before, you have the second prize, and you only missed two votes for the first. When M. Dupont had sung your cantata, they began to write their bulletins and I brought the *hurne*. There was a musician on my side, who spoke low to an architect and who said to him: You see, this one will never do anything; don't give him your voice, he's a lost young man. He admires only Beethoven's shamelessness; we will never get him back on the right track.
'You think so, said the architect?' However...
'Oh! It is very certain; moreover ask our illustrious Cherubini. You do not doubt his experience, I hope; he will tell you, like me, that this young man is mad, that Beethoven has troubled his brain.

the Prologue to the dramatic symphony *Roméo et Juliette*, on 24 November, 1839. In August, 1844 – three years after his retirement – Dupont joined Duprez when supporting Berlioz as one of 100 tenors in the chorus conducted by the composer at his "*Monstre*" concert in August, 1844, with 1,025 performers.[32] During his two decades at the Opéra-Comique and the Opéra, Dupont created numerous roles for Rossini (*Moïse et Pharaon, Le comte Ory* and *Guillaume Tell*), Auber (*La muette de Portici*), Halévy (*La tentation*), Meyerbeer (*Les Huguenots*) and Louise Bertin (*La Esmeralda*). He did so using *falsetto* for everything above an A4, and then with an often choking weight of floridity. His voice was described (after retirement) by Charles Hervey as a "sweet but delicate organ ... drowned by the orchestra of the Académie Royale ...". This absence of vocal heft might, of course, have been a consequence of the often *very* large orchestras in Paris, notable for their alimentary wind sections. More probably, lightness of tone was compensated for by the use of declamatory techniques – a kind of emphatic projection, analogous to a tonally centred *sprechgesang* that can be heard in its "driest" form in the recorded performances of Sarah Bernhardt.

When Debussy was setting Baudelaire's "*Spleen*" from *Les Fleurs du Mal* ("*Quand le ciel bas et lourd pèse comme un couvercle*"[33]), his amendments and variations over the course of different versions of the song reflected the evolution of the developing approach to articulation during the latter stages of the French nineteenth century. The difference between the two declamatory styles – *parlée* and *chantée* – amplified the significance of performance within the versification of French poetry as song,[34] something remembered by the conductor Désiré-Émile Inghelbrecht when retained as chorus master for the first performance of Debussy's *Le martyre de Saint Sébastien*. In 1913 he was appointed director of the new Théâtre des Champs-Élysées, and in 1921 he conducted the premiere of *Les mariés de la tour Eiffel*, a ballet by five of "Les Six." He was engaged as music director of the Opéra-Comique in 1924, and in 1933 he recalled how, when working with Debussy

> the performers would often benefit from sometimes saying the text, before adding the Debussy-ist melody intended to poetize it afterwards."[35]

'Pardon me,' said Pingard, interrupting himself, 'but what is this Monsieur Beethoven? He is not from the Institute, and everyone is talking about him.

'No, he's not from the Institute. He's a German: continue.'"

32   The *London Times* reported on 5 August, 1844 that: "The most remarkable effect produced by this colossal union of voices and instruments was the full chorus in a hymn to France, composed by Berlioz for this occasion, and the effect of the words *Dieu protège la France!* which forms the refrain, was positively electric... the air which received the most enthusiastic applause was not for any beauty in the composition, or the execution, but simply because it exhibits an anti-English feeling—this was Halévy's "*Chant National*" from the opera of *Charles VI*, in which the now well-known couplet, "*Jamais en France*"/"*Jamais l'Angleterre ne regnera!*" was followed by rapturous and long-reiterated plaudits…"

33   'When the low heavy sky weighs like a lid.'

34   Dubiau-Feuillerac, Mylène (2013). "*Verlaine/Debussy: la 'mise en sons' de 'Spleen'*. " *Dix-Neuf* (Journal of the Society of Dix-Neuxiémistes), 17:1. pp.57–77.

35   "*Les interprètes gagneraient souvent à dire parfois le texte, avant d'y ajouter la mélodie debussyste destinée à la poétiser ensuite.*" Inghelbrecht, Désiré-Émile (1933). *Comment on ne doit pas interpréter 'Carmen,' 'Faust' et 'Pelléas'*. Heugel. See also Abbott, Helen (2013). "Poetry, Performance, Music in Nineteenth- Century France. " *Dix-Neuf* (Journal of the Society of Dix-Neuxiémistes), 17:1. pp.1–8; p.3

Linguistic emphasis was especially valuable when the majority of French tenors were slow to adopt Duprez's ringing *do di petto*. So too was line. Much can be learned of 19th century practice in France from the surviving recordings of Victor Capoul[36] – both of them of his own "*Oh! Ne t'éveille pas encore*" from Godard's *Jocelyn*, a role he created in 1868. Four sides were recorded for Fonotipia in Paris in 1905 (of which two are lost); he was 66 years old and almost entirely deaf. Although Capoul's resources are diminished, his singing on the unreleased take is exquisite. The tone is light and the *vibrato* quick; he employs a *voix-mixte* above the stave (a kind of half *falsetto,* between chest and head voices) and his phrasing is the model of *charme* and *souplesse,*[37] qualities for which he was renowned. The performance is striking also for Capoul's dynamics, and some stunning *diminuendi*. His use of *portamento* is balanced by a clear sense of dramatic attack – as a function of melodic shape and emphasis. Most telling is the absent masculinity, which speaks to emotional availability and intuition, qualities better serving of romantic fantasy than the clichés attaching more commonly to tenors.

Capoul was a celebrity as well as a singer, having created Horace in the two-act version of Gounod's *La colombe* on 7 June 1866, Le Marquis de Kerdrel in Massenet's *La grand'tante*[38] (opposite Marie Heilbronn) on 3 April, 1867, Gaston de Maillepré in Daniel Auber's *Le premier jour de bonheur* on 15 February, 1868, and Valentin in Offenbach's *Vert-Vert* on 10 March, 1869. Karen Henson has written beautifully of Capoul's status:

> Henry Bauer of *Le Reveil-Matin* described him as "once the prettiest man in Paris... more famous, in the end, for his gallantry than for his art, and for his elegant plumage more than his warbling." At the tenor's death in 1924, apparently embittered and penniless, another writer reported that he had been turned down by the army at the time of the Franco-Prussian war because they did not need 'a ladies' man' ('un homme a femmes'). When not being catty about Capoul, men tried to imitate him: the 'coiffure a la Capoul,' a short wavy haircut with a pronounced middle parting, was fashionable until 1900 ... At the peak of his career, Capoul ties, tiepins, jackets, and 'redingotes' (more formal jackets) were the rage. He was naturally supposed to have had many lovers.[39]

Capoul's on-stage colleague for the first production of Offenbach's *Vert-Vert* in 1869 was the tenor Joseph-Antoine-Charles Couderc.[40] He had a light and reedy voice, characterised by extreme crispness of delivery, with little warmth or roundness of tone. He created numerous roles over a lengthy career, notably Daniel in Adolphe Adam's *Le chalet* (1834), George in Halévy's *L'éclair* (1835), Horace de

---

36 27 February, 1839 – 18 February, 1924. See also Chapter 1 above.
37 'Flexibility.'
38 'The Grand-mother.'
39 Henson, Karen (1999). "Victor Capoul, Marguerite Olagnier's Le Saïs, and the Arousing of Female Desire." *Journal of the American Musicological Society*, Vol. 52, No. 3. pp.419–463; p.428.
40 10 March, 1810 – 16 April, 1875.

Massarena in Auber's *Le domino noir*[41] (1837), Shakespeare in Ambroise Thomas' *Le songe d'une nuit d'été*[42] (1850), Clifford in Halévy's *Le nabab* (1853), Laerte in Thomas' *Mignon* (1866), and Baladon in *Vert-Vert*. Couderc was a renowned actor and a master of declamation – a skill in which he was said to have been bettered only by Gustave-Hippolyte Roger,[43] another star of the Opéra-Comique. Roger was greatly prized by Halévy, Auber and Thomas and in 1846 he created the role of Faust for Berlioz – contributing much to the work's instant success. Having toured England with Jenny Lind in 1849, Roger was invited by Meyerbeer to appear as Jean de Leyden in the first production of *Le prophète*, a role that most considered beyond his means. He shared the first night with a younger tenor, Louis Guéymard,[44] who created the role of Jonas. Two years later, Gounod chose Guéymard to sing Phaon at the premiere of *Sapho* and, in 1854, the first Rodolphe in *La nonne sanglante*.[45] Verdi heard him in Paris and accepted the Opéra's recommendation that he sing Henri at the first staging of *Les vêpres siciliennes*[46] in 1855.

Guéymard was one of Duprez's many "successors." When he was painted by Courbet as Robert (*le Diable*) in a dramatic canvas first shown at the Salon in 1857, the painter chose for his theme the final scene of Act 1, in which Robert plays a game of dice with two knights in service to the Devil. While Robert's wicked father looks on, he sings of the dangers of lusting after gold ("*L'or est une chimère... O fortune! à ton caprice*"[47]). It's obvious that Courbet knew the opera, and Guéymard's lionised triumph in the title role. Noting Robert's words "*Le vrai bien sur la terre n'est-il pas le plaisir?*"[48] it's no less probable that Courbet painted Guéymard with purpose; his legs are open and the singer's generously proportioned leather belt is placed exactly where it was most likely to be seen for what it represented.

The lingering appeal of vocal acrobatics stylised for the violin by Paganini, and by Jenny Lind *et al.* in the opera house, was a feature of Meyerbeer's work even into the 1850s. "*O fortune! à ton caprice*," for example, is a simple enough 6/8 *Sicilienne* in F major – but the composer marked the scene "*léger et détaché*,"[49] and throws in a number of extremely difficult phrases, with a host of grace notes designed to amplify passages of alliteration (such as "*ah n'est il pas, n'est il pas le Plaisir*"[50]). Runs of chromatic semi-quavers, demi-semi-quavers (for one bar marked *cadenza ad libitum*) and three high Cs are followed by a trilled C5 that would challenge a *coloratura* soprano. The resolving cadence is preceded by a five-bar passage in which Meyerbeer openly invites the tenor to show off his highest notes by adding the indication "*Au choix du Chanteur*."[51] Duprez did not, as a rule, sing Meyerbeer's music, and his

---

41 'The Black Domino.'
42 'A Midsummer's Night Dream.'
43 17 December, 1815 – 12 September, 1879.
44 17 August, 1822 – July, 1880.
45 'The Bloody Nun.'
46 'The Sicilian Vespers.'
47 'Gold is an illusion... O fortune! At your whim.'
48 'Isn't pleasure the greatest good on Earth?'
49 'Light and detached.'
50 'Ah, isn't it, isn't it pleasure?'
51 'At the singer's discretion.'

stentorian *spinto* (or *ténor fort*) would have brought little or nothing to such overtly acrobatic music. Guéymard would probably not have been able to sing the role as it was first performed by Nourrit in 1831. During the two decades separating Nourrit's performances from those by Guéymard the taste for "empty" vocal acrobatics had declined, to be replaced by an insatiable hunger for outré theatrical licence. This shifting dialectic was driven by the fashion among French writers for pushing boundaries.

When Duprez bid farewell to the stage in 1851 he sang the role of Edgardo in *Lucia di Lammermoor* at the Théâtre des Italiens. Gustave Flaubert's debut novel, *Madame Bovary: Mœurs de province*,[52] was published in two volumes five years later. The author was prosecuted for obscenity and tried in January, 1857 – which helped make the book a huge success. In chapter 15, at the end of Part II, Charles and Emma Bovary attend a French-language production in Rouen of *Lucia* (staged as *Lucie de Lammermoor*) – with Emma still recovering from illness and the rejection of her lover Rodolphe. Emma relates inevitably to Lucia and her prefigured tragedy; her focus during the performance is on the celebrated tenor Lagardy, however, whom Flaubert based loosely on Duprez. When describing Emma's first sight of the singer, Flaubert characterises Lagardy's

> splendid pallor which lends something of the majesty of antique marble to the passionate races of the Midi. His manly physique was held firm in a brown tunic; a little chiselled dagger knocked against his left thigh, and he gazed languorously about him while baring his white teeth. It was said that a Polish princess, listening to him sing one evening on the beach where he used to mend the launches had fallen instantly in love. She had ruined herself because of him. He had abandoned her there for other women.... A fine organ, imperturbable aplomb, more temperament than intelligence, and more bombast than lyricism rounded off this wonderful charlatan character, in whom there was something of the hairdresser and the toreador.[53]

Lagardy was renowned as a lover off stage as well as on it, and the effect of the music and the power of the words – which Emma remembers from having read Walter Scott's novel – inspire her to dream again of romance. So complete is Emma's identification with the intensity of the stage lovers' feelings that the music's climax is

---

52 'Madame Bovary: Provincial Manners.'
53 '*pâleurs splendides qui donnent quelque chose de la majesté des marbres aux races ardentes du Midi. Sa taille vigoureuse était prise dans un pourpoint de couleur brune; un petit poignard ciselé lui battait sur la cuisse gauche, et il roulait des regards langoureusement en découvrant ses dents blanches. On disait qu'une princesse polonaise, l'écoutant un soir chanter sur la plage de Biarritz, où il radoubait des chaloupes, en était devenue amoureuse. Elle s'était ruinée à cause de lui. Il l'avait plantée là pour d'autres femmes, et cette célébrité sentimentale ne laissait pas que de servir à sa réputation artistique. Le cabotin diplomate avait même soin de faire toujours glisser dans les réclames une phrase poétique sur la fascination de sa personne et la sensibilité de son âme. Un bel organe, un imperturbable aplomb, plus de tempérament que d'intelligence et plus d'emphase que de lyrisme, achevaient de rehausser cette admirable nature de charlatan, où il y avait du coiffeur et du toréador.*'

mirrored in her own:"⁵⁴ "*elle jeta un cri aigu, qui se confondait avec la vibration des derniers accords.*"⁵⁵ Many tenors entered Duprez's slipstream, as lovers as well as artists.

Emma Bovary's overt sexuality and Flaubert's clear narrative and symbolic parallels with Donizetti's opera in its performance in French by French artists on a French stage resonated at a time when French composers were beginning to emerge from under the "curse" of Italian lyric oppression – even noting Verdi's irrepressible ascendence. With Spontini, Cherubini and Berlioz failing as competing cultural *imprimaturs*, it fell to a romantic satirist of the classical to find a French voice that *le tout Paris* wanted to hear.

Jacques Offenbach traded in a coruscating and joyful mixture of the comic, the ambiguous and the mundane, and his balletic navigation of high art and low comedy was tailored perfectly to the pleasure-markets spreading across France during the 1850s. His complicated background as the German-born[56] son of a Synagogue musician who was trained as a cellist by an Italian composer (Cherubini) living in Paris equipped Offenbach to speak to more of his "own" people than any composer before him. When *Orphée aux enfers* was first performed on 21 October, 1858, Offenbach gave the role of Pluton to Achille-Félix Montaubry,[57] a fellow 'cellist who turned to singing relatively late in his career as a musician. The title role was created by Henri Tayau, a violinist who had received no voice training before Offenbach engaged him on the basis of an audition that consisted of a single popular song. It may now seem extraordinary for a culture in which vocal tuition can occupy a student for a decade, but many of Offenbach's amateur vocalists were cast in operas and operettas that would now be thought almost impossibly challenging for professionals. Montaubry, for example, signed a five-year contract at the Opéra-Comique in 1858 (generating fees of 40,000 francs per year[58]), and he performed leading roles in *Fra Diavolo*, *Le songe d'une nuit d'ete*, Ferdinand Hérold's *Zampa*, and Adam's *Le postillon de Longjumeau*. On 9 August, 1862, he sang the first Bénédict in *Béatrice et Bénédict* for Berlioz in Baden-Baden. In 1866, he was described as having

> played in the provinces and abroad before coming to Paris. A great cunning and a perfect knowledge of his art. The first string I know. At the bottom, he has few or no notes, he speaks, he eludes, he does everything except sing. His high notes have grace, always finesse, often lively and fiery: then he shouts. He says dialogue equates to meaning, it's the pretty ruin of a drawing-room. On stage, with few outfits, he has fun. He leads his song and his shoes at the same time. Every morning, after the dumbbells and hydrotherapy, he walks for two hours in his room to break his boots and find his feet.[59]

---

54 See generally Williams, John R. (1992). "Emma Bovary and the Bride of Lammermoor'" *Nineteenth-Century French Studies*, Vol. 20, No. 3/4. pp.352–360.
55 'She gave out a shrill cry, which merged with the vibrations of the final chords…'
56 He would often sign himself "O de Cologne."
57 12 November, 1826 – 2 October, 1898.
58 Approximately $450,000 – $500,000 in 2020.
59 '*débuté par jouer du violon dans quelques orchestres de petits théâtres. Entré au Conservatoire dans les classes de chant, il a joué en province et à l'étranger avant de venir à Paris. Une grande rouerie et une connaissance*

It might now seem extraordinary that Berlioz relished a singer with "few or no notes" in his lower register, who was either forced or chose to speak, elude and do "everything except sing." He did so, regardless, with grace and finesse when singing above the stave – which explains, in part, why his tendency to "ruin a drawing-room" when shouting worked more effectively in the theatre. Tayau was less equipped still as a "classical" tenor; he was nonetheless a huge draw throughout the 1860s as a *tenorino*, achieving notable successes as Flavio/Florville in Offenbach's production of Rossini's *Il signor bruschino* at the Bouffes in 1858. His talents as a comic and physical actor were legendary, and his skill with Offenbach and Halévy's often challenging patter songs ensured that audiences accepted his limitations as a "pure" vocalist. Tayau's crystalline articulation was of acute value when performing *chansonettes* (French popular song) for the *Sociétés savants* – a tradition that filtered into the *mélodies* and *chanson* (French art songs) that transferred over time to the concert hall.

Offenbach's comic genius was distinguished from the "comedy" of many other *opera buffo* composers. For a start, his works are genuinely funny; more importantly still, he pursued the sounding of each and every word because his settings were designed to do more than feed the vanity and technique of peacocks. Offenbach's settings frequently attached one syllable to a single note, a concision that valued diction above tone. Offenbach's equivalence was transformative of the culture of French lyric theatre, where performances of new works were often singular and always expensive. His democratic instincts kept costs down and ticket sales high. Volume was a metric for sales, not sound.

Because Offenbach did not expect his almost 100 operettas to remain in repertory, he required a first performance to turn a profit because there was every possibility that there might not be a second. Even accounting for Offenbach's extravagant conflation of profligacy and generosity, his success was financial as well as artistic – an achievement that helped deliver and demarcate an absolute separation between the "popular" and the "serious." Many "serious" composers rejected this division as undermining of Offenbach's talent and skill (including Debussy and Ravel). For French tenors, however, the separation of interests favoured the primacy of intelligibility over beauty.

Montaubry and Tayau were popular also in London where, in 1874, the manager of the Royalty Theatre, Richard D'Oyly Carte, commissioned William Gilbert to write a short libretto for an opera to be played as an afterpiece to Offenbach's *La Périchole*. He approached the composer Arthur Sullivan to write the music. *Trial by Jury* – the first collaboration for "Gilbert & Sullivan" – was composed and staged in a matter of weeks in 1875. The tenor roles of The Defendant (and Piquillo in *La Périchole*) were both played by Walter H. Fisher[60] – an actor who made his London Stage debut as Ambroise in the play *Broken Spells* at the Court Theatre in 1872. After

---

parfaite de son art. Le premier ficelier que je connaisse. Dans le bas, peu ou point de notes, il parle, il élude, il fait tout, chanter excepté. Dans le haut, de la grâce, toujours de la finesse, souvent de l'entrain et du feu : alors il crie. Il dit le dialogue à côté du sens, c'est une jolie ruine de salon. En scène, peu de tenue, il s'amuse. Il mène de front son chant et ses chaussures. Tous les matins, après les altères et l'hydrothérapie, deux heures de promenade dans sa chambre pour briser ses bottines et se faire le pied.' Rambaud, Yveling and Coulon, E. (1866). *Les Théâtres en robe de chambre*. Achille Faure. p.49.

60   1848 – 1 January 1893.

several performances in a range of spoken comedy roles, Fisher appeared for the first time in light opera as Marasquin in *Giroflé-Girofla*, an opéra bouffe by Charles Lecocq. Fisher was able to sing both tenor and baritone roles, and for D'Oyly Carte he appeared as Archibald Grosvenor in *Patience* (1883), Captain Corcoran in *H.M.S. Pinafore* (1887–1888), Samuel *and* Frederic in *The Pirates of Penzance* (1888) and Nanki-Poo in *The Mikado* (1888). He could sing neither Mozart nor Wagner, and there was no need for him to do so. As such, the creation of the artful "popular" tenor voice in English light musical theatre was a by-product of Offenbach's *bouffes* in Paris. The emergent species of light tenor that became so valuable to satirical music-theatre in France, England and the United States remained *en vogue* until well into the 20th century – when the "popular" voice and microphones picked up where *The Grand Duke* left off.

The Grand Duke was Gilbert and Sullivan's fourteenth and last opera together; it was premiered at the Savoy Theatre on 7 March, 1896. Eight years later (in April, 1904) Ernest Pike[61] made the first of his hundreds of recordings, "Take a Pair of Sparkling Eyes" (from Gilbert and Sullivan's *The Gondoliers*) for the Gramophone & Typewriter Company. Pike first performed for D'Oyly Carte in 1887, at the age of 16 (using the pseudonym Herbert Payne); he later toured with the "B" Company, playing one of the ghosts of the ancestors in *Ruddigore*. His singing in 1904 is typical of the English tradition of light music during and after the 1870s, and entirely awful – save that every single word is perfectly enunciated. Pike's absent technique, constricted tone and uneven pitching are typical of many French light opera tenors of the time also; these were sacrifices accepted by Offenbach at the Théâtre des Bouffes-Parisiens and by Sullivan at the Savoy, tiny theatres with small orchestras where clarity, wit and amenity were better appreciated than resonance, floridity and pitch.

Expectations were different at the Opéra after Gounod's *Faust* was first performed to huge acclaim at the Théâtre Lyrique on 19 March, 1859. The title role was given initially to Hector Gruyer who proved ill-equipped and was replaced during rehearsals by Joseph-Théodore-Désiré Barbot, a principal of the Opéra-Comique. Having come from the Opéra-Comique, Barbot's voice was not large, and in any event he was praised for his ability to draw out beautiful high notes softly.[62] Though his innate musicianship and use of dynamics was prized by Gounod, he turned to Romé Pierre-Jules Michot for the first production of *Roméo et Juliette* on 27 April, 1867. Eight years later, when staging the first production of *Carmen*, Bizet gifted the role of Don José to Paul Lhérie,[63] a dashing tenor who had achieved critical acclaim as the first Charles II for Massenet's *Don César de Bazan* (1872), Kornélis in Saint-Saëns' *La princesse jaune*[64] (1872) and Benoît in Delibes' *Le roi l'a dit*[65] (1873). Lhérie had a powerful voice by French standards and he transitioned just seven years later to a baritone – enjoying huge success as Posa at the first staging of the Italian revision of

---

61   1871 – 4 March, 1936.
62   Barbot's wife, Caroline, was a popular soprano, with an international career. She is best remembered for having created Leonora for Verdi in St. Petersburg at the first performance of *La Forza del Destino* in 1862.
63   8 October, 1844 – 17 October, 1937
64   'The Yellow Princess.'
65   'The King Has Spoken.'

Verdi's *Don Carlos*, as Zurga at the Covent Garden premiere of *Les pêcheurs de perles*[66] in 1887, and the first Rabbi David in Mascagni's *L'amico Fritz* on 31 October, 1891.

None of these singers made recordings, but much can be presumed of their voices from their repertoire, which was predominantly French and none of it heroic. Since the 1960s, the roles of Don José and Faust have been sung and recorded by increasingly dramatic voices – with Franco Corelli doing irrevocable violence to both. With the decline of the French tenor after WW2, and the ubiquity of emphatically internationalist, non-French tenors – most obviously Plácido Domingo – it is easy to forget that the established repertoire from the middle of the 19th century was almost entirely light in form and texture – even Don José. The opera's best-known aria for tenor, Act 2's "*La fleur que tu m'avais jetée*"[67] is now routinely belted – though it was written for a light voice. The opening five-note motif descends from an F4 to an E3; it is marked *piano*, with the accompanying flutes, cor anglais, clarinet, trombone and cellos in *pianissimo*. The aria remains attached to *piano* markings, with a handful of hairpins, *crescendi* and *diminuendi* until, finally, for the words "*un seul désir, un seul espoir*"[68] Bizet allows a *forte* and then a *fortissimo* for the articulation of his wish "*Te revoir, ô Carmen.*"[69] The aria returns to shades of quiet reflection when Don José sings the cumulative phrase "*Et j'étais une chose à toi*"[70] – which crests with a *diminuendo* B flat 4 of supreme delicacy. In theory, at least. Even when, at the end of Act IV, he threatens Carmen "*Pour la dernière fois, démon, veux-tu me suivre?*"[71] the score is written so that the high B flats of "*démon*" are snatched, rather than sustained for show.[72]

The ethereal sensibilities of the Opéra and the quotidian immediacy of the Bouffes were confronted with equal force by the arrival of Richard Wagner. When the Prelude to *Tristan* was first heard in Paris during his three concerts at the Théâtre-Italien in January and February, 1860, no one – including Berlioz – could grasp what was being attempted. Incomprehension yielded to outright hostility when Wagner presented his revision of *Tannhäuser* in Paris on 13 March, 1861.[73] The Franco-Prussian War of 1870–71 amplified the German composer's status as an invading force – particularly at the Conservatoire, where there was a natural disconnect between the training of singers to perform French work and the increasing popularity of Wagner's emblematically Teutonic music dramas. In the wake of Berlioz's settings of Gautier's verses in 1841 as *Nuits d'été*, the emergence of the *mélodie* as a conscious reaction to the German *Lied* became a political weapon after France's defeat by Prussia.[74]

For the singers themselves, of course, the Wagner-effect was a challenge of characteristically epic proportions. Berlioz wrote frequently for a huge orchestra, but he

---

66 'The Pearl Fishers.'
67 'The flower that you threw at me.'
68 'a single desire, a single hope.'
69 'to see you again, O Carmen.'
70 'and I was a thing of yours.'
71 'For the last time, you devil, will you come with me?'
72 The word is scored as a semi-quaver-crotchet.
73 The anger of the audience's reaction was such that the run had to be cancelled after just three performances.
74 See generally Faure, Michel and Vivès, Vincent (2000). *Histoire et poétique de la mélodie française*. CNRS Editions.

did so with sensitivity to his singers. The same was not true of Wagner. The first French production of *Tannhäuser*, for example, did not feature a single French-born singer in the main cast,[75] and Wagner's operas remained a difficult proposition for French-trained voices while singers, teachers, academies and composers acclimatised to the new aesthetic. Even (or particularly) when performed in French, the scale of Wagner's demands outstripped the supply of suitable voices in an operatic culture where the heroic was embraced fully by a single composer, Berlioz. Even then, Berlioz's dramatic sensibilities were diaphanous compared to those of his younger German rival. A more robust vocal hue was advanced by Camille Saint-Saëns in 1877 with *Samson et Dalila*.

Shortly after the premiere of Saint-Saëns' second opera, *La princesse jaune*, the composer travelled to Weimar for the first revival of *Das Rheingold*, conducted by Liszt – who persuaded Saint-Saëns to finish *Samson*. Act 1 was performed in isolation in 1875 at the Théâtre du Châtelet; it was received harshly by critics and public alike. The work was completed in 1876 – after Saint-Saëns attended the first *Ring* Cycle. There was no desire in France to stage it, however. Liszt came to the rescue and arranged for the first performance in Weimar on 2 December, 1877.[76] The role of Samson was created by Franz Ferenczy,[77] the leading tenor at the Grossherzogliches Theater (now the Staatskapelle Weimar) and one of the first internationally successful Wagner tenors not to pass through Bayreuth. Ferenczy studied initially in Milan, with Francesco Lamperti,[78] an illustrious miserabilist and professional augur of the decadence and ruin of contemporary singing. For all his prominence, Lamperti was not close to Verdi, and in tandem with the musicologist Abramo Basevi (who dismissed Verdi's innovations as "*l'effetto e nient'altro che l'effetto*"[79]) he considered the cheapening appeal of overly dramatic vocal mannerisms to be the undoing of the lyric tradition as it had been memorialised by Rubini. Lamperti and Basevi were repulsed by the overwhelming tendency towards heightened dramatic character in its operation at the expense of pure melody.

Ferenczy was contracted to Graz and Berlin (where he was all but adopted by Giacomo Meyerbeer), Moscow, and London. He joined the Wiener Hofoper in 1864, with whom he toured Scandanavia. He sang fluently in German, Italian and French and traded in a repertoire that spanned Adolar in *Euryanthe*, Arnoldo in *Guillaume Tell*, Eléazar in *La Juive*, Jean de Leyden and Jonas in *Le prophète*, Raoul de Nangis in *Les Huguenots*, Vasco da Gama in *L'Africaine*, the Duke, Manrico, Loge and Siegmund. Ferenczy was not a "French tenor," therefore; rather, he was a polyglot troubadour, after the fashion (if never the reputation) of Jean De Reszke. He too could sing pretty much everything – as a dramatic tenor capable of lightening his tone, including Saint-Saëns' Samson, the first vocally "heroic" role in French opera.

---

75 A technicality for some, perhaps, but Marie Constance Sasse – who sang Elisabeth – was Belgian.
76 Liszt did not conduct, however. The baton was passed to Eduard Lassen, Liszt's successor as music director in 1858 (and until 1895). Lassen also conducted the first performance in Weimar, and the first outside Munich, of *Tristan und Isolde* in 1874.
77 1835 – 27 February, 1881.
78 11 March, 1811 or 1813 – 1 May, 1892. A legendary teacher at the Milan Conservatory from 1850, whose students included Italo Campanini and the sopranos Teresa Stolz and Emma Albani.
79 'The effect and nothing but the effect.'

The score was written at a time when there were few native-French heroic tenors, so the work's second production was, again, in Germany – at the Hamburgische Hofoper in 1882. French audiences were not introduced to Samson until 3 March, 1890, when the Théâtre des Arts in Rouen presented the national premiere with Emmanuel Lafarge and Carlotta Bossi.[80] Lafarge studied at the Conservatoire in Paris before making his debut in Rouen in 1889. From 1890 to 1892 he was engaged at the Théâtre Royal de la Monnaie in Brussels, from where he moved to Lyon Opera and, for the season 1894–95, to La Scala, where he sang Samson as well as the title role in Ernest Reyer's love letter to Wagner, *Sigurd*. He sang Siegmund at the Opéra on 31 July, 1896. Lafarge was best known as a singer of Wagner, and it is as a Wagner tenor that he can be heard on some early cylinder recordings, most notably "*L'entrée du cygnet*" from *Lohengrin* and "*Nothung! Nothung!*" from *Siegfried* (which he introduces as "*Couplets de la forge*"). He recorded both in French, without accompaniments. The former is remarkable for its phrasing, which accounts for the peculiarities of the French language when sung. Though nasal on occasion, his tone is open and warm. It is coloured more by *portamento* (rising and falling) than *vibrato*, of which there is almost none. Even 120 years later, every word is delivered with perfect clarity, with some fascinating "spreading" of syllables. When speaking to introduce his recording, he announces the opera as "*Loh-en-ger-in*". Lafarge employs *gruppetti* in both Wagner excerpts, and with considerable flamboyance for "*Nothung*," which he delivers in a vibrant form of *sprechgesang* that was plainly in accord with *fin de siècle* French tastes.

The richness and rotundity of pronunciation as it is captured on record around 1900 was suggestive of John Cleese's axiomatic declaration in the *Holy Grail*, "I'm French. Why do you think I have this outrageous accent, you silly King?" Word use was then far more expressive, both when sung and spoken, and then to a point of apparent artificiality. Louis Becq de Fouquières attempted to explicate the scansion of French verse using musical notation in 1879, with his *Traité général de versification française*,[81] and while his codification of poetic reading practices through music was embraced as necessary performance in French was too supple and flexible to be notated precisely.

The best and clearest evidence for French tenor style during the last two decades of the 19th century is Lafarge's recording of "*Esprits, gardiens de ces lieux vénérés*"[82] from *Sigurd*, with piano.[83] The singing is nothing short of sublime; the languid phrasing and resplendent B4s are markedly superior. The voice would now be considered "small" and unsuited to Siegmund, far less Siegfried, but contemporary expectations were defined by the pre-eminent virtues of word-colour and expression – over and above amplitude. Lafarge's example appears to have aligned him with Jean-Alexandre Talazac,[84] who sang the role of *Samson* at the first Parisian production (at the recently constructed Éden-Théâtre) on Rue Boudreau on 31 October, 1890. Talazac was an

---

80   8 July, 1862 – 1911.
81   'General Treaty of French Versification'. Abbott, Helen (2013). "Poetry, Performance, Music in Nineteenth- Century France." *Dix-Neuf* (Journal of the Society of Dix-Neuxièmistes), 17:1. pp.1–8; p.3.
82   'Spirits, guardians of these venerated places.'
83   It still seems bizarre that so many early recordings were produced with badly maintained pianos. This is one of the worst.
84   16 May, 1853 – 26 December, 1892.

obvious choice, having established his reputation as a singer of acute musical sensitivity with atypical power and resonance in creator roles for Offenbach (as the first *Hoffmann* in 1881), Delibes (as the first Gérald in *Lakmé* in 1883), Massenet (as the first Des Grieux in *Manon* in 1884) and Lalo (as the first Mylio in *Le Roi d'Ys*[85] in 1888). With 4,000 seats and a huge stage, the Éden was one of Europe's largest theatres.[86] It presented the city's infamous first production of Wagner's *Lohengrin* on 30 April, 1887 – in French with Ernest van Dyck in the title role, and Charles Lamoureux conducting – as well as numerous ballet spectaculars. The colossal theatre was notoriously difficult to fill – acoustically and commercially[87] – and Talazac was one of the first French-born and trained tenors with genuinely stentorian resonance. While doing justice to the floated introspection of Des Grieux's "*Ah! Fuyez, douce image,*"[88] Talazac was equally equipped to sing Hoffmann's "*Il était une fois à la cour d'Eisenach*"[89] and Samson's "*Israël! romps ta chaîne.*"[90]

The Paris Opéra finally staged *Samson* on 23 November, 1892, in a performance supervised by Saint-Saëns, conducted by Édouard Colonne and directed by Alexandre Lapissida,[91] a retired tenor and the Opéra's pre-eminent *régisseur general*. The role of Samson was performed by Edmond-Alphonse Vergnet,[92] one of the earliest Third Republic tenors to specialise in contemporary French repertoire. At the Théâtre de la Monnaie in Brussels, Vergnet created the roles of John the Baptist in Massenet's *Hérodiade* in 1881, Shahabarim in Reyer's *Salammbô* in 1890, Zarastra in Massenet's *Le mage*[93] in 1891, and Dominique in Alfred Bruneau's *L'attaque du moulin*[94] in 1894.

During the ten years either side of 1900, Wagner's influence on music in France was as seismic for singers as it was for composers. Until Debussy broke ranks with *Pelléas et Mélisande* on 30 April, 1902, French composers struggled to isolate a post-Wagnerian voice, even with a number of exceptional tenors capable of ensuring the promotion of national identity through the French language as compensation for the often derivative sound world. It's no exaggeration to observe that French opera would have struggled but for the talents of the tenors Pierre-Émile Engel,[95] Adolphe Maréchal[96] and Charles Rousselière.[97] Engel created major roles for Emmanuel Chabrier (*Gwendoline* in 1886), Pierre-Louis Deffès (*Les noces de Fernande* in 1878[98]), Henry Litolff (*Les templiers* in 1886), Benjamin Godard (*Jocelyn* in 1888 – with a libretto by Victor Capoul), Emile Mathieu (*Richilde* in 1888) and Gustave Charpentier (*Louise*

---

85 'The King of Ys.'
86 By contrast, the Palais Garnier (first opened in 1875) seats fewer than 2,000.
87 The theatre's financial difficulties caused it to close in 1894. It was demolished in May, 1895.
88 'Ah! Flee, sweet image'.
89 'Once upon a time at the court of Eisenach.'
90 'Israel! break your chains.'
91 9 March, 1839 – 16 February, 1907.
92 4 July, 1850, Montpellier – 15 February, 1904.
93 'The Wizard.'
94 'Attack on the mill.'
95 15 February, 1847 –18 July, 1927.
96 26 September, 1867 – 1 February, 1935.
97 17 January, 1875 – 11 May, 1950.
98 'Fernande's wedding.'

in 1900). Charles Rousselière created roles for Saint-Saëns (*Les Barbares* in 1901[99]), André Messager (*Béatrice* in 1914), Gabriel Fauré (*Prométhée* in 1900 and *Pénélope* in 1913), Massenet (*Cléopâtre* in 1914[100]) and Charpentier (*Julien, ou La vie du poète* in 1918[101]), while Adolphe Maréchal also created roles for Charpentier (*Grisélidis* in 1901) and Massenet (*Le jongleur de Notre Dame*[102] in 1902).

Though each performed a range of contemporary French-Wagnerian repertoire, as well as Wagner, none of these fine singers was a *heldentenor* by international standards – as their recordings testify. Rousselière (a student of Vergnet) was admired at the Opéra as Samson, Faust, Roméo, Sigurd and Canio; he also sang the title roles in *Otello, Don Carlo, Siegfried* and *Parsifal*. Rousselière took on the most demanding tenor roles in all opera but was "dramatic" by French standards only. His legacy of nearly 140 recordings (the majority of them produced during his first sessions for the Gramophone & Typewriter Company in 1903) amplify his lyrical sublimation of pure tone to word sounding. His 1903 recording of a French translation of "*Winterstürme*" from *Die Walküre* is a case in point. The voice is pure elegance but almost clipped in its articulation. It's beautiful – but in an idiosyncratically French way.

Each of these tenors was renowned for working closely with French composers at a time when French music was enjoying a period of unprecedented renaissance. The Academies were churning out talent in which the public was genuinely interested, and publishers were making a fortune from the sale of songs and music for the home, the integrity of which operated in perfect confluence with the art-music being performed in opera houses and concert halls. For all its popularity, however, contemporary music continued to be played in tandem with the established repertoire, and where opera houses were concerned that meant the works of Verdi and Wagner. Inevitably, therefore, it was possible, for the first time, for singers to attach themselves to "historical" repertoire where the *spinto, ténor fort, héroïque* and *heldentenor* roles had to be performed in French.

Léon Escalaïs[103] was among the first to make a virtue of power in isolation; his reputation survives on the back of a capacity for pure tone that was largely alien at the time. He was one of the first to achieve success despite generally distancing himself from contemporary composition. Escalaïs made his debut at the Théâtre du Château in Paris in 1882; only six years later he appeared for the first time at La Scala. He first sang at the Opéra on 12 October, 1883, in what would become his signature role, Arnold; in 1892 a dispute with the Opéra's management led to him transferring his talents to far-flung theatres in Dijon, Lyon, Marseille and, eventually, Italy, where he spent most of the ensuing 16 years. He was popular as Eléazar, Robert (*le diable*), Raoul, Le Cid and Sigurd, and in demand also as Manrico, Radamès and Otello. Escalaïs returned to the Paris Opéra in 1908 and retired four years later, heavy with honours, awards and titles. Unlike the tall, athletic and polished Charles Dalmorès, Escalaïs was given to fat and *very* short, at around five feet in height. He was described

---

99   'The Barbarians.'
100 *Cléopâtre* was first performed at the Opéra de Monte-Carlo on 23 February, 1914 – nearly two years after Massenet's death.
101 'Julien, or The Poet's Life.'
102 'The juggler of Notre Dame.'
103 8 August, 1859 – 25 August, 1940.

as "dwarfish," "stumpy," "ungainly," and a "barrel". Others compared him unkindly to a basset hound. It's obvious from his recordings that he compensated for his physical disadvantages by yelling in a manner that suggests he might well have lived up to his title as the "French Tamagno." Of one performance, the critic of London's *The Era* stated:

> M. Escalais has been condemned by the composer to scream at the top of his voice from end to end, an ordeal that must be as trying to the artist as it is disagreeable to his hearers.

On 29 November, 1909, the critic of the New Orleans *Times-Democrat* recorded his astonishment when Escalaïs sang "*Di quella pira*" (as "*Supplice infâme*") no fewer than six times, hurling out a total of 18 high Cs. Such vulgar feats were inconsistent with the French tradition, which is not to suggest that Escalaïs was unable to thrill when at full tilt. Indeed, his 1906 recording of "*Supplice infâme*" is octane entertainment even if it owes nothing to the traditions into which the singer had been born.

Those traditions – typified by the *ténor de grâce* and the *haute-contre* – were unaffected by the shift towards Teutonic grandeur. Many of those who indulged in *Wagneriana* continued to create works that played to the strengths of a native word-sensitive style of projection that favoured refinement of phrasing over bug-eyed howling. Albert Vaguet[104] is widely admired for his glorious body of recordings, many of which he made while a member of the Opéra (having given the first of more than 300 performances as Faust in 1890), but it is the effortless languidity of Louis Delaquerrière[105] that became the model of Gallic expressive sensibility. At La Monnaie, Delaquerrière created the role of David for the Belgian premiere of *Der Meistersinger* (translated by Victor Wilder as *Les maîtres chanteurs de Nuremberg*) in 1885. He sang in Geneva for a season and then settled at the Opéra-Comique where he excelled in *Mignon, La dame blanche, La traviata, Carmen, Le postillon de Lonjumeau* and as *Le Barbier de Séville*, the 100th performance of which (at the Opéra-Comique) he performed on 25 February, 1887. Delaquerrière created roles for Chabrier (*Le roi malgré lui*[106] in 1887), Charles-Édouard Lefebvre (*Le trésor* in 1884[107]) and André Messager (*Madame Chrysanthème* in 1893), and he was admired by every composer with rooms in Paris. His son, José Delaquerrière,[108] was a talented tenor also, although he specialised in operetta, with a gift that many considered greater even than his father's. Certainly, José's recording from 1924 of Paul Bernard's "*Ça fait peur aux oiseaux*"[109] (from the operetta *Bredouille*) is a miraculous example of French style at its most aristocratic. The balletic rhythmic delicacy makes a mockery of the bar-lines, such that the music's momentum is propelled as much by his treatment of

---

104 15 June, 1865 – 22 February, 1943.
105 24 February, 1856 – 11 September, 1937.
106 'King in Spite of Himself or The Reluctant King.'
107 'The treasure.'
108 16 September, 1886 – 10 April, 1978.
109 'It scares the birds.'

the words as by the music. His animation of the repeating line "*Aimez-moi sans me le dire*"[110] has much to teach anyone hoping to perform a *chanson*.

One of the few French tenors able to reconcile stye and articulation to raw vocal power was Charles Dalmorès,[111] the creator of the title role for Ernest Chausson of *Le roi Arthus* in 1903. He was born Henri Alphonse Brin and began his musical career as a horn player with the Colonne and Lamoureux orchestras. He took singing lessons in Paris, without revealing this fact to his colleagues; he made his stage debut on 6 October, 1899 – when he was almost 30. Dalmorès chose for his first appearance the role of Siegfried, at the Théâtre des Arts in Rouen – where Charles and Emma Bovary had attended the production of *Lucie* starring Lagardy. His success was immediate, and within just six years he was invited to New York for a production of *Faust* by the Manhattan Opera Company. Between 1906 and 1910 he spent long seasons in the United States, specialising in French roles – including many he was the first to perform. He excelled as Julien in *Louise*, Jean Gaussin in Massenet's *Sapho* and as *Pelléas* for Debussy. In 1910, Dalmorès was engaged by the Chicago Grand Opera Company, with whom he performed until 1914; three years later he appeared in Chicago for the first time as Parsifal and Tristan. Dalmorès also visited Germany and Austria prior to the outbreak of World War I – where he performed Wagner in German. In 1908 he appeared as *Lohengrin* at the 1908 Bayreuther Festspiele.

Although Ernest van Dyck was better known – and more popular in Germany – Dalmorès was the finer musician, and more faithful to his native traditions. His voice was richer than van Dyck's and he was admired universally for his impressive stage presence and acting ability. Between 1907 and 1912, he made numerous recordings, the best of which attest to the declamatory power of his singing as well as an exceptional sensitivity for line and phrasing. The opening notes of the duet "*O merveille!*" from *Faust*, for example, speak to an exceptional technique and sensibilities better suited to Mozart and Gounod than to Wagner, in whose music such rarefied expressive plasticity was considered out of place at Cosima's Bayreuth. His 1907 recording of "*Ah! si, ben mio*" (in Italian) is delivered across a highly unusual span of tone and expression, with only a hint of the sobbing and empty effect reviled by Lamperti and Basevi. On record, at least, Dalmorès' voice had great warmth and there is a hint of power also; it is only ever hinted at because he exercised unfailing judgment so that even when throttling up for his 1911 recording of Lohengrin's "*Atmest du nicht mit mir die sussen Dufte*" – in German – his *legato* and placement remain flawless.

The different schools of French tenor singing after 1900 were embodied by *fort-héroique* singers like Agustarello Affre,[112] Mario Gilion,[113] Paul Franz,[114] and Cesar Vezzani[115] – all of them belters, one way or another – and *ténors de grâce* like

---

110 'Love me without telling me.'
111 1 January, 1871 – 6 December, 1939.
112 23 October, 1858 – 27 December, 1931.
113 1870 – 24 November, 1914.
114 30 November, 1876 – 20 April, 1950. Franz was born François Gauthier. He changed his family name to Franz because of the tenor Jules Gautier, who was already known in France. Some references cite Jules Gautier as being Franz Gautier. They were different people.
115 8 August, 1888 – 11 November, 1951. Incredibly, Vezzani appears never to have performed in a major opera house.

Valentin Duc,[116] Edmond Clément,[117] Lucien Muratore,[118] and David Devriès.[119] Clément's recording of "*En fermant les yeux*"[120] from *Manon*, and Paul Franz's recording of "*La fleur que tu m'avais jetée*" – both from 1911 – highlight the disparity between them. The former floats the music; the latter all but shouts it. During the first decade of the century Caruso's vast vocal resources and the ubiquity of his recordings widened the divide between schools and regions of singing. Just as orchestras began to conform to international standards, so too did the tenor. The impossible weight of changed expectations fostered by Caruso and the gramophone was compounded by the steady decline in new music. In this respect, France was one of the last bastions of resistance through a song-based culture that prevailed through the Gallo-centrality of language and poetry. The great flowering of French song and opera during the first third of the 20th century was driven by a concentration of national and cultural identity unprecedented in French musical history. It was built initially on the achievements of Gounod, Massenet and Debussy; after 1900 it was mastered by Gabriel Fauré, Georges Auric, Maurice Ravel, Albert Roussel, Francis Poulenc, Erik Satie, Henri Dutilleux, Reynaldo Hahn, *les soeurs* Boulanger, Arthur Honegger, Jacques Leguerney, Darius Milhaud, Déodat De Séverac and Olivier Messiaen.

Among the most influential – if least prolific – composers of *mélodies* and *chanson* was Gustave Charpentier, the author of *Louise*. He studied with Massenet (winning the *Grand Prix de Rome* at the age of 27 for his cantata, *Didon*) but later claimed to have been a student also of Montmartre and the 18th Arrondissement,[121] where he lived in the shadow of the Basilique du Sacré-Cœur.[122] Despite living beneath the Church, he joined instinctively with his neighbours – a collection of bohemians, poets, artists and anarchists with whom he claimed to be an anti-intellectual, more comfortable in the company of "instinctive" artists rather than the establishment figures who otherwise dominated Paris' Conservatoire mentality.

---

116   24 January, 1858 – 23 February, 1915.
117   28 March, 1867 – 24 February, 1928. To give some idea of the extraordinary vitality of Parisian musical culture around the turn of the century, it is worth noting just *some* of the roles created by Clément, and how few of them are by composers remembered beyond their deaths: Andrea in Diaz's *Benvenuto* (1890), Sentinel in Bruneau's *L'Attaque du Moulin* (1893), Jacquemin in Cui's *Le Flibustier* (1894), Georges in Godard's *La Vivandière* (1895), Landry in Dubois' *Xavière* (1895), Loti in Hahn's *L'Île du Rêve* (1898), Christian in Erlanger's *Le Juif Polonais* (1900), Pedrito in Dupont's *La Cabrera* (1905) and Jean-Simon in Silver's *Le Clos* (1906). Clément also sang in the Parisian premieres of Saint-Saëns' *Hélène*, Verdi's *Falstaff* and Puccini's *Madama Butterfly*.
118   29 August, 1876 – 16 July, 1954.
119   14 February, 1881 – 17 July, 1936.
120   'On closing the eyes.'
121   So great was his attachment to the district that, when having to take his train to the Villa de Médicis in Rome, he kept walking back to his home, only to be turned around by his friends. On another occasion, he "fled" back to Paris, only to be discovered near the Eiffel Tower by Massenet – who compelled him to return to Italy. At the age of ninety-one he conducted a concert of his own works in front of Sacré-Coeur; he died just a few months before the thousandth performance of *Louise* at the Opéra Comique. See Foley, Ruth Iona. "The Songs of Gustave Charpentier" (2000). *ETD collection for University of Nebraska - Lincoln*. AAI9967370. pp.7–14; also Abbott, Helen (2017). *Baudelaire in Song: 1880–1930*. Oxford University Press.
122   Begun in 1875 when Charpentier was 15 and completed in 1914 – forty-two years before his death at the age of 95.

Charpentier was a proponent of *"naturalisme,"* an aesthetic that many compare unhelpfully to *verismo*. If it's true that his instincts were for the "real," his music is absent the unimpeded dramatic momentum by which the music of his Italian peers was defined. Instead, his naturalist tendencies drew him to isolate emotional and pictorial clarity in poetry that amplified what he considered to be a "human" fusion of speech and harmony. His chromatic freedom was married perfectly to the poetry for which he felt such proximity when writing for *"le Peuple,"* primarily Verlaine and Baudelaire. Charpentier's twenty songs published as *Poèmes chantés*, *Les Fleurs du Mal*, and *Impressions Fausses* (1885 – 1895) are exquisite in their setting of Baudelaire's perfumed language; they make great demands of singers when balancing the differing needs of text and music. In his introduction to the published score of his setting of *"Parfum exotique"* (1893) Charpentier wrote:

> During a trip to the Eastern Islands and the Indies, completed during his youth, Baudelaire retained an unforgettable emotion. It seems that he suddenly understood all that his great tragic soul could ask of life: the modern refinement, the noble and intellectual profundity that he would become, never forgot the ardent and melancholy Oriental who had divined himself eternally.[123]

The composer's ambition was to isolate an accessible route to Baudelaire's verse while allowing the singer and the audience ready access to poetry that Debussy had, in Charpentier's view, placed beyond reach when writing his *Cinq poèmes de Charles Baudelaire* in 1889. Rather than yield like Debussy to Wagner's influence, Charpentier pursued a vernacular that was technically accessible. His setting of *"Parfum exotique,"* for example, is in D flat and sits without any awkward intervals within the span of D flat 3 and E4. It begins:

> *"Quand, les deux yeux fermés, en un soir chaud d'automne, Je respire l'odeur de ton sein chaleureux."*[124]

The song places no obstacles before the singer; it might be performed easily by an amateur or in a café or cabaret. Living just a few minutes' walk from Moulin Rouge, which first opened when Charpentier was 29 in 1889, the composer was open to the belief that his music, like all *good* art, should reach further than the concert halls and opera houses. *Louise* was much influenced by cabaret culture and the concomitant rise of syndicalism, musician unions, and "universités populaires" for the working classes. Charpentier was inclined emotionally and creatively, therefore, to the emerging culture of *Chanson réaliste* which dominated Montmartre during the 1880s and which he had come to know while working at the arts journal *Chat Noir*. Though

---

123 *'D'un voyage aux iles orientales et aux Indes, accompli dans sa jeunesse, Baudelaire garda une émotion inoubliable. Il semble qu'il ait compris là-bas subitement tout ce que sa grande âme tragique pouvait demander a la vie: le moderne raffiné, l'intellectuel noble et profond qu'il fut par la suite, n'oublia jamais l'ardent et mélancolique Oriental qu'il s'était diviné pour toujours.'*
124 'When, with both eyes closed, on a hot autumn night, I breathe the perfume of your heated breast.'

the genre was dominated by female artists like Aristide Bruant, and despite most *chanteuses réalistes* performing songs of hopelessness and abandonment (with texts by writers instinctively distant from Baudelaire), Charpentier related emotionally to the real as it was experienced by most of those living in the *faubourgs*. The rising popularity of naturalist theatre, championed by Émile Zola and staged by André Antoine at his Théâtre-Libre, added to the increasing delamination of the boundaries between art and entertainment. For Charpentier and most of the composers to follow him into the 20th century, the blurring of these once absolute boundaries meant that tenors, in particular, were required to appeal to audiences at the *cabarets* as well as the *salles des concert*, with high and low art fused in a manner that enabled singers to achieve success in both.

It was soon common for cabaret singers to relocate to the opera houses, and *vice versa*. The once impermeable barriers between serious and popular began to break down even in the United States. The American lyric tenor Orville Harrold[125] began his career in 1906 as a performer in operetta, cabaret, musical theatre and vaudeville; he later transitioned to contemporary opera. In Chicago, between 1912 and 1922, he appeared as Des Grieux, Dimitri in *Boris Godunóv*, Don José, Faust, Gérald, Pinkerton, Rodolfo, Win-San-Lui in Franco Leoni's *L'oracolo*, and in the title roles of Offenbach's *Hoffmann* and Mascagni's *L'amico Fritz*. He returned to vaudeville in 1915, performing *operetta* and arias in a variety show at the Palace Theatre in New York while creating the role of the "Hero" in the original cast of the musical *Hip! Hip! Hooray!* at the Hippodrome. He returned to opera, at the Metropolitan, in 1919, singing Prince Leopold in *La Juive* opposite Caruso as Eléazar and Rosa Ponselle as Rachel. The following year he created the role of Meïamoun in the first production of Henry Hadley's *verismo* opera *Cleopatra's Night* in 1920, in addition to numerous other Met premieres, memorably Korngold's *Die tote Stadt* (1921, opposite Maria Jeritza), Rimsky-Korsakov's *The Snow Maiden* (1922) and Charpentier's *Louise* (1921, with Geraldine Farrar in the title role). He was famed also as the Italian Singer in *Rosenkavalier*, Nicias in Massenet's *Thaïs* and, somewhat bizarrely perhaps, as Parsifal. In 1922 he sang in the New York premiere of Mahler's *Das Lied von der Erde*, conducted by Artur Bodanzky – while continuing to perform in vaudeville. His last appearance on Broadway was in 1925, when he starred as Peter Novak in the musical *Holka Polka* at the Lyric Theatre.

Just as it became "normal" for opera singers to moonlight as Kabaret performers in Germany during the Weimar Republic, so in France the novelty of cultural ambidexterity was embraced by tenors like André Goavec,[126] Henri Legay,[127] and Hugues-Adhémar Cuénod,[128] each of whom excelled in both arenas. For the French tenor during the 1920s and 30s the blurring of boundaries was a value in which the text remained primary – even when performed by Maurice Chevalier and Tino Rossi. The "high" art of the French tenor remained, of course, a pre-eminent consideration

---

125   17 November, 1877 – 23 October, 1933.
126   6 February, 1897 – 17 February, 1947.
127   1 July, 1920 – 16 September, 1992.
128   26 June, 1902 – 6 December, 2010.

in the opera house, not least for Charpentier, who conducted a still unrivalled recording of *Louise* in 1935 with arguably the most gifted French tenor of the 20th century.

Georges Thill[129] was a star of the Opéra (where he made his debut in 1924) and the Opéra-Comique for more than two decades; his huge repertoire included all the standard fare, and little contemporary work. He did, however, perform songs in recital and on record, featuring popular music like "*Chansons de Paris*" as well as *melodies* and *chansons* by colleagues, notably André Messager. His enormous discography included a heavily edited *Louise* and a nearly complete performance of *Werther* (1931). Thill appeared also in several filmed scenes and French-language movies, including a version of *Louise* (1939) with Grace Moore in the title role, directed by Abel Gance. Thill was the very model of the effortless tenor *en plus d'élégance* – the gain being the vibrancy, clarity and masculinity of his tone, and his ringing top notes and crystalline word-placement. His voice was overwhelmingly luscious and gleaming in its expressive reach, with none of that nasal quality that many non-natives find distasteful in French singing. The "openness" of his sound was atypical, therefore. Thill did not indulge the fluency and richness of the instrument but applied instead a fine musical intelligence to preserve the greatest refinement of style *and* substance. Employing a perfect admixture of *portamento* and *rubato*, his work was always in the service of the words, to which end he employed his consistently expressive diction to deliver whatever he was singing with equal consideration for the poet and the composer.

Thill's pre-eminence was absolute throughout the 1930s, although many talented singers dipped in and out of his shadow (including René Maison[130]). Inevitably, however, the number of French tenors committed to new music by French-born composers was in mutual decline after 1935. A memorable exception to this rule was Paul Derenne[131]. He took singing lessons in private while studying as an architect, and made his debut under Charles Munch in the French premiere of Hindemith's "operatic sketch" *Hin und Zurück*[132] – alongside Hugues Cuénod – in 1927. He began to work closely with Nadia Boulanger (who introduced him to the madrigals of Monteverdi) and in 1937 he sang for the first time at the Opéra Comique, where he appeared in the French premieres of *Le testament de la tante Caroline*[133] by Albert Roussel and Strauss' *Ariadne auf Naxos*. After the war he sang in the first performance of surviving fragments of Chabrier's *Vaucochard et Fils* and during the Occupation he became friends with Henri Sauguet, for whom he created the role of Détieulette in the 1944 premiere of the composer's setting of Michel-Jean Sedaine's 1768 comedy *La Gageure imprévue*,[134] as well as the song cycle *Les Pénitents en maillot rose*.[135] Derenne was introduced by Sauguet to Jacques Leguerney (whose *Poèmes De La Pléiade* he premiered in Paris in 1944) and other members of "Les Six," for whom

---

129 14 December, 1897 – 17 October, 1984.
130 24 November, 1895 – 11 July, 1962.
131 Born René Bouvier (1907– 18 April, 1988). Reynaldo Hahn suggested his stage name based on his home town.
132 'Back and forth.'
133 'Aunt Caroline's Will.'
134 'The Unexpected Challenge.'
135 'The Penitents in pink jerseys.'

he became a muse as well as an advocate. In Italy he appeared at La Fenice and La Scala in early performances of Ravel's *L'heure espagnole* and *L'Enfant et les sortilèges*, which he later recorded with Ernest Ansermet in 1953. With Henri Sauguet he gave numerous radio concerts celebrating the *mélodie*.

With the rise of popular song and the emergence of an increasingly stark vernacular among *les modernes*, French repertory and its performance collapsed during the 1940s and 50s to an irresistible internationalism, with French works performed routinely in Italian and German outside France and the converse being accepted inside France, with Italian and German works being performed as their composers *and poets* intended. More damaging for French music was the tacit acceptance that non-French speakers were at liberty to perform French works *in French*. It follows that Helge Rosvaenge[136] – a Danish tenor of exceptional talent – could routinely be mistaken as a French singer, while the two most recorded "French" tenors of the 20th century were both Spanish – Alfredo Kraus and Plácido Domingo. Neither was a "French" tenor, and neither sang anything in accordance with French traditions. There were, of course, French tenors whose work preserved the finest of the native school, the best of whom, during the 1950s and 60s, were Canadian: Leopold Simoneau,[137] Raoul Jobin,[138] and Richard Verreau.[139]

Simoneau was a lyric tenor of exceptional grace and elegance, and peerless in Mozart. Jobin's rich and resonant voice was singular for its grainy texture, power and lyricism. He was a star of the Opéra and the Opéra-Comique and greatly admired by Beecham, Inghelbrecht and Cluytens. With the latter he made landmark recordings of *Les contes d'Hoffmann* in 1948 and *Carmen* in 1950 – both with the Opéra-Comique – as well as a still peerless recording of *Roméo et Juliette* with the Opéra, conducted by Alberto Erede in 1953. Jobin recorded only excerpts from *La Damnation de Faust* (for Decca, conducted by Anatole Fistoulari), a role that was perfected, on record at least, by Jobin's pupil, Richard Verreau in 1959, conducted by Igor Markevich. This extraordinarily febrile, brooding performance was made exceptional by Verreau's performance of the title role. His voice is more textured and beautiful than that of anyone else to have recorded the work (nearly) complete; his delivery of Berlioz's language is infinitely characterful, and the absolute model of French singing and diction at their finest. The roundness and power of the timbre, the graceful line and the ease of delivery are haunting – particularly when the drama is at its most intense. In short, Verreau had one of the most beautiful, expressive French voices of the century. Aside from some albums of arias and songs, he made no other significant recordings.

After studying with Jobin, and some successful performances in Canada and France, he travelled to Rome for lessons with Gigli and his daughter Rina, following which, in 1956, he appeared at the New York City Opera as Wilhelm Meister in Thomas' *Mignon*. Together with his fellow Canadians, Jon Vickers and Joseph Rouleau, Verreau was engaged by Covent Garden for 20 performances of three roles

---

136 Born Helge Anton Rosenvinge Hansen (29 August, 1897 – 17 June, 1972).
137 3 May, 1916 – 24 August, 2006.
138 8 April, 1906 – 13 January, 1974.
139 1 January, 1926 – 6 July, 2005.

during the 1956–57 season (singing Rodolfo in *La Bohème*, the Duke in *Rigoletto and* Aeneas in *Les Toyens*). Verreau appears to have clashed with Rafael Kubelik, music director at the time, as he did with other conductors elsewhere. At a concert performance of *Rigoletto* in Montreal in December, 1966, his voice began to fail, and the following year he underwent throat surgery that ended his career. Verreau was 40 years old. The loss to music was appalling, and it remains one of the greatest tragedies to befall the history of the tenor.

The creep of internationalism during the 1970s collided with the promotion of the entirely misplaced belief that French opera could be performed by anyone, no matter their origins or training. This fallacy was escalated by anti-nationalist sentiments that dismissed localism as small-minded or, worse, xenophobic – even though French singing was as ineluctably nativist as Italian and German. A number of French tenors survived through the 1970s, notably Alain Vanzo,[140] Gilbert Py,[141] Charles Burles,[142] and Guy Chauvet[143] – the latter standing out as that most unusual of creatures, a French *heldentenor* – but with them passed the tradition of honeyed, elastic and evocative French tenor singing that blossomed through the 18th and 19th centuries. By 2000 the "French" tenor in its evolution produced as its last alleged exponent Roberto Alagna.

The history of the tenor is not an entirely happy one. As the once and future *gloire de la musique française*, it ended in tragedy.

---

140   2 April, 1928 – 27 January, 2002.
141   9 December, 1933 –
142   21 June, 1936 –
143   2 October, 1933 – 25 March, 2007.

Chapter Sixteen

Sons of Father Russia

For anyone engaging in word-association, "Russian Opera" triggers commonly the image of Fyodor Chaliapin, or the sound more generally of a bass. Uniquely in the history of opera, Russia's vocal tradition in its relationship with native composition is linked inextricably to the lowest and darkest of the human voices. It's a cliché with much to recommend it. The low bass tradition nurtured by the Russian and Greek Orthodox Churches (which produced the freakish, but still-robust skill of "oktavism"[1]) remains a prominent feature of Russian musical and religious life, as it does for many other countries east of western Europe's borders. The emphatically patriarchal structure of Russian society codified masculinity by *fach*, with the leading roles in many Russian operas being scored automatically for baritones and basses. The prominence and availability of bass voices in Russia during western music's emergence as currency during the second half of the 18th century was problematic for composers because low-pitched singing is difficult to score against anything larger than a chamber orchestra; it is no coincidence that most Greek Orthodox music continues to be performed unaccompanied.

The prominence of bass roles across the emerging repertoire contributed exponentially to the weighting of maleness towards depth of pitch as the primary indicator of masculinity. High male voices suffered by association with the social and cultural prejudices that painted Tchaikovsky into the famously unhappy corner wherein he appears to have committed suicide by drinking cholera-infected water. With a few exceptions – most obviously Hermann, the tragi-toxic "hero" of Tchaikovsky's *Pikovaya dama*[2] – the majority of Russian operas disavowed the Western identification of the tenor voice with heroism, strength and vitality. The list of Russian operas necessitating a tenor capable of singing dramatic repertoire after the manner and fashion of Verdi, Wagner, Puccini and Strauss is *extremely* limited – an anomaly for a culture celebrated for its attachments to priapic and heterosexual masculinity.[3]

The issue is complicated further by the codification of the Russian tenor as the only culturally distinct voice within the operatic canon to resist analysis other than through the filter of national identity. Italian, French and German opera can be sung by "everyone"; it is often performed by "anyone." The same is not true of Russian opera, which admits not only significant issues as concerning the language but also a performing style that is given often and easily to the lachrymose and the sentimental.

---

1 Singing an octave *below* the bass *fach*.
2 'Queen of Spades'; also *Pique Dame*.
3 Especially so when noting how the contemporary Russian attitude towards homosexuality in the 2020s is less progressive even than it was in the 1890s.

No-one listening to an Italian tenor born during the thirty years following unification in 1861 appreciates their work through a filter of cultural-identity politics, and yet the entire history of Russian opera and singing continues to be heard and studied within what Richard Taruskin construed as the Russian nationalist discourse.[4]

As Marina Frolova-Walker asked of the "Russianness" of Glinka's five-act opera of 1842, *Ruslan i Lyudmila*:

> is there some peculiar shortcoming afflicting Russian music that prevents us from discussing except in terms of nationality? So much critical writing, so many articles, monographs and textbooks of the last 150 years cannot blithely be set aside: they continue to feed programme and liner notes, encouraging and reinforcing audiences' fond belief in an intrinsic Russianness that mysteriously subsists beneath every note of this perennially popular repertoire.[5]

Part of the problem for any student of the tenor voice in particular is the unavoidable perpetuation of maleness as a construction of complex issues of gender, freedom, labour and class. For Russians, the roots of patriarchy were secular as well as religious. Peter I's vaunted reforms introduced many western values and fashions to Russia – including Italian music and musicians – and he emancipated the young and the male by exception. By order of a 1722 decree, forced marriage was regulated to require a bride and a groom to consent,[6] with men being entitled uniquely to end a marriage by the lawful dispatching of wives to nunneries.[7] An adulterous wife could be sentenced to forced labour, while men who killed their spouses were flogged. Even after the death of the relatively progressive Peter, law and custom in Russia gave yet greater power within a marriage to men, and in 1782 civil law reinforced a woman's responsibility to obey her husband. In 1832, the Digest of laws amended this obligation as "unlimited obedience." In 1818, the Russian Senate forbade the separation of married couples – further excepting, of course, the right of an aristocratic family to exercise its privilege. Pressure from within the nobility was fundamental to the minor adjustment of restrictions against Russian women owning property; in 1753 a decree ensured that noble families could secure a daughter's inheritance by making it a part of her dowry. Even so, they could not inherit *their* property until married – which created the added spice for women that on their deaths, their husbands would retain anything they brought with them to the husband's family. Under such circumstances, obedience was commonly assured.

---

4   Taruskin, Richard (1984). "Some Thoughts on the History and Historiography of Russian Music," *Journal of Musicology*, 3.4. pp. 321–39.
5   Frolova-Walker, Marina (1997). "On Ruslan and Russianness." *Cambridge Opera Journal*, 9, 1. pp.21–45; p.21.
6   The law required parental permission – a policy that aligns closely with the contemporary position in the United States of America where many states require parental permission before an abortion can be authorised as lawful.
7   It should be noted that when Hamlet tells Ophelia to "get thee to a nunnery," he was employing a word with a well-known slang meaning. At the turn of the 17th century a nunnery was known to signify a brothel also.

During the latter half of the 19th century the appropriation of women as unpaid workers to their husbands and children fostered the perpetuation of labour, family and the state as expressions of patriarchal power. The fecundity of the intelligentsia's ambition for the emancipation of women saw Marx align with Engels, Feuerbach, Bebel and Kollontai[8] when promoting female "equivalence," but the ideologues of Marxism and Leninism overlooked the influence of private property on the changing relationship between men and women as it was represented in music and drama.

The chronology of Russian opera is well known. Maksim Berezovsky (1745–1777), Dmitri Bortniansky (1751–1825), Vasily Pashkevich (1742–1797), and Yevstigney Fomin (1761–1800) all composed operas – in French and Italian. The first opera to be written and performed in Russian, *Tsefal i Prokris,*[9] was by an Italian composer, Francesco Araja. It was premiered at St. Petersburg in a wing of the Winter Palace in 1755 – with Russian singers. Whatever else may be said about the evolution of Russian operatic vernaculars, opera came to exist in Russian twenty years before the Italian grip on German musical theatre was loosened by Abel Seyler and his work with Hiller, Benda and Schweitzer. The latter's *Alceste*, premiered in 1773 in Weimar, is considered to be the first serious "German" opera. The use of the Russian language in Russia was neither ubiquitous nor especially textural until another Italian composer, Catterino Cavos (1775 – 1840) created a series of important works for the stage, including *Knyaz-nevidimka*[10] (1805), *Ilya Bogatyr*[11] (1807), *Zephyre et Flore* (1808), *Ivan Susanin* (1815), and *Zhar–ptitsa*[12] (1822). Cavos contributed to the second part of the opera tetralogy *Rusalka* (1803–1807), which had a huge impact on Alexey Verstovsky (1799–1862), whose grand opera *Askoldova mogila*[13] (1835) was performed on hundreds of occasions throughout St Petersburg and Moscow.

Despite being performed in Russian, there was little sign in the theatre of native Russian cultural characteristics, practices and vernaculars until Glinka composed his Russian-language operas *Zhizn' za tsarya* [14] and *Ruslan*. He employed conventional Italian and French structural models of the period while making prominent textural use of distinctively Russian folk songs and idioms, foundations that sustained the ensuing generation of Russian nationalistic and historical operas, most famously Serov's *Rogneda*, Mussorgsky's *Boris Godunóv*, Rimsky-Korsakov's *Pskovityanka*,[15] Tchaikovsky's *Oprichnik* and *Mazeppa*, and Borodin's *Knyáz Ígor*.

It follows that while the Russian vernacular of music drama *in Russian* may be said to have crystalised in 1842 with *Ruslan*, singing in Russian was well established long before Lev Leonov[16] created the role of Finn the sorcerer for Glinka at the St

---

8   Articulated variously in Engels' *The Origin of the Family, Private Property and the State*; August Bebel's *Woman and Socialism*, Kollontai's *The Social Bases of the Woman Question*, and a variety of articles and speeches by Lenin.
9   'Cephalus and Prokris.'
10 'The Invisible Prince.'
11 'Ilya the Hero.'
12 'The Firebird.'
13 'Askold's Grave.'
14 'A Life for the Tsar.'
15 'Maid of Pskov.'
16 *circa* 1813 – October, 1872.

Petersburg premiere on 27 November, 1842.[17] Leonov also created the role of Bogdan Sobinin at the premiere of *A Life for the Tsar* in 1836. He is not, however, the first tenor to warrant mention within the development of Russian opera. In Italy, Nikolay Ivanov[18] was sufficiently well-regarded to be chosen by Rossini to sing the solo tenor part in the Italian premiere in Bologna of his *Stabat Mater* in March, 1842 – a "role" created by Mario at the Paris-premiere two months earlier. Donizetti conducted the performance, and reported the public's enthusiasm as being

> impossible to describe. Even at the final rehearsal, which Rossini attended, in the middle of the day, he was accompanied to his home to the shouting of more than 500 persons. The same thing the first night, under his window, since he did not appear in the hall.[19]

Ivanov studied with famed bari-tenor Andrea Nozzari in Naples, and made his début at the San Carlo in 1832 as Percy in *Anna Bolena*. He appeared at the Théâtre Italien in Paris in 1833 as Gianetto (*La gazza ladra*) and the following year he was engaged in London (again as Percy) at the King's Theatre. In 1840 he sang Arnold in *Guillaume Tell* (given as *Rodolfo di Sterlinga*) in Bologna. In 1843, Ivanov created Riccardo in the première of Pacini's *Maria, regina d'Inghilterra*, in which role he appeared for the first time at La Scala later the same year. He became close friends with Rossini, who introduced him to Verdi, and Donizetti regarded him as one of the finest tenors of his generation. Ivanov was not a Russian tenor, however – any more than was Leonov, who was born Leon Charpentier[20] in 1813 and raised within a predominantly French culture by his mother, despite being born and living in Russia. Leonov was given his mother's name because his father, the Irish composer and pianist John Field, was married to another woman at the time.[21] Field spent 29 years of his remarkable life in Russia, shifting like most others between the court-dominated musical centres of Moscow and St Petersburg. In May, 1832, the now single Field[22] left Moscow to perform his last musical tour – in the company of the teenage Leon. Field barely knew his son, but Leonov's mother implored that he promote the young man's talent as a singer. It was plainly considerable, since Glinka (himself a tenor) preferred Leonov to all others, and gave him both of the leading tenor roles in his most celebrated operas – including Sobinin – when the tenor was in his early twenties.[23]

---

17   The Moscow premiere in 1846 was conducted by the Russian-born conductor, Ivan Iogannis.
18   10 / 22 October, 1810 – 7 July, 1880.
19   Gossett, Philip; Ashbrook, William; Budden, Julian; Lippmann, Friedrich; Porter, Andrew; Mosco Carner, Mosco (1997). *The New Grove Masters of Italian Opera*. W. W. Norton & Company. p.59.
20   Charpentier took the name Leonov after turning 18 years of age.
21   His wife, Adelaide Percheron, was a highly regarded French actress. Their son Adrien became a pianist of note.
22   Adelaide grew tired of waking up scratching next to someone who drank so much that he was frequently unable to remember "the month before". Field observed famously that he was a "*better pianist drunk than everyone else sober.*" This was less bold a claim in Russia than it would have been anywhere else.
23   Forshaw, Juliet (2014). *Dangerous Tenors, Heroic Basses, and Non-Ingénues: Singers and the Envoicing of Social Values in Russian Opera, 1836 – 1905*. PhD thesis. Columbia University. p.95.

The adherence of Sobinin's writing to concomitant French-Italian heroic clichés provoked criticisms of Russian inauthenticity. The high-note ballistics, spitting brass and *bel canto* sensibilities sailed too close to a sound that a prejudiced community was swift to diminish as feminised. In modern (post-1900) performances of Sobinin's infamous cloud-catching aria from Act IV, "*Brattsi! v metyel*"[24] the C5s are sung routinely (though not always) in full voice (*do di petto*); the first few decades of performances likely employed *falsetto*, however. It's not known whether Leonov utilised Duprez's C5 in full voice, and while the prevalence of high Cs might suggest they were imported for that reason it's worth recalling that *Guillaume Tell*'s acrobatics were written for a voice in *falsetto*. Moreover, when presented with the role of Sobinin, Leonov was still very young. Attempting such vocally reckless feats when noting the addition of C sharps to "*Brattsi! v metyel*" would likely have caused terrible damage to an immature voice; and yet, ten years after Leonov created Sobinin in 1836 he was Glinka's first choice to sing Finn in the first Moscow production of *Ruslan*. If Leonov's undoubted vocal talents were not *au monde moderne*, then his acting most certainly was. One review by Tchaikovsky's collaborator and on-and-off friend, Prince Vladimir Odoyevsky, isolated the apparent restraint with which he approached his role:

> Some listeners, used to the layout of ordinary operas, inevitably wanted to see Sobinin as some kind of hero, rather like Tancredi or Orbazzano[25], and were annoyed that Leonov didn't resort to the frightful gesticulations by which operatic lovers distinguish themselves. This bridegroom was like all the bridegrooms in our villages, that is, bold in a fight but artless, bashful, and to some extent a carefree youth.[26]

Leonov's pre-eminence was not unrivalled. The first Sobinin at the Moscow premiere in 1842 was Alexander Bantyshev, [27] a chorus member discovered by Alexey Verstovsky and promoted at the Bolshoi Theatre in Moscow, where he was established in competition with Leonov. Bantyshev was known throughout the city as the "Moscow Nightingale," which gives some idea of the kind and type of voice for which he was celebrated. His sobriquet speaks directly to the value of those lyrical characteristics for which Russian tenors were known more commonly by their repertoire. In the wake of Glinka's successes, and with nativist ambitions escalating the value and necessity of a uniquely Russian musical culture – as distinct from the foreign influences that had coloured domestic musical life until the turn of the 19th century – composers tapped into Russia's uniquely complex body of folksong. Disavowing the abstemious "dryness" of liturgical tradition, the music written for tenors by the generation immortalised by the *Kuchka* or "The Mighty Five" (Balakirev,

---

24 'Into the blizzard, lads.'
25 Both characters from Rossini's *Tancredi*.
26 Forshaw, Juliet (2014). *Dangerous Tenors, Heroic Basses, and Non-Ingénues: Singers and the Envoicing of Social Values in Russian Opera, 1836 – 1905.* PhD thesis. Columbia University. p.95.
27 1804 – 1860.

Rimsky-Korsakov, Mussorgsky, Borodin and Cui) did nothing to heat up a voice that could be heroic only when singing music that had been composed outside Russia.

With the exception of Rimsky-Korsakov's *Snegúrochka–vesénnyaya skázka*[28] and *Sadko*, the best of the operas composed by the Five all contained parts for tenor that disavowed the passion, sanguinity and bravura for which music in Italy, France and Germany was increasingly typical after 1840. *Boris Godunóv*, *Knyáz Ígor*[29] and *Khovanshchina* all made virtues of native history, folk tales, and modern literature – as masterpieces of romantic nationalism – before they did anything for the Russian tenor as a species distinct from the artists without whom Verdi and Wagner could not have prevailed.

As Juliet Forshaw put it:

> The question of what defines a tenor hero, and what defines a proper Russian tenor hero as opposed to an exaggeratedly demonstrative Franco-Italian one, would gain urgency later in the century as upwardly mobile young men and tenor characters all over Europe redefined mid-century conceptions of youthful masculinity. In 1836, it was evidently not necessary for a tenor to be a hero at all; indeed, for Odoyevsky,[30] a realistically depicted young bridegroom in a Russian village could not be heroic in the confident and bombastic mold of an Italian tenor. The mantle of the hero went to the bass Ivan Susanin, and tenors would not lay claim to it until much later in the century.

The character of the Russian tenor underwent no material changes as it did in Europe. The *fach* and its constitution were typified by the ubiquitous Fyodor Komissarzhevsky,[31] a leading tenor at the Mariinsky Theatre in St Petersburg. Komissarzhevsky studied in Italy (arriving in time to contribute to the hysterically anti-Catholic Garibaldi's rebellion) and he toured widely across Europe and South America before making something of a hero's return to Russia. He sang the first Lohengrin at its Russian premiere in 1873, and created many of the most important roles in 19th century Russian opera, including Don Juan in Dargomyzhsky's *Kamennyj gost'*,[32] the Pretender in Mussorgsky's *Boris Godunóv*,[33] Prince Sinodal in Rubinstein's *Demon*,[34] and the title role in Tchaikovsky's first opera, *Kuznéts Vakúla*[35] – something of which Tchaikovsky complained vociferously when writing to his patron Nadezhda von Meck about the premiere of *Yevgény Onégin*[36]:

28　'The Snow Maiden.'
29　'Prince Igor.'
30　One of the leading Russian dramatists of the 19th century (1823 – 1886).
31　1832 – 14 March, 1905.
32　'The Stone Guest'; on 16 February, 1872.
33　On 27 January, 1874.
34　On 25 January, 1875.
35　'Vakula the Smith'; on 11 February, 1869.
36　'Eugene Onegin.'

Later on I am prepared to present it in a State Theatre, but only if they ask me, because only in this way shall I be able to demand conditions of production which are essential for *Onegin* to have any success. If I don't take the initiative myself, they will behave with the lack of ceremony displayed in the production of previous operas. I must be fair to the management of the St Petersburg theatres. *Vakula* was performed with great care and the production was not miserly, but there were so many things wrong, so many anachronisms, so much worn-out routine in the grouping of the choruses, and, most important, such miscasting! Komissarzhevsky as Vakula!! Quite dreadful, of course, yet they insisted that the part should be given to him. In general, in the production of *Vakula* I had to submit to every instruction of the conductor and the producer, who answered every observation of mine with: 'It can't be done any other way.' I don't want this from now on. If they ask me to present *Onegin* there, I shall make the conditions.[37]

Tchaikovsky dedicated his song "*Skazhy o chom v teni vetvej,*"[38] Op. 57, No. 1, to Komissarzhevsky – in 1884, six years after the tenor's retirement from the stage. During his 14 years as first tenor at the Mariinsky (from 1863), Komissarzhevsky developed a reputation as an actor of unusual sophistication, and it's clear he was able to raise the status of the tenor as a feature of theatrical life in Russia through force of intellect rather than (or in addition to) *mere* voice.[39] When accepting a professorship at the Moscow Conservatory, he taught acting as well as singing; one of his students was Konstantin Stanislavsky, and Komissarzhevsky later became the first head of the operatic and musical section of Stanislavsky's Society of Art and Literature in 1888. The tenor was famed also for his scandalous private life, which involved a host of mistresses, wives and children – most of whom became successful actors and directors.[40] When finally he retired he settled on the Ligurian coast, in Sanremo, wedded emotionally to a culture that tolerated or failed to register his instinctive defiance of class and sexual and moral etiquette. He died while tending his Italian roses, six

---

37   von Meck, Galena (trans). Eds. Garden, Edward & Gotteri, Nigel (1993). '*To My Best Friend'; Correspondence Between Tchaikovsky and Nadezhda von Meck, 1876–1878*. Clarendon Press; letter 89.
38   'Oh say, what is it, in shady branches.'
39   Komissarzhevsky's status within the wider community of artists and writers made him a celebrity even after he had emigrated to Italy. In 1904, Anton Chekhov incorporated a fictionalised account of the drowning of Komissarzhevsky's six-year-old son, Grisha, into *The Cherry Orchard*.
40   Komissarzhevsky's story, and that of his family, is fascinating. In 1880, he abandoned his wife (Mariya Nikolaevna Shulgina) and children for a mistress, Princess Maria Kurtsevich – a former pupil (like his wife). In 1882 she became pregnant with their son, Fyodor. His first wife agreed to divorce as the guilty party so that the child could be legitimised through marriage. Fyodor went on to become one of the world's most celebrated theatre directors, as "Theodore" Komissarzhevsky after emigrating to Britain in 1921 and, later, the United States, where he died in 1954. Fyodor's younger brother Nikolai, who became a writer, remained in Russia and was executed during Stalin's Great Purge in 1938. In the US, Theodore came to represent the camp in opposition to Stanislavsky. Among those who worked for him was Christopher Plummer, who later recalled a production of *Cymbeline*, in which he appeared alongside an equally young William Shatner. At the end of the production, Komissarzhevsky decided that the entire cast should leave the stage singing "*We're off to see the Wizard,*" from the *Wizard of Oz*. Plummer admitted that he had no idea why, but concluded regardless that Komissarzhevsky was a genius of the theatre.

weeks into the First Russian Revolution of 1905. He was buried in Rome's Protestant Cemetery, where his gravestone continues to read:

Teodoro Komissarzhevsky di Pietro. Artista lirico dell'opera italiana e dell'opera imperiale a Pietroburgo, professore al conservatorio di Mosca e combattente nelle legioni garibaldine, morì sul suolo della sua amata Italia.[41]

Komissarzhevsky represented the maturation of a distinctively Russian approach to singing and acting, through which filter of repositioned priorities he was able to achieve much for singers with limited vocal resources. In his memoirs, one of Komissarzhevsky's students, Vasily Shkafer, recalled him saying of one unusually stentorian tenor: "He's such a dimwit, but his voice is splendid; it's a true operatic voice, but what can you do with him? He doesn't understand a damn thing."[42]

The Russian approach to opera as lyric theatre ensured that sung-sound for its own sake was less meaningful than it was in Europe, where the taste for "frightful gesticulations" remained *en vogue* until well into the 20th century. Certainly, the evidence suggests that tenors more than any other voice-type took to theatrical pedagogy in Russia, for which a best-fit explanation is that most female opera singers sacrificed their careers for family, while baritones and basses were able to persuade in roles that were frequently written as mature or elderly.[43]

The tenor's limited function as central casting was not improved by the success and popularity of Rubinstein's *Demon* (in which Prince Sinodal – a role created by Komissarzhevsky – is killed off in the first act) and the controversy provoked by *Boris Godunóv*, which portrayed the failure of the establishment and the ascent of a revolting commoner (the Pretender). The absence of native heroic parts for tenors – and the dearth of *echt* romantic narratives – was exacerbated by the prevalence of characters that required tenors to be placed in a subservient or even deviant relationship with some better, stronger, older and more powerful man. The air of the ineffectual and the apathetic climaxed in the role of Lensky, the tenor lead in Tchaikovsky's *Eurgne Onegin*; there were anti-heroic stepping stones *en route*, however, including Dargomyzhsky's *Rigoletto*-esque *Rusalka*.[44] This provided Komissarzhevsky with the role of a seducer, for which he was well-equipped, having been the first tenor in Russia to perform the role of the Duke in Rigoletto at the Mariinsky.[45]

With the operation of theatres in Russia during the 1870s allowing singers little say in repertoire and casting, Komissarzhevsky's celebrity gave him *some* latitude, which led to his singing heavier-weight operas by Verdi for which (contra-Tamberlik) he was unequipped. The critical dismissal of Komissarzhevsky as an Italianate singer

---

41 'Teodoro Komissarzhevsky di Pietro, artist of the Italian opera and the Imperial Opera of Petersburg, professor at the Moscow Conservatory, and a soldier in Garibaldi's legions, died on the soil of his beloved Italy.'
42 Forshaw, Juliet (2014). *Dangerous Tenors, Heroic Basses, and Non-Ingénues: Singers and the Envoicing of Social Values in Russian Opera, 1836 – 1905*. PhD thesis. Columbia University. p.122.
43 Ibid.
44 Premiered on 4 May, 1856.
45 The role of the Prince was created by Pavel Bulakhov, who was praised (again) for his lyricism, but criticized for his limited range as an actor.

was nurtured by nationalist sentiments and the perennial prejudice for the perceived limitations of any light voice characterised by a limited technique. One critic observed simply that he "sang skillfully, but absolutely in the Italian manner, thus greatly detracting from the Russian character."[46] What that character was meant to entail is not clear; in any event, the raising of text and sentiment above tone and amplitude inspired Dargomyzhsky to create one of Komissarzhevsky's most successful roles, Don Juan, in *Kamennyj gost'*. The tenor's part is an almost constant *arioso*, set plumb centre in the tenor range and requiring primarily shades of declamation – and little or nothing from above the stave.[47]

The resolution of *Kamennyj gost'* in a duel between the tenor (as perennially young) and an elder statesman further alluded to the critical dynamics in which duelling was an inherent act of rebellion because it provided an anti-institutional and unorthodox route for young men to resolve personal conflicts – outside the influence and authority of the establishment.[48] In all but a handful of cases, the tenor dies – paradigmatically in *Yevgény Onégin* and *Mazepa* – and takes little or no sympathy with him when leaving. Even Lensky's duel is petulant, and then with his superior best friend – played by a baritone.

Dargomyzhsky's vocal range for Don Juan is almost baritonal, which represented a break with the high-voice traditions otherwise promulgated by Russian tenor roles. With Tchaikovsky's operas, and excepting Hermann in *Pikovaya dama,* Russian tenors after 1870 were either in or pursuing sincere, stable relationships. The earnestness of the Russian tenor as opposed to the routinely transgressive baritone and the authoritarian bass did not, of course, determine the sound of all tenor singers, even if the common currency was lyric and elegiac. The names of the tenors on whom the Five and their peers relied are forgotten outside Russia: Pyotr Inozemtsev, Yekab Karklin, Anton Sekar-Rozhansky, Mikhail Vasilyev, Anton Bartsal, Aleksandr Davïdov and Vasiliy Vasilyev. Even Mikhail Medvedev,[49] the first tenor to sing Lensky for Tchaikovsky, in Moscow on 29 March, 1879, survives only as a footnote, while Dmitri Usatov,[50] who sang the role at the Bolshoi premiere two years later,[51] is remembered chiefly as the teacher, patron and *pater familias* of Fyodor Chaliapin.

The first Russian tenor to become widely recognised, and then outside Russia, was also one of the first to make recordings. Nikolai Figner[52] was chosen by Tchaikovsky to create arguably the greatest role for tenor in 19th century Russian opera, Hermann (in *Pikovaya dama*, in St Petersburg on 19 December, 1890),[53] as well as Count Vaudémont in *Iolanta* on 18 December, 1892. Tchaikovsky created the roles of

---

46   Forshaw, Juliet (2014). *Dangerous Tenors, Heroic Basses, and Non-Ingénues: Singers and the Envoicing of Social Values in Russian Opera, 1836 – 1905*. PhD thesis. Columbia University. p.109.
47   See Taruskin, Richard (1981). "The Stone Guest and Its Progeny." *Opera and Drama in Russia as Preached and Practiced in the 1860s*. UMI Press.
48   Reyfman, Irina (2008). *Ritualized Violence Russian Style: The Duel in Russian Culture and Literature*. Stanford University Press.
49   1852 – 1925.
50   22 October, 1848 – 23 August, 1913.
51   On 23 January, 1881.
52   21 February, 1857 – 13 December, 1918.
53   Medvedev sang the role at the Bolshoi premiere in Moscow on 4 November, 1891.

Hermann and Liza for Figner and his wife Medea Mei, whose career was yet more celebrated, in part because she excelled in repertoire from outside Russia. Italian-born and trained, Mei was admired by Verdi, Boito and Puccini – with whom she studied the role of Mimi, which she was the first to sing in Russia. In 1949, in her 90th year, she was interviewed in French about her life and experiences, which included detailed and fascinating reminiscences of Tchaikovsky and Toscanini, among others. She can be heard also singing the first and last phrases from Liza's Act 3 aria, "*Uzh polnoch blizitsya,*"[54] music she was the first to sing for Tchaikovsky 59 years previously. Her voice, like her memory, is bewilderingly fresh; it seems incredible that she should have died just three years later.

Nikolai's repertoire was dominated reputationally by the music of Tchaikovsky, and the composer was famously grateful to the tenor for his efforts, writing after the premiere of *Pikovaya dama* that "Figner and the Saint Petersburg orchestra ... worked true miracles." His actual repertoire was dominated by well-worn imports like *Guillaume Tell* and *Lucia di Lammermoor* and more recent Italian operas – notably *Aida*, *La traviata* and, in 1889, the Russian premiere of *Otello*. Figner was also the Russian creator of Turiddu in *Cavalleria rusticana*, Canio in *Pagliacci* and Cavaradossi in *Tosca*, from each of which he recorded arias during the first few years of the 20th century. His 1902 Russian-language recording of Otello's "*Ora e per sempre addio,*" with piano accompaniment, is fascinating for its contemporaneity. The voice is young (he was only 45 at the time) but some distance from being a *tenore di forza*. The tone is overly bright, and thin on occasion; his pitching and placement are wayward and he is prone to yelling – characteristics that colour his recordings of "*Plus blanche que la blanche hermine*" from *Les Huguenots*, "*Che gelida manina*" from *La bohème*, and "*Ah! lève-toi*" from *Roméo et Juliette*. They are a feature also of his recording of "*vesti la giubba*" – an aria that Figner was the first to sing on stage in Russia. His approach to this most emotive of *verismo* arias is typical of Figner's work on record more generally; it is unsentimental, dry even, with little joined-up thinking in the phrasing and *legato*. His *portamento* yields routinely to swooping, which suggests a less than resolute technique, and his infrequent use of *rubato* is far from natural. The voice may well have filled the theatres in Moscow, St Peterburg, Madrid, Bucharest and London – where he made a number of well-reviewed appearances at Covent Garden; it cannot have been thought beautiful, however, when compared to the best of his European contemporaries.

Aesthetics were a secondary concern for many in Russia who regarded Figner and his family with political suspicion. His sisters played a pivotal role in the anti-tsarist cabal[55] that led to the assassination of Alexander II in 1881,[56] and Figner's progressive sensibilities were blamed for his decision to sing almost nothing by the Five – even after Alexander III initiated an aggressive programme of support for Russian music. Figner's self-evident preference for "foreign" repertoire was perceived as reactionary and stifling of modern Russian music – a construction that appears with hindsight to be more than a little ironic. His singing of "foreign" music as evidenced by his

---

54 'Midnight is Approaching.'
55 "Narodnaya Volya" ['People's Will'].
56 His eldest sister, Vera, was a member of the executive committee and sentenced to death.

recordings was anything but Italianate, while his performances of Tchaikovsky's work were positively Mediterranean by contemporary standards.

More tolerable to the orthodoxy – and the first truly dramatic Russian tenor to make records – was Ivan Yershov.[57] He recorded "*Ora e per sempre addio*" a matter of months after Figner, again in Russian. That is the only point of comparison between the performances, in no small part because Yershov enters half a bar early when singing "*dardi volanti, e volanti corsier.*" Instead of re-taking the side, Columbia released it – as one of fewer than a dozen '78s recorded by Yershov for the Gramophone & Typewriter Company and Columbia. Unlike Figner, Yershov's tone is coincidentally brilliant and rich – a classically clarion sound for Otello – which is supported by superb breath control, text book diction and some splendid articulation. If it's more histrionic than modern tastes might prefer then that is a construction of taste; the theatrical instincts and the thrilling timbre are timeless, and he must have been sensational in the theatre.

Yershov's coincident recording of "*Plus blanche que la blanche hermine*" is special also, notwithstanding an atypical tendency to sing sharp; he produces a genuine *legato*, and manages his trumpet-like sound to achieve that magnificent fusion of lyricism and power for which the best of his Italian contemporaries and successors were celebrated.[58] His reputation travelled widely outside Russia even if he didn't. Notice was certainly taken of his exceptional resonance and line as it was captured so memorably on his Russian-language recording of "*Nothung, nothung, neidliches Schwert.*" Three years before making that recording Yershov created the roles of Loge, Siegmund and Siegfried in the country's first Russian staging of the *Ring* Cycle.[59] He was also the first Tristan. Inevitably, and despite the prevailing fashion for declamation at Bayreuth, Cosima Wagner invited Yershov to sing at the 1901 Festival. Yershov declined. He was then the leading tenor in St Petersburg, if not the entire of Russia. The prospect of travelling to Northern Bavaria to re-learn the Wagner canon in another language was sufficiently unappealing for Yershov to turn down the House of Wahnfried. Moreover, he was lionised at the Mariinsky, where his pre-eminence as the leading dramatic tenor was unchallenged. In addition to Lensky and Hermann, Yershov paid careful homage to the Russian establishment by making regular appearances as Sobinin, the Pretender and Prince Vasily Golitsyn in *Khovanshchina*, and also to the Five when making himself available to Rimsky-Korsakov's boiler-room work ethic. He excelled as Tsar Berendey in *Snegúrochka–vesénnyaya skázka*, Grishka in *Skazániye o nevídimom gráde Kítezhe i déve Fevrónii*,[60] Mikhail Tucha in *Pskovityanka*,[61] and the title roles in *Kashchéy bessmértny*[62] and *Sadko*. Yershov was the first tenor to live up to Rimsky-Korsakov's ambitions. Apparently for the first time, his *heldentenorial* timbre and sensibility injected *echt* Wagnerian tone into the construction and conception of the Russian tenor voice as heroic. His sensibilities appear to have remained avowedly

---

57 8 November, 1867 – 21 November, 1943.
58 It is worth noting also that his arsenal included a ballistic high C, as can be heard on his recording of "*Versez! que tout respire*" from Act V of *Le prophète*.
59 See Bartlett, Rosamund (1995). *Wagner and Russia*. Cambridge University Press.
60 'The Legend of the Invisible City of Kitezh and the Maiden Fevroniya.'
61 'The Maid of Pskov.'
62 'Kashchey, the Deathless.'

Russian, however, and thoroughly in keeping with the Dostoevskyan supplanting of the individualistic Nietzschean-Wagnerian ideal with a pure fool defined by selfless idealism. According to the critic M. S. Shaginian, where German Siegfrieds "always stressed courage and joyfulness":

> "[Russian heroism] is nothing like that: we have Ivanushka the fool, Prince Myshkin, the Poor Knight; our popular imagination loves the wisdom in foolishness. And lo, Yershov takes this child-hero and makes him simpler and more folksy, makes him gentle, wise, charmingly ingenuous, an artless and clumsy person with the striking honesty of a child who approaches us openly." [63]

In Juliet Forshaw's compelling analysis:

> Yershov's interpretation of Siegfried gives us the key to Sadko and the other heroic Rimsky-Korsakov roles he created or helped propagate.... None of them is a hero according to the Western European chivalry-inflected model of warriors who slay dragons or rescue damsels in distress. This chivalric model can easily be detected in Italian and German tenor heroes such as Manrico and Siegfried. The Western European expectation that the hero earn his success and the love of the heroine through arduous struggle may explain why characters like Sadko have not particularly engaged Western audiences. Sadko doesn't earn his wealth or the love of Volkhova by battling evil; indeed, the story contains no villains. His one heroic gesture is sacrificial: when his ships get stuck in the doldrums, he throws himself overboard as a sacrifice to the underwater king in the hopes of generating a favorable wind and meeting Volkhova. (At no point does he think his life is in danger, which dilutes the power of the gesture.) After she expresses her love and returns him safe and sound to mundane Novgorod, it is hard to avoid the impression that Sadko's successes stem more from a divine handout than his own efforts. But Yershov's interpretation of Siegfried provides insight into this character, and into one Russian model of heroism.[64]

The Russian predilection for the phlegmatic and the anti-heroic as it was revealed by Dostoevsky, Tolstoy, Vladimir Solovyov and Vyacheslav Ivanov presented little with which Russian composers were able to work. Ennui and passivity were ill-suited to dramatic translation and downright antithetical to the traditional conception of masculinity in Russia. Even if many of Rimsky-Korsakov's tenor characters carry music that gains from resonance and amplitude, they are often feeble, decadent, wicked or emasculated. The most striking example of the disparity between vocal resources and character was Grishka Kuterma, a role created by Yershov at the St

---

63   Forshaw, Juliet (2014). *Dangerous Tenors, Heroic Basses, and Non-Ingénues: Singers and the Envoicing of Social Values in Russian Opera, 1836 – 1905*. PhD thesis. Columbia University. pp.146–147.
64   Ibid.

Petersburg premiere on 20 February, 1907, of *Skazániye o nevídimom gráde Kítezhe i déve Fevrónii*. A demonically possessed drunkard, Kuterma betrays Kitezh to the Tatars – a crime for which he frames Fevroniya. He is the negative of the Holy Fool, and one of the most awful tenor-scored characters in all of opera. Kuterma presents huge opportunities for a character-tenor; some of the music rewards a singer with Yershov's resources; analogous to Siegfried it most certainly isn't.

After Rimsky-Korsakov's death in 1908, Yershov remained a formidable presence on the Russian stage (and thereafter as a teacher). His last significant new role was Truffaldino in the Russian premiere of Prokofiev's *L'amour des trois oranges*[65] (as *Lyubov' k tryom apel'sinam*) in February, 1926, at the Mariinsky.[66] Yershov was also key to Rachmaninov's modest success as a composer of opera, creating the role of the Young Gypsy at the St Petersburg premiere of *Aleko* on 27 May, 1899 (with the composer conducting, and Chaliapin in the title role). He was not, however, chosen for the Moscow premiere – which went to Lev Klementiev.[67] Neither was Yershov Rachmaninov's first choice when casting Dante Alighieri for the premiere of *Francesca da Rimini* on 24 January, 1906. That role was given by the composer to Dmitri Smirnov,[68] a *spinto* tenor with a highly distinctive tone, a spectacular technique, and a passport.

Five years after making his Russian debut, Smirnov appeared for the first time at the Paris Opéra on 19 May, 1908, as the Pretender in *Boris Godunóv*. So great was his success that he was invited by the Metropolitan Opera's newly-installed Intendant, Giulio Gatti-Casazza, to join the company in New York. He arrived to find himself in competition with Enrico Caruso and John McCormack. Never can the gods have seemed so unkind. Despite achieving excellent notices as Rodolfo, Roméo, Alfredo and the Duke, Smirnov survived only three seasons, and was gone by 1912. He returned to Russia, but left again after the Revolution of 1917, preferring to continue his career in the West. In 1932 he took Estonian citizenship and later taught singing in London and Athens before he retired to Riga, where he died at the age of 61.

Smirnov was one of the first Russian tenors of note not to build his career around new music, or the music of Russian composers. He was also the first to record extensively. His approximately 90 recordings (produced over 20 years from 1909) are consistently impressive. He was essentially a *lirico-spinto* tenor, with a flame-proof technique that enabled him to achieve Di Stefano-type effects without damaging his voice, even when taking every opportunity to fire off high notes where none were available. For his otherwise magnificent Italian-language recording of "*Giunto sul passo estremo*" from *Mefistofele,* he added a pointless albeit impressive C5, his *diminuendo* on which is nothing short of miraculous. It is a technical feat unique to performances of the aria on record, and wholly absurd.[69] Smirnov also contributed two entirely vandalising interpolations to his (Italian language) recording of "*Donna non vidi mai,*" something Puccini may well have lived to regret. On the other hand,

---

65 'The Love for Three Oranges.'
66 Now renamed the *Leningrad State Academic Theatre for Opera and Ballet.*
67 1868 – 1910.
68 19 November, 1882 –27 April, 1944.
69 If the reader knows of any other, the author will welcome hearing about it.

his recording of Manon's "*En Fermant Les Yeux*" (in Italian, as "*O dolce incanto*") is sublime in the delicacy of its phrasing, dynamics and line, and proof that Smirnov was one of the most gifted and musical tenors of the first quarter of the 20th century.

Smirnov's primary rivals were Leonid Sobinov[70] and Andrey Labinsky.[71] Their voices were lighter than Smirnov's and dwarfed by that of Yershov. It is for this reason that Sobinov and Labinsky's repertoire attached them natively to Jontek in Stanisław Moniuszko's *Halka*, Lensky, Sobinin, and Vladimir Igorevich in Borodin's *Knyáz Ígor*.[72] Labinsky was popular, and as something of a lothario the object of at least one public assassination attempt by an angry husband. He was also limited as a singer and an actor – particularly when compared to Sobinov – and like many others in Russia he didn't travel, dividing his professional life exclusively between Moscow and St Petersburg. Sobinov took a different path. Shortly after making his debut he appeared for the first time with Chaliapin, in 1899, and this inspired him to focus on his approach to stagecraft. His training brought the gravity of a singing-actor to the core lyric repertoire of Faust, Des Grieux, the Duke, Gérald (*Lakmé*), Wilhelm Meister (*Mignon*), Lyonel (*Martha*), Alfredo, and, famously, Lohengrin. He was unhappy with his technical limitations vocally, however, and three years later he travelled to Italy for study and so as to better analyse what qualified as authentic in Europe. During the seasons 1904–06 (and again in 1911) he made successful appearances at La Scala, which led to performances at the Opéra, Covent Garden, the Opéra Monte-Carlo, the Hofopers in Berlin and Vienna, and the Teatro Real, Madrid. Sobinov sang in French, German and Italian as well as Russian. In 1914 the War sent him back to Russia. Following the 1917 Revolution, he was appointed director of the Bolshoi Theatre, and in 1918 he was appointed Chairman of the musical committee of the all-Ukrainian Division of Arts in Kiev. Sobinov returned to the Bolshoi in 1921. Having sung for the last time in 1933, at a Bolshoi gala held in his honour, he accepted a post in Stanislavsky's studio.

Sobinov's talents as a singer are well served on many fine recordings, most of which speak to excellent musicianship and consistent judgment – although his range was limited when compared with Smirnov, whose voice was palpably easier above the stave. Sobinov's recordings cannot, of course, convey his skills as an actor, which were considered by many to be comparable to those of Chaliapin. In Russia he was a hero of the people as well as the State, while in Europe he was celebrated for bringing a measured, Russian seriousness to light-lyric repertoire that suffered on occasion from the reductionism of isolated vocalism.

His commitment to the Communist system fomented personal tragedy, with the death in 1920 of his son Yuri while serving with the White Army near Melitopol, and the emigration of his other son, Boris, to Germany. It did not, conversely, draw him to the music of contemporary composers, from whom, like every other star tenor of the day, he remained at arm's length. The distance of Russia's "greatest" tenors from native culture exacerbated the decline of Russian opera for young composers. Indeed, following in the wake of the Five, many of those who committed to the

---

70   7 June, 1872 – 14 October, 1934.
71   20 August, 1871 – 8 August, 1941.
72   'Prince Igor.'

Russian stage did so infrequently or without lasting success, while those who elected to serve the Stalinist regime were compromised or terrorised. Stravinsky left Russia for Paris in 1920, and his constantly evolving musical language adhered throughout to librettos in French for performance outside Russia; this lowered the burden of the Russian operatic tradition almost entirely onto the shoulders of two composers, Sergei Prokofiev and Dmitri Shostakovich. Between 1911 and Prokofiev's death in 1953, they completed ten operas between them, with Shostakovich finishing only three works sufficient for staging, despite working on more than a dozen projects and scores. Their celebrity globally ensured that each completed opera was an international event, whether for musical or political reasons, and they occupied a narrative space that left little room for anyone else. On point: each of the following Russian composers composed (and saw staged) operas during Shostakovich's lifetime:[73] Eduard Nápravník,[74] Vladimir Rebikov,[75] Vano Muradeli, Yuri Shaporin, Visarrion Shebalin,[76] Isaak Dunayevsky,[77] Alexander Mossolov,[78] Dmitri Kabalevsky,[79] Veniamin Fleishman,[80] Tikhon Khrennikov,[81] Grigory Frid,[82] Mieczysław Weinberg,[83] Vladimir Shcherbachev, Sergei Vasilenko, Vladimir Fere, Vladimir Vlasov, Kirill Molchanov, and Alexander Kholminov.

It is not an overstatement to say that only two of these composers, Rebikov and Prokofiev, wrote anything featuring a tenor part that required more than what might generically be considered a "character" voice.[84] This is not to diminish the quality of the invention or the art; it is simply to acknowledge that Russian tenors during and after the 1930s adhered through choice to repertoire that pre-dated them, and then for the most part within the lyrical, lighter end of the vocal spectrum, for which there was the greatest supply of voices, most notably Sergei Yudin,[85] Georgy Vinogradov,[86]

---

73   In many cases, each composed as many as six or seven fully-orchestrated, multiple-act works.
74   Nápravník was one of Russia's leading conductors, renowned for his work at the Mariinsky Theater in St Petersburg. He composed four operas, each in the shadow of Nápravník's idol, Tchaikovsky. For his most successful work, *Dubrovsky*, he secured a libretto from Tchaikovsky's brother Modest – like *Eugene Onegin*, after Pushkin.
75   1866 – 1920; composed more than ten operas, of which only one, *Yolka*, survived.
76   1902 – 1936; composed three operas, notably a setting of *The Taming of the Shrew* (1957).
77   1900 – 1955; composed 14 operettas, most successfully *White Acacia* (1955).
78   1900 – 1973; composed four operas, including *The Barrage* (1930).
79   1904 – 1987; composed seven operas, including *Colas Breugnon* (1936–1976).
80   1913 – 1941; composed only a single opera, *Rothschild's Violin* (1941), which was completed and orchestrated by Shostakovich.
81   1913 – 2007; composed five operas, including *Into the Storm* (1939).
82   1915 – 2012; composed two chamber operas, including *The Diary of Anne Frank* (1968).
83   1919 – 1996; composed seven operas.
84   Rebikov wrote in an expansive late romantic style, while Prokofiev's *Duenna* contains some very fine lyrical writing (for Antonio) as does the title role of *Semyon Kotko*.
85   8 July, 1889 – 5 May, 1963.
86   16 November, 1908 – 12 November, 1980. Vinogradov never performed on the opera stage (and he never joined an opera company), but he participated in many radio performances, including Don Giovanni, Manon, Mignon, and numerous Russian operas.

Pyotr Slovtsov,[87] Vladimir Rosing,[88] and Vitaly Kilchevsky.[89] It is generally accepted that the best of them were Sergei Lemeshev[90] and Ivan Kozlovsky.[91]

For admirers of tenor singing since the invention of recording, Lemeshev and Kozlovsky remain the greatest Russian exponents to have made records. Kozlovsky, in particular, developed an extraordinary technique[92] and a reputation for *bel canto* extravagance that should probably have caused official censure. On a 1943 broadcast recording of "*Ecco ridente*" he threw in a high C, followed by an easy D, which would have satisfied the majority of those relishing high-note interpolations for the sake of it. He nonetheless ends the performance with a lightning-bolt E5 from which he pushes through "E sharp" into an F5 in full voice before dropping through the scale to a D2. The whole thing is entirely silly, and thrilling for being done at all. The *coloratura* is far from perfect, however, and his style is often hard, if not downright brutal; vulgarity was no bar to popularity. Kozlovsky enjoyed a lifelong but friendly rivalry with Lemeshev,[93] whose artistry was incomparably more refined.[94] For most Russian singers, the language dictates the sound that can be produced; the timbral range is markedly different from that of their Western peers insofar as it is darker, with more "closed" vowels such as "y" and a series of much harder consonants; the voice is forced commonly to the back of the mouth and down into the chest. Lemeshev was one of very few to transcend these peculiarities, and despite singing *almost* everything in Russian,[95] he produced when young one of the most beautiful *legatos* of any tenor since the invention of recording.

His tone was light, eternally warm and easily placed. The tenderness of his singing was made sweeter still by his exceptional breath control and an exquisite sensibility that shielded him from the high-kicking crudities for which Kozlovsky was renowned. Both singers engaged in sentimentality and the lachrymose, but Lemeshev brought unshakeable integrity to decisions that often sounded cheapened when adopted by Kozlovsky. There is compelling evidence for his gifts in a 1941 film released (originally) as *Kino-kontsert*.[96] Made up of a collection of musical and dance numbers (featuring performances by Yevgeni Mravinsky and Emil Gilels, among others), Lemeshev was filmed as the Duke, singing "*Questa e quella*" and "*La donna è*

---

87   30 June, 1886 – 24 February, 1934.
88   23 January, 1890 – 24 November, 1963.
89   1899 – 1986. A student of Sophia Akimova – Mrs. Ivan Yershov.
90   10 July, 1902 – 26 June, 1977.
91   24 March, 1900 – 21 December, 1993.
92   Kozlovsky continued to sing while teaching at the Moscow Conservatory (from 1956 to 1980); he gave his last concert in 1989, at the Central House of Writers in Moscow – four years before his death at the age of 93.
93   Their rivalry was whipped up by fans who were either "Lemeshistki" or "kozlovityanki".
94   Lemeshev was married six times, in part because of his serial adultery – a weakness made much worse by his status as a (reluctant) idol.
95   There is a single recording in Italian of "Una furtiva lagrima" from after 1941 – when, during an evacuation, he caught a very bad cold which resulted in two attacks of pneumonia, complicated by pleurisy and tuberculosis of the right lung. His treatment caused the collapse of one of his lungs – and the loss of much of his once easy projection. He nonetheless went on to record *Lakmé, Snegúrochka–vesénnyaya skázka* and *Les pêcheurs de perles*.
96   Known also as *Russian Salad*.

mobile" from *Rigoletto*. He enters in traditional costume – an androgynous vision in ruffs, cuffs and puffed-out sleeves – and assumes the posture of a dilettante; he is as sexually ambiguous in his vocal manner as in his appearance. The effortlessness of his placement and projection are wondrous, such that he almost speaks the music. For "*Questa e quella*" he swells each phrase, finding a magical harmoniousness of line to convey the character's essential flippancy; his gestures and expressions add gloriously to the sense of decadent self-assurance, and because of (rather than despite) the tenderness and elegance of line, and the foppishness of his postures and movements, he creates an almost evil presence. The articulation of "*La donna è mobile*" is remarkable, as is the technical bravura of the dynamic changes (which make use of his infamously silken *diminuendo-pianissimo*), the word use and *rubato*; rarely does the music that precedes the concluding C5 render that note perfunctory. The looks on the faces of his female admirers are entirely believable.

Lemeshev and Kozlovsky were both lifelong supporters of Stalin, although the General Secretary's preference for Kozlowsky appears to have been unshakable. He was made a People's Artist of the USSR in 1940;[97] Lemeshev was denied the same title until a few weeks after Stalin's death on 5 March, 1953. In a televised interview, filmed some years after 1953, the bass Ivan Petrov observed without smiling that "Stalin greatly loved opera. You can accuse him of many terrible things, but he was knowledgeable about art." It's not clear whether Uncle Joe encouraged the performance of musical theatre at the salt mines of Siberia; it seems unlikely. "You can ask me anything," he once said to Kozlovsky, "but I will not let you travel abroad." Stalin's control of Soviet art and artistry is well-known. The life and work of Nikolai Pechkovsky is not.[98] Stalin and his Soviet "editors" removed him from the official record because he was said to have collaborated with the German army during the siege of Leningrad. He was rumoured also to be gay, a greater crime for anyone with low enemies in high places. There is scant evidence for either "disgrace"; in fact the alleged collaboration involved Pechkovsky doing little more than attempting to care for his sick mother. During the summer of 1941, she was recovering from illness in the tenor's dacha in Kartashevskaya, 40 miles south of Leningrad. Having surrounded the city, the German army severed the railroad line from Kartashevskaya to Leningrad, stranding Pechkovsky and his mother behind enemy lines. Pechkovsky had to earn money to keep them both alive and so he sang in local clubs where Germans mixed with Russians. He eventually made his way to the Baltic States, where he gave concerts. On 12 November, 1945, he attempted to return to the Soviet Union and was arrested in Moscow; in the usual way, he was sentenced without a trial. Pechkovsky was sent to a Gulag camp, north of the Arctic Circle, for ten years. As for his sexuality, it was rumoured that Pechkovsky's marriage to a female admirer after his release from prison was strategic.

In 1956, Pechkovsky was 60 years old, and his career as one of the most gifted dramatic Russian tenors of the 1930s was over. He was "rehabilitated" and had his status as a People's Artist of the USSR returned to him; he was forbidden from singing at

---

97   The title "Hero of the Soviet Union" was the highest distinction of the Soviet Union. It was awarded on 12,775 occasions.
98   1896 – 1966.

the Bolshoi, the Kirov or the Mariinksy, however. He committed his time to teaching instead; it was in the company of his students that he gave his final performance as Hermann, in private in 1965, a year before his death. Pechkovsky's greatest roles were Hermann and Otello. Shostakovich greatly admired a production of *Otello* starring Pechkovsky, which the tenor also directed. Coincidentally he loathed the conducting of Sergey Yeltsin, about whom he fired off an especially bad-tempered review.[99] Shostakovich rated Pechkovsky as superior to his only rival in the weightier repertoire, Georgii Nelepp.[100] Nelepp's voice was shrill by comparison, and coloured by a dreadful wobble. On one occasion, Nelepp was called upon to replace an indisposed Pechkovsky as Hermann. A large proportion of the audience returned their tickets to the box office and left. Nelepp gained inevitably from Pechkovsky's imprisonment and subsequent eradication. There is a complete recording of *Pique Dame* in circulation, with Pechkovsky as Hermann, and it's claimed there is also an uncut *Otello* – in Russian. There is little else to which reference can be made; the best of what survived the tenor's purging is some excerpts as Hermann, conducted by Yevgeny Wolf-Israel in Moscow in 1937, which speak to a fine, ringing voice and intelligent, thoughtful musicianship.

Like Lemeshev and Kozlovsky, Pechkovsky sang little or nothing by living composers. Celebrated tenors were not troubled with new music, excepting the promulgation over the radio of traditional folk song and flag-waving propaganda during and immediately after the war. Every leading tenor in Russia sang regularly for the troops, events for which art was rarely a criterion beyond its service to the State. The common reluctance to engage with the contemporary was exacerbated by the popularity in Russia of broadcasting and recording, and it was equally certain that graduates sought out opera houses and companies with programmes that provided, first and foremost, easy opportunities for display. The restrictive cultural environment fostered a host of syntactical dilemmas, wherein everything that wasn't political was either irrelevant or dismissably western. A prominent exception to this rule as it applied to tenors was Aleksei Maslennikov,[101] one of the most important singers for Russian composers during the Cold War. Throughout the 1950s, 60s and 70s, Maslennikov made his lyric tenor available to a host of composers and a section of repertoire that brought neither fame nor fortune. His commitment to the State brought him into service to (or direct collaboration with) Prokofiev, Shostakovich, Stefania Zaranek, Tikhon Khrennikov, Yuri Shaporin, Ivan Dzerzhinsky, Rodion Shchedrin, Vano Muradeli, and many others whose work was restricted to the Soviet Union. Like his contemporaries Rostropovich, Oistrakh and Richter, Maslennikov performed the music of Benjamin Britten, including the role of Lysander in *A Midsummer's Night Dream*. He did so without leaving the USSR, and always in Russian.

Consistent with the Russian tenor tradition, Maslennikov was light-voiced, as was his colleague, the Latvian-born Mikhail "Mischa" Alexandrovich.[102] The latter

---

99   Glikman, Isaac (1993) *Story of a Friendship: The Letters of Dmitry Shostakovich to Isaak Glikman with a commentary by Isaak Glikman*, trans. Anthony Philips, Cornell University Press. p.xlii.
100   20 April, 1904 – 18 June, 1957.
101   9 September, 1929 – 30 November, 2016.
102   23 July, 1914 – 3 July, 2002.

was hugely popular in Russia, where he sold around 20 million recordings. Because he too was not allowed to travel out of the Union, he didn't make his western debut until 14 December, 1972, at the age of 57, when he sang a concert of arias with piano in New York's Town Hall. The sharp-toned, lyric tradition remained largely undisturbed throughout the 1950s and 60s, until the emergence of Vladimir Atlantov,[103] the most successful dramatic Russian tenor of the 1970s and 80s. Atlantov is unusual for a variety of reasons, the first of which (by way of a question for the Met's Opera Quiz) is that he is probably the only tenor to have spent his entire life from birth until retirement in an opera house. Atlantov's father was the bass Andrey Petrovich; his mother a soprano, Maria Yelizarova. Both were long-serving performers at the Kirov and Mikhailovsky Theatres in Leningrad; Atlantov's earliest memories were of voice-training, rehearsals and operas starring his parents. By the age of six he was a member of the Glinka Choir and in 1957 he enrolled at the Leningrad Conservatory. Five years later he was awarded the silver medal at the Glinka vocal competition and – remarkably, given the political tensions between Europe and Russia – allowed to travel to Milan for studies at La Scala.

Upon returning he was engaged by the Kirov as Alvaro in *La forza del destino*. Among the audience was the Russian-born *uber*-impresario Sol Hurok, who invited Atlantov to sing at the Metropolitan in New York. Unfortunately, the authorities did not on this occasion allow him to travel, so he remained in the Soviet Union, winning prizes at the Tchaikovsky Competition in Moscow and the 3rd International Competition in Sofia. He was scouted by the Bolshoi, with whom he toured to Milan – where he was considered as thrilling for the West as Bergonzi had been for the East when touring Russia in 1964 with La Scala.[104] Atlantov sang 18 roles at the Bolshoi, including the two that would define his career on stage: Hermann and Otello. His voice had fantastic *squillo*, which cut through the largest of orchestras, and he could act – a quality not always paramount among his Italianate peers. He was inarguably something of a shouter, however, and amplitude preoccupied him rather more than line and phrasing. His repertoire was broad – from Glinka, Rimsky-korsakov and Mussorgsky (notably *Khovanshchina*[105]) to Don José, Canio and Cavaradossi. He took a swing at Siegfried and missed; neither was he persuasive when transitioning to light-baritone roles (as Rodrigo in *Don Carlo*, for example). Atlantov made only a few recordings – among which his performance as Hermann for Seiji Ozawa in Boston (RCA) is very fine. For anyone with a taste for such things, his album of Italian *canzone* ("Serenade") is a thing of unique perversity. It's best compared to staring into a violently powerful shower-head at full pelt with one's eyes open. The arrangements add to the horror as among the worst ever captured and released on record. In particular, and for hearing just once, the arrangement of "*L'alba sepàra dalla luce l'ombra*"[106] (featuring rhythm drum, harps, *Mantovani* strings, and what

---

103   19 February, 1939 –
104   With La Scala, in the company of Freni, Scotto, Simionato, Cossotto, Tucci, Nilsson, Price, Raimondi, Prevedi, Cappuccilli, Gavazzeni and von Karajan.
105   Deutsche Grammophon released a fine recording of a performance from the Staatsoper production in Vienna in September, 1989, with Atlantov as Prince Andrey Khovansky, conducted by Claudio Abbado.
106   'Dawn separates the light from the shadows.'

appears to be Sinatra's touring band) is almost certainly the most awful thing ever done to a song by Tosti.

Far more musical, if not as resonant, was Sergei Larin,[107] a tragically short-lived Russian tenor from Lithuania who, like Atlantov, ended his career in Vienna, where he was prized for his unusual musical intelligence and expression. He was pre-eminent for more than a decade as the leading Russian *lirico-spinto* tenor, and his death at the age of 51 denied him at least another decade on the international stage. He might have lasted longer still, since he had a superb technique which he used with unfailing judgment. Larin also made very few recordings, the best of which is a badly engineered[108] but still impressive collection of songs by Rachmaninov. His performance of "*Vessenniye Void*,"[109] Op.14, No.11 memorialises his splendid voice placement, expressive colouring and word-use. The performance of "*Son*,"[110] Op.8, No.5 reveals exceptional dynamic control and a rare feeling for dramatic-*legato*. These qualities did not always survive in the theatre, where some of his roles were vocally beyond his natural limits – notably *Don Carlo* and Calàf in *Turandot*.

The same could not be said of Vladimir Galouzine,[111] a once-in-a-lifetime force of nature, whose titanic dramatic voice was promoted fanatically by Valery Gergiev at the Mariinsky as the most compelling of his age. Gergiev was spot-on, insofar as Galouzine's voice was truly colossal, and a match for the largest of orchestral forces. The tone was huge but bright when it needed to be, and he had a B4 and a C5 that could cause subsidence – famously so when hammering out "*No, No, Principessa Altera*" in *Turandot*. It was in the middle range of his voice that Galouzine was at his most formidable. The power of the instrument was ferocious and unsettling in its intensity, which generated an almost Gothic psychological presence. He was at his greatest in the role of Hermann, which he performed for the first time in 1993. Tchaikovsky did not create the role for a voice anything like Galouzine's. Indeed, as a construction of dramatic capacity, and by comparison with Nicolai Figner, Galouzine's voice would have operated in the 1890s as a baritone, emboldened by the addition of a third above the stave. Even for modern audiences he was sufficiently upholstered to sing the majority of baritone roles. Between 1995 and 2008, however, he was the most complete dramatic tenor on the world stage – albeit in *certain* roles only. The enormity of the voice and the diabolical power of the man wielding it left him unsuited to a span of repertoire for which he was theoretically ideal by *fach*,[112] particularly after his *vibrato* began to spread.

Galouzine's life before turning to opera full time is unique in the history of the tenor. He served in the army for a number of years before being introduced to opera, and the work of Chaliapin in particular. Like the best of his predecessors, he was drawn to the theatre as an actor as well as a singer, and like many other Russians he turned automatically to the many bass roles for which by scale he was inclined.

---

107 9 March, 1956 – 13 January, 2008.
108 Chandos released the album, with Eleonora Bekova as accompanist. The piano is horribly prominent, and destructive of much of Larin's phrasing and diction.
109 'Spring Waters.'
110 'The Dream.'
111 11 June, 1956 –
112 Including Cavaradossi, Don Carlo, Radamès and Des Grieux.

Having learned each of Chaliapin's roles, his professional life as a singer began with him singing as a bass, but his studies at the Novosibirsk Conservatory did not go as intended, so he pivoted as a baritone. When these studies failed to result in graduation, he joined the Novosibirsk Musical Comedy Theatre, where he performed as many as two shows daily, across numerous different productions. He worked for eight years in Russian musical comedy before making his way finally to small roles at the Novosibirsk Opera House in 1988. He was already 32 years old, and even at this stage in his career unable to gain regular work in an opera house. In consequence he relocated to St Petersburg and Yuriy Alexandrov's Chamber Music Theatre. He came eventually to the attention of Valery Gergiev, who invited him to sing Otello at the Mariinsky Theatre. His success threw him to the spotlight, and after the collapse of the USSR at the end of 1991 he relocated to Belgium, from where he was invited by the world's leading opera houses to perform his signature roles, Hermann, Otello, Prince Vsevolod and Sadko.

When singing his first Calàf at the Chorégies d'Orange in 1997, and despite being past his 40th birthday, the power of the voice and his fearsome dramatic focus were for many a revelation. It came at cost, however, and the effort invested made demands that shortened his vocal lifespan. His singing was never beautiful, in any formalistic sense, and it would have been impossible to continue performing as he did in the 1990s for more than a handful of appearances annually, but he was possessed of a Stakhanovite work ethic. This sustained him physically, but within a decade his massive voice became declamatory and absent anything passing for a *legato*.

Between 2005 and 2008 Galouzine performed in productions of *Pique Dame* that survive on film as the most compelling ever recorded. It's conceded that Domingo's performances at the Met with Gergiev in the late 1990s were unrivalled for many; they were sensational for the conducting as well as for Domingo's extraordinary acting and singing (even when noting his downward transposition of the "storm and oath" scene). Galouzine's performances (filmed with Gergiev in St Petersburg and Gennady Rozhdestvensky in Paris) revealed something else in the character entirely that Domingo could not. The Russian's confidence in the role was not merely vocal; he embodied that elemental defiance that makes Hermann so compelling; he was more than a tragic, pathetic caricature, whose suicide can seem inevitable from the first. Galouzine's Hermann is unhinged by circumstance, not by insanity – even when he admits to madness during the final scene. Galouzine's power transcended the solipsism that so often determines the role in performance; his immersion in the tragi-comic was fed by that peculiarly Russian flair for revealing suffering as normal. In this respect, and uniquely since the end of the Soviet Union, Galouzine embodied a definitive Russian masculinity in sound and appearance, as a truly heroic singer who represented the wholescale transformation of two centuries of gender-reductive clichés without yielding to compromise.

The social and demographic traditions established by Lev Leonov and transformed by Vladimir Galouzine have stalled. The handful of internationally-recognised Russian tenors are now, for the most part, light or lyric in voice, tone and repertoire – most prominently Maxim Mironov.[113] With masculinity continuing to represent a

---

113   30 September, 1981 –

serious issue within modern-day Russia, and State-authorised and sponsored attacks on gay men and women on the increase, the febrile and politically and socially unstable conception of masculinity in Russia continues to occupy a cultural space within which the tenor still has much to say.

CHAPTER SEVENTEEN

Sacred and Profane

Between 1970 and 2010, the Royal Opera House, Covent Garden, presented twelve world premieres on its Main Stage:

Victory (Richard Rodney Bennett, 1970)
The Knot Garden (Michael Tippett, 1970)[1]
Taverner (Peter Maxwell Davies, 1972)
We Come to the River (Hans Werner Henze, 1972)
The Ice Break (Michael Tippett, 1977)
Thérèse (John Taverner, 1979)
Gaiwan (Harrison Birtwistle, 1991)
Arianna (Alexander Goehr, 1995)
Sophie's Choice (Nicholas Maw, 2002)
The Tempest (Thomas Adès, 2004)
1984 (Lorin Maazel, 2005)
The Minotaur (Harrison Birtwistle, 2008)

Other notable productions, again on the Main Stage, included:

Owen Wingrave (Benjamin Britten, 1973)
Death in Venice (Benjamin Britten, 1973)
Donnerstag aus Licht (Karlheinz Stockhausen, 1981)
The King Goes Forth to France (Aulis Sallinen, 1984)
Un Re in Ascolto (Luciano Berio, 1984)
Mary Seacole (Richard Chew, 2000)
Jane Eyre (Michael Berkeley, 1948);
House of the Gods (Jayne Plowman, 2006)
Monkey - Journey to the West (Damon Albarn, 2007)

Between 2001 and 2010, the following composers presented operas for staging at the Linbury Studio: Graham Preskett, John Browne, Errolyn Wallen, Nigel Osborne, Stephen McNeff, Dominique Le Gendre, Stuart Macrae, Edward Rushton, and Michael Berkeley. This is not the forum to take up arms for or against contemporary music. It is appropriate, however, to conclude that the tenor as a voice and a cultural phenomenon has formed over time in a crucible of compositional form and content, fired at all times by popular taste. Even that most "difficult" of 19th century

---

1 It was re-staged in a reduced version in 1983.

composers, Wagner, was a global celebrity by reason of his work. The myth of the unrecognised genius is at its most fantastical when applied to composers, whose reputations for the most part were consistent with their achievements; even Mozart and Schubert's compositions were performed widely during their lifetimes. There is a navigable difference between success and prosperity however, something for which Richard Strauss was damned by those with less commercial sensibilities. If the evolution of the tenor as a construction of social, cultural, architectural and economic influences is self-evident, then so too is the disconnect between contemporary music after 1960 and the tenor voice to that date. Many gifted tenors like Robert Tear and Philip Langridge adhered manfully to the principle that contemporary invention will always be the lifeblood of musical art. They were right to think so; for opera to survive it is vital that young composers be encouraged to write music that is not only new but fresh in its thought and feeling. The question arising is whether they have any right to expect to hear it performed. This is especially true of opera.

But for works by Britten, the operas staged by Covent Garden since 1970 are not popular and are never going to be. Neither are they performed regularly. Whether they should be is a matter for critical judgment; whether they *can* be falls to the capacity and willingness of singers to meet the considerable challenges of performing music that is rarely tonal and frequently outside the parameters of expression as it is taught by singing coaches and music academies around the world. Langridge,[2] for example, sang Monteverdi and Mozart while committing to the music of Britten who was, during the first fifteen years of Langridge's career, a living, breathing cultural force. The tenor later gave his time and talent to Harrison Birtwistle, for whom he created the roles of Orpheus The Man in *The Mask of Orpheus* in 1976 (the year of Britten's death), Kong in *The Second Mrs Kong* in 1994, and Hiereus in *The Minotaur* in 2008. Each of these roles is technically and expressively challenging; they are not easy for audiences, either. This serried dispute has been raging for centuries. Beethoven's music was impossible for many during his lifetime, and the same was true of most every musical titan until Schoenberg took the ultimate leap of faith when observing that "one day people will be whistling my music in the streets." They are not, and they never will be. Schoenberg's tonal compositions are popular contextually – with *Gurre-Lieder* a perennial favourite whenever funding warrants the extravagance. He emancipated the dissonance well over a century ago, however, and that is surely long enough for posterity to resolve itself into *adieu*.

Langridge was a master of the English songbook, a vast catalogue that includes the wonderful but sadly forgotten work of C. W. Orr. Langridge's performances of Orr's ravishing "Housman Songs" were highlights in a career littered with achievements, but his capacity for expression when singing "*Is my team ploughing*" (1925) was precluded by *The Mask of Orpheus* (1986). He sang it anyway, and he did so while admitting the application of A. E. Housman's lecture in 1933 that

> Poetry is not the thing said but a way of saying it. Can it then be isolated and studied by itself? For the combination of language with its intellectual content, its meaning, is as close a union as can well be imagined.

---

2 16 December, 1939 – 5 March, 2010.

Is there such a thing as pure unmingled poetry, poetry independent of meaning? Even when poetry has a meaning, as it usually has, it may be inadvisable to draw it out. 'Poetry gives most pleasure' said Coleridge 'when only generally and not perfectly understood'; and perfect understanding will sometimes almost extinguish pleasure. The Haunted Palace is one of Poe's best poems so long as we are content to swim in the sensations it evokes and only vaguely to apprehend the allegory. We are roused to discomfort, at least I am, when we begin to perceive how exact in detail the allegory is; when it dawns upon us that the fair palace door is Roderick Usher's mouth, the pearl and ruby his teeth and lips, the yellow banners his hair, the ramparts plumed and pallid his forehead, and when we are reduced to hoping, for it is no more than a hope, that the winged odours have no connexion with hair-oil. Meaning is of the intellect, poetry is not.[3]

In Tom Stoppard's *The Invention of Love*, Charon informs Housman of the imminent arrival of two fares, "*A poet and a scholar.*" Housman replies "I think that must be me." "Both of them?" asks Charon. "I'm afraid so...." The battle identified by Schoenberg as between "heart and mind" rumbles on, but it does so at a cost to performers as well as audiences. The smear of anti-intellectualism attaching to the whispered suggestions that human expression remains a function of poetry rather than (or at least in addition to) intellect can be countered by a cursory analysis of the real-world status of any of the composers promoted by Convent Garden, with the singular exception of Britten. Does it matter that whenever Stockhausen and Berio wrote for the tenor voice (or voices more generally) the music operated to negate the essential lyricism of the instrument? Does the "modernity" of the *Licht* cycle bear on the distance that each of the seven operas places between the composer and the performer and those paying to hear them?

Berio's most accessible work for the stage is a completion of Puccini's *Turandot*. That fact alone would occupy analytical space only if the rest of Berio's work was accessible at all. By contradistinction, Mahler completed Weber's unfinished score for *Die drei Pintos* while working on his First Symphony. 21 years later, when completing the manuscript of *Das lied von der Erde*, Mahler's music was written as clearly for the art of Fritz Wunderlich as for William Miller when he took part in the first performance on 20 November, 1911. Conversely, Berio's *Melodrama* for tenor and eight instruments (1970) was not written for the same tenor voice that might have sung the role of Calàf. Berio was able to straddle the tonal-traditional and the contemporary (as he did with his *Folk Songs*); he did so because there were singers like Cathy Berberian willing and able to adhere to the "new" as it was conceived by John Cage and others. Without them the "modern" would not have been heard at all. It's an unpalatable truth for defenders of the faith that Cage was at his most accessible when writing parodies of the popular (as he did for his *Song Books* of 1970). Even Maxwell Davies abandoned his *credo* when embracing the universal and expressive potential of "singing" with *An Orkney Wedding With Sunrise, Farewell to Stromness*

---

3   Housman , A. E. (2010). *The Collected Poems of A.E. Housman*. Penguin, p.xxx.

and the latter three symphonies. His reversion during the last two decades of his life to the tonal and the conventionally beautiful was not denounced as a compromise, even accepting the radicalist dogma of *Eight Songs for a Mad King*. This "challenging" 40-minute monologue for male voice (a tenor as easily as a baritone or a bass, considering the notation and its advocacy of *falsetto* shrieking) has George III rant and howl his way through "songs" that are inherently unsingable. The score's references to the King's failed efforts to teach caged birds to sing are arguably more absurdist than Sir Arthur Streeb-Greebling's desperate attempts to teach ravens to fly underwater.[4] They are both, in any event, as anachronistic as the *Eight Songs*' quotations from Handel's *Messiah*. Characterisations of the composer's brutalist sound-world as representative of mental distress are unpersuasive. Whither the "mad" scenes of 19th century opera, or the cultivation of displacement achieved by Schoenberg with *Erwartung*?[5]

Is a "modernist" composer presumed to equate the tonal and the lyrical to the casual? How was Philip Langridge to approach a composer who would write *for* his voice when otherwise conspiring *against* it? There were militant exceptions. The angry old man of British modernism, Harrison Birtwistle, was never less than certain of the value of his creative voice, indecipherable though it was for anyone thinking in 12 tones. His stage works adhere to the vernacular of a defiant youth that celebrated the negation of a language to which he nonetheless turned for his own pleasure. When asked by the BBC to choose his "Desert Island Discs," Birtwistle nominated the Tudor composer Robert Fayrfax's *Aeternae Laudis Lilium*, Schubert's Symphony No. 8 in B minor, Mozart's Clarinet Quintet in A major, and the "Funeral Music" from Wagner's *Götterdämmerung* – as well as Stravinsky's Symphonies of Wind Instruments and Stockhausen's *Gruppen*. Birtwistle was apparently keen to preserve the diatonic for himself while denouncing its atavism as a composer. As Schoenberg was always quick to concede, there is yet a great deal of music to be written in C major.

The post-War rejection of pre-War sensibilities did not begin with *Peter Grimes* – though it was first performed just one month after Churchill announced Victory in Europe, on 7 June, 1945[6]. Britten's first major opera was the last to achieve world-wide popularity – by anyone, including Britten. He composed a further fourteen operas and music dramas, a body of work to compare in its significance with the 16 operas completed by Richard Strauss. Where Strauss tailored his scores to a constantly changing panoply of singers, Britten wrote nearly everything with a single voice in mind – that of his partner for almost forty years, the tenor Peter Pears.[7]

The tradition of the English tenor stretched back to Michael Kelly and Charles Incledon in the 18th century; John Braham,[8] Sims Reeves,[9] and Edward Lloyd[10] in

---

4 See, generally, Peter Cook on this, and much else.
5 'Expectation,' Op. 17.
6 8 May, 1945.
7 22 June, 1910 – 3 April, 1986.
8 1774 – 17 February, 1856.
9 John Sims Reeves (21 October, 1821 – 25 October, 1900).
10 7 March, 1845 – 31 March, 1927.

the 19th, and Gervase Elwes,[11] Walter Widdop, and Joseph Hislop[12] in the 20th. Each of these singers performed in Italian, French and German, as well as English; with the exception of Lloyd, their repertoire reached well beyond the British *oratorio* tradition. Elwes was the leading British-born performer of Schubert and Brahms *lieder*, in which repertoire he toured Germany with great success in 1907.[13] In January, 1913, he gave the British premiere of *Das lied von der Erde* with Doris Woodall and Sir Henry Wood. Elwes made a huge contribution to the English song tradition also, working closely with Roger Quilter, Thomas Dunhill, Charles Villiers Stanford and Britten's teacher, Frank Bridge. Elwes was the dedicatee and first performer of Ralph Vaughan Williams' setting of Housman's verses *On Wenlock Edge*, which the tenor recorded with the London String Quartet in 1917. Though he was in his 60s, age had not wearied him, and the recording attests to a warm and easy tone as well as a natural, if overly dry performing style. The Quartet utilises considerably more *portamento* than does Elwes.

Peter Pears was raised in Elwes' song-form tradition, and his earliest work (as recorded in the late 1930s) had a Cathedral-choir purity to it that made him ideal for Britten's idiomatic compositional voice. The composer's earliest works for Pears were mostly isolated songs, an evolving platform that reached its first maturity in 1943 when Britten composed the *Serenade for Tenor, Horn and Strings*, Op. 31, at the request of Dennis Brain. He did so while working at the same time on *Peter Grimes*. Pears and Brain gave the first performance of the *Serenade* at the Wigmore Hall on 15 October, 1943; they recorded it, with the Boyd Neel Orchestra, in October the following year. The premiere of *Peter Grimes* at Sadler's Wells on 7 June, 1945[14] (conducted by Reginald Goodall), secured Britten his first international success. After years of halting theatrical efforts by Stanford, Ethyl Smyth, Gustav Holst, Rutland Boughton, Frederick Delius and Vaughan Williams, Britten's genius operated as a lightning conductor across Europe and the United States, transforming not only his career but that of Pears also. Over the next three decades, Pears served as muse to the most important British composer of music drama since Purcell, which is not to detract from Pears' status as the tenor of choice for a host of concert works also, notably the *War Requiem*. Spanning his work between Grimes and Aschenbach (*Death in Venice*, 1973), Pears was Britain's leading tenor internationally, and a major figure in the nation's musical life – a status that embraced important relationships with Sviatoslav Richter and, after Britten's death, Murray Perahia. Notwithstanding his primacy and celebrity, Pears was singularly divisive. His characteristically reedy timbre and effete style were satirised beautifully by Dudley Moore in *Beyond the Fringe* when he performed "*Little Miss Muffet*," a biting parody of Britten and Pears as indivisible partners.[15] Pears' voice was nothing like that of Elwes. It was tight and

---

11 Gervase Henry Cary-Elwes (15 November, 1866 – 12 January, 1921).
12 5 April, 1884 – 6 May, 1977.
13 With the pianist Fanny Davies, a pupil of Clara Schumann.
14 The author's grandfather played trumpet in the orchestra at that performance.
15 Pears appreciated Moore's routine. Britten's reaction was quite different. As one of the prickliest pears in the history of music, he did not see the funny side, and was apparently furious. Nothing can be presumed of Weill and Beethoven's probable reactions to Moore's equally savage (and accurate) parodies of their music.

colourless, with little warmth. He was nonetheless subtle and sensitive as a performer of Britten's settings, and his poetic evocation of atmosphere (rather than feeling) became the benchmark for generations of "English tenors," of which Pears' predecessors would almost certainly not have approved.

Britten and Pears were the last composer-tenor relationship of note. With their work done, the tenor voice was enshrined absolutely to re-creative impulses, with students drawn to the singing of idols immortalised on recordings of music by long-dead composers. As far as opera was concerned, the abstruse direction in which contemporary music headed during the 1960s saw an absolute and irrecoverable split between the arts of performance and the apparent science of composition. In an interview in 1987, James King was asked about the state and health of the tenor voice in modern opera. He responded:

> Unless people get more aware of the value of theatre and the musical arts, we're heading for more trouble. I don't think our pop culture is doing anything for us, really, except giving people certain diversion. I can't see much in it, although I do like pop music of the past ... Opera is entertainment, too; there's no doubt about that. Wagner wanted that himself. Even with *Parsifal*, as serious as that was, he still was cautious to make the thing something that the people would enjoy seeing as well as philosophizing about. There has to be the element of entertainment in any opera ... Even in a town of one million here, it's hard to find an opera house. But this critic said that it's very, very hard to find anybody that's exceptional today; they're all sort of mediocre. Wagner said an interesting thing about this idea. He said, 'The bad is really not bad, because we all know what bad is. It's the mediocre that's really bad, because everybody thinks it's good'. I think that's one of the greatest things he ever said, and he said so much! We should all read more of what Wagner has written. Whether you agree with it or not, there's still something enormous to learn from it. He was something. He was really something, that old rascal! I can't get over it.

The art of the tenor was spared mediocrity by a flourish of talent, spanning multiple languages and cultures, on stages, records and television. Technology provided small compensation for the ubiquity of alternative forms and sources of entertainment. Where *Tristan und Isolde* and *Madama Butterfly* once sated the popular taste for public expressions of love and lust, the 1960s and 70s fostered the emergence of films by Russ Meyer and sexploitation movies. Grindhouse cinemas outpaced Paris' Le Théâtre du Grand-Guignol, with "Playhouses" during the 1960s showing overt sexual acts that had once been simulated only in music and art. Where intercourse, as a feature of the intricate philosophy of lovemaking, had been characterised in the "outrageous" Prelude to *Der Rosenkavalier*, the 1970s saw unchecked and adulterated pornography screened for audiences formed of grubby men in grubbier theatres. The ambiguities of Mozart's socially and emotionally complex stage works had now to compete with the explicit banalities of the blatant and the gynaecological. How might a tenor seduce when Steve McQueen and Faye Dunaway could play chess, and

R v Penguin Books Ltd[16] freed Mellors to traduce the Obscene Publications Act as well as Lady Constance?[17]

The 1970s did not invent pornography, and Russ Meyer did not cause the decline and fall of western civilisation. The conflation of sex and violence is older than both. Spoken theatre pushed the boundaries of "taste and decency" long before the building of the first cinema. In Frank Wedekind's play, *Der Kammersänger* – translated commonly as 'The Tenor'[18] – Gerardo receives a series of unwelcome guests in his hotel room: a 16-year-old female admirer, an aging composer anxious to see his opera produced, and a married woman who, rejected by the tenor, commits suicide. Wedekind's *Frühlings Erwachen*[19] was more shocking still, partly for its condemnation of his hypocritical society's flawed sense of moral probity (a corruption that inspired Monet when painting *Le Déjeuner sur l'herbe*[20]) but primarily because the play's brooding satire portrayed adolescence as decent, likable and engaged, and the "wisdom" of maturity as ignorant, stubborn and callous. Violence and an overtly sexual complexion were more explicit still in Wedekind's *Der Erdgeist*[21] and *Die Büchse der Pandora*[22] – to both of which Alban Berg turned when composing *Lulu*.[23]

Which was the more shocking: the first public screening of a toilet by Alfred Hitchcock in 1960,[24] Herschell Gordon Lewis' *Two Thousand Maniacs!* (1964), Bertolucci's *Last Tango in Paris* (1972), or *Lulu*, in which Jack the Ripper washes his hands after murdering the opera's heroine ("*Ich bin doch ein verdammter Glückspilz!*"[25]) only to complain of the lack of a towel? Composers of opera did their best to shock, but cinema offered more, with less singing.[26] The popularity of film musicals declined during the 1960s and 70s, just as opera became glamorous and relevant for the last time. The primacy of performance in the absence of composition was adequate for the majority of the world's Houses, and for opera enthusiasts more generally. This terminal shift in values coincided with the emergence of three singers whose careers would transform the status and currency of the tenor as a cultural and musical commodity. The "Three Tenors" was a phenomenon of the 1990s, but each had to earn their spurs before riding Grane into the sunset. They did so within an extravagantly well-serviced tenor-culture.

---

16   [1961] Crim LR 176.
17   What was shocking for the 1960s and 70s is, of course, innocuous when compared with the material made routine by the internet.
18   1897. The literal translation is 'The Chamber Singer,' but the play's hero is a tenor. Published also as 'The Singer.'
19   'Spring Awakening' (1891).
20   '*Lunch on the Grass*' (1865–1866).
21   'Earth Spirit' (1895).
22   'Pandora's Box' (1902).
23   1928 – 1935 (unfinished). Premiered (incomplete, in its 2-Act form) by Zurich Opera on 2 June, 1937.
24   *Psycho*.
25   'I am just the luckiest of men!'
26   It's notable that the first public representation of "gore" outside the *Guignol* can be traced to D. W. Griffith's *Intolerance* (1916), which features numerous gruesome moments, including two onscreen decapitations, and a scene in which a spear is slowly driven through a soldier's naked abdomen, causing blood to pour from the wound.

The leading French-Italian tenor during the 1960s (and into the 1990s) was Spanish. Alfredo Kraus[27] was born in Gran Canaria and began his career singing Zarzuela in Madrid and Barcelona. He made his operatic debut in Cairo as the Duke in 1956. Two years later he sang Alfredo opposite Maria Callas' Violetta in Lisbon, causing a sensation. He appeared for the first time at the Met in 1966, again as the Duke, in which role he bid farewell to New York in 1994. Kraus sang a wide range of Italian and French repertoire, all of it lyric. He was – and remains – an important figure in the history of the tenor because he understood, and accepted more importantly, his vocal form and character for what it was. Where Di Stefano's voice survived for little more than five years, Kraus was able to record the role of Alfredo in the studio forty years into his career.[28] He was 65 years old and sounded half his age. Like every other tenor of note, Kraus' voice was individuated, with a distinctive tone and even delivery. His formidable technique equipped him to sing music that was subjected increasingly to shouting. Kraus is often damned with the faint praise that he was a singer characterised by "good taste," which is to underestimate the theatricality of instincts that gave him access to a valuable palette of measured vulgarity. His facility for plangent, long-held phrases did not prevent him from exploiting his technique to indulge stupendous, effortless high notes, unnecessary longueurs and dynamic phrasing for its own sake. Because he applied his talents to music that warranted it he remained throughout his career one of opera's few tenor aristocrats, a singer bound by tradition and history to values that overreached his inarguable vanity. Kraus' performances in lyric Italian opera (of Bellini and Donizetti primarily, with Almaviva his solitary Rossini role) would have remained unrivalled during the 1970s but for the appearance during the 1960s of Luciano Pavarotti. Like his more famous Italian rival, Kraus was a splendid Tonio in *La fille du régiment* – in which opera he had no difficulty navigating the infamous run of nine high Cs. Unlike Pavarotti, however, he was pre-eminent in French repertoire also, excelling as Massenet's *Werther*[29] and Des Grieux in *Manon*; as Nadir in Bizet's *Les Pêcheurs de perles*; as Gounod's *Faust* and *Roméo*, and as Offenbach's *Hoffmann*. Kraus was equally unusual in being one of the few tenors during his era (other than the obvious Three) to be engaged regularly to make studio recordings.

Though integrity and cultivation were hallmarks of Kraus' work, he was not alone in his elevation and discretion. Luigi Alva[30] was born seven months *before* Kraus (and is still alive at the date of publication); he occupied a position of near-unique pre-eminence during the 1960s in the Rossini *coloratura* repertoire in which Kraus took no interest. He was acquainted also with his limits, and despite the extreme lightness of his voice he sang with memorable clarity and laudable diction, qualities captured on many fine recordings of Rossini and Mozart. Renato Cioni[31] was another light-voiced Italian tenor who strayed with mixed success into middle-weight repertoire, including Pinkerton and Pollione. Alva and Cioni were succeeded by Giuseppe

---

27   Alfredo Kraus Trujillo (24 November, 1927 – 10 September, 1999).
28   With Kiri Te Kanawa and Dmitri Hvorostovsky, conducted by Zubin Mehta (1992).
29   There are at least 17 recordings of Kraus in *Werther*, made between 1966 and 1991. The only studio recording dates from 1979, conducted by Michel Plasson, with Tatiana Troyanos as Charlotte.
30   Luis Ernesto Alva y Talledo (10 April, 1927).
31   15 April, 1929 – 4 March, 2014.

Sabbatini[32] and Salvatore Fisichella.[33] The former was successful as *the* Rossini tenor of the 1980s and '90s (partnering often with Cecilia Bartoli) while the latter never enjoyed anything like the success to which he was entitled by talent and training. Like Kraus, Fisichella forged a resolute technique when young, which enabled him to continue singing well into his 60s. His breakout moment – recording Rodrigo with Carreras in the title role of Rossini's *Otello* for Philips in 1978 – established his credentials as a *virtuoso* lyric tenor with thrilling *spinto* sensibilities. Apart from a studio recording as Aronne in *Mosè in Egitto*, however, he was not engaged by any of the studios to build on his flawless foundations. It was a sign of the times as they were in the 1970s and 80s that Fisichella was surplus to requirements and unable to persuade A&R departments to take their eyes off the usual suspects. Had he made his debut 20 years later, things would have been very different indeed. If Fisichella was not the most subtle of vocalists then his clear and open tone, focussed *vibrato*, and brilliant high notes (which reached D5 without loss of line or tone) set him apart. His fluency when singing Bellini in particular made him the only tenor to rival Pavarotti during the decade when the big man focussed on *bel canto* repertoire.

The heavier end of the Italian dramatic repertory after Del Monaco's retirement was inherited by a coterie of big voices, none of which was sufficiently merchantable to warrant more than infrequent recording. Carlos Cossutta[34] is remembered for having sung *Otello* for Decca, with Solti, in 1977[35] – one of just two studio recordings by the tenor – while Nicola Martinucci[36] and Lando Bartolini[37] made almost none. Though Martinucci had a big voice, it was heavy-set and lacked personality. Bartolini appeared, on the other hand, to be channelling his idol, Del Monaco. He made his debut in 1973, just as as Del Monaco's career was coming to an end, and many thought him an imitator of the fading warhorse, so similar are their voices in the resonance of their lowered larynxes. In fairness to Bartolini, he was in many respects a finer artist; he used his large and resonant heroic-*spinto* voice with greater refinement, as is obvious from some of his live recordings as Andrea Chénier. There is pirate footage of him in circulation, recorded in Marseille in 1991, that is entirely magnificent. Other than because taste was changing, it is difficult to know why Bartolini wasn't more successful. He was not engaged to record a complete opera in the studio until 1983, when he sang Giosta Berling (a role created by Franco Lo Giudice) in Riccardo Zandonai's *I Cavalieri Di Ekebù*.[38] He can otherwise be heard at his most thrilling on live recordings, many of them sadly hard to find. Bartolini worked in Europe for almost his entire career before the age of 50,[39] during which period he developed a reputation as one of the world's small coterie of singers able to do justice to Calàf.

---

32 11 May, 1957 –
33 15 May, 1943 –
34 8 May, 1932 – 22 January, 2000.
35 Cossutta made only one other complete studio recording of an opera – as Paco in *La vida breve* by Manuel Falla, conducted by Rafael Frühbeck de Burgos, for EMI in 1965.
36 28 March, 1941 –
37 11 April, 1937.
38 Conducted by Gianandrea Gavazzeni, with Fiorenza Cossotto as La Comandante ('The Commander'). The opera was premiered on 7 March, 1925, conducted by Arturo Toscanini.
39 He made his debut at the Metropolitan Opera in 1988 – when he was 51 years old.

He was one of a handful globally with the weight and power necessary to make the best of a role that was shortly to become associated eternally with a *lirico-spinto* tenor who sang it on stage on only a handful of occasions. The best of Bartolini's *many* live recordings as Calàf are from 1987 (conducted by Giuseppe Patanè, at the Bayerischen Staatsoper) and 1993 (conducted by Nello Santi, at the Teatro Colón).

Equally overlooked was Maurice Stern,[40] an American-born tenor raised in the Cantorial tradition who, like Jan Peerce before him and Neil Shicoff after him, survives in the Pantheon as one of the most talented Jewish-American tenors of the 20th century, a star of whom the general public remains almost entirely in ignorance. Readers of different ages and inclinations will know his work as a celebrated sculptor,[41] while others may know of his daughter, the rock-Goddess Jennifer Rush (born Heidi Stern). Both of these considerable achievements warrant commentary, but they pale beside what little can be said of his abilities as one of the most thrilling dramatic tenors of his age. Only little can now be said because Stern made almost no recordings, and none in the studio of a complete opera. This is a tragedy considering the sensational mix of resonance and artistry for which his work during the 1970s and 1980s is remembered by those privileged to hear it.

Like Peerce, Stern's technique was military by discipline and supine in its *apparent* ease. He played the long game while young, specialising in lighter lyric repertoire before morphing effortlessly into dramatic roles that spanned Manrico, Radamès, Don Alvaro, Otello, Samson, Tannhäuser, Lohengrin, Canio, Dick Johnson, Andrea Chénier and Bacchus. He sang across the United States, Canada, Mexico, South America, Europe and China – but was overlooked by the Met (despite being booked to appear in the1989–90 season as cover for Domingo and Gary Lakes in *Samson et Dalila*). The live recordings in circulation of his performances in *Otello*,[42] *Turandot* and *La fanciulla del West* suggest he was barely rivalled in these roles during the early 1980s – when he should have been admitted to the first rank of dramatic tenors.

His career as an anomaly was evidenced by his appearance as Johnson for the Spoleto Festival in 1985 in a production by the film director Bruce Beresford, with designs by Ken Adam. On 30 May, Will Crutchfield wrote for the *New York Times* a review of the second of four performances in Charleston, in which the critic's isolated commentary on Stern's performance as Johnson was that he was "security itself on the top notes, but his tone is hard and dry, and his style fiercely uningratiating." There is a recording and a telecast of this production which suggests that Crutchfield had been spoiled on this occasion by the privilege of his experience.[43] Stern's performance

---

40 22 October, 1928 –
41 His sculpture of a seated Dustin Hoffmann was shown at the Coronet theatre on the debut of Mike Nichols' romantic comedy *The Graduate* in 1967.
42 Stern's first performances as Otello (conducted by Alberto Erede) were in 1982; his last were in 1992 – when he was ten years older than he appeared. Stern's abilities past the age of 60 would have been remarkable had he been 45, in which respect he stands in equivalence with the equally ageless Jan Peerce.
43 Crutchfield's standards were of the highest, of course, as the *Times*' critic; it would be interesting to know what he thinks of Stern with thirty years' hindsight, and how he would respond to such a voice as the Artistic Director of the Teatro Nuovo. In any event, the remorseful, bitter aspect of Stern's portrayal as Johnson was recognised by Harold Farwell in *Opera News* for October, 1985. He wrote that ".... Maurice Stern's stoical bandit complemented this. His '*Or son sei mesi*' was an explanation, not an apology, with singing that was Eastwood steel, not Italian sobs."

is outstanding. The voice is that of a dramatic tenor, rather than a lifted baritone, and it is rich and easy – with not the slightest "hardness." The extension is, as Crutchfield acknowledges, superb, but it is Stern's phrasing and articulation that set him apart. The empathy generated by his performance of *"Ch'ella mi creda"* attests to an ideal theatrical sensibility and a musician of rare insight. He is entirely persuasive and makes a glorious sound, the focus of which does much to highlight the quality of Civinini and Zangarini's often-overlooked verse.

So why did Stern's career fail to match his talent? The explanation provides no excuse. Stern began life as a character tenor, chiefly for the New York City Opera, in which capacity his success and popularity combined to trap him in roles for which he was suited ideally but not creatively. His debut as the Emperor Altoum at New York City Opera was singled out by Eric Salzman for the *New York Times*,[44] whose recognition of Stern's ability as an actor was shared by the Company's Viennese management, John White, Felix Popper and Julius Rudel. They did all they could to hold onto him, and Stern waited too long to break into the repertoire for which he was technically and emotionally ideal. In this respect he was either too early or too late, having been born just seven years after Corelli and only seven years before Pavarotti. He reached his maturity as a singer at the same time as Domingo, in much the same repertoire. His evolution as one of the finest dramatic tenors of the century occurred too late for him to compete with the Manrico and Chénier of Corelli and Tucker, and by the time his Otello blossomed, as undeniably it did, he had been overtaken by the lighter-voiced Domingo. It grieves that Domingo was able to sing and record the role as often as he did while Stern was neglected entirely. His decision during the 1960s to change his professional name to "Mauro Lampi"[45] attests to frustrations that are easy to understand. Stern was born under an evil star of bad timing, one that saw him, like so many others, lost to the brilliance of the *holy trinity*.

Less naturally gifted than Stern, but better known thanks to a small catalogue of recordings sufficient for posterity to form a view, was Giuseppe Giacomini.[46] He made his debut in 1966 as Pinkerton and was acclaimed soon after as Turiddu in Parma and Modena. His first triumphs were outside Italy, in Berlin (1970), Lisbon (1971), Barcelona (1972) Vienna (1973), Munich (1973) and Buenos Aires (1974). When returning to Italy, Giacomini triumphed as Alvaro and Rodolfo at La Scala, and established himself as one of the first-rank dramatic-*spinto* tenors to rival Pavarotti and Domingo as Macduff, Don Carlo, Manrico, Cavaradossi, Canio and Des Grieux. For all his achievements, however, Giacomini was little more than a solid performer; his powerful voice lacked character and excitement, and it was given also to thickness. His appearance compounded his unsuitability as a bill-board artist to rival the prevailing triumvirate.

---

44 Stern's portrayal as the old and frail Altoum was so convincing that Felix Popper, standing at the bottom of the tall platform on which the tenor was seated, demanded that someone clamber up a ladder to deliver him water. Popper feared that Stern was suffering a seizure, and an ambulance was called. When the perfectly healthy Stern descended at the end of the act, a party had gathered to deliver him to hospital.
45 On the "advice" of the conductor Anton Guadagno.
46 7 September, 1940 –

Excitement was in ready supply whenever Franco Bonisolli[47] took to the stage, though not always for the right reasons. His unpredictability and unprofessionalism attached him to the eccentric and tragic conventions embodied by Antonio Arámburo a century earlier. It's important to recognise that Bonisolli had a fine voice, particularly in his 30s. At its best, it was powerful, richly coloured and thrilling above the stave. He had tremendous lungs and worked them like an 18th century organ, efforts that coloured his performances on record and in the theatre with a pronounced sense of unease, wherein he joined with audiences in an unspoken suspicion that he was never more than a high C away from a Sbigolian embolism. To make matters worse, as plainly it did, Bonisolli had a Gatsbian impulse for self-destruction – which led to his mostly affectionate nickname, "*Il pazzo.*"[48] His most celebrated episode of presumably sober delirium occurred in 1978, during a public dress rehearsal of *Il trovatore* in Vienna, under the typhlotic gaze of Herbert von Karajan. When disagreeing over their different approaches to "*Di quella pira,*" Bonisolli reacted by throwing his sword at the conductor as a prelude to leaving the stage. One can admire the confidence of anyone willing to stand up to the most powerful musician in the history of art music, even if there were better ways of representing his interests to a conductor who was famed for collaborating well with singers. His recording of *Il trovatore* for EMI from the previous year in Berlin, again with Karajan, gives a good impression of what Bonisolli might have achieved had he exercised some self-control and accountability. Instead, there are some 50 live recordings and eight produced in the studio that attest to a career better remembered for eccentricity than for art and artistry. The stub is formed of distended high notes, unhinged *ad libs* (famously his three repeated high Cs at the end of "*No, no, Principessa alterà*" in *Turandot*) and inappropriate encores. The Arena in Verona saw less violence during the first century AD than during Bonisolli's many ill-judged appearances as Manrico (recorded in 1979 and 1985), *Aida* (recorded in 1986 and 1989) and *Turandot* (recorded in 1979). In his urgent but unrealistic determination to outdo Franco Corelli when singing "*Di quella pira*" and "*Nessun dorma,*" Bonisolli failed on every occasion to recognise that it was his idol's phrasing and his submission to the essential melancholy of his characters that made Corelli's singing of those arias, and his work more generally, definitive. That Corelli *could* hold onto notes did not compel him always to do so. In fact, "*Di quella pira*" was the only *scena* in which Corelli routinely declared his superiority. Bonisolli was profoundly affected by the "circus" of the Three Tenors, about which he spoke obsessively when proving that he was in no way jealous or angry for having been overlooked. He would delight anyone willing to listen by observing that he was the "One Tenor."

For all their imperfections, had any of these singers made their debut in 2000 they would have been elevated to the first rank within a single performance. Each was cursed to be competing with the three most successful and popular operatic singers of

---

47 25 May, 1938 – 30 October, 2003.
48 'The Madman.'

the 20th century. Luciano Pavarotti,[49] Plácido Domingo[50] and José Carreras[51] dominated opera during the latter third of the 20th century as demi-gods. The summit of their celebrity brought them together as the "Three Tenors," after Pavarotti's 1972 recording with Zubin Mehta of "*Nessun dorma*" was chosen by FIFA as the theme song for televised broadcasts during the 1990 World Cup finals. When it was decided to present the "football mad" tenors in concert on the eve of the competition's final, on 7 July, 1990, no one anticipated a global television audience of 800 million, or the creation by Decca of the best-selling classical recording in history. The Trio subsequently sang together in 33 concerts, with events promoted to coincide with three further World Cups – in Los Angeles in 1994, the Champ de Mars (under the Eiffel Tower) in 1998, and in Yokohama in 2002.[52] The sums of money generated – initially for charity – were sensational, with the already wealthy singers entering the league of the super-rich in consequence. Much has been written about the commerciality of the "Three Tenors" phenomenon; none of it has added greatly to an understanding of how, and why, these particular singers became famous in the first place, sufficient to warrant a TV audience for the 1994 "World Cup" concert of 1.3 billion – only 200 million fewer than watched "Live Aid" in 1985.

Their achievement was, of course, economic in scale and effect; a lot of people became very wealthy through their collaboration. The sale of millions of recordings and DVDs does not explain their pop-cultural apotheosis globally, however, or how they ended up populating *Seinfeld, The Simpsons, Frasier, Friends, Yu-Gi-Oh!* and MTV's clay-mation *Celebrity Deathmatch* – in their episode of which the tenors battled with Larry, Moe and Curly, better known as *The Three Stooges*.[53]

At the time of the first "Three Tenors" concert, Pavarotti and Domingo were approaching the thirtieth anniversary of their debuts in 1961; Carreras had celebrated his twentieth anniversary in January, 1990. They were the only tenors during the 1970s and 80s to be recorded and filmed routinely, with each of them securing first refusal on any front-line project for which they were broadly suited. It's difficult to convey their influence from *before* 1990 because they were unrivalled in their repertoire, with the singular exceptions of Alfredo Kraus and Neil Shicoff. Opera

---

49 12 October, 1935 – 6 September, 2007.
50 José Plácido Domingo Embil (21 January, 1941 –).
51 Josep Maria Carreras (5 December, 1946 –).
52 A side letter to the contract between Warner and PolyGram placed restrictions on the marketing of the first two concert albums, which led to a controversial investigation and Anti-Trust decision by the FTC. Pavarotti's exclusive contract with Decca, a PolyGram subsidiary, prevented Warner from securing the rights to the concert without PolyGram's approval. The deal struck with the promoter gives an indication of the value of the "Three Tenors" phenomenon. The contract called for an $18 million advance, half from each label. They divided the world market and agreed to a 50-50 split of profits and losses. As it turned out, there were substantial losses.
53 The episode (first broadcast on 15 July, 1999) involves the *Three Stooges* making use of a time machine, with which Moe reduces Domingo to bones and dust. Carreras has his head crushed by Curly, who in turn rips off Pavarotti's face. For the sake of completeness, Larry inadvertently transforms himself in the time machine into a spermatozoa, while Moe Howard is impaled through the eye with the handle of a sink plunger. The champion and sole survivor is Curly. Such was MTV in the '90s. Of course, what makes the whole thing completely absurd and unbelievable is the wearing by the tenors of Wagnerian helmets. As everyone plainly knew in 1999, only Domingo had ever (or would ever) sing the music of Richard Wagner.

has always amplified the exceptional – it is, after all, the most competitive of the arts – but the part played by Pavarotti, Domingo and Carreras in the history of opera, and the evolution of the tenor voice more specifically, is unique because of the coincidence of "their" decades with the exponential growth in technology and media. The launching of opera festivals, the building of new theatres, and the formation of record companies, radio stations and TV channels devoted to opera and classical music fostered a demand for singers, whose performances of the same roles over and over again created a Groundhog Day in which the same three tenors were always headlining. The pressure to meet a demand that escalated exponentially with the Compact Disc should, in normal circumstances, have led to the promotion of rivals, of competing talents made glorious by the habitual appetite for novelty. It didn't. There were necessarily hundreds of tenors working on thousands of stages around the world between 1970 and 1990; while the best of them serviced the major Houses, only three met the requirements of the dominant record labels (EMI, Decca, Philips, Deutsche Grammophon and RCA), each of which operated from just three cities – London, Berlin and Manhattan.

Between 1969 and 1994, there were nine complete studio recordings released internationally of *Il trovatore*. Two of them were produced with Bonisolli singing Manrico. All but one of the remaining performances was produced with Pavarotti, Domingo or Carreras.[54] Five studio recordings of *Rigoletto* were produced between 1971 and the beginning of 1988 – one with Alfredo Kraus, two with Pavarotti, one with Domingo, and one with Neil Shicoff.[55] Between 1970 and 1996 there were four recordings of *La forza del destino*; three of them starred Domingo or Carreras.[56] *Un ballo in Maschera* was recorded and released internationally on six occasions between 1969 and 1990. Every single one of them featured one of the "Three Tenors."[57]

A wealth of cynicism and expert derision clouded the "Three Tenors" sensation; the resulting arguments across various international courts to resolve who owed what to whom led to costly litigation. Dark men were fined and sent to prison for tax evasion, and it was concluded by those with axes to grind that Art had grabbed its ankles for an ungrateful, eternally priapic Mammon. Pavarotti became a cliché, celebrated for his girth, his handkerchief, his "friendships" with Princess Diana and Bono, and his larger-than-life appetites, all of which occluded any consideration of his actual work as a tenor beyond (or beneath) "that" single high B4. The gossip columns fed greedily from his affairs, his abandonment of his wife of thirty years for a woman more than thirty years his junior, and tax affairs that were scandalous even by Italian standards. Domingo's unique career was damaged badly in 2020 by nasty allegations concerning his behaviour towards female colleagues over time; he apologised, and much of his diary (and his reputation) survived. Carreras had scant

---

54   Domingo, Mehta (RCA, 1969); Pavarotti, Bonynge (Decca, 1976); Carreras, Davis (Philips, 1980); Domingo, Giulini (DG, 1983); Pavarotti, Mehta (Decca, 1990); Domingo, Levine (Sony, 1991).
55   Pavarotti, Bonynge (Decca, 1971); Kraus, Rudel (EMI, 1978); Domingo, Giulini (DG, 1979); Shicoff, Sinopoli (Philips, 1984).
56   Bergonzi, Gardelli (EMI, 1969); Domingo, Levine (RCA, 1976); Carreras, Sinopoli (DG, 1985); Domingo, Muti (EMI, 1986).
57   Pavarotti, Bartoletti (Decca, 1970); Domingo, Muti (EMI, 1975); Carreras, Davis (Philips, 1978); Domingo, Abbado (DG, 1979–80); Pavarotti, Solti (Decca, 1982–83); Domingo, Karajan (DG, 1989).

reputation as a singer to preserve after 1990, and but for marrying his mistress – a pale crime contextually – he lived his private life beyond the reach of public audit. After his death in 2007, Pavarotti's estate was settled at a declared $474.2 million. It was presumed unofficially, and with good reason, to be worth twice that sum. It follows that a tenor – a private citizen who did nothing more than sing for his supper, and who designed no cars, and operated no steel corporations, and published no newspapers, or produced even a single Oscar-winning movie – was within reach of being a dollar billionaire at the time of his death.

Why did these three particular tenors become *the* "Three Tenors"? The answer can be traced on record to their talent. Comparable to the chronicled episodes processed by the "machine" in Alex Garland's *DEVS*, posterity is able to walk in the shoes of the happy few who were present at Pavarotti's debut as Rodolfo on 29 April, 1961. The performance was recorded, and it remains widely available. He was 25 years old at the time, and barely trained; his performance for Francesco Molinari-Pradelli at the Teatro Municipale di Reggio Emilia of "*Che gelida manina*" resonates as one of those perfect moments where history and posterity can share in an equivalence of wonder and emotional fulfilment. The tenor's phrasing, his use of the poet's words, and the shameless, unthinking sensuality of his line resolve in a high C of such effortless, erogenous wonder that past and present coalesce in the audience's audible intakes of breath and spontaneous gestures of wonder. Pavarotti sang many better high Cs; this – the first – was the most perfect because it came without thought of fame or glory. It operated outside the parameters of expectation, free of the vulgarities of the ancillary and the mercantile. It is a voice of effortless, guileless youth, and one of the most beautiful sounds ever produced by a human being.

The audience's reaction to Pavarotti's glistening C5 and the aria's concluding *mezza voce* was redolent of the popular appreciation of Rubini's singing, typified by Richard Wagner's review for Schlesinger's *Gazette Musicale* of a performance of *Don Giovanni*. Of the Italian's singing of Don Ottavio's Act II aria, "*Il mio Tesoro,*" Wagner wrote:

> 'Ottavio' was left alone on the stage; I believed he was about to make an announcement, for he came right up to the prompter's box: but there he stayed, and listened without moving a feature to the orchestral prelude to his B flat aria. This ritornel seemed to last longer than usual; but that was a simple illusion: the singer was merely lisping out the first ten bars of his song so utterly inaudibly that, on my discovery that he really was giving himself the look of singing, I thought the genial man was playing a joke. Yet the audience kept a serious face; it knew what was coming; for at the eleventh bar Rubini let his F swell out with such sudden vehemence that the little reconducting passage fell plump upon us like a thunderbolt, and died away again into a murmur with the twelfth. I could have laughed aloud, but the whole house was still as death: a muted orchestra, an inaudible tenor; the sweat stood on my brow. Something monstrous seemed in preparation: and truly the unhearable was now to be eclipsed by the unheard-of. The seventeenth bar arrived: here the singer has to hold an F for three bars long. What can one do with a simple F? Rubini only becomes divine on the high B flat: there must he get, if a night at

the Italian Opera is to have any sense. And just as the trapezist swings his bout preliminary, so "Don Ottavio" mounts his three-barred F, two bars of which he gives in careful but pronounced crescendo, till at the third he snatches from the violins their trill on A, shakes it himself with waxing vehemence, and at the fourth bar sits in triumph on the high B flat, as if it were nothing; then with a brilliant roulade he plunges down again, before all eyes, into the noiseless.... This was the trick for which one had assembled... and felt richly rewarded by the coming-off of this one wondrous moment when Rubini leapt to B flat.[58]

Wagner's equation of the "art" of Rubini's B flat 4 with the virtuosity of a trapeze act was typical of his (largely political) hostility for Italian opera. It's possible his reference to the "wondrous moment" was sincere, of course – because he plainly admired Rubini's gifts as a vocalist, particularly when singing Bellini. A similar element of the circus attached to Pavarotti in his youth, and the expectations fostered by his stupendous upper register; it remained with him for the duration – and until his gloaming. The B4 of "[vin]*ce*[*ro*]" became the driver of his brand and the common denominator for all tenors, no matter their *fach*, nationality or talent. Pavarotti's re-casting of "*Nessun dorma*" as a short-hand for *all* Opera allowed for the aria's routine abuse by tenors ill-equipped to sing the role of Calàf, or Italian opera, as well as by Aretha Franklin and Michael Bolton. The path to this vertiginous process of *reductio ad absurdum* began in April, 1961, with *that* C5 and its rapid consequences. There were tenors in operation at the time with an Italianate head voice – Mario Filippeschi and Cesare Valletti most obviously. With Di Stefano's early demise, however, there was no one equipped to make the best of repertoire then returning to vogue with the supremacy of Callas, Sutherland and Caballé. It was during the "revival" of what became known as *bel canto* that Pavarotti promised an embarrassment of riches. His early success with Mozart's *Idomeneo* led to a decade-long specialisation in the music of Bellini and Donizetti (but not Rossini, whose *Guillaume Tell* he sang only in the studio). His first two studio recordings – both of them conducted by Richard Bonynge in 1967 – were as Orombello in Bellini's *Beatrice di Tenda* and Tonio in Donizetti's *La fille du régiment*. The latter caused a sensation wherever he sang it, thanks to his narcotic charm and because of the magnificent tone, line and word-use with which he glorified Donizetti's sumptuous melodies. The apparent ease with which he was able to fire off high notes allowed for his comparison with Di Stefano, into whose shoes he stepped more than once to secure acclaim as well as gratitude when the older singer was "unable" to perform. His next recording (a rare appearance for a label other than Decca[59]) was in the title role of *L'amico Fritz*, opposite Mirella Freni; EMI's recording ranks among the most perfect of anything in Italian – eclipsing as it does the recording by the opera's creator, Fernando de Lucia. What sets it apart serves to define everything that transformed Pavarotti from Poseidon into Zeus. First and foremost, he is in absolute control of his voice. This is not a given – as anyone watching

---

58   Wagner, Richard (1966). "The Virtuoso and the Artist," in *Richard Wagner's Prose Works*. Trans. and Ed. William Ashton Ellis. Broude Bros. p.115.
59   This was released by HMV/EMI.

or listening to Franco Bonisolli will testify. Pavarotti's command is so complete that his singing unfolds as if he is speaking Nicola Daspuro's words.[60] Indeed, it is in the beauty and elegance of his diction that Pavarotti was definitive. More so, even, than Tito Schipa, Pavarotti was a master of speech-song, of that objectively indulgent, creative exploitation of the conjunction of words and music to which every composer of opera, including Wagner, attached their ambition. Pretty much everything surviving on record by Pavarotti from between 1967 and 1982 is miraculous for this reason, with 113 available recordings of complete works (27 of them produced in the studio) to trace his evolution as one of opera's supreme artists. The inseparable force of his enunciation, and his construction of an idealised sound-world, after the philosophy (if not the style) of Sarah Bernhardt and Albertine Zehme, resulted in a projection as immediately recognisable as that of Caruso, Corelli and Wunderlich. The man's personality was huge; the character of his voice greater still.

In 1971 he toured Japan with Oliviero De Fabritiis, giving performances as the Duke, with Peter Glossop as Rigoletto, Louise Russell as Gilda, Anna Di Stasio as Maddalena, and Ruggero Raimondi as Sparafucile. One of the performances was filmed and recorded. Pavarotti's part in the quartet "*Bella figlia dell'amore*" illustrates the clear difference between his singing and everyone else's. The words are well known:

"*Bella figlia dell'amore, Schiavo son dei vezzi tuoi;*
Con un detto sol tu puoi, Le mie pene consolar.
Vieni e senti del mio core, Il frequente palpitar."[61]

Pavarotti anticipates the first syllable of "*Bella*" (on an unaccompanied A flat) with a short phonemic "ah," which aids him as he slides into the drawn-out A flat, holding onto the dotted quaver so that the resolving semi-quaver allows for greater emphasis on the first syllable of "*figlia*," and the opening of the tone on the third syllable D flat. The vowels are gloriously free and round, a quality amplified by Pavarotti's natural use of *portamento* and a variable *vibrato* for the descending F – D flat – A flat of "[a]*more*," which he delivers with a clear *diminuendo*, designed to amplify the Duke's consideration of love (and his seduction more generally) as tender and sensual. The phrase is repeated; the words are not. Pavarotti emphasises the "*a*" in "*schiavo*,"[62] revealing to the audience (if not Maddalena) the truth of his misogyny. He mirrors only the shape and phrasing of the F – D flat – A flat so that when singing the repeating D flats of "*detto un detto*" his clear articulation draws attention to Verdi and Piave's construction of speech and truth, and the Duke's darkly purposeful manipulation of both. Pavarotti adds an unwritten note and a syllable (an E flat with an "*eh*" sound) to "*sol*" (and before "*tu*"), which goes beyond Verdi's score to create an erotic, expressive rush as he ascends easily to the A flats of "*tu puoi*" (the second of which he ducks into by a quarter-tone, facilitating the enunciation of a syllable lost commonly to literalism). The libertine approach to the precisely crafted rhythms of

---

60 Written as "P. Suardon," and based on *L'Ami Fritz* by Émile Erckmann and Pierre-Alexandre Chatrian.
61 'Beautiful daughter of love, I am a slave to your charm, with but a single word you could relieve my every pain. Come, touch me and feel how my heart races.'
62 'Slave.'

"*puoi, Le mie pene*" places him again in conflict with the composer, but the resulting tension ensures that "*pene consolar*" is delivered almost flippantly – ensuring by its clipped delivery that the audience is able to appreciate how consolation is the last thing on the Duke's mind.

"*Vieni e sienti*" is moulded well beyond the confines of the dotted D flat – C – F as written, and when singing "*del mio core il frequente*" in a single, uninterrupted phrase not a single note is delivered without *rubato-portamento*, so that the two bars of music are heard (in expressive terms) as one. The crowning phrase to the high B flat (for "*palpitar*") resolves without audible *passaggio* on an A flat to which Pavarotti introduces yet another unwritten syllable (a pronounced quaver "*eh*" at the end of "*palpitar[e]*"), which adds yet another beat to his already racing heart. This allows in turn for the Gigli-esque racheting of "*con un detto, un detto*" under the pressure of his own *rubato* – the effect of which is spine-tingling. It's a testament to Anna Di Stasio's professionalism that she remembers to join with the ensemble. How much of this did Pavarotti plan? It's impossible to know. By his own admission he was an innate, instinctual singer. For many who heard him live, his talent was God-given because it was presumed with good reason that he had over-thought very little before simply being and "speaking" as himself. During his *bel canto* years he produced a body of work in the studio that remains incomparable. His recordings with Richard Bonynge of operas by Bellini and Donizetti between 1967 and 1974 are especially priceless: *Beatrice di Tenda* (1967), *L'elisir d'amore* (1970), *Lucia di Lammermoor* (1971), *La fille du régiment* (1972), *I puritani* (1973) by Vincenzo Bellini, and *La favorite* (1974).

They remain important historical and musical artefacts because no other tenor has approximated what is suggested by the music's complexion of the singing of Giovanni Rubini. It's certain that Pavarotti's singing was more brilliant, being that he employed the *do di petto*, and Rubini appears to have indulged greater dynamic and temporal extremes than Pavarotti. In the elegance and sweetness of the phrasing, however, and because of the ease of his projection – which features not a hint of tension or strain in the voicing – Pavarotti established himself as the *sine qua non* of *bel canto* tenors. In this repertoire, he really was the most complete tenor of the century. As the years passed, he moved into heavier, roles – with inconsistent success. He was one of that rare breed of tenor whose voice did not darken with maturity, so there was a necessary and larcenous discrepancy between his studio recordings and his work in the theatre – especially at the Met in New York, where he struggled to be heard. Pavarotti was always *leggiero* and unsuited in consequence to Calàf, Andrea Chénier and Otello (his performance/recording of which was a folly). If his voice weakened over time he never lost it – a considerable achievement over more than 40 years of committed work.

Strength and staying power are also key characteristics of Domingo's still-vibrant career. The date of his first appearance depends on whether one counts his early work as a baritone in Zarzuela, his backing vocals for the rock-and-roll band *Los Camisas Negras*, or his *comprimario* roles as a tenor.[63] Either way, his first performance as

---

63 It's hard to credit, but Domingo sang his first operatic role, Borsa (*Rigoletto*) on 23 September, 1959 in the same decade as Franco Corelli made his debut. His roles thereafter, and prior to singing Alfredo, were *Le père confesseur du couvent* (*Dialogues des Carmélites*) on 21 October, 1959; Danilo (*Die lustige*

Alfredo on 19 May, 1961, is cited by the tenor as his debut. Domingo's diary for 2020 (as a baritone) included *Simon Boccanegra* in Vienna for 9, 12, 15 and 18 September; *Nabucco* in Florence on 4, 7, 10 and 13 October; *Traviata* and concerts in Milan in November; *I due Foscari* in Monaco and a concert in Belarus, both in December. Most of January, 2021, was to have been occupied by his 80th birthday celebrations and multiple performances as *Nabucco*, in Vienna. Had he fulfilled his engagements, Domingo would have celebrated additionally his 60th anniversary as a performer. It is to state the obvious that there has never been anyone like him; it's equally certain that a career like his can never happen again.

Domingo is often said to have started his operatic life as a baritone. This is incorrect. His first performances in opera were as a tenor, and he remained a tenor until announcing in 2007 that he would be performing the title role of *Simon Boccanegra* in 2009. He has continued to perform as a baritone (and on occasion as a conductor) ever since. His voice has always been difficult to categorise, in part because he sang almost everything – more than 150 roles, a greater number and diversity than any male singer in the history of music theatre. That does not mean he sang everything well, or to the best of his own considerable ability; he was his own worst enemy when accounting for himself in equivalence as Almaviva, Nemorino and Otello in Italian; Hippolyte (Rameau), Faust and Werther in French; Shuysky (*Boris Godunóv*), Lensky and Hermann in Russian; Parsifal, Alfred (*Die Fledermaus*), and Der Kaiser (*Die Frau ohne Schatten*) in German – as well as an unprecedented range of Spanish-language Zarzuela and opera. He was frequently caught up in the tricky question of pronunciation and language-use (in which consideration he fell far short of Pavarotti and Carreras in their shared repertoire). He was especially problematic for many in German music (spanning *Oberon*, *Fidelio*, everything by Wagner except *Rienzi* and *Siegfried*, and Mahler's *Das lied von der Erde*[64]), which was a shame considering the value gained from his often polished line and tone. The only major tenor role within his gift that he chose not to sing, even in the studio, was Peter Grimes.

Unlike most tenors, he was cursed with an exceptional musical facility, a near-photographic memory, endless curiosity and a Stakhanovite work ethic. He was also a tenor without a high C, or even an easy B4 – which did not prevent him from singing repertoire that called for both. His inevitable categorisation as a jack-of-all trades was compounded by an essential vocal inflexibility, and a sense of effort – which is unfortunate since he had (and has still) a resolute technique. Domingo's portrayals were somewhat generalised, such that the voice, while rich with individuality, never carved into the soul as did the best of the work by his "Three Tenor" colleagues. At his finest he was exceptional when singing Verdi,[65] and also as Don José, Cavaradossi and Dick Johnson – roles that made the best of his formidable talents as a dramatic stage and singing actor. His most celebrated roles were Andrea

---

Witwe [performed in Spanish]) in 1960; Imperatore Altoum (*Turandot*) on 11 September, 1960; Pang (*Turandot*) on 1 October, 1960; Normanno (*Lucia di Lammermoor*) on 5 October, 1960; Gastone (*La traviata*) on 8 October, 1960; Remendado (*Carmen*) on 15 October, 1960; and Cassio (*Otello*) on 17 October, 1960.

64   In the studio and/or on stage.

65   Each of his many recordings of Verdi's middle and later period works are valuable, particularly *La forza del destino*, *Un ballo in Maschera* and *Don Carlo*.

Chénier (as whom he excelled, most famously perhaps in Vienna in 1981) and Otello – of which he made three studio recordings. For all that is remembered of his Moor, however – and it was vocally and dramatically a consummate achievement – his finest work was probably as Don Alvaro in *La forza del destino*. There are four recordings in circulation, two of them live. The second, from 1972, was taped at the Teatro Colón in Buenos Aires, conducted by Fernando Previtali. Domingo was in blistering form, and his performance as Alvaro is arguably the finest of any recorded complete. The tenor's voice is ideal in its brightness and lyricism – with a powerful middle register. It is not an especially large instrument, but it is resonant and thrilling and he uses it with consistent intelligence, insight and art – making much of a character that is difficult to believe and almost impossible to like. The audience's response to "*O tu che in seno agli angeli*" is almost as haptic as the singing that precedes it.

Domingo's place in the Pantheon of tenors is assured, despite and not because of his ubiquity. The position occupied by José Carreras is more problematic. By the time of his first appearance as one of the "Three Tenors," his instrument was a ruin, a splinter of something of which the majority of the 800 million who heard him murder "*Un di all'azzurro spazio*" in Rome in 1990[66] knew nothing and were never likely to. Carreras had nonetheless once been the best of them, if not actually the most gifted lyric-dramatic tenor of the 20th century. He was born with talent hardwired to his voice. At the age of eight he gave his first public performance, singing "*La donna è mobile*" accompanied by Magda Prunera on Spanish National Radio. A recording of the performance is widely available and makes for jaw-dropping listening. In fact, it is barely credible. His treble has the force of an English cathedral boys' choir, with a significantly greater emotional reach. The phrasing is fluent, mature even – and positively surreal for a child some years from puberty. In 1958 he appeared as an eleven-year old at Barcelona's Gran Teatre del Liceu, singing the soprano role of Trujamán in Manuel de Falla's *El retablo de Maese Pedro*. Though born eleven years after Pavarotti, he made his first professional appearance some three years before him.

Carreras' debut as an adult was as Flavio in *Norma*, on 8 January, 1970. This brought him to the attention of his fellow Catalan, Montserrat Caballé, who invited him to sing Gennaro in *Lucrezia Borgia*. The production opened on 19 December, 1970 – two weeks after his 24th birthday; Carreras' triumph was absolute. There is a recording from that run, which confirms the improbability of his talent. It's trite that few tenors are able to perform to any realistic standard of vocal maturity in their 20s; Carreras emerged fully-formed as a voice and as an artist. This is evidenced across a collection of more than 170 complete (live and studio) recordings, the best of them produced between 1970 and 1979. The first of the twenty-three studio recordings from this time was made in 1973;[67] the last four were released in a single year, 1979.[68]

---

66 He sang it again for the "Three Tenors" concert in London in 1996, when he had to transpose the aria down a semi-tone, so that the two written B flat 4s were sung as A naturals.
67 His breakout studio recordings did not appear until 1974–75: as Nicias in *Thaïs* (in 1974) for RCA, conducted by Julius Rudel; as Corrado in *Il Corsaro* (in 1975) for Philips, conducted by Gardelli; and as Leicester in Rossini's *Elisabetta regina d'Inghilterra* (in 1975) conducted by Gian-Franco Masini.
68 *Cavalleria rusticana* (conducted by Muti); *Pagliacci* (conducted by Muti); *Stiffelio* conducted by Gardelli); and *Tosca* (conducted by Karajan).

His most important work was captured between 1973 and 1978. It follows that Carreras' career in the studio was over in just five years, midst a career spanning more than thirty. Much like the brightest candle that burns for half as long, his performances during this period rank among the most important in the recorded history of the tenor voice.

Carreras was the definitive article from the start, as can be heard from the recordings made during the "Voce Veriane" competition in Parma in 1971. His singing (with piano) of "*Quando le sere al placido*" from Verdi's *Luisa Miller* attests to a bizarre radiance, wholly unfettered by restraint or self-awareness; it provoked an entirely appropriate frenzy from the competition audience. Soon after, he was presented at the Royal Festival Hall in London in four performances of three operas – Donizetti's *Maria Stuarda* (18 July, 1971, with Caballé)[69]; Boito's *Mefistofele* (2 and 25 May, 1972, both with Carol Neblett); and Donizetti's *Caterina Cornaro* (10 July, 1972, with Caballé). Three of the evenings were recorded; each evidences the decadent luxury of his tenor in its callow indulgence. The thrice-cooked warmth and opulence of tone set it apart from the metallic, sometimes effortful Domingo, and the lighter-voiced Pavarotti – who, by compensation, had the high notes that Carreras did not. As sound alone, his intonation was rivalled in its richness only by Bergonzi's. It's accepted that there was little *squillo* above the stave, certainly when compared to Corelli, but neither was there any registrable *passaggio* or any hint of industry. The quintessence of his difference was isolated in his phrasing and voice-placement, qualities that explain not only the miracle of his instrument to 1978, but also the velocity of its demise thereafter.

In March, 1976, Carreras recorded an album of arias in London with the Royal Philharmonic Orchestra, conducted by Roberto Benzi – another child star turned musician.[70] The repertoire was populated by arias made famous by Gilbert Duprez. Duprez created the role of Gaston in Verdi's *Jérusalem*[71] in 1847; the opera features one of the composer's most beautiful arias, "*L'infamie... O mes amis, mes frères*"[72] from Act 3. Carreras ignores most of the music's carefully prescribed dynamics (which span *pianissimo* to *forte*). He uses no mid-phrase *messa di voce*, routinely overlooks the written hairpins, and adds *fermatas* where none are indicated – even though many are. And yet. The singing is miraculous in its beauty because of how he phrases it, and by reason of his uniquely creative use of *vibrato* and *portamento*. The second phrase, marked *piu lento* ("*Ah! C'est la pitié, c'est la pitié, que je reclarme...*"[73]), begins on an F sharp, from which Carreras descends an octave using a *tremelo-portamento* to introduce the dramatic change in pace as he sings the repeating words "*C'est la pitié,*" which Verdi sets to music that spans only a minor third, but from which Carreras draws staggering emotional force. He achieves this by filtering his glorious, expansive

---

69 The London performance was not recorded, but a later performance at the Salle Pleyel, Paris on 26 March, 1972 was.
70 Benzi acted in films as a teenager and studied music with André Cluytens as a ten-year-old.
71 *Jérusalem* was based on Verdi's *I Lombardi alla prima crociata* of 1843, and his recital recording features a sublime performance of the earlier opera's most famous tenor aria "*La mia letizia infondere*" ['My heart is full of joy'].
72 'Infamy... O my friends, my brothers.'
73 'Ah! It's pity, pity that I reclaim.'

tone through an ever-changing palette and word-directed *vibrato*, the colour and shape of which is unlike anything produced by anyone else since the invention of recording.

For the phrase "*Ah, laissez moi mourire, ah, parpitié, sans mefletrir*,"[74] Carreras glides from an A sharp 3 to an F, with which he pre-empts a climb up the scale to a B4 of bizarre resonance. He doesn't abuse the apex; instead, and despite milking the note for longer than the written dotted crotchet, he tumbles through the octave, maintaining the line and the drama with such idiomatic, golden intensity that one simply wants him to get to the double-bar and do it all again. The sensuality of his application of *vibrato* as a permutable feature of expressive complexion (rather than as a fixed construction of technical necessity and fashion) is almost embarrassing in its calculation. Except, of course, it wasn't calculated. It was the product of a singer wholly lacking in artifice or design; it speaks to the articulation of an artist who delighted no less than his audience in being able to sing as he did. With the quivering tail of each beautifully delivered line and phrase, and the attachment of a variegated *vibrato* to an innately fluent, eternally expressive *portamento*, Carreras conveys breath-catching humanity through music that might otherwise simply be sung. The album features additionally two arias by Mercadente for which Duprez was also celebrated, *Il giuramento's*[75] "*La Dea di tutti i cor*"[76] from Act 1, and "*Bella adorate incognita*"[77] from Act 2. Carreras' madly beautiful singing of these arias compels the question: is this what Gilbert Duprez sounded like? Can he have been this good? It is easy for romantics dreaming of idealised perfection to settle on Carreras' singing in 1976 as equal to the fantasy.

Unfortunately, Carreras' open-throated abandon necessitated an equivalently passionate disregard for the mechanics and limitations of the human. Like Di Stefano before him, he threw his all into everything and it was recklessness, not repertoire, that proved his undoing. The common suggestion that Carreras' shift towards heavier roles led to the loss of the strength of the physical structures that allowed him to sing as he did in his youth is a myth. His diary for 1972 proves the point beyond dispute. Between 28 September and the end of the year, he gave multiple performances in productions or concerts of *Madama Butterfly*, *La bohème*, *Lucia di Lammermoor*, *Adriana Lecouvreur*, *I Lombardi*, *Un ballo in maschera*, *La pietra del paragone* (Rossini), *Traviata* and *Don Carlo*. He did so in the company of "big" voiced colleagues like Caballé, Scotto, Plishka, Dimitrova, Stratas and Cappuccilli. In 1978, his diary included performances in productions of *La bohème*, *Don Carlo*, *Adriana Lecouvreur*, *L'elisir d'amore*, *Tosca*, *La battaglia di Legnano*, *Luisa Miller*, *Un ballo in maschera*, *Lucia di Lammermoor*, *Otello* (Rossini), *Werther* and *La forza del destino*. He sang multiple performances of *Tosca* every year between 1973 and 1979.

The beginning of the end can be traced to his first performances as Alvaro in *La forza del destino* at La Scala in 1978 with Caballé, Cappuccilli and Ghiaurov,

---

74 'Ah, let me die, ah, please, without withering.'
75 'The Oath.' This is a glorious opera, and it's a great shame that Carreras' concert performances with Baltsa and Albrecht in 1974 did not lead to its renaissance.
76 'The Goddess of all hearts.'
77 'Unknown beauty worshipped.'

conducted by Patanè. The recording from that run is stupendous. He holds nothing back, as usual; for the first time, however, he can be heard to struggle. His studio recording of *Don Carlo* for EMI with Karajan in Berlin (5 – 20 September, 1978) is thrilling also but his Otello for Philips in London with Jesús López Cobos (produced the same month) is pressured, loud and absent finesse – failings made explicit by the sublime Desdemona of Frederica von Stade. There is a live recording from April, 1979, of Carreras singing "*O amore, o bella luce del core*" from *L'amico Fritz*, conducted by López Cobos, which traces the point at which the game was up. It should be noted that this was *years* before the tenor's widely reported battle with leukaemia. His subsequent work during the 1980s and 90s was lamentable when compared to the artistry that proceeded it. His once precious *vibrato* degenerated into an incessant wobble, and necessity compelled him to shout his way through everything.

There were good lessons to be learned from Carreras' throttling of one of history's most beautiful tenor voices. Some were willing and able to learn from them. Francisco Araiza[78] adhered to his natural base of Mozart and Rossini until his late 30s, when he transferred with infrequent success to middle-weight and *spinto* repertoire. Carreras' fellow Catalan Giacomo Aragall[79] suffered from grievous nerves and stage anxiety, none of which was improved by his tendency to oversing. An exception to the rule, and the best of the Three Tenors' rivals during the 1990s, was Neil Shicoff,[80] an outstanding American-born musician with a beautiful, technically perfect tenor voice which he used with intelligence over the course of a long and productive career. His relatively few recordings are highly collectible, with standout performances as the Duke for Sinopoli (who denied him the unwritten high C of "*la donne mobile*") and a splendid Edgardo for Bonynge – both with Edita Gruberova. Shicoff's Lensky for Bychkov is peerless and recommended to anyone yearning to hear this difficult role sung by a lyric tenor with compelling dramatic sensibilities. Shicoff's origins in the Cantor tradition are obvious and communicated through a plangent, yearning vocal sensuality that should have been better exploited by record companies. His now legendary performances from 1999 as Eléazar at the Wiener Staatsoper were taped – on video as well as audio – and it's not hyperbole to observe of Shicoff's portrayal of this complex role that it is by some way the finest to be recorded. His physical and spiritual immersion in the character dissipated Eléazar's fanaticism, creating a profound vulnerability that resolved with almost shocking force in a vocally exceptional but tortured "*Rachel, quand du siegneur.*" Shicoff is celebrated as a teacher. It is reassuring to reflect that a tenor with his talent and insight is helping to marshal the next generation.

Though under-represented on record, Dennis O'Neil[81] and Richard Leech[82] enjoyed long and successful careers, particularly during the 1980s. O'Neil's performances as Faust alongside the immortal Mefistofele of Samuel Ramey for the San Francisco production of Boito's masterpiece will survive him. Richard Leech was

---

78   José Francisco Araiza Andrade (4 October, 1950 –).
79   Jaume Aragall i Garriga (6 June, 1939 –).
80   2 June, 1949 –
81   25 February, 1948 –
82   26 March, 1957 –

consistently (and reliably) the Met's go-to lyric tenor for almost 200 performances, while Jerry Hadley's[83] charisma and talent made him something of a poster-boy for American opera at the end of the 20th century. He had a wide repertory that spanned Mozart and Stravinsky, *bel canto* and Bernstein, and at his best he sang beautifully if never with much character. The 1990s saw a flourish of talent in Frank Lopardo[84] and Ramón Vargas[85] – both gifted lyric tenors with international careers – and some disappointing, forced vocalising from Vincenzo La Scola;[86] much worse was heard from Tito Beltrán.[87] The 1990s also saw the rise to stardom of Roberto Alagna[88] and José Cura.[89] The latter failed to learn from Carreras' mistakes; he forced his instrument far too early and developed a spectrum of ugly vocal habits, the worst of them his need to anticipate any rising interval above a third with a brutalist flick that killed the line and its phrasing. Cura had a large voice, and he sang Otello far too often; the instrument was never given a chance to settle and his career ended soon after it began.

The French-born Alagna had a much longer career – initially as the husband (and frequent onstage partner) of Romanian soprano Angela Gheorghiu. He was the only tenor to enjoy a multi-platform contract with EMI, for whom he recorded extensively. His good looks and easy stage manner, and the Burton-Taylor dynamic of his marriage (which ended only with a single divorce), helped bring him considerable fame. His voice, however, was perennially under pressure. From the start he forced the tone, singing sharp routinely in consequence of his manifest efforts to exceed the limits of his naturally-formed voice. His voice had obvious, distinguishing character, but his phrasing was square and lacking from *portamento*. In lighter repertoire, such as Alfredo and Nemorino, he was very fine. Like so many others he was drawn to the weightier, darker end of the spectrum, which resulted in an early and significant vocal decline. His decision to gravitate to *Andrea Chénier* and Verdi's *Otello* was as misguided for Alagna as it had been for Di Stefano, although that is the only arena in which these tenors were comparable when at their best.

Alagna's primary rivals during the 1990s were the Argentian Marcelo Álvarez[90] and the Italian Salvatore Licitra.[91] Neither was ever more than solid, with essentially bland lyric voices conspicuous for ringing high notes and *cantabile* PR machines. Rolando Villazón[92] was something else entirely. He can be considered with premature hindsight to be the first and most impressive Italo-French tenor of the 21st century. Born in Mexico, he was discovered by the baritone Arturo Nieto, the friend of a neighbour who heard him singing in the shower. Nieto invited him to his music academy, where he trained formally. In 1999 he won second prize in the Operalia competition patronised by Domingo, followed shortly after by his Italian debut in

---

83   16 June, 1952 – 18 July, 2007.
84   23 December, 1957 –
85   11 September, 1960 –
86   26 January, 1958 – 15 April, 2011.
87   Ernesto Beltrán Aguilar (1 July, 1965 –)
88   7 June, 1963 –
89   José Luis Victor Cura Gómez (5 December, 1962 –).
90   27 February, 1962 –
91   10 August, 1968 – 5 September, 2011.
92   Rolando Villazón Mauleón (22 February, 1972 –).

Genoa as des Grieux in *Manon*. The following year he sang Macduff in Berlin, before branching out into footlight roles like Rodolfo, Rinuccio in *Gianni Schicchi* and Hoffmann. His debuts in the latter role at the Royal Opera House in London, and as Alfredo at the Met in New York, were hailed universally as the most important by any tenor for decades. This energised his celebrity internationally, and with it his willingness to force his diary as well as his voice. In 2004, he sang the title role in Willy Decker's magnificent staging in Amsterdam of the revised 4-act version of *Don Carlo*, alongside Dwayne Croft's Rodrigo, Amanda Roocroft's Elisabetta di Valois, and Robert Lloyd's Filippo II. Within a span of less than 24 months, Villazón was crowned universally as the real deal – a genuine *lirico-spinto* tenor with a brain to match his burnished, beautifully placed and easy tenor voice. Publicity helped make him popular; it was not required to make him talented. Many compared him to the young Domingo and Carreras, which was asinine even by the standards of the post-Three-Tenors dialectic. Villazón was plainly his own man, with an easy extension, some fascinating word-use, and a ringing, effortless high C. He was the first Villazón, not the fourth tenor.

His work in the studio was formed initially of collections of arias, to which he added performances in *L'elisir d'amore*, *La bohème* and *Traviata* – the latter two with the controversially successful Russian superstar, Anna Netrebko. Villazón also recorded Claudio Monteverdi's *Il combattimento di Tancredi e Clorinda*, shortly before his voice began to fail him. Anyone who heard Villazón in the theatre during his first seven years on stage will attest to how he hurled himself and his voice into everything with comparable force and energy. No one left a performance by Villazón feeling as if they had been cheated of their money. He failed nonetheless to learn from the mistakes of his forebears, and in 2007 his exertions led to the formation of a congenital cyst on one of his vocal cords – which necessitated surgery and a long period of silence. When returning to the theatre and studio he did so in the company of Handel and Mozart rather than Verdi and Puccini. Because he is now approaching his 50th birthday, Villazón will not be adding meaningfully to what will be perceived with time, and intense sadness, as a woefully inchoate talent.

Carreras made his debut two years before Villazón was conceived; he gave his final performance in a fully-staged opera just five years before Villazón's enforced sabbatical.[93] Pavarotti died in the same year as Villazón's voice. Domingo's candle continues to burn at both ends, as it will until his death in 30 or 40 years' time. Long before their elevation as personalities, each of the big Three was well-established as one of the finest Italo-French tenors of their generation. The admixture of charisma, charm, talent and individuality transcended their subordination to the media's ravenous agenda, so that while the "Three Tenors" phenomenon remains their defining legacy, it qualifies as little more than a footnote to their actual achievements. Of course, the gaudy and the vulgar have been pillars of the theatre's *res publica* since the 18th century, and the art, science and religion of opera survived its ontological crisis; it will continue to do so for as long as the wealthy view opera as a priority. Dissemination and inclusion are values to which the guardians of the art failed to turn in time, particularly in the dimming light of opera's decline as a platform for contemporary

---

93 In Tokyo, in the title role of Wolf-Ferrari's *Sly*, on 12 July, 2002.

music. And yet, the drawing of even one young man in the 21st century to art-song by the excesses of Big Top thinking is a triumph for the continuity of the Pantheon. What is less certain is whether the use and abuse of three singers in particular to achieve a point of definitive absolutism for the tenor as an archetype has damaged the popular and professional expectations of what a tenor is supposed to sound like.

Chapter Eighteen

How to Fake a Tenor

In 2013, the TV talent show *America's Got Talent* sought to prove the merit of its rationale by presenting Branden James to the public for the first time. He was to be judged by a panel of apparent "experts," none of whom was a professional singer, or indeed a professional in any meaningful sense of the word: Heidi Klum (a model); "Mel B" (a "Spice Girl"); Howie Mandel (a comedian and game show host); and "shock jock" Howard Stern. During the course of his "segment," the producers sought to explain how James, a Chicago native, had been raised by a conservative family with "traditional" values, without ever establishing that this environment had not contributed directly to James being (in his own words) "openly gay."[1] His family was apparently "disapproving" of his sexuality, a deprecation of which James' sexuality had taken little notice.

In mortifying scenes of emotional terrorism, James and his mother Lynda spoke of their differences for the entertainment of a gruesomely invested TV audience. "Singing has always been my dream," announced 34-year old James, before adding "I have been learning to be who I am." While sharing his "journey," James' ashen-faced mother stared at her shoes before informing 20 million Americans that "I think every parent has dreams and their ideals, and that just doesn't [sic] what you put in the formula. So it was a real difficult time." James continued "My mother wishes and prays every day that my situation was different", to which Mrs James responded "all I can do is just continue to express my love." And I hope a wonderful future for him. As any mother would for their child." On the basis, presumably, that her son agree not to live a sexually fulfilling life in the loving company of another man.

The programme then cut to Howard Stern. Having confirmed for the sybaritic DJ that he was a tenor, the "Judge" asked whether that meant he was "an opera singer?" James confirmed that this was indeed the case, to which Stern replied "Oh-oh." Drawing on his celebrated reserves of humanity and compassion, Stern enquired, "so what makes you so special?" James answered "the passion in [sic] which I sing." The crowd was encouraged to approve of this answer, contributing a smattering of applause and some light whistling. While cutting to footage of Lynda either praying or wishing for her son's success (it was unclear which), James was invited to "show us what you got."[2]

---

[1] To quote the modern-day prophet George Carlin: the adverb "openly" is applied only to gay people: "You wouldn't say that anyone was 'openly black'; well, maybe James Brown ... Colin Powell is not openly black. Colon Powell is openly white. He just happens to be black."

[2] An injunction later adopted almost verbatim by the geniuses behind *Rick & Morty* (Justin Roiland and Dan Harmon) for an episode in which an alien "floating head" appears on Earth to judge an inter-planetary talent show (Episode Five, Season Two, "*Get Schwifty*").

He obliged by singing a heavily edited version of "*Nessun dorma*" – transposed down a semi-tone from G major – in which he demonstrated the limited reach of his talent as a singer of opera. The use of a backing group with rather more cymbal than Puccini would have liked added to the unreality of the performance. Surprisingly, considering his obvious suspicion of opera, Howard Stern appeared to like what James had got and began to applaud. As James struggled with the resolving B flat 4, the audience leapt cheering to its feet. James' mother was seen to do the same before the camera cut to the now-tearful panel joining with the ovation. Somebody called Nick Cannon commented that the performance had been "amazing." Once the cheering subsided, Stern informed James that "Chicago knows talent, and I think this town just got really excited about your skill." The former statement may well have been true; the latter was not. James enjoyed little attention subsequently.

This submission of the vulnerable to the acumen of the inadequate is perverse at the best of times. Television has done much to compress the horror. The format is designed by its nature for limited spans of attention – which is not to say that everyone watching *America's Got Talent* is unable to focus for more than five minutes at a time; it is merely to say that the programme's producers assume this of their audience. Cynicism has always nourished talent shows. The modern form is separated from its antecedents only because the final judgment is left to the general public. In Britain the laurel wreath was given in 2012 to a woman and her dancing dog.[3] The fifth season of *Arabs Got Talent* (2017) was won by another "opera singer" – an eight-year old girl called Emanne Beasha.

Since 2000 there has been a steady shift in attention away from a competitor's abilities to the necessary drama of their personal journeys. The popular appetite for ugly ducklings and fairy tales has fostered a gruesome dialectic in which the stable and the capable have been replaced by a lumpen *pas de deux* starring the traumatised and the traumatising. Where once a contestant's talent was expected to speak, sing or juggle for itself, an individual's narrative now holds as much value as their act. Indeed, no one asked by a "Judge" to account for their submission to the bear-pit of public opinion, in any of the dozens of countries in which talent is alleged to reside, will reach much further than "it's my dream." It is here that the trite collides with the offensive.

The word "tenor" identifies the register of a voice. The words "opera singer" can refer only to a person who sings in performances of opera, not a singer of arias and art songs in concerted or recorded isolation, such as Kathryn Jenkins. On television, however, and across the globe, the title "opera singer" has begun to mean anyone who sings "*Nessun dorma*" – an aria that is now the go-to for any performer wishing to approximate cultivation.

The third season of *Australia's Got Talent* (2009) was won by Mark Vincent, a 15-year old "opera singer"; the third season of българия търси талант (Bulgaria; 2014) was won by Thomas Tomov, a 17-year old "opera singer"; seasons three and four of *Česko Slovensko má talent* (Czech Republic & Slovakia; 2012 and 2013) were both won by "opera singers," Jozef Pavlusík (aged 24) and Miroslav Sýkora (aged 25).

---

3 A "woman preaching" was presumably unavailable. Ashleigh Butler and her dog Pudsey received a prize of £100,000 for performing a "Mission Impossible" routine lasting 1 minute and 40 seconds.

Got Talent series in Germany, Indonesia, Italy, Netherlands (twice), Norway, Romania (twice), Slovenia, South Africa, Spain, Sweden, Switzerland, the UK, and Vietnam have also been won by "opera singers." A disturbing number of the winners was under the age of 20; the youngest was 9, the oldest 57. None of them was an opera singer. Many sang "*Nessun dorma*"; all of them did so badly, insofar as there *is* a metric for considering the objective quality of a performance. Had any of the Judges wanted for more than a sustainable human narrative they might have focussed on the tone of a singer's voice, the service of that tone to the shape and character of the music; the singer's phrasing, breathing and enunciation; the use (if any) of *vibrato* and *portamento*, the application of articulation and attack, of the existence (if any) of applied dynamics or *any* discernible expressive feature as emerged over the previous 300 years of the lyric tradition. None of these criteria even once featured in a televised judges' commentary when evaluating a performance by an (alleged) "opera singer" appearing on a TV talent show. Ever.

Neither has a panel addressed the question of amplitude, because everyone singing on a talent show and on television is singing into a microphone. Performances are relayed through speakers for a "live" audience and through cables for broadcasting thereafter. The same is true of any "opera singer" appearing other than in a concert hall or an opera house. Even when singing outdoors, as at the Festival Puccini at Torre del Lago in Viareggio (but not, conversely, the amplified Bregenzer Festspiele on the Austrian part of the Bodensee), opera singers have to project over a large orchestra if they are to be heard at the back of a raked arena seating 3,400. In Verona, singers have to reach audiences of 15,000. Anyone performing at the Wigmore Hall in London or the Liszt Hall in Raiding in Austria has little need for stentorian force because of the exceptional acoustics; singers with small voices, like the English tenor Ian Bostridge[4], can be heard with crystal clarity without resorting to microphones and speakers. The process of amplification distorts the mechanics of vocal projection and also the acoustical relationship between a singer, a chorus, an orchestra and a conductor. It's true that Caruso had the lungs necessary to perform for thousands of admirers in the open air, using only a horn and, where available, stage shells; Corelli sang unamplified at the Albert Hall in London with Renata Tebaldi – with only a piano for accompaniment. One attendee, sitting near the back of one of the farthest tiers observed many years later that both singers had been in magnificent voice, while regretting that Corelli was "simply too loud" for the 5,000-seat venue.

The ills of the microphone and the camera are relevant because they force a destructively artificial construction of sound and projection for singers trained and raised in a natural acoustic. Anyone who has been present when a large voice is performing unamplified in a "small" room will know how thrilling and oppressive the experience can be. Rehearsal spaces are especially problematic for singers when practicing because "self-hearing" in a small space can do nothing to prepare a singer for performing in a larger space, where reverberation times are considerably greater, and the opportunity for self-correction is curtailed. It can be just as difficult in a badly-designed opera house or concert hall – of which there are many. Modern producers, directors and designers are also at liberty to make preposterous demands

---

4 25 December, 1964 –

of singers that compel amplification. The Royal Swedish Opera, for example, was criticised for using speakers on stage for Aegisthus' scene at the end of Strauss' *Elektra* – an artifice compelled in part by the designer's decision to construct a set where the entrance to the castle was at the end of a long corridor towards the very back of the stage. When entering, Aegisthus was behind a wall and around 40 meters distant from the orchestra. James King would have been audible, as would his friend Fritz Wunderlich; neither tenor would have accepted the Swedish Opera's solution, which was to "enable" the tenor singing the role by amplifying him over Strauss' orchestrations. The use of amplification was criticised for undoing the atmosphere of the moment, and for humiliating a singer who was presumed inevitably (albeit unfairly) to be under-resourced vocally. Similar "tricks" were utilised for a Swedish production of *Rigoletto*, albeit for more tenable artistic and dramatic reasons and to a specific narrative end. Even so, there was no denying the negative construction of having an "enhanced" voice infect the parity of an otherwise natural acoustic experience. For a production of Karol Szymanowski's *Król Roger*, amplification was used throughout – ostensibly to support the dramatic proposition that the story takes place in Roger's head rather than 12th century Sicily (as written).

In a modern musical – whether on Broadway or the West End – *everyone* on stage is amplified. Singers of musicals are not expected to meet the challenges of a natural acoustic because the majority of lyric theatres have no acoustic at all, and because pit bands are now made up of fewer than 15 musicians, the limitations of which compel amplification. Performers of non-operatic music are not taught to project on the stage of the New York Met with an orchestra of 100 in the pit. Modern popular singers perform routinely with an "in-ear monitor," an electronic device that allows a singer to hear exactly (and only) what they need to when performing with a band before an audience in excess of 10,000. Many now do so with the additional support of "auto-tuning," a depressing technology that allows singers without a reliable sense of pitch (such as Madonna and Katie Perry) to be able to concentrate on the business of the stage show rather than the art of singing. Florence (Welch) and her Machine would consider auto-tuning an imposition and an impudence, as would Maria Reining and Lisa della Casa, both of whom employed glorious palettes of *portamento*, the "pitching" of which would have created overwhelming obstacles for the software.

Why does any of this matter, and then for tenors? The evolution of the tenor voice over time has compelled and embraced technical and methodological changes, the secrets of which have been passed down through singers, composers, teachers and, most recently, conductors – with music schools, colleges and academies formalising the training of singers so that some of the most important music of the past 700 years can continue to be performed in *broad* accordance with the composer's wishes. Each of the singers memorialised in this book trained, studied and worked with religious zeal. The extent of their sacrifices would discourage all but the most committed. Most of those who succeeded endured worse poverty than was romanticised by Puccini's La bohème, and the *vast* majority never managed to leave it behind. Some, like Di Stefano, were gifted nascently, but most relied on the rigours of training to better appreciate how important it is to protect and nurture an art that can be achieved only at the greatest cost. There are no short cuts to singing well without a microphone. Opera singers and performers of art song have, in every case, committed thousands of hours to the study of music – semantically, technically and aesthetically. They have had to master multiple languages, in their sung and spoken forms, while re-learning how to breathe so as to project to the back of the largest of acoustic spaces. They must acquire a diverse and sonically plastic range of expression that has by design to allow for the most tender and complicated of emotional states, as well as the fire and brimstone of climax and catastrophe. The technical expertise required of a tenor learning to sing a high C, and the discipline necessary for its preservation over decades, is merely one element within a regime that serves the greater arts of phrasing and articulation – the isolation of character through *cantabile*, emphasis and tone. These are skills that bind a singer to a culture that reaches back centuries.

The art of singing becomes a science whenever a voice operates within the expanse of a room without amplification. This is true also for chorus members, who often have to rehearse and perform several productions at the same time. Even before a singer is able to find work, they will have adopted a regimen of practice that extends to vocal exercising for as much as six hours a day. When not singing, most train physically for at least two or three hours to maintain the musculature necessary to support the technical "bellows" of the diaphragm. When in work, a rehearsal day will operate according to a daily schedule that requires three to four hours of singing – with an evening performance running from 90 minutes to five hours, on and off the stage. Chorus members are expected to give five or six performances a week, with stage rehearsals necessitating the study and retention of dramaturgy and stagecraft, and the physical mastery of each movement as it has been prescribed by design and rehearsal. Near-constant focus is required by the hell of waiting time and enforced silence. For every ten minutes a singer in session is not singing, their body will be recovering from the previous 20, a vagary that necessitates constant breathing and musculatory exercise until around 10–11pm on *every* performance day. When not performing, singers have to return to exercise and practice and, in many cases, teaching, while having to study and master their craft as actors. When Carlo Bergonzi was in his late 60s and early 70s, he submitted to four hours of practicing daily. Corelli would become a nervous wreck if he was unable to rehearse, even in a hotel room, so that he could reassure himself that his voice was "working." The paranoia and fear engendered by the threat of illness was equal to the terror of an audience's expectations; few can appreciate the pressure suffered by tenors, in particular, when having to prepare to sing so often above the stave. Indeed, no-one buys a ticket to an opera by Bellini, Rossini or Donizetti without thinking first and foremost of the *tessitura*. The psychological strain for a singer when anticipating the autocracy of conjecture is brutal; for many it can be ruinous. Most professional singers are now presumed to train (and perform only rarely) during their first ten years – a decade of effort, endurance and sacrifice. Some are well paid once they graduate; the majority are not. The actual cost of an evening's appearance by a tenor singing Tonio or Cavaradossi cannot be measured strictly in terms of the performance's length: the audience is paying for the 15 or 20 years of time and discipline invested before the curtain rises. The curse of a talent that has been formed through such sacrifice is that it will survive only on the terms by which it was gained in the first place.

There are, globally, dozens of professional singing competitions that have to account for these privations, as well as the pressures on the culture of modern performance practice, to ensure that young talent is not lost to greed, impatience and poor decision-making. The best of the established competitions can serve as platforms for the discovery of world-class talent. Cardiff Singer of the World, for example, launched the careers of Anja Harteros, Bryn Terfel, Katarina Karnéus, Lisa Gasteen, Dmitri Hvorostovsky and Karita Mattila. Since 1983, however, only a single tenor, Marius Brenciu, has won the competition; Andrew Kennedy is the only tenor to have been awarded the Song Prize. Neither enjoyed notable careers. Since the audience was given a right to an opinion in 2003, two tenors have received the "Dame Joan Sutherland Audience Prize": Giordano Lucà, in 2009, and Ben Johnson, in 2013.

Singing competitions like Cardiff are not looking for overnight stars, because that is not how professional singers operate; they live within a world where bookings are made many years in advance. With recordings in decline, the opportunity for promotion is limited, at best. The disparity between the media's appetite and the world of opera and art song is shown most clearly in the fact that anyone trained as a singer cannot register to appear on *Britain's Got Talent*, or any of its global siblings. The culture, as it has formed since the "Three Tenors," separates the amateur from the professional without appreciating how, little more than a century ago, everyone was an amateur until they were paid. The 18th and 19th centuries attached no value to training unless it resolved in a performance worth hearing. Rosa Ponselle had no formal tuition before Gatti-Casazza offered her a contract for the 1918/1919 season at the Met. She was 21 years old when signing it.

TV talent shows celebrate the amateur in its disjunction with the professional, a perverse dialectic which allows for the "discovery" of singers and of "tenors" in particular who have neither trained nor sacrificed anything save for their dignity when revealing their bathetic journey to the stage. The audience for a TV talent show knows as little of singing as the judges, and the competitors have only to emote to ensure their adoption by a culture for whom talent is as transitory as the breaks made necessary by advertising. In Britain, there have been two celebrated discoveries of "operatic tenors" since the 1990s. Russell Watson[5] was a part-time performer of popular songs in working men's clubs in the north of England. In 1990, during an engagement at a club in Wigan Road, it was suggested that he "have a go" at singing "*Nessun dorma*" – a "song" then all the rage thanks to the World Cup and the ubiquity of Pavarotti's 1972 recording. A few months later he won a "Search for a Star" contest organised by Manchester's Piccadilly Radio, which brought him to the attention of managers who were able to recognise that he had "a voice"; in 2001 his first album was released with Watson being promoted as "The Voice." The success of this album helped drive what has since become known as "crossover."[6] Watson was not an opera singer, but rather "the People's Tenor," a self-styled gesture towards the egalitarianism of the average. Watson's voice was formed by the microphone and it could be heard only with amplification. His performances of anything in Italian were poorly enunciated, badly phrased and strained. Anyone trained to sing – as Watson

---

5   24 November, 1966 –
6   Fryer, Paul (2014). *Opera in the Media Age: Essays on Art, Technology and Popular Culture.* McFarland. p.128.

admits he was not – would recognise the poor placement and absent diaphragm control, virtues that otherwise define the art of singing as it is taught professionally. Because he was hugely popular with those who would not otherwise be interested in, or aware of, opera as an "elitist" distraction, he prevailed as the popular face of the tenor voice in Britain. He sang for the people as one of the people. Watson's status as a lounge singer from the North of England was adopted enthusiastically as a form of social activism for a culture defined by class-warfare; it was made merchantable by skilful promotion and the increasingly populist appetite for "art made accessible." Watson's attachment to the anti-intellectualism caricatured by Mario Lanza was distinguishable from his predecessor because Lanza did not need a microphone, and he was highly trained as a vocalist. The principle remained the same, with Watson holding onto Pavarotti's enormous coat tails, just as Lanza sought to align himself with Caruso 40 years earlier. The circus surrounding Watson, however, was antithetical to the principle of *l'art pour l'art*, wherein the intrinsic value of art was best appreciated when separated from its didactic and utilitarian function. Watson's repudiation of the autotelic was not his intention or his doing because he was being promoted as the right product for the right time; instead of art for art's sake, the metric for success was now unashamedly *l'art pour de l'argent*.

In November, 1996, The "Three Tenors" sold approximately 1.6 million copies of their latest album. Yo-Yo Ma's coincident album release, 'Appalachia Waltz,' sold 29,000 copies, sitting at Number One on the Billboard Classical Chart.[7] The "Three Tenors'" concert tours adhered in form, logistics, promotion, economics and spirit to concerts by *Muse*. A press release before one stadium event announced that "[the Tenors'] new production will be the most visually stunning and technologically advanced to date... with dazzling lighting providing a visual feast for every member of the audience." Of course, the crossover market reached much further than singing. There was room for the Finnish cello quartet *Apocalyptica* performing arrangements of songs by *Metallica* and for Linda Lampenius, a famously beautiful violinist who played an electric instrument painted white. The Anglo-Singaporean violinist Vanessa Mae was pictured on the cover of one of her "pop" albums standing in a wet T-shirt in the sea while holding her electric violin. One all-female quartet from Australia decided to skip to the chase by calling themselves *Fourplay*.

Crossover was not always so reductively commercial. Kurt Weill's collaborations with Bertolt Brecht, for example, were purposeful gestures towards the reconciliation of the popular and the avant-garde (an instinct that resulted in his writing Broadway musicals such as *Knickerbocker Holiday* and *One Touch of Venus*); and more than a decade before Louis Clark and the Royal Philharmonic Orchestra launched the *Hooked on Classics* series of albums, the Brazilian jazz composer Deodato released an inspirational funk version of the theme from Richard Strauss' *Also sprach Zarathustra* on his 1973 album *Prelude*. This re-imagining of Strauss' best-known music realised nine minutes of glorious invention that was transformative of the source material. The use of Deodato's music for the "Wanderer" scene in Hal Ashby's film version of Jerzy Kosiński's novel *Being There* in 1979 made perfect sense, particularly in the light of the film's portrayal of the Christ-like Chauncy Gardner's revelatory emergence.

---

7   A., Kozinn. 'A Once Proud Industry Fends Off Extinction.' The New York *Times*, 8 December, 1996.

This was not crossover as it would become; it did not replicate the source material badly or add a drum-beat simply to make it relatable. Russell Watson, however, was giving performances of standard operatic repertoire in chunked form, using production techniques developed uniquely for popular musical culture. His career was formed around record releases and tours, and not even once through an unassisted performance in a natural acoustic. His audiences did not resent this or reject him for it, because he was performing *against* the traditions established over hundreds of years of cultural continuity. The millions who bought his recordings and the thousands who attended his shows knew nothing of the voices of Caruso, Gigli, Di Stefano, Bergonzi and Corelli. They were not comparing Watson to masters of the art of tenor singing because there was nothing appropriate for comparison. Watson was not *really* an opera singer; he was "The Voice." For "The People."

The clichéd portrayal of opera singers in the light of the "Three Tenors'" phenomenon highlighted the extrinsic white-tie formalities of an art form that was anathema to arena-based performances. The nadir of this process of normalisation – whereby the exceptional was made normal for popular tastes – was broadcast during the first season of *Britain's Got Talent*, in 2007, when Paul Potts[8] was crowned the first winner. Potts had worked at supermarkets, and at the time of his first appearance on television he was employed by The Carphone Warehouse. His "arc" was determined on the basis that whatever he did as a singer was made special because he was an "ordinary man" doing something apparently extraordinary. Except it wasn't. The standing ovation received by Potts when singing "*Nessun dorma*" for the first time at the Millennium Centre in Cardiff was given by an audience of 2,000 people encouraged by production staff to agree that his performance warranted the approbation. A video clip of that performance has received more than 180 million views on YouTube at the time of publication. For his semi-final performance on 14 June, 2007, Potts performed the main verses of "*Time To Say Goodbye*" – a tediously repetitive song made famous by another tenor, Andrea Bocelli. Potts reverted to "*Nessun dorma*" for his final performance on 17 June, 2007, receiving the greater percentage of the popular vote (cast by more than two million viewers) and was awarded £100,000. Six months later, he performed in front of Queen Elizabeth II at the Royal Variety Performance, just as Mario Lanza had sixty years earlier. Unlike Lanza, of course, Potts was another "tenor" with little or no voice, who would have been inaudible but for the use of amplification. It didn't prevent him from becoming popular, and his life story was filmed in 2013 as *One Chance*, starring James Corden, Julie Walters, Alexandra Roach, Colm Meaney and Mackenzie Crook.

Subsequent series of *Got Talent* have featured counter-tenors and male sopranos, including Greg Pritchard (for Britain in 2009) and Andrew-De-Leon (for America in 2012). Some have performed "*Nessun dorma*"; none of them sang "I know a bank" from Britten's *A Midsummer Night's Dream* or Purcell's "Here the deities approve." Talent shows and the "Three Tenors" "inspired" many others to pursue careers as crossover tenors, as soloists and in groups. Il Divo, Il Volvo, Forte, The Kingdom Tenors, and G4 have all sold a lot of records and filled numerous stadiums. They have done so with none of their number excelling vocally so as to compare to the third

---

8   13 October, 1970 –

rank of their predecessors. Il Divo has had number one hits in 33 countries – including Italy, Spain and France. They have sold 15-and-a-half million albums, eclipsed Led Zeppelin's 25-year standing record of being the only group to achieve a Number One album without first releasing a commercial single, and produced an album, *Ancora*, that went to Number One in the United States after selling 150,000 copies in its first week. These "acts" are manufactured. The oft-repeated allegations of cynical "conveyor-belt" production thinking are impossible to rebut; even when many of the performers have been trained, it is equally certain that each has been chosen for their appearance as well as their capacity to hold a note.

In 2006, Il Divo toured the United States with Barbra Streisand – a popular singer of exceptional talent and musicality, who was able to transition to Schumann and Schubert without throwing either of them under the bus. She had no classical training, and performed art song with respect, and in the spirit of its conception. She was not seeking to outdo or imitate Victoria de los Angeles, Lucia Popp or Susan Graham; neither was she claiming to be an "opera singer" or a "classical" artist. Her talent was embedded in integrity, so that her performances of "*Auf dem Wasser zu singen*"[9] and "*Mondnacht*" adhere strictly to the tradition of German *lieder*, at least to the 1920s. The same was not true of Susan Graham singing "*La vie en rose*," for which she employed an operatic tone and "comic effects" which added nothing to the song and its sentiments. Streisand's judgment was perfect even if her voice was not; she was happy to be heard according to her elevation of the genius of Schumann and Schubert, just as she had when performing Sondheim. Graham, though one of the finest singers of her generation, chose to overreach her limitations, demanding to be considered equally with Piaf, Louiguy and Monnot.

These considerations matter because expectation and ambition are determined by supply. With opera's currency in decline, the need for standards to be raised, or at the very least maintained, is pivotal to the prospect and probability of tenor voices being salvaged for future – generations who may never get to hear (or be introduced to) the best that might be achieved. This is especially troubling when noting the terminal collapse in church and synagogue attendance throughout Europe and large parts of the United States – the crucible for every leading tenor until the 1960s. It's self-evident that when almost every child born between 1700 and 1945 attended a church, they sang also as part of a choir or the congregation. It was statistically probable that talent would emerge from within so vast a sample, whereas children since the 1970s have had much else to distract them. The place of singing has been subsumed into the popular and the amplified, leaving the tenor voice in its acoustic formulation marginalised by the irredeemably vulgar. The potential for a singer to find introspection when plugged into banks of amplifiers and speakers is limited, at best, whereas Reynaldo Hahn can be heard from more than a century ago singing his own songs (as he recorded them between 1909 and 1919) into a horn without assistance or intervention.

Hahn was not a vocalist after the fashion of Caruso or Georges Thill. He was a composer who performed his own music – fostering an instant and physically immediate dynamic idealised by Marcel Proust, who wrote:

---

9 'To sing on the water.'

From the first notes of *Cimetière*, the most frivolous audience members and the most rebellious listeners were tamed. Not since Schumann has music that depicts pain, tenderness and the peacefulness of nature had so many characteristics of human truth and absolute beauty. Each note is a word – or a cry! His head slightly thrown back, his mouth melancholy and a bit disdainful, lets the rhythmic flow forth from the most beautiful, the saddest and warmest voice that has ever been. This 'instrument of musical genius' named Reynaldo Hahn grips our hearts, moistens our eyes. In the thrill of admiration that engulfs us and makes us tremble, we bend, one after the other, like a silent and solemn undulation of wheat in the wind.[10]

Proust's commentary was written having sat a matter of feet from the composer while he sang. Hearing Hahn performing "*L'Énamourée*" is profoundly moving because of the intimacy of the process; the composer was sat beside a primitive horn in a tiny room doing no more nor less than what Proust reported when describing his art. The substance of that art was captured in the authenticity of its performance, not its glamour.

Hahn was a professional composer, but he was (by his own admission) an amateur singer. Many French composers during the first third of the 20th century preferred amateurs over the conventionally trained. The critic Louis Aguettant, for example, remembered how

Fauré spoke to me about his performers—amateurs like Bagès[11], Mme Bardac, Mlle Girette, and others—who, he said, came closer to realizing his musical intentions than the professionals did. The professional singers want to 'exteriorize' everything. They remove the charm of intimacy from music."[12]

The concept of the amateur did not necessarily mean that a performer's skills were inferior to those of a professional. As Jean-Michel Nectoux has demonstrated:

it is essential to understand that the line between amateur and professional was not clearly drawn in the nineteenth century. Indeed, this distinction was only consistently made after the First World War. It was a common practice for amateurs— whether singers or instrumentalists— to appear in public concerts alongside professionals."[13]

---

10   Dominique [Marcel Proust], "Le cour aux lilas et l'atelier des roses," *Le Figaro*, May 11, 1903, 3.
11   Maurice Bagès Jacobé de Trigny (1862–1908) was a Parisian bureaucrat and a noted amateur tenor. Fauré gifted him the premieres of some of his most important song cycles, including Cinq mélodies "de Venise" (1892) and, in a private performance, La Bonne Chanson (1894).
12   Hubbell, Mary (2019). *Early Twentieth Century Vocal Performance Practice and The French School: An Exploration of the Lectures and Selected Songs by Reynaldo Hahn*. The City University of New York. p.20.
13   Nectoux, Jean-Michel (1999). "Fauré: Voice, Style and Vocality," in *Regarding Fauré*. Ed. Tom Gordon. Gordon and Breach. pp.370.

The times have changed. For as long as the second and third-rate are presented as genuine by those who know no better there is little hope for the probability of talent maturing other than in the teeth of decline. Many will leap to defend the ubiquity of compromise as a price worth paying for accessibility, but at what cost should accessibility be achieved? It's accepted that modern greats like Juan Diego Flórez and Jonas Kaufmann have let their hair down in concert, and there is *nothing* wrong with them doing so when the art and their vocalism survive temporary re-positioning. The value of accessibility becomes problematic only when singers fail to live up to the normative expectations of the art in whose service their voices have evolved. This sorry declination is embodied at its worst by Andrea Bocelli,[14] a "celebrity" tenor with an easily relatable story, formed primarily of the loss of his sight at the age of 12. Bocelli went on to graduate as a lawyer, but in 1992, at the age of 34, he was "discovered" by the Italian rock star, Zucchero, who was looking for a tenor to make a demo-recording of his song "*Miserere*," to send to Pavarotti in the hope of persuading him to take an interest. Pavarotti urged Zucchero to engage Bocelli; Zucchero persuaded Pavarotti to record the song with Bocelli. It became a huge hit and helped launch Bocelli into a career of concerts and recordings as an "opera star," after the fashion but without anything like the talent of Mario Lanza.

Bocelli has performed in complete operas, for the first time as Rodolfo in *La bohème* in 1998; apart from a small number of lessons from Franco Corelli, he is untrained. Compared to Villazón or Piotr Beczała – the world's two leading Rodolfos after 2000 – Bocelli has almost no projected voice, such that he is barely audible without amplification. In an interview with Kevin Berger for the Los Angeles *Times*,[15] Bocelli's conductor and friend Steven Mercurio addressed the issue of the tenor's tone and amplitude by suggesting that

> Andrea's voice is similar to the way people sang *bel canto* at the time *bel canto* was written ... it was a chest voice admittedly up to G, maybe A-flat. Everything after that, basically from A-flat or A on, goes into a mixed voice. It's half head, half chest. Andrea can get to a G, maybe an A-flat, in that full voice. After that, which was b*el can*to tradition, they turned it into, if not a real *falsetto*, a mixed voice. If you look at some of these old Donizetti things, written up to high Bs, by the time they were singing that high, they were singing in a *falsetto*. Andrea has always had this sort of half voice. Now, if you're trying to sing B flat and Cs, which opera singers like the Marcello Giordanis of the world do, well, they're singing those high notes in full voice. And when they sing over an orchestra, they cut glass. In other words, it gets really exciting. Whereas Andrea's voice, amplified, is just fine. Singing that stuff on stage unamplified is where the issue is.

These admissions by Bocelli's conductor are confirmed routinely by everything he has done since 1992. The tone is very light, with little edge and no depth of tone; he

---

14   22 September, 1958 –
15   8 December, 2010

sings with almost no articulation. This would be fine, but for his repertoire choices when recording works such as *Il trovatore* – for which amplitude and phonetic inflection are a pre-requisite. Bocelli's indulgence of "amplified reality" would make more sense if the voice being amplified had any discernible character. Unfortunately, the instrument is as bland as the music of Ludovico Einaudi, and instantly recognisable for what it lacks. Because Bocelli's singing is without *l'impostazione* – the Italian construction of vocal placement – he is unable to draw on the chest, throat and head resonating chambers. The absence of *squillo* leaves him unable to sing in the "Maschera" (the mask), which means he is unable to make use of the bones and sinus cavities above and around the eyes. The resulting tone is vapid and colourless. None of this has prevented Bocelli from becoming the world's highest paid and most successful tenor by record sales. His wealth and celebrity have seen him attend on the Pope and a host of major royalty and celebrity (including an appearance at the wedding of Princess Eugenie of York in 2018). In 2020, he was invited to give an online concert at Milan's empty Duomo during the Covid-19 lockdown.

A classically-trained tenor voice is expected to create sentiment, beauty and effect through an admixture of register, tone and inflection. The lack of drama in Bocelli's singing is in stark contradistinction with the impulses that drive much of his repertoire; his audience appears not to care. If Bocelli's singing ever raises the temperature in the room it does so only because listeners are unaware of how hot it can get. For modern audiences, the thrill once engendered by the tenors of old was registered by an altogether different kind of mercury.

Chapter Nineteen

Glory's Small Change

It's probably best to establish at the outset that Freddie Mercury[1] was one of the most talented and important tenors of the 20th century. Admirers of the traditions celebrated throughout the greater part of this book may take issue with the correlation of a pop singer with the likes of Donzelli, Duprez and Mario, but Mercury's status as the most famous tenor in the world-history of music probably warrants more than a passing reference, especially when noting his coincident standing as a composer of one of the most significant song-books of the 20th century. Mercury composed fewer than 70 individual works (as lyricist, composer or both), and though limited in number his song-book attaches to the traditions mastered by Schubert, another composer whose contribution to contemporary local and national culture was fundamental to the evolving *zeitgeist*. Unlike Schubert, Mercury was renowned for singing his own music. Most would agree that he sang it better than anyone else. He was key also to the aesthetics of his music in its sound and performance – as distinct from its appearance in written form. Schubert was not a vocalist, and so submitted necessarily (and for the most party happily) to the enthusiasms of others, most notably the baritone Johann Michael Vogl.

Vogl's influence over Schubert's *lieder* was judged by virtually everyone to be malignant. He is said to have persuaded the composer to make changes to his songs when preparing them for publication, and he certainly altered them in performance, introducing a host of antithetical ornaments and effects that served more often that not to infect the purity of Schubert's invention; his re-drafting of *Die schöne Müllerin* was particularly controversial. Schubert's debt to Vogl was considerable, however. The singer's declamatory style introduced an operatic flair to the *lied* that intensified the power of a form that was experienced almost exclusively in small rooms in private houses, accompanied (mostly) by a fortepiano in isolation. His emphasising of words as speech as well as song, and his predilection for sudden outbursts, notes in *falsetto*, extremes of dynamic effect and expressive hyperbole caused many to consider him wildly flamboyant, if not something worse. Vogl's vocal affectations were anathema for many, in part because Schubert appears to have represented Christ-like restraint. In his *Notizen zur Biographie des Franz Schubert*, Leopold von Sonnleithner recalled:

> As regards the manner in which Schubert's songs should be performed, there are very strange opinions today among the great majority of people.... I heard [Schubert] accompany and rehearse his songs more than a hundred times. Above all, he always kept the most strict and even time,

---

[1] Farrokh Bulsara (5 September, 1946 – 24 November, 1991).

except in the few cases where he had expressly indicated a ritardando, morendo, accelerando, etc. Furthermore, he never allowed violent expression in performance.... Michael Vogl, it is true, overstepped the permissible limits more and more as he lost his voice, but nevertheless he always sang strictly in time; and where his voice and strength did not suffice, he merely helped himself out as well as he could in the manner of an experienced opera singer. Schubert would certainly not have approved his manner of performance as it developed in his last years.[2]

Josef von Spaun remembered Vogl as an especially "sensitive" performer – a characterisation that did not translate automatically into "emotion" but which attached the expressive *locus* for a song to its musico-poetic structure. The cloth was cut for the model, therefore – an axiomatic validation of the dialectic that would be used commonly to validate Freddie Mercury's extravagances during his lifetime, and ever since. Of course, Mercury's achievements are not obviously analogous to those of Schubert and Vogl, particularly for those who see the popular and the serious as distinct and irreconcilable. Do the words of Heine's poem *"Der Atlas,"* when set to music by Schubert, reach further than the words and music of Mercury's "We Are the Champions" – simply because the classical tradition admits more complexity than the popular?[3]

Schubert's opening chords for *Der Atlas*, rendered ponderous by *tremolo*, announce the vocal articulation of Heine's ironic self-conception as a Promethean hero, lost to the hyperbole of conceit and delusion. Heine's Atlas carries his own suffering, as its presumed cause as well as its solitary agent; the pathos is narcissistic – coincidentally bombastic and self-piteous. Schubert omits *"der Schmerzen"*[4] from the repeated second line, so that it is performed as *"Die ganze Welt muss ich tragen"*[5] – a savage gesture towards the solipsism of the text in its setting. Schubert's song invites aggrandisement; as much is delivered enthusiastically by those who sing it – including Vogl when accompanied by the composer. In his memoirs, Eduard von Bauernfeld recalled of Vogl that the

> alterations and embellishments which this skilful singer, a past master of effect, allowed himself, received the composer's consent to some extent, but not infrequently they also gave rise to friendly controversy.[6]

---

2 Deutsch, Otto Erich (1958). *Schubert: Memoirs by his Friends*. A. & C. Black. pp.111–116.
3 "*Der Atlas Ich unglücksel'ger Atlas! eine Welt / Die ganze Welt der Schmerzen, muss ich tragen, Ich trage Unerträgliches, und brechen / Will mir das Herz im Leibe. Du stolzes Herz, du hast es ja gewollt! Du wolltest glücklich sein, unendlich glücklich / Oder unendlich elend, stolzes Herz, Und jetzo bist du elend.*" 'The atlas I unfortunate atlas! a world / the whole world of pain, I have to bear, I bear the unbearable, and I want to break / my heart in my body. You proud heart, you wanted it! You wanted to be happy, infinitely happy / Or infinitely miserable, proud heart, And now you are miserable.'
4 'The pain.'
5 'I have to carry the whole world.'
6 Dürr, Walther. "Schubert and Johann Michael Vogl: A Reappraisal." *19th Century Music* Vol. 3, No. 2 (Nov. 1979). pp.126–140; p.127.

Schubert was approving, writing to his brother, Ferdinand, in 1825:

> The manner in which Vogl sings and I accompany, how we appear in a given moment to be united into one, is something quite new and unheard-of for these people.[7]

Vogl's "controversial" use of improvised embellishments was advocated widely in contemporary songbooks, such as Anna-Maria Pellegrini Celoni's *Grammatica o siano regole di ben cantare* (printed in Leipzig in 1813); Vogl was sufficiently motivated to copy out the melodies and accompaniment for multiple-verse songs for which Schubert had provided only the first stanza. In writing out each line he was able to anticipate variations of statements that might otherwise simply be repeated. Vogl did not seek *merely* to repeat what was repeated; he brought his own considerable identity and personality to the composer's music – whether or not Schubert was playing the piano. The self-promotion of the performer was an accepted construction of virtuosity – Schubert could not, after all, sing many of his songs, even to disappoint – and his peers were equally accepting of the dynamic in which the recreative was tolerated as transcendent of its source. Schubert is remembered in isolation as the "father" of the *lied*, but there were many others for whom the song compelled the intervention of the singer.[8]

The *lied* is now "high art." For many, it is the highest. The words for "We are the Champions"[9] would not be thought creditable when compared to those penned by Heine. They are purposively crafted for the sentimentality of a musical setting that was inspired by a concert at Bingley Hall, Stafford, in which the audience began to sing along to Rodgers and Hammerstein's "You'll Never Walk Alone." Where Schubert's two-minute setting of *Der Atlas* was a purposefully satirical miniature, designed to prick the vanity of the inflated (and then for performance in the company of the uneasy), Mercury's three-minute "Champions" was a dissolute, anthemic tribute to the collectivist values of a post-*Star Wars* society recoiling from the deceit of Nixon and the death of Elvis. Stadium rock was incomparable to a Schubert lied, but the forms themselves were not meaningfully distinct other than by context. Indeed, Mercury's voice was extremely powerful without amplification; even if the scale and theatricality of Queen's performance at Vienna's Stadthalle on 12 May, 1982, would have knocked Schubert's wig from his head, Mercury was sufficiently confident in his voice to be able to perform in the same rooms and halls in which Vogl and Schubert had collaborated.

Mercury was more than a singer, of course. He was a gifted composer and his songs work perfectly well at the piano, with or without a voice; many of them have

---

7   *Ibid.* p.128.
8   A *very* modest sample would include Carl Loewe, Louis Spohr, Ludwig Berger, Franz Paul Lachner, Václav Tomášek, Sigismund Neukomm, Stephan Franz, Johann Vesque von Püttlingen, Conradin Kreutzer and Anselm Hüttenbrenner.
9   "I've paid my dues, Time after time / I've done my sentence, But committed no crime / And bad mistakes, I've made a few / I've had my share of sand kicked in my face / But I've come through / We are the champions, my friends / And we'll keep on fighting 'til the end / We are the champions / No time for losers / 'Cause we are the champions of the world."

been orchestrated, some of them on hundreds of occasions. The asinine prejudice that holds against pop songs because they last only two or three minutes while being prone to banality and vapidity would denigrate a 200-year-old European and American tradition of art music that began with Goethe. On 19 October, 1814, the not-yet eighteen year-old Schubert composed a scene from *Faust* as "*Gretchen am Spinnrade,*"[10] his first published score.[11] Certainly, the emotional and intellectual context for appreciating Schubert's music drama is greater than it is for a song by Freddie Mercury. The subtlety, text and subtext, of *Nacht und Träume* (D827; 1825) reaches further and admits more complexity than anything written or performed by *Queen*, without this warranting or sustaining criticism of a composer – and a group – who were clearly not writing songs for domestic living rooms filled to bursting with society's most educated men and women. The music and sensibilities of *Queen* were purpose-built for a singer with a voice and a charisma sufficient to warrant the interjection of giga-watt amplifiers and speakers. Performances by Mercury and *Queen* were designed consciously to reach tens of thousands of people at the same time, and millions through their recordings. It's reasonable for Sting to lean on John Dowland for credibility when down-sizing, but it would be wholly perverse to expect a singer-songwriter like Freddie Mercury to have re-fashioned his instincts after the Schubertiade during a very different time, when social convention was subject to near-constant challenge.

Order during the 1820s was determined by political and economic instability, and the imposition of civil metrics and manners that tolerated only passing insubordination. The 1970s allowed for Mercury's flaunting of a sexually ambiguous, socially deviant and musically extravagant vernacular that animated a culturally latent romanticism in an otherwise grimly unromantic age. Mercury's magnificent vulgarity separated him from the *nuages gris* of Schubert's eternally stratified sensibilities. The unspoken was paradoxically articulate, therefore, whereas Mercury's work on stage and as a composer left nothing to ambiguity. *Queen* tore off the paper lampshades fitted by Schubert and his peers as standard. As an artist devoid of introversion, Mercury's performances repudiated those internalised, damaged states captured by so much *lieder* – operating outside the bourgeois parameters of what was considered by the establishment to be civilised. It helped that Mercury's often lurid *persona* spoke as clearly to his own time as had Goethe's gruesomely self-absorbed *Werther* when tracing the onset of romanticism two centuries earlier. Unlike his sorrowful predecessor, however, Mercury's value as a rock deity (rather than as someone writing *An Gott*[12]) was isolated in what he gained from being Freddie Mercury rather than what he lacked by not being Schubert.

On the face of it, Vogl's abuses of artistic convention cannot compare to Mercury's hair, make-up, outfits, stage persona and choreography. In their admixture of poetic licence and creative impatience, however, Mercury and Vogl were both exemplars of theatrical cultures that simultaneously established and undermined convention. "We are the Champions," for example, begins in C minor, followed by a B flat / C with

---

10 'Gretchen at the Spinning Wheel'.
11 It was nonetheless published as his Op. 2.
12 D.863.

a G added – as C minor before resolving as Eb, the tonic of the relative major. The song develops along a progression to increase its momentum (as E flat – B flat / D – Cm – F7 – B flat; a B flat / D inverted V chord). Tension is maintained by adherence to this chord, but – instead of resolving to the tonic – Mercury introduces a sun-lit C major, serving as the dominant of F major, in which key the repeating choruses are performed throughout, saturated with four and five-part vocalised harmonies. The lead vocal rises to the song's challenge by compelling a resonant high C from Mercury. In the studio he managed such notes in full voice as well as *falsetto*. At *Live Aid* in London in 1985, and again at Wembley in 1986, he sang *ossia* versions of the chorus, extemporising and interjecting after the manner (if not the presumed delicacy) of Vogl. In performance he would deliver the words "You brought me fame and fortune and everything that goes with it; I thank you all" in spoken word, or as a *sprechstimme*, and across the range of available recordings it's clear that the *fach* of the song suited his voice perfectly. His irregular and rapid *vibrato* is audible in higher and sustained notes, and it was certainly one of the hallmarks of his vocal complexion. On a more general level, the power and resonance of his voice are often startling, and so bizarrely idiomatic that the instrument sustains comparison, if only for this reason alone, with the most important tenor voices ever recorded.[13] Mercury's vocal placement is entirely untrained, and a hostage to good fortune; no-one would advocate singing as he did. He was further separated from any comparator by his personality – a supernova of theatrical and musical intensity that shone through everything he did, no matter how cheesy or questionable. The celebrated performance of "Champions" in Montreal in 1981 is the go-to for sheer bravura, with Mercury evincing more confidence, invention and charm than it is fair or reasonable to find in any one person.

The oft-repeated consideration of Mercury as "a force of nature" captures the primary distinction between the classical tenor and the popular. He can be identified immediately as the performer within a single bar. The same is true of Reynaldo Hahn, Maurice Chevalier[14] and the Corsican-born tenor Tino Rossi,[15] whose ethereal recording of "*J'attendrai*" memorialised the sound of the crooner for a generation transitioning from acoustic opera and art song to amplified populism. Only thirty-five years before Mercury began to perform in public, the oil and water sound of Rossi characterised the musical tastes of a generation for whom ease, elegance, *legato* and the art-sciences of *rubato* and *portamento* were definitive – as they had been for Tito Schipa when singing on the stage of the Palais Garnier, a ten-minute walk from Rossi's Casino de Paris in Rue de Clichy. During the 1850s, the French *mélodie* replaced the romance, with Gounod and Massenet mastering a form in which the vocal line began to imitate spoken language. Massenet was the first to create a true melodic cycle based on recurring motifs ("*Poèm d'avril*," 1866), approximating the free verse poetry being written by Paul-Marie Verlaine, Arthur Rimbaud and Stéphane Mallarmé; between the 1880s and 1940s the French tenor was required to alternate

---

13 For an ambitious, if somewhat bizarre acoustic analysis of Mercury's voice see: Herbst, Christian T.; Hertegard, Stellan; Zangger-Borch, Daniel; and Lindestad, Per-Åke (2016). "Freddie Mercury—acoustic analysis of speaking fundamental frequency, vibrato, and subharmonics." *Logopedics Phoniatrics Vocology*. pp.1651–2022.
14 12 September, 1888 – 1 January, 1972.
15 29 April, 1907 – 26 September, 1983.

between the classical forms memorialised by mainstream opera and the increasingly popular salon-repertoire mastered by Massenet's pupil,[16] Reynaldo Hahn, during the first quarter of the 20th century.

The blurring of the lines between "popular" and "serious" was, for a time, more contextual than cultural – since both Schipa and Rossi were able to sing Mozart with comparable elegance. It was a matter of choice for Rossi that he did not. On the other hand, Stéphane Grappelli and Sidney Bechet were both equipped to perform Mozart and Brahms, but their decision not to was formed more obviously by cultural and technical differences – of taste as much as origin.[17] Mercury could *not* have sung Mozart, other than badly – although his range would have allowed him to get through the *Rhapsodie*, "für eine Altstimme."[18] The merging of once absolute polarities across Europe (even after the levelling influence of *Neue Sachlichkeit*[19]) led to the splaying of the "crooning" tenor voice in the United States through the work of the baritone Bing Crosby and the tenors Bobby Darin,[20] Tony Bennett,[21] and Marvin Gaye.[22] In France, Georges Brassens,[23] Charles Aznavour,[24] Serge Gainsbourg,[25] Yves Montand,[26] Jacques Brel,[27] and Gilbert Bécaud[28] aligned the popular with the country's poetic-philosophical left wing, language-driven lyric tradition. Crosby could never have sung Schubert; he was incapable of doing justice even to "Brother, Can you Spare me a Dime?" which he sang like a man wearing $1,000 loafers. The French popular school remained within reach of the classical tradition well into the 1960s, when its finest practitioners could (and in some cases did) perform songs by Weil, Hahn and Hollaender without even one of them being able to sing the music of Rossini, Berlioz, Wagner or Strauss. Freddie Mercury was a contemporary of Jon Vickers, Pavarotti *and* Brel. He shared nothing with any of them – save that he exercised an equivalent degree of vocal character and personality to distinguish him from his peers.

With the widening divergence between the popular and the serious, the potential for crossover was enormous and, for the most part, calamitous. Mercury was willing to tolerate the blurring of the lines while doing nothing to promote it, even though many have presumed he must have done so with his masterpiece, "Bohemian

---

16 ·Hahn dedicated his gorgeous operatic fantasy *L'île du rêve* (1898) to Massenet.
17 It's reasonable to conclude that both would have done considerably more with Brahms' music than the majority who have been playing it "straight" since 1900.
18 Alto Rhapsody, Op.53.
19 Though remembered primarily for its impact on painting and design, 'New Objectivity' made a significant contribution to music also, by encouraging the rejection of late Romantic sentimentality and the emotional unease of Expressionism. Paul Hindemith is probably its best-known proponent, with the opera *Neues vom Tage* ['News of the Day'; 1929] its most successful product. Other prominent adherents to the movement included Ernst Toch and Kurt Weill.
20 14 May, 1936 – 20 December, 1973.
21 August 3, 1926 –
22 2 April, 1939 – 1 April, 1984.
23 22 October, 1921 – 29 October, 1981.
24 22 May, 1924 – 1 October, 2018.
25 2 April, 1928 – 2 March, 1991.
26 Born Ivo Livi (13 October, 1921 – 9 November, 1991).
27 8 April, 1929 – 9 October, 1978.
28 24 October, 1927 – 18 December, 2001.

Rhapsody." In truth, there is nothing "operatic" about this unique song except for some basic call-and-response antiphony, a meaningless "plot," some distorted phrasing and distended high notes. Attempts at identifying "underworld" motifs in imitation of the tropes of opera as captured in Monteverdi's *L'Orfeo*, *Don Giovanni*, *Der Freischütz* and *Der Ring der Nibelungen* fail routinely. Similarly tenuous is the isolation of moral transgression in the bisecting worlds of opera and rock,[29] which isn't, of course, to suggest that Mercury didn't know what he was doing. Indeed, Queen's producer, Roy Thomas Baker, recalled how Mercury played the opening ballad on the piano only to announce: "this is where the opera section comes in!" They left immediately afterwards for dinner.

The *Rhapsody's* glorious invention was no sop to the past, as it had been for Strauss and Stravinsky; instead, Mercury absorbed almost apocryphally the vernacular of "serious" opera as it was perceived during the 1970s, with glam-rock and Joan Sutherland dancing on the head of a pin on which there was plainly insufficient room for both. The extravagance of "Bohemian Rhapsody" was neither pastiche nor parody. To suggest otherwise is to undermine and misunderstand the originality of the song's fantasy – which is, at its most outré, *pseudo*-operatic only. Mercury's fondness for the glamour of the "operatic" was hard-wired to his act and his personality; it was ancillary to David Bowie's more structured narrative-identification as "Ziggy Stardust." It aligned him to a theatricality that owed nothing to opera whatsoever.

It was a logical fit for many when he was invited to record "Barcelona" with the legendary *bel canto* soprano Montserrat Caballé. Mercury relocated from one camp to another with the lightest of steps, while the Spanish soprano looked like a whale out of water. The "Barcelona" project joined Mercury's powerful rock tenor to Caballé's soaring but ageing soprano, a synthesised fusion of rock and orchestral "textures" and a vaguely operatic chorus. It proved to be Mercury's final solo release. The song was first revealed during a televised concert in Ibiza on 29 May, 1987, in celebration of Barcelona's hosting of the 1992 Summer Olympic Games. Both singers mimed, as always they did whenever "performing" together. "Barcelona" was one of two songs launched officially by the Barcelona Olympic committee; the other was a predictably soul-crushing production by Andrew Lloyd Webber, "*Amigos Para Siempre,*" sung by Sarah Brightman and José Carreras. Plans for Mercury and Caballé to open the Olympics had to be re-drafted after Mercury died in 1991. A video montage featuring the song was broadcast during the opening ceremony on 25 July, 1992.

"Barcelona" is a miserable affair, even with Mercury hammering out some spectacular high notes and generally giving his all. Caballé's warbling added nothing to the tenor's still-charismatic turn, although the critical reception did, at least, appreciate how the song's creators had attempted to "be" operatic, rather than merely toy with mephitic theatrical clichés. *Entertainment Weekly* held that

> All the material in *Barcelona* (cowritten by Mercury) is penned in a style meant to snub rock in favor of 'real' opera, but likable pop hooks keep peeking through. The stuff lands somewhere between Andrew Lloyd

---

29   McLeod, K. (2001). "Bohemian Rhapsodies: Operatic Influences on Rock Music." *Popular* Music 20 (2). pp.189–203; p.194.

Webber and 'Climb Ev'ry Mountain'. Such a goofy context ultimately makes Caballé seem less like Maria Callas and more like Yma Sumac. But then, Mercury's reverence for the star and his flair for kitsch make this a novelty item too cracked to resist.[30]

When the *Barcelona* album was re-released in 2012, with an upgraded orchestral package, another reviewer celebrated

> "the weirdest combo in pop history: the flamboyant Queen frontman Freddie Mercury and opera superstar Montserrat Caballé certainly hit the world between the eyes with their *Barcelona* album 25 years ago. To mark its quarter century, this special edition has been reworked.... You can tell the difference: big and lush and sweeping, it makes the previous version seem a little on the cheap side. Whether you can handle that eccentric vocal pairing, mind you, is quite another matter."[31]

Of course, *Barcelona* was padded with tracks laden with operatic clichés (such as "*Overture Piccante*"), and the pair sang in English, Spanish and Japanese. Caballé remains an opera singer throughout; she indulges in some spectacularly arcane vocalising while Mercury attempts to shift his vocal production towards classical discipline with "*Ensueño*" and the culturally suspect "*La Japonaise.*" He sounds more often than he can have wanted like Andrea Bocelli. Mercury's vocal tone when restraining himself speaks always to his musicality; his projection is fragile, however – hinting at vulnerabilities that separate him as the leading vocalist of his generation from those of his "popular" predecessors who were raised at home or at school on art song. *Barcelona* is operatic as affectation only; it's a dessert without an aperitif.

Mercury's final song with Queen, "The Show Must Go On" (1991), reverted to the band's circus-top stage tradition, fusing sentimentality, extravagance and bravura with unimpeachable sincerity. After the singer's death, Queen made the tactically logical and infinitely depressing decision to use other singers, notably Adam Lambert,[32] a lacquered product of reality TV and blind ambition. Lambert achieved nascent fame in 2009 as the runner-up of Season 8 of *American Idol*, and a debut album released with the temerarious title *For Your Entertainment*. Lambert is widely admired for the range of his voice and its stentorian power; both Brian May and Roger Taylor were vociferous in their praise when touring together. His tenor lacks personality, however, and he is first and foremost a simulacrum, a post-modern confection with a "big" voice and a grandiose stage persona, constructed from a miscellany of clichés articled by predecessors who did it better. His absent authenticity, as someone approximating Freddie Mercury, places him in a Looking Glass world in which he is, in real terms, a cover-band singer working for the original band. If Lambert's *chutzpah* in stepping

---

30 Klein, Eve (2018). "When Divas And Rock Stars Collide: Interpreting Freddie Mercury and Montserrat Caballé's Barcelona". In *Popular Music, Stars and Stardom*. Eds. Stephen Loy, Julie Rickwood and Samantha Bennett. ANU Press. p.122.
31 *Ibid.*
32 29 January, 1982 –

into the breach is admirable, his status as a gun for hire (as distinct from an "original" artist) isolates him from the late 20th century tradition of singer-songwriters. His polish as an artist is the product of commercial necessity rather than cultural agency, and to a limited extent he perpetuates the force of Queen's influence during the 1970s, when Freddie Mercury hummed as a gay icon speaking for the voiceless. The developed world's embrace of gay values, identity and independence fifty years later is very different indeed. For similar reasons, Brian May's indelible contribution to the counter-cultural revolution, as the composer of some of Queen's best songs, was dissipated by his appearance on the roof of Buckingham Palace in 2002 – a disconnect that amplified the evolving conception of voices as cultural *imprimaturs* (rather than "mere" singers) after 1950.

If it can be agreed that Mercury's voice was never "beautiful" (when compared to the established *schema* as it prevails in the opera house and the concert hall), then neither would it be deemed meritable by the anodyne standards of the modern TV talent show. Indeed, Mercury would fail to secure a pass for a British ABRSM[33] Grade 6 vocal exam, with the repertoire lists in 2021 dominated by art composers writing in English, French, Italian and German. The large body of obligatory pieces includes works by Gibbons, Purcell, Beethoven, Schubert, Bellini, Donizetti, Ravel, Quilter, Britten and others. There are a small handful of representative "popular" works by Loewe, Porter and Menken – all of which would be expected to adhere in performance to the same broad criteria as are applied to songs by Brahms and Chausson. The ABRSM's published criteria for "interpreting the score" provides that

> Printed editorial suggestions such as phrasing, metronome marks, realization of ornaments etc. need not be strictly observed. Whether the piece contains musical indications or not, candidates are always encouraged to interpret the score in a stylistically appropriate manner. Ultimately, examiners' marking will be determined by consideration of pitch, time, tone, shape and performance, and how control of these contributes to the overall musical outcome.

There is nothing in the list of obligatory works by Mercury; no student at Grade 6, or beyond, is entitled to have a crack at "Fat-Bottomed Girls." Instead, and to secure even a pass, a student must satisfy an examiner, when meeting the undefined and unsettling criterion of "overall musical outcome," that they have produced:

> highly accurate notes and intonation; Fluent, with flexibility where appropriate; Rhythmic character well conveyed; Well projected; Sensitive use of tonal qualities; Expressive, idiomatic musical shaping and detail; Assured; Fully committed; Vivid communication of character and style.

It may be presumed that each of these requirements would have been met at some level by Sid Vicious when singing "God Save the Queen" with the Sex Pistols,

---

33 The Associated Board of the Royal Schools of Music is a British examination board that provides more than 650,000 music exams and assessments annually in 93 countries.

noting the sophistry of a "stylistically appropriate manner" and the apparent need for "vivid communication of character and style." What might an examiner have made of David Bowie performing almost any of the music he produced with Tin Machine? Or Roy Orbison?[34] What of Robert Smith[35] when singing with The Cure, or Nate Ruess[36] when fronting the band Fun? Smith had one of the most striking tenor voices to make records; his idiosyncratic tone and plangently wayward delivery were nonetheless antithetical to the sound and style recommended (and presumed) by the ABRSM for performances of William Walton's "Under the Greenwood Tree."

The post-war democratisation of singing allowed for difference to be determined by an absence of training, which was re-positioned as a function of individuality. Bowie and Smith did not sing as they did because they were taught to do so; they couldn't help sounding as they did, any more than they could help being who they were. Paul McCartney's[37] expressive high tenor is as recognisable to most of the planet as the sound of a mother's voice, and yet the Liverpool Institute for Performing Arts, founded by McCartney, now teaches students to sing and perform what he learned to do in his bedroom. The arch dissimilarities between formative experience and the language of expression compels students and graduates alike to question at what point anything is good enough for a "Distinction" when there is no measurable standard to which to aspire. If the axiom "be yourself" was sufficient for McCartney, Bowie, Mercury and Smith, then how might universal measures of technical and artistic excellence be determined and applied?

During the "Jonny B Goode" scene in *Back to the Future*, when Marty McFly "invents" Chuck Berry's "sound" for him in 1955, Marty McFly slays his guitar into extreme sonic dissolution, a moment of brilliant narrative repositioning by Robert Zemeckis and Bob Gale because Marty McFly would have been the *last* man on Earth to play like that in 1985. Marty was as "square" as his father had been in 1955 and as "clean" as Hendrix was presumed to be dirty when burning the "Stars and Stripes" in 1969.

The pressure on singers of art song to conform culturally is not a societal expectation, as it had been for Vogl; it is, instead, a technical construction formed of aesthetic continuity. French *chanson*, German *lieder*, Italian *canzone* and the American songbook all require a co-ordinated approach, so that a student studying notes on a page in Tokyo can be presumed to know how to sing them when attending for a concert in Oslo with others expecting to play the same score. The opposite is true of singers of contemporary popular music, for whom difference is commonly the *solitary* measure of quality – an eternally vanishing horizon for those thinking further than the soporific infusions of Ed Sheeran.

Sheeran's music can be performed by anyone with a guitar and an averagely dull voice; the music of AC/DC cannot. Brian Johnson,[38] the band's lead singer for more than thirty years, had a tenor voice comparable to the feeding of burning-hot coal

---

34   23 April, 1936 – 6 December, 1988.
35   21 April, 1959 –
36   26 February, 1984 –
37   18 June, 1942 –
38   5 October 1947 –

into the turbine of a 747. It was primeval in its force and effect, redolent of Joshua's choir of ram's-horn trumpets at full tilt, and equally inexplicable. Johnson himself could never explain how he sang as he did; in an interview with *Fox News* in 2012 he admitted

> I don't know. People ask me how I prepare for a show which I don't at all. I just go into the bathroom, make a big loud noise and then come back into the boys and say, 'Well that's me ready.' I try to give as much passion up there and as long as I can keep in tune for the band I'm happy. It's just a very singular band with very singular members.[39]

Notwithstanding the gross irresponsibility of the many and various online promises offering to teach "how to sing like Brian Johnson," there is no prospect of anyone achieving the sound he did by training. Johnson's "method" would have horrified Manuel García and Jean De Reszke – or *anyone* equipped to sing even a scale in accordance with ABRSM dogma. That he managed to do so for 36 years joins the miraculous to the incautious. There have been many other tenor "screamers" – as anyone with an ear for Scandinavian "metal" will attest. Johnson was extremely musical, however, with a fantastic pair of ears – before an accident (rather than his experience of being on stage and in the studio for decades with Angus Young) caused him to lose much of his hearing.[40] Others have capitalised on the thrill of high-note tenor voices in popular music, most obviously Prince[41] and Michael Jackson,[42] of whose "star status, effeminate appearance and *falsetto* voice" Ken McLeod observed that they appeared "to mimic conventions previously only observed in baroque *castrati* such as Farinelli."[43] Jackson's tenor has been much considered elsewhere, as has Jackson. The essence of his vocal significance can be traced to the exceptional talent of his youth, defined as it was by a vocal fluency that he largely jettisoned for the Tourette's that characterised his work after "Billie Jean" in 1983.

Less successful, and describably awful, was Michael Bolton,[44] a mullet-haired lothario with a chalky, high-lying tenor voice who sounded forever like he was either clutching a single red-rose or about to clamp one between his teeth. The low point of Bolton's lactose-tolerant career occurred in 1992 when he struck the motherload of vanities with his album of opera arias to which, pre-Jeffrey Epstein, Sony gave the title "My Secret Passion."

This monstrous folly appealed neither to fans of Bolton's work to date nor to anyone interested in opera. The majority recognised his attempt to mount the "Three Tenors" bandwagon as an artless lunge towards the validation of his voice and his

---

39 https://bravewords.com/news/ac-dc-singer-brian-johnson-talks-about-his-voice-surviving-canons-and-bells-doubts-if-there-will-be-another-big-tour#:~:text=Johnson%3A%20%22I%20don't,the%20band%20I'm%20happy.
40 As of early 2021, it has begun to return, gradually.
41 Prince Rogers Nelson (7 June, 1958 – 21 April, 2016).
42 29 August, 1958 – 25 June, 2009.
43 McLeod, K. (2001). "Bohemian Rhapsodies: Operatic Influences on Rock Music." *Popular Music* 20 (2):. pp.189–203; p.199.
44 26 February, 1953 –

artistry, such as it was. After 1,000 performances of "When a Man Loves a Woman," Bolton can be forgiven for having felt jaded; rather than crossing over, however – as he might have done after sharing the stage more than once with Pavarotti – he determined on an album of eleven of the most important and challenging arias in the canon, accompanied by the Philharmonia. In addition to the obligatory "*Nessun dorma,*" he laid waste to "*Una furtiva lagrima,*" "*Che gelida manina,*" "*O soave fanciulla*" (with Renée Fleming), "*Vesti la giubba,*" "*È la solita storia,*" and "*Celeste Aïda.*" The performances are excrescently bad. His singing takes no account of any of the fundamental structural elements within the music; there is no attention to phrase length, shape or line, and he has neither the insight nor the technique necessary to articulate music that is difficult to place even for decade-trained tenors. When singing the arias live, as he did for a toe-curling TV production with a sad-faced orchestra and a microphone, he took such rhythmic liberties with the music that the conductor can have done nothing less than close his eyes. The performance, in particular, of "*Che gelida manina*" is like watching a suspension-bridge twist in the wind.

Bolton's assault on art song did not equate to Pavarotti's inappropriate advance on "*Singin' in the Rain*" – which was clearly delivered with a glint in his eye. The only thing captured in Michael Bolton's eye when performing Puccini was Michael Bolton. Hubris being what it is, Bolton was unaware of (or deaf to) the cultural and social norms that rendered the operatic tenor thrilling in the first place. He failed to grasp what it was that caused the finest classically trained tenors to sound so remarkable, namely their absolute and unshakeable discipline, as vocalists and as artists. The thrill attaching to any note above an A4 when sung by a man (whether a baritone or a tenor) is the sense shared by almost everyone that there is a lot to get through before a climax can be achieved. The high notes that crown many arias are cumulative of tensions created and released, a state of flux that calls invariably on often *very* long phrases. The metric for Wagner's writing for tenor is, of course, entirely different because he rarely places dramatic valves where they might most obviously serve a purpose. Bolton's crimes were at their most egregious when approaching every phrase prior to the concluding high note as an encumbrance. It would seem that no-one bothered to point out that the art in art song is located not in its meridian – no matter how thrilling that can be – but in the event horizon of precision and power that precedes it. The tenor voice at its most emotional requires a singer to traduce the natural shocks that flesh is heir to by the application of gymnastic discipline to the overcoming of physical tension. The magic is in making it *sound* easy; not in making it easy.

Bolton's meagre abilities were eclipsed entirely by someone with considerably fewer record sales and infinitely greater talent. David Phelps[45] is a Texan tenor with a once-in-a-lifetime voice, extraordinary musical sensibilities, and an attachment to contemporary gospel that has ensured his relative concealment outside the United States. He nonetheless possesses one of the most eye-popping voices of the 21st century, with a stupendous *legato*, a continent-wide range of expressive colour and an effortless and mostly uncovered D5; its use for a dispensable body of music is nothing less than a tragedy. As with all of the greatest singers, Phelps' brilliance is best

---

45   21 October, 1969 –

experienced live. For anyone who has not heard him sing before, there is a widely available recording of a now-legendary performance of "O Holy Night," filmed on 30 August, 2000, for a Christian TV spectacular titled "Christmas in the Country." The event was hosted by Phelps' long-time ecclesiastical patrons, Bill and Gloria Gaither, and staged in the Alabama Theatre, a Terry Gilliam-esque cinema built in 1927, seating 2,500. For his performance of Adolphe Adam's touching carol, Phelps was joined on stage by a frantically energetic pianist, the Gaithers, and some of their more visibly devout friends. It is obvious from the start that Phelps has an extraordinary voice; he phrases the opening verse and chorus with immense delicacy and a faultless beauty of line. So great is the fluency of his shaping of the music, and such is the intensity of his articulation, that one can easily overlook the bloated vulgarity of the setting and its bug-eyed religiosity.

One can certainly imagine the faithful becoming more so when Phelps hits a tuning-fork D5 that quite properly causes everyone to stand up. It's at this point that the worthies on stage get to join in and raise their hands, while the Wurlitzer organ and supporting band attempt to keep up with what is plainly one of the most completely impressive voices of any century. There is more colour in this one performance than in the entire careers of many still-working operatic tenors; his breathing, turns, ornaments, variegated *vibrato*, *mezza-voce*, *rubato* and dynamic articulation are not always used tastefully – a necessary penance when in Alabama – but the performance is as close to perfect technically as it is possible to get. Certainly, the three electrifying C sharp 5s with which it ends are among the most thrilling ever recorded; by anyone. Midst all the teeth, hair and posturing on stage behind him, Phelps threw down a gauntlet that has not been picked up by anyone since. What makes it all so entirely compelling is the sincerity of his performance amid so much artifice; indeed, while his authenticity was informed by personal beliefs that are doubtless easier to nurture when singing Adam's infamously emotive music, there is a sense also that his decisions artistically are logical.

The power of conviction is part of the tenor mythology. If the worst are full of passionate intensity, then the best may be said to be those whose belief in their voices legitimises the ignorance of convention. This explains why opera and rock music share in the extravagance of excess and spectacle – functions of luxury without which it would be difficult to suspend disbelief. As Suzanne Aspden observed:

> Luxury was the vice that defined operatic deviance. In modern discussions of the significance of luxury in opera, the vast amount of money spent on opulent sets, and on fees and gifts for singers, along with the sexual perversions that were imagined to spread from singers to audience, define luxury as the wasteful extravagance of a commercial society fascinated with the foreign.[46]

Luxury is a construction of exceptionalism, which is itself a formulation of eternally shifting interactions between technique and expression. This difficult balancing

---

46   Aspden, S. (1997). "An infinity of factions: Opera in eighteenth-century Britain and the undoing of society." *Cambridge Opera Journal*, 9/1. pp.1–19; p.13.

act was typified by the antinomies of Bob Dylan[47] and George Michael[48] – two of the most successful artists of the post-war era. Few singers have been more polarising than Dylan. An atavistic attachment to the origins of blues-country legitimised his nasal, purposefully anti-lyrical disavowal of traditional vocal mechanics, which in turn helped shape his worth as a social critic and commentator.[49] The preternatural fear that beauty might undermine the sincerity of a message played no part in the evolution of George Michael's[50] routine detachment from complex political and philosophical concerns. Although this balance of priorities was never absolute,[51] his remarkably expressive tenor voice was subject perennially to the infinite distraction of his status as a pop star. Michael was separated, in consequence, as a "song bird" from the "serious" *sprechstimme* vocalising idealised by Dylan and, later, Thom Yorke[52] of *Radiohead*. Their absolution of intellect has been much exploited by singers like Tom Waits and Leonard Cohen (neither of them tenors, of course), for whom "beauty" in its formality was conceptually and practically meaningless.

An individual's identification psychologically with the voice of a singer is a plainly complex process, admitting as it does a vast range of emotional, educational, cultural and social factors and appetites. The "guilty pleasure" of "*Nessun dorma*" for those who would never listen to an opera is analogous to the delight taken by "serious" musicians in Katie Perry's "Roar," a thing more infectious than anything found in nature. No one would identify Katie Perry as an intellect, certainly not Katie Perry, and there is nothing wrong with liking her songs unless an attachment to her music speaks to the vulnerability of the attached. It's well worth remembering that Escoffier admitted a weakness for beignets while Brahms adored the music of Johan Strauss; neither craving undermined the credibility of their work in isolation. The tenor has become a thing of luxury, however – an accoutrement that can be tolerated by many only when a singer is able to abandon or undermine their lyricism, for fear that the artificiality of elegance might corrupt the integrity of thought. Has there been a more beautiful, affecting and unsettling song than "Fake Plastic Trees"? It need not be asked whether it has been sung more "beautifully" than by Thom Yorke on record and in concert.

As with the reconciliation of surface and substance, the ambition of heart and mind has been well-served by popular music. The fascism of technique continues nonetheless to characterise considerations of tenor voices, just as surely as it feeds the polarising of visual artists debating the axiomatic assertion that "my child could have painted that." Where voices are concerned, the popular choice settles frequently on Adam Lambert and the legions of the auto-tuned because boy-bands sound pretty enough, and no more distract the barber from his work than would the violin concertos of Paganini. Gord Downie from the Tragically Hip, Jack White (of Stripes fame) and Anthony Kiedis from the Red Hot Chili Peppers are not celebrated as

---

47 24 May, 1941 –
48 25 June, 1963 – 25 December, 2016.
49 A cultural position undermined somewhat by the sale of his catalogue of songs for around $300m in 2020.
50 25 June, 1963 – 25 December, 2016.
51 His acutely affecting performances in concert of "*Brother can you spare me a dime*" made Bing Crosby's recording sound like an outtake from a "Road" movie.
52 7 October, 1968 –

"singer-songwriters"; neither would anyone invite them to sing Gounod's "*Ave Maria*" at their daughter's wedding. Kurt Cobain's voice fell broadly within the nomenclature of "tenor," a definition he would not have appreciated because of the concomitant expectations of fidelity and discipline.

The gulf separating capability from quality has not been traversed routinely. Modern exceptions are Bruno Mars[53] and Matt Bellamy of Muse. Both are talented musicians and vocalists – notable for their transcendence of compromise. Mars affirmed his credentials when unintentionally humiliating the hip-hop dancing Chris Martin during the half-time show for the Super Bowl in 2016. Mars did not need Martin to amplify his ingenuity and expertise; his set nonetheless provided valuable context. Bellamy's synaesthetic slice of gamy theatre has been well-served on record and in concert by a voice that is fizzing with character and expression, while also being capable of startling beauty. The power of his tenor and its dramatic complexion have not come at cost to the primacy of the band's music, however; he remains an ideal exemplar for those fearful of the corruption of technique and training. A *fach* will always summon the better devils of skill and precision, so that the converse realities of "serious" and "popular" will collide only rarely, particularly where the tenor voice is concerned. One of the few to have achieved this alchemic ideal is Stevie Wonder.[54]

Blind from shortly after his birth, Wonder is a 19th century talent, comparable in ability to most of his classically trained predecessors, including Schubert. As a tenor vocalist, the effect of his performances in concert warrant analogous references to Johann Vogl. That he sings his own songs merely adds to the extravagance of his gifts as they were first revealed as a child, when he signed with Motown's Tamla label at the age of 11. Wonder achieved his first success in 1963 with the single "Fingertips." By the end of 1971 he had recorded twelve award-winning albums. In 1972 he released his 14th and 15th albums, *Music of My Mind* and *Talking Book*, embarking on what is now considered to be his most creative period. This included *Fulfillingness' First Finale*, a darkly introspective collection of ten songs released in 1974. Many of them are spartan and bleak, the most affecting being "They Won't Go When I Go," the only track that Wonder composed in collaboration (with Yvonne Lowrene Wright).

"They won't go" is a funeral lament, in F sharp minor,[55] with a fixed bass equivalent to a *passacaglia* or a *chaconne*. The song alludes openly to the 19th century German chorale "*O mein Jesu*" and Thomas Kelly's 1805 Protestant hymn "Stricken, smitten, and afflicted" – the last lines of which are "Lamb of God, for sinners wounded, Sacrifice to cancel guilt! None shall ever be confounded Who on him their hope have built." The song's prosody is achingly beautiful, as articulate an expression in words and music as exists anywhere in any songbook, in any language, from any time. Wonder employs extended sequences to convey the experience of a journey, with a

---

53 8 October, 1985 –
54 Stevland Hardaway Morris; né Judkins (13 May, 1950 –).
55 When George Michael covered the song, he did so having transposed it down to F minor. F sharp minor is the most obsidian of keys, employed most powerfully by Mahler for the trumpet-stated "fate" motive in the *Trauermarsch* (Funeral March) that is the opening movement of his Fifth Symphony. It is a rarely employed key, with the best-known examples probably being Schubert's unfinished Piano Sonata, D 571; Chopin's Polonaise in F-sharp minor, Op. 44; Nocturne, Op. 48, No. 2; Mazurka, Op. 59, No. 3; and Rachmaninov's Prelude in F-sharp minor No. 1, Op. 23.

series of falling-fifths capturing the sinner's progress when ascending and descending Jacob's Ladder. The judgment to which the song refers is both "away from tears" and also from "lying friends, wanting tragic ends" whose day is yet to come. The falling-fifths progressions are formed of an interval pattern of connected tenths to sevenths, consecutive major-minor seventh chords, and an extended sequence that connects the tonic chords at each end of the progression – forming a circular architecture that codifies closure for the penitent.

The studio performance is very fine, even accepting Wonder's questionable use of synthetic instrumental commentaries; his scoring for a chorus of heavily accented, *vibrato*-rich voices attaches the song's origins to the gospel roots of slavery. His lyric tenor is charismatic and instantly identifiable. At his peak, Wonder's tessitura gave him access to two octaves (F3 – E flat 5), although his lower register was always light, with an unmistakably nasal colour. The voice is striking still for its superb diction and diverse colouring, which includes a fluent *falsetto* that breaks high, at around E4, and a palette of effects, *coloratura* and phrase-shaping – all conveyed through a wide *vibrato* which Wonder uses with obvious calculation.

On 7 July, 2009, he performed "They won't go" at Michael Jackson's memorial service in California, with piano only – leaving out a verse that may well have been considered politically imprudent or too close to home for some of those in the audience.[56] Wonder's singing was articulate in its integrity and sincerity; it spoke for the tragically flawed Jackson as well as those who knew just enough of the truth of his damaged and exploited life to feel compassion as well as unease. The emotional range and reach of Wonder's voice – which concluded with a series of blistering C sharp 5s – hammered home the complicated sentiments being experienced by everyone inside the Staples Centre, as well as the unique capacity of a tenor to capture the most profound and acute of feelings. Wonder's miraculous talent spoke for generations of African-Americans unaware that they mattered; it continues to speak through recordings and performances that have led to his routine imitation, such that many of those who now "do" Stevie Wonder fail routinely to appreciate the true significance of a singer whose unique sound was formed by equally unique experiences.

The passage of time between Vogl and Wonder has seen more continuity and fewer changes than many might realise. Not quite two hundred years before Wonder sang "They won't go" for Michael Jackson, the *Taschenbuch fur Schauspieler und Schauspielfreunde auf das Jahr 1821* published an essay by Ignas Franz von Mosel,[57] a theorist known to Schubert (with whom he studied Handel's scores), in which Mosel petitioned as his ideal a singer

> who on the one hand embellishes a simple melody with taste, adding a turn or two to the original form to produce a pleasing variety but who, on the other hand, does not succumb to licentious fantasy or to a desire

---

[56] "Gone from painful cries; Away from saddened eyes; Along with him I'll bide; And they won't go when I go; Big men feeling small; Weak ones standing tall; I will watch them fall; 'Cause they won't go when I go; And I'll go where I've longed; To go so long Away from tears."

[57] Titled "*Ober die gewohnliche Anwendung der Worter: Methode und Kunst auf die Leistungen dramatischer Singer.*"

to excel by cheer mechanical ability; instead he relies on reason, sensibility and taste, which are the prerequisites for every dramatic singer. Frequently, a single suspension, a well-expressed mordent, an ornament of three, four, or at most six notes, every time new and gracious in its form, every time appropriate to the sense of the text, to the character of the song, the singer, and the accompaniment – these may genuinely embellish the melody, intensify its expression and increase the overall effect.[58]

---

[58] Dürr, Walther. "Schubert and Johann Michael Vogl: A Reappraisal." *19th Century Music* Vol. 3, No. 2 (Nov. 1979). pp.126–140; p.136.

Chapter Twenty

Epilogue: A View from the Pit

The history of the tenor is a tableaux of religious, cultural, and societal practices, the consistency of which explains the supply of great voices until late into the 20th century. The decline of the West's attachment to Christianity (and church attendance more generally) and the rise in alternatives to music and theatre escalated the declining supply of talented tenors – which is not to say that the modern absence of a Caruso or a Corelli can be attributed uniquely to the trans-national emergence of atheism and agnosticism because both singers were *extreme* outliers for their own times. But there were *many* superb tenors to compete with Caruso and Corelli throughout their careers, and it cannot be denied that this concentration of talent has diminished dramatically since the 1990s. Whither progress in the absence of continuity? Of course, progress has always been problematic conceptually, but when attached to the arts, and to painting, sculpture and music in particular, it is illusory. Was Van Gogh an improvement on Van Eyk? Is Gentileschi's painting of *Judith Slaying Holofernes*[1] "better than" Caravaggio's imagining of the same subject?[2] Does Gentileschi's canvas qualify as progress at all? Is Michelangelo's *Pieta*[3] inherently superior to Brâncuși's *Kiss*[4] or one of Giacometti's *L'Homme qui marche*[5] sculptures simply because it speaks more obviously to the expertise and flamboyance of its creator's technique? Can the narrative of Friedrich's *Wanderer*[6] survive comparison with Picasso's *Guernica*[7] – when both are as political as they are beautiful?

The impulse to confuse the principles of change and progress is well-documented. Voltaire's scientific rationalism and Kant's flight from barbarism towards enlightenment collided with education, which raised as primary the mutualised virtues of training and effort. A century later, Nietzsche promoted the miserabilist conviction that progress operates only as a "weakling's doctrine of optimism." These extremes of hope and despair continue to inform the research, policy and thinking in consequence of which enlightenment values can cause more division than unity because every enlightened society introduces those values to the few rather than the many. Of course, Voltaire, Kant and Nietzsche were not thinking of the art of singing when writing as they did – though each sang and played the keyboard with skill. Nietzsche even composed his own songs – for others to sing. They each conspired as devotees

---

1 1614 – 1620.
2 1598 – 1599; or 1602.
3 1499.
4 1909.
5 1961.
6 *Der Wanderer über dem Nebelmeer* [Wanderer above the Sea of Fog] (1818).
7 1937.

of opera to the presumption of progress within an open system – in which one singer was exposed necessarily to the influence of every other. That system worked only for as long as everyone was able to agree on what qualified as archetypical.

Progress began to fail on the altar of technique. How might the metrics for quality isolated in this book be applied to a singer like Paolo Conte?[8] Hearing Conte mumble and rasp his way through a song like "*Via Con Me*"[9] (with its magnificent refrain "Chips, chips, do, du, du, du, di bum ci bum bum") is a rare pleasure but it fails as a performance when compared to Rubini's presumed singing of "*Vieni fra questia braccia*" from Bellini's *I puritani*. Neither, of course, can the benchmarks applied to Rubini be adapted to the singing of Pavarotti or his "successor," Juan Diego Flórez.[10] Conte's active rejection of technical skill as a singer does not signal incompetence. He was merely different, a word that many who write about classical voices disavow because it admits anything by everyone. The legitimisation of difference equates to the abandonment of "better" and "best." Whether one can ever "be best" without first resolving what that means is a question only for those who can answer it. When, for example, Hans Bülow was presented with one of Nietzsche's compositions, he dismissed it as "the most undelightful and the most anti-musical draft on musical paper that I have faced in a long time." von Bülow was still able to read it. He did not assert that the music was unintelligible or incompetent in its writing; Nietzsche had plainly mastered the fundamentals of pitch, rhythm and harmony, and he was able consequently to speak through music, even if Bülow hated what Nietzsche had to say. He didn't question his capacity to say it. In doing so, the spectrum for analysis was reduced to a score-card heuristic that resolved in a gun fight between two equivalently capable slingers – one in which taste was the sole arbiter of quality.

It follows that everything is good, and nothing is truly bad, until a singer is required to spin a line by Rossini or seduce as Don José or cry out in the darkness for Leonora. Different can then become dissonant, or something worse. For admirers of singing, this hot-tin roof reached boiling point[11] thanks to the American online video-sharing platform YouTube. For more than two decades YouTube has allowed for the posting of hundreds of thousands of important recordings, while inviting coincidentally the opinions of its subscribers, many of whom have taken full advantage of their First Amendment rights to say whatever they like about singers and their performances. This democratisation of opinion has enabled people to become acquainted with just about every singer to have made a professional recording; many speak their minds with alarming candour; most of those with the ripest opinions hide behind pseudonyms, commonly with good reason. Few of those who comment on the art and the artist have been trained as musicians or as singers.

In May, 2020, one particularly angry poster published recordings of performances by the little-known Bulgarian-born *lirico-spinto* tenor, Nicola Tagger,[12] with the

---

8   6 January, 1937 –
9   'Away with me.'
10 13 January, 1973 –
11 4,716° F (2,602°C).
12 30 May, 1930 –

heading "So much better than the overrated Flórez!!! Nicola Tagger sings four bel canto arias. THIS IS OPERA!" The poster introduced the recordings by writing:

> Nicola Tagger sings four arias from *I Puritani, Il barbiere di Siviglia, La favorita and Zelmira (!)*, his voice is well-developed, so dark and resonant, not nasal and constricted, this is opera.

Tagger's career after his debut in Rome in 1956 was concentrated in Bulgaria, Israel and Italy; he built a repertoire of around eighty roles – many of them in forgotten works by Donizetti and Rossini; he was never out of work. To say that his singing as evidenced by these recordings was "so much better" than that of the Peruvian Flórez is as absurd as the reference to Flórez being "overrated." The same poster had it in for Flórez; in another video, a studio performance by Flórez of "*Ecco ridente*" from *Il barbiere* is compared to a live recording by Franco Bonisolli. The banner for this less-than-rigorous analysis was: "Flórez = NO VOICE, Bonisolli = OPERA!!! Bad VS Great Rossini singing." One of the many to comment on this comparison asked "Do you think florez [sic] ever realise [sic] he doesn't sound like a opera singer?" The poster replied unhelpfully: "No." Another wrote that he was no longer able to engage in exchanges concerning "good and bad singers" because "I got so burned and insulted that I had to give up." In the same chain a different commentator announced without prompting:

> In terms of Arnoldo from *Guglielmo Tell*, I can never go wrong with Giacomo Lauri-Volpi, Mario Filippeschi, Antonio Salvarezza, Gianni Raimondi, Gianni Iaia, Luigi Ottolini, Franco Bonisolli, Kurt Baum, Salvatore Fisichella, and Chris Merritt.

The poster's conclusion was that "Flórez is an undeveloped tenor. Bonisolli is a real tenor." No one contributing to these exchanges identified what qualified as a "real tenor" – other than that Tagger and Bonisolli were preferable because of their richer, darker voices. When analysing the recordings on which the poster relied, however, Bonisolli is unable to navigate Rossini's *fioriture* and Tagger oversings everything above the stave. Neither of them produces a true *legato*, none of which concerns the poster, for whom amplitude is apparently everything. These exchanges are calm and rational by the standards of YouTube's community of posters and subscribers, many of whom appear to be obsessed with criticising Flórez and many other high tenors because they are said to compare unfavourably with their predecessors, all of whom worked apparently during some halcyon period of perfection that occurred after the invention of recording.

Flórez's persecution is perplexing because he is one of the most gifted tenors of the 21st century and the finest lyric Italian-repertoire tenor since Pavarotti transitioned to *verismo* during the 1980s. As a *coloratura* tenor, he numbers among the most gifted since Rossini's lifetime, an assessment that would doubtless infuriate many using YouTube. Flórez made his formal debut in 1996[13] at the Rossini Opera Festival in

---

13 In the same year that Cecilia Bartoli made her debut at the Metropolitan Opera.

Pesaro, having been called upon to replace an indisposed Bruce Ford in Rossini's *Matilde di Shabran*. He was 23 years of age. Later the same year Flórez appeared for the first time at La Scala, as the Chevalier Danois in Gluck's *Armide*, and between 1997 and 2002 he appeared on every major world stage, including now legendary premieres at Covent Garden, the Wiener Staatsoper and the New York Met. His more than fifty studio and broadcast recordings of arias and complete operas by Rossini, Bellini and Donizetti cemented his reputation for unrivalled technical fluency and musical intuition. On this evidence, Flórez and his mezzo-soprano colleague Cecilia Bartoli can lay claim to having made a unique contribution to the recalibration of contemporary taste, insofar as they made popular that which had fallen from popularity.[14]

But for a few exceptions, Flórez and Bartoli did not partner as had Callas and di Stefano; instead, they danced around each other's huge celebrity, collaborating rarely in the studio. Their 2009 recording of Bellini's pastoral romance *La sonnambula* contains some miraculous artistry, with highlights including the duets "*Son geloso del zefiro*" and "*Prendi l'anel ti dono*," in which Flórez demonstrates the core values of his art – unfailing warmth of tone and ease of placement. His light, variegated *vibrato*, crisp articulation and endless, lung-busting *legati* are fused to an outstanding musical judgment that makes equal room for exquisite *piano* passagework, dynamic contrasts and impassioned vigour. His word-use is unfailingly clear though not as expressive as that of Pavarotti or Schipa; unlike his predecessors, however, Flórez's head and chest registers join without *passaggio*, enabling him to reach high C sharp 5s, D5s and E flat 5s with an undimmed sweetness of tone unique in modern times. High notes became his calling card because no other tenor has been able to make the tenorial stratosphere sound so effortless. Although the beauty of his voice would be enough in and of itself, Flórez's skills extend to a technically flawless *coloratura*, which equips him to fire off fusillades of ornaments, including trills, chromatic runs and aspirate-free articulations that outstrip many sopranos specialising in the same repertoire. Franco Bonisolli could not have dreamed of such refinement. Indeed, there was more art in one of Flórez's 2006 performances as Ernesto at the Zurich Opera than the entire of Bonisolli's *pazzo* career. Has anyone sung "*Povero Ernesto*" with such grace and sincerity? Certainly not Bonisolli or Tagger.

Flórez's eventual emergence from Pavarotti's shadow was achieved by his sensational appearances as Tonio in *La fille du régiment* – a role he helped return to the main stage after decades in abeyance. The joy and thrill of his skipping through "*Ah mes amis*"[15] was greatly enhanced by audiences' unshakeable confidence that Flórez was never going to miss any of those high Cs. Indeed, part of Flórez's problem as the pre-eminent *bel canto* tenor of his generation was the absence of that guillotine of ambition into which most of his predecessors and rivals placed their heads by necessity.

---

14   In tandem with the phenomenon that was Bartoli.
15   On 20 February, 2007, when performing the opening night of the season production of *La fille du régiment* at La Scala, Flórez defied the theatre's 74-year tradition of denying encores when he repeated "*Ah! mes amis*" in consequence of the audience's unquenchable clamour. Flórez repeated the encore at the Metropolitan on 21 April, 2008 – the first singer to do so since 1994.

Flórez's performances admit no danger; for all his thrill and artistry he makes easy what is known to be difficult.

The pyrotechnic repertoire has been well-served since 2000 by a stable of (mostly) North American tenors. The torch was re-lit initially during the 1990s by Rockwell Blake,[16] Chris Merritt,[17] Gregory Kunde,[18] John Osborn,[19] and Bruce Ford[20] – each capable of reaching past the clouds, albeit none as them as easily as Flórez. Some of these capable tenors were more capable than others. Blake, in particular, had a superb breathing technique and a diaphragm from which NASA might have launched the Shuttle; he suffered from a spreading *vibrato*, however, and was given too often to yelling. His range to an E5 was impressive but fleeting, after the fashion of a knife-throwing act. Merritt, Osborn and Ford have lighter voices still, and none of them was as musical or as characterful as their repertoire required; the high-note and *coloratura* repertoire compels exceptional phrasing. Bullets fired into the mouldings do not, in and of themselves, make a *bel canto* tenor, any more than does a talent for "high winds" acting make an actor.[21]

It is unusual to have so many tenors capable of navigating the *bel canto* repertoire consistently. Indeed, those for whom our modern times pale automatically when viewed with rose-tinted hind-sight cannot point to a time when so many were capable of so much. If there has been progress, and there has, it is in the consistency of an approach to the *bel canto* tenor repertoire that idealises technique as a means towards expressive ends – values which have most recently been adopted by Michael Spyres.[22] Spyres is particularly interesting because he is one of the few high tenors able to sing in French – a body that includes a number of French-born singers. He made his debut at La Scala, in *Il viaggio a Reims*, in 2009, in which year he triumphed also as Raoul in *Les Huguenots* at Bard SummerScape in New York. He is pre-eminent as Arnold in *Guillaume Tell* and Raoul in *Les Huguenots* (sensationally so in 2009), and splendid also in the title roles of *La Damnation de Faust* (in which role he first appeared at the Metropolitan) and *Les Contes d'Hoffmann*. More recent standout performances have included Vasco da Gama in *L'Africaine* at the Frankfurt Opera (2018) and Chapelou in *Le postillon de Lonjumeau* at the Opéra-Comique in 2019. His forays into darker Italian repertoire have not been so successful. His appearance in June, 2019, as Pollione in Zürich (in Robert Wilson's ludicrous staging of *Norma*) saw him interpolating high notes without musical or dramatic purpose, including an entirely pointless high C in "*Me protege, me difende.*" He would have achieved more by concerning himself with the fundamentals of phrasing and vocal character. The inclination among lyric tenors to transition to heavier-weighted repertoire is fatal, in most cases. Sadly, Spyres appears to have determined on this course also.

---

16   10 January, 1951 –
17   27 September, 1952 –
18   24 February, 1954 – . Bizarrely, Kunde has turned at the end of his career to the role of Otello.
19   16 May, 1972 –
20   15 August, 1956 –
21   Cognoscenti will appreciate the priceless value of the lesson taught so brilliantly by Matt Berry as Steven Toast, and Terry Mynott as Axel Jacklin, in season two, episode four of *Toast of London* (Channel 4 (UK), 2014).
22   1980 –

One of those to get it right, and consistently, is Lawrence Brownlee,[23] the only other high lyric tenor with the technique and the tone to rival Flórez. His voice is one of the most beautiful on the modern stage, and more than sufficient to warrant admission to the tenorial hall of fame. That he is an African-American makes his achievement all the more enjoyable because opera has struggled for many years, as it will for many more to come, to engage with black communities across the West. The experiences and achievements of Marian Anderson, Leontyne Price, Grace Bumbry, Jessye Norman and Kathleen Battle were exceptional and categorically singular, insofar as they were all sopranos. The depressing absence of black male classical voices – and particularly tenors – capable of meeting the "blind" expectations of music directors and producers is an obstacle that must be overcome. Even now, the attainments of Paul Robeson, Willard White and Vinson Cole[24] are perceived to be singular (though they are not), and Brownlee's status as "the" black tenor of the 2020s is as unpalatable as Halle Berry's still-anomalous recognition by the Oscars in 2001.[25]

The tone of Brownlee's tenor is honeyed and rounded, with little strain and a fine *squillo* ping that promises to darken with time, assuming he is able to exercise patience. During his run in Paris at the Opéra as Ramiro in *Cenerentola* in 2018/19, his performances brought the audience to its feet. The highlight for most was Brownlee's riotous vanquishing of "*Si, ritrovarla io giuro,*" which he delivered with exceptional vibrancy, pathos and power. Every note sounded within its phrase as written, with a palette of colour and expression that would have staggered audiences during the early 20th century. A clip from the production, published subsequently on YouTube, provoked some generous comments. Not everyone agreed, of course; one viewer complained:

> All the vowels are in some language other than Italian and there's also that *caprino*. Pretty provincial/chorister singing. Also nasal, horrible.

The term "*caprino*" was not intended as a compliment. It means "little goat," and was employed to attack Brownlee's *vibrato*, which is by no means overly fast or nervous. In fact, it is one of the most natural of any modern tenor – striking for its expressive force and those magical shifts in emphasis that enable him to vary the sound and the form through which he characterises both the words and the music. His *cantabile* suffers from none of those potentially ugly and intrusive elements formed by an overreliance on decoration, and the discipline with which he creates shade and shape is a model of its type and kind. Brownlee is a musical and gifted artist, and any century would have pushed him to the footlights. Which, again, raises the spectre of progress, and how the spiteful and unwarranted comments of opera trolls survive the test, even, of comparisons with singers from earlier times on record. But whether Brownlee is as good as any of the best of his 20th century predecessors matters less than whether he is as good as Giacomo Guglielmi, the first Don Ramiro.

---

23 1972 –
24 21 November, 1950.
25 She won the Oscar for Best Actress in a Leading Role for her performance in *Monster's Ball*.

It's impossible to know, of course, but it's reasonable to analyse the requirements of the role in its post-Duprez fullness. In this context, one cannot imagine it being done much better.

We are living, in short, through a golden age of lyric Italo-French repertoire tenors, in which the likes of Javier Camarena[26] can *almost* be considered second rank. Fifty years earlier, Luigi Alva was the first rank. Is Camarena a finer Rossinian tenor than Luigi Alva? Very probably – and yet he makes no records and enjoys little celebrity outside his native Mexico. That fact alone is shocking when considering how it was once considered proportionate and responsible to cast Bonisolli as Almaviva. Of course, none of these lyric voices is capable of singing *verismo,* and it is across the *spinto* and dramatic repertoire that the best of all possible worlds has fallen to profit-less sacrifice. In that sense, what Nietzsche considered necessary for the magnitude of progress has failed to crystallise either in hope or fruition, so that there is almost no one on the world stage to stand in the shoes left empty in the late 1990s by Domingo.

The burden of expectation fell initially on the uneven shoulders of Carl Tanner,[27] Marcello Giordani[28] and Johann Botha.[29] The latter two died young, having given too much time to repertoire for which neither of them was suited. Giordani was a lyric tenor who ended up singing Calàf at the Metropolitan; Botha was perennially miscast. Barely equipped to sing Cassio, far less Otello, he was as fat as his voice was thin, and incapable of persuading on stage, being that with every step he threatened to pass through it. Far more compelling as an actor, and a very fine singer also, was the Polish-born Piotr Beczała.[30] He was fortunate to study with Sena Jurinac, one of the finest sopranos of the post-war generation, and herself a student of Anna Bahr-Mildenburg. Jurinac taught Beczała to conserve his resources and to reconcile the competing needs of line and language.

After ten years as something of a journeyman, Beczała's career blossomed after 2004, with successes as the Italian Tenor, Faust and the Duke at Covent Garden, Lensky in San Francisco, and the Duke at La Scala. *Rigoletto* was the opera in which he made his Metropolitan debut on 19 December, 2006. Like so many before him, he sang too often, and with ever increasing force. By 2013 his voice was tiring early, and the limpid, effortless grace with which he had once seduced audiences began to yield to strain and a widening *vibrato*. The *loggionisti* at La Scala ripped into him during the opening night of the 2013/14 season, when he struggled audibly as Alfredo – which provoked him to announce that he would thereafter blacklist the theatre. Milan learned to cope with its loss. Beczała remains popular at the Metropolitan, where he has achieved success as Edgardo (2009), Des Grieux (2012), the Duke (2013), Lensky (2013), The Prince in *Rusalka* (2014), Vaudémont in *Iolanta* (2015), Rodolfo in *Luisa Miller* (2018), and Maurizio in *Adriana Lecouvreur* (2019). The last of these roles is the heaviest to which he has turned on stage, although his 2020

---

26 March 26, 1976.
27 1962 –
28 25 January, 1963 – 5 October, 2019.
29 19 August, 1965 – 8 September, 2016.
30 28 December, 1966 –

album *Verismo* (released mid-pandemic) suggests he is planning to end his career singing dramatic repertoire. The performances as they have been recorded further suggest that this is as much a folly for Beczała as it was for every other essentially lyric tenor who tripped when turning to the dark side. His singing of "*Amor ti vieta,*" from Giordano's *Fedora*, by way of example, is grimly uneasy, with a notable wobble, forced amplitude and little feel for dramatic architecture. The elegance of form and articulation that defined his work a decade previously is gone, and whatever was taught him by Jurinac has been forgotten. The album captures just another anonymous tenor over-singing his heart out.

The predictability of Beczała's choices has not been observed by younger singers like Massimo Giordano[31] and Vittorio Grigolo[32], both of whom have attempted *spinto* without success. The shadows thrown by Beczała and Corelli in their gravitational interaction have fallen over the young British-Italian Freddie De Tommaso[33], a light-lyric tenor with ambitions to sing heavier repertoire. The voice is pretty enough, but his technique is far from secure, which fact did not dissuade Decca from signing him as a declared "vocal phenomenon" in 2021. His first album, *Passione*, is an interesting collection of Italian songs with arrangements of wildly varying quality. De Tommaso was said by Decca to be "arguably the most exciting lyrico spinto tenor to emerge in over a decade," an argument they would have struggled to evidence. Decca was comfortable reporting that *Passione*, paid "homage to [de Tommaso's] great hero Franco Corelli, born a century ago in Ancona, Italy on 8th April 1921".[34] The homage to Corelli was misplaced because the singers' voices are incomparable, and Corelli did not perform most of the repertoire chosen for the album. Even so, it is clear from the forced effects, unnaturally darkened tone and general sense of effort that De Tommaso has his eyes on the *spinto* repertoire, to which he was attached by Decca's PR department. On current evidence, this would be a mistake – particularly when noting his youth and musicianship. He is artful – as the jury at the 2018 Francisco Viñas International Singing Competition recognised – but his repertoire should be limited to the scale of his debut role at Covent Garden in December, 2019 (Cassio). The talent is obvious, but so is his ambition – and this threatens to disable a voice and a musical intellect that are worth protecting.

Similarly gifted, with a naturally impressive instrument, is the handsome, tall and athletic Chilean-born American Jonathan Tetelman. His powerful, essentially lyrical voice is well-suited to the *spinto* repertoire, but he appears determined to yell himself into silence before the age of 35. He is a potential star, for certain, but since he is given routinely to shouting, he threatens to burn brightly and briefly. Tetelman's successes in Europe as Pinkerton, Rodolfo and Cavaradossi have been warranted, and he has an inarguable dramatic sensibility, but someone needs to intervene before he treads the same, sorry path as those who failed to marshal their resources and bide their time as did their ancestors. Tetelman has to develop *a* voice, as well as *his* voice, so that

---

31 19 February, 1971 –
32 19 February, 1977 –
33 20 January, 1993 –
34 Noting that fact, Decca released the album on 9 April (a Tuesday).

his character and personality can feed the development of those identities he is being asked to play on stage. His singing currently has little style, such that he would not be recognisable to most when heard blind – a characteristic of two another American *spinto* tenors, Bryan Hymel[35] and Michael Fabiano.[36] Both have fine techniques, with excellent placement, some power and unusual amounts of *squillo*. They have made good choices, and – unlike the much younger Franco Farina,[37] whose voice was ruined by too many Calàfs before his 40th birthday – both have adhered to repertoire for which they are well-suited. Fabiano's turn as Poliuto for Glyndebourne in 2015 was wildly impressive, even if he too was given to barking what might otherwise have been phrased. His covered tone in head voice is too often vinegar-bright. When he sings at 60%, however, he reveals a voice that is more beautiful than he allows. That said, his closing C5 at the end of Poliuto's Act Two scena, "*Sfolgoro divino raggio*," was extraordinarily thrilling, and should have provoked more than the polite applause it received from the picnic-scoffing audience.[38]

Each of these singers suffers to varying degrees from the same ineluctable problem – that the root of vocal personality is located in the phrasing of the words, rather than tone in isolation. Orchestras have, of course, become much louder over time, and that has had an inevitable effect; the *spinto* and dramatic repertoire is not inherently *anti*-lyrical, however. Instead it requires an admixture of qualities that stand collectively on a platform of style *and* substance. On the contemporary stage, two Italo-French tenors have achieved this balance, with varying degrees of popularity and success: Joseph Calleja[39] and Jonas Kaufmann.[40]

Calleja was born in Malta and made his stage debut as Macduff at the age of 18. He should in consequence have been done before the age of 25. He survived, however, to develop one of the most elegant, sweet-sounding *lirico-spinto* tenors of the new century. His artistry has been embraced globally, thanks to a voice of caramel-warmth and a thick slice of personal charm that makes him ideal for light romantic repertoire such as his signature role, Rodolfo in *La bohème*.

Rodolfo was created in 1896 by Evan Gorga[41] – just two years after his first appearance as Ernani (when called on to replace an indisposed Francesco Tamagno). Gorga's repertoire in 1895 included Wilhelm Meister in Thomas' *Mignon*, des Grieux in Manon and the title role of *L'amico Fritz*. He was admired by Mascagni and Verdi (who heard him in *I Lombardi alla prima crociata* at the Teatro Costanzi in Rome in September, 1895). A year after his triumph in *La bohème*, Gorga was hailed for performances at La Fenice of Leoncavallo's *La bohème*. He remained unavoidably associated with Puccini's opera, however, and this dominated his schedule for the following two years. In January, 1899, Gorga sang Rodolfo at Verona; despite receiving ecstatic reviews, he never sang on stage again. He was retired at the age of 34.

---

35 8 August, 1979 –
36 8 May, 1984 –
37 16 September, 1986 –
38 More than one of those who attended the run was reminded of Corelli's reception at Covent Garden as Cavadossi in 1958, which is not to compare the singers, but rather the audiences.
39 22 January, 1978 –
40 10 July, 1969 –
41 6 February, 1865 – 5 December, 1957.

Frustratingly, despite living for more than nine decades, and then through the age of the gramophone and into that of the LP, he made no recordings and instead devoted his life to collecting antiques and musical instruments. Gorga's career was short and, while no-one can say for certain why he walked away at the height of his career it has been suggested that he was bored, and feared season after season of repetition. This seems unlikely, in isolation, when noting his popularity and the ubiquity of new work at the time. It is equally possible that his voice began to fail him – even though his final performance was hailed as exceptional. More probably he yielded to a combination of both influences – in which respect Gorga's experience has much to teach those standing in his shoes. Joseph Calleja is, in this respect, a case in point.

Calleja's repertoire on stage hinges on a small number of roles, which he rotates carefully, including Faust, Hoffmann, Alfredo, Adorno in *Simon Boccanegra*, Roberto in *Maria Stuarda*, Riccardo in *Un ballo in maschera* and Ruggero in *La rondine*. During the season 2018/19, he sang Rodolfo in *Luisa Miller* in Hamburg; Cavaradossi at the Metropolitan and the Festival International d'Art Lyrique d'Aix-en-Provence; Pollione and Don José in Munich; Edgardo and Don José at the Deutsche Oper in Berlin; and the Duke in Vienna. Throughout this seam of stage work Calleja has performed a large number of concerts, many of them amplified, and he has made a good number of recordings also – most of them recitals. It is a feature of the record industry as it has devolved since 2000 that Calleja has made almost no complete opera recordings;[42] the few that have been released feature him in every case in small print: *Maria Stuarda* (2013); *I Capuleti e i Montecchi* (2009); and *Simon Boccanegra* (2013). For arguably the most gifted *lirico-spinto* tenor of his generation, this is more than troubling. Calleja's recitals on record have included generic collections (such as *Verdi*) and cynical cross-over albums like *Be My Love* (his *Tribute to Maria Lanza*) and the implausible *Magic of Mantovani* – which anticipated the album's vanishing soon after its first appearance. Of course, Calleja's judgment and intelligence have prevented him from making the sort of catastrophic mistakes for which Vincenzo La Scola, for example, became celebrated. La Scola's performance as Radamès for Nikolaus Harnoncourt's predictably atrocious production of *Aida* typifies the sort of lunatic casting decisions for which the major labels became infamous at the beginning of the 21st century. Calleja knows his limits as a tenor in his early forties, and he has quite properly remained true to the parameters of a voice that is more beautiful than it is dramatic. Just because he can sing Manrico – with a "*pira*" in key, and not *come è scritto* – should not warrant his doing so because he lacks that resonant ping that would justify taking on such an infamously stentorian role. His record company, Decca, has opted regardless to record nothing of value either for sale or for posterity, which is a disaster for the finest tenor specialising in his repertoire since the Big Three.

As anyone who has heard him live will attest, Calleja's art is his voice, which he uses with affecting elegance. He looks set to enjoy a long and memorable career, even if it appears there will be little by which to remember it in the decades to come. What seems certain is that he will never appear as Otello, Andrea Chénier or Dick Johnson.

---

42   This does not account for DVD releases of live performances, namely *Mefistofele*, *Macbeth*, *La traviata* and *Simon Boccanegra*.

Part of his talent is knowing that he's not meant to. Which leaves the question: who is?

During the 1960s and 1970s there was a surfeit of big voices capable of performing Otello as well as Siegfried. In addition to Vickers *et al*, there were less well known, albeit talented tenors like Charles Craig,[43] John Mitchinson,[44] and Alberto Remedios[45] – each of whom carved out excellent careers as dramatic tenors spanning Italian, French and German repertoire. The Russian and former Eastern Bloc school threw large voices into the ring also. In the wake of Vladimir Atlantov and Galouzine, the Latvian Aleksandrs Antonenko[46] has rattled the chandeliers, albeit rarely in service to musical art. His repertory is dominated by standard Russian fair, memorably so at the Metropolitan, but he has nonetheless become the go-to tenor for middle-weight French and Italian roles spanning Des Grieux, Cavaradossi, Dick Johnson and, bizarrely, Don José. He sings this repertoire with power, but little or no style. The worrying absence of Italian or even Italianate dramatic tenors since 2000 has left certain corners of the repertoire unperformable, other than in the broken teeth of compromise. *Verismo* has been difficult to cast, with works like *Andrea Chénier* and *La fanciulla del West* being staged only rarely and often unhappily. At Covent Garden, for example, *Chénier* was staged for Carreras in 1984, and then shelved for 30 years until Antonio Pappano conducted a new production in 2015 by David McVicar. The star of that show was Jonas Kaufmann, the über tenor of the 21st century – and, for many, the true heir to the first Chénier, Giuseppe Borgatti. Like his predecessor, Kaufmann is as popular in Italian as German music, with a voice that qualifies at its best as one of the most impressive to be recorded. That might be enough, in and of itself; for many it is. Kaufmann's glorious, sonorous and deep-toned tenor is a modern phenomenon that places him among the pantheon of dramatic voices. Stylistically, however, Kaufmann is a German tenor who happens to sing Italian and French repertoire also. It is in this tension – between voice and repertoire – that Kaufmann's career is at its most revealing.

In the United States and across Europe, it is now routine for the politics of cultural appropriation to determine who may do what, and with whom, on stage and screen. The binary simplicity of *Otello* no longer tolerating "blackface" has admitted *finally* the liberation of a woman playing "the Moor" for Shakespeare, but not for Verdi of course. These are difficult waters to navigate. Female parts were played by male actors when Shakespeare was alive. Male parts were played by men or boys. On 8 December, 1660, Anne Marshall appeared at the Vere Street Theatre to perform Desdemona in a production of *Othello*; 60 years later, Charlotte Charke[47] played numerous male characters, including Hamlet, since which time Sarah Bernhardt made the role her own in 1899, as she did everything to which she turned her Leviathan

---

43   3 December, 1919 – 23 January, 1997.
44   31 March, 1932 –
45   February 1935 – 11 June, 2016.
46   19 February 1939 –
47   née Cibber, also Charlotte Secheverell, aka Charles Brown.

talent. Bernhardt's performances in Paris and London were divisive, of course, with one London critic opining in disgust:

> A woman is positively no more capable of beating out the music of Hamlet than is a man of expressing the plaintive and half-accomplished surrender of Ophelia.[48]

Mozart invested in "breeches" roles long before Bernhardt became the first woman to play Hamlet on film in 1900, and Richard Strauss' Octavian seduced in 1911 as one of the greatest "trouser" roles in staged drama. Gender fluidity after 1911 became politically and culturally relevant when Ellen Terry gave her talent to the "Shakespeare Hut," in satisfaction of a debt owed to the playwright "for his vindication of women in [his] fearless, high-spirited, resolute and intelligent heroines." Terry played the cross-dressing Portia of *The Merchant of Venice* while younger actresses performed scenes from *Henry V*. The Danish star Asta Nielsen played Hamlet as a woman raised as a boy for a silent film in Germany in 1920, which laid the foundations for gender as a metric, so that critics in 1979 focussed on the quality of Frances de la Tour's performance as Hamlet rather than her sex. Ruth Mitchell played *Hamlet* in an all-female production at the Warehouse in Croydon in 1992, as did Angela Winkler at the Edinburgh Festival in 2000, and Abke Haring at the Toneelgroep Amsterdam in 2014. Maxine Peake was revered universally as the Dane at the Royal Exchange Manchester in 2014; Michelle Terry was less successful in her first season as artistic director of Shakespeare's Globe in 2018. Ruth Negga was a triumph for Yaël Farber at the Dublin Theatre Festival in 2018, while Tessa Parr was the most feminine of Hamlets for Amy Leach at Leeds Playhouse the following year. For a 2018 production of *Troilus and Cressida* the roles of Thersites, Agamemnon, Ulysses, Aeneas and Calchas were all played by women. Phyllida Lloyd directed an all-female production of *Julius Caesar* at the Donmar Warehouse in 2012 in which Frances Barber took the title role and Cush Jumbo played Mark Antony opposite Harriet Walter's Brutus.

In Shakespeare's play, Othello demands:

> "Villain, be sure thou prove my love a whore;
> Be sure of it. Give me the ocular proof,
> Or, by the worth of mine eternal soul
> Thou hadst been better have been born a dog
> Than answer my waked wrath!"[49]

Neither Verdi nor Boito made a bid for "auditory proof" of the authenticity of the tenor performing the title role, a construction of evolving practice that shifted the burden onto the vocal character of the tenor playing the role. This feature of the currency of performance is not easily dismissed for a developing praxis in which a character who is gay or Jewish can now be played only by an actor who is gay or

---

48 The Athenaeum, 17 June, 1899.
49 III.iii.

Jewish. It is quite properly unacceptable for a tenor to appear in "blackface," although it *is* appropriate for an Anglo-Indian to play the prescriptively Caucasian David Copperfield – as Dev Patel did for Armando Iannucci's film *The Personal History of David Copperfield* in 2019. The need for a role to be performed in alignment with its performer's cultural and racial legitimacy fosters equivalent expectations among tenors, where a German singer might well be capable of performing a role in (and as an) Italian while adhering to none of the cultural idiosyncrasies by which his role and its articulation are defined. Such things did not matter until recently, so that tenors were able to sing Otello with corked faces and in any language without the slightest regard for the musical and poetical features of the role as it was written and designed by Verdi and Boito. That such things might not have mattered to the composer and his publishers is palpably irrelevant; they matter politically and culturally unless politics and culture are themselves dispensable.

Dietrich Fischer-Dieskau sang Italian repertoire as well as German; few considered this a good idea – including, for the most part, Dietrich Fischer-Dieskau. Domingo sang Rossini, which even he must have conceded was an imperfect fit. Before cultural appropriation became an issue it was routine for Italian opera to be sung in German in German-speaking territories, and for everything in France to be performed in French. Every other country with a native tongue performed opera in that language until relatively late into the 20th century. The change in tone, metre, weight, articulation and emphasis for music when translated – into any language – makes a vast difference to a composition, as anyone who has attended English National Opera will know. The virtue of doing so is challenged routinely by the imperfection of diction and word use, across every type and *fach* of voice. ENO even admits to it, publishing on its website that:

> Here at ENO we believe opera exists for everyone, so don't worry if you don't know all the words. In our productions we project English surtitles (not to be confused with subtitles, although they are more or less the same thing) above the stage so that your eyes can pick up what your ears might have missed.

Any reader comfortable with more than one language will know how imperfectly they adapt to translation, and how uneasy it can make the performance of a score that was designed specifically around its poetry. Wagner's *stabreim* does not translate, even if the words do; *Pelléas et Mélisande* cannot properly be performed other than in French. The effect of Maeterlinck's verse on Debussy survives both men because of the manner in which the composer formed his music around the peculiarities of the poet's words; the opera was a construction of the phonetic and syntactical properties of the French language as Debussy and Maeterlinck heard, spoke and imagined it. If cultural appropriation is the improper adoption of the customs, practices and ideas of one people or society by members of another (whether or not the one doing the appropriating is more dominant than the other) then the singing of music in French by a tenor trained in (and as) a German has to qualify as inappropriate. If not, then the entire value and virtue of a country's national-cultural identity as it is expressed in matters of performance falls either to irrelevance or imitation.

These issues preoccupy the many and various guardians of national language and cultural tradition as they operate to determine and inform identity. The *Académie française*, for example, defines its mission as the "*Défense de la langue française*". It is confident of its purpose when asserting:

> *Du haut Moyen Âge au début du xviiesiècle, le français passe lentement de l'état de langue du vulgaire (ou vernaculaire) à celui de langue égale en dignité au latin. Cette maturation est jalonnée de repères, dont deux méritent d'être cités: 842, date du Serment de Strasbourg, premier texte écrit en français; 1539, date de l'édit de Villers-Cotterêts, par lequel François Ier fait du français la langue administrative et judiciaire commune à l'ensemble du royaume, en remplacement du latin. Au début du XVIIe siècle, cette langue est encore en pleine évolution, très fluctuante sur certains points : verbes passant d'une conjugaison à une autre (recouvrer/recouvrir), genre des mots non fixé, morphologie flottante (*hirondelle, arondelle *ou* erondelle*), prononciation variable. Si le XVIe siècle s'accommodait de ces variantes et flottements, la tendance au XVIIe siècle est à l'unification dans un langage « moyen », qui soit compréhensible par tous les Français et par tous les Européens qui adoptent de plus en plus souvent le français comme langue commune. Ce dessein, exprimé par le poète Malherbe, est repris par de nombreux grammairiens et gens de lettres (Vaugelas), qui se rencontrent pour œuvrer en ce sens.*[50]

There are numerous other organisations across Europe, including Germany's *Gesellschaft für deutsche Sprache*, the *Language Council of Sweden*; and Italy's *Società Dante Alighieri*,[51] founded in 1889 by the poet Giosuè Carducci, the ambition of which is to

> preserve and spread the Italian language and culture throughout the world, rekindling the spiritual connection of compatriots abroad with their homeland, and instilling in foreigners love and passion for Italian culture.

---

50 'From the early Middle Ages to the beginning of the seventeenth century, French passed slowly from the status of a vulgar (or vernacular) language to that of a language equal in dignity to Latin. This maturation is marked by landmarks, two of which deserve to be mentioned: 842, the date of the Strasbourg Oath, the first text written in French; and 1539; the date of the Edict of Villers-Cotterêts, by which Francis I made French the administrative and judicial language common to the kingdom, replacing Latin. At the beginning of the 17th century, this language was still evolving, fluctuating on certain points: verbs passing from one conjugation to another (to recover/to cover), the gender of words, floating morphologies (*hirondelle, arondelle or erondelle*) and variable pronunciation. If the 16th century accommodated itself to these variations and uncertainties then the tendency during the 17th century was towards the unification of an "common" language, comprehensible to all French people, and by all Europeans who increasingly use the language. French as a universal language. This design, expressed by the poet [François de] Malherbe, has been adopted by many grammarians and men of letters ([Claude Favre de] Vaugelas), who continue to meet to work towards this ambition.'

51 Intriguingly, the Dante Society is alone among the three highlighted here to provide its website with an English translation.

Epilogue: A View from the Pit

Linguistic independence and tradition are acutely significant when languages are recognisably in a state of constant flux. What that means is the subject of equally enduring debate and research. In November, 2019, Vladimir Putin proposed that Wikipedia be banned in consequence of its "littering" of the Russian language with foreign words and influences. A spokesman for the President observed that:

> The level of command of the mother tongue precisely reflects the level of education and intellectual development of any society.

Everyone from Beethoven to Balthus has said something similar, and it remains a pressing issue. Most of the discourse concerning interculturality and language fails to appreciate the extent to which performance vernaculars exercise their own *imprimaturs*, no less than do the aesthetics cultivated by the period performance movement. If, for example, an historically informed interpretation of a work by Bach holds more value because it is played on gut strings, with wooden flutes and narrow-bore brass – all of it without *vibrato* and *portamento* – then why does the performance of an opera by Gounod not compel at least an equivalent recognition of the virtues and values of French vocal style as it can be heard on cylinders and '78s, without the need for metatextual reconstruction? An "authentic" performance of a work from before 1800 will adopt routinely crisp rhythms, stringent tone and unsentimental articulation as evidence of a vernacular unsullied by romanticism. What of music from the late 19th and early 20th centuries? Does the performance of music composed for the flute by Tomasi, Poulenc and Ibert gain from imitations of the *vibrato* and phrasing employed by the flautists Philippe Gaubert, Adolphe Hennebains, Paul Taffanel and Marcel Moyse? We can hear the string players Joseph Joachim, Arnold Rosé and the Flonzaley Quartet on record, and yet no one – literally no one – now plays their repertoire in an equivalent style.

The quest for dialectical personality is an inevitable function of exhaustion. There is now so much music available that the curious and the enthusiastic can hear hundreds, and in many cases thousands, of performances of the same work with the click of a mouse. The expanding surfeit of opera houses in which modern tenors compete for roles and opportunities are added to almost annually by concert halls, radio stations, on-line posters, bloggers and, even, record companies. Where once a "new" tenor had to be heard in the flesh to warrant a recommendation to a conductor or an intendant, decisions are now made almost automatically by reference to recordings. Differences have to be overt when there is *very* little to distinguish one singer from another.

Outside the opera house, variance is a more obvious virtue. A Moldovan gypsy band like *Fanfare Vagabontu*, or a Tuvan throat singer performing *Khoomei* in Mongolia, can be appreciated for their distinguishing cultural, musical and linguistic characteristics, while similarly idiosyncratic features of a performance of "*Salut demeure chaste et pure*" from *Faust* are wilfully and blithely de-acculturated by every modern singer for whom the French tradition is ignored or deemed irrelevant. The isolation of "world music" from that of western Europe warrants no comment; the inclination to dissipate those features by which the performing traditions of the primary operatic nations were once differentiated is to strip them of a valuable palette of colour and identity. Neither Corelli nor Bergonzi sang well in French – if "well" is to qualify as something more than a formulation of *le ton pour le ton*. For the same reason, few would consider Russian opera to be authentic when performed in Paris by non-Russian speakers unused to the unique metrical and phonetic qualities of the Russian language.

Much of this will fall to interrogations of taste and prejudice; it is inarguable, regardless, that performances of operas written in Italian, French, German, Czech, Hungarian, Russian *etc.* were formed of nativist traditions and idiosyncrasies that manifested themselves in the sound of instruments, orchestras and voices, and in the manner and style of performance – all of which has largely disappeared. These fingerprints were once an unblinking preoccupation of most voice and instrument teachers regionally. They are not, as a rule, taught any more.

Despite the global cultural rush back to Babel, these questions are not without consequence for the preservation of national performing styles where pitch and instrumentation have become standardised. For the tenor voice, there are profound differences between Italian, French, German, Spanish and Slavic languages in their pronunciation and musical complexions – but the majority now sing everything in almost precisely the same amorphic way. Which gets us back to Jonas Kaufmann, the "World's Greatest Tenor."

In 1995, having graduated from the Hochschule für Musik und Theater München, Kaufmann suffered a vocal "crisis" born of physical and psychological tension. He was helped by the American baritone Michael Rhodes to relax, and soon after began to make a name for himself as a Baroque and Classical tenor, albeit an unusually well-upholstered one. In 2001/2002 he made his first recordings (on CD and DVD), as Franz in *Der Vampyr*, as Telemaco in Monteverdi's *Il ritorno d'Ulisse in patria,* and as Lindoro in Paisiello's *Nina* (with Cecilia Bartoli). Between 2004 and 2006 he recorded his first *Fidelio, La clemenza di Tito, Carmen,* Schubert's *Fierrabras* and a collection of Strauss *lieder*. In 2004 he scored a widely reported theatrical success as Ruggero in *La Rondine* at Covent Garden; two years later he created a sensation as Don José. After adding Alfredo to his repertoire (in which role he made his Metropolitan debut) it was clear that Kaufmann's days as Belmonte and Ferrando were behind him. He added Cavaradossi, Don Carlo and Maurizio to his schedule, and from 2010 it was obvious that he had re-invented himself as a *spinto*-dramatic tenor of unrivalled power and resonance. After performing *Lohengrin* at the Bayerischen Staatsoper, he was booked to open the Bayreuther Festspiele in 2010 – in which year he also appeared in *Werther* at the Opéra Bastille in Paris. In 2011 he appeared at the Metropolitan as Siegmund and Faust. Two years later he made his debut as Parsifal, again in New York. Since 2010, Kaufmann has been the most prolific male opera singer on DVD and CD, appearing in a huge number of recordings, spanning complete operas, song recitals (notably *Winterreise*), galas and concert work (including Mahler's *Das Liede von der Erde*). He has presented a rare commercial advantage, well taken by his label, Sony, who is to be commended for having captured the best of the tenor in his youth as well as his maturity.

It is telling that Kaufmann has appeared on more DVDs of complete operas than studio recordings. He is a fine actor, of striking physical intensity, whose beauty and masculinity have added considerably to his appeal as a performer. Listening to his work on record between 2006 (when he produced one of the *very* finest collections of Strauss songs) and 2019 (prior to his studio recording of the title role of *Otello*), Kaufmann bestraddled the world as very possibly the finest German *lyrischer-dramatischer-heldentenor*[52] since at least 1900. To say that he represented "progress" for those with an ear for recordings would suggest that Kaufmann emerged from the same cultural tradition that produced the generations of great German tenors identified in previous chapters. To argue against that assertion when applied to his work in the theatre would necessitate the longest of living memories. Whether the trolls online like it or not (and there are *many* who appear determined not to) Kaufmann is an outlier whose talent is as rare as the rainbow eucalyptus. His voice is uncommonly rich and firm, defined as it is by a darkly resonant tone and a sophisticated eloquence that marginalises even the best of his forebears. James King was thrilling and a superb artist, but for all his power and resonance he lacked Kaufmann's mellifluence. Siegfried Jerusalem was barely precedented, and yet Kaufmann's dynamic and expressive range is preternatural even among a fantasy league of dramatic tenors. Melchior was a miracle also, but his diction and attention to the score pale beside Kaufmann's often transcendental application of *lieder*-like sensibilities to music that is commonly roared, barked or shrieked.

Over hundreds of performances as Florestan, the Tenor/Bacchus and, more recently, Parsifal and Siegmund, Kaufmann has produced performances that can have been imagined only by those reaching for ideals of sound and style. Anyone who heard him as Parsifal in New York, or his concert performance of the Second Act of *Tristan und Isolde* in Boston, will attest that there is no one alive today who has heard this music more completely fulfilled by another tenor. Kaufmann's capacity to breathe the duet, without rendering it breathless was matched by a blazing richness of tone that allowed him actually to collaborate with Andris Nelsons and the Boston Symphony. It was nothing short of a revelation.

If Kaufmann's diction and dynamic-tonal range are unique on the modern stage, they are also rare historically. His capacity when singing *lieder* and opera are otherworldly, and serve commonly to free the music to a point where technique and tone are transcended by expression. In this respect, Kaufmann is analogous to the two finest poetic-baritones of the post-war generation: Tito Gobbi and Fischer-Dieskau. Kaufmann might easily have trained (and may yet retrain) as a baritone. His voice has an equivalent depth and profundity; like Gobbi and Fischer-Dieskau, and unlike most other "German" dramatic tenors, he is so gifted technically that he is able to focus on the articulation and sounding of *every* syllable – a facility that produces sensational rewards in German repertoire where the poetry warrants the attention.

Of course, Kaufmann also sings a great deal of repertoire in French and Italian, and it is here that his talents are emblematic as well as problematic. Kaufmann made his name singing Italian and, to a lesser extent, French repertoire. He has the technical and vocal resources to perform just about anything, having fostered a range that encompasses an easy and splendid high C,[53] but his voice is antithetical in matters

---

52 Clearly, there is no such *fach*, but for Kaufmann's adoption of it.
53 The power of Kaufmann's extension is much evidenced. Arguably the most thrilling example on record is the closing of "*Das Lied vom Leben des Schrenk*" ['The Life-Song of Shrenk'] from *Die große*

of style to Italian repertoire, for which he is unsuited. His appearance as Andrea Chénier in London was a case in point. McVicar's beautifully costumed production[54] benefitted from having a singer in the title role who was able to fill the poet's britches and persuade as Giordano's romantic hero; it was unusual also to have access to a tenor capable of producing the tone and facility necessary to give voice to the high-octane music. Indeed, his performances were lean and irrepressibly tasteful – remarkable for the new-found attention to the score as it was written. And yet, with little of that destabilising *rubato* for which *verismo* is uniquely well-suited, and with a palette of unwritten dynamic shadings that cannot have occurred to (and were certainly not annotated by) Giordano, the role was robbed of much of its necessarily hysterical power. Particularly during the *parlando* of "*Un di*" he stripped the writing of its expressive intensity because he sang it as a German artist, raised in German traditions, with German instincts. The absence of Latin frenzy and phrasing failed to open that sanguinous emotional vein for which Kaufmann's "covered" voice was an imperfect fit. The absence of *squillo* – typical of the voice for which the role (and all *verismo*) was designed[55] – and the surfeit of discretion denuded *Chénier* of that curtain-tearing intensity from which it gains its greatest traction.

The same could have been said of Kaufmann's Cavaradossi, which was characterised in all regards by Teutonic sensibilities. While a great deal was made of his Otello, it too was ponderous in its articulation and thick in tone. Tragically, by the time he came to record the role in the studio, the once concrete security of placement for which his voice had been remarkable had deteriorated audibly. For the first time, on record at least, Kaufmann's creative *vibrato* degenerated into a painful wobble. The tone was still present but his word-use as a German allowed him none of that *attaco* intensity necessary for *Otello* and Italian opera more generally after 1880. These flaws (such as they are) have been evident throughout his performances in *Il trovatore* (his appearances in Munich in 2013 left the opera sounding as if two baritones had been cast as Manrico and the Conte di Luna), *Don Carlo*, *La forza del destino*, *Adriana Lecouvreur*, *Manon Lescaut*, *Cavalleria rusticana* and *Pagliacci*. The incongruity of Kaufmann's work in Italian opera is more audible still in his performances as Faust and Werther. His singing in French is astylistic; there is no shaping of the music around the text, as romance languages require it, and his phrasing is positively static; particularly in Gounod's opera, Kaufmann's performances have generated little sense of the sung-line being determined by the words. The richness of Kaufmann's voice almost diminishes the intimacy of the writing – something for which *mezza voce* and *diminuendi* cannot compensate in isolation.

Kaufmann's enormous ability demonstrates the extent to which singers and voices can (and do) appropriate cultural metrics for which they are paradigmatically unsuited. That this would not have mattered fifty years ago is irrelevant, as is the willingness of critics to characterise the theft by Elvis and Eminem of African-American

---

Sünderin ['The Great Sinner'] (1935) by Eduard Künneke, on the Sony album *Du bist die Welt für mich* ['You are the World to Me'].
54 Costumes by Robert Jones and Jenny Tiramani. The stars of this production were the orchestra and chorus of the Royal Opera – and Antonio Pappano. Some may have disliked his urgent *tempi* but his theatrical logic and mastery of orchestral dynamics are unrivalled on the contemporary stage.
55 This survives the incongruity of Fernando de Lucia's part in proceeding.

culture as "learning from each other."⁵⁶ What deniers of cultural appropriation most fail to appreciate is that the "learning" process can cause the diminishing of its source material. To that end, Deutsche Grammophon's great "French" hope – the tenor, Benjamin Bernheim – is not, by previous standards, an especially *French* tenor. He has a sweet enough voice but his pronunciation and diction are no more Gallic than is his singing of Italian music especially Italianate. In consequence it may be concluded that the erosion of those characteristics by which the tenor voice was once defined was too great a price to pay simply for a paradigm defined by tone *in absentia*.

Judging by his most recent endeavours, Kaufmann may well have undone his voice – before being able to sing *Tristan* (ideally at Bayreuth). He claimed he would take up the role for the Season 2020/2021, a promise that Covid-19 may yet cause him to break. Like so many others before him, Kaufmann appears to have succumbed to the ruin of over-singing and overwork. Because he is now past 50, it seems likely that his Tristan and Siegfried will be heard in the gloaming. For the most complete *heldentenor* of the 21ˢᵗ century, that is a tragedy. Certainly, there doesn't appear to be anyone else on the horizon capable of mining Kaufmann's admixture of judgment, artistry and tone.

Wagner's operas continue to be performed regardless. The *heldentenor* landscape since 2000 has been uneven, at best. The lighter end of the Wagner-Strauss *fach* (for roles like Alberich and Mime) was served to perfection by the finest character-actor of his generation, Graham Clark⁵⁷ – who completed 16 seasons at Bayreuth – and by Peter Bronder⁵⁸ more recently. The reality of the Wagnerverse, however, is that anyone interested primarily in the *helden* end of the tenor spectrum has spent the last two decades in something of a wilderness. As Siegfried Jerusalem neared the end of his career, a number of emergent "German" tenors inspired hope; none of them had the vocal resonance necessary for anything more robust than Lohengrin, Tannhäuser and Walther. Paul Frey⁵⁹ was possessed of a beautiful voice, which survives memorably on a splendid recording of *Ariadne auf Naxos* with Jessye Norman in the title role, conducted by Kurt Masur. The German-named Frey was born into a Mennonite farming family in Ontario; after working as a truck driver, he enrolled to read music at university when still unable to read music. In 1987 he was spotted by Wolfgang Wagner and recommended to Werner Herzog, who cast him as Lohengrin for a production that was recorded and released by Philips. Frey was talented and musical; he was nonetheless unable to do justice to Siegmund, Siegfried, Tristan or Parsifal – far less Strauss' Der Kaiser, Menelas and Apollo.

Another natural Lohengrin was Peter Seiffert,⁶⁰ who established himself during the 1990s as a first rank light-romantic German-repertoire tenor over numerous productions (and on many recordings) of Mozart, Weber and Strauss. He was extraordinary as Matteo in *Arabella*, and proved his worth on a memorable recording that achieves more with the role than anyone before or since.⁶¹ Seiffert was an unusually

---

56   Chiefly the Canadian commentator Jordan Peterson.
57   1941 –
58   22 October, 1953 –
59   20 April, 1941 –
60   4 January, 1954 –
61   The recording was released in 1988, conducted by Jeffrey Tate, with Kiri Te Kanawa in the title role.

thoughtful artist, with a flexible, tonally focussed and sweeping voice. It darkened with time, but not so much that it equipped him to relocate as a *heldentenor*. He proceeded nonetheless to carve out a career after 2010 singing Tristan. His performance at the Teatro Colón in Buenos Aires in 2018, conducted by Barenboim, was below par at a time when par has never been lower. What was Barenboim to do? How is any conductor to approach repertoire that cannot be performed other than in compromise? Seiffert's strained and oscillating voice is no more cut out for Tristan than was Poul Elming[62] fit to take on Siegmund, and yet Barenboim cast him for his *Ring* at Bayreuth knowing that there was no-one else available. Elming's tone was essentially gaunt, but at least he employed it without that terrible *vibrato* by which Lars Cleveman's singing was luridly coloured. His performances as Tristan at Covent Garden in 2009, as Tannhäuser at Bayreuth in 2011 and as Siegfried at the Metropolitan in 2013 were choked and brittle[63] – with the primary effect being thinness of tone. This has been a ubiquitous characteristic of *heldentenors* since 2000, so that strain and effort have come to occupy the musical and interpretative space. Jay Hunter Morris,[64] for example, is a renowned Siegfried in New York; it is unclear why because his merit appears to be located solely in his capacity to get through the role(s) without collapsing. Among modern Wagner tenors, however, Morris' diction is exceptional, and a model of its kind even if his voice is anything but pretty and often painfully constricted.

That Max Lorenz was able to help James King become a world class *heldentenor* had no bearing on James King's capacity to do the same for someone else. Proximity is rarely productive, which explains, in part, why so few great singers have produced children with talents comparable to their own. For every family García or Serafin, there are a thousand Enrico Caruso Juniors and Rolf Björlings – as the best-known examples of apples falling a long way from their trees.

A sense of bargaining has come to characterise the casting of roles for *heldentenor*, which has seen the rise to prominence of vocalists who would not have been considered fit for task by earlier generations. The Canadian Ben Heppner[65] is the best-known example of this appropriation of the Peter Principle, whereby a competent individual will earn promotion to a more senior position requiring skills they do not have. Heppner was a lyric tenor of skill and excellent musical judgment. He was certainly not without style, and when singing the right repertoire he was terrific to hear. He was less compelling to see because of his size, but the ringing fervour of his voice at its best gave fantastic bang for buck. Heppner was said for more than a decade to be the leading *heldentenor* of the first decade of the 21st century, when quite plainly he warranted the sobriquet only because there was no one else to challenge the assertion. Heppner was a *spinto* tenor at best – and a good one at that; his status as a *heldentenor* was pure invention. He sang *Tristan* many times, albeit never with the power, fervour or resonance that the role necessitates. On his recording of excerpts from the *Ring* he is barely distinguishable, when singing Siegfried's forging song, from the tenor playing Mime, Burkhard Ulrich. That was not the composer's intention or

---

62 21 July, 1949 –
63 16 June, 1958 –
64 3 July, 1963 –
65 14 January, 1956 –

expectation. Heppner did not make a habit of Siegfried, of course, and in 2011 he withdrew from the Metropolitan's productions of *Siegfried* and *Götterdämmerung* – announcing coincidentally that he was withdrawing the role from his repertory.

While it would be wrong not to stage these works simply because they cannot be cast as once they were, the message that has been sent by the dearth of *heldentenors* since 2010 should compel some reflection among those whose responsibility it is to train the next generation. Outside Germany, the American tenors Gary Lehman and Stephen Gould[66] have enjoyed solid careers as Wagnerians, and Gould has at least had the vocal presence to go toe to toe with Siegfried. Both tenors are also to be commended for having coped manfully on stage (and on record) with Violetta Urmana's Kundry and Brunnhilde.[67] The British-born Christopher Ventris,[68] a stalwart at Bayreuth and Vienna for years, is not a true *heldentenor,* while the Australian Stuart Skelton[69] has a big voice but is something of a blunt instrument, with neither the style nor the line that Ventris brought to his best work. Skelton is a barker by comparison, with none of Ventris' crystalline diction.

The most recent stock of Wagner tenors were all born after Kaufmann. Klaus Florian Vogt[70] is a lyric tenor incapable of wrestling a bear, forging a sword, or killing a dragon; the American Brandon Jovanovich[71] and the Swedish Daniel Johanson[72] promised much and failed to deliver. The New Zealand-born Simon O'Neill[73] is another *spinto* tenor who has managed to make a little go a long way, achieving success in repertoire for which he is vocally ill-equipped, notably *Verdi's* Otello. He has a superb command of German and he sings with great expression – as he demonstrated when making his debut at Bayreuth as Lohengrin in 2010. The following year he took the bold step of agreeing to sing Parsifal for the Festival. He did not return in 2012. O'Neill's replacement – Burkhard Fritz – is similar in terms of tone and phrasing.

Andreas Schager's essentially lyric voice has some fibre to it; it is hard in its texture, however, which suffers further from an inveterate and inexpressive *vibrato*. He is given moreover to opening his tone too widely and his word-use is surprisingly poor for an Austrian-born singer – as was demonstrated throughout his exhausting appearance as Tristan at l'Opéra Bastille in 2018.

The Canadian Lance Ryan[74] was Bayreuth's Siegfried in 2010, 2013 and 2014 – in both operas. He should not have been. *Force majeure* being what it is, divine intervention is rarely kind, and the latest crop of *heldentenors* does not promise any significant improvements – although the current decade has seen Germany return to the fore as a source for their supply. The most high-profile talent at the time of publication is Stefan Vinke. The latter made his debut as Siegfried in 2006 for Cologne Opera, since when he has sung every major Wagner tenor role pretty much everywhere, including Bayreuth, Vienna, Munich, Berlin, Stuttgart, Cologne, London, Zurich,

---

66   1962 –
67   Urmana's fearsome wobble is among the worst captured on record. It cannot otherwise be contained.
68   1965 –
69   1968 –
70   12 April, 1970 –
71   5 October, 1970 –
72   4 August, 1980 –
73   1971.
74   1 May, 1971 –

Budapest, Venice and Barcelona. He has also sung Bacchus in *Ariadne*, Paul in *Die tote Stadt* (memorably so at La Fenice), the Drum Major in *Wozzeck* and Menelas in *Die ägyptische Helena*. His appearance as Siegfried at Bayreuth in Frank Castorf's reviled (and famously booed) production of the *Ring* was considered one of the few vocal highlights, while his performances as Tristan at Bayreuth in 2019 with Christian Thielemann (a role he shared with Stephen Gould) were acclaimed.

The most complete talent at the time of publication is Daniel Kirch, an alumni of the Komische Opera in Berlin. Like Kaufmann, he began life as a lyric German-repertoire tenor, with acclaimed early performances of Mozart, most famously his appearances in 2003 as Belmonte for Christof Loy's celebrated production in Frankfurt. Kirch made his debut at the Opéra de Lyon as Tristan in 2017 – to universal acclaim. He is a genuine *heldentenor*, with a powerful, richly centred voice that gains palpably from its ringing *spinto* top. His acute sense of line is well-supported by a disciplined and creative *vibrato* and he phrases with striking musical and poetic intelligence reminiscent of Kaufmann. Also like Kaufmann, Kirch is a gifted *lieder* and concert singer; his quiet obsessions with Schubert's *Winterreise* and Schönberg's Waldemar (*Gurre-Lieder*) have yielded much of value.

At the time of publication, Vinke and Kirch have both celebrated their 50th birthdays. Kaufmann is older than both of them. The threat of tumbleweed is certain when the same singers continue to monopolise a handful of roles for more than 500 Houses globally. Were even a quarter of the world's intendants to think to cast a new production of *Parsifal* in the same week of the same season, there would be a run on the *heldentenor* market, and the majority of theatres would go dark. The situation is not greatly improved where Manrico and Alvaro are concerned. Whither progress? In the Preface to his 1930 book *Culture and Progress*,[75] Wilson D. Wallis inferred that the times were changing – while identifying a still relevant cultural fascism whereby

> Other civilisations and times are utilised mainly as a means of reflecting light upon our own time and civilisation.

Just three years before Hitler secured absolute power in Germany, Wallis admitted further that

> The culture changes in Western civilization, or in all historical civilizations taken in their totality, constitute a unique event in a unique culture world. The thing which has been has never been before, and there is no basis for the induction that it will be again, or that it will persist.[76]

Many have anticipated the decline and fall of music as a classical art. Many more have announced its failure. The critic Henry Pleasants devoted an entire book to how awful everything was in 1961.[77] There's no arguing with much of what Pleasants

---

75   Wallis, D. Wilson (1930). *Culture and Progress*. McGraw-Hill.
76   *Ibid.* p.463.
77   Pleasants, Henry (1961). *Death of a Music? The Decline of the European Tradition and the Rise of Jazz*. Gollancz.

had to say, but it's equally true that his prognostications were misplaced analytically because he was starting from a position of inherent and admitted prejudice. Merely observing the decline in the number of tenors who compare with the best of the past does not address the issues as they have evolved. For a start, it is absurd to argue that the absence of a Caruso, a Melchior or a Corelli in 2021 is indicative of failure or collapse, when each of those singers was unprecedented for their own times. Moreover, comparison was not an option until recording enabled it. The nature of the art as it evolves after 2021 may yet be nurtured by a return to 19th century values, since almost none of those singers identified in this chapter makes records or is likely to make them on anything more than an *ad hoc* basis. Some will be filmed in central Europe – and live broadcasts of opera around the world have increased steadily since 2000. Even so, the screening of productions from Covent Garden and the Met are unlikely to reverse the decline in the interest among young people for art music and singing.

It is easy for many to dismiss the "Three Tenors" circus as a "moment," and it survives memetically because of its transference of a "serious" art form to a "popular" arena. The truth, however, is that the most famous totems of heroic, dramatic and romantic art until the 1960s were as often singers of opera as they were actors. Lawrence Tibbett, Maria Callas and Mario Del Monaco were as celebrated in their day as any scion of Hollywood, which explains why Charlton Heston and John Wayne made regular visits to the Met when in New York. One cannot imagine that "Chuck" and the "Duke" were especially interested in Mozart and Da Ponte's lyrical dissections of European social demography; but they knew better than anyone that the sweet smell of success was enhanced by high-cultural attachments that enabled relevance at a time when opera was still definitively contemporary.

As a function of "progress," it is now possible to compare anyone to everyone else – as long as they have been recorded. It is easier, of course, to compare Beczała with Corelli when they are singing the same repertoire than it is to measure Picasso against Renoir. The platform on which one art survives in parity with another is *not* the same as can reasonably (and unreasonably) be said of singers performing *exactly* the same music. That splinter of contextualisation is venal and destructive. In 2015, for example, Beczała was recorded using 1920s technology – to make a point that no one seemed able to agree upon. If nothing else, his singing of an aria by Verdi did much to amplify the miracle of Caruso's voice for anyone compelled to doubt it.

Rather than focussing on progress, it might be better to embrace the less inflammatory ambition of change. Most of Caruso's stage productions in New York, for example, and nearly everything outside Germany until after the Second War, were parochial and literal. Set design, and dramaturgy more generally, admitted little more than the least that was necessary for singers to exhibit their art. The standard of stage production and design has evolved since the 1980s to a point of skill and sophistication that renders memories of Melchior and his canvas sets and spot-lights cartoonish. This does not exonerate the guilty of "produceritis" at its worst, wherein European stagecraft, in particular, has endured determined efforts at cultural, social and psychological redemption and regeneration. Where once the appearance by singers of note would justify spending everything on a cast, the slide into obsolescence of soloists qualifying for stardom has shifted the focus onto stage-craft, symbolism and the collegial work of the chorus and the orchestra. This is problematic when someone attends the staging of an opera in which the quality of the ensemble as vocalists has *almost* to exceed any other consideration. If, for example, *Il trovatore* requires *only* the "four best singers on Earth,"[78] then *Ariadne aux Naxos* needs at least three of its own to survive the probability of compromise. When the least has also to be enough, the decline in supply becomes an issue only because the world's most celebrated Italian-repertoire dramatic tenor is also the world's finest *heldentenor*.

There are solutions, none of which owe anything to banning international flight – to which development many continue to attribute the failure of supply to meet the market's rapacious demands. Singers have been travelling globally since shipping and aviation first allowed it. The value of the *stagione* system is self-evident but impractical, should a company wish to perform operas in multiple languages with anything approximating vocal and linguistic authenticity. The root of any solution vests with training, and the manner in which "voice" is taught and studied. The primary duty of any teacher is to submit their '78s, LPs and CDs to a bonfire of certainties sufficient to dissuade anyone hoping to speak through music from standing on the shoulders of giants. Personality will always trump imitation, and any process of individuation must compel an absolute and ruthless reversion to the text as grail. The curse of studio recording in particular is its re-casting of the exceptional as routine, just as the attachment of normalcy to the abnormal flattens the bell-curve. The score and its crafting allow for every individual to read what they find, and to find only what they read. For all the joy to be gained from recordings, the hearing of a voice in anything other than a live and natural acoustic is to cheat and dissemble, with editing, engineering and technology infecting the realistic expectations of singers as well as audiences. The acoustics of La Fenice, for example, suit the music of Rossini better than they do the work of Puccini – with the stone, wood and plaster of the building influencing the interaction between the orchestra and a voice – a consequence that, again, steers the perception of the singer as well as the audience towards the truth that one size can never fit all.

Teachers of singing have also to compel their students not to overuse whatever voice they discover for themselves. Singers should reach only for repertoire to which they are by nature inclined because the lifetime of a tenor is too often short, especially in the theatre. Of course, many have enjoyed viable careers lasting more than two decades, with Domingo performing without amplification into his 80s. Though he is unusual even by the standards of the outlier, many others have been able to perform well into their 60s without diminishing their tone, placement or line. Judgment and discretion must also be taught as rigorously as breathing and diction. The spitting of consonants and the exposing of vowels can be overcome so as to allow for a natural and sustainable *cantabile* – from which it follows that colour, nuance and character should be prioritised over tone in isolation. Drama begins and ends with the human; singers are not in and of themselves instruments after the fashion of Rachmaninov's *Vocalise*; the value of the word and its articulation must determine the study and formation of technique so that the apparent ambitions of *bigger*, *louder* and *higher* can be prevented from doing violence to organs that are defined by their delicacy. Neither

---

78 A quote attributed to Toscanini, Serafin and others.

should amplitude exclude nuance and dexterity; while the use of turns by tenors when performing Wagner's music would now be rejected, they should still be known even if they are no longer employed. Barking and *legati* are mutually exclusive, save for moments of the greatest dramatic intensity or when a composer has excluded the lyrical intentionally. The curating of talent must compel a process that begins at the very latest with Mozart – so that shape and line remain determinative of voice. The soprano that sings Elektra should also be able to sing Donna Anna – even if not on the stage; a tenor singing Tristan should be able to perform Don Ottavio in the shower when resting. There needs to be a hard-turn on the belief that volume equates to resonance; shouting cannot compensate for articulation and character.

Perhaps the greatest of modern sins is the appropriation of repertoire. Nothing is gained through an obeisance to globalisation, no matter the force of its tide. French, Italian, German and Russian vocalism are irreconcilable in their demands, and the place and primacy of the word when presented through music must be approached with the respect and identification they deserve; *every* language has formed its own discreet expressive vernacular and that is captured unavoidably in any concomitant musical setting. It follows that the serious and solemn values formed by art music over the centuries have to be cherished and understood in their historical, psychological and cultural place. The interaction between the classical tradition and philosophy, history, language, religion and societal narratives and dialogues is necessarily complex, meaning that accessibility can be promoted as meaningful only where its absence is proscriptively damaging or isolationist. It cannot supplant the ambition of the art and the artist when committing to a narrative that compares better to a millefeuille served at Les Deux Magots than to candyfloss consumed on Coney Island. Few would disagree that the crisis is to an extent statistical; the majority of young people are now unaware even of opera's existence. In Italy, every café, bar and restaurant now plays pop music ubiquitously; even in Venice, the majority of classical music and opera is performed by fading talents in hour-long concerts with poorly-tuned pianos for tourists feeding their social media profiles. That might be better than nothing, but it's not the best it might be.

When Laura Bretan performed "*Nessun dorma*" on *America's Got Talent* (eliciting, as of right, a standing ovation and a shower of gold confetti), the celebrated bass Samuel Ramey railed that "she has no business" singing the aria. The voice coach Heidi Moss circulated an open letter explaining what a performance of opera *actually* entailed, while the soprano Helen Hassinger launched a GoFundMe campaign to "Send Simon Cowell to the Met." The blogosphere reached for its thesauruses. By reduction, these allegedly stuffy and arrogant elitists[79] were invited to self-harm in increasingly inventive ways. Their criticism was perceived as hostility for a 13-year old girl rather than as an expression of concern for a culture under attack.

Ultimately, any preservation of objective musicianship and diction when employed in the service of dramatic art and emotional truth requires the prioritisation of standards best evaluated in the same acoustics in which the art was first established. That remains the test for anyone singing in the same buildings as Donzelli, Rubini, Nourrit, Duprez, Mario, De Reszke, Winkelmann, Tamagno, Caruso, Lorenz, Thill,

---

79 Among the least troubling terms employed commonly in responses online.

Bergonzi and Carreras. The isolation of performing ethics formed in halls and theatres that have changed little over centuries allows for a measure of continuity that has to be respected or abandoned. By this reasoning there was nothing elitist in Sam Ramey's dismay – any more than a surgeon might be criticised for demanding proper technique when operating to save the life of a patient. Elitism is the preservation of ambition at its most definitive, not the suppression of difference.

More than anything else, the teaching of a young man drawn to sing in an opera house or a concert hall requires guardianship. The larynx and vocal folds undergo dramatic developments with puberty, changes that continue into a singer's late twenties. The cultivation of clarity of tone and intonation, the eradication of physical tension and the development of a technique capable of facilitating modulations in registration, originate in the maturity of the vocal folds and culminate in an evolved psychological conception of the art to which singing contributes. The German pianists Josef Hoffmann and Walter Gieseking and the violinist Jascha Heifetz would invite potential students carrying cases stuffed with music to perform nothing more than scales. Each was able to know within a few notes whether there was anything with which to work; that "simple" test needs to be carried through to the art of the tenor as it was promoted and characterised by Manuel García, Alceste Gerunda and Antonio Cotogni. Anyone dreaming of playing Tristan, Cavaradossi or the Drum Major has first to employ a seamless and uninfected four-bar *legato* before thinking to do battle with an orchestra and a score.

That process is one of labour, coloured by the awareness that for every Giuseppe di Stefano there are 100 Jonas Kaufmanns. The effort invested by the best of those celebrated in this book is either audible or easily imagined; the cost to them is not. Either way, the outcome is consistent, as it has been for every composer when pursuing an emotional, psychological and cultural connection capable of speaking to the many. If a singer in the 21st century is not expected to preserve a composer's sound-world as they imagined it, then there exists a prevailing obligation to adhere to the principles that cultivated composition through performance. Those principles have not yet surpassed the music and the drama as it was written down as a primary source. A tenor doesn't have to sing the B4 *come è scritto* at the end of "*Nessun dorma,*" but he will remain forever obliged to shape, colour and articulate the phrases that precede it. If there is to be progress then it is isolated in continuity, wherever and however it can be achieved in service to the art.

Acknowledgements

This book began in the early 1990s, at the piano with Neil Vint and Angelo Villani, both of whom tolerated my sledgehammer attempts at "*Niun mi tema*" and "*Non piangere, Liù*" with unfailing patience. Angelo's knowledge of singing resonates throughout his performances as one of the finest pianists I have known; what he taught me as a young man has been a constant influence across the decades since, and throughout the researching and writing of this book. I remain eternally in his debt. I learned much also from my eighteen months as John Ogdon's amanuensis, and it continues to surprise me how the finest instrumentalists are often more attuned to the art of singing than are many singers. The gratitude I owe to my formative influences compels me to pay tribute once more to Jonathan Buckley, a remarkable writer and man of letters, whose talents are captured only lightly by his many novels.

    I am especially grateful to my editor, Mike Purswell, for his erudition, insight and humour, and also to Lee Haynes, my publisher at Ragueneau Press, for producing such a beautiful book, and for doing all that he does. Huge thanks are owed to the infinitely patient Jill Sweet, the designer of the manuscript. During the writing process I have gained considerably from the support and advice of numerous friends and colleagues at the Goethe Institute (London), the National Portrait Gallery (London), the British Library, the Imperial War Museum, the New York Public Library, L'Opéra de Paris, La Monnaie (Brussels), the New York Metropolitan Opera, the Teatro Regio Torino, the Gran Teatro La Fenice, the Teatro dell'Opera di Roma, the Komische Oper, Deutsche Oper and Staatsoper, Berlin, and the Staatsoper, Vienna. The records and resources to which I have been given access have made the research process an unusual pleasure; I look forward to returning for the sequel to this volume, *The Soprano – a Cultural History* (2023). In no particular order, I'd like thereafter to express profound affection and gratitude to the following associates, assistants, colleagues and friends in the United States and Europe: Christopher Plaas (for being the first to read the manuscript, and for his insights as a singer), Molly and Maurice Stern, Will Crutchfield, Brian Wilson, Josh Reisberg, John Pennino and Peter Clark, Jilly Cosgrove, David Mills, Sam Morgan, Bruce Barnard, Ian Pumfrey, John Franklyn, Ashley Dawes, Alex Smith, Juliette Smith, James Aveyard, Robert Saville, Graham Postles, Henry Box, Matthew Taylor, Donal Thorburn-Muirhead, Pietro di Maria, Duccio ("Il") Re, Maddalena Cataldo, Alessandro Re, Michail Favro, Stefano Monelli, Paola Monelli, Gabriele Monelli, Fabrizio Zanca, Roberto Nicoloso, Caterina Clemente, Alberto Favro, Andrea Zuccato, Cesare Bondio, Reece Whittington, Ian Brooks, Tom and Georgie Reed (and the little Reeds, Henry and Jack), Dan Maker, Miles Slover, Adam Davis, Simon Stanley, Karen Wright, Simon

Dalton, Simon Kendrick, Greg Moore, Matt Riley and Richard Norman. As usual, I could have done nothing without the support, patience and inspiration of my children: Joachim, Lucia, Amelie, Octavia and Atticus. *Padre augusto...Conosco il nome dello straniero! Il suo nome è...Amor!*

I should like finally to pay inadequate tribute to Rachel Slover, whose brilliant mind and perfect heart continue to inspire me more than anything or anyone identified in this book. But for her, it would have been finished in half the time; it would not have been half as good.

Bibliography

Abbott, Helen. "Poetry, Performance, Music in Nineteenth-Century France." *Journal of the Society of Dix-Neuxiémistes,* No. 1 Dix-Neuf (2013).
Abbott, Helen. *Baudelaire in Song: 1880–1930.* Oxford University Press (2017).
Adorno, Theodor. *Introduction to the Sociology of Music,* trans. E. B. Ashton. Seabury Press (1976).
Aldrich, Perley Dunn. "Reminiscences of Celebrated Singers: A Conversation with Signor Sbriglia." *Etude Magazine.* (August 1906).
Allgemeine Musikalische Zeitung, Jg. 6, No. 45 (8 August 1804).
Allgemeine Musikalische Zeitung, Jg. 8, No. 15 (8 January 1806).
André, Naomi. *Voicing Gender: Castrati, Travesty, and the Second Woman in Early-Nineteenth-Century Italian Opera.* Indiana University Press (2006).
Aspden, S. "An Infinity of Factions: Opera in Eighteenth-Century Britain and the Undoing of Society." In *Cambridge Opera Journal,* vol. 9:1 (1997).
Bailey, Lucanne Magill. "The Effects of Live Music versus Tape-Recorded Music on Hospitalized Cancer Patients." *Music Therapy,* Vol.3, Issue 1 (1983).
Barbier, Patrick. *The World of the Castrati: The History of an Extraordinary Operatic Phenomenon.* Souvenir Press (2001).
Bartlett, Rosamund. *Tchaikovsky and His Contemporaries: A Centennial Symposium,* ed. Alexander Mihailovic. Greenwood Press (1999).
Bartlett, Rosamund. *Wagner and Russia.* Cambridge University Press (1995).
Bauerle, Ruth. "Caruso's Sin in the Fiendish Park: 'The Possible Was the Improbable and the Improbable, the Inevitable.'" *James Joyce Quarterly,* Vol. 38, No. 1/2, (Fall, 2000 – Winter, 2001).
Benton-Cohen, Katherine. *Inventing the Immigration Problem: The Dillingham Commission and Its Legacy.* Harvard University Press (2018).
Berenak. Leo. *Music, Acoustics, and Architecture.* John Wiley & Sons, Inc. (1962).
Berlioz, Hector. *La Critique Musicale*, ed. Cohen and Bongrain, 4 vols. Buchet/Castel (1996–2003).
Berlioz, Hector. *Evenings with the Orchestra,* trans. Jacques Barzun. University of Chicago Press (1999).
Berlioz, Hector. *Mémoires.* Adamant Media Corporation (2000).
Berlioz, Hector. *Les Soirees de l'Orchestre,* trans. C. R. Fortescue (London, 1963).
Berlioz, Hector. *Correspondance Générale I: 1803–May 1832 (nos. 1–273)*, Ed. Pierre Citron (1972).
Bernardoni, Nathalie Henrich. "Mirroring the Voice from Garcia to the Present Day: Some Insights into Singing Voice Registers." *Logopedics Phoniatrics Vocology.* 31: (February, 2008).
Bernhardt, Sarah. *My Double Life: The Memoirs of Sarah Bernhardt.* State University of New York Press (1999).

Bernheimer, Martin. "The World of Wagnerian Tenors," Los Angeles *Times* (March 10, 1966).
Bing, Rudolf. *5000 Nights at the Opera*. Hamish Hamilton (1972)
Bloch, Gregory W. "The Pathological Voice of Gilbert-Louis Duprez." In *The Divo and the Danseur: On the Nineteenth-Century Male Opera and Ballet Performer*. Cambridge Opera Journal, Vol. 19, No. 1, (Mar., 2007).
Boagno, Marina and Starone, Gilberto. *Corelli: a Man, a Voice*. Atlantic Books (1996).
Boyd, William. *An Ice-Cream War*. Penguin Books (2011).
Boyden, Matthew. *Beethoven and the Gothic*. Verba et Musica (2018).
Boyden, Matthew. *Richard Strauss*. Weidenfeld & Nicolson (1999).
Boyden, Matthew. *Rough Guide to Opera*. Penguin (4 Eds. 1996–2004).
Branscombe, P. *W. A. Mozart: Die Zauberflöte*. Cambridge University Press (1991).
Budden, Julian. *The Operas of Verdi*. Cassell (1978).
Burke, Edmund. *A Philosophical Enquiry into the Origin of our Ideas of the Sublime and Beautiful*. Second edition. Routledge Classics (2008).
Byron, Avior. "The Test Pressings of Schoenberg Conducting *Pierrot lunaire*: Sprechstimme Reconsidered." *Society for Music Theory*. Volume 12, Number 1. (2006).
Caruselli, Salvatore, ed. *Grande Enciclopedia Della Musica Lirica*. Longanesi & C. Periodici S.p.A. (1980).
Caruso, Enrico Jr. and Farkas, Andrew. *Enrico Caruso: My Father and My Family*. Amadeus Press (1990).
Castellani, Giuliano. *Ferdinando Paer: Biografia, Opere e Documenti Degli Anni Parigini*. Verlag Peter Lang (2009).
Celletti, Rodolfo. *A History of Bel Canto*. Clarendon Paperbacks (2001).
Cesari, Armando. *Mario Lanza: An American Tragedy*. Baskerville (2008).
Chorley, Henry F. *Modern German Music, 2 vols*. Vol. 1. Reprinted Da Capo Press (1973).
Chorley, Henry F. *Thirty Years' Musical Recollections*. Reprinted by Knopf (1926).
Chouquet, Gustave. *Histoire de la Musique Dramatique en France*. Didot (1873).
Christensen, Kenneth A. *The Toscanini Mystique: The Genius Behind the Music*. Xlibris (2014).
Civiltà. *Rivista dell'Esposizione Universale di Roma*. Bompiani (1941).
Clapton, Nicholas. *Moreschi and the Voice of the Castrato*. Haus Books (2008).
Clapton, Nicholas. "Carlo Broschi Farinelli: Aspects of his Technique and Performance." *British Journal for Eighteenth-Century Studies*. (2005).
Comte de La Garde-Chambonas, Auguste Louis Charles. *Anecdotal Recollections of the Congress of Vienna*. Andesite Press (2015).
Cone, John Frederick and Moran, William R. *Adelina Patti: Queen of Hearts*. Amadeus Press (1993).
Coward, Noel. *The Noel Coward Diaries*. Macmillan (1983).
Crutchfied, Will. "Verdi: The Phonographic Evidence." 19th Century Music, 7 (1983).
Culshaw, John. *Ring Resounding*. Viking Press (1967).
D'Orazio, Dario and Nannini, Sofia. "Towards Italian Opera Houses: A Review of Acoustic Design in Pre-Sabine Scholars." *Acoustics*. (2019).
De Clerville, J. "Verdi and the Two Operas." *The Musical World*. (April 29, 1848).
de la Grange, Henry. *Gustav Mahler, Volume 2, Vienna: the Years of Challenge*. Oxford University Press (1995).
Delacroix, Eugène. *Selected letters, 1813 – 1863*. MFA Publications (2011).
Dermota, Anton. *Tausendundein Abend: Mein Sängerleben*. Paul Neff Verlag (1978).
Deutsch, Otto Erich. *Schubert: Memoirs by his Friends*. A. & C. Black (1958).
Dictionary of National Biography, 1885–1900, Volume 44 (1900).
Diday, H. and Pétrequin, J.E. "Mémoire sur une nouvelle espèce de voix chantée." *Gazette médicale de Paris, viii* (1840).

Donati, P. *Descrizione del Gran Teatro Farnesiano di Parma e notizie storiche sul medesimo di Paolo Donati parmigiano architetto teatrale e accademico di Bologna e professore della Reale Accademia di Firenze* (1817).
Dorfmüller, Kurt. *Beiträge zur Beethoven-Bibliographie* (1978).
Drake, James A. "*Ecco! Il Leone!*: Giacomo Lauri-Volpi and the Metropolitan Opera, 1922–32." *Italian Americana*, Vol. 7, No. 1. (1981).
Dubiau-Feuillerac, Mylène. "Verlaine/Debussy: la 'mise en sons' de 'Spleen.'" *Dix-Neuf. Journal of the Society of Dix-Neuxiémistes*, 17:1 (2013).
Duffett, Mark. "Caught in a Trap? Beyond Pop Theory's 'Butch' Construction of Male Elvis Fans." *Popular Music*, 20:3 (2001).
Dunham, Arthur. "How the First French Railways Were Planned." *Journal of Economic History*, 1:1 (1941).
Dürr, Walther. "Schubert and Johann Michael Vogl: A Reappraisal." *19th-Century Music* Vol. 3, No. 2 (Nov. 1979).
Ehrlich, Cyril. *The Piano: A History*. Clarendon Press (1990).
Ellmann, Richard. *James Joyce*. Oxford University Press (1959).
Emmons, Shirlee. *Tristanissimo: The Authorized Biography of Heroic Tenor Lauritz Melchior*. Schirmer Books (1990).
Emmons, Shirlee (December / January 1990 / 91). "Lauritz Melchior: Heldentenor for the Ages." *American Music Teacher*, Vol. 40:3 (December/January 1990/91).
Everist, Mark. *Music Drama at the Paris Odéon, 1824–1828*. University of California Press (2002).
Faure, Michel and Vivès, Vincent. *Histoire et Poétique de la mélodie Française*. CNRS Editions (2000).
Favia-Artsay, Aida. *Caruso on Records: The Historic Record*. Valhalla (1965).
Fenner, Theodore. *Opera in London: Views of the Press, 1785–1830*. Southern Illinois University Press (1994).
Ferris, George T. *Great Singers: Malibran To Titiens, Vol. 2*. D. Appleton and Company (1891).
Foley, Ruth Iona, "The Songs of Gustave Charpentier." *ETD collection for University of Nebraska – Lincoln* (2000).
Forbes, Elizabeth. "Davide (David), Giacomo." In *The New Grove Dictionary of Opera*, Ed. Stanley Sadie. Oxford University Press (1997).
Ford, Charles. *Alban Berg's Letters Music and Letters, Volume Li, Issue 1*. (1970).
Formes, Karl. *My Memoirs. Autobiography of Karl Formes*. James H Barry (1891).
Forshaw, Juliet (2014). *Dangerous Tenors, Heroic Basses, and Non-Ingénues: Singers and the Envoicing of Social Values in Russian Opera, 1836–1905*. PhD thesis. Columbia University.
Forster, E. M. *Howard's End*. Penguin Books (2000).
Freitas, Roger. "Towards a Verdian Ideal of Singing: Emancipation from Modern Orthodoxy." *Journal of the Royal Musical Association*, Vol. 127:2 (2000).
Frolova-Walker, Marina. *On Ruslan and Russianness*. Cambridge Opera Journal, 9, 1, 21 – 45 (1997).
Fryer, Paul. Opera in the Media Age: Essays on Art, Technology and Popular Culture. McFarland & Company (2014).
Führer, Karl Christian. "German Cultural Life and the Crisis of National Identity during the Depression, 1929–1933." *German Studies Review*, Vol. 24:3 (2001).
Furtwängler, Wilhelm. *Ton und Wort: Aufsätze und Vorträge 1918–1954*. Brockhaus (1955).
Furtwängler, Wilhelm: *Notebooks, 1924–1954*. trans. Shaun Whiteside. Quartet Books (1995).
Garcia, Manual. *Traité Complet de l'Art du Chant*. Brandus et Cie (1840).
Gelatt, Roland. *The Fabulous Phonograph*. Collier Books (1977).

Gerdes, Daniel. *"The Legacy of Fritz Wunderlich: One Performer's Perceptions of Selected Discography."* A Treatise submitted to the College of Music in partial fulfilment of the requirements for the degree of Doctor of Music. Florida State University, College of Music. (2011).

Giles, Peter. *The History and Technique of the Counter-Tenor.* Scolar Press (1994).

Goebbels, Joseph. *Die Tagebücher von Joseph Goebbels*, ed. Jana Richter, Part 1, 1923–1941, Volume 3 (March 1936 – February 1937). K.G. Saur Verlag GmbH (2001).

Glikman, Isaac. *Story of a Friendship: The Letters of Dmitry Shostakovich to Isaak Glikman with a commentary by Isaak Glikman*, trans. Anthony Philips, Cornell University Press (1993).

Goethe, Katharina Elisabeth. *Die Briefe Der Frau Rath Goethe.* Volume 1. Palala Press (2005).

Goldstein R.J., Need, A.M., eds. *Political Censorship of the Visual Arts in Nineteenth-Century Europe.* Palgrave Macmillan (2015).

Gossett, Philip. "Becoming a Citizen: The Chorus in 'Risorgimento' Opera." *Cambridge Opera Journal*, Vol. 2:1 (Mar, 1990).

Gossett, Philip; Ashbrook, William; Budden, Julian; Lippmann, Friedrich; Porter, Andrew; Mosco Carner, Mosco. *The New Grove Masters of Italian Opera.* W. W. Norton & Company (1997).

Gray, Dave and Shami, Jeanne. "Political Advice in Donne's Devotions." *Modern Language Quarterly*. Duke University Press (1989).

Gresinger, G. *Biografische Notizen über Josef Haydn.* Reclam (1975).

Grey, Thomas S., ed. *Richard Wagner and His World.* Princeton University Press (2009).

Hailey, Christopher, ed. *Alban Berg and His World.* Princeton University Press (2010).

Hanslick, Eduard. *Hanslick's Musical Criticism*, Ed. Henry Pleasants. Dover Publications (1988).

Harari, Yuval. *Homo Deus.* Vintage Publishing (2018).

Harrington, Judith. "Mario: The Tenor of His Times." *James Joyce Quarterly*, Vol.38:1:2 (Fall, 2000 – Winter, 2001).

Hastings, Stephen. *The Björling Sound: A Recorded Legacy.* Boydell & Brewer (2012).

Henrysson, Harald. *A Jussi Björling Phonography.* Svenskt Musikhistoriskt Arkiv (2014).

Henson, Karen. "Victor Capoul, Marguerite Olagnier's Le Saïs, and the Arousing of Female Desire." *Journal of the American Musicological Society*, vol. 52:3 (1999).

Henson, Karen. *Opera Acts: Singers and Performance in the Late Nineteenth Century.* Cambridge University Press (2015).

Hepokoski, James A. *Giuseppe Verdi: 'Falstaff'.* Cambridge Opera Handbooks (1983).

Herbst, Christian T.; Hertegard, Stellan; Zangger-Borch, Daniel; and Lindestad, Per-Åke. *Freddie Mercury—Acoustic analysis of Speaking Fundamental Frequency, Vibrato, and Subharmonics.* Logopedics Phoniatrics Vocology (2016).

Hey, Julius. *Richard Wagner als Vortragsmeister.* Breitkopf & Härte (1911).

Hitler, Adolf. *Mein Kampf.* Houghton Mifflin (1943).

Hochmuth, Michael. *Chronik der Dresdner Oper.* Verlag Dr. Kovač (1998).

Horace and Dryden, John. *The Satires of Decimus Junius Juvenalis, Volume 3.* Nabu Press (2012).

Horace. *Ars Poetica (ii.132, 135.)* Quoted by Burke in *On Taste.* (1759).

Howard, Patricia, ed. *C. W. von Gluck: Orfeo.* Cambridge University Press (1981).

Huebner, Steven. "Opera Audiences in Paris 1830–1870." *Music & Letters*, Vol. 70: 2 (1989).

Huxley, Aldhous. "Silence is Golden." *Vanity Fair* (July, 1929).

Inghelbrecht, Désiré-Émile. *Comment on ne doit pas interpréter 'Carmen', 'Faust' et Pelléas.* Heugel (1933).

Iverson, John R. "Voltaire's Militant Defense of the French Language." *Romance Notes*, Vol. 40:3. (Spring, 2000).

Jones, Robert. "The Authenticity of the Alleged Strauss-accompanied Tauber Records." *The Record Collector*, Vol. 19. (June 1970).
Joyce, Stanislaus. *The Complete Dublin Diary of Stanislaus Joyce*, ed. George Harris Healey. Cornell University Press (1971).
Jung, Uli and Schatzberg, Walter. "The Silent 'Rosenkavalier:' A Film by Hugo von Hofmannsthal, Richard Strauss and Robert Wiene." *Modern Austrian Literature*, Vol. 27: 2 (1994).
Kahane, Martine. *Robert le Diable: Catalogue de l'exposition Théâtre National de l'Opéra de Paris 20 Juin – 20 Septembre 1985*. Bibiloteque National (1985).
Kelly, George A., Ed. *Addresses to the German Nation*. Harper Torch Books (1968).
Kelly, Michael. *Reminiscences of Michael Kelly: Of the King's Theatre, and Theatre, Volume 1*. H. Coburn (1826).
Kildea, Paul. *Chopin's Piano: A Journey Through Romanticism*. Allen Lane (2018).
Klein, Eve (2018). "When Divas and Rock Stars Collide: Interpreting Freddie Mercury and Montserrat Caballé's Barcelona." In *Popular Music, Stars and Stardom*. Eds. Stephen Loy, Julie Rickwood and Samantha Bennett. ANU Press (2018).
Klein, Herman. "Jean De Reszke and Marie Brema: Some Reminiscences." *The Musical Times*, Vol. 66, No. 987 (May 1, 1925).
Klein, Herman. *Thirty Years of Musical Life in London*. The Century Co. (1903).
Klein, W. "Verdi's 'Otello' and Rossini's." *Music & Letters*, vol. 45:2 (1964).
Kraemer, Richard H. *The Secret War in the Balkans: A WWII Memoir*. Author House (2010).
Krehbiel, Henry. "Caruso Sings in *La Juive*." *New York Tribune*.
Krones, Hartmut, "'Wiener' Symbolik? Zu musiksemantischen Traditionen in den beiden Wiener Schulen" in *Beethoven und die Zweiten Wiener Schule. Studien zur Wertungsforschung* 25. Otto Kolleritsch (Ed.) Wien-Graz (1992).
Lajosi, Krisztina and Stynen, Andreas. *Choral Societies and Nationalism in Europe*. Koninklijke Brill (2015).
Lang, Paul Henry. *Music in Western Civilization*. W. W. Norton & Co. (1941).
Laver, James. *Drama: its Costume and Decor*. The Studio Publication (2015).
Leiser, Clara. Jean De Reszke and The Great Days of Opera. Sagwan Press (2015).
Lickint, Fritz. *Tabak und Tabakrauch als ätiologischer Factor des Carcinoms*. Zeitschrift für Krebsforschung (1929).
Liszt, Franz. "Revue musicale de l'année 1836." *Le Monde*. (8 January, 1837).
Locke, John. *Two Treatises of Government*, Ed. Peter Laslett. Cambridge University Press (1967).
Lopez, Jesus M. *Antonio Paoli: El Leon de Ponce*. Ediciones Liricas Puertorriqueñas (1997).
Lorenz, Alfred. "Betrachtungen über Beethovens Eroica-Skizzen (Ein Beitrag zur Psychologie des Schaffens)." *Zeitschrift für Musikwissenschaft*, Vol. 7. (1924–1925).
MacDonald, Hugh. "To Repeat or Not to Repeat?" *Proceedings of the Royal Musical Association*, CXI (1985).
Mackenzie, Sir Compton; and Stone, Christopher. "Antonio Cotogni's description of his training." *The Gramophone*, 2 (1924).
Mangini, Nicola. *I teatri di Venezia*. Mursia (1974).
Mann, Thomas. *Pro and Contra Wagner*. trans. Allan Blunden. Faber and Faber (1985).
Mannering, Derek. *Mario Lanza: Singing to the Gods*. University Press of Mississippi (2005).
Mapleson, James, H. *The Mapleson Memoirs: the Career of an Operatic Impresario*. Ed. Harold Rosenthal. Putnam (1966).
Marek, Dan H. *Giovanni Battista Rubini and the Bel Canto Tenors*. Scarecrow Press (2013).
Martland, Peter. *Recording History: The British Record Industry, 1888 – 1931*. Scarecrow Press (2013).

Martland. S.P. "Caruso's First Recordings: Myth and Reality." *ARSC Journal XXV* I:ii (1994).
McInerney, Jay. "Milan Notebook: A Night at La Scala." *New Yorker* (Dec. 25, 2000 & Jan. 1, 2001).
McIver, Stuart B. *Dreamers, Schemers and Scalawags*. Pineapple Press (1993).
McLeod, Hugh. "Christianity and Nationalism in Nineteenth Century Europe." *International journal for the Study of the Christian Church*, 15:1 (2015).
McLeod, K. "Bohemian Rhapsodies: Operatic Influences on Rock Music." *Popular Music* 20:2 (2001).
Mendelsohn, Gerald A. "Verdi the Man and Verdi the Dramatist." In *19th-Century Music*, Vol. 2:2 (Nov, 1978).
Meyerbeer, Giacomo (2001). *The Diaries of Giacomo Meyerbeer: Volume 1. 1791–1893 & Volume 2. The Prussian Years and "Le prophète", 1840–1849*. Trans., Ed. and Annotated by Robert Letellier. Fairleigh Dickinson University Press (2001).
Michotte, Edmond. *Richard Wagner's visit to Rossini, and An Evening at Rossini's in Beau-Sejour*. University of Chicago Press (2016).
Migliavacca, Giorgio. "Gaetano Fraschini: il tenore della transizione da Donizetti a Verdi." in *Moderne Sprachen* 44 (2000).
Miller, James. *Flowers in the Dustbin: The Rise of Rock and Roll, 1947–1977*. Fireside (2000).
Miller, Richard. "The Role of Language in National Pedagogies." In *National Schools of Singing*. Scarecrow Press (1997).
Misch, Rochus. *Hitler's Last Witness: The Memoirs of Hitler's Bodyguard*. Frontline Books (2014).
Morse, Peter. *Richard Strauss's Recordings: A Complete Discography* (2020).
Moscheles, Charlotte. *Life of Moscheles, with Selections from his Diaries and Correspondence, by his Wife*, tr. A.D. Coleridge, vol. 1 (London, 1873).
Mosco, Carner. "Alban Berg in His Letters to His Wife." *Music & Letters* Vol. 50:3. Oxford University Press. (July, 1969).
Münch, Paul. "Homines tertii generis: Gesangskastraten in der Kulturgeschichte Europas." *Essener Unikate*, 14 (2000).
Murphy, Agnes G. *Melba: A Biography*. Palala Press (2016).
Nagel, Thomas. "The Absurd." in *Mortal Questions*. Cambridge University Press (1979).
Newman, Ernest. *The Life of Richard Wagner, Volume IV: 1866–1883*. Cambridge University Press (1978).
Nicoli, Giuseppe (2015). "Romano e la sua storia ... sulle orme di Damiano Muoni." http://www.comune.romano.bg.it/attachments/article/539/Romano%20e%20la%20sua%20storia...pdf.
Nuzzo, Ferruccio. "Mario Del Monaco." In *Tenors in Opera*. Opera Magazine Ltd (2003).
Osborne, Richard. *Herbert Von Karajan: A Life in Music*. Chatto & Windus (1998).
Ozouf, Mona. *La Fête révolutionnaire (1789–1799)*. Edition Gallimard (1976).
Parker, David L. "Golden Voices, Silver Screen: Opera Singers as Movie Stars." *The Quarterly Journal of the Library of Congress*, Vol. 37: 3/4. (Summer/Fall 1980).
Parr, Sean M. "Wagnerian Singing and the Limits of Vocal Pedagogy." *Current Musicology* (2019).
Pearse, Cecilia M., and Hird, Frank. *The Romance of a Great Singer: A Memoir of Mario*. Smith, Elder & Co. (1910).
Peschel, Enid Rhodes and Peschel, Richard E. "Medical Insights into the Castrati in Opera." *American Scientist*, Vol. 75: 6 (November–December 1987).
Pleasants, Henry. *The Great Singers*. Gollancz (1974).
Pleasants, Henry. *The Great Tenor Tragedy*. Amadeus Press (1995).
Pleasants, Henry, Ed. *Hanslick's Musical Criticism*. Dover Publications (1988).

Potter, John. "The Tenor-Castrato connection, 1760–1860." *Early Music*, Vol. 15:1. Oxford University Press (2006).
Potter, John. *The Tenor: History of a Voice*. Yale University Press (2010).
Rambaud, Yveling and Coulon, E. *Les Théâtres en Robe de Chambre*. Achille Faure. (1866).
Ravens, Simon. *The Supernatural Voice: A History of High Male Singing*. Boydell Press (2014).
Reeves, Simms. *On the Art of Singing* (1900).
Rene, Schoen and Eugenie, Anna. *America's Musical Inheritance – Memories and Reminiscences*. G.P Putnam (1941).
Reichardt, Johann Friedrich, ed. *Berlinische musikalische Zeitung* (1969).
Reyfman, Irina. *Ritualized Violence Russian Style: The Duel in Russian Culture and Literature*. Stanford University Press (2008).
Robledo, Julio Enciso. *Memorias de Julián Gayarre*. Laida Edición e Imagen (1990).
Roche, Jerome. "Giovanni Antonio Rigatti and the Development of Venetian Church Music in the 1640s." *Music & Letters* 57:3 (1976).
Rogers, Francis. "Adolphe Nourrit." *The Musical Quarterly,* 25 (1939).
Rogers, Francis. "America's First Grand Opera Season." *The Musical Quarterly*, Vol. 1, No. 1 (Jan., 1915).
Rosen, Charles. *Freedom and the Arts: Essays on Music and Literature*. Harvard University Press (2002).
Rosselli, John. *The Opera Industry in Italy from Cimarosa to Verdi: The Role of the Impresario*. Cambridge University Press (1984).
Rosselli, John. *Singers of Italian opera: the history of a profession*. Cambridge University Press (1995).
Sataloff, Robert Thayer. *Clinical Assessment of Voice*. Plural Publishing (2017).
Scarry, John. *James Joyce and John McCormack*. Revue belge de philologie et d'histoire, tome 52, fasc. 3. Langues et littératures modernes (1974).
Schönberg, Arnold. *Sämtliche Werke: Pierrot lunaire*. Josef Rufer (ed.). Universal Edition AG and Schott Music International, Section 6, series B, 24/1 (307) (1995).
Schonberg, Harold C. *Facing the Music*. Summit Books (1981).
Schopenhauer, Arthur. "On the Sufferings of the World." in *The Meaning of Life*, ed. E.D Klemke. Oxford University Press (1981).
Scott, Michael. *The Record of Singing to 1914*. Duckworth (1977).
Seghers, René. *Franco Corelli: Prince of Tenors*. Amadeus Press (2008).
Seligman, Vincent. *Puccini Among Friends*. Macmillan (1938).
Senner, Wayne M., Wallace, Robin, Meredith, William. *The Critical Reception of Beethoven's Compositions by his Compositions by his German Contemporaries, Vol. 2*. University of Nebraska Press. No.240 (2001).
Shaman, William. *More EJS: Discography of the Edward J. Smith Recordings – Unique Opera Records Corporation*. Greenwood Press (1999).
Shaw, Bernard. *Shaw's Music: The Complete Musical Criticism of Bernard Shaw*. Ed. Dan H. Laurence. The Bodley Head. Vol. I (1876–1890) (1981).
Simms, Bryan. *The Atonal Music of Arnold Schoenberg, 1908 – 1923*. Oxford University Press (2000).
Skelton, Geoffrey, ed. *Cosima Wagner's Diaries: 1869 to 1877*. Yale University Press (1997).
Smith, Micheal Lee Jr. *Adolphe Nourrit, Gilbert Duprez, and the high C: The influences of operatic plots, culture, language, theater design, and growth of orchestral forces on the development of the operatic tenor vocal production*. UNLV Theses, Dissertations, Professional Papers, and Capstones. 1273 (2011).
Solomon, Maynard. *Beethoven*. Schirmer Books (1998).

Sorba, Carlotta. "To Please the Public: Composers and Audiences in Nineteenth-Century Italy." *The Journal of Interdisciplinary History*, Vol. 36, No. 4, Opera and Society: Part II (2006).
Sorba, Carlotta. "National Theater and the Age of Revolution in Italy." *Journal of Modern Italian Studies* 17 (2012).
Taruskin, Richard. "The Stone Guest and Its Progeny," in *Opera and Drama in Russia as Preached and Practiced in the 1860s*. UMI Press (1981).
Taruskin, Richard. "Some Thoughts on the History and Historiography of Russian Music," *Journal of Musicology*, 3.4 (1984).
Trenner, Franz, ed. *Cosima Wagner – Richard Strauss: ein Briefwechsel*. Verdffentlichungen der Richard Strauss Gesellschaft. Schneider (1978).
Trippett, David. *Wagner's Melodies: Aesthetics and Materialism in German Musical Identity*. Cambridge University Press (2016).
Vennard, William. *Singing: The Mechanism and the Technic*. Carl Fischer LLC (1967).
Verdino-Süllwold, Carla Maria. *We Need a Hero! Heldentenors from Wagner's Time to the Present*. Weiala Press (1989).
Vest, Jason. *Adolphe Nourrit, Gilbert-Louis Duprez, and Transformations of Tenor Technique in the Early Nineteenth Century: Historical and Physiological Considerations* (DMA dissertation, University of Kentucky) (2009).
von Czartoryski, Konstantin. *Recensionen und allgemeine Bemerkungen über Theater und Musik*, (1853 – 1855). Bei J. F. Greß (2010).
von Meck, Galena (trans). Eds. Garden, Edward & Gotteri, Nigel. *'To My Best Friend'; Correspondence Between Tchaikovsky and Nadezhda von Meck, 1876–1878*. Clarendon Press (1993).
Wagner, Richard. *Richard Wagner's Letters to his Dresden Friends*, trans. J. S. Shedlock. Vienna House (1972).
Wagner Handbook, Ed. Ulrich Müller and Peter Wapnewski, trans. John Deathridge. Harvard University Press (1992).
Wagner in Performance. Eds. Millington, Barry and Spencer, Stewart Yale University Press (1992).
Wagner, Richard. "The Virtuoso and the Artist," in *Richard Wagner's Prose Works*, trans. and ed. William Ashton Ellis. Broude Bros (1966).
Warrack, John; and West, Ewan. *The Oxford Dictionary of Opera*. Oxford University Press (1992).
Watson, Brian James. *Wagner's Heldentenors: Uncovering the Myths*. University of Texas (2005).
Weininger, Otto. *Geschlecht und Charakter: Eine prinzipielle Untersuchung*. Wilhelm Braumüller (1903).
Weinstock, Herbert. *Donizetti and the World of Opera in Italy, Paris, and Vienna in the First Half of the Nineteenth Century*. Methuen (2000).
Whittall, Mary and Gray, Andrew, eds. *Richard Wagner: My Life*. Cambridge University Press (1983).
Williams, Jeannie. *Jon Vickers: A Hero's Life*. UPNE (2007).
Williams, John R. "Emma Bovary and the Bride of Lammermoor." In *Nineteenth-Century French Studies*, Vol. 20, No. ¾ (1992).
Winokur, Mark. "Improbable Ethnic Hero: William Powell and the Transformation of Ethnic Hollywood." *Cinema Journal*, 27.1 (1987).
Zicari, Massimo. *Verdi in Victorian London*. Open Book Publishers (2016).
Zosimus. *The Decline of Rome*. Trinity University Press (1967).
Zweig, Stefan. *The World of Yesterday*. Cassell (1947).

Index

Abbado, Claudio   372, 389
Abendroth, Hermann   194, 272
Abenteuer am Lido (film)   237
Abott, Bessie   145
AC/DC   423–424
Acerbi, Giuseppe   172
Ackermann, Otto   278
Acoustics   8, 25, 49–51, 53, 57, 65, 67, 103, 109, 163, 166, 169, 173, 178, 207, 248, 257, 258, 262, 276–277, 294, 344, 404–405, 408, 410, 418, 454–455
Adam, Adolphe   128, 277, 287, 335, 338, 385, 421, 426–427, 457
  Works by:
    Brasseur de Preston, Le   128
    Chalet, Le   335
    Fidèle berger, Le   128
    Postillon de Lonjumeau, Le   287, 338, 346, 435
    Serment, Le   128
    Minuit, chrétiens! (O Holy night)   177, 257, 426
Adam, Ken   385
Adams, John   xxi
Adès, Thomas   376
  Works by:
    Tempest, The   376
Adorno, Theodor   93, 106, 192, 440
Aelia Eudoxia   1
Apollo Space Programme   xv
Arcadius, Emperor   1
Affre, Agustarello   56, 347
Aguilera, Christina   14
Akimova, Sophia   369
Al diavolo la celebrità (film)   224
Alagna, Roberto   162–163, 353, 399
Albanese, Francesco   279
Albanese, Licia   222, 252, 274, 292, 295
Albani, Carlo   172, 178–179
Albani, Emma   42, 149, 153, 172, 175, 342
Albarn, Damon   376
  Works by:
    Monkey – Journey to the West   376
Albertazzi, Emma   100
Albrecht, Gerd   397
Alda, Frances   217
Aldenhoff, Bernd   310
Aldrich, Perley Dunn   145, 147–148, 187
Aleotti, Giovanni Battista   50
Alexandrovich, Mikhail   371
Alexandrov, Yuriy   374
Alfano, Franco   188
Alfieri, Vittorio   31
Allegri, Gregorio   4–5, 7
  Works by:
    Miserere   4–5, 7
Althouse, Paul   292
Alvarez, Albert   112
Álvarez, Marcello   399
Amaury-Duval, Eugène Emmanuel Pineux   332
Allen, Woody   111, 247
  Works by:
    Bullets Over Broadway   111
    Midnight in Paris   247
Allgemeine Musikalische Zeitung   57, 115, 120–121
American Idol   421
American in Paris, An (film)   247
Anchors Aweigh (film)   246
Anders, Peter   203, 205, 311, 313, 320
Anderson, Marion   248, 436
Andry, Peter   269
Anelli, Angelo   32
Anema e core (film)   224
Ángeles, Victoria de las   272, 274–275, 287
Angelo, Gianna D'   203, 296
Animal Crackers (film)   215
Annie Get your Gun (film)   247
Ansani, Giovanni   38
Anselmi, Giuseppe   177–179
Ansermet, Ernest   271, 352
Antonęnko, Aleksandrs   441
Antonicelli, Giuseppe   279, 292

Aprile, Giuseppe   17
Aragall, Giacomo   398
Araia, Francesco   13
Araiza, Francisco   398
Araja, Francesco   356
  Works by:
    Tsefal i Prokris   356
Arámburo, Antonio   112, 175–177, 179, 387
Argento, Dominick   xxii
Arlen, Richard   214
Arnim, Achim von   115
  Works by:
    Knaben Wunderhorn, Des   115
Ashby, Hall   408
Aspden, Suzanne   426YO
Astaire, Fred   247
Atlantov, Vladimir   372–373, 441
Atonality   24, 192, 230
Auber, Daniel-François-Esprit   52–53, 66, 69, 194, 221, 288, 334–336
  Works by:
    Domino noir, Le   336
    Fra Diavolo   221, 224, 338
    Muette de Portici, La   52–53
    Premier jour de bonheur, La   335
Auer, Leopold   xvi, 43–45
Augér, Arleen   26
Auric, Georges   348
Avalon Boys, The   220
Ave Maria (film)   221
Avenarius, Ferdinand   125
Aznavour, Charles   419

Bach, Johann Sebastian   xx, 6, 71, 118, 133, 209, 287–288, 445
Bachrich, Ernst   191
Back to the Future (film)   423
Bacon, Francis   xv
Bader, Carl Adam   124–125
Bahr-Mildenburg, Anna von   305–307, 437
Baillot, Pierre   44, 333
Baker, Josephine   111
Baker, Roy Thomas   420
Balakirev, Mily Alexeyevich   271, 358
  Works by:
    Tamara   271
Balfe, Michael   78, 83, 91, 221
  Works by:
    Bohemian Girl, The   221
    Falstaff   83
Balthus (Balthasar Klossowski de Rola)   445
Baltsa, Agnes   397

Balzac, Honoré de   20–21
  Works by:
    Comédie Humaine, La   20
    Sarrasine   20–21
Band Wagon, The (film)   247
Bandiera Brothers   32
Bantyshev, Alexander   358
Barbaia, Domenico   35–36, 46, 67, 77
Barber, Frances   442
Barber, Samuel   xxii, 183, 288, 315
  Works by:
    Antony and Cleopatra   29 30, 215
    Vanessa   183, 288
Barber, Frances   442
Barbiere di Siviglia, Il (film)   224
Barbieri, Fedora   44–45, 72, 274
Barbirolli, Sir John   272, 286, 297
Barbot, Joseph Théodore Désiré   340
Barenboim, Daniel   326, 450
Barioni, Daniele   279
Barrymore, Ethel   245
Barrymore, John   215, 235
Barthes, Roland   20
Bartoli, Cecilia   13, 34, 384, 433–434, 446
Bartolini, Lando   282, 384–385
Bartsal, Anton   362
Basevi, Abramo   342, 347
Bastianini, Ettore   256, 260, 274, 281, 296
Battistini, Mattia   237
Baucardé, Carlo   87–88, 91, 259
Baudelaire, Charles   334, 348–350
Bauer, Harold   216, 223, 335
Bauernfeld, Eduard von   415
Baum, Kurt   250, 279, 292, 323, 433
"Because You're Mine"   252
Bay, Michael   viii
Bayreuther Festspiele (Bayreuth Festival)   xxii, xxvi, 48–49, 52, 87, 95, 126, 132, 134–136, 140–143, 155–157, 173, 194, 199, 202, 206, 217, 223, 288, 292, 301, 303, 306, 310–315, 317–320, 324–326, 342, 347, 364, 446, 449–452
BBC (British Broadcasting Corporation)   x, 379
"*Be My Love*"   246
Beasha, Emanne   403
Beatles, The   277
Beaumarchais, Pierre-Augustin Caron de   65
Bécaud, Gilbert   419
Bechet, Sidney   419
Beck, Karl   132–133
Beckett, Samuel Barclay   viii

Beczała, Piotr   269, 412, 437–438, 453
Beecham, Sir Thomas   201, 222, 256, 272, 274, 301, 304, 314, 320, 352
Beerbohm, Max   22
Beethoven, Ludwig van   6, 13, 16, 20, 24, 28, 31–32, 46–47, 56,   63, 68, 84, 114–125, 138, 142
  Works by:
  Adelaide   122
  Christus am Ölberge   6
  Eroica (Symphony No.3 in Eb)   312
  Fidelio   xxi, 13, 16, 17, 86, 115–119, 121–124, 126, 128, 133, 138, 205, 229, 249, 273, 303, 317–321, 323–324, 394, 432, 446–447
  Symphony No.5 in C minor   63
Being There (film)   408
Bekova, Eleonora   373
Bell Telephone Hour   256
Bellini, Vincenzo   28–29, 35, 38–39, 45, 60, 62, 76–79, 81–84, 91–92, 99–100, 103, 105, 107, 112, 129, 164, 174, 179, 224, 259, 262, 288, 332, 383–384, 391, 393, 406, 422, 432, 434
  Works by:
  Adelson e Salvini   77
  Beatrice di Tenda   76, 82, 92, 391, 393
  Bianca e Fernando   77
  Bianca e Gernando   77
  Briganti, I   84
  Capuleti e i Montecchi, I   76, 77, 440
  Norma   28, 43, 45, 77, 81–82, 92, 99, 122, 175, 183, 255, 259, 279, 280, 383, 395, 435, 440
  Pirata, Il   60, 77–79, 81, 92, 259, 263
  Puritani, I   40, 76–81, 84, 87, 101, 190, 227, 239, 257, 263, 279–280, 286, 393, 432, 433
  Sonnambula, La   43, 62, 77, 101, 434
  Straniera, La   77
  Zaira   77
Beltrán, Tito   399
Bennett, Richard Rodney   376
  Works by:
  Victory   376
Bennett, Tony   251, 419
Benzi, Robert   396
Beowulf   27, 314
Berberian, Cathy   378
Berchet, Giovanni   31
Beresford, Bruce   385
Berezovsky, Maksim   356

Berg, Alban   xxii, 25, 191–193, 195, 197, 208–209, 319, 321, 382
  Works by:
  Lulu   321, 382
  Wozzeck   ix, xxii, 191–195, 319, 452
Berger, Ludwig   416
Bergonzi, Carlo   xvii–xix, xxvi, 60, 93, 104, 171, 190, 263, 272, 281, 294–299, 304, 372, 389, 396, 406, 409, 446, 456
Berio, Francesco Maria   36–37
Berio, Luciano   376, 378
  Works by:
  Folk Songs   378
  Melodrama   378
  Re in Ascolto, Un   376
Bériot, Charles-Auguste de   333
Berkeley, Busby   220, 239, 376
Berkeley, Michael
  Works by:
  Jane Eyre   376
Berlioz, Hector   xx, 40, 53–56, 61, 63–66, 69–70, 74–75, 83, 96, 101–102, 111, 119, 123–124, 127, 156, 222, 288, 330–334, 336, 338–339, 341–342, 352, 419
  Works by:
  Béatrice et Bénédict   332, 338, 345
  Benvenuto Cellini   53, 83, 133, 288, 331
  Damnation de Faust, La   65, 156, 268, 288, 336, 352, 435
  Grande Messe des morts   69, 127
  Marseillaise, La   75
  Mort d'Orphélie   333
  Nuits d'été   341
  Symphonie fantastique   xx, 63
  Te Deum   69–70
  Troyens, Les   133, 317–318, 353, 442
Bernard, Paul   346
  Works by:
  Bredouille   346
Bernardi, Francesco ("Senesino")   3
Bernhardt, Sarah   22–27, 45, 65, 160–161, 251, 316, 334, 392, 441–442
Bernheim, Benjamin   8, 449
Bernheimer, Martin   327
Bernstein, Leonard   242, 268, 288, 399
  Works by:
  Candide   11, 288
Berry, Chuck   xix, 423
Berry, Matt   435
Berry, Halle   436
Bertin, Louis-François   66, 334

Bertin, Louise 96
    Works by:
        Esmeralda 334
Bertolucci, Bernardo 382
Beyoncé (Knowles) 14
"*Billie Jean*" 424
Bing, Sir Rudolph 266, 268, 274, 279, 281, 289, 291, 316, 318
Birtwistle, Sir Harrison 376–377, 379
    Works by:
        Gaiwan 376
        Mask of Orpheus, The 377
        Minotaur, The 377
        Second Mrs Kong, The 377
Bist mein Glück, Du (film) 221
Bispham, David 161
Bixio, Cesare A. 226
Bizet, Georges 52, 111, 212, 288, 340–341, 383
    Works by:
        Carmen ix, xxi, 154, 175, 177, 208, 212, 255–256, 268, 284, 288–289, 292, 318, 334, 340–341, 346, 348, 352, 394, 446
        Djamileh 52
        Pêcheurs de Perles, Les ix, 341, 369, 383
Björling, Gösta 273
Björling, Jussi xvi, 250, 272–277, 280, 289, 294, 297, 309, 450
Björling, Olle 273
Blake, Rockwell 434–435
Blanc, Dominique 23, 45
Blanc, Mel 300
Blech, Leo 193, 194, 200, 202, 233
    Works by:
        Aglaja 200
        Versiegelt 202
Blossom Time (film) 233
Bocelli, Andrea xxvi, 409, 412–413, 421
Bodanzky, Artur 186, 223, 301, 350
Boero, Felipe
    Works by:
        Tucuman 230
Bohemian Girl, The (film) 221
"*Bohemian Rhapsody*" 419–420
Böhm, Karl xxii, 26, 203, 205–206, 249, 272, 289, 317, 319, 321–322, 325–326
Boieldieu, François-Adrien 122
    Works by:
        Béniovski ou les Exilés du Kamchattka 120
Boito, Arrigo xxiv, 106, 109–110, 177, 230, 255, 363, 396, 398, 442–443
    Works by:
        Mefistofele 177, 255, 366, 396, 398, 440
        Nerone 230
Boldrey, Richard viii
Bolton, Michael 391, 424–425
Bonaparte, Napoléon viii, 10, 33, 53, 114, 122–123
Bonci, Alessandro 80, 172, 183
Bonisolli, Franco 175, 289, 326, 387, 389, 392, 433–434, 437
Bonnard, Mario 226
Bonoldi, Claudio 38
Bonynge, Richard 299, 389, 391, 393, 398
Bordogni, Giulio 44–46, 96
Borgatti, Giuseppe xxi, 88, 168, 172–173, 177, 441
Borkh, Inge 284–285
Borodin, Alexander 356, 359, 367
    Works by:
        Knyáz Ígor 356, 359, 367
Borosoni, Francesco 16
Bortniansky, Dmitri 356
Bosetti, Hermione 194
Bostridge, Ian 404
Botha, Johann 437
Boughton, Rutland 380
Bouilly, Jean-Nicolas 116
Boulanger, Nadia 348, 351
Boulanger, Lili 348
Boulez, Pierre 25, 325
Boult, Sir Adrian 288
Bow, Clara 239
Bowie, David 86, 420, 423
Boyd, William 144–145
    Works by:
        Ice-Cream War, An 145
Boyd Neel Orchestra 380
Braham, John 18–19, 379
Brahms, Johannes xxi, 40, 290, 302–303, 380, 419, 422, 427
    Works by:
        "*Feldeinsamkeit*" 303
        Hungarian Dance No.5 290
        Concerto for Violin in D minor 290
        Liebeslieder-Walzer 302
        Rhapsodie für eine Altstimme 40, 419
Brâncuși, Constantin 431
    Works by:
        Kiss 431
Brand, Max
    Works by:
        Maschinist Hopkins 199

Brando, Marlon   244–245
Branzell, Karin   243
Brassens, Georges   419
Brazzi, Rossano   251
Brecht, Bertolt (Friedrich)   196–197, 244, 408
Brel, Jacques Romain Georges   419
Breme, Ludovico di   31
Bremner, Robert   43
Brenciu, Marius   406
Brentano, Clemens   115
   Works by:
      Knaben Wunderhorn, Des   115
Bretan, Laura   455
Bréton, Tomás
   Works by:
      Dolores, La   40
Bridge, Frank   380
Brightman, Sarah   420
Brignone, Guido   226
Brison   1
Britten, Benjamin   ix, xxi–xxii, 318, 371, 376–381, 409, 422
   Works by:
      Death in Venice   376, 380
      Midsummer's Night Dream   336, 371, 409
      Owen Wingrave   376
      Peter Grimes   ix, xxii, 318, 379–380, 394
      Serenade for Tenor, Horn and Strings   380
Broadbent, Jim   247
Bronder, Peter   449
Broschi, Carlo ("Farinelli")   3, 267
"*Brother, Can you Spare me a Dime?*"   419
Brownlee, Lawrence   435–436
Bruant, Aristide   350
Bruckner, Anton   313
Brunacci, Angelo   91
Bruneau, Alfred   344, 348
   Works by:
      Attaque du moulin, L'   344, 348
Büchner, Georg   254
Buckley, Jeff   xxviii
Bulakhov, Pavel   361
Bullets over Broadway (film)   247
Bülow, Hans von   229, 432
Bumbry, Grace   268, 436
Bungert, August   200
   Works by:
      Nausikaa   200
      Odysseus Tod   200
Buñuel, Luis   111
Burbage, Richard   293

Burgess, Anthony   301
   Works by:
      The Worm and the Ring   301
Burgos, Rafael Frühbeck de   384
Burian, Karel   200–202
Burke, Edmund   xii, xv
Burles, Charles   353
Burney, Charles   1, 5, 266
Burroughs, Edgar Rice   214
Burton, Richard   86, 293, 316, 399
Busby Berkeley's Gold Diggers of 1935 (film)   220
Busch, Ernst   196
   Works by:
      Silbersee, Der   196
Busch, Fritz   194, 196–197, 272, 310, 314
Busoni, Ferruccio   165, 167, 191, 194
   Works by:
      Doktor Faust   194
Butler, Ashleigh   403
Buys, Jan Brandts   208–209
Bychkov, Semyon   398
"*By the Waters of the Minnetonka*"   217
Byron, George Gordon   20, 36–37, 95
   Works by:
      Childe Harold's Pilgrimage   36
      Manfred   20

Caballé, María de Montserrat   391, 395–397, 420–421
Cabaret   197, 349–350
Caffetto, Carlo   166
Cabinet des Dr. Caligari, Das (film)   231
Calamity Jane (film)   247
Callas, Maria   xii–xiv, 54, 86, 181, 255, 258–260, 262–264, 272, 274, 279–281, 284–287, 292– 293, 383, 391, 421, 434, 453
Calleja, Joseph   252, 439–440
Callinicos, Constantine   252
Calvé, Emma   167
Camarena, Javier   437
Campanini, Cleofonte   171
Campanini, Italo   175–176, 180–181, 183–184, 342
Camussi, Ezio   181
   Works by:
      Dubarry, La   181
Candia, Giovanni Matteo De (see "Mario")   95, 97
Cantelli, Guido   272

Cantors   137, 154, 185–186, 202, 232, 234, 291–292, 309, 385, 398
Capelli, Obelissima   172
Capocci, Gaetano   6
Capoul, Victor   xx, 335, 345
Capponi, Giuseppe   89
Cappuccilli, Piero   372, 397
Capuana, Franco   xxiii
Caravaggio, Michelangelo Merisi da   214, 254, 290, 431
  Works by:
  Death of the Virgin   290
  Judith Slaying Holofernes   431
  Pieta   431
  Supper at Emmaus   214
Carducci, Giosuè   444
Carelli, Beniamino   43
Carelli, Gabor   222
Carey, Clive   145
Carey, Mariah   14
Carmen (film)   211
Carnegie Hall   xix, 219, 234, 248, 269, 295
Carolsfeld, Schnorr von   136, 138–140, 266, 304
Carosone, Renato   xiv
  Works by:
  Maruzzella   xiv
Carpi, Fernando   172
Carousel (film)   247
Carreras, José   xvi, xix, 60, 149, 190, 253, 295, 384, 388–389, 394–400, 420, 441, 456
Carroll, Harry   220
Caruso, Enrico   vii, xiv, xix, xxi, 7, 9, 24, 80, 88, 93, 110, 145, 161–168, 171–172, 174, 176–178, 180–188, 190, 201–203, 208–209, 212–215, 218–221, 233, 235, 242–243, 250–251, 253, 255, 257, 273, 291–292, 294, 297, 308, 348, 350, 366, 392, 404, 408–410, 431, 450, 453, 455
Casa, Lisa della   25, 164, 221, 405
Casa Lontana (film)   221
Casablanca (film)   237
Casanova, Giacomo Girolamo   11–12
Casati, Gabrio   34
Casella, Alfredo   165, 191
Cassilly, Richard   313
Castelnuovo-Tedesco, Mario   191
Castrati   1–6, 9–16, 18–21, 27, 33, 34–35, 46, 51, 54, 58, 71–72, 75, 77, 83–84, 88, 257, 263–264, 267, 329, 333, 424
Catalani, Alfredo   191
Cavaliere del sogno, Il (film)   226

Cavalli, Francesco   xxi
Cavos, Catterino   356
  Works by:
  Bogatyr   356
  Ivan Susanin   356
  Knyaz-nevidimka   356
  Ilya Bogatyr   356
  Rusalka   356
  Zephyre et Flore   356
  Zhar–ptitsa   356
Cavour, Camillo   95
Cebotari, Maria   210
Celebrity Deathmatch (MTV)   388
Celoni, Anna-Maria Pellegrini   416
Chabrier, Emmanuel   156, 344, 346, 351
  Works by:
  Gwendoline   356
  Roi Malgré Lui, Le   346
  Vaucochard et Fils   351
Chaliapin, Fyodor   166–167, 354, 362, 366–367, 373–374
Chandos   288, 373
Chaplin, Charles   214, 235, 313
Charke, Charlotte   441
Charlemagne   71
Charpentier, Gustave   165, 345, 348–351
  Works by:
  Didon   348
  Fleurs du Mal, Les   348
  Grisélidis   345
  Impressions Fausses   348
  Julien, ou La vie du poète   165, 345
  Louise   345, 347–351
  Poèmes chantés, Les   348
Charpentier, Marc-Antoine   329
Charpentier, Leon (see Leonov, Lev)   357
Chassériau, Théodore   254
Chatrian, Pierre-Alexandre   392
Chaucer, Geoffrey   328
Chausson, Ernst   347, 422
  Works by:
  Roi Arthus, Le   347
Chauvet, Guy   353
Chekhov, Anton   360
Chéreau, Patrice   23
Cherubini, Luigi   66, 331, 333, 338
  Works by:
  Medea   331
Chevalier, Maurice   239, 251, 418, 350
Chew, Richard   376
  Works by:
  Mary Seacole   376
Chimay, Princess   66

Chi è più felice di me! (film)   226
Chizzola, Gaetano   37–38
Chopin, Frédéric   40, 56, 66, 96, 428
Chorley, Henry   54, 77–78, 93–94, 100–101, 104–105, 127
Christoff, Boris   256, 274, 287
Churchill, Sir Winston   379
Ciaffei, Francesco   146
Ciaroff-Ciarini, Romano   172
Ciccimarra, Giuseppe   37–38, 127–128
Cigarettes   144–145, 179, 189
Cilea, Francesco   164–165, 171
   Works by:
     Adriana Lecouvreur   40, 112, 165, 269, 299, 397, 437, 448
     Arlesiana, L'   164–165, 252
     Gloria   171
Cimarosa, Domenico   17, 26, 35, 68, 94, 99
Cinthio (Giovanni Battista Giraldi)   37
   Works by:
     Capitano Moro, Un   37
Cioni, Renato   383
Civinini, Guelfo   386
Clairval (Jean-Baptiste Guignard)   329
Clark, Louis   408
Clarke, Graham   449
Cleese, John   343
Clément, Edmond   348
Cleva, Fausto   269, 272, 298, 314
Cleveman, Lars   450
"Clouseau, Inspector"   249
Cluytens, André   272, 288, 325, 352, 396
Coates, Albert   301
Cobain, Kurt   428
Cobos, Jesús López   398
Cohen, Leonard   xxviii, 427
Colbran, Isabella   18, 35–37, 76
Cole, Vinson   436
Colonne, Édouard   229, 344, 347
Como, Perry   251, 253
Condell, Henry   293
Conried, Heinrich   183, 237, 291
Constantinides, Dinos   xxii
Constantino, Florencio   40, 43, 230
Cook, Peter   379
Cooper, Gary   228, 239, 256
Cooper, Emil   292
Corbiau, Gérard   257
Corden, James   409
Cordero, Antonio   175
Corelli, Franco   vii, xxi, xxvi, 13, 21, 54, 78, 90, 94, 96, 229, 255–270, 272, 277, 280–281, 284, 289, 292–294, 297–298, 304, 315, 341, 386–387, 392–393, 396, 404, 406, 409, 412, 431, 438–439, 446, 453
Corena, Fernando   280, 296
Corneille, Pierre   26
Cornelius, Peter   288
Corsi, Rina   274
Cossotto, Fiorenza   372, 384
Cossutta, Carlos   384
Cotillard, Marion   112
Cotogni, Antonio   146, 155, 227, 456
Cottone, Salvatore   167, 177
Couderc, Joseph-Antoine-Charles   335–336
Courbet, Gustave   336
Cowell, Simon   455
Coughlin, Charles Edward   241
Cox, Jean   313
Craig, Charles   441
Cremonini, Giuseppe   168
Crescentini, Girolamo   10, 17, 88
Crivelli, Gaetano   44–45
Croft, Dwayne   400
Croiza, Claire   145
Crook, Mackenzie   409
Crooks, Richard   249
Crosby, Bing   236, 419, 427
Crossover   407–409, 419
Cruise, Tom   214
Cuénod, Hugues-Adhémar   350–351
Cui, César Antonovich   348, 359
Culshaw, John   284, 324–325, 327
Cura, José   399
Cure, The   423
Curioni, Alberico   82
Curtis, Ernesto de   251, 269
Czartoryski, Count Konstanin von   122
Czinner, Paul   307

D'Albert, Eugen   208
   Works by:
     Toten Augen, Die   208
     Tiefland   208, 306
Dalí, Salvador   86, 111, 294
Dallapiccola, Luigi   165, 191
Dalmorès, Charles   346–347
Damrosch, Walter   160–161, 223, 291
Dani, Carlo   172
"*Danny Boy*"   217
Dante Alighieri   328, 366, 444
Darby, W. Sinkler   6, 166
Dargomyzhsky, Alexander   359, 361–362
Dark Knight, The (film)   26

Works by:
   Kamennyj gost 359
   Rusalka 361
Darrin, Bobby 251
Daspuro, Nicola 392
David and Bathsheba (film) 250
Davïdov, Aleksandr 362
Davies, Fanny 380
Davis, Sir Colin 288, 389
Davy (film) 190
Day at the Races, A (film) xxii
Debussy, Clause Achille 6, 156, 271, 288, 334, 339, 344, 347–349, 443, 357, 444
Works by:
   Cinq poèmes de Charles Baudelaire 349
   Enfant prodigue, L' 156
   Fleurs du Mal, Les 334
   Martyre de Saint Sébastien, Le 271
   Pelléas et Mélisande 325, 334, 344, 347, 443
Deffès, Pierre-Louis
Works by:
   Noces de Fernande, Les 344
Degas, Edgar 66
Delacroix, Ferdinand Victor Eugène xiv, 34, 56, 73–75, 331
Works by:
   Grèce sur les Ruines de Missolonghi 74
   Mort de Sardanapale, La 74
   Liberté guidant le people, La 34, 74
Delaquerrière, José 346
Delaquerrière, Louis 346
Delavigne, Casimir 27
Delibes, Clément Philibert Léo 52, 111, 340, 344
Works by:
   Lakmé 344, 367, 369
   Roi l'a dit, Le 52
   Source, La 52
Delius, Frederick 380
Demmer, Ignaz Anton 119–120
Dench, Judy 316
Deng, Xiao-Jun 190
Deodati, de' Tovazzi 328
Deodato, Eumir de Almeida 408
Works by:
   Prelude 408
Dermota, Anton xxiv, 206, 210, 320–321
Dessau, Paul
Works by:
   Verhör des Lukullus, Das 194
Destinn, Emmy 172, 217, 306
Deutekom, Cristina 265

Devil's Brother, The (film) 221
Devriès, David 348
Dibdin, Charles 19
Works by:
   Cabinet, The 19
Dickens, Charles 5
Works by:
   David Copperfield 442–443
Diday, S. H. 59
Dillingham Immigration Commission 184
Dimitrova, Ghena 397
Divo, Il 409–410
Dix, Otto 198
Dobrowen, Issay 287
Dolce Vita, La (film) 283
Domingo, Plácido 54, 60, 109, 111, 152, 157, 166, 190, 253, 273, 289, 291, 295, 314, 341, 352, 374, 385–386, 388–389, 393–396, 399–400, 437, 443, 454
Domino, Fats 241
Don Juan (film) 215
Donizetti, Gaetano xviii–xix, xxi, xxiii, 29, 35, 38–39, 45–46, 53, 58, 61, 64–65, 69, 76–78, 83, 85, 91–93, 95, 97, 99–100, 103, 107, 111–112, 119, 122, 132, 164, 178–179, 226, 231, 258–259, 262, 286, 288, 332, 338, 357, 383, 391, 393, 396, 406, 412, 422, 433–434
Works by:
   Anna Bolena 76, 78, 80, 92, 286, 357
   Betly, ossia La capanna svizzera 85
   Caterina Cornaro 92, 396, 457
   Don Pasquale ix, xxiii, 93, 95, 99, 218, 239, 261
   Duca d'Alba, Il 179
   Elisabetta, Regina d'Inghilterra 18, 35, 39, 395, 400
   Elisir d'amore, L' ix, xvii, xviii, 84, 99, 173, 178, 187, 244, 278, 280, 369, 393, 397, 400
   Elvida 78
   Fille du regiment, La 58, 60–61, 68, 92, 104, 231, 396, 434
   Gianni di Calais 78
   Gianni di Parigi 85
   Giove di grasso, Il 78
   Lucia di Lammermoor 64–65, 68–69, 82–83, 92–93, 99, 107, 160, 173, 175, 178, 244–245, 268, 280–281, 286–287, 298–299, 337–338, 363, 369, 393–394, 397–398, 425, 437, 440
   Lucrezia Borgia 97, 99, 176, 181, 395

Maria Padilla 77
Marino Faliero 77–78
Martyrs, Les 53
Paria, Il 78
Parisina 64
Poliuto 107, 175–177, 258–259, 262–263, 265, 439
Roberto Devereux 92
Rosmonda d'Inghilterra 64
Zoraide di Granata 46
Donna è mobile, La (film) 224
Dont, Jakob xvi
Donzelli, Domenico 18, 45–46, 57, 60–61, 78, 81–82, 84, 110, 119, 258, 298, 414, 455
Dorfmüller, Kurt 119
Dostoevsky, Fyodor 365
Dowland, John 417
Downie, Gord 427
Doyle, Sir Arthur Conan 28
  Works by:
    "*The Adventure of Black Peter*" 28
D'Oyly Carte, Richard 339–340
Draghi, Antonio xxi
Dreyfus, Alfred 55
Dryden, John 11
Duc, Valentin 348
Duchamp, Marcel 290
  Works by:
    Fountain 290
Dunaway, Faye 381
Dunayevsky, Isaak 368
Dunhill, Thomas 380
Dubois, Théodore 348
  Works by:
    Xavière 348
Duponchel, Henri 57, 66–67
Dupont, Alexis 333–334, 348
  Works by:
    Cabrera, La 348
Duprez, Gilbert 42, 52, 54, 58–70, 77–78, 82–84, 90– 91, 97, 99, 104–105, 110, 226, 229, 263, 298, 333–338, 358, 396–397, 414, 436, 455
Durante, Jimmy 251
Dutilleux, Henri 348
Dvořák, Antonin 111, 222, 302–303
  Works by:
    Cigánské melodie 302
Dyck, Ernest van 156–157, 185, 294, 344, 347
Dylan, Bob (Robert Allen Zimmerman) 427
Dzerzhinsky, Ivan 371

Eames, Emma 180
Eastwood, Clint 246
Eberl, Anton xx
Ed Sullivan Show 256
Edison, Thomas xvi, 22, 215, 231
Edvina, Louise 145
Eggerth Marta 328
Eiffel, Gustave 145, 348, 388
Einaudi, Ludovico 412
Einem, Gottfried von xxii, 311, 321
  Works by:
    Dantons Tod 321
    Prozess, Der 311
Elgar, Edward 6
Eliot, T. S. 111
Elman, Mischa 184, 207, 237
Elmendorff, Karl 206, 301, 310
Elvey, Maurice 238
Elwes, Gervase 379–380
Elming, Poul 450
Eminem (Marshall Bruce Mathers III) 448
Endrèze, Arthur 145
Enesco, George (Enescu) 288
Engel, Pierre-Émile 344
Engels, Friedrich 356
"*Ensueño*" 421
Entartete Musik 25, 241
Entertainer, The 25
Epstein, Solomon xxii
Erb, Karl 195–196, 320
Erckmann, Émile 392
Erede, Alberto 272, 274, 352, 385
Erlanger, Camille 348
  Works by:
    Juif Polonais, Le 348
Escalaïs, Léon 56, 345–346
Eschenbach, Christoph 26
Escoffier, August 427
"*Estrellita*" 217
Ettore, Guglielmo D' 16
Eulenburg, Prince Philipp of 30
Eunuchs 1–3, 4, 6, 8, 11, 268
Eutropius 1
Eyk, Jan van 431
Eysler, Edmund 232
  Works by:
    Künstlerblut 232
    Exotischer Fürst, Ein (film) 233

Fabiano, Michael 439
Fabritiis, Oliviero de 272, 279, 392
Faccio, Franco 110
Fairbanks, Douglas 214

"*Fake Plastic Trees*" 427
Falcon, Cornélie 55
Falla, Manuel De 384, 395
  Works by:
    Retablo de Maese Pedro, El 395
    La vida breve, La 384
Fancelli, Giuseppe 89, 91
Fanfare Vagabontu 445
Farber, Yaël 442
Farina, Franco 439
Farinelli (Carlo Broschi) 3, 6, 11, 15–18, 21, 84, 91, 257, 263–270, 424
Farinelli, Il Castrato (film) 257
Farnese, Odoardo 50–51
Farnese, Elizabeth 266
Farrar, Geraldine 165, 212–213, 350
Farrell, Charles 214
Farrell, Eileen 319
"*Fat-Bottomed Girls*" 427
Fauré, Gabriel 345, 348, 411
  Works by:
    Pénélope 345
    Prométhée 345
Fayrfax, Robert
  Works by:
    Aeternae Laudis Lilium 379
Federici, Vincenzo 33
  Works by:
    Conquista delle Indie Orientali, La 33
Fellini, Federico 251, 283
Felici, Alessandro 17
  Works by:
    La cameriera astute 379
Ferdinand, Ludwig 138
Fere, Vladimir 368
Ferenczy, Franz 342
Ferraris, Franco 257
Ferrer, Cardinal Luis Ladaria 2
Ferrier, Kathleen 322
Ferris, George T. 101
Fétis, François-Joseph 39, 54, 125
Fiakerlied (film) 232
Fichte, Johann Gottlieb 114, 123
Field, John 357
Fielding, Henry 329
  Works by:
    Tom Jones 329
Fields, Gracie 144
Figner, Nikolai 166, 362–364, 373, 441
Figner, Medea 166, 363
Filippeschi, Mario 78, 279–280, 391, 433
Finck, Henry T. 158

Fine, Larry 388
"*Fingertips*" 428
Fino, Giocondo 181
  Works by:
    Festa del Grano, La 181
Finzi, Gerald 222
Fioravanti, Valentino 6, 91
Fischer, Wilhelm 133
Fischer-Dieskau, Dietrich 286, 313, 323, 443, 447
Fisher, Walter H. 339–340
Fisichella, Salvatore 384, 433
Fistoulari, Anatole 352
Fitzgerald, F. Scott 111
Fitzgerald, Zelda 111
Flagstad, Kirsten 304, 310, 313
Flaubert, Gustave 337–338
  Works by:
    Madame Bovary 337–338, 347
Flaubert, Valentino 337–338
Fleischer, Hanns 196, 208
Fleishman, Veniamin 368
Fleming, Renée 425
Fleta, Miguel 183, 188–190
Flonzaley Quartet 445
Flórez, Juan Diego 34, 61, 411, 432–435
Flotow, Friedrich, Freiherr von 99, 165, 237
  Works by:
    Martha 99, 165, 237, 367
Floyd, Carlisle xxii
Flying Deuces 221
Flynn, Errol 235, 257
Fodor-Mainvielle, Joséphine 21
Folignato, Pietro Paolo 2
Follie per l'opera (film) 226
Fomin, Yevstigney 356
Fontaine, Joan 252
Ford, Henry 241
Ford, Bruce 433, 435
Forget Me Not (film) 221
Formes, Karl 127–128
Forster, E. M. 162
  Works by:
    Howard's End 162
Foscolo, Ugo 31
Fossataro, Marcello 15
Fouquières, Louis Becq de 343
Franchetti, Alberto 9, 165–167, 171, 180
  Works by:
    Cristoforo Colombo 180
    Germania 9, 165–166
Franchi, Nazzareno 166

Francis, Pope (Jorge Mario Bergoglio)   2
Francis I of Austria   31
Francis, Connie   251, 304
Francis, Kay   279
Franklin, Aretha   xxvii, 391
Franklyn, Milt   300
Franz, Paul
Franz, Stephan   416
Fraschini, Gaetano   91–95, 105, 107, 110, 189
Frasier (television series)   388
Frazzoni, Gigliola   256
Freimüller, Ignaz   84
Freni, Morella   264–265, 268, 286, 372, 391
Frey, Paul   449
Freycinet, Charles de   145
Fricsay, Ferenc   272
Frid, Grigory   368
Frieberth, Karl   16
Friedman, Arthur L.   1Z8
Frittoli, Barbara   86
Froment, Louis de   288
Frühbeck de Burgos, Rafael   384
Fulfillingness' First Finale   428
Fun   423
Funny Face (film)   247
Fuolega, Mauro   87
Furtwängler, Wilhelm   xxii–xxv, 222–223, 229, 320, 324–325
Fusati, Nicola   xx
Fuscati, Chamaemelo   172

Gabrilowitsch, Ossip   223
Gainsbourg, Serge   419
Gaisberg, Frederick   xvii, 5, 8–9, 11, 109, 166–167, 177, 180, 218
Gaisberg, William   5, 8
Gaither, Bill   426
Gaithers, Gloria   426
Gaito, Constantino   230
  Works by:
    Ollantay   230
Galouzine, Vladimir   373–374, 441
Galuppi, Baldassare   xxi
Gance, Abel   351
Garbin, Edoardo   91, 109, 180–181
García, Manuel   38–43, 45, 53, 59, 78–80
García, Manuel *fils*   xix, 40, 41, 42–43, 78, 79, 91, 113, 164, 330, 424, 450, 456
Gardelli, Lamberto   272, 288, 299, 389, 395
Gardoni, Italo   91
Garibaldi, Giuseppe Maria   359, 361

Garland, Alex   390
Garner, James   256
Garnier, Charles   53
Gasteen, Lisa   406
Gatti, Carlo   105
Gatti-Casazza, Giulio   185, 220, 229, 366, 407
Gaubert, Philippe   445
Gautier, Franz   348
Gautier, Jules   348
Gautier, Jules   341, 347
Gavazzeni, Gianandrea   xvii, 104, 272, 281, 284, 295, 372, 384
Gay, John   186
  Works by:
    Beggar's Opera, The   186
Gay Desperado, The (film)   239
Gay, Maria   239
Gayarre, Julián   112, 150–151, 180
Gaye, Marvin   419
Gazzaniga, Giuseppe   33
  Works by:
    Due gemelli, I   33
Gedda, Nicolai   183, 272, 280–281, 287–292, 294
Gehört mein Herz, Dir (film)   221
Geminiani, Francesco   43
Gencer, Leyla   259, 265
Genina, Augusto   220
Gentil, Serafino   33–34
Gentile, Serafino   33
Gentileschi, Artemisia   431
  Works by:
    Judith Slaying Holofernes   431
Gentlemen Prefer Blondes (film)   247
Gentner, Karl   196
George White's 1935 Scandals (film)   220
Gergiev, Valery   373–374
Géricault, Jean-Louis André Théodore   114
  Works by:
    Radeau de la Méduse, Le   114
Gerron, Kurt   197
Gerstl, Richard   254
Gheorghiu, Angela   399
Ghiringhelli, Antonio   xii
Ghiaurov, Nicolai   397
Giacomelli, Gerolamo
  Works by:
    Merope   17
Giacometti, Alberto   431
  Works by:
    L'Homme qui marche   431

Giacomini, Giuseppe 386
Gibbons, Orlando 422
Gibson, Sir Alexander 261
Gielgud, Sir John viii, 22, 25
Gieseking, Walter 456
Giesen, Hubert 324
Gigli, Beniamino xvi, 9, 78, 174, 183, 215, 218–225, 228–230, 239, 243, 259, 278, 352, 393, 409
Gilbert, John 214
Gilbert, William 339–340
Gilels, Emil 369
Gilion, Mario 348
Gillion, Ode 172
Giordano, Massimo 438
Giordano, Umberto xii–xiv, 83, 164–165, 167, 171–173, 182, 191, 407, 438, 448
 Works by:
  Andrea Chénier ix, xii–xiv, xxvi, 83, 109, 164–165, 167, 171–173, 177, 178, 182, 191, 227, 244, 256, 259, 264, 279, 284, 293, 295, 384–386, 393, 395, 384–386, 393, 395, 407, 438, 440–441, 448
  Fedora 164, 252, 259, 438
  Madame Sans-Gêne 182
  Siberia 171, 370
Giordani, Marcello 412, 437
Girardi, Alexander 232
Giraud, Albert 24, 177–178
Girl from Utah, The 245
Gitlis, Ivry 290
Giudice, Franco Lo 189, 384
Giulini, Carlo Maria 272, 295, 317, 389
Giuseppe Verdi (film) 221
Glass, Philip xxi
Glazunov, Alexander
 Works by:
  Stenka Razin 271
Glaub' nie mehr an eine Frau, Ich (film) 233
Glinka, Mikhail 179, 355–358, 372
 Works by:
  Ruslan i Lyudmila 355, 358,
  Zhizn' za tsarya 179, 356–357
Glossop, Peter 392
Gluck, Christoph Willibald (Ritter von) 10, 16–17, 26, 30, 49, 51, 53, 68, 71, 119, 165, 259, 262, 288, 329–333, 433
 Works by:
  Alceste 17, 224, 330, 356, 456
  Armide 165, 330, 433
  Echo et Narcisse 330
  Iphigénie en Aulide 259, 329

Iphigénie en Tauride 53, 68, 119, 330, 333
Orfeo ed Euridice 10, 329
Goavec, André 350
Gobbi, Tito 224, 274, 280, 287, 447
"*God Save the Queen*" 422
Godard, Benjamin xx, 335, 345, 348
 Works by:
  Jocelyn xx, 335, 345, 348
  Vivandière, La 348
Goebbels, Joseph 222, 233, 311, 324
Goehr, Alexander 376
 Works by:
  Arianna 376
Goethe, Johann Wolfgang von 20, 28, 119–120, 127, 231, 254, 289, 417, 457
Gogol, Nikolai 168
 Works by:
  Taras Bulba 168
Goldberg, Albert 244
Goldmark, Karl 165, 302
Goldberg, Reiner 326
Goldmark, Rubin 223
 Works by:
  Königin von Saba, Die 302
Gomes, Carlos 107
 Works by:
  Maria Tudor 302
González, Irma 242
Goodall, Reginald 380
Gorga, Evan 439–440
Goring, Marius 294
Göring, Hermann 311
Got Talent (series) 403–409
Gould, Stephen 451–452
Gounod, Charles xx, 6–7, 25, 40, 53, 99–100, 111, 167, 169, 231, 237–238, 265, 268, 288, 335–336, 340, 347–348, 383, 418, 428, 445, 44
 Works by:
  Ave Maria 6, 428
  Colombe, La xx, 335
  Faust 6, 20, 25, 40, 53, 99, 146, 154, 167–169, 181, 202, 208, 231, 237, 244, 249–250, 254, 273, 279, 288, 334, 340–341, 345–347, 350, 367, 383, 394, 398, 417, 437, 440, 445–446, 448
  Nonne Sanglante, La 336
  Reine de Saba, La 53
  Roméo et Juliette ix, 100, 154–155, 160, 265, 268, 334, 340, 345, 352, 366
  Sapho 53, 336, 347
Goya, Francisco xxi

Gozlan, Leon   161
   Works by:
      Pluie et le Beau Temps, La   161
Grade, Leslie   252
Graener, Paul   194, 196, 199, 208
   Works by:
      Don Juans letztes Abenteuern   208
      Hanneles Himmelfahrt   199, 208
      Prinz von Homburg, Der   194
      Theophano   196, 208
Graf, Herbert   xxii
Graham, Susan   410
Granada   324
Granados, Enrique   182
   Works by:
      Goyescas   182
Grappelli, Stéphane   290, 418–419
Grassi, Celeste   172
Grayson, Kathryn   245–247, 251
Graziani, Lodovico   91
Great Caruso, The (film)   250
Greebling, Sir Arthur   379
Green, Johnny   245
Green, Mitzi   239
Grenzebach, Ernst   307
Grétry, André   xxi, 329
   Works by:
      Huron, Le   329
      Zémire et Azor   329
      MariaGes samnites, Les   329
      Amant jaloux, L'   329
      Aucassin et Nicolette   329
Griffith, David Wark   382
Grigolo, Vittorio   438
Grillparzer, Franz   31, 324
Grindhouse   381
Grisi, Giulia   82, 84, 97, 100
Gros, Jean   114
   Works by:
      Bonaparte visitant les pestiférés de Jaffa   114
Gruber, Franz   195
Gruberova, Edita   398
Guadagni, Gaetano   10, 329
Guadagno, Anton   386
Guasco, Carlo   91
Gudehus, Heinrich   135, 140, 142
Gueden, Hilde   280
Guerrero, Jacinto   287
   Works by:
      Huésped del sevillano, El   287
Guéymard, Louis   91, 336–337
Guglielmi, Giacomo   436

Guglielmi, Pietro Alessandro   xxi, 17, 91
Gui, Vittorio   272
Guichandut, Carlos   xxiii, 286
Guignard, Jean-Baptiste   329
Günther, Carl   237, 324
Guridi, Jesús   287
   Works by:
      El caserío   287
      Guys and Dolls (film)   247

Hadley, Henry
   Works by:
      Cleopatra's Night   350
Hadley, Jerry   399
Hahn, Reynaldo   288, 348, 351, 410–411, 418–419
   Works by:
      "*Énamourée, L'*"   411
      Île du rêve, L'   348, 419
Haines, William   214
Halévy, Jacques-François-Fromental-Élie   52–55, 66, 69, 99, 128, 185, 187, 334–336, 339
   Works by:
      Éclair, L'   335
      Guido et Ginevra   53, 128
      Juive, La   52–55, 66, 107, 128, 165, 183–188, 185–187, 232–233, 292, 298, 342, 345, 350, 398, 458
      Tentation, La   334
      Nabab, Le   336
Hammerstein, Oscar   80, 178, 416
Handel, Georg Frideric   xx–xxi, xxi–xxii, 16, 26, 102, 112, 219, 236, 259, 262, 379, 400, 429
   Works by:
      Giulio Cesare   259
      Hercules (Eracle)   259
      Messiah   102, 379
      Tamerlano   16
Hanslick, Eduard   304, 309
Harari, Yuval   xix–xx
Hardy, Oliver   220–221, 271
Harlow, Jean   220
Harnoncourt, Nikolaus   440
Harrold, Orville   350
Harteros, Anja   406
Hassinger, Helen   455
Hauptmann, Elizabeth   196–197
Haydn, Joseph   4, 13, 15–16, 18, 71, 118, 222, 288
Hayward, Thomas T.   250
Hazzan   234

Hazzunah 292
Heger. Robert 205, 322
    Works by:
    Verlorene Sohn, Der 205
Heifetz, Jascha 456
Heilbronn, Marie 335
Heine, Heinrich 56, 76, 96, 128, 415–416
Hellmesberger, Joseph xvi
Helmholtz, Hermann von 30, 56
Hemingway, Ernest 111
Henderson, W. J. 136, 158–159, 308
Hendrix, Jimmy 14, 423
Henke, Waldemar 193–194, 196, 208
Hennebains, Adolphe 445
Henrysson, Harald 275
Henson, Karen 110, 137, 158, 335
Henze, Hans Werner xxi–xxii, 376
    Works by:
    We Come to the River 376
Heppner, Benjamin 450–451
Herbert, Victor 235
    Works by:
    Natoma 235
Here's to Romance (film) 239
Hérold, Ferdinand 338
    Works by:
    Zampa 338
Herold, Vilhelm 301
Hertz, Alfred 201–202, 223
Herzog, Werner 449
Heston, Charlton 453
Heut' ist der schönste Tag in meinem Leben (film) 234
Hicks, Betty 243
Hidalgo, Elvira de 181–182
High Society (film) 247
Hillary, Edmund 138
Hiller, Ferdinand 56, 78, 356
Himmler, Heinrich 197
Hindemith, Paul xxii, 196, 351, 419
    Works by:
    Hin und Zurück 351
    Neues vom Tage 196
Hines, Jerome 292
Hislop, Joseph 379
Hitchcock, Alfred 382
Hitler, Adolf 132, 222–223, 232–233, 310–311, 313, 320, 452,
Hobbes, Thomas 235, 338
    Works by:
    Leviathan 235, 338
Hoffmann, E. T. A. 56, 125, 320, 344, 350, 352, 383, 385, 400, 435, 440, 456

Hoffmann, Josef 456
Hofmann, Peter 119, 326
Hofmannsthal, Hugo von 24, 165, 231
Hoiby, Lee xxii
Holka Polka 350
Hollaender, Friedrich 419
Hollreiser, Heinrich 126
Holst, Gustav 380
Honegger, Arthur 348
Hopf, Hans 119, 324
Hooked on Classics 408
Horace (Quintus Horatius Flaccus) xii, xx, 11, 199, 335
Ho tanta voglia di cantare (film) 224
Horne, Marilyn 318
Hotter, Hans 304, 313, 315
Housman, A. E. 377–378, 380
    Works by:
    On Wenlock Edge 380
Howard, Curly 388
Howard, Moe 388
Hudson, Rock 257
Hugo, Victor 75
    Works by:
    Notre-Dame de Paris 75
Hüttenbrenner. Anselm 416
Humperdinck, Engelbert 24, 202, 208
    Works by:
    Hänsel und Gretel 202
    Königskinder 24
Hunchback of Notre Dame, The (film) 26
Huneker, James Gibbons 186
Hurok, Sol 372
Hutt, Robert 206
Hüttenbrenner, Anselm 416
Huxley, Aldous 216–217
Hvorostovsky, Dmitri 383, 406
Hymel, Bryan 439

Iannucci, Armando 442
Ibert, Jacques 445
Ibos, Guillaume 156–157
Ibsen, Henrik 24
Illica, Luigi xiii–xiv
In cerca di felicità (film) 226
Incledon, Charles 18–19, 379
Inghelbrecht, Désiré-Émile 334, 352
Ingres, Jean-Auguste-Dominique 66, 331–333
Ingris, Eduard xxi
Inozemtsev, Pyotr 362
INRI (film) 232
Iogannis, Ivan 357

IRCAM (Institut de Recherche et
    Coordination Acoustique) 25, 257
Isouard, Nicolas xxi–xxii, 189, 191
  Works by:
    Cendrillon 122
Iturbi, José 245–246
Ivanov, Nikolay 357, 365

Jackson, Michael 424, 429
Jadlowker, Herman 202–203
Jäger, Ferdinand 140
Jäger, Rudolf 200
Jailhouse Rock (film) 242
Jaione, Clara
  Works by:
    La Postina della val Gardena xiv
Janáček, Leoš 194
  Works by:
    From the House of the Dead 194
    (Z mrtvého domu)
    Jenůfa (Její pastorkyňa) 194
"Japonaise, La" 421
Jazz Singer, The (film) 183, 216
Jelinek, Elfrede 301
  Works by:
    Rein Gold 301
Jélyotte, Pierre 330
Jenkins, Florence Foster 177
Jenkins, Kathryn 403
Jeritza, Maria 203, 292, 350
Jerusalem, Siegfried 119, 122, 142, 325–327,
    447, 449
Joachim, Joseph 43, 445
Jobin, Raoul 352
Jochum, Eugen 314, 325
Johanson, Daniel 451
Johnson, Ben 198, 407
Johnson, Brian 423–424
Johnson, Edward 238, 249
Johnson, John "Jack" 172
Johnson, Robert 254
"Jonny B Goode" 423
Johnson, Dr. Samuel 172
Jones, Allan 220
Jones, Chuck 221, 300
Jones, Inigo 50
Jones, Robert 448
Jones, Sidney 245
Jonson, Ben
  Works by:
    Epicoene, or the Silent Woman 198
Jörn, Carl 165
Jousse, John 44

Jovanovich, Brandon 451
Joyce, James xix, 96, 98, 162, 176, 213, 236
  Works by:
    Dead, The 176
    Finnegans Wake 213
    Ulysses 213, 236, 301
Joyce, Nora 236–237
Jullien, Louis-Antoine 229
Jurinac, Sena 437–438

Kabalevsky, Dmitri 368
Kahn, Percy 184
  Works by:
    "Ave Maria" 184
Kaiser, George 196, 200, 204, 394, 449
Kalmanoff, Martin xxii
Kálmán, Emmerich 288
Kanawa, Kiri Te 383, 449
Kant, Immanuel 116, 431
Karajan, Herbert von 61, 268–269, 272,
    276, 280–281, 283–288, 297–299,
    314–315, 322, 325, 372, 387, 389, 395,
    398
Karklin, Yekab 362
Karnéus, Katarina 406
Kaskel, Karl von 200, 208
  Works by:
    Sjula 200
Kaufmann, Jonas xvi, 25, 119, 122,
    142–143, 203, 302, 412, 439, 441,
    446–449, 451–452, 456
Kaun, Hugo 200, 208
Kean, Edmund 39, 63
Keats, John 254
Keilberth, Joseph 314, 319, 323, 325
Keiser, Rheinhard xxi
Keizer, Jan 321
Kelly, Michael 17, 86, 114, 329, 379, 428
Kelly, Thomas 428
Kempe, Will 293
Kholminov, Alexander 368
Khoomei 445
Khrennikov, Tikhon 368, 371
Kid Creole (film) 242
Kiedis, Anthony 427
Kiepura, Jan 237–238
Kilchevsky, Vitaly 369
King and I, The (film) 247
King, James 313, 315, 317–320, 327, 381,
    404, 450
King, Thomas A. 267
King, Walter Woolf 88, 220–221
Kiss Me Kate (film) 247

481

Kitzke, Jerome P. xxii
Klarwein, Franz 205
Kleiber, Carlos 321, 325
Kleiber, Erich xxii, 191, 193–194, 272
Klein, Fritz Heinrich 191
Klein, Hermann 42–43, 152–153, 159–160
Kein, Yves 43
Klementiev, Lev 366
Klemperer, Otto 272, 288, 317, 322
Kloiber, Rudolph viii
Klum, Heidi 402
Ku Klux Klan 241
Kmentt, Waldemar 313
Knappertsbusch, Hans 249, 272, 312, 314–315, 317, 325
Knickerbocker Holiday 408
Kniese, Julius 141
Koestenbaum, Wayne 265
Kollo, René 119, 326
Kollontai, Alexandra 356
Komissarzhevsky, Fyodor (Theodore) Fyodorovich 359–362
Konetzni, Anny 310, 312
Konwitschny, Franz 322
Korda, Alexander 220
Korngold, Erich Wolfgang 195, 208–209, 237–238, 288, 301, 319–320, 350
  Works by:
    Kathrin, Die 238
    Lied der Liebe, Das 208
    Ring des Polykrates, Der 195, 208
    Tote Stadt, Die 195, 208–209, 221, 319, 350, 452
    Violanta 195
    Wunder der Heliane, Das 237, 301
Környey, Béla von 203
Kosiński, Jerzy 408
Koss, John C. 272
Koussevitzky, Serge 223, 242
Kozlovsky, Ivan 369–371
Kozub, Ernst 324
Kraus, Alfredo 281, 352, 383–384, 388–389
Kraus, Karl 24, 193
Kraus, Richard 320
Krauss, Clemens 26, 272, 314, 325
Krehbiel, Henry 159, 184, 187
Krenek, Ernst 194
  Works by:
    Zwingburg, Die 194
Kreutzer, Conradin 416
Kreutzer, Rodolphe 56, 216
Krips, Josef 210, 288

Krismer, Giuseppe 172
Krushelnytska, Solomiya 173
Kubelik, Rafael 272, 314, 317, 353
Kuffner, Christoph 32
Kullman, Charles 249–250
Kunde, Gregory 435
Künneke, Eduard 448
  Works by:
    Große Sünderin, Die 447–448
Kurtsevich, Princess Maria 360

Labinsky, Andrey 166, 367
LabLache, Luigi 84, 97, 126, 147
Lache Bajazzo (film) 221
Lachner, Franz Paul 416
Lafarge, Emmanuel 343
Lahee, Henry C. 183
Lahr, Bert 105
Lakes, Gary 385
Lakmé 344, 367, 369
Lalo, Édouard-Victoire-Antoine 344
Lalo, Pierre 78
Lamarr, Hedy 250
Lambert, Adam 421, 427
Lamoureux, Charles 344
Lampenius, Linda 408
Lamperti, Francesco 342, 347
Lampi, Mauro (see Stern, Maurice) 386
Land des Lächelns, Das (film) 233
Landry, Martin 177
Lang Lang xxvi
Lang, Fritz 238
Langridge, Philip 377, 379
Lanza, Mario vii, viii, 91, 242–253, 255, 277, 408–409, 412, 440
Lanzinger, Hubert 311
Lapissida, Alexandre 344
Lara, Agustín 324
  Works by:
    "*Granada*" 324
"*Last Rose of Summer, The*" 217
Larin, Sergei 373
Lasky, Jesse 211–212, 239, 250
Last Dogie, The (film) 239
Last Tango in Paris (film) 382
Lathrop, Isabel Stevens 145
Laughton, Charles 26
Laurel, Stan 220–221
Lauri-Volpi, Giacomo 9, 174, 227–230, 243, 255, 259, 263, 279, 433
Lawrence, Carol 251
Lawrence, Rosina 221

Index

Lawrence, Walter   10
Lean, David   viii
Lecocq Charles   340
   Works by:
      "*Giroflé-Girofla*"   324
Ledger, Heath   26
Ledner, Emile   185
Ledoux, Nicolas   48–49, 51–52
Leech, Lloyd Thomas   214, 398
Legay, Henri   350
Legge, Walter   xvii, 272, 280, 287, 308, 322
Legros, Joseph   10, 329–330
Leguerney, Jacques   348, 351
   Works by:
      Poèmes de La Pléiade   351
Lehár, Franz   207, 209, 281, 288, 313
   Works by:
      Friederike   207
      Giuditta   207
      Land des Lächelns, Das   207, 209, 233, 281
      Lustige Witwe, Die   288, 394
      Paganini   207
      Schön ist die Welt   207
      Zarewitsch, Der   207
      ZigeunerLiebe   207
Lehman, Gary   451
Lehmann, Henry   331
Lehmann, Lilli   136, 150
Lehmann, Lotte   24, 136, 209, 272, 307, 331
Leighton, Lord Frederic   98
Leinsdorf, Erich   249, 272, 275, 289, 299
Leiser, Clara   150, 154, 161
Lelio, Loretta Di   257
Lemeshev, Sergei   369–371
Lennon, John   241
Leoncavallo, Ruggero   ix, 107, 163–164, 167, 178, 180, 215–216, 439
   Works by:
      Bohème, La   439
      "*Mattinata*"   163
      Medici, I   107
      Pagliacci   ix, 133, 164, 169, 171, 174, 177, 182, 183, 187, 190, 194, 202, 212, 215, 216, 221, 233, 242, 256, 259, 274, 280, 285, 293, 298, 306, 309, 317, 319, 345, 363, 372, 385–386, 425, 448
      Zazà   180
Leonov, Lev   356–358, 374
Lesley, Cole   264

Levi, Hermann   133, 140, 229
Levine, James   326, 389
Lewis, Herschell Gordon   382
Lhérie, Paul   340
Liadov, Anatoly   271
   Works by:
      Baba-Yaga   271
Libanius   198
Liberace, Władziu Valentino   242
Licette, Miriam   145
Licitra, Salvatore   86, 88, 90, 113, 399
Liddell, Eric   317
Life and Death of Colonel Blimp, The (film)   238
Liebermann, Rolf   288
Lied geht um die Welt, Ein (film)   233
Ligeti, György Sándor   290
   Works by:
      Macabre Grand, Le   290
Lima, Edna de   145
Limarilli, Gastone   255
Lind, Jenny   40, 92, 336
Lisle, Rouget de   75
Liszt, Franz   5, 13, 27, 56–57, 66, 68–69, 78, 96, 132–133, 143, 167, 229, 332, 342, 404
Litolff, Henry Charles   345
   Works by:
      Templiers, Les   345
Ljungberg, Göta   301
Lloyd, Edward   379–380
Lloyd, Phyllida   442
Lloyd, Robert   400, 420
Lloyd-Webber, Andrew   420
Locke, John   266
Loeffler, Charles   223
Loewe, Carl   416
Loewe, Frederick   422
Long-Haired Hare (film)   221
Longobardi, Luigi   172
Lopardo, Frank   399
Lorenz, Max   119, 142, 301, 303, 307, 310–313, 318–320, 326, 450, 455
Lorre, Peter   219
Lortzing, Gustav Albert   194, 288
   Works by:
      Zar und Zimmermann   194
Louiguy (Louis Guglielmi)   410
"*Loveliest Night of the Year, The*"   252
Lied geht um die Welt, Ein   233
Love Never Dies (film)   236
Lucà, Giordano   407

483

Luccioni, José   286
Lucia, Fernando de   8–9, 43–44, 168–169, 172, 178–179, 230, 391, 448
Lucioni, Luigi   174
Lully, Jean-Baptiste   29, 329–330

Maazel, Lorin   376
  Works by:
    1984   376
MacNeil, Cornell   297
Macrae, Stuart   376
Madelaine, Stéphen de La   69
Madonna   405
Maeterlinck, Maurice   443
Mahler, Gustav   xix, xxii, 6, 202, 217, 232, 305–308, 322–323, 350, 378, 394, 428, 446
  Works by:
    Drei Pintos, Die (Weber)   378
    Lied von der Erde, Das   322–323, 350, 378, 380, 394, 446
Maison, René   351
Makart, Hans   313
Malibran, Maria   21, 39, 80–81, 85, 97–98, 101, 147
Malipiero, Gian Francesco   165, 191
Mallarmé, Stéphane   418
Mallory, George   138
Malvezzi, Settimio   91
Mamma (film)   221
Mancinelli, Luigi   169
Mancini, Giovanni   267
Mandel, Howie   402
Maniacci, Michael   9
Mann, Thomas   127, 254, 300–301, 311
  Works by:
    Tod in Venedig, Der (Death in Venice)   380
    Doktor Faustus: Das Leben des deutschen Tonsetzers Adrian Leverkühn, erzählt von einem Freunde   254
    Wälsungenblut   300–301
"*Magic of Mantovani, The*"   440
Manzoni, Alessandro   31, 226
  Works by:
    Promessi Sposi, I   31
Mapleson, James H.   140, 147, 153, 159, 169, 175
Maréchal, Adolphe   345
Marchesi, Luigi   14
Marchi, Emilio De   xx, 168–169
Marcolini, Marietta   33
Marconi, Francesco   181
Maréchal, Adolphe   344–345

Marelli, Marco Arturo   26
Marette, De   49
Marie, Rose   251
Mario (de Candia)   95–101, 105, 107, 110–113, 127, 147, 153–154, 263, 357, 414, 455
Marionette (film)   221
Mary Poppins (film)   294
Monaco, Mario Del   xii–xv, xxiii–xxvi, 179, 191, 222, 224, 226, 255, 259–260, 280, 282–284, 287, 314, 317, 453
Markevich, Igor   287, 352
Marliani, Marco Aurelio   91
Marriner, Sir Neville   22
Marschner, Heinrich   19, 103, 125
  Works by:
    Hans Heiling   125
    Vampyr, Der   19, 125, 446
Marshall, Anne   441
Martin, Chris   428
Martin, Dean   251, 253
Martin, Freddie   246
Martinelli, Giovanni   xvi, xxi, 25, 94, 111, 174, 182–183, 214–217, 219, 228, 291
Martínez, Iride   26
Martini, Nino   239
Martini, Padre   4
Martinucci, Nicola   384
Martland, Peter   166
Marvin, Lee   246, 419
Marx Brothers   88, 220–221
Marx, Harpo   215
Marx, Karl   356
Mascagni, Pietro   164–165, 169, 179, 181–182, 190–191, 199, 218, 224, 230, 341, 350, 439
  Works by:
    Amico Fritz, L'   169, 230, 241, 341, 350, 391, 398, 439
    Cavalleria rusticana   164, 174, 179–180, 190, 202, 235, 259, 274, 280, 291, 293, 298, 363, 386, 395, 448
    Guglielmo Ratcliff   182
    Iris   164
    Lodoletta   165
    Nerone   230
    Piccolo Marat, Il   199
Masini, Angelo   9, 180, 286, 395
Masini, Galliano   286
Masini, Gian-Franco   395
Maslennikov, Aleksei   371
Massenet, Jules   28, 107, 111, 150–152, 156–157, 182, 224, 268, 288–289, 335,

340, 344–345, 347–348, 350, 383,
    418–419
Works by:
Cid, Le   151, 159, 345
Cléopâtre   345
Don César de Bazan   340
Grand'tante, La   335
Hérodiade   107, 109, 150–151, 344
Jongleur de Notre Dame, Le   345
Mage, Le   344
Manon   ix, 278, 344, 348, 350, 367, 368,
    373, 383, 400, 439
Panurge   182
Thaïs   350, 395 53, 128, 130–132, 179,
    200, 205, 306–307, 314, 317, 320,
    341–342, 385
Roi de Lahore, Le   107
Werther   155–156, 268, 272, 279,
    288–289, 351, 383, 394, 397, 417,
    446, 448
Massey, Raymond   144
Massini, Galliano   286
Masur, Kurt   449
Matačić, Lovro von   288
Materna, Amalie   140
Mathieu, Emile   345
Works by:
Richilde   345
Matisse, Henri   112
Mattei, Gennaro   237
Matter of Life and Death, A (film)   238
Mattila, Karita   406
Maturin, Charles   20
Works by:
Melmoth the Wanderer   20
Mauldin, Steve   177
Maurel, Victor   52, 150–151
Maw, Nicholas   376
Works by:
Sophie's Choice   376
May, Brian   xxvii, 421–422
Mayer, Louis B.   244–245
Mayr, Simon   33, 36, 82, 91, 118
Works by:
Amor congiugale, L'   33
Fanatico per la musica, Il   82
Sogno di Partenope, Il   36
Maxwell Davies, Peter   376, 378, 380
Works by:
An Orkney Wedding With Sunrise,
Farewell to Stromness   378
Eight Songs for a Mad King   379
Taverner   376

Mazzini, Giuseppe   95
McCartney, Paul   423
McCormack, John   146, 235–236, 366
McCracken, James   286
McGonagall, William   325
McLeod, Ken   423
McNeff, Stephen   376
McQueen, Steve   381
McVicar, David   441, 448
Meaney, Colm   409
Meck, Nadezhda von   305, 359–360
Medvedev, Mikhail   362
Mehta, Zubin   383, 388–389
Mein Herz Ruft Nach Dir (film)   238
Melba, Nellie   159–160, 167, 188, 201,
    235
Melchior, Lauritz   119, 142, 148, 272,
    301–304, 307–310, 312, 316, 319,
    326–327, 447, 453
Melocchi, Arturo   255, 258, 282
Melton, James   239
Mendelssohn, Arnold   200
Works by:
Elsi, die seltsame Magd   200
Mendelssohn, Felix   5, 71, 98, 134, 154
Menken, Alan   422
Menotti, Gian-Carlo   xxi, 288
Works by:
Last Savage, The   288
Menuhin, Yehudi   290
Mercadante, Saverio   32, 35, 78, 84, 91–92,
    111, 397
Works by:
Donna Caritea   32
Giuramento, Il   397
Mercury, Freddie   xxvii–xxviii, 271, 414–423
Mérimée, Prosper   212
Merli, Francesco   xx, 111, 190, 285
Merrill, Robert   272, 274, 291, 292
Merritt, Chris   433, 435
Meschke, Michael   290
Messager, André
Works by:
Béatrice   345
Madame Chrysanthème   346
Messiaen, Oliver   348
Metallica   408
Metastasio (Pietro Antonio Domenico
    Trapassi)   26
Metropolis (film)   238
Metternich, Klemens von   31
Meyer, Kerstin   203
Meyer, Russ   381–382

Meyerbeer, Giacomo   37, 40, 52–54, 56,
    65–66, 68–69, 96, 98–99, 111–112,
    126, 132, 134, 159, 185, 263, 288, 334,
    336, 342
  Works by:
    Africaine, L'   53, 107, 154, 159, 165,
      175, 181, 183,   233, 234, 273,
      342, 435
    Huguenots, Les   40, 52–54, 66–69, 97, 99,
      107, 128, 154, 159, 165, 169, 194,
      228, 263, 305, 334, 342, 345, 346,
      352, 363, 364, 435
    Prophète, Le   53, 99, 109, 154, 165, 174,
      185, 336, 342, 364
Michaelis, Alfred   167
Michelangelo di Lodovico Buonarroti
    Simoni   xix, 431
Michot, Pierre-Jules   340
Mihalovici, Marcelay   xxii
Milanov, Zinka   272–274, 281
Milhaud, Darius   194, 348
  Works by:
    Christophe Colomb   194
Milhoff   144–145
Miller, William   378
Millhoff, J.   144
Millionenonkel, Der (film)   232
Milnes, Sherrill   142, 295
Miraglia, Corrado   91
Mirate, Raffaele   91, 221
Mironov, Maxim   374
Misch, Rochus   233
Misteri di Venezia, I (film)   226
Mitchell, Ruth   442
Mitchinson, John   441
Mitchum, Robert   214
Mitropoulos, Dimitri   272, 288
Moffo, Anna   292, 295, 298
Mohaupt, Richard   205
  Works by:
    Wirtin von Pinsk, Die   205
Moissi, Alexander   24
Molchanov, Kirill   368
Molière (Jean-Baptiste Poquelin)   20, 65
Molinari-Pradelli, Francesco   256, 272, 288,
    292, 390
Mollo, Nicola   37
Monaco, Mario Del   60, 94, 105, 110, 170,
    179, 255, 259–260, 272, 279–286,
    288–289, 291, 293–295, 297, 304, 314,
    317, 384, 394, 453
"*Mondnacht*"   410
Monet, Claude   382

Works by:
    Déjeuner sur l'herbe, Le   382
Mongini, Pietro   91
Moniuszko, Stanisław   367
  Works by:
    Halka   367
Monjauze, Jules-Sébastien   91
Monnot, Margerite   410
Montand, Yves   419
Montaubry, Achille-Félix   338–339
Monte, Carlo Del   287
Montecchi   76–77, 440
Montemezzi, Italo   165, 180
  Works by:
    Amore dei tre re, L'   165
    Héllera   180
Montesanto, Luigi   278
Monteux, Pierre   249
Monteverdi, Claudio   30, 50–51, 351, 377,
    400, 420, 446
  Works by:
    *Combattimento di Tancredi
    e Clorinda, Il*   400
    Mercurio e Marte   51
    Orfeo, L'   50, 420
Monti, Vittorio   290
  Works by:
    Czardas   290
Moore, Dudley   380
Moore, George   xvii
Moore, Grace   234–235, 351
Moore, Thomas   74
Morelli, Mario   164
Morère, Jean   91
Moreschi, Alessandro   2, 5–11, 14, 17,
    21, 31, 50, 78, 80, 172, 181, 190,
    263–264
Morlacchi, Francesco   91
Morris, Emannuale   174
Mosca, Jacopo   91, 361
Moscheles, Ignaz   80–81
Mosel, Ignas Franz von   429
Moshinsky, Elijah   318
Moss, Heidi   455
Mossolov, Alexander   368
Mottl, Felix   156
Moyse, Marcel   445
Mozart, Wolfgang Amadeus   xix–xx, xxvi,
    4–5, 7–8, 10, 16–17, 26, 29, 39, 44,
    49, 51, 68, 82, 84, 88, 91, 94, 99, 103,
    112, 119–120, 132, 192–193, 195, 202,
    208–209, 236–237, 254, 273, 288–289,
    302, 315, 322–323, 326, 331, 340, 347,

352, 377, 379, 381, 383, 391, 398–400,
  419, 442, 449, 452–453, 455
Works by:
  Così fan tutte ix, 68, 224, 293
  Clemenza di Tito, La 446
  Don Giovanni 38–39, 118, 139, 147, 208,
    210, 210, 215, 239, 249–250, 267,
    285, 288, 390–391, 420, 455
  Entführung aus dem Serail, Die ix, 119,
    194, 288
  Idomeneo
  Mitridate, re di Ponto 16
  Nozze di Figaro, Le 10, 17, 38, 40
  Re di Creta ossia Ilia e Idamante 132, 203,
    233, 288, 391
  Zauberflöte, Die ix, 17, 119–120, 123,
    192, 194, 208–209, 288, 293, 320,
    322, 324
Mozzoni, Maria 34
Mravinsky, Yevgeni 369
Muck, Karl 194
Mulè, Giuseppe
Works by:
  Dafni 189
Müller, Heiner 326
Müller, Wenzel xxi
Munch, Charles 272, 351
Misteri di Venezia, I (film) 226
Muppets, The 266
Muradeli, Vano 368, 371
Murat, Joachim 31
Muratore, Lucien 348
Murray, John 36, 98, 380
Music for Madame (film) 239
Music of My Mind 428
Musica di sogno (film) 221
Musset, Alfred de 96
Mussolini, Benito 222–224, 226–227, 229
Mussorgsky, Modest 287–288, 356, 359, 372
Works by:
  Boris Godunov 287, 350, 356, 359, 361,
    366, 394
  Khovanshchina 359, 364, 372
Mustafà, Domenico 6, 10
Muti, Riccardo 40, 61, 86–90, 113, 389, 395
Mutterlied (film) 221
Muzio, Claudia 285
Mynott, Terry 435
My Cousin (film) 211–213
My Song for You (film) 238

Nachod, Hans 196
Nagel, Thomas 289–290

Nápravník, Eduard 368
Nash, Heddle 112–113
Nast, Minnie 201, 207
Neblett, Carol 396
Nectoux, Jean-Michel 411
Negga, Ruth 442
Negri, Giovanni Battista De 112, 182, 285
Negrini, Carlo 91
Neitzel, Otto 194
Nelepp, Georgii 371
Nelson, Chris 213, 424
Nelson, Prince Rogers (see "Prince") 424
Nelsons, Andris 447
Netrebko, Anna 400
Neufeld, Max 228
Neukomm, Sigismund 416
Neumann, Josef Angelo 134
Newman, Ernest 133, 138, 217, 328
Nezhdanova, Antonina 166
"*Core 'ngrato*" (Salvatore Cardillo) 261
Nichols, Mike 385
Nicolai, Otto 183, 237, 242, 280, 287, 290,
  373
Works by:
  Lustigen Weiber von Windsor, Die 242,
    376
Nicolini, Giuseppe 31
Nicoloso, Roberto 457
Nielsen, Asta 442
Nielsen, Carl 6
Niemann, Albert 136, 140
Nietzsche, Friedrich Wilhelm 365, 431–432,
  437
Night at the Opera, A (film) 88, 220
Nikisch, Arthur 229
Nilson, Christina 40
Nilsson, Birgit 106, 263–264, 269, 272, 275,
  289, 298, 304, 325–326, 372
Nimoy, Leonard 186
Nixon, Richard 416
Non ti scordar di me (film) 221
Nordica, Lillian 147–149, 158–161
Norman, Jessye 319, 326, 436, 449, 457
Nourrit, Albert 52–57, 61, 63–70, 79, 82,
  110–111, 229, 259, 263, 298, 337, 455
Novak, Peter 350
Novarro, Ramon 214
Nozzari, Andrea 18, 35–39, 44, 357
Nureyev, Rudolf 256

Oakie, Jack 239
Offenbach, Jacques xx–xxi, 28, 111, 288,
  335, 338–340, 344, 350, 383

Contes d'Hoffmann, Les 287, 288, 320, 344, 350, 352, 383, 400, 435, 440
Orphée aux enfers 338
Périchole, La 339
Vert-Vert xx 335
Oestvig (Østvig), Karl Aagard 204
Oistrakh, Igor 371
Oklahoma (film) 247
Oldman, Gary 26
Olivero, Magda 282
Olivier, Sir Laurence 25, 293, 316
One Touch of Venus (film) 408
Onofrio, Vincent 15
Orbison, Roy 423
Orfei, Don Sebastiano 72
Orff, Carl 321
Ormandy, Eugene 244–245, 249
Orr, C. W. 377
Osborn, John 435
Osborne, John 25
Osborne, Nigel 376
Osten, Eva von der 207
Oswald, Richard 233–234, 237, 311
Ottolini, Luigi 433
Oxberry, William 19
Oxilia, Giuseppe 112
Ozawa, Seiji 372

Pabst, Georg Wilhelm 197
Pacchierotti, Gaspare 17
Pacini, Giovanni 45, 78, 92, 111, 357
  Works by:
    Cesare in Egitto 45
    Fidanzata Corsa, La 92
    Maria, regina d'Inghilterra 357
    Merope 92
    Regina di Cipro, La 92
    Romilda di Provenza 92
    Saffo 92
    Stella di Napoli, La 92
Paer, Ferdinando 35, 91,116–119
Paganini, Niccolò xxv, xxviii, 13, 27, 143, 207, 254, 331–333, 336, 427
Pagliacci, I (film) 221
Paint Your Wagon (film) 246
Paisiello, Giovanni xxi, 17, 35, 91, 94, 446
  Works by:
    Giochi di Agrigento, I 17
    Nina 446
Palet, José 172
Palma, Piero de 275, 296
Pancani, Emilio 91

Panerai, Rolando 274
Panizza, Ettore 111, 249, 273–274
Paoli, Antonio 112, 181–182
Pappano, Antonio 268, 441, 448
Paramount on Parade (film) 239
Pardon Us (film) 221
Parin, Gino 222
Parr, Tessa 442
Pasatieri, Thomas xxii
Pascal, Blaise 254
Pashkevich, Vasily 356
Pasta, Giuditta 28, 46, 80–81
Patanè, Giuseppe 385, 398
Patel, Dev 442
Patti, Adelina 28, 42–44, 100, 149
Patti, Amalia 28
Patti, Salvatore 61
Patzak, Julius 205–206, 320–322
Paulsen, Harald 196–197
Pavarotti, Luciano viii, xi, xiv, xix, 21, 58, 60–61, 149, 190, 219, 268, 291, 295, 297, 383–384, 386, 388–396, 400, 407–408, 412, 419, 425, 432–434
Pavlusík, Jozef 403
Peake, Maxine 442
Pearse, Cecilia M. 98–99
Pearman, William 19
Pears, Peter ix, 188, 318, 379–381
Pechkovsky, Nikolai 370–371
Pedrotti, Carlo 107
Peerce, Jan 241, 243, 248–250, 385
Pellegrini, Anna-Maria 416
Pellico, Silvio 31
Penno, Gino 286
Perahia, Murray 380
Percheron, Adelaide 357
Perelmuth, Jacob Pincus 248
Pergolesi, Giovanni 15
Peri, Jacopo 50
  Works by:
    Dafne 50
    Euridice 50
Perrin, Pierre 329
Perry, Katie 405, 427
Persichini, Venceslao 181
Pertile, Aureliano xxi, 174, 228, 230
Peters, Roberta 292
Peterson, Jordan 449
Petit, Philippe 61
Pétrequin, J. E. 59
Petrov, Ivan 370
Petrovich, Andrey 372

Pfitzner, Hans   194, 196, 199, 208, 288, 322
    Works by:
    Herz, Das   194, 199
    Palestrina   194, 196, 199, 322, 324
Phelps, David   425–426
Philidor, François-André   329
Philips, Sam   241
Phillips, Peter   8
Piaf, Edith   410
Piave, Francesco Maria   103, 392
Picasso, Pablo   86, 111–112, 431, 453
    Works by:
    Guernica   431
Piccaver, Alfred   237
Piccinni, Niccolò   xxi, 331
Pinto, Amelia   166
Pinza, Ezio   248
Pisaroni, Benedetta   58
Pitt, Brad   214
Plançon, Pol   147, 149, 160
Plasson, Michel   383
Plautus, Titus Maccius   24, 198
    Works by:
    Casina   24
Pleasants, Henry   36, 57, 60, 65, 67, 105, 138–139, 304, 309, 452
Pleasantville (film)   242, 253
Plishka, Paul   397
Plowman, Jane   376
    Works by:
    House of the Gods   376
Poe, Edgard Allan   378
Poell, Alfred   210
Poggi, Antonio   91
Poggi, Gianni   279
Pohl, Richard   135
Pollert, Karoline   84
Polverosi, Manfredo   172
Polzelli, Luigia   4
Ponchard, Louis   96
Ponchielli, Amilcare   107, 111, 168, 179–180, 218
    Works by:
    Gioconda, La   168, 179, 183, 218–219, 279, 281, 284, 292–293, 299
    Figliuol prodigo, Il
    Marion Delorme
    Promessi Sposi, I   180
Ponselle, Rosa   186–187, 228, 350, 407
Pope Leo XIII   5
Pope Sixtus V   2
Popp, Lucia   322, 410

Popper, Felix   386
Porpora, Nicola   15–17, 38
    Works by:
    Polifemo   17
Porrino, Ennio   165
Portamento   xxviii, 7, 16, 41–43, 45, 65, 80, 104, 110, 141, 157, 160, 163, 173, 178, 182, 187, 191, 201, 203, 208, 219, 228, 237, 260, 267–268, 285, 289, 292, 295–296, 303, 306–307, 315, 325, 335, 343, 351, 363, 380, 392–393, 396–397, 399, 404–405, 418, 445
Porter, Cole   111, 422
Potts, Paul   409
Poulenc, Francis   xxii, 288, 348, 445
Powell, Michael   294
Powell, William   239
Prandelli, Giacinto   286
Preskett, Graham   376
Presley, Elvis   241–242, 416, 448
Pressburger, Emeric   238, 294
Prêtre, Georges   262–263, 288, 298–299, 322
Prevedi, Bruno   286, 372
Previtali, Fernando   284, 395
Price, Vincent   252
Pritchard, Sir John   298, 409
Profili, Ettore   91
Prokofiev, Sergei   288, 366, 368, 371
    Works by:
    Amour des trois oranges, L' (*Lyubov' k tryom apel'sinam*)   366
    Duenna (*Betrothal in a Monastery*)   368
    Semyon Kotko   368
Promessi Sposi, I (film)   226
Proust, Marcel   410–411
Prunera, Magda   395
Provost, Jean-Baptiste   27
Puccini, Giacomo   6, 9, 26, 29, 103, 164–165, 167–169, 171–173, 178, 183, 189–191, 199, 224–225, 235, 237, 268, 273, 280, 288, 297, 315, 323, 348, 354, 363, 366, 378, 400, 402, 404–405, 425, 439, 454
    Works by:
    Bohème, La   viii, ix, xxi, 40, 44, 60, 164, 173, 180, 199, 201–202, 203, 229, 242, 245, 249, 273–274, 281, 283, 288, 293, 296, 323, 353, 363, 390, 412, 439, 425
    Fanciulla de West, La   165, 171–172, 182, 183, 201–202, 217, 273, 284, 293, 385, 394, 440, 441

Gianni Schicchi 279, 287, 400
Madama Butterfly ix, 165, 170, 171–173, 202, 217, 218, 244–245, 249–250, 275, 280, 287, 288, 296, 297, 348, 350, 381, 386, 397, 438
Manon Lescaut 180, 183, 274, 280, 281, 293, 366, 448
Rondine, La 165, 225, 440, 446
Tabarro, Il 273, 278
Tosca ix, xi, 7, 26, 40, 164–165, 168–172, 182, 202, 238, 242, 252, 256, 259, 261, 263, 263, 272, 274, 280–281, 293, 363, 372–373, 386, 394, 395, 397, 406, 438–440, 446, 448, 456
Trittico, Il 165
Turandot viii, ix, 165, 171, 183, 189–191, 199, 228, 238, 256, 259, 263, 269, 275, 279, 284–285, 288–290, 319, 373–374, 378, 384–385, 386, 387–388, 391, 393, 394, 402–403, 407, 409, 425, 427, 437, 439, 455–457
Pudsey 403
Purcell, Henry 16, 245, 247, 380, 409, 422
Works by:
Dido and Aeneas 16, 245
"*Here the Deities Approve*" 409
Putin, Vladimir 445
Püttlingen, Johann Vesque von 416
Puzzi, Giovanni 80–81
Py, Gilbert 353
Pynchon, Thomas 242
Works by:
The Crying of Lot 49 242

Queen xxv, xxvii, xxviii, 277, 416–417, 420–422
Queler, Eve 152, 295
Quilter, Roger 380, 422
Quo Vadis (film) 250

Raabe, Peter 195
Rabbit of Seville, The (film) 221
Rachmaninov, Sergei xxv, 288, 366, 373, 428, 454
Works by:
Aleko 366
Francesca da Rimini 366
Prelude in F-sharp minor, No. 1, Op. 23 428
"*Vocalise*" 454
"*Vessenniye Vodi*" 373
"*Son*" 373

Racine, Jean-Baptiste 22–23, 26–27, 65
Works by:
Iphigénie 27
Phèdre 22–23, 26–27, 65
Radichi, Giulio (Julius) xxi, 120–121
Radiohead 427
Raimondi, Gianni 286, 372, 433
Raimondi, Ruggero 392
Raisa, Rosa 189
Ralf, Torsten 204–205, 310
Ramann, Lina 56
Ramanujan, Srinivasa 254
Rameau, Jean-Philippe 288, 329–331, 394
Works by:
Hippolyte et Aricie 394
Platée 329
Ramey, Sam 398, 455–456
Rangström, Ture 194
Works by:
Die Kronenbraut 194
Raskolnikow (film) 231
Rathbone, Basil 235
Rauzzini, Venanzio 17
Ravel, Maurice 6, 29, 339, 348, 352, 379
Works by:
Enfant et les sortilèges, L' 379
Heure espagnole, L' 352
Ray, Man 111
Rebikov, Vladimir 368
Reckless (film) 220
Red Hot Chili Peppers 427
Red Shoes, The (film) 238
Reeves, Simms 65, 379
Reid, Walllace 213
Reinhardt, Max 24
Reining, Maria 25, 313, 405
Relph, Michael 190
Remedios, Alberto 441
Renaud, Maurice 166
Renoir, Pierre-Auguste 453
Rescigno, Nicola 283, 314
Reszke, Édouard De 145, 147, 150, 153, 161
Reszke, Jean De 95, 108, 112–113, 144–161, 184, 188, 227, 229, 263, 276, 342, 344, 346, 424, 455
Révial, Louis Benoît Alphonse xx
Reyer, Ernest 156, 343–344
Works by:
Salammbô 344
Sigurd 156, 343, 345
Ricci, Federico 91
Works by:
Duello sotto Richelieu, Un 91

Richelieu 92
Richepin, Jean 26
Richter, Hans 173, 229, 371, 380
Richter, Sviatoslav 371
Rick & Morty 402
Ricordi, Giulio 89, 106, 180, 281
Ricordi, Tito 110, 169, 281
Ridder, Anton De 26, 60, 321
Riesenfeld, Hugo 212
Righini, Vincenzo Maria 124
Rigoletto (film) 221
Rimbaud, Arthur 418
Rimsky-Korsakov, Nikolai 250, 350, 356, 359, 364–366, 372
   Works by:
   Antar 271
   Kashchéy bessmértny 364
   Pskovityanka 356, 364
   Sadko 359, 364–365, 374
   Skazániye o nevídimom grade Kítezhe i déve Fevrónii 364, 366
   Snegúrochka–vesénnyaya skázka 364–365
Ripa, Antonio 38
Ritter, Rudolf 133, 195
Roach, Alexandra 409
Robeson, Paul 436
Robinson, Francis 304
Röckel, Joseph August xxi, 120
Rockwell, Norman 294
Rodgers, Richard 416
Roger, Gustave-Hippolyte 336
Rogers, Will 235
Röhm, Ernst 311
Roman Holiday (film) 251
Romani, Felice xviii
Romberg, Sigmund 246
   Works by:
   Student Prince, The 246
Romero, Jose 269
Ronzi de Begnis, Giuseppina 92
Roocroft, Amanda 400
Rooney, Mickey 220
Roosevelt, Theodore 213, 240
Roppa, Giacomo 91
Rosalba (film) 226
Rosati, Enrico 243
Rosé, Arnold 445
Rosen, Charles 126
Rosenkavalier, Der (film) 231
Rosing, Vladimir 145, 369
Ross, Gary 242
Rossellini, Roberto 251
Rossi, Tino 350, 418–419

Rossini, Gioachino xx, 2, 10, 14–15, 17–18, 21, 27–30, 32–40, 44–47, 51–54, 58, 60–61, 66, 68–69, 71, 76–77, 80, 82–84, 88, 90–92, 94, 99–100, 103, 105–107, 111–112, 122–124, 129, 164–166, 179, 202, 224, 258, 262, 273, 280, 286, 288, 295, 330–334, 339, 357–358, 383–384, 391, 395, 397–398, 406, 419, 432–434, 443, 454
   Works by:
   Armida 35, 38, 286
   Aureliano in Palmira 10, 34, 83
   Barbiere di Sivglia, Il 28, 38, 40, 44–45, 72
   Cenerentola 99, 436
   Comte Ory, Le 334
   Crociato in Egitto, Il 10, 18, 35, 39, 45, 80, 82–83, 384
   Demetrio e Polibio 35
   Donna del lago, La 18, 35, 82, 99
   Ermione 18, 35
   Gaza Ladra, La 99, 357
   Guillaume Tell 28, 31, 47, 52–53, 57–58, 60, 62, 63, 68, 76, 87, 156, 288, 334, 342, 357–358, 363, 391, 435
   Italiana in Algeri, L' 32–34, 39, 99
   Matilde di Shabran 433
   Maometto II 18
   Moïse et Pharaon 53, 334
   Otello 18, 28, 35–37, 39, 57, 60, 82–83, 85, 89–90, 92, 99, 106, 133, 384, 394, 398
   Pietra del Paragone, La 397
   Ricciardo e Zoraide 18, 35, 39, 82
   Semiramide 39, 60
   Signor Bruschino, Il 339
   Siège de Corinthe, Le 53, 330
   Stabat Mater 100, 357
   Tancredi 35, 358, 400
   Torvaldo e Dorliskj 39
   Turco in Italia, Il 18, 35, 280
   Viaggio a Reims, Il 45–46, 96, 435
Rostand, Edmond Eugène Alexis 10, 36, 161
   Works by:
   Cyrano de Bergerac 10, 36, 161, 235
Rostropovich, Mstislav 288, 371
Rosvaenge, Helge 203, 352
Rota, Nino 165
Rothko, Mark xix
Rothschild, Alfred de 153–154
Rouleau, Joseph 352
Roxas, Emanuel 147
Rousseau, Jean-Jacques 331

Roussel, Albert   348, 351
  Works by:
    Testament de la Tante Caroline, Le   351
Rousselière, Charles   344–345
Rozhdestvensky, Gennady   374
Rubato   40–42, 44, 157, 177, 178, 191, 201, 206, 208, 219, 221, 225, 261, 289, 296, 351, 363, 370, 393, 418, 426, 448
Rubens, Peter Paul   73, 245
Rubini, Giovanni   18, 73, 77–85, 91, 94, 97–101, 105, 110, 147, 158, 227, 229, 279, 342, 390–391, 393, 432, 455
Rubinstein, Anton   78, 359, 361
  Works by:
    Demon   359, 361
Rudel, Julius   386, 389, 395
Ruffo, Titta   163, 181
Rush, Jennifer   385
Russell, Anna   300
Russell, Louise   392
Rushton, Edward   376
Ryan, Lance   451
Rykkvin, Aksel   10
Rysanek, Leonie   203

Sabajno, Carlo   218–219
Sabata, Victor de   86, 272, 280, 301, 313
Sabbatini, Giuseppe   383–384
Saint-Saëns, Camille   40, 52, 107, 111, 136, 185, 340, 342–345, 348
  Works by:
    Barbares, Les   345
    Hélène   348
    Samson et Dalila   40, 107, 109, 185, 250, 317, 342–345, 385
Sakall, S. Z.   237, 251
Salfi, Saverio   34
Salieri, Antonio   xxi, 17, 26, 29, 121, 198, 330–331
Salignac, Thomas   160
Sallinen, Aulis   376
  Works by:
    King Goes Forth to France, The   376
Salvarezza, Antonio   433
Salvatini, Mafalda   145
Salvi, Lorenzo   85, 91–92, 105, 110
Salzman, Eric   386
Samara, Spiro   180
  Works by:
    Rhea   180
Sammarco, Mario   166
Samson, Joseph   27

Sanderson, Sybil   147
Santi, Nello   385
Santini, Gabriele   272, 275, 287, 314
Sarcey, Francisque   27
Sardou, Victorien   26
Sargent, John Singer   40
Satie, Erik   348
Sattler, Joachim   206, 310
Sauguet, Henri   351–352
  Works by:
    Gageure imprévue, La   351
    Pénitents en Maillot Rose, Les   351
Sawallisch, Wolfgang   314, 325
Sayão, Bidu   145, 239, 250
Sbigoli, Amerigo   45–46, 266, 387
Sbriglia, Giovanni   145, 147–150
Scampini, Augusto   285
Scaravelli, Carlo   255
Scarlatti, Domenico   xxi
Schack, Benedikt   17
Schager, Andreas   451
Schalk, Franz   160, 203
Schattmann, Alfred   199
  Works by:
    Die Hochzeit des Mönchs   199
Schauerroman   114
Schenoni, Luigi   172
Scherchen, Hermann   282
Schetky, Johann   43
Schiele, Egon   xv
Schiller, Friedrich   48, 127, 229, 305
Schillings, Max von   204
Schindler, Anton   46
Schipa, Tito   xix, 39, 60, 174, 218, 224–229, 239, 243, 392, 418–419, 434
Schippers, Thomas   284, 288, 297, 299
Schlosser, Max   137
Schmedes, Erik   301, 305–307, 309, 324, 326
Schmidt, Franz   194
  Works by:
    Fredigundis   194
Schmidt, Joseph   228, 233–235, 239, 246
Schmidt-Gentner, Willy   231
Schmitz, Ettore   236
Schnittke, Alfred   290
  Works by:
    Life with an Idiot   290
Schnorr von Carolsfeld, Ludwig   136, 138–140, 304
Schnorr von Carolsfeld, Ludwig Ferdinand   138

Schock, Rudolf   203, 320
Schoeck, Othmar   199, 205
   Works by:
    Massimilla Doni   205
    Venus   199
Schoenberg, Arnold (Schönberg)   xxii, 6, 23–25, 191–192, 194, 196, 208, 230, 292, 377–379, 452
   Works by:
    Erwartung   79
    Gurre-lieder   196, 292, 377, 452
    Pierrot lunaire   23, 24, 191, 216
Schöffler, Paul   210
Schonberg, Harold C.   308
Schopenhauer, Arthur   114, 118, 229
Schorr, Friedrich   307–308
Schreker, Franz   195–196, 208
   Works by:
    Ferne Klang, Der   195–196
    Gezeichneten, Die   196
Schröder-Devrient, Wilhelmine   126, 128, 130–131, 195
Schröder, Karl   195, 204
   Works by:
    Zwerg, Der   195, 204
Schubert, Franz   xv, 28, 71, 98, 209, 217, 230, 233, 254, 288, 303, 324, 377, 379, 380, 414–417, 419, 422, 428–430, 446
   Works by:
    "*Am Meer*"   303
    "*Atlas, Der*"   415–416
    "*Erlkönig, Der*"   217
    "*Fruhlingstraum*"   209
    "*Gretchen am Spinnrade*"   417
    "*Nacht und Träume*"   417
    "*Schöne Müllerin, Die*"   324, 414
    "*Schwanengesang*"   303
    Symphony No.8 in B minor   379
    "*Winterreise*"   452
Schubert, Richard   195
Schuch, Ernst von   217, 305
Schuh, Oscar   xxii
Schuh, Willi   194
Schumann-Heink, Ernestine   160, 217
Schumann, Clara   138, 380
Schumann, Robert   229, 324, 410
   Works by:
    "*Dichterliebe*"   324
Schünzel, Reinhold   311
Schwaiger, Egloff   323
Schwarzkopf, Elisabeth   x, 210

Schweitzer, Anton   356
   Works by:
    "*Alceste*"   356
Schwind, Moritz von   276
Sciutti, Graziella   255–256
Scott, Sir Walter   xv, 337
   Works by:
    Bride of Lammermoor, The   356
Scotti, Antonio   167, 172
Scotto, Renata   xvii, 264, 281, 297, 372, 397
Scribe, Eugène   66
Sebestova, Jana   457
Secombe, Sir Harry   190
Sedaine, Michel-Jean   351
   Works by:
    Gageure Imprévue, La   351
    Pénitents en Maillot Rose, Les   351
Seider, August   310
Seidl, Anton   134, 142–143, 158
Seiffert, Peter   ix, 302, 449–450
Seinfeld, Jerry   388
Sekar-Rozhansky, Anton   362
Sembach, Johannes   203, 305, 309
Sembrich, Marcella   149
Senesino (Francesco Bernardi)   3, 6, 263
Serafin, Tullio   109, 272, 274, 279–280, 286–287, 292–293, 296–298, 317, 450, 454
Sereni, Mario   275, 287
Serov, Alexander   356
   Works by:
    Rogneda   356
Seven Brides for Seven Brothers (film)   247
Seven Hills of Rome (film)   252
Séverac, Déodat De   348
Severi, Giovanni   91
Seyler, Abel   356
Sex Pistols   422
Shakespeare, William   2–3, 13, 22, 26, 36–37, 245, 293, 336, 441–442
   Works by:
    Antony and Cleopatra   2–3, 8, 10, 22, 442
    Cymbeline   360
    Hamlet   22, 53, 248, 355, 441–442
    Henry V   442
    King Lear   284
    Macbeth   25–26
    Merchant of Venice, The   442
    Othello   36, 37, 39, 106, 441–442
    Troilus and Cressida   441–442
Shaporin, Yuri   368, 371
Shatner, William   360

Shaw, George Bernard 95, 100, 105–108, 110, 112, 135, 157–158, 169, 179, 247–248, 264, 316, 328
   Works by:
      Man and Superman 247
      Perfect Wagnerite, The 95
Shchedrin, Rodion 371
Shcherbachev, Vladimir 368
Shebalin, Visarrion 368
Sheeran, Ed 423
Shelley, Mary 36
Shelley, Percy Bysshe 254
Sheridan, Margaret 285
"September in the Rain" 239
Sherwood, Robert E. 215
Shicoff, Neil 385, 388–389, 398
Shkafer, Vasily 361
Shostakovich, Dimitri 368, 371
   Works by:
      Lady Macbeth of Mtsensk 288
Show Boat (film) 247
"Show Must Go On, The" 421
Shulgina, Mariya Nikolaevna 360
Sidney, Sylvia 218
Siegel, Benjamin 291
Siems, Margarethe 207
Siepi, Cesare 296
Silenzio, si gira! (film) 221
Simionato, Giulietta 54, 263–264, 297, 372
Simoneau, Leopold 352
Simpsons, The 388
Sinatra, Frank 240, 246, 251, 373
Singende Tor, Der (film) 221
Singende Stadt, Die (film) 238
Singin' in the Rain (film) 247
Sinopoli, Giuseppe 389, 398
Skelton, Stuart 451
Slezak, Leo 145, 238, 301, 305, 307, 326
Slovtsov, Pyotr 369
Smareglia, Antonio 171
   Works by:
      Oceàna 171
Smetana, Bedřich 111, 140
   Works by:
      Bartered Bride, The (*Prodaná nevěsta*) 200, 202
      Dalibor 140
Smirnov, Dmitri 366–367
Smith, William 314,
Smith, Robert 423
Smyth, Ethyl 380
Sobinov, Leonid 166, 367

Soho Conspiracy (film) 226
Solomon, Maynard 116
Solovyov, Vladimir 365
Sondheim, Stephen 410
Song o' My Heart (film) 236
Song of Scheherazade (film) 246
Sonnenfeld, Barry viii
Sonnleithner, Leopold von 414
Sontag, Henrietta 21, 97
Sorba, Carlotta 34, 77
South Pacific (film) 247
Spaun, Josef von 414
Spielmann, Julius 306
Spohr, Louis 36, 103, 123, 126, 416
   Works by:
      Faust 123
      Jessonda 123
      Zemire und Azor 123
Spoliansky, Mischa 207, 238
Spontini, Gaspare 259, 331, 338
   Works by:
      Agnese di Hohenstaufen 259
      Vestale, La 255, 259–260, 280
Sprechgesang 130, 141, 156, 171, 192, 334, 343
Sprechstimme xxiv, 23–24, 192–193, 197, 202, 311, 418, 427
Spyres, Michael 435
Stabile, Mariano 278
Stagno, Roberto 179–180
Stalin, Joseph 360, 370
"Star Spangled Banner, The" 14, 214
Stanford, Charles Villiers 362, 380
Stanislavsky, Konstantin 360, 367
Star is Born, A (film) 247
Stars Over Broadway 239
Steane, John 313, 316
Steber, Eleanor 292
Stefano, Giuseppe Di vii, xix, 259–260, 272–274, 277–282, 284, 287–289, 294, 297, 366, 383, 391, 397, 399, 405, 409, 434, 456–457
Stegmann, Matthias von 126
Stein, Gertrude 111, 319
Steinberg, William 319
Stendhal (Marie-Henri Beyle) 14, 88
Stern fällt vom Himmel, Ein 228, 234
Stern, Howard 402
Stern, Maurice 385–386
Stevens, Risë 292
Stiedry, Fritz 292–293, 314
Stimme des Herzens, Die (film) 221
Stockhausen, Karlheinz 376, 378–379

Works by:
Donnerstag aus Licht 376
Gruppen 379
Stokowski, Leopold 245, 269, 289, 292
Stoppard, Tom 378
Works by:
Invention of Love, The 378
Storace, Nancy 19
Stradivarius, Antonio 15
Strakosch, Maurice 28
Stratas, Teresa 397
Strauss, Johann II 230, 232, 288
Works by:
Fledermaus, Die 232, 250, 272, 288, 394
Zigeunerbaron, Der 326
Strauss, Josef 305
Works by:
"*Komm doch*" 305
Strauss, Richard ii, xxi–xxii, 6, 10, 13, 25–26, 29, 59, 101, 103, 137, 165–166, 173, 191–196, 198–201, 203–209, 223, 230–231, 273, 288, 290, 303, 305, 307, 310, 312–314, 318–321, 324, 327–328, 351, 354, 377, 379, 404–405, 408, 419–420, 427, 442, 446–447, 449
Works by:
Aegyptische Helena, Die 198, 200, 452, 313–314
Alpensinfonie, Eine 13
Also Sprach Zarathustra 408
Arabella 25, 59, 198, 200, 203, 273, 449
Ariadne aux Naxos 198, 200, 203, 205, 207, 249, 313–314, 319, 351, 385, 447, 449, 452, 454
Capriccio xxii, 26, 199, 205–206, 322
Daphne ix, 59, 200, 204–205, 319, 322
Elektra 18, 35, 101, 166, 191, 193–194, 200, 203–204, 217, 290, 305, 328, 404, 455
"*Enoch Arden*" 318
Frau ohne Schatten, Die ix, 24, 160, 199–200, 204, 313–314, 319, 322, 394, 449, 452
Friedenstag 205, 320–321
Guntram 200
"*Heimliche Aufforderung*" 209
Liebe der Danae, Die 206
"*Morgen!*" 206, 209
Rosenkavalier, Der x, 10, 165, 194, 199, 201, 203, 207, 231, 250, 252, 279, 305, 314, 315, 321, 350, 381, 442

Salome 137, 151, 166, 191, 194, 199–201, 206, 207, 289–290, 305
Schweigsame Frau, Die 198, 321
Rosenkavalier, Der 10, 165, 192, 194, 199, 203, 231, 250, 252, 279, 305, 314–315, 321, 350, 381
"*Zueignung*" 201, 204, 307
Stravinsky, Igor xix, xxii, 6, 277, 288, 368, 379, 399, 420
Streisand, Barbra 410
Strepponi, Giuseppina 91
Striggio, Alessandro 50
Strokes, The 186
Student Prince, The (film) 251
Suchet, David 284
Suetonius 198
Sullivan, Arthur 256, 266, 339–340
Works by:
Gondoliers, The 340
Grand Duke, The 340
Mikado, The 340
Pirates of Penzance, The 340
Ruddigore 340
Trial by Jury 339
Sumac, Yma 421
Suppé, Franz von 220
Works by:
Light Cavalry 220
Sutermeister, Heinrich 205
Works by:
Zauberinsel, Die 205
Suthaus, Ludwig 310
Sutherland, Joan 263, 391, 407, 420
Svanholm, Set 119, 309–310
Swiss Miss (film) 221
Sýkora, Miroslav 403
Szell, George 209
Szymanowski, Karol 405
Works by:
Król Roger 405

Taddei, Giuseppe xvii, 281
Tadolini, Giovanni 80, 91
Taffanel, Paul 445
Tagger, Nicola 432–434
Tagliabue, Carlo 293
Tagliavini, Ferruccio 223–224
Talazac, Jean-Alexandre 344
Talking Book 428
Tallis, Thomas 8, 13
Works by:
Spem in alium 13

Tamagno, Francesco   9, 91, 93, 106–111, 113, 140, 153, 160, 180, 182, 259, 285, 346, 439, 455
Tamberlik, Enrico   xvi, 38, 58, 89–91, 97, 104–106, 111, 176, 216, 222, 242, 248, 259, 263, 304, 310, 319, 323, 334, 361, 378–379, 428, 447
Tamburini, Antonio   81, 84, 97, 100
Tardieu, André   185
Tartakov, Joachim   166
Taruskin, Richard   355, 362
Tarzan the Ape Man (film)   214
Tate, Sir Jeffrey   449
Tauber, Richard   25, 183, 188, 190, 207–210, 233, 236–237, 239
Taubmann, Horst   206
Taucher, Kurt   196, 199, 208
Taverner, John   376
  Works by:
    Thérèse   376
Tayau, Henri   338–339
Taylor, Elizabeth   86
Taylor, Deems   224
Taylor, Estelle   215
Taylor, Roger   xxvii, 421
Tchaikovsky, Pyotr   246, 288, 304–305, 354, 356, 358–364, 368, 372–373, 441
  Works by:
    Yevgény Onégin   359–362, 364, 367, 368, 394, 398, 437
    Iolanta   362, 437
    Kuznéts Vakúla   359
    Oprichnik   356
    Mazepa   356, 362
    Pikovaya dama (Pique Dame)   ix, 354, 362–363
    "*Skazhy o chom v Tenivetvej*"   360
Tear, Robert   377
Tebaldi, Renata   256, 264, 272, 274–275, 279, 284–286, 296–297, 404
Telemann, Georg Philipp   xxi
Tennyson, Jean   243
Terfel, Bryn   406
Terra di fuoco (film)   226
Tetelman, Jonathan   438
Tetrazzini, Luisa   167, 191, 227
Teyte, Maggie   145
That Midnight Kiss (film)   245
Thebom, Blanche   248
Thielemann, Christian   452
Thill, Georges   60, 272, 351, 410, 455
Thomas, Ambroise   303, 336

Works by:
  Mignon   176, 208, 279, 303, 336, 346, 352, 367–368, 439
  Songe d'une nuit d'été, Le   336
Thomas, Jess   203, 313–314, 317
Thorborg, Kerstin   248
Thorpe, Richard   251
Three Coins in the Fountain (film)   252
Three Stooges, The   388
Thuille, Ludwig   202
  Works by:
    Lobetanz   202
Tibbett, Lawrence   250, 453
Tiberini, Mario   91
Tichatschek, Josef   119, 127–133, 138, 155
Tietjens, Heinz   176
Tintoretto (Jacopo Robusti)   73
Tippett, Sir Michael   376
  Works by:
    Ice Break, The   376
    Knot Garden, The   376
Toast of London   435
Toast of New Orleans, The (film)   246
Toklas, Alice B.   111
Tolstoy, Leo   28, 365
  Works by:
    "*Anna Karenina*"   28
Tomášek, Václav   416
Tomasini, Luigi   13
Tommasini, Vincenzo   191
Tommaso, Freddie de   438
Torelli, Giuseppe   266
  Works by:
    "*Tu lo sai*"   266
Toscanini, Arturo   xx, xxii–xxiii, 9, 40, 89, 165, 167–169, 172–173, 182, 188–189, 202, 222–223, 229–230, 243, 248–249, 272–273, 292, 304, 306, 312, 314, 363, 384, 454
Tosti, Paolo   6, 8, 176, 180, 217, 288, 373
  Works by:
    "*Alba Sepàra dalla luce L'ombra, L'*"   372
    "*Ideale*"   6–7, 176–177
Toulouse-Lautrec, Henri   112
Tragically Hip   427
"*Trail of the Lonesome Pine, The*"   220
Tourte, François Xavier   333
Tovazzi, Deodati de'   328
Tozzi, Giorgio   275
Traubel, Helen   248, 314
Tre uomini in frak (film)   225
Treitschke, Heinrich von   116
Treptow, Günther   324

Trigny, Maurice   411
Troyanos, Tatiana   383
Tucker, Richard   241, 248–249, 272, 280, 291–294, 297, 386
Turgenev, Ivan   40
Two Thousand Maniacs (film)   382
Tyson, Alan   116

Uhl, Fritz   326
Ullman, Bernard   28
Unger, Georg   135, 140
Urlus, Jacques   301
Urmana, Violetta   86, 451
Usatov, Dmitri   362

Vagabond Bien-Aimé, Le (film)   251
Vaguet, Albert   346
Valente, Alessandro   190–191
Valentino, Rudolph   6, 213–216, 240
Valero, Fernando   180
Valletti, Cesare   39, 279, 391
Van Gogh, Vincent   254, 431
Vanzo, Alain   353
Vargas, Ramón   399
Varischino   72
    Works by:
       L'Odoacre   72
Varnay, Astrid   142
Vasilenko, Sergei   368
Vaughan-Williams, Ralph   380
Veidt, Conrad   311
Velasquez, Diego Rodríguez de Silva y   290
    Works by:
       Pinturas Negras   290
Velluti, Giovanni Battista   10, 14–15, 30, 34, 45, 54, 83–84, 264
Vento di Primavera (film)   224
Ventris, Christopher   451
Verdi, Giuseppe   xix, xxiii–xxiv, 9, 28, 36, 52–53, 58, 61, 68, 83, 85–95, 99–111, 113, 132, 139–140, 151, 155–156, 164–165, 174–175, 177–178, 180, 182, 191, 217, 221, 224, 237, 239, 243, 259, 262, 271, 273, 275, 281, 283, 288, 290, 292, 294–295, 299, 309–310, 323, 336, 338, 340–342, 345, 348, 354, 357, 359, 361, 363, 392, 394, 396, 399–400, 439–443, 451, 453
    Works by:
       Aïda   ix, 14, 52, 89, 102, 105, 106, 107, 111, 152–155, 166, 169, 172, 177, 179, 183, 190, 238–239, 255, 259, 263, 268, 274, 279, 280, 292, 295, 297, 310, 319–320, 345, 363, 373, 387, 425, 440
       Alzira   92
       Attila   299
       Ballo un Maschera, Un   93, 95, 99, 107, 154, 249, 263, 273, 281, 293, 298–299, 389, 394, 397, 413, 440
       Battaglia di Legnano, La   93, 397
       Corsaro, Il   93, 395
       Don Carlos   53, 89, 102, 293, 298, 317, 341
       Due Foscari, I   93, 99, 295, 394
       Ernani   87, 93, 132–133, 169, 182, 271, 299, 439
       Falstaff   ix, 91, 109, 164, 180, 202, 279, 348
       Forza del destino, La   ix, xvi, xviii, 38, 57, 88, 90, 93, 102–105, 107, 176, 180, 183, 187, 188, 256, 259, 280–281, 292–293, 295, 299, 340, 372, 385–386, 389, 394–395, 397, 448, 452
       Jérusalem   90, 104, 396
       Lombardi alla Prima Crociata, I   93, 99, 244, 283, 396, 397, 439
       Luisa Miller   93, 292, 298, 396, 397, 437, 440
       Macbeth   90, 440
       Masnadieri, I   93, 299
       Nabucco   394
       Oberto, Conte di San Bonifacio   85, 89–93, 90, 91, 92, 93, 299
       Otello   ix, xix–xx, xxii–xxv, 36, 83, 89, 90, 106–112, 139–140, 155, 171, 179, 181–183, 202–203, 205, 217, 230, 243, 252, 259, 268, 280–281, 283, 285, 295, 314, 317–320, 345, 363–364, 371–372, 374, 385, 386, 393–395, 399, 435, 437, 440–441, 443, 447–448, 451
       Rigoletto   ix, xxv, 40, 90, 99, 101, 111, 175, 178, 221, 227, 231, 249, 262, 274, 278, 280–281, 284, 286–288, 323, 353, 361, 370, 389, 392–393, 405, 437
       Simon Boccanegra   93, 106, 244, 293, 295, 394, 440
       Stiffelio   93, 95, 395
       Traviata, La   40, 99, 153, 168, 225, 244–245, 249–250, 278–279, 281,

286–287, 291, 299, 346, 363, 394, 397, 400, 440
Trovatore, Il ix, xxvi, 58, 86–88, 90, 86, 93, 95, 99, 106–107, 112, 113, 169, 175, 178, 183, 228, 250, 259, 261, 263, 269, 274, 283, 287, 289–290, 298, 319, 342, 345, 346, 365, 385–387, 389, 440, 448, 452
Vêpres Siciliennes, Les 53, 93, 336
Vergiss mein nicht (film) 220
Vergnet, Edmond-Alphonse 150, 344–345
Verne, Jules 28
Works by:
"*The Village in the Treetops*" 28
Veroli, Manlio Di 190–191
Verreau, Richard 352–353
Verschwender, Der (film) 232
Verstovsky, Alexey 356, 358
Works by:
Askoldova mogila 356
Vezzani, Cesar 347
Viardot, Pauline 40, 96, 305
Viardot, Louis 66
Vickers, Jon ix, xiv, 111, 119, 286, 313, 315, 317–318, 327, 352, 419, 440
Vieuxtemps, Henry 333
Vignas, Francisco 172
Villazón, Rolando 399–400, 412
Viñas, Francisco 285, 438
Vinay, Ramón xvi, xx, xxiii–xxvi, xxviii, 111, 286, 289, 314, 317–318
Vinci, Leonardo 18
Works by:
Il medo 18
Vinci, Leonardo da 162
Works by:
Mona Lisa 162
Vinogradov, Georgy 368
Viotti, Giovanni Battista 333
Visconti, Luchino 255, 286
De Vito, Danny viii
Vitruvius (Marcus Vitruvius Pollio) 49
Vivaldi, Antonio 29, 72
Vivere Ancora (film) 226
Vives, Amadeo 287
Works by:
Maruxa 287
Vlasov, Vladimir 368
Vogl, Heinrich 133–136, 142–143, 302, 414–418, 423, 428–430
Voglio vivere così (film) 224
Vogt, Florian 451
Voice of Firestone 249, 256

Völker, Franz 119, 132, 142, 303, 307, 310–311
Volkmann, Johann Jacob 4
Voltaire (François-Marie Arouet) 11, 328, 431
Votto, Antonino xiii, 272, 279
Vyacheslav, Ivanov 365

Wachtel, Theodor 106
Wagner, Cosima 126, 141–143, 156, 173, 193, 199, 217, 306, 310–311, 318, 347, 364
Wagner, Minna 132
Wagner, Richard ix, xix, xxv–xxvi, 6, 14, 30, 48–49, 52–53, 56, 84–85, 90, 95, 111–112, 119–120, 125–143, 154–157, 173, 179, 194–195, 199–202, 206, 208, 232, 237, 246, 248, 282, 288, 292, 300–306, 308–320, 322, 324–327, 340–345, 347, 349, 354, 359, 364, 376, 379, 381, 388, 390–392, 394, 419, 425, 443, 449–451, 455
Works by:
Fliegende Holländer, Der 128, 130, 138–139, 194, 196, 300, 301, 305, 307, 322, 348
Götterdämmerung 136, 155, 194, 306, 379, 451
"*Judenthum in der Musik, Das*" 134
Liebesverbot, Das 84, 126, 128, 141
Lohengrin 40, 128, 132–133, 138, 140, 146, 155–§156, 159–160, 165, 179, 194, 200, 202, 205, 288, 302, 305–307, 310–311, 314, 319–320, 322, 324–326, 343–344, 347, 359, 367, 385, 446, 449, 451
Meistersinger, Die 134–135, 137, 139–141, 168, 194, 303, 305, 307, 309, 312, 317, 320, 322, 346
Parsifal ix, 6, 130, 133, 140, 142–143, 315, 451
Rheingold, Das 134, 137, 139, 302, 326, 342
Rienzi 119, 126–130, 132, 282, 300, 312, 394
Ring des Nibelungen, Der ix, 6, 52, 119, 134, 300–301, 303, 420
Siegfried ix, 129, 131–137, 139 –141, 155, 158 –159, 194, 206, 300, 303, 310–311, 312, 315–317, 324, 325–327, 343, 345, 347, 364–366, 372, 394, 440, 449–452

Tannhäuser 138, 140, 250, 300, 310–311, 322, 324, 449–450
Tristan und Isolde ix, 119, 129, 130, 132, 135–140, 155–160, 173, 183, 194, 200, 202, 205–206, 301–302, 304–306, 307, 309–314, 316–317, 319, 321, 324–327, 341–342, 347, 364, 381, 447, 449, 449–452, 455–456
Walküre, Die ix, xxvi, 132, 134, 136–137, 139, 140, 156, 161, 194, 205, 272, 300, 302–303, 305–307, 310–311, 314–317, 319–320, 324–326, 342–343, 345, 364, 446–447, 449–450
Wagner, Wieland xxvi, 314–315, 318, 324–325
Wagner, Wolfgang 288, 449
Waller, Lewis 25
Walter, Bruno xxiii
Walton, Sir William 22, 423
  Works by: 22
    "*Under the Greenwood Tree*" 423
    Hamlet (music for) 22
Warner Brothers 215, 252, 300, 327
Warren, Leonard 250, 274, 281
Watson, Russell 407–408
Way Out West (film) 221
Wayne, John 453
"*We are the Champions*" 415
Weber, Carl Maria von 103, 123–126, 128, 142, 288, 342, 378, 449
  Works by:
    Euryanthe 123, 125, 127–128, 342
    Oberon 123–125, 288, 306, 394
Webern, Anton Friedrich Wilhelm von 25, 208–209
Wedekind, Frank 24, 382
  Works by:
    Büchse der Pandora, Die 382
    Erdgeist, Der 382
    Frühlings Erwachen 382
    Kammersänger, Der 382
Weill, Kurt 196–199, 208, 380, 408, 419
  Works by:
    Dreigroschenoper, Die 196–198
    Aufstieg und Fall der Stadt Mahagonny 196
    Protagonist, Der 199
Weinberg, Mieczysław 368
Weinberger, Jaromír 194, 199
  Works by:
    Schwanda der Dudelsackpfeifer 194, 199

Weininger, Otto 137, 311
Weisgall, Hugo xxii
Weissmuller, Jonny 214
Weissenborn, Hermann 233
Wellington 1st Duke of (Arthur Wellesley) 97, 101
Wendt, Amadeus 115–118
Wenkoff, Spas 326
Wenn du jung bist, gehört dir die Welt (film) 234
What's Opera, Doc? (film) 221
Wharton, Edith 28
  Works by:
    "*Age of Innocence, The*" 28
"*When a Man Loves a Woman*" 424
Merry Widow, The 238
White Christmas (film) 247
White Stripes, The 427
White, Jack 427
White, Michael xxii
White, Willard 436
Widdop, Walter 379
Wieck, Friedrich 138
Wiene, Robert 231–232
Wieniawski, Henryk xxv
Wilde, Oscar xvii, xix, 20–21, 23, 25, 28
  Works by:
    Picture of Dorian Gray, The xvii, 21, 28
Williams, Tennessee 244
  Works by:
    Streetcar Named Desire, A 244
Wilson, Woodrow 184
Winchell, Walter 226–227
Winckelmann, Johann 311, 327
Windgassen, Wolfgang 119, 142, 315, 324–327
Wings of the Morning (film) 236
Winkelmann, Hermann 140–143, 302–303, 306–307, 326, 455
Winkler, Angela 442
Witt, Joseph 206
Wo Die Lerche Singt (film) 232
Wolf, Hugo 136
Wolf-Ferrari, Ermanno 165, 191
  Works by:
    Donne Curiose, Le 202
    Piccolo Marat, Il 199
    Sly 230, 400
Wolf-Israel, Yevgeny 371
Wollfit, Donald 284
Wollstonecraft, Mary 20
Woodall, Doris 380

Wonder, Stevie   428,
Wray, Fay   239
Wright, Yvonne Lowrene   428
Wunderlich, Fritz   319, 321–324, 326, 378, 392, 405
Wyeth, Andrew   xix
  Works by:
    Christina's World   xix

Yeend, Frances   243–244
Yelizarova, Maria   372
Yeltsin, Sergey   371
Yershov, Ivan   364–367, 369
Yorke, Thom   427
"*You'll Never Walk Alone*"   416
Young, Angus   423–424
Yudin, Sergei   368
Yvan   163
Youtube   8, 26, 177, 409, 432–433, 436

Zanasi, Mario   279
Zandonai, Riccardo   165, 183, 189, 191
  Works by:
    Cavalieri di Ekebù, I   189, 384

Francesca da Rimini   165
Giulietta e Romeo   183
Zanelli, Renato   285, 301
Zangarini, Carlo   386
Zaranek, Stefania   371
Zarzuela   287, 383, 393–394
Zauberlied, Das (film)   232
Zuccato, Andrea   457
Zucchero   412
Zueignung   201, 204, 307
Zukor, Adolph   211
Zweig, Stefan   197–198
Zeffirelli, Franco   286
Zehme, Albertine   24, 45, 392
Zemeckis, Robert   423
Zemlinsky, Alexander von   204, 208, 306
Zenatello, Giovanni   111, 171, 239
Zeno, Apostolo   17
Ziegler, Karl   196, 238
Zimbalist, Efrem   216
Zola, Émile   28, 334, 344, 350, 392
  Works by:
    "*Nana*"
Zuying, Song   xxvi